Books by Joseph C. Grew

Sport and Travel in the Far East
Report from Tokyo
Ten Years in Japan
Turbulent Era

Turbulent Era

A Diplomatic Record
of Forty Years

1904 – 1945

VOL.
I

Joseph C. Grew, 1902

Turbulent Era

A Diplomatic Record
of Forty Years

—————————— 1904–1945 ——————————

Joseph C. Grew

〰〰〰〰〰〰〰〰〰〰〰〰〰〰〰〰〰〰〰〰〰〰〰

EDITED BY WALTER JOHNSON

Assisted by Nancy Harvison Hooker

VOLUME I

HOUGHTON MIFFLIN COMPANY BOSTON

𝕿𝖍𝖊 𝕽𝖎𝖛𝖊𝖗𝖘𝖎𝖉𝖊 𝕻𝖗𝖊𝖘𝖘 𝕮𝖆𝖒𝖇𝖗𝖎𝖉𝖌𝖊

Library of Congress Catalogue Card No. 52–5262

The quotations from Ten Years in Japan, *Copyright, 1944, by Joseph C. Grew, are reprinted by the courtesy of Simon and Schuster Inc. The quotations from* The Memoirs of Cordell Hull *are reprinted by the courtesy of the MacMillan Company.*

The Riverside Press
CAMBRIDGE · MASSACHUSETTS
PRINTED IN THE U.S.A.

To the Foreign Service of the United States at whose birth I assisted and whose development and welfare have been my greatest interest in life

Foreword

THIS IS the record of one lifetime, spent in the Foreign Service of the United States. As history must be built upon contemporary comment, presented as accurately as surrounding circumstances permit, I have felt an obligation to keep a diary during most of my service. Such daily comments, recorded at given posts at given times, can, of course, deal with only very small segments of the world picture and cannot presume to record more than a fraction of political and diplomatic developments observed from those points of vantage. They can, however, piece out and add atmosphere to the official correspondence and press comment which must be the working material of historians. In publishing this book I am therefore trying to discharge what I have always conceived to be an obligation to the accurate recording of history.

The story of any man's life, however close its contacts with important events in history and with some of the outstanding people of his day, can be but a cold and colorless thing if it affords no intimate glimpse of the personalities involved. Biography and autobiography have always been my favorite form of reading, and I well know that the portrayals which stand out in memory are those in which the element of human interest is intimately woven into the narrative.

Thus, in culling from my diary and letters the material for this book, my editor and I have not hesitated to draw freely on comments of a purely personal or descriptive nature. Candid-camera shots, let us call them. Even the recording of history needs atmosphere and color to vitalize the tale. Especially in the earlier years, when, as a younger officer, my work and responsibilities were of no great moment, and when our country was still a country young in international affairs, this part of the record contains less of historic importance than the later years.

My career took me from the early days of the nation as a great power to the close of World War II. The peaceful world of diplomacy that I knew in my early experience was shattered by two world wars. It was a diplomatic life, then, catapulted from a world of serenity into one of turbulence and distress.

This much may be said. I recorded from day to day what I saw and thought at the time of writing, and that record has not been altered. As to the accuracy of my records, no diplomatic observer anywhere can at any one time and place see the whole scene. His observation may be at fault, for it is a truism that two or more observers of an event at a given spot may honestly report that event with wide discrepancy. How much more difficult it is to report with accuracy a political situation! It shocks me profoundly to remember that on the outbreak of war in 1914, most of us in the Embassy in Berlin accepted the German point of view, hook, bait and sinker, for in those dramatic days we were unused to war and war propaganda, and we were, for a time at least, cut off from all other points of view. But the record stands here as originally written. Only the historians, with their access to the general and detailed records of what has occurred, can reproduce something approaching the full picture.

I wish to say a word of special appreciation of the helpfulness of Count A. Kabayama during my mission to Japan. Count Kabayama's greatest interest in life was the maintenance and development of mutually helpful relations between Japan and the United States. He had been educated in our country, at school and later at Amherst College. For some time he was President of the America Japan Society in Tokyo. With entire loyalty to his own country he kept me informed, especially during our early years in Japan, of developments behind the scenes and thus assisted me in keeping my finger on the pulse of Japan's political life. The outbreak of war between our two countries was a terrible shock to him, upsetting as it did the major part of his life's work. For his helpfulness and that of other far-sighted Japanese friends, among whom I include the present Prime Minister, Mr. Shigeru Yoshida, during those prolific years, I shall always be truly grateful.

My editor and I have quarreled on only one point. It troubles me to have to publish diary and letters written some thirty or forty years ago in the immature style of youth with all its tendency to redundancy and superlatives. I would be happier if some of these early documents could have been more simply, briefly, and conservatively phrased, as I believe they would have been phrased today. But on this point Professor Walter Johnson, Chairman of the Department of History of the University of Chicago, has been adamant. He would not hear of my changing a word, save to correct misspellings and a few grammatical errors which interfered with the clarity of the text. Thus the historian. Of course, I ceded the point.

Incidentally, I feel that Dr. Johnson has done a superb job of editing, not only in his selections from the original material but also in the helpfulness of his footnotes and his comments at the beginning of chapters. This has involved a great amount of research and a thoroughness of method which should render the book of far greater value to historians than my original text ever could have been. I highly appreciate the way in which the usefulness of the manuscript has been developed in Dr. Johnson's skillful hands.

The relief at getting this book finished is very great. I have constantly felt the urge to make available to historians and to the public at least the high spots of my experiences, and while this book contains only a very small part of my records, the entire collection will go in due course to a well-known library. Anyway, here is the story, for what it is worth.

JOSEPH C. GREW

Table of Contents

List of Illustrations

1. Joseph C. Grew, 1902, *frontispiece*

following page 70

2. The Author's bungalow in Cairo, 1904
3. Honeymoon in the Maine woods, 1905
4. Mrs. Grew in Cairo, 1905
5. A diplomatic reception in Mexico, 1906
6. Mrs. Grew in Berlin, 1909
7. Mrs. Grew and the children about 1913
8. Austrian note from Count Czernin, breaking diplomatic relations, 1917
9. Note from Colonel House to the Author
10. Signing of American-Turkish Treaty, Lausanne, 1923
11. Reception of American flyers by Kemal Atatürk in Turkey, 1931
12. Kemal Atatürk, his adopted daughter and the Author

VOLUME II

13. Joseph C. Grew, 1952, *frontispiece*

following page 858

14. The American Embassy, Tokyo — the Residence
15. The American Embassy, Tokyo — the Chancery
16. At the graves of the sailors of Perry's Expedition
17. The Author speaking at a dinner of the America-Japan Society

Joseph C. Grew's Four Decades
in the Foreign Service

WHEN Joseph C. Grew retired from the Foreign Service, the *New York Times* observed on August 20, 1945:

> After more than twoscore years of what State Secretary Byrnes rightly characterized as distinguished and devoted public service, Joseph C. Grew has resigned as Under Secretary of State at the height of his career. He rendered this service in many diplomatic posts and held important positions in both Berlin and Vienna during the last war. But it was his special fortune to play a major role in the events which led up to the war in the Pacific and its present grandiose climax. As Ambassador to Tokyo for ten years preceding Pearl Harbor he fought valiantly to preserve the peace while warning the American Government of the possibility of Japanese treachery. Japanese treachery won out, and Mr. Grew felt that his lifework had crashed all about him. It must, therefore, have given him special satisfaction to help preside over the liquidation of Japan's ambitions, and his counsel contributed much to the speedy end of the Pacific war through the utilization of the Japanese Emperor. His policy both before and after Pearl Harbor has sometimes been subject to criticism, but if he erred he erred on the side of humanity. . . .

Mr. Grew was an active participant in many of the vital developments in American diplomacy from the presidency of Theodore Roosevelt to the opening days of the Administration of Harry S. Truman. From 1904 to 1945, Mr. Grew's career mirrored the stress and strains that accompanied the emergence to world power of the gigantic new nation of the West.

Drew Pearson and Robert S. Allen observed in "The Merry-Go-Round" on October 28, 1939:

When [the] time comes, he can write a diplomatic record unique in recent history: from the old days in Vienna when he waltzed with the Countess Montgelas; through the World War, the Versailles Treaty, the Lausanne Conference, at which single-handed he virtually brought peace between the Turks and the Greeks; and on down to the diary of his seven years in Japan.

It was a career that took Mr. Grew to many sensitive posts. As a young officer he witnessed the breakup of the peaceful world of the late Victorian age. Later, in important positions, he saw the turmoil of the world through two great international conflicts. His despatches from such posts as Germany, Switzerland, Turkey, and Japan were influential in the shaping of American foreign policy. Twice as Under Secretary of State, first under President Calvin Coolidge and later under Presidents Franklin D. Roosevelt and Harry S. Truman, he not only exerted a significant influence in many diplomatic decisions, but he also contributed greatly to the development of a professional Foreign Service.

Mr. Grew was first appointed to the Foreign Service in 1904 as Deputy Consul General in Cairo. Nearly two years later he was transferred to Mexico as Third Secretary of Embassy. After a short tour of duty in the Mexico of the closing years of the Díaz regime, he was sent to St. Petersburg as Third Secretary of Embassy. During his work in Russia in 1907–8, he was to see something of the social and political forces at work which in a few years would lead that country into revolution.

The next nine years, 1908–17, Mr. Grew had two terms of service in both Berlin and Vienna. He witnessed the gay social life of these two imperial capitals and then saw the world plunged into a war that was to end for Vienna its role as the center of an important empire. Throughout the years of American neutrality, 1914–17, Mr. Grew was in a strategic position as First Secretary of Embassy and as Chargé d'Affaires, when Ambassador Gerard was away from Germany, to explain American policy to the German Government and to report on conditions within the leading nation of the Central Powers.

During America's participation in the war, Mr. Grew served in Washington as Acting Chief of the Division of Western European Affairs. In October, 1918, Colonel E. M. House took Mr. Grew to Versailles to be Secretary to the American delegation to the pre-Armistice negotiations. Then, at the Peace Conference, he was Secretary-General of the American Commission to Negotiate Peace and American Secretary on the International Secretariat of the Peace Conference. Although heavily involved in administrative work, he did have the opportunity of seeing the inside of the Peace Conference and of observing the major forces that shaped the Treaty of Versailles.

In the spring of 1920, Mr. Grew was appointed Minister to Denmark, a most pleasant tour of duty and one of considerable importance as a listening post on developments in the Soviet Union. The following year he was transferred to Switzerland, where he was to serve until 1924. The ministership to Switzerland gave Mr. Grew an important vantage point from which to watch the struggles of the League of Nations. While in Switzerland he served as American representative at the Lausanne Conference, where he saw the leaders of the new Turkey successfully negotiate with the Allied Powers. With these same Turkish leaders, Mr. Grew drafted a treaty between Turkey and the United States, which later was to fail of ratification in the Senate.

After his experiences in Switzerland, Mr. Grew returned to Washington to serve as Under Secretary of State from 1924 to 1927. It was during these years that the Atlanta *Constitution* referred to him as "the most widely experienced diplomat in the American service."

In 1927, Mr. Grew was sent to Istanbul as the first American Ambassador to the new Turkey. For five exciting years he saw that country, led by Kemal Ataturk, undergo vast changes which were to make Turkey a modern republic. His diary faithfully records Turkey in the years of transition from the Ottoman theocracy to the westernized state. As he wrote in his diary on April 27, 1931:

While away on our trip I thought a good deal of abandoning
the diary permanently, realizing the triviality of many, indeed
most of the comments which it contains. But I'll try to continue
it, at least for a while, because some day in future it may be possible to separate the wheat from the chaff and perhaps to find in
it a certain amount of useful "contemporary comment" throwing
light on this particular period of the early days of the Turkish
Republic and America's relations thereto — for if the Turkish
Republic continues to exist, these will some day be looked upon
as its "early days" and history is built upon contemporary comment.

The year after Japan invaded Manchuria, Mr. Grew went
to Tokyo as Ambassador. For nine hectic years he was to
represent the United States in one of the most difficult assignments in the Foreign Service. "Professional diplomat of the
finest vintage, he has brains, and character," *Ken* Magazine
commented on June 2, 1938. "If he had less, his country might
pay dearly for the lack." The Tokyo correspondent of the
New York Times observed on May 19, 1939:

The Japanese press reveals public sentiment here in its customary topsy-turvy way by telling its readers that Mr. Grew, when
home, will help Americans understand Japan's true policies
better.

This is a pleasant but entirely illusory view. The fact that it
can be presented to the populace after seven years, during which
Japanese-American relations have been uniformly bad, testifies to
the skill with which Mr. Grew has handled his mission. Neither
during the Panay incident nor on any of the numerous similar
occasions did Mr. Grew omit to state American policy and defend
American rights in forthright language. Well-qualified observers
here deem Mr. Grew's tenure one of the most successful as well
as one of the most important in the history of the American
Embassy here.

Mr. Grew's capacity for going straight toward the American
goal, which the Japanese realize is usually an unselfish one, has
made him one of the greatest instruments of America's Far
Eastern policy today.

Time Magazine commented on May 29, 1939: "Already rated one of the best career diplomats in the U.S. Foreign Service when Herbert Hoover sent him to Japan in 1932, Ambassador Grew by general consensus has done a bang-up job of pleasantly conveying unpleasant news to the Nipponese." And the Japan *Times Weekly* stated on May 18, 1939: "He has served his Government and his own nation faithfully, honestly and unswervingly, and has acted as friend to Japan in so doing . . . Mr. Grew's personal popularity not only with his own countrymen but, more important, with the people of Japan is great indeed."

After the Japanese attack on Pearl Harbor and the subsequent months of detention in Japan, Mr. Grew returned to Washington to become Special Assistant to the Secretary of State. Early in 1944 he was appointed Director of the Office of Far Eastern Affairs and late that year was made Under Secretary of State. Secretary of State Edward R. Stettinius, Jr., in urging the Senate Foreign Relations Committee to recommend confirmation of Mr. Grew's appointment, said:

He has devoted 40 years to serving our country with great distinction and honor in the conduct of our foreign relations in all parts of the world. He has served three years as Under Secretary of State and nine years as Ambassador to Japan. He knows at first hand both fascism and aggression and hates them both. As Under Secretary he would be a strong right arm in the tasks of building now for a more democratic world after victory and of making peace secure.

As Under Secretary of State he was to have considerable influence in the decision to retain the Japanese Emperor after Japan surrendered. He was, also, to deal with and influence a wide variety of diplomatic policies when he was Acting Secretary of State over a period of several months.

When President Truman assumed office, Mr. Grew submitted his resignation. It was not accepted, however, until August 16, 1945. By this date Mr. Grew had reached the retirement age

of sixty-five, and he had completed forty-one years of service
in the field of American diplomacy.

The Washington *News* commented on his resignation that
"Under Secretary of State Grew will be missed in American
diplomacy," while the Salt Lake City *Tribune* remarked:

> Mr. Grew has been a faithful servant of the public in the
> field of foreign relations for 41 years — long enough to become
> thoroughly familiar with all the details and formalities of that
> institution and to be of valuable assistance to political appointees
> of changing administrations. . . . He was regarded as one of the
> most efficient ambassadors of his time.

During his forty-one years in the Foreign Service Mr. Grew
collected one hundred and sixty-eight bound volumes of his
papers in addition to some unbound papers in the period from
1941 to 1945. Of the volumes thirty-nine are diary, and the
remainder include records of conversations, speeches, carbons
of letters, despatches, and press clippings. The bound diaries
usually run to one thousand typewritten pages per volume.

There were a number of years when Mr. Grew was unable to
keep his diary. In the place of a diary, therefore, the editor has
utilized records of conversations, letters, or despatches. In many
chapters, too, diary, letters, records of conversations, and despatches were all utilized to present the events covered.

Through the years Mr. Grew occasionally set forth in his
diary or letters his view as to why it was important for a diplomat to maintain such a record of activities. In 1915, for instance, he wrote to a friend:

> I hope you have been keeping a diary since the beginning of
> the war, for it is a duty for every one of us to record even the
> smallest points, which may seem to us now unimportant but
> which may subsequently, in connection with other points, throw
> valuable light on dark corners in history. Occasionally facts of
> the greatest importance are let drop in a casual conversation, of
> which I have had many instances. The more one reads the docu-
> ments of the war, the more insatiable does one become for in-

formation and evidence on the points that have not been cleared up or which have been withheld from publication.

In 1932 he wrote in his diary:

I think a diary should set forth, more or less, what one is thinking at the time it is written. History is a continually unfolding panorama and in later years it may be valuable to be able to furnish a little color and atmosphere to a particular scene of the past.

He wrote to another friend in 1924:

A diary is of no real value unless it is thoroughly indiscreet, and mine, in Berlin, at Lausanne, and elsewhere, left nothing to be desired in that respect.

When it came to writing despatches, Mr. Grew in 1933 set forth his attitude by observing to a friend:

If you happen to recollect certain pages of the 1916 War Supplement, notably pages 129, 300, etc., you will perhaps have gathered that in writing despatches I constantly have the historical record in mind and have turned in a good many which were intended much more for the record than for their current importance, summarizing matter which had been dealt with piece-meal in cablegrams.

The Grew diary was more than a record for Mr. Grew's own perusal. Over the years copies of various entries went to members of his family, to colleagues in the Foreign Service, and to certain friends back in the Department of State. On December 14, 1929, for instance, Mr. Grew writing from Turkey to Wallace S. Murray, Assistant Chief of the Division of Near Eastern Affairs, said:

From now on, in accordance with my promise, I will inflict you with the diary fortnightly. You will, I fear, have to wade through — or around — a good deal of personal and family stuff, because I haven't time to make an "expurgated" copy. There is nothing in it that I have the slightest objection to your seeing; I merely don't want you to bore yourself and I have no doubt that with your long experience of reading masses of documents, you will be quite able to sift the wheat from the chaff very rapidly. Much of it is trivial. I send it on only because here and there things get into it which may help to give you a little more background of affairs in Turkey than may appear in our despatches. Please remember that it is a sort of slapdash affair and that I am likely to make a statement in it one day which may have to be withdrawn or modified the next. Do not therefore attach too much importance to its contents. That is why I do not want it to appear on the official files of the Department or the Division as Admiral Bristol's diary did. But you may always show it to Howland Shaw or to Bill Castle — if either or both of them desire to see it — and you may in your own good discretion show any part of it to any officer of the Department to whom you think that particular part might be of interest or assistance. Of course you will keep it safely locked up.

Among others outside the family who often received diary excerpts were William R. Castle, Jr., Howland Shaw, and Stanley Hornbeck. The diary, therefore, at times probably had an influence in policy determination.

The Grew papers contain a storehouse of informative material. The volume presented here is obviously a highly selected portion of the total collection. Mr. Grew sent his entire collection to the University of Chicago, where Mrs. Nancy Harvison Hooker and I made the selections and did the editorial work. This manuscript was then submitted to Mr. Grew for approval. In general, only two restrictions were placed on our editorial work. Mr. Grew asked that none of the reports that he had written on the members of his staff be utilized and that no personal criticisms of the Ambassadors or Ministers under whom he served in his early years be used, except in cases where such comment threw light directly or indirectly on current developments. The manuscript was, also, submitted for security clearance.

Chapters I to IV of this volume were written by Mr. Grew.

He started the first draft of these chapters in 1938, and they were considerably revised in 1950. Mr. Grew selected, also, the material that appears in Chapters XXX, XXXI, XXXII, and XXXIV. The rest of the chapters in both volumes were selected by Mrs. Hooker and by the editor. Whenever Mr. Grew has written a footnote comment on the text the initials J.C.G. appear at the end of the comment. All the other footnotes are the responsibility of Mrs. Hooker and the editor, except in Chapters XXX, XXXI, XXXII, and XXXIV, where the special situation involved is explained in the foreword to the chapters.

The diary, letters, and other papers reproduced in these volumes were often written at top speed and misspellings and grammatical errors occasionally crept in. Misspellings, in the few places where they occur, have been corrected, and other changes have been made in grammar and punctuation, when such errors obscured the sense of the original text. When names first occur in the manuscript, full names and identifying material have been added to the text.

Mr. Grew and I are indebted to Simon & Schuster for permission to reprint an occasional passage that first appeared in *Ten Years in Japan;* and to D. Appleton-Century Co., Ernest Benn, Ltd., The John Day Co., Doubleday & Co., E. P. Dutton & Co., Inc., Harper & Bros., The Johns Hopkins Press, Houghton Mifflin Co., B. W. Huebsch, Little, Brown & Co., Atlantic Monthly Press, Longmans, Green & Co., *Look,* McGraw-Hill Book Publishing Co., The Macmillan Co., *The New Republic, The New York Herald Tribune, The New York Times,* Princeton University Press, *The Saturday Evening Post,* The University of Chicago Press, D. Van Nostrand Co., Inc., The Viking Press, World Peace Foundation, and Yale University Press for permission to quote from material which was first published by them.

Mr. Grew and I are deeply grateful to the following people who read all or portions of the manuscript and who offered us valuable suggestions: Ellery Sedgwick, Professor Donald Lach, Eugene H. Dooman, Joseph W. Ballantine, Charles E. Bohlen,

Herbert Feis, and others. Mr. Grew's appreciation of the constant interest and helpfulness of Mrs. Marion Arnold Johnston in typing and assembling his diary and letters over many years is enduring.

I am indebted to Alma Lach for the typing of the manuscript.

WALTER JOHNSON

PART ONE

Diplomacy Before an Age of Conflict
1904–1914

THE THIRTY YEARS prior to 1914 seemed, on the surface at least, to be years of stability, security, and progress. Europe, in these years, dominated the world. That continent had more than doubled its own population between 1815 and 1914; it had helped to people the plains of the United States and Canada; it had colonized Australasia, and had partitioned Africa. Great Britain had extended its rule over India, and nations nominally independent, like Turkey, Persia, China, and Japan, had felt the impact of an industrialized Europe.

In the closing decade of the nineteenth century, Great Britain, France, Russia, and Austria had to share world power with four new nations — Germany, Italy, Japan, and the United States. A century before, Germany and Italy had not yet become united nations; Japan was still closed to the outside world; and the United States was on the threshold of its western expansion and its industrial development.

Germany and Italy greatly increased their power following unification in the eighteen-seventies, while Tsarist Russia and Imperial Austria gradually fell into a state of decay. At the same time, the emergence of Japan and the United States as world powers signified, in the long run, that Europe would no longer be able to dictate to the rest of the world. World control now would have to be shared with the Western Hemisphere and the Far East.

1

Throughout most of the nineteenth century, the United States had concentrated on settling the West, fighting a great civil war, and building an industrial society. In this era, since world relations did not bulk large, the country, as a relatively isolated power, developed no strong foreign policy, and the Department of State remained a neglected branch of the Government. Until the Spanish-American War, the President and the Secretary of State, with the aid of a few experts and clerks, were able to deal with the problems of foreign policy.

After 1898, however, the United States proclaimed the Open Door policy in China, President Theodore Roosevelt concerned himself with the problem of helping to maintain peace in Europe, and the nation greatly extended its control and influence in Latin America. The Department of State, then, expanded its operations, although inadequately, to meet its new obligations. In 1898 salaries for Departmental officers, for instance, amount to $118,038.50, while by 1908 they had increased to $228,386.85; the employees on the Department's payroll in 1898 numbered 82, and this increased to 167 by 1908; American foreign trade in 1898 totaled $1,847,531,984, and by 1908 it amounted to $3,055,115,138.

In spite of the larger role that the United States Government was playing in world affairs, Congress and the American people relegated world politics to the sidelines, while the Progressive Movement dominated the center of activity. American newspapers, furthermore, seldom had correspondents in Europe, and European events were either ignored or buried in the back pages of the newspapers. Writing from Vienna in 1911, Mr. Grew said of American newspapers: "I have almost given up reading them now, for even the best of them are filled with page after page of murder and suicide accounts, while the most important political matters of world interest are given short paragraphs and sandwiched in where one can scarcely find them."

Although rivalry among the great powers was intense, and two localized Balkan wars occurred in 1912 and 1913, the general impression one received of European life was of its sta-

bility and permanence. People did not speak, then, of an impending crisis in civilization which might threaten the destruction of man. It seemed to be rather a world of rich promise, hope, and accomplishment — a world evolving continually toward a better and better day.

I

Choice of a Profession
1880 – 1904

THE CHOICE of a life's profession becomes a matter of moment even to the child. While some imaginative youngsters in our day and age, especially if city- and movie-bred, no doubt see in the big shots of gangsterdom the highest form of heroism, others aspire to a life-job on the police force, and I well remember passing through that healthy stage when first impressed with the majesty of the law as personified by the cop on the local beat. "Coppie Doyle," incidentally, was a benevolent old Irish gentleman, but his job was no sinecure so far as we urchins had anything to do about it. We took good care to keep him busy.

But once emerged from childhood, it was the call of the sea that predominated all other aspirations and led me, almost as soon as I was out of apron strings, to spend the free hours rambling among the vessels at the docks in Boston. Indeed, even today the smell of hemp and tar poignantly recalls that early love of ships and the youthful visions of foreign seas and ports and the spice-laden romanticism of unknown lands beyond the horizon. My uncle, Henry Sturgis Grew, as a member of Russell and Company, had sailed in his youth on the old China tea clippers, and the treasures that he had brought home from the Far East were to me a never-failing attraction, for they stirred the imagination.

Ships to me were indeed personified; I knew them intimately by sight and name, and many were the old friends that I met in foreign ports on later travels. Old friends might change with the years, but seldom could they lose their characteristics and personalities. No daydreams possessed for me greater allure

than the thought of "those that go down to the sea in ships
and do their business in great waters," and it was this longing
for the sea and for distant travel that undoubtedly played its
part in leading me eventually to the Foreign Service as a profession.

Yet another allure was equally strong in youth — the woods.
Stevenson's lines "of green days in forests and blue days at
sea," and "Home is the sailor, home from the sea, And the
hunter home from the hill," and Kipling's "Who hath smelt
wood-smoke at twilight? Who hath heard the birch-log burning? Who is quick to read the noises of the night?" held for
romantic youth an indescribable appeal and gave concrete expression to the perpetual urge, especially in spring, to get far
away from the prosaic surroundings of city life. Poetry, particularly romantic poetry — Keats, Shelley, Byron, Wordsworth,
the *Rubáiyát,* which I could repeat by heart, Shakespeare —
and music, were always running through my thoughts; mem-
orization came easily, and the vast store that was available to
suit every mood was constantly called upon to make the time
pass rapidly on subsequent travels and on long climbs and
treks in many lands, a never-failing treasure-house which
yielded on all occasions its stimulus or balm.

But to return to the sea and the woods. Fortunate is the
youth who can satisfy those longings. From the age of fifteen,
no summer vacation went by without a camping and shooting
or fishing trip somewhere — in the Maine Woods, year after
year, with long canoe trips down the west branch of the Penob-
scot through the lovely lake country, still undisturbed by the
advance of civilization, where one tasted the true joys of the
forest primeval; elk-hunting in Jackson's Hole in Wyoming;
moose and caribou-shooting in New Brunswick. All of these
experiences whetted the wanderlust, enhanced the call of the
wild, and led in due course to the hunting trip around the
world which ultimately rendered a sedentary life at home unthinkable. The sea, also, became as familiar as the woods, and
summer after summer, glorious weeks were spent cruising in
my tiny yacht up and down the New England coast, every nook

and cranny of which was intimately known to me, as was every mood of the ocean. When a heavy sou'easter suddenly rolls in with high seas and fog, even the amateur must know what he is up against and he must be prepared with chart and compass and conch horn to dig through difficult situations. I had my fill of them. Such experiences build character and, more, develop a sound philosophy and a healthy outlook on life.

Returning from a year and a half of distant travels,[1] I was met at the railway station in Boston by my dear father, Edward Sturgis Grew, who was a great gentleman of the old and ultra-conservative school. The occasional bulletins of my wanderings and sometimes vivid experiences of hunting big game and climbing mountains had already contributed almost the last white hairs to his magnificent silver-topped head; yet there was still room for a few more, dutifully supplied by his errant son in due course. One or two of them must have attained their final hue right there, when he saw me arriving with twenty-two pieces of baggage, some of which broke open, depositing a pair of dilapidated slippers on the station platform, and a Japanese servant. W. S. Suzuki, by the way, completely won my mother's heart and he subsequently became the family butler, serving efficiently until he had learned fluent English and then returning to Japan where he became a well-known guide in Yokohama.

As gently as possible the bad news was broken to Father. He had raised his boy to be a banker, but the boy had now developed other views. The fact that all previous males of the family had settled down respectably in Boston and had one and all gone into respectable business and had become respectable citizens registered not a whit with this headstrong youth. The

---

[1] Leaving Marseilles on September 15, 1902, Mr. Grew had taken an extensive tour of the Far East, hunting big game in such places as the Malay jungle, Kashmir, Baltistan, and China. He also traveled in Australia, New Zealand, Tasmania, and Japan. See J. C. Grew, *Sport and Travel in the Far East* (Boston: Houghton Mifflin Co., 1910). He returned to Boston on December 15, 1903.

only field that interested him was the Foreign Service, and willy-nilly a Foreign Service man he would be. Often have I thought how at that pregnant moment Father must have realized the full implication of his one big strategic mistake, in letting me go abroad instead of clamping me into business the moment my college diploma was in my pocket. But I was not wholly undutiful; the plea that this step would permanently separate our lives counted, and I agreed to a compromise; the only form of business that interested me was publishing, for I loved literature and everything that pertained to it; if Father would get me a job in a publishing house, I would stay. He agreed and began looking around, but no vacancies were in sight anywhere. I stayed in Boston through the winter, accomplishing two things of somewhat varied aspect: I learned typewriting professionally in a business school, and I laid the foundations for an unusually happy married life.

For those who contemplate a professional life, especially the Foreign Service, let me say here that the ability to typewrite, as rapidly and accurately as any stenographer, has been the greatest of boons. The touch system employing all ten fingers can be learned so easily, even without going to a school at all, and so rapidly, that I often wonder why more men don't take the trouble to acquire it. With the Corona in front of me, my thoughts fly forward and take shape on paper even as they fly; with the pen I am hopelessly cramped, physically and mentally. Perhaps that is merely a personal idiosyncrasy but in the drafting of despatches, reports, official telegrams, diary, letters, I know that many hours have been saved and that literary construction has been far more facile than if those documents had been composed by pen or pencil.

The matrimonial episode came about through a concatenation of circumstances just as unusual as various other unusual circumstances in a not altogether humdrum life. At the very first dance after returning home I was promptly swept off my feet, metaphorically if not quite actually, by the vision of a lovely creature dancing like a dream and looking like a dream too. Inquiries elicited the fact that the young lady had just returned from Japan. "Why, I have just returned from Japan too," I said to my informer. "Lead me to her." But my friend, pleading that he had that dance engaged, asked me to find someone else to make the introduction. Accosting another friend I asked if he knew the young lady who had just returned from Japan. "Certainly," he said. "Come on." But instead of taking me up to the vision, he led me to quite a different lady. Truthfulness requires me to say that she was a vision too, but in my surprise at the substitution I'm quite sure that my jaw dropped and that my expression must have clearly intimated: "Hasn't there been some mistake?" Vision No. 2 had also just returned from Japan. She was Alice Perry, a direct descendant in fact of Oliver Hazard Perry, renowned brother of the Commodore Matthew Calbraith Perry who originally opened Japan to the western world, and she was also a great-great-granddaughter of another fairly well-known diplomatist, Benjamin Franklin. Her family had recently spent three years in that lovely country, Japan, where her father, Thomas Sergeant Perry, filled the chair of English literature at Keio University. The crosscurrents of life, or shall we say the schemes of Dame Fortune who, I think, does a little discreet wirepulling in the side wings, are sometimes passing strange. At any rate, Vision No. 2 became Mrs. Grew in due course, while Vision No. 1, the lovely Maya Lindsley, married Bertie Poole and settled down in Yokohama where, thirty years later, we met and I had the fun of telling her what a close call she had had at that Boston dance.

At the end of three months in Boston I felt that professionally I was getting nowhere and when the old spring fret came on, as it always has come on every year of my life, and when reading Kipling simply made it worse, the announcement was communicated to my respected but bewildered sire that I proposed to go abroad to study French while still awaiting that mythical job in a publishing house.

Once again Dame Fortune was clever and kind. She put me in a French family in Tours composed of a gentle widowed mother and a son of about my own age, a medical student, whose character was anything but gentle. In fact he was one of the most opinionated, argumentative and obstinate youths that I've ever run across and, as necessity is ever the mother of invention, it became essential for me to invent a sufficient stock of quantitative if not qualitative French to hold up my end in those almost constant arguments. When a Frenchman tells an Anglo-Saxon that the latter is bordering on idiocy because he sleeps with his window open and thus "dares the vile contagion of the night" at supreme risk to his health if not his life, and in the next breath derides all Anglo-Saxons for wasting valuable time on the football and cricket fields instead of spending those hours in elevating study, as the Frenchman does, or did in those days, the youthful Anglo-Saxon must take his choice between adequate riposte or apoplexy, and as the former alternative requires some kind of noise, preferably comprehensible noise, in the language of his opponent, it readily appears that the incentive to learn French rapidly was overwhelming. André and I argued at breakfast and luncheon and dinner and in the afternoons we took long bicycle rides together, still arguing. In three months I had acquired a very fair smattering of solid if not always idiomatic French, and the latter came readily enough when our future life was largely thrown among French-speaking people. André became a distinguished physician. I met him in Paris many years later and our greeting was full of affection and mutual esteem.

While I was still in Tours, and with plans made to spend the summer in the University of Grenoble, a telegram came from Professor Archie Coolidge saying that Fred Morgan, Edwin's brother, our Vice Consul General in Cairo, wanted a young man to go out with him to Egypt as a sort of private secretary, although the position technically would be that of clerk to the Consulate General at a salary of $600 a year. It was added in view of certain impending changes, I could count on being promoted shortly to the position of Vice Consul General. Would I accept? My reply was on the wires within ten minutes: "I must have two weeks to consider." My initial thought was that I must dash home to Boston to talk the matter over with my father.

But here again Dame Fortune interceded; she walked me up and down the boulevards in Tours for four full hours that afternoon, putting winged thoughts into my fallow mind, and at the end of those four hours she sent me once again to the telegraph office and guided my hand while I wrote the most pregnant telegram of my life: "Accept unconditionally." Opportunity generally knocks but once. Later I learned that had the second telegram not been sent, I would have lost the job.

A discreet veil had perhaps better be drawn over those last weeks at home. Parental displeasure was exceeded only by parental disappointment at having produced an idiot son. My father, conservative and brought up in a different groove, unquestionably believed that I was throwing my life away by embarking upon such uncharted seas as the Foreign Service, and my argument that American public life, ruled as it then was by politics, needed men of principle and education fell on deaf ears. My dear mother, Annie Crawford Clark Grew, aided and abetted me in every way, for she believed in my plans, and it is doubtful if they would ever have been carried out had it not been for her staunch if tacit support. I owe her much and revere her memory. Father came down to the station to see me off for Cairo and his last words, as I swung on to the train, were: "Since you have chosen, my blessings go with you." But there was a pretty big lump in my throat all the same.

Those last weeks were well employed in other respects, too, and on the evening of Class Day at Harvard, somewhere in the Yard not far from the President's house, observations were exchanged which made it fairly certain that Miss Alice Perry would some day become Mrs. Grew.

Before passing on to the next two years of life in Cairo we must jump ahead a bit because the process of "breaking and entering" into the Diplomatic Service was not yet complete and we had better get all this straightened out right here. As a matter of fact I wasn't in the Diplomatic Service, nor in any service at all, and the "impending changes" which Fred Morgan had mentioned to Archie Coolidge, which would have made me a Vice Consul General, never did materialize, because Morgan's hopes to be appointed Diplomatic Agent and Consul General fell through. Within a few months the State Department did appoint me a Deputy Consul General,[2] a high-sounding title which permitted the signing of official documents with no salary attached, but this didn't fill the bill of my ambitions by any means. I well knew that when Fred Morgan left, I would probably have to leave too, and I wanted some more substantial outlook for the future. Bellamy Storer, a friend of the Perry family, who was then Ambassador to Austria-Hungary, asked for me as one of his official secretaries and I had high hopes which were sadly dashed when one day the press announced the appointment of the son of a prominent politician to the vacancy. This is what counted in those days — political pull. Profound discouragement. Then Alford Cooley, Assistant Attorney General and a friend of my family, who was close to President Theodore Roosevelt and a member of his celebrated "Tennis Cabinet," spoke to the President of my ambitions. The reply was always the same: "Too much political pressure. I can't do it." One day Cooley had a brilliant thought. He went out for a hike with the President and told him of my adventure with the tiger in China.[3] Mr. Roose-

---

[2] Mr. Grew was appointed Deputy Consul General at Cairo on November 3, 1904, an unsalaried position. From July 19, 1904, until March 1, 1906, he held the position of clerk of the Consulate General at a salary of $600 a year.

[3] Mr. Grew shot his tiger in the hinterland behind Amoy on October 3, 1903. Having placed goats around a village he waited ten days, until the tiger came, ate the goats and went to a cave to sleep off his gorge. Tracking the tiger to his lair, Mr. Grew and his Chinese hunters found it impossible to dislodge him, so that after four hours the sportsman had to go in. The entrance was a narrow, horizontal, rock tunnel leading to a subterranean cave, where the tiger lay on a rock ledge facing the tunnel. When Mr. Grew had wriggled with difficulty to the end of the tunnel, dragging his gun after him, the tiger's face was not four feet from his, but the tunnel had so narrowed as to prevent a charge. The hunters had meanwhile lit up the cave by inserting long bamboo torches through crevices in the rock. From his cramped position Mr. Grew had to fire from the hip, and he missed the tiger. The explosion, however, extinguished the torches, leaving the tiger and the sportsman in complete darkness. In the black of the cave Mr. Grew fired two more shots and killed the tiger. The animal measured ten feet six inches from nose to tip of tail.

velt listened with interest and finally pulled out his notebook, saying: "By Jove, I'll have to do something for that young man," and the very next day, March 1, 1906, my appointment as Third Secretary of Embassy in Mexico City was announced. That tiger-shooting was the only examination I ever took, and what fun I had some twenty years later when, as Chairman of the Examining Board for the Foreign Service, I used to say to the candidates: "You gentlemen have a very easy time entering the Service. All you have to do is to answer a few questions. I had to shoot a tiger."

When later I saw President Roosevelt in Washington in 1906 he said: "I have put you in the Service because I believe in you, but I can't recommend it as a permanent career. There is no career; it's all politics. I will keep you there as long as I am President but my successor will in all probability throw you out to make way for political henchmen, and then where will you be?" I replied: "Mr. President, I'll take the chance. We *must* develop a career. As a great nation with steadily expanding interests abroad we must, if only as a simple business proposition, develop and maintain a professional service. Otherwise we shall be steadily handicapped in competition with other nations." Within a year President Roosevelt had submitted and had put through Congress legislation placing the Diplomatic Service on a Civil Service basis up to and including the grade of First Secretary.[4] My vision of the future

4 On November 10, 1905, Theodore Roosevelt issued an Executive Order to the effect that vacancies in the offices of Secretary of Embassy or Legation were to be filled by transfer or promotion from some branch of the Service or by appointment upon examination. U.S. Congress, Senate, *Rules and Regulations Governing the Department of State*, Senate Document No. 359, 59th Cong., 2d Sess. (Washington: Government Printing Office, 1907), pp. 9–10. On April 5, 1906, an act was approved by Congress grading and classifying consular officers which made practical the extending of the Civil Service system to the whole Consular Service. This was done by Roosevelt in an Executive Order of June 27, 1906. *Ibid.*, pp. 15–16. Three years later on November 26, 1909, the success of the operation of Civil Service within the consular branch prompted President Taft to issue an Executive Order placing the Diplomatic Service under the same system. J. Rives Childs, *American Foreign Service* (New York: Henry Holt & Co., 1948), pp. 9–10; Graham H. Stuart, *The Department of State* (New York: The Macmillan Co., 1949), pp. 205, 219.

was no chimera. My appointment was, I think, the last under the old political system, and I was certainly the last to slip through without examination. Heaven knows whether I could ever have passed one! At any rate, we can now move on from this preamble to the life in the Service and to some of the great experiences which it entailed, for the process of breaking and entering was at last complete.

II

Cairo

1904 – 1906

EGYPT! What memories that lovely name recalls! Memories of the palm-lined streets of Cairo of deep red earth, which have now alas given place to asphalt boulevards and Parisian shops, and the clop-clop of the ponies with their snappy dogcarts, now superseded by the honking of myriad motorcars.[1] Memories of the Kasr-el-Nil bridge over the gently flowing Nile with the picturesque sails of the *dahabeahs* passing below: the lovely verdure and color of Ghezireh, the long road out to the Mena House on the edge of the desert and the never-failing inspiration of the Pyramids. Or should I qualify that remark? In the tourist season, with the raucous cries of the guides and vendors and donkey owners and the visions of portly females being pulled from in front and pushed from behind up the ledges of the big Pyramid of Cheops, I must admit that there may be moments when inspiration falters. But to me the Pyramids will always be associated with the summer nights when the tourists had gone and we had Egypt

---

[1] When Mr. Grew visited Cairo in 1931, he wrote in his diary: "Cairo at 3.15 — good old Cairo but, alas, no longer our Cairo. No more quiet streets and peaceful gardens; the old *arabiehs* and the clop-clop of their nags on the reddish earth, the smart dogcarts, white-gowned *syces* and snappy little Arab ponies — all are gone or nearly gone. In their place the raucous honking of motor horns, the wild dashing of Arab-driven taxis, Parisian shops, tall modern buildings. Sad, sad. But once at the Semiramis, whence we were driven by our Minister, William Jardine, President Coolidge's Secretary of Agriculture, things were somewhat different. Here we looked from our rooms directly on the Nile with its *dahabeahs* and lateen-sailed *feluccas,* the Kasr-el-Nil bridge and the British barracks — where I have passed many a happy evening with the old Royal Inniskillings — palm-horizoned Ghezireh opposite, and to the left the eternal Pyramids in the distance. The passing years cannot change that scene."

to ourselves, when to escape the fearful heat in town I used to take a camp bed out on the desert and sleep directly under those wonderful monuments, fanned by a breeze as cool and sweet as on a liner's bow at sea. It was easier, then, to merge one's self with the historic past, and inspiration was not lacking.

One of the Pyramids, I think it must be Mena, is smooth at the top, just as all the Pyramids were originally built, flat and smooth from base to apex until the coverings were removed, leaving great ledges which simplify the ascent. This smooth covering at the top of Mena must extend some twenty or thirty feet or more down from the apex and then, like a big candle extinguisher, ends abruptly and gives place to the uncovered ledges below. I once climbed that Pyramid to the top. The Arab who went with me as far as the jutting-out extinguisher said that no foreigner had ever done it before. That, of course, was "exaggerated," but it is probably not done often because the job of getting one's body onto the overhanging smooth cap by a process of very careful sinuous wriggling, and with quite a drop below, is a little like getting over some of the difficult overhanging places on the Matterhorn and with no chains to help. And once the overhang is safely negotiated, only one's bare toenails afford any sort of grip on the almost crackless and sensationally inclined surface that leads to the pointed top. Coming down is infinitely more difficult than going up. I claim no Richard Halliburton feats, but that climb was not worth doing twice. My relief at getting safely off that cap was great.

One other American once tried it and was killed. His name, I believe, was Rand Herron. He already had a splendid climbing record and was a member of the German-American attempt on Nanga Parbat in the Pamirs. The expedition was unsuccessful, but on his way home Herron stopped in Cairo and having climbed one Pyramid, was enthusiastic enough to do the second, Mena, also. On the way down, after all difficulty was over, he started to run, tripped in some way and fell to his death.

In our roving life in the Service we meet many conditions of life and reside in many surroundings, some congenial, some quite the reverse, but my habitation during that first year in Cairo stands out in memory as the nearest approach to Elysian perfection that we can ever expect to meet here below. It was nothing but a rather unprepossessing cement bungalow with two small rooms and a minute kitchen, but in what surroundings! In those days one of the old khedivial palaces on the island of Ghezireh had become the Ghezireh Palace Hotel which for seven or eight months of the year was closed and empty. It stood in the midst of a great park which for sheer loveliness would be hard to exceed anywhere and the park was full of flower beds, mostly full of great long-stemmed roses which, in the off-season, run in wild profusion. My bungalow was in that park and there was no other building near it, and on returning from the office I used to find it filled with those magnificent roses which would make even an American Beauty blush for shame. Those days and nights in that little bungalow brought a spiritual joy, a feeling of restfulness and a sense of peace and beauty, which can never be reproduced anywhere. Alas, it's all gone now. I visited Cairo a quarter of a century later and found the garden built up with private residences. My bungalow of course had disappeared, but the memory of it can never fade.

There was no gradual acclimatization on arriving in Cairo. It was on a very hot day of a very hot summer, July 19, 1904, to be precise, and the glass, as I now remember it, registered 118° Fahrenheit in the shade. One's eyes burned in the street and during the first few months I lived in town where the only relief lay in those occasional nightly excursions to the desert. But the heat bothered me not at all; my new surroundings, work and friends were far too interesting to let weather conditions intrude. Daily I played tennis at the club in Ghezireh and after a cold shower drove back in my little pony trap in the scented twilight to the club in town, feeling that life was marvelously good and that the world was mine.

But what of the diplomatic life? Well, I was still a clerk and my principal jobs, among other duties, were making out invoices and superintending the disinfection of evil-smelling hides. Fred Morgan was the Vice Consul General. He was finicky and fussy but a pleasant enough chief. When he took me to my first audience with the Khedive, Abbas Hilmi Pasha, he guessed at the appropriate costume without inquiring and we were a little chagrined to find ourselves quite inappropriately dressed.

John W. Riddle was the Diplomatic Agent and Consul General and, as it happened, one of our first career officers, if the holding of several successive posts could in those days be so construed.[2] Tall and lean, with a sweeping black moustache, he was a great gentleman and possessed an Old World courtliness of manner which immediately clothed him with distinction. He wrote in a clear, painstaking hand and, as I remember it, his drafting was clear and to the point, but I am quite sure that he never wrote or did anything that he did not actually have to write or do. His, I think, was a laissez-faire policy and in those olden days in the Service, when politics ruled, it was generally a very sound policy to follow. His desk was always piled high with unsorted papers and I could not help wondering how it was that urgent documents did not sometimes get lost in that mountain. I used to have the feeling that a disordered desk was indicative of a disordered mind, but that theory, I find, doesn't really hold water in practice because the desks of some of the ablest men I have known have been kept in just the same chronic confusion as that of my first chief. Personally I find it impossible to work in such conditions. Another quality of Mr. Riddle was great economy of words. Sometimes in Cairo he took me out for an afternoon's drive; in the beginning I used to burble like the brook, even in the face of monosyllabic replies, but soon learned to respect his silences and to restrain, albeit with difficulty, my impetuous chatter during long and what seemed to me grimly silent outings. In the way of instructing the aspiring neophyte in the intricacies of diplomacy, he did very little. But I liked and respected

2 Riddle had served as Secretary to the United States Legation in Turkey and to the United States Embassy in Russia before coming to Cairo.

him and was delighted to serve under him again in St. Petersburg a few years later. We always remained good friends until his death.

Ellery Sedgwick, who knew Riddle well, tells the following story to illustrate his precise type of mind. Sedgwick came on him one day poring over a book on his desk which proved to be the *Encyclopaedia Britannica.* "What on earth are you doing?" asked Sedgwick. "Well," replied Riddle, "when there is no bridge to play I enjoy hunting out errors in the *Encyclopaedia.*" "Catch any fish today?" "Yes," said Riddle, "three errors so far!"

Among the other diplomats in Cairo were several with whom we became intimate. The French Diplomatic Agent, Monsieur de la Boulinière, and especially his charming wife and four attractive daughters, became very good friends; we made frequent excursions and picnics together and kept in touch with them for many years, always calling on the family at their home in Buc near Versailles when passing through Paris.

Baron Rücker-Jenisch, the German Diplomatic Agent, was a distinguished and attractive man and a close friend of the Kaiser; we ran into him occasionally during our later days in Berlin. And the famous Baron Max Oppenheim was on his staff. Oppenheim was generally supposed to represent in Egypt the type of, shall we say "internationalist," so often portrayed by another Oppenheim in some of his most lurid stories of Continental life. As Oriental Secretary of the German Diplomatic Agency, he spoke Arabic fluently and his contacts were wide and varied.

But of course it was Lord Cromer [British Agent and Consul General, Minister Plenipotentiary in Egypt] who stood out among the diplomats, if so mighty a figure could even be classed with the diplomats. His position in those days was much more nearly that of a viceroy, and he exercised it to the full. Once, and I think only once, I had to beard the lion in his den, having been left for some six weeks as Chargé d'Affaires (although my high-sounding title was that of Deputy Consul General in Charge) and being obliged to discuss some point, now long

forgotten but probably connected with missionaries and schools.
My knees literally trembled as I entered the great man's study,
for he was, both in person and in fact, an awesome figure. But
the yawning chasm was successfully negotiated and I retired with
just a trifle more self-confidence merely for having gone through
the ordeal undaunted and, so far as I can now recollect, un-
dented. Incidentally, Lord Milner's book, *England in Egypt*
— published in New York in 1894 — was then my bible and
vade mecum and I knew it pretty well by heart which greatly
added to the interest of watching and studying current developments both in Egypt and the Sudan.

Slatin Pasha, who had been held for ten years in captivity
by the Mahdi and had ultimately escaped, was then at the
height of his fame and prestige, a gentle, fat little man, with
upturned moustaches and plastered with medals when in uniform. Later we came to know him well in Vienna during the
World War. Although Austrian by nationality, he refused to
fight against England on account of his old associations and
simply worked for the Red Cross during that trying time. How
he used to love Ambassador Penfield's suckling pigs at luncheon
in Vienna! But that is anticipating the story by many, many
years.

I was far from idle that first, terrifically hot summer. One
summer afternoon, several years later but still several years
before the war, in the good old times when our chanceries
generally closed at one o'clock for the day, a colleague from
another post wandered into the chancery in Berlin and found
me alone, hard at work. His amazement was quite genuine.
"What on earth are you doing?" he asked. "Oh," said I rather
shamefacedly, "I'm getting up a résumé of all the military
cases involving Americans of German birth since the beginning
of the Empire, so as to be able to show by graphs the percentage
of cases in which we have been able to get our naturalized citizens out of the German Army and the particular circumstances
which have brought failure or success. It may be useful as a
future guide." My colleague regarded me with real pity. "Cut
it out," he said (how well I remember his words because they

certainly cut me at the time), "work won't get you anywhere. Only politics count in our Service. Better enjoy yourself while you're in it." That was the guiding spirit in those days. But still, I felt differently. I had no political backing. I enjoyed work and it seemed to me that a reputation for hard work could not come amiss if we were ever to develop a professional Service. That colleague, incidentally, didn't last very long in our Service.

During that first summer in Cairo I gave up all thought of enjoying the night life and returned each evening to the chancery, first to study Arabic and secondly to bring some order out of chaos in our archives. In those days we had no general filing system whatever; all papers were filed chronologically and unless one happened to remember a previous document and its date there was no possibility of piecing out the background of any issue or of any case. So I bought a simple card catalogue and in three months of night work managed to index every paper on file for ten years back with cross references. My new chief, Lewis Iddings [American Agent and Consul General at Cairo] arrived in the autumn and I took him with pride to show him my handiwork.[3] But, alas, there was no "Well done thou good and faithful servant." He simply snorted and said: "You can put that thing down in the cellar; even if you have the energy to keep it up, your successors won't," and he left me alone with my shattered dream. In such devastating moments one has to take refuge in the lines of an old song which Billy Chilton [Sir Henry Getty Chilton], who later became an Ambassador in the British service, used to sing:

> The building of ambition
> Is fraught with strife and pain,
> But if your castle tumbles down,
> Just build it up again.

[3] Iddings had been on the staff of the *New York Tribune* and the *Evening Post* before starting on his career in the Foreign Service in 1897. He had served as Secretary and Chargé d'Affaires at Rome before coming to Cairo.

But in the face of such opposition there wasn't any earthly use in building up that catalogue, and down to the cellar it duly went. I suppose it's still there. The profit, be it said, was mine and mine alone. I dare say I would do it again under similar circumstances.

Iddings was a good chief. He also was fussy and something of a martinet, but he gave me a background of written English, from the point of view of composition, rhetoric and style, which far surpassed all my school and college training. When I drafted a letter or note or despatch, he would take up a blue pencil, reminiscent of his former days as a newspaperman, and with a few deft strokes would turn it into a concise, graceful, literary presentation. I profited greatly and remembering my appreciation of his helpfulness, I have tried in later years to render similar assistance to my own secretaries.

In spite of that summer night-work in the chancery it would be false to give the impression that life in Cairo was all work and no play. During the tourist season from November till April there was an almost constant round of gaiety including dinners, dances and picnics on the desert, and many pleasant friendships were formed with charming visitors. How can one ever forget the far-famed and lovely Hurly girls of Lynn, Massachusetts, both of whom soon embarked on romances with dashing British officers whom they later married? Or my attractive cousins, the Dangerfields? And many, many others. Cecil Higgins, of the British diplomatic service, was one of our group and later married one of the Cryder triplets of New York. Big towering Findlay [Mansfeldt de C. Findlay] was Counselor of the British Agency, Frank Lindley [Francis Oswald Lindley, Second Secretary] and Horace Rumbold [Horace George Montagu Rumbold, First Secretary] secretaries. Rumbold and I were again colleagues in Berlin and Berne and at the Conference of Lausanne; together we sealed up the archives of the British Embassy in Berlin on August 4, 1914, when our Embassy took over British interests during the war, and throughout the first three years of the war we constantly corresponded

because he, in the London Foreign Office, had to do with
questions involving prisoners of war. Good old Lindley and I
met again as Ambassadors in Tokyo some thirty years later.
One of the pleasantest aspects of our profession lies in the
warm friendships formed with colleagues, both in our own and
in foreign services. When we meet again at other posts we do
not have to get to know each other all over again, and the
mutual liking and mutual trust formed between diplomatic
officers of different nations is one of the most important and
valuable assets in our profession. Men who play a great deal
together get to know each other far better than those whose
relationship is confined to official contacts; confidence is often
developed and thus, without injury to any national interest,
information is mutually exchanged which helps governments
to piece out the international picture. In our various posts,
my wife, Alice, and I have formed many intimacies and many
permanent friendships both with Americans and foreigners
which have contributed greatly to the joy of our work and
will always remain wherever we may be.

In looking back on the social life of Cairo it is difficult
after all these years to recollect particular events, but I do
remember very clearly the visit of the then Prince and Princess of Wales, later King George V and Queen Mary, who
were entertained by Mr. and Mrs. Iddings at a big afternoon
reception. My wife has cause to remember it too, because she
was placed by Mrs. Iddings behind her and so close to the
wall that she found considerable difficulty in curtseying without losing her balance and falling ignominiously on the polished floor of the ballroom. I myself have cause to remember
a certain musicale at the British Agency because the virtuoso
of the occasion was late and my hostess, knowing that I had
a way of strumming, albeit inadequately, on the piano, suddenly approached me in front of the multitude of guests and
begged me to play something by way of a prelude to the great
man's arrival. I weakly consented and managed somehow to
accomplish an awful rendering of the "Frühlingsrauschen" by

Sinding. Just as I finished, the maestro was announced; he bowed to the guests, opened the piano top, adjusted the music stool with utmost care and then, after a few preliminary chords, proceeded to play, with many flourishes, magnificent sentiment, fire and brilliant execution, Sinding's "Frühlingsrauschen."

But music, dancing and dining were not the only form of sport of those halcyon days. We played tennis daily on the excellent courts at Ghezireh, and another form of sport once led me, unconsciously, into a situation of gravest danger. In the small native villages were erected towers of dried mud which served to attract the multitudes of wild pigeons and were so constructed that the natives could collect and use the guano for fertilizing their fields. But among the wild birds were many domestic pigeons which belonged to the villagers and were carefully protected. It was a usual form of sport among the officers of the resident British regiments to organize shooting parties to these villages and occasionally I was included. I did not know, however, that acute opposition to these shoots had been gradually mounting among the natives who resented the fact that their domestic pigeons, difficult sometimes to distinguish from the wild ones, were killed, and towards the end of my assignment in Cairo this feeling had approached the boiling point. It must have been but a few weeks before our final departure from Egypt that I joined one of these shooting parties to a village called Denshawi. No outward sign of mutiny among the natives was then visible, but my horror was great when a few weeks later, in France, I read of the historic and terrible "Denshawi Incident" in which the villagers mobbed just such a shooting party as those I had so recently participated in, killed a British captain, and, as I remember it, either killed or seriously injured several other officers.[4] Lord Cromer was absent at the time and Findlay was in charge. His responsibility was great, for he had to make an example of the murderers or risk further disturbances. I think that four men were

---

[4] On June 13, 1906, five British officers went to Denshawi to shoot pigeons. They were attacked by a group of the natives of the village. One officer lost his life and two others were injured. *The Times* (London), June 15, 1906, p. 5.

hanged and four flogged, alternately, on a scaffold erected in the village where the assault had taken place.[5] It was a grim reprisal and it excited grim repercussions in England. Upon the wisdom of the sentence, I do not presume to pass judgment. Presumably the officers knew something of the risk they were incurring in carrying on those shoots, and perhaps I, albeit unwittingly, had shared in a provocation which never ought to have been permitted. It was many years before I could forget the shock of that terrible news.

But those British officers were attractive fellows; the Inniskilling Fusiliers, the King's Royal Rifles and later the Rifle Brigade were stationed there in my time and often I messed with them on guest nights, always impressed by the solemn ceremony of drinking the King's health when the port came on: "Mr. Vice, the King! Gentlemen, the King! The King — God bless him!"

They taught me poker too, all one lurid evening. It cost, and how! Mother had to come to the rescue that time. I abjured that most fascinating of all games for many, many years. Considering that I was supposed to be living on a salary of $600 a year, and that I allowed myself a ten-cent instead of a five-cent cigar only on Saturday nights, it was slightly out of proportion to embark at that particular epoch on a gambling game of which I knew nothing whatever. I did learn it later but must frankly acknowledge that I am of far too curious a disposition ever to become a good poker player. Like the man from Missouri I always want to know, and in poker that is likely to become a very expensive tendency. In poker, patience is a virtue, possess it if you can, seldom found in woman and never (says Alice) found in man. Maybe she's right.

I have left till the last the really important event of my stay in Egypt: my parents came to visit me bringing with them Miss Alice de Vermandois Perry, their future daughter-in-law.

[5] The sentences passed by the special tribunal were carried out on June 28, 1906. One man was hanged first and left hanging while two others were whipped, another hanged and two more whipped, two others hanged and the final two whipped. *The Times* (London), June 29, 1906, **p. 5.**

They stayed at the Ghezireh Palace Hotel, directly opposite my bungalow. The reader will observe that the hotel was opposite the bungalow and not vice versa. I had the same feeling about that bungalow that the Englishman has about England, and I have always been able to understand how *The Times* of London, when once a fog covered the Channel for three days, reported in headlines: "Continent Isolated." So far as I was concerned, the hotel was merely an appendage, but it became a very attractive appendage when my fiancée came to it. Those were happy days. That summer I took a month's leave and went on an excursion to Turkey, Syria and the Holy Land. Peter Jay was Chargé d'Affaires in Constantinople at that time, and he kindly arranged for me to attend one of the Friday *selamliks*, where I was able to catch a hurried glimpse of Sultan Abdul Hamid as he drove in his open barouche the short distance from his palace to the mosque. It was a colorful scene. Good old Peter Jay! How we loved him and how greatly we enjoyed a visit to him and Susan in Rome many years later when we took a fiendish delight in plaguing our abstemious wives by calling frequently for our fictitious morning absinthes. Later I shall probably "extend," as the *Congressional Record* puts it, my observations concerning alcohol and its uses. But for the present let me merely say, with Omar Khayyám, that the grape, when properly used, is a gift of God and I have always felt, and still feel, that those organizations which call themselves Christian Temperance Unions are sailing under radically false colors. Rubbish! There's no temperance whatever in their doctrine and their preaching. Temperance means moderation and the term has become, by usage, clothed with a connotation entirely unjustified by its literal derivation. If prohibition is meant, why not say it? I have never been able to square the two terms as analogous. And I do, most profoundly, believe in temperance just as strongly as I disbelieve in prohibition.

Then in September I set sail for home and on October 7, 1905, Alice and I were married on a gorgeous autumn day at the country home of Mrs. Samuel Cabot, Alice's aunt, in Ponkapog, Massachusetts. Very early in the morning of the big day I arose and took a ten-mile run across country, so that by the time of the wedding my nerves were under perfect control. I wanted to be sure to avoid the situation of certain friends of mine who had been obliged to lie on the couch and take deep breaths for half an hour before their own ceremonies. Edward Everett Hale, famous author of *The Man Without a Country* married us. Dr. Hale was a splendid old man, with a long beard and a face full of wisdom. When I asked him in advance just what I was to do about the ring, he regarded me gravely and said: "Young man, I will tell you at the appropriate moment." My honored and sportive father-in-law, Mr. Perry, rapidly took the sting out of this rebuff. He beckoned me into an adjoining room just before the ceremony, opened a window and said: "Your last chance, and I won't say a word!" Few men have been blessed with such a father-in-law as Tom Perry; his deep erudition, his brilliant conversation, his sparkling humor into which no dirt was ever allowed to penetrate, made him the most congenial of companions, and while enjoying the privilege of that companionship I sat at his feet and learned.

After our honeymoon in the Maine woods, we returned to Cairo. That winter of 1905–1906 we spent in an apartment in the old khedivial harem belonging to Colonel Jimmie Watson, a congenial officer in the Egyptian army. Apart from the happiness of that first year of married life my thoughts turn irresistably back to our Arab cook. Bakr was his name, black as original night, with a flashing celestial smile, whose *oeufs à la tripe* I have never managed to have even approximately duplicated anywhere.

I must not leave Cairo without a word about our kawasses, those gorgeously costumed diplomatic guards with their fezzes, gold-embroidered jackets, tremendous bloomers, sashes and businesslike swords. I won't say much about our head kawass. He hadn't been there as long as the others, I believe. Once, when I wanted to buy a pony for my trap, he had one of his friends bring around a splendid little beast which I bought and paid for on the spot, but when I looked for the pony the next day the kawass came with outspread hands, that all-expressive gesture: "Allah be his witness, the dealer had gone with both money and pony and completely disappeared into the desert." The pony never, never came back. The kawass didn't last very long. But kawass No. 2, old Ali, was a perpetual joy. He must have been well over six feet tall, black as ebony, with an inherent dignity but a dazzling smile and a spirit of ever-ready helpfulness which endeared him to all of us. I was happy many years later — in 1937 — to receive a letter from the then American Minister, Mr. Bert Fish, asking for a small contribution from all former officers in Cairo to buy a testimonial for Ali on the twenty-fifth anniversary of his service. He highly deserved it.

But all good things must end. We had loved our stay in Egypt, for it was a perpetually romantic, always congenial post. We had learned perhaps not very much, but still a little of diplomatic life and work. It had certainly whetted our eagerness to follow the career. Towards the end of that winter came the news of my appointment by President Theodore Roosevelt as Third Secretary of Embassy in Mexico City which filled me with great joy. The future looked rosy and full of happiness. Perhaps it is as well that we cannot pierce the veil of future events too soon, for had we known what the Mexican assignment had in store, our satisfaction would have been all too grimly curbed. The *Caledonia* had brought us to Egypt; the *Cleopatra* took us away, in April, 1906, and later to our surprise it was the very same old *Cleopatra* that took us from Italy to my first ambassadorship in Turkey, twenty-one years later.

Thus the perfumed romance of Egypt fades, and the rugged mountains of Mexico swing gradually into the picture of our roving life.

III

Mexico

1906 – 1907

*En route from Cairo to Mexico, the Grews visited Venice,
Paris, and Giverny-par-Vernon in Normandy, where Mrs.
Grew's parents were spending the summer. Mrs. Grew remained at Giverny to have her first baby. "My own problem
was expeditiously settled," Mr. Grew later wrote. "There was
not a shadow of a doubt that I must 'proceed to my post' forthwith, nor did I feel that in my situation as a neophyte not yet
firmly located even on the first rung of the ladder of the
Service I could afford to explain to Washington by cable or
letter our family circumstances and ask for leave even before
assuming the job to which the President had most considerately appointed me. So I took the very first ship to America,
the old* Kaiser Wilhelm der Grosse *I think it was, and promptly
reported at the State Department as on my way. Robert Bacon
was then Assistant Secretary of State under Elihu Root. If the
incumbent of that position had been anyone less full of human
sympathy than Bob Bacon it is doubtful whether I would have
been permitted to attend the arrival of our first-born, but
Bacon didn't hesitate a moment; he simply said: 'You go back
to your wife until the baby is there, and we'll attend to Mexico
and will keep the place for you.' Bless him for what Solomon
called an understanding heart. That sort of thing wouldn't
be so simple nowadays, especially in the case of a young officer
just entering the Service, but in those old days the regulations
and discipline were less strict and the work, if not a sinecure,
at least far less heavy. I met Elihu Root, too, just as I had
met John Hay who was Secretary of State when I went to
Cairo. Then, by the first ship, back to Giverny." During the*

29

summer, Mr. Grew wrote Sport and Travel in the Far East, *which was published in 1910. Edith Agnes Grew was born on September 24, 1906. Soon after her birth Mr. Grew left for his post in Mexico where his position was that of Third Secretary of Embassy at a salary of $1200 a year. There were then no extra allowances whatever. Officers were obliged to pay their transportation expenses to and from their posts.*

I CAME to Mexico in November, Alice and the baby arriving a month or so later. The then chancery entirely occupied a large and modern building of residential type on one of the quiet streets in the residential quarter, and my own office, even as Third Secretary, the lowest form of official if not of human life, was a splendid big room with a luxurious rug, very large windows and a businesslike roll-top desk. The Ambassador's house was some distance away. So far as I am aware, it is only in the American Foreign Service that the chancery is called the embassy or legation, as distinguished from the ambassador's or the minister's residence. Sometimes, of course, the chancery or office is in or adjoining the ambassador's or minister's residence, so that the same term covers both, but then when they are separate it is the residence and not the office that in other services is called the embassy or legation, while the office or office building is officially termed the chancery or chancellery. As the United States comes to possess its own official diplomatic residences in the various capitals, I think that this discrepancy in terminology will, perhaps gradually, disappear. It is often a source of misunderstanding in foreign countries where visitors or guests are frequently directed to the wrong address, and since in some capitals the residence and chancery are widely separated in distance, embarrassments occur. It seems to me that the foreign terminology is more appropriate than ours. An ambassador is the personal representative of his sovereign or chief of state, and just as the White House, as distinguished from the Executive Offices, is the official center of the President's representative life, so the ambassador's residence, as distinguished from the chancery, is the official center of his representative life. This argument seems to me to be logical, and I think it should equally apply in the case of ministers and legations, for, while a minister does not represent the person of his sovereign or chief of state, he is nevertheless just as much an official representative of his country as is an ambassador.

My new chief was David E. Thompson, a rugged, self-made man in the best sense of our American tradition, for he had begun life as a truckman and brakeman on a railroad, had risen to the job of superintendent and thence to higher positions whence he exerted influence and power in the railway world; he became Minister and then our first Ambassador to Brazil and ultimately moved by promotion to Mexico. I should not call him an easy chief; there was no reason in the world why he should look on his Secretaries of Embassy as in any way different from his former railway employees, and quite properly he was exacting. One day when I had been in the Embassy but a few weeks I asked to see him, said that I had always been dependent on regular exercise and asked whether, in view of the early winter darkness, he would have any objection to my slipping out occasionally in the middle of the afternoon, when my work was up to date, to get a game of tennis. That was a very, very unwise step. I can see him even today, sitting like a great shaggy lion at his desk, the vein on his forehead swelling with anger until it had become quite purple, regarding me first with amazement and then with uncontrollable fury, smashing his great fist on the blotter and shouting: "By no means. You will stay in your office every day until five, including Saturdays." Yes, that was an unwise and, as it turned out, a quite unnecessary step, because, as the Ambassador gradually found that I worked hard and was fond of hard work, I slipped quietly out whenever I pleased and he said not a word. He had a very human and gentle streak, too, and whenever he saw my wife or the baby, and during Alice's subsequent illness, that delightfully gentle side expressed itself in full measure. We became very fond of him, although we were not with him long. Many years later in July, 1912,

he called at our Embassy in Vienna at a time when I was Chargé
d'Affaires to ask that I find him a reliable chauffeur to take
the place of one whom he had discharged for drinking while
he was touring Europe. He had recently lost his wife and was
sad and dejected. I found for him a good man, and for years
afterwards he used to send us Christmas postcards, or a box
of cigars.

Fenton McCreery, an old hand in the Service, was First
Secretary, a splendid fellow of gentle mien and speech and with
a goatee which inevitably associated him with the southern
title "Colonel." He ultimately became Minister to Honduras
and then dropped out of the ranks. But he, even with his
gentle personality, could become, as the speaker at his farewell banquet put it, "a man of Flint (Michigan)." Paxton
Hibben was Second Secretary, and on one occasion McCreery,
then Chargé d'Affaires, had gone away for the weekend and
had given Hibben explicit instructions to send no telegrams to
Washington until his return, but came back to find that Hibben had done just the contrary and had sent a long telegram
airing his own views on a certain political question. I happened to be present at the McCreery-Hibben interview on the
afternoon of the former's return; he was in riding togs and
punctuated his coruscating observations with his riding whip,
not on Hibben but on the desk, but the verbal lashing the
latter received was just about as effective as if the punishment
had been physical instead. The usually gentle volcano had exploded, and most effectively. I saw it happen only once, and
once was enough.

After looking around for a few weeks we found what proved
to be one of the most attractive habitations we have ever dwelt
in, and in that respect, considering our many posts, fourteen
in forty years, and the rapidity of many of our transfers, we
have been extraordinarily lucky. This particular house was
in a suburb of Mexico City, Tacubaya by name; the rooms
opened on to a wide verandah which in turn gave on a lovely
garden full of great tropical trees, shrubs and flowers, and although the taste of its interior furnishings was pretty awful,

Alice, as she has always done in every post, soon had at least a room or two tidied up in presentable style, leaving only one "chamber of horrors" to which we relegated the antimacassars and other atrocities. Alas, the lovely pieces of Spanish furniture then acquired disappeared between Mexico and our next post and we never saw them again.

I can never think of that old house in Tacubaya without remembering Bully. Bully went with the house. He was a fat and waddly bulldog with a face that would have made Cerberus look like a friendly kitten in comparison, but his heart and nature were of pure gold. Whenever we came home from the city, there was Bully, craning what neck he had, which was practically nil, around the corner waiting for us and wagging, not just his tail, but his entire ungainly self in one big wag. Alice and I agree that when (and if) St. Peter decides in due course at the appropriate moment to throw open the golden gates for our triumphal entry, there will be Bully, just one big wag, craning his neckless neck around the corner waiting for us with his hideous seraphic smile, and behind him, if we guess aright, will be all the others whom we have so dearly loved, Jimmie and Danny, Kim and Sambo, Micky and Sasha and Sailor, and all the rest of them. Our dogs have been just as much members of the family as the family itself; the joy of companionship and the strains of parting have been just as intense. It simply cannot be that such vivid personalities can ever sink into utter oblivion. No, we must and shall meet again to renew and to treasure permanently the old association and affection. Bully's sudden taking off was a wrench that we shall never forget. Our Mexican chauffeur, a mere boy, used to take him into town in the car sometimes, and one day he returned without Bully. I hurried back along the road and found him, run over and quite dead. How it happened, we never knew. Indeed our sorrow was such that we didn't care very much about the details, but we did care very much that that wretched boy had left Bully's beloved body uncared for in the dusty road as unworthy of respect.

There was another incident on that dusty road that led into

the city, but its results were far from regrettable. We had bought our first automobile, a necessity for commuting. It was a sort of prehistoric two-cylinder Cadillac. Think of it. Two cylinders! It chugged and it smelt and we used to call it the two-candle-power stinkomobile. But still, it went — sometimes. That winter a new vision appeared in one of the shop windows downtown. It was one of those magnificent chariots, high off the ground and painted a gorgeous and vivid light and dark green, known as a Pope Hartford. I coveted that Pope Hartford with all my mind and with all my heart and with all my soul, but its price was far, far beyond my meager competence. And then my dear mother came down to visit us. Alice was driving her into town one morning when (no, Gentle Reader, it was not prearranged) both front wheels of that two-candle-power stinkomobile flew off at precisely the same moment, throwing Alice, who was talking, with her teeth clenched into the front seat while Mother flew gracefully over the radiator into the dusty road. Mother picked herself up, unhurt but very, very, indignant, and said with emphasis: "Alice, you must never ride in that car again. Joe must get a new one this very afternoon." Joe, being the most dutiful of sons, obeyed, and thus the Pope Hartford came into the family and remained there for many years, going with us to Russia and then to Germany and serving faithfully for a long, long time. And how I loved that old Cadillac for its noble self-sacrifice and its perfectly timed suicide! That was really one of the most magnificent acts of devotion I've ever witnessed.

My work in the Embassy was steady but not exhilarating. I had to deal with some of the miscellaneous correspondence, but most of it was simply making neat typewritten copies of outgoing documents for the permanent files. We never made carbon copies in those days; the outgoing documents were moistened and impressed on tissue pages in a copybook and then again typed for the bound archives. This, of course was a tremendous waste of time and labor, and the risk of errors in typing was ever present while carbon copies cannot go wrong. I don't remember why carbon paper wasn't used. Perhaps in

those days the results were smoochy and unneat. Or perhaps it
was due just to the old conservatism which looks askance at any
change in system. I remember very well that one British Ambassador in Paris absolutely refused to allow a typewriter in his
chancery at first, insisting that every document must be written
in longhand according to sacred tradition, but even he had to
give in at last although, as I remember it, he strictly limited
this infamous intrusion of mechanized diplomacy to a single
machine. How I wish he could have seen, and heard, the big
ballroom in our Embassy in Berlin along about 1915 which
sounded something like a boiler factory with thirty or forty
typewriters banging away at the same time.

Our life during those comparatively few months in Mexico
was socially rather quiet, for we went out but little. I remember once meeting at the opera Porfirio Díaz, that fine old
rugged dictator who had ruled Mexico so long and, probably,
so wisely, because at least there were no revolutions for a
longer period than perhaps ever before; and we occasionally
met some of the older Mexicans whose distinction and culture
could hardly be surpassed in any country. Old white-headed
José Yves Limantour, the Minister of Finance, was always a
prominent figure both in the official and social world.

Among the diplomats, Baron Hans von Wangenheim, the
German Minister, and his beautiful statuesque wife, stood out
with distinction. He was a devotee of music and played
Wagner magnificently on the piano, a characteristic which
seemed to belie his rough and rugged manner and personality.
He later rendered important service to his country in Constantinople in the early years of the First World War. He is buried
there in the summer Embassy park overlooking the Bosporus.
Johanna, the Baroness, we knew in Berlin in later years.

Reginald Tower was the British Minister to Mexico. He was
very tall and thin and the tale is told of an occasion, when the
diplomats were being entertained on a government trip to
southern Mexico, how he became separated from his colleagues
and rode hither and yon on his diminutive donkey, his long
legs touching the ground, inquiring plaintively, "Donde está

el cuerpo diplomatico?" a cliché which always mightily amused me.

But a young Third Secretary, with a wife whose main interests just then centered around that blessed baby, was not likely to make much of a splurge in the social world even if he had been thus inclined, which he wasn't at all. The home life appealed mightily. We had our American friends, of course, and I especially remember the Seegers, who had long lived in Mexico City, in the motorcar business I think, and of knowing as a boy young Alan who later wrote that inexpressibly beautiful poem "I Have a Rendezvous with Death" and himself went to the meeting place, head high and unafraid.

Mexico City itself is a lovely place. The air, as I remember it, was almost always crystal clear; Chapultepec Castle built on a high isolated rock and its surrounding park, through which we passed on our way to Tacubaya, and the Paseo de la Reforma, that majestic avenue leading out to Chapultepec through geometrically regular blocks of the great city, were beautiful, and the snow-covered mountains in the distance, Popocatepetl and Ixtaccihuatl, lent an impressive background to the far-flung city. But what we most enjoyed was a trip down into the valley to Cuernavaca, the old capital, luxuriant in jungle growth and vivid tropical flowers and the red and yellow walls of its ancient Spanish buildings, where picturesque scenes of great beauty and the balmy air of the lowlands gave a most welcome change from the high-strung atmosphere of Mexico City.

And now we must lower the curtain on a grimmer note to terminate this brief period of our career. I know not whether it was that high-strung atmosphere, for Mexico City is over seven thousand feet high, or some other fundamental or abetting cause which led to the trouble which now beset my wife. The first symptom I noticed was loss of taste; she began to complain that the food had lost its savor, while to my own sensitive palate the high spices of Mexican cooking, especially the omnipresent chile con carne, had lost nothing whatever of their redhot hotness. Then her eyesight began to go, her sense of touch and her sense of balance. Let us draw a veil over those awful last few days, for all this developed within a single week. The doctors failed to diagnose the trouble and only advised getting her down to sea level as soon as possible. The parting on the night train to Vera Cruz, with a handful of friends to see us off, was strange and very sad. On the ship to New York, with a trained nurse in charge, there was little improvement. She was carried on a stretcher into our house in Boston and two of the foremost physicians in Boston, Alice's uncle, Arthur Cabot, and Dr. Frederick Shattuck were called. They told me afterwards that when I described the symptoms before they saw the patient, both mentally agreed that she could not live.

But she lived. This was in November, 1906. I had been in Mexico eight months, and Alice six. Towards spring, when her health began to show improvement, I went down to Washington and saw the authorities who very considerately arranged an early transfer, and on May 7, 1907, my appointment as Third Secretary of Embassy at St. Petersburg, Russia, was announced.

So another chapter in a very different scene now opens. It was a scene which we shall never forget, for it enabled us to participate in almost the last days of a mighty but crumbling empire before the cataclysm of the great war shattered the old order beyond repair.

IV

St. Petersburg
1907 – 1908

BY EASY STAGES we went to St. Petersburg, Alice and the baby
waiting in Paris until I could find an apartment. Never shall I
forget that journey into, for me, the unknown. A day or two
in Berlin were rendered delightful by the hospitality of John
Garrett and Basil Miles, respectively the Second and Third
Secretaries in the Embassy. As a matter of fact I had asked for
the third secretaryship in Berlin, hoping to be able to serve
under Charlemagne Tower, Ambassador to Germany, whose
reputation in the Service stood very high, but Miles was moved
to Berlin and I took his place in St. Petersburg. As things
turned out it was a fortunate development because we were
thus able to see Russia while the old Tsarist Court was still
carrying on, and Berlin came later. That year in Russia
rounded out a career of varied and rich experiences. But for
the present, my impressions were vividly centered on the journey, the crossing of the frontier at Wirballen, presenting a passport for the first time at any frontier and then, on the broad-
gauge railway and in the wide comfortable Russian sleeper,
disappearing at an unhurried pace into the seemingly endless
stretches of the dense forest while the sparks from the broad
funnel of the wood-burning engine drifted past the window.

Alice enjoyed the same journey a few weeks later, and the
ordeal of the frontier was entirely simplified by the courtesy of
a Russian gentleman traveling on the same train who presented
her passport to the authorities and saw her through without
any of the usual formalities. Indeed, she and the baby were
the first to get on the other train. Just before reaching the end
of the journey he said to her: "I hope we meet often in St.

Petersburg," and Alice replied that she knew I would wish to thank him for his helpfulness and, with what I am sure must have been a proud flourish, gave him my official visiting card, just lithographed at Brentano's in Paris, bearing the imposing title "Third Secretary of the American Embassy." She put his own card into her bag and didn't look at it until we both examined it later. It read "The Grand Duke Nicholas Michaelovitch"! How we laughed!

I had taken an unfurnished apartment in a splendid new building at Kamennoostrovsky Prospect, on Kamennoostrov Island, not far from the Troitsky Bridge across the Neva to St. Petersburg proper and nearly adjoining the big villa of the famous ballet dancer Ksessinskaya, the favorite of the Tsar and of many of the Grand Dukes. We saw her sometimes, a lovely creature. Directly above us was the apartment of Baron Ramsay, one of the Masters of Ceremony at Court, who had married Fanny Whitehouse of New York, a sister of Sheldon Whitehouse, long in our Service. There were many American women married to Russians, among whom Princess Serge Belosselsky, née Susie Whittier of Boston, and Princess "Mike" Cantacuzène, née Julia Grant of New York, stood out prominently as among the most charming and beautiful. Princess Orloff, a younger sister of Belosselsky, was another very attractive friend of ours. They were all lovely and our memories of St. Petersburg, even if somewhat blurred by time, is one of many beautiful women.

Perhaps I ought to draw a discreet veil over the two or three months after Alice's arrival, for they reflect little credit on the spirit of co-operation in the Service as it existed in those old days. But first I must go back and record the troubles of our arrival in Mexico. We had sent our heavy baggage ahead from Cairo, and when I found that we were to spend the summer in France a telegram was sent to our Embassy in Mexico City requesting that on arrival it be stored until we should come. But it wasn't stored. It lay out on the open docks in Vera Cruz all summer in the tropical rains and sun. On arriving I asked an express company to bring it to Mexico City. The authorities there requested my keys for customs examination to which we replied that owing to our diplomatic privilege the trunks should be passed without examination. But they weren't. The customs authorities, without waiting for our keys, tore open every trunk, unpacked every article and stuffed our possessions back as if loading potato sacks. Then they gave the baggage to a common carter to drive it to our house in Tacubaya. The carter must have taken it to his own house first, because when we came to unpack, more than half of our wedding-present silver and certainly more than half of Alice's wardrobe, just fitted out in Paris, had disappeared. She couldn't find a complete dress of which either skirt or blouse hadn't gone. I duly sued the Mexican Government and several years later lost the case and had to pay the costs. So much for the co-operation of the Embassy.

That astonishing lack of co-operation was now once again to cause us great and needless expense and infinite hardship. Immediately on learning of our appointment in Russia in May, I had sent a telegram to the Embassy in Mexico asking that our baggage and furniture be promptly shipped to St. Petersburg. It was two full months before we took our apartment and, since the hotels were fearfully expensive, we bought some kitchen utensils and moved in to camp there until our things should arrive. We expected them daily. I well remember that our salon furnishings during that cheerful period consisted exclusively of a grand piano and two kitchen chairs. When three months had gone by since my telegram to the Embassy I wired the Ambassador: "When were our effects shipped?" He replied: "Effects not yet shipped. Awaiting your keys for final customs examination"! My reply to the Ambassador I believe holds the Service record for official profanity. Well, the baggage came, two months later, five months in all, but the furniture never came and has never been heard of since. I never even received a bill of lading and subsequent correspondence failed to produce one. That's enough of that episode. An officer who didn't like an assignment once said to me, when I was serving as Chairman of the Personnel Board

many years later: *"You* don't know what it means. You have
never had to rough it in the Service!" No, it is not a bed of
roses. But it's the most splendid, exhilarating, stimulating,
satisfying and withal useful form of service I can imagine. The
difficulties and handicaps that one inevitably meets are a thousand times worthwhile. Had I to choose all over again, I would
make precisely the same choice determined on that momentous
day in Tours.

The impressions of that summer and winter in St. Petersburg, recollected even through the haze of the many intervening years, still form in our minds a vividly colored mosaic.
First of all were the white nights, so light that one could read
in the street at midnight, and the clop-clop of the droshky
horses as they plodded over the wooden pavements. Then
came winter and the long, long daily walks from our house
to the chancery at Galernaya 45 (how well I remember that
number, *sorrok-pyat,* and our prodigious telephone number,
dvaisti-pedissiat-pyat-vwossimdisit-vwossim, and how, incidentally, the St. Petersburg telephone system, installed by an American company, was one of the very best in the world). That
daily walk was just about three miles. It led me across the
Troitsky Bridge over the Neva and along the long Naberezh-
naya or quays, facing the river and with some of the finest
houses in the city set back from the waterfront, with the big
fortress and prison island of St. Peter and St. Paul lying omin-
ously on the opposite side of the Neva. Then the tremendous
Winter Palace, the fatal spot where, only two years earlier,
the Cossacks had charged and killed a great number of peasants
coming to the Palace under the leadership of Father Gapon —
Georgii Gapon, Russian Orthodox priest and revolutionary —
to present a petition to the Tsar, which started the sporadic
revolution of 1905, and so past The Admiralty and through
the big Issachievskaya Ploshad or square with the great St.
Isaac's Orthodox Cathedral standing out in commanding im-
pressiveness under its enormous dome, its beautiful bells chim-
ing through the city on religious holidays, of which there were
very many throughout the year. In midwinter I used to cross

the bridge with the sun just rising, somewhere between nine and ten o'clock in the morning (we didn't have to keep very long hours in the office in those comparatively idle days), and returned about three, with the sun already on the verge of disappearance. But those three miles were covered quickly enough; one had to move rapidly or risk freezing to death. The inside of one's nose quickly froze up, rendering breathing difficult, and there were big charcoal braziers on every other street corner where passers-by could warm themselves a little before dashing on to the next.

John Riddle, who had been our chief in Cairo, was the Ambassador, Montgomery Schuyler, First Secretary, and Irwin Laughlin, Second Secretary. There was little enough official work, and once again my own duties dealt largely with miscellaneous correspondence and typing the permanent records. After several months in the Embassy I persuaded the Ambassador as to the patent advantages of the carbon-copy system, both from the point of view of laborsaving and of accuracy, and he gave orders that the new system would be adopted on January 1st. But, alas, I had failed to observe one of the rudiments of tact; the First Secretary was my senior and chief of the chancery and I had not won him over first; in fact, I had gone over his head, perhaps well knowing that a suggestion from a mere Third Secretary would have been highly out of order and peremptorily discarded. So my victory was short-lived, our charming but complacent chief bowed to the storm which then broke about his ears and back we went to the old, old system of permanent transcription of every document which must have accorded with diplomatic usage ever since Noah made out his inventory for the ark.

EXCERPTS FROM LETTERS HOME

June 2, 1907

Petersburg was reached on Friday afternoon, May 31st, in a half rain half snow storm.

The first two days of my stay were bitterly cold, very un-

usual for May as it is usually a warm month, but today, Sunday,
is beautiful, cold and crisp but clear and sunny and I feel
as if I could walk ten miles and enjoy them. The most extraordinary thing about the place is that now it is hardly ever dark
during the 24 hours; last night I went to a reception at ten; it
was then light enough to read, and when I came out at one,
it was daylight again. The whole darkness of the night had
taken place within those three hours. But how will it be in
winter when there are only about three hours of daylight?
Our electric light bill will ruin me.

Later when I have begun to meet people I shall tell you
what I can of them, but for the present my impressions are
confined to the city itself. It is a fine city in that the official
buildings are magnificent; the Winter Palace is the most imposing edifice I have certainly ever seen, but it looks as dead
as it is, with all the curtains down and no sign of life about
it; the Emperor, Nicholas II, lives out at Tsarskoye Selo and
never comes to the city now, so of course there is no court
life whatsoever. I was disappointed in the famous Nevsky
Prospect — it is merely a very long business street like the
Calle San Francisco only of course much broader. But the
quays along the river Neva are really beautiful; the fashionable
drive runs along the river and the finest houses front on it.

You would be much amused, as of course you will be some
day, to see the *izvostchiks* or cabs here; they are tiny little open
carriages with barely room for two people to sit side by side,
and the driver placed about a foot from your nose, padded out
to about three times his natural size, with a funny little hat and
bushy hair and beard. You see thousands of them everywhere
— very much more numerous than in Mexico or even in
Cairo — dashing along as if each had the whole road to himself.
The more padded the driver, the more fashionable the carriage, and the drivers of really swell private turnouts are padded
so enormously that you can scarcely find the driver in his uniform.

June 17, 1907

. . . I have been doing nothing exciting since my arrival and have seen few people except at the Polo Club where we play tennis three times a week. The Grand Duke [Uncle of Tsar Nicholas II] and Duchess Vladimir were there the first time we went and we were duly presented; being a little rusty on just what to do, Curtis [Charles B. Curtis, secretary to Ambassador Riddle] and I bowed formally from a distance of about ten feet, but to our surprise the Grand Duchess helped us out by saying, "Oh come on, boys, shake hands," which we accordingly did. . . .

I was fortunate to see the Duma before it was dissolved; in fact I was there at its last session. It is indeed an interesting body, being made up as it is of so many different races — Mohammedans, Chinese, Finns, Poles, Jews, etc., and many representatives of the peasant class, with great shocks of hair, collarless, and with their great cowhide boots coming up to their knees. Yesterday the manifestoes dissolving the Duma were posted in every street; the Government had demanded the surrender of 55 Social Democrats for punishment for revolutionary propaganda, which of course was refused, this being merely a pretext to prorogue the Duma.[1] The city is still quiet but there seems to be a possibility of trouble as the people are very discontented. The city is heavily guarded with troops, all stations, post offices, banks, etc. Last Wednesday a bank was robbed in broad daylight and several innocent people shot in the fight which ensued between the soldiers and the looters, and the same day an official in the Admiralty was assassinated. But these events were not at all connected with the dissolving of the Duma. It is exceedingly interesting to see just what will happen. I dine every night with the various newspaper correspondents here and so hear at first hand what is going on, and what is likely to occur. . . .

[1] The second Duma had assembled March 5, 1907. It was dissolved on June 16, 1907, after the Duma had refused to take away the privilege of immunity from and surrender the Social Democrats, a revolutionary party accused by the police of planning to stir mutiny in the army. Bernard Pares, *The Fall of the Russian Monarchy* (London: Jonathan Cape, 1939), pp. 100–102.

June 26, 1907

I have little news to tell you for my life is a simple and quiet one. I find the Russian language fascinating, and am putting in some really hard work on it. I find the best way to grasp it is to learn by heart little Russian fables and stories; this fixes the words in one's mind and gradually the grammatical forms begin to assume shape and mean something to one. At first it is like bucking up against a stone wall, for it seems to resemble nothing that one has ever learned before. I have an excellent teacher, a woman who teaches many of the various other secretaries in the Diplomatic Corps, and am much encouraged by her telling me that if I continue to work hard as I am now working, I shall begin to express myself in three months.

I have joined an excellent tennis club, called the Krestovsky Club, out on the islands near the Polo Club; they have the best courts of any club I have ever seen, being literally perfect; the standard of tennis there is very high and they send teams all over the country, to Moscow, Stockholm, the Riviera, etc. I shall enjoy it greatly. At present I am playing in a tournament, in which I won a match yesterday and play another today. . . .

I dined one night last week with the British Ambassador and Lady Nicolson. A few nights later I went out to a *datcha* or country house owned by Czekonics, an Austrian, and Nevile Henderson, a British secretary, and had a most pleasant evening. . . .[2]

---

2 It is interesting to look back on the later careers of some of my St. Petersburg diplomatic colleagues, several of whom worked up to the highest places in their respective services. Nevile Henderson, a young secretary in the British Embassy, later became Ambassador to Germany just prior to the Second World War and wrote the well-known book *Failure of a Mission* — New York, 1940. Hugh O'Beirne, Counselor of the British Embassy, was lost with Lord Kitchener in the First World War in the sinking of the cruiser *Hampshire*. Cerutti, Italian secretary, later became Ambassador to France; Czekonics, Austrian, also became an Ambassdor. Paravicini, Swiss secretary, became Minister to Great Britain, Djevad Bey, Turkish secretary, was later Ambassador to Great Britain. Baron von Schoen, secretary of the Bavarian Legation, became a German Ambassador. Count Leopold Berchtold, Counselor of the Austro-Hungarian

July 20, 1907

I greatly hope you will see St. Petersburg some day soon; you must visit us if it is possible; the beauty of the city grows on one and it must be fascinating in winter. The view which we get as we cross the Troitsky Bridge to our apartment is very lovely, especially at night when the spires of the many great churches in the city are half wrapped in haze; these "white nights" are truly beautiful. The Neva is always full of interest and very busy; all the wood that is burned throughout the long winter must be brought in during the very short summer; it comes in great barges from Finland and lies along the quays while being unloaded, thousands and thousands of tons of it. The principal streets are formed of octagonal blocks of wood fitted together and resting on a concrete bed — an ideal system, for it is soft to the horses' feet and deadens the noise — but it has to be renewed every two years, and during the summer all the principal thoroughfares are in a state of upheaval which is very annoying. Of course the small cost of wood and labor is the only reason for such a system. There are always many large ships in the Neva too; often private yachts come in and anchor right off the quays and Russian warships are generally in evidence; their navy is slowly being rebuilt (since the losses in the war with Japan); a few weeks ago a fleet of 28 brand-new torpedo-boat destroyers anchored in the heart of the city; they had been built from the school taxes and the Government wanted to show the people what they had got for their money; so they lay off the quays for several days, covered with flags, their officers holding continual receptions on board and thousands of people coming down to the river to see them at all hours.

Whatever interest you have in the political state of the country can be easily satisfied by the papers, for they are generally pretty full of Russian topics. There has been a

Embassy, returned to St. Petersburg as Ambassador after a year's absence and was subsequently Foreign Minister in Vienna at the time of my own later service in that capital. All of us young secretaries played around together in St. Petersburg, and the friendships then formed were very helpful at other posts in later years. — J. C. G.

good deal of outcry against the dissolving of the Duma and the Government is even less popular than before; but there are so many clashing factions that no one sentiment prevails. Over 1000 political prisoners have been taken and shipped off to Siberia in the last fortnight and every prison here is full.

Did I tell you that I saw the Tsaritsa, Alexandra, the other day? She had come in from Peterhof, the summer palace, for the day and happened to cross the Troitsky Bridge almost beside my carriage; she was going into the fortress of Peter and Paul which lies very close to our apartment; I should have recognized her by seeing everyone taking off their hats as she passed if by no other means. The Tsar never comes in to the city now; it would be the height of folly if he values his life; I am going to send this letter by the pouch today, so there is no harm in speaking openly. I am told that all letters in the ordinary mails are opened by the Russian authorities and that they are very clever in removing the seals and replacing them; but I don't know how much faith to put in such a statement. I should say that it would better be taken with a grain of salt, especially in the case of English letters. But I should not like to have a letter of mine fail to reach you because the Russian officials found revolutionary expressions in it! [3]

August 3, 1907

We had a thoroughly delightful little trip to Moscow. . . . There you feel as if you have been carried back into the midst of medieval times; it was, of course, the capital of Russia up

[3] The story is told of an enterprising and imaginative young American in Russia who wrote to a well-known professor of entomology in the United States that he was enclosing three Russian fleas for the professor's collection. He enclosed no fleas but sealed the envelope and sent it off through the open mails. When the professor received the envelope, however, the three fleas were all there — and very active. Clearly the Russian censors, after reading the letter, supposed that the fleas had escaped when the envelope was steamed open in their own office, and as this would have been an embarrassing give-away of their supposedly secret methods, they conscientiously enclosed the three fleas before resealing and forwarding the letter. The vision of those deluded censors painstakingly interrupting their work until they could catch threes fleas always brought a laugh when the story was told. — J. C. G.

to a comparatively recent date, and everything that has to do
with the ancient tsars is preserved there, chiefly in the Kremlin
or great walled city in the center of the present town. The
palace is about the most magnificent in the world; all the
Russian tsars are still crowned there and the coronation hall
is wonderfully imposing; it was as late as 1895[4] that the present
Emperor went down to crown himself there. What strikes one
more than anything else is the number and richness of the
churches throughout the city. I believe there are more in
Moscow than in any other city in the world; certainly as you
look from the battlement of the Palace you see nothing but
spires in every direction and domes too, for the Russian
churches are more like Turkish mosques and very flamboyant,
so that the effect of color and shape as you look across the city
is truly extraordinary. Inside they are decorated with gold,
pearls, diamonds, emeralds and all sorts of precious stones,
paid for mostly I suppose from the money wrung from the
poor for ages back. We spent one day going out to the hills
from which Napoleon first looked down on the city before
entering, where one gets a splendid idea of its effect. But there
is little use in trying to describe it all to you, for you will
have to see it for yourself before long. . . .

August 27, 1907

We are both busy with German lessons and I with Russian as well. I am beginning in a very hesitating fashion to
read the Russian newspapers, for I have been working at the
language for nearly three months now, pretty hard, and have
quite a fair vocabulary. But it is almost hopeless to grasp the
grammar and I wonder if I shall ever be able to speak fluently
as I should so much like to. If we stay here for two years I
think I shall be able to in a modest way for I am already holding short conversations with my teacher who is an excellent
one. One thing I have eventually grasped and that is the
handwriting, and it is very necessary as we are continually
receiving bills and letters in Russian which Alice would have

---

[4] Nicholas II was crowned in Moscow on May 14, 1896.

a hard time to make out without me. I have written out such quantities of exercises that it now comes almost as easily to me as writing English. The print, of course, offers after a month of study no difficulty at all. All my spare time is devoted to it and I find it fascinating.

September 3, 1907

I must tell you about the very interesting experience I had on Sunday. The big new Church of the Resurrection which was erected on the spot where Alexander II was murdered by a bomb in 1881 was to be consecrated and among the very few people invited outside of the Russian court and army and navy officials were the Diplomatic Corps. We were told beforehand that the service would last for at least three hours and that no one would be able to sit down during the whole time, so though she was much disappointed it seemed better for Alice not to go. There had been a rumor that the Tsar and Tsaritsa might possibly be present, but it was kept very quiet and as he has not been inside St. Petersburg since the opening of the first Duma over two years ago it seemed rather doubtful. However, as we got out of our carriage and walked across the big open space where all comers could be carefully inspected to see that they did not conceal bombs under their coats, the soldiers who surrounded the church began cheering, and there walking slowly around inside the hollow square formed by the troops, and at the head of all the Grand Dukes, was the Little Father himself, acknowledging with bows the very hearty applause. He entered the church immediately behind us and walked past us with the Empress, who is a very beautiful and dignified-looking woman, and they took their places just opposite the Diplomatic Corps. It was one of the most imposing scenes I have ever witnessed: in the chancel was the magnificent choir of men and boys, all in rich scarlet uniform, and all the archbishops of St. Petersburg, robed in gowns of solid embroidered gold; then, just below the chancel the Emperor and Empress, and behind them the Queen of Greece — the former Olga Constantinovna, Grand Duchess of Russia —

visiting them, and behind her all the Grand Dukes in magnificent uniforms; then came the entire suite of the Tsar and all the court officials, in more brilliant and varying uniforms than you have ever imagined existed, and across the aisle representatives from all the Russian regiments and fleets and training schools, and next to them the Diplomatic Corps, no less gorgeously arrayed than the rest. The service was very impressive, at one time the whole royal family and the court forming a procession and walking around outside the church while its walls were consecrated. The interior of the church shows that nothing has been spared to make it the very finest in Russia; the frescoing on the walls is magnificent and many of the ikons are embroidered solid with great pearls. It was rather tedious standing still for three full hours, for as the Tsar and Tsaritsa do not sit down during service, no one else can do so, and I admired the way in which she stood stock-still without budging an inch during it all and held herself so straight and proudly. The Emperor looks much as I had imagined him, though with the distinctive Russian features rather more marked than I had supposed from his pictures; he has a great sweeping blond moustache and his eyes are of the Russian distinctive type; it is not a face that shows much strength, but he is very handsome and kind-looking, and he walks in a slow and graceful manner. The Tsaritsa is an empress in her looks and bearing from head to heel; she was dressed simply in white with a white feather hat and a light blue ribbon around her shoulder; she carries herself superbly and seemed to enter into the service with much fervor and piety; she is exceedingly handsome, but looked worried and rather sad. They say that the continual terrorist plots have made her melancholy, and I do not doubt that she was praying that her husband would get safely back to Peterhof that day after the service. The greatest precautions were taken; they came up the Neva in a launch and all the bridges were closed to traffic so that bombs could not be thrown down upon them; the route from the landing to the church kept as much as possible to open squares which were all heavily guarded with troops, and where the procession had to traverse streets, a soldier was placed in every window of every house and a fine of 3000 rubles imposed on anyone who even opened one. Thank heaven they did get back safely.

There are a good many tales relative to the building of this church which I will tell you some day but they are too long to write; I don't know how much faith is put in the story, but when it was half done the funds, which had been generously supplied by the people, suddenly disappeared, and the architect in charge was exiled to Siberia. But scandal has it that the Grand Duke . . . who had been made president of the committee, had put them into his own pocket and caused the blame to fall on the unfortunate architect. He was there on Sunday, the Grand Duke . . . superintending the arrangements, and I must say, he looks as if he were capable of anything — a terrible old reprobate. You remember I met him soon after my arrival. . . .

October 26, 1907

Two days ago a young woman gained access to Alexander Maximovsky, the Director of Prisons with whom we have more or less to do ourselves, and shot him dead in his office. She was then seen to be fumbling with a string beneath her clothes, and on being arrested and searched, she was found to have 13 pounds of dynamite packed about her person with an arrangement for setting it off by pulling a string. Luckily she failed to do this for the charge would have blown up the entire building and killed everyone outright. She was tried by court-martial yesterday and hanged this morning, within 48 hours of the perpetration of her crime. This sort of thing happens continually and terrorism is by no means on the wane, though it is perhaps less active in St. Petersburg, on account of the extra vigilance of the police, than in the south of Russia and the Caucasus, and especially in Poland.

November 16, 1907

I attended the opening of the Third Duma on Thursday,

November 14. There was absolutely no excitement; the formal opening was preceded by a mass in which there was the most beautiful singing; Russian choirs are superb and in important events of this kind all the best voices in the city are brought together, and above them all you hear the splendid deep bass of the Metropolitan Antony, the head of the Russian Church, who also officiated at the consecration of the Church of the Resurrection a month or so ago. He intones the service in the most marvelous voice you have ever heard. After the mass they sang the Russian National Anthem three times; the music is that of the hymn "Rise, Crowned with Light, Imperial Salem Rise" and it is very fine. I saw Stolypin — Peter Stolypin, Chairman of the Council of Ministers, Minister of Interior — for the first time, seated in the Ministerial benches; he ought to be pretty proud of his triumph in the make-up of this Duma, as it is pro-Government by a very large majority.[5] But whether it will accomplish anything is quite another matter. It has taken other countries centuries to perfect their legislative bodies, and when a new one is started for the first time, one cannot expect it to jump into a state of perfection at once. If these Dumas accomplish nothing else, they are at least learning a little more all the time in matters of procedure, so they cannot be said to be utterly useless.

November 20, 1907

Yesterday morning when I walked across the Troitsky Bridge to the Embassy the most remarkable change had taken place in the Neva overnight: the day before it had been a broad sheet of open water with ferryboats dashing around in all directions and big steamers plying up and down: now it was completely frozen from shore to shore, great quantities of ice having come down from a big lake far above and jammed and frozen solid.

[5] Of the 429 members of the first session of the Third Duma, the parties of the Right with 49 members, the National Group with 26, the Moderate Right with 69, and the Union of 17 October with 148, comprised a pro-Government majority. Warren B. Walsh, "Political Parties in the Russian Dumas," *Journal of Modern History,* June, 1950, p. 148.

Every ferryboat landing had been towed away for the winter, the steamers had all disappeared and the big bridge which runs across in front of the Winter Palace supported on pontoons had been swung downstream, and in their place platforms had been put alongside the quays in places from which to run tramcars across the ice. Winter had come with a vengeance at one fell swoop. I don't know of any place in the world where the transformation is so sudden and so unexpected. It is getting very cold, but I find I like it immensely, and after my long walk to the Embassy in the morning I am warm for the rest of the day. For the last week the temperature has been hanging around 6° below zero Reaumur, but what that is in Fahrenheit I haven't the slightest idea. . . . Lately for a change we have been having the sun — the first time in many weeks — only a very little above the horizon even at midday, to be sure, but still it is a pleasure to know that it still exists. It sets at shortly after three and one cannot read in the house without artificial light after 2.30. We get up at 8 in almost total darkness and when I start for the office between 10 and 11 the sun is just appearing. That is why people get up so disgracefully late here, but we are early birds and cannot shake off the habits of generations so easily even though we have to breakfast by electric light.

I cannot tell you how we love the city; its beauty grows on one continually. The colors on the Neva just before dark are really superb, sometimes a pink and sometimes a delicate blue haze covering it, from which the spire of the church in the Peter and Paul fortress rises indistinctly and the lights all down the river mark the quays and the bridges across it. When you have seen the Neva just before dark on a winter afternoon and again at midnight in the middle of summer you will have seen two of the most beautiful effects to be beheld in any city in the world. If you ask if we are contented here I should answer infinitely more than in any other post I can imagine. I am now so pleased that we did not go to Berlin for its interest and charm would not begin to compare with that of St. Petersburg.

December 3, 1907

I have just had the interesting experience of being the only one to see a meeting between two of the most prominent of the statesmen of the world today, Mr. Taft and Mr. Stolypin: [6] I happened to be in Mr. Taft's room going over some official papers with him when Stolypin came in and though I discreetly withdrew, it was interesting to see the cordial greeting between the two men. Secretary Taft is a thoroughly charming person, cordial even to the most humble, and I am glad to have seen so much of him during his short visit here.

I could not go down to Moscow to meet Secretary Taft, but since he arrived here two days ago we have been busy every minute. Yesterday we went to the Duma and last night a big dinner was given for him by the American colony, at which he made an important speech, and a very good one, denying all the absurd newspaper rumors that he was traveling on a diplomatic mission. His only duty, he said, was to open the Assembly in the Philippines and to see for himself certain conditions in the Islands. Tonight we go to a reception given for him by Mr. Izvolsky [Alexander Izvolsky, Minister of Foreign Affairs]. The evening before Mr. Taft came I was especially fortunate in going to the annual Krestovsky Tennis Club dinner and sitting opposite Baron Alexander Meyendorff, the Vice-President of the Duma, with whom later I played billiards all the evening and had a long talk about American and Russian affairs. He is a delightful man . . . and a prominent influence in the Duma.

December 3, 1907

I have recently sprung into unpleasant prominence in Russia through no fault of my own. A rumor had gone around that the United States was on the verge of war with Japan and was

[6] Taft had promised the Filipinos to be present at the opening of their first Assembly. In the course of a three-month trip around the world he paused long enough in the Philippines to fulfill this promise and then continued across Siberia to Moscow and St. Petersburg. Mrs. William Howard Taft describes the journey in detail in *Recollections of Full Years* (New York: Dodd, Mead & Co., 1914), pp. 313–23.

eager to have Russian officers, the natural enemies of Japan, enlist in our army in the Philippines.[7] We were besieged by officers and correspondents and Schuyler instructed me to see them as they came and simply state that as yet we knew nothing about the matter though that the question seemed to us too improbable for consideration. We could not say more than this as the State Department had given us no instructions to emphatically deny the rumor. The result was that the whole Russian press came out with my words, but omitting to say anything about my statement that "the Embassy considered the whole matter too improbable for consideration" and included only the first part of my statement, saying "Mr. Grew acknowledges that great quantities of Russian officers are coming daily to the Embassy." This entirely distorted the sense of the information which I was instructed to and did convey, and made it appear that we were welcoming the officers who wished to enlist. The consequence has been that we have been flooded with letters from all over Russia from officers begging to enlist and they have been coming around in batches to the Embassy and even dogging me in the street to have their names entered for enlistment, and the worst of it is, all these letters have been directed to me personally. We gave up trying to read them long ago, as of course they are all in Russian, and have simply thrown them into a basket, and today they are to be answered through the papers. Mr. Taft of course put an end to the business by denying the rumors in a strong speech at the

[7] The tension created between the United States and Japan over racial conflicts on the west coast of the United States had led to the circulation in both countries of war rumors which reached their height in the latter part of September or early October, 1907. See Thomas A. Bailey, *Theodore Roosevelt and the Japanese-American Crises* (Stanford University, Calif.: Stanford University Press, 1934), pp. 123–260. This war scare coupled with the fact that some Russians sincerely wished for Japan to engage in and be defeated in war, as a sort of retribution for Russia's defeat in the Russo-Japanese War, served as the background from which the rumored need of the United States for Russian soldiers arose. Before Taft's visit to St. Petersburg the significance of his position as Secretary of War in Roosevelt's Cabinet was emphasized, and he was said to be coming to plan for the stationing of two Russian army corps in the Philippines and one American army corps in Vladivostok. *New York Times,* November 29, 1907, p. 8; November 24, 1907, pt. III, p. 2.

American colony dinner and when this appears in the press the incident will be finished. But to me personally it has been exceptionally annoying.

December 6, 1907

I hope you are not putting faith in the newspaper reports of interviews with me which are appearing in America. The *New York Times,* November 24, 1907, reported that when Secretary Grew was asked by the reporter what Mr. Taft had been doing in the Philippines the American diplomat's face clouded; "Hush," he said, "that's a diplomatic secret." I have never heard anything so ridiculous; of course I said nothing of the kind, as it was well known to us that Taft's only object in visiting the Philippines was to open the Assembly there and to inspect the Islands. It is annoying to have it made to appear that we were making a state secret out of it. . . .

December 6, 1907

The reception at Mr. Izvolsky's the other night was brilliant and I greatly enjoyed it. All went well except for Mr. Taft's being half an hour late owing to his having split his trouser leg in going downstairs in the hotel; Mrs. Taft had packed his other suit and so he had to wait to be sewed up. General Clarence Edwards who was in the room at the time, regarded the Secretary waiting in his drawers and dress coat and with tears of merriment streaming down his cheeks begged Mr. Taft to go just as he was as he looked so distinguished that way. Mr. Taft for once lost his temper and said unprintable things.

January 16, 1908

On the Russian New Year's Day the Diplomatic Corps went out to Tsarskoye Selo and we all were presented to the Tsar and the Empress Dowager Marie, his mother, the Empress herself being ill and not able to be present. We were taken out in a splendid private train and driven up to the palace two by two in the court carriages, and finally assembled in the

audience hall of the palace. All the Embassies and Legations
stood in little groups according to seniority, that is, the Embassy whose Ambassador had been here longest at the head
and so down to the latest arrival, and then the senior Minister
and so down through the Legations; that brought the Embassies in this order: Turkish, French, Italian, British, Austrian, American, Spanish and German. The Emperor and Empress Dowager with their suites then came in and beginning
with the Turks stopped for five minutes or so talking with
each mission; after a few minutes' chat with the chief, the new
secretaries would be presented and after a few words with
each, the Tsar would pass on to the next. I am sorry to say
that Mr. Riddle seemed very nervous, for he introduced Captain Slocum [Captain Stephen L'H. Slocum, American Military
Attaché at St. Petersburg] as Major Gibson [Major William W.
Gibson, former American Military Attaché at St. Petersburg]
and then presented all of us secretaries one after the other without waiting a little between each so that the Tsar could speak a
few words to everyone. Accordingly we were the only secretaries
in the room whom the Emperor merely shook hands with,
without speaking to. However, it made no great difference. I
was glad to see him so close; he has a distinctly Russian face
and Slavic features; his eyes slope up almost like a Japanese's,
though he would probably not be glad to hear it said. He is
handsome and kind-looking, but shows no great strength; he
speaks English well, but with an accent of course. I was sorry
for him, for he had to speak to 27 different *chefs de mission,*
besides a few words to each secretary, and it must have required
some ingenuity to think of appropriate things to say in each
case, besides being rather fatiguing. It took a long time for
him to make the round and it was weary work for the rest of
us too. The Empress Dowager is a pleasant little woman,
rather dowdily dressed, with a little turned-up nose and
screwed up features, which however give her a pleasant and
cheery appearance when she talks; she is, you know, the sister
of the Queen of England, and somewhat resembles her. She
talked for some time with the Ambassador and we were all

duly presented, kissing her hand as is the custom. Next came Princess Galitzine, the *Grande Maîtresse de la Cour,* an old lady of some eighty summers (in Russian, after a person has attained to the age of five years, you say no longer years but summers) who closely resembles Joanna, our old nurse, who chatted merrily with us for some ten minutes, asking as to the relative severity of the Russian and American winters and telling us that she was much interested in Canada as the best seeds used for sowing in Russia came from there. The whole scene was a very brilliant one; there were an enormous number of officials present, dressed in the inimitable Russian uniform, and many young *dames d'honneur* and gentlemen-at-arms, who stood close to the Emperor wherever he moved. Speaking about the Russian uniform, Ramsay, who is in the Department of Ceremonies and who ran the whole thing on New Year's Day, told me the other day that he had to have three separate uniforms, one of which alone costs $500 and the hat $125 more, and it all comes out of his pocket. Of course the result is that the splendor of the Russian court ceremonies is unsurpassed. A rather significant and interesting fact concerning the reception was revealed by Agüera, the Spanish secretary, who stood next to me and was taken suddenly ill during the reception and was obliged to be let out of the room by a door which opened directly behind us. He told us afterwards that he was led along a passage which completely surrounded the reception hall and was absolutely packed with soldiers and secret police, so that by no possible chance could any outsider get into the room, even by breaking through the wall. After the reception, the Emperor withdrew, bowing genially to us all, and then tea was served and we returned to Petersburg as we had come. This is a lot of gossip, is it not? — but I hope it may interest you. . . .

January 16, 1908

I do not by any means agree . . . that the Russian you see in the street looks sad; the *muzjik* is an eminently cheery person, generally wears a broad grin and looks as if he lacked nothing to make him happy. Frequently my *izvostchik* driver turns around and engages in genial conversation with me, remarking on the excellence of his horse or the change in the weather and grins from ear to ear when I jolly him back and tell him that his old sawbones of a horse ought to have been buried long ago and that the idea of giving him a *polteenik* or half-ruble as fare would be an outrage to humanity. The middle class perhaps look more serious, but I think not more so than the middle class in any other country. I do not call Russia a sad country if one can judge at all by its outward aspect; Petersburg is a very cheery, lively city and gives one the impression of gaiety rather than of depression. Of course one does not see much of the undercurrent of political persecution or of the imprisonments and banishments to Siberia for political offenses. . . .

May 19, 1908

Speaking about Russian society, Paravicini [C. R. Paravicini, Swiss Secretary of Legation at St. Petersburg], Seymour [Richard Sturgis Seymour, British Second Secretary at St. Petersburg] and I were discussing it today, and all agreed that it was without exception the most formal and least cordial society of any capital in the world. One spoke of having brought three letters of introduction from . . . people in Paris to three Russians; in each case he called, leaving the letter of presentation with his own card, and in each case nothing resulted except that each of the three Russians sent his man around to leave a card, where the matter ended, no invitation to lunch, which in any other country would be expected, being forthcoming. Paravicini came with an excellent letter to a Russian lady; as she paid no attention to his first call he presumed that she had failed to receive his card or had forgotten it and called again; nothing happened until several weeks later when he finally met her at a dinner and told her who he was, she said, "Ah oui, vous êtes excessivement bien recommandé, Monsieur Paravicini," and turned her back on him.

There is one embarrassing thing about the Yacht Club; when

one enters one must go up to every man present, no matter
what he is doing or whether one knows him, and shake hands;
according to our notion it seems the height of presumption to
go up and shake hands with men you don't know and have
never seen, but the Russians are deeply offended if anyone
omits the ceremony, so it has to be gone through religiously.
It is a pleasant outward sign of cordiality, but it means nothing.

Ramsay was summing up the characteristic traits in the home
life of various nations and he hit the thing pretty well on the
head when he said that the Anglo-Saxon's first lookout was for
his personal comfort, the Frenchman's for his food, and the
Slav's for the impression of luxury he could make upon his
guests. The Anglo-Saxon loves above all his bath and clean
clothes, the Frenchman his dinner, while the Russian will
live in a few wretched little back rooms in order to fit out his
drawing room superbly and will dine on bread and butter
six days in the week in order to afford a mighty banquet and
make a brave show to his guests on the seventh. As Ramsay
put it, the Russian does not understand the luxury of personal
comfort, and that is why most Russian apartments sacrifice
everything to the reception rooms and those parts of the house
which his guests will see. This is evident everywhere.

V

Berlin

1908 – 1910

After having spent more than a year as Third Secretary of the Embassy at St. Petersburg, Mr. Grew was appointed Second Secretary of the Embassy at Berlin on June 10, 1908, at a salary of $2000. In his new post, he served under Ambassador David Jayne Hill. Ambassador Hill had formerly been president of Bucknell and Rochester Universities, Assistant Secretary of State from 1898 to 1903, and Minister to Switzerland and the Netherlands. The Grews' second daughter, Lilla Cabot, was born in St. Petersburg on November 30, 1907, and their next child, Anita Clark, was born in Berlin on May 27, 1909. Elizabeth Sturgis, the fourth daughter, was born in Vienna on April 25, 1912. From this chapter to the end of these volumes, the selections from Mr. Grew's papers were made by the editor.

To my mother, Christmas Eve, 1909

. . . We have just had a very successful Christmas Tree for the children . . . the tree looked very well in the dining room, all lit up and the electric lights out, and everybody received presents of one kind or another. Yesterday was the Durham [1] tree and tomorrow is the Hitts' [2] and we all dine with the Hitts afterwards.

Of course you have heard of Hitt's promotion to be Minister to Panama: the news came very unexpectedly for only a fortnight or so ago the State Department had told Dr. Hill that none of his staff would be moved for at least a year. We shall miss them greatly in more ways than one and Alice is

[1] James A. C. Durham, Honorary Attaché of the British Embassy at Berlin.
[2] R. S. Reynolds Hitt, First Secretary of the American Embassy at Berlin.

desolate at the prospect of Mrs. Hitt's departure for they have become very good friends. . . . I don't mind telling you in the strictest confidence that the Ambassador did his best in Washington to insure my being appointed 1st Secretary in the event of Hitt's promotion and of Scholle's [Gustav Scholle, Third Secretary of the American Embassy at Berlin] moving up to my place, and he seems more disappointed about the matter than either of us. Huntington Wilson, Assistant Secretary of State, who has entire charge of the personnel of the Diplomatic Service, said that the Department did not want to promote men in the same post but to move them on elsewhere when the time for promotion came. In spite of the fact that several 1st secretaryships have just become vacant by the shake-up in the Service,[3] we seem to have escaped being moved on and I am happier than I can say that we are to remain here for the present. It would have been heartbreaking to have had to break up our household now even for a promotion, and the next best thing to being appointed 1st Secretary here is to stay on as 2nd. I am entirely satisfied and have told Dr. Hill so in all sincerity. . . .

To Edward Bell, Vice Consul General in Egypt, January 4, 1910

. . . I am very sorry for your sake to see that they have stiffened the entrance examination to the Service before you have taken it, though as a principle it is a splendid thing.[4] Of

3 Secretary of State Philander C. Knox and Assistant Secretary Huntington Wilson undertook in 1909 the most extensive reorganization of the Department of State in almost forty years. New offices, such as Counselor of the Department and Resident Diplomatic Officer, were created. The divisions of Western European, Near Eastern, and Latin American Affairs were established. Personnel changes were made, and many men in the field were appointed to the new positions, creating vacancies abroad. Graham H. Stuart, *The Department of State* (New York: The Macmillan Co., 1949), pp. 212–20.

4 President Taft's Executive Order of November 26, 1909, listed such fields as international law, diplomatic usage, a modern language in addition to English, economic resources of the United States, American history, modern history of Europe, Latin America, and the Far East which were to be tested by examination. The oral examination was to determine the candidate's general contemporary knowledge, alertness, and suitability for a Service career. U.S. De-

course you won't have any trouble with it, but you had better
bone up on European history since 1850: if you want me to I
can get Dr. Hill to recommend a good book. . . . I see that the
next exams are set for the beginning of March: hadn't you
better apply for leave in order to be there at that time? The
sooner you get in, the better, for once this house-cleaning is
over and the rotten boughs are all weeded out, there won't
be so many vacancies occurring. In old days they used to let
men into the Diplomatic Service from the Consular Service
without examination, but this doesn't hold good any more unfortunately.[5] I shall be awfully glad to see you in. . . .

To my mother, February 6, 1910
    . . . We are right in the thick of the social season now. . . .
On the 2nd was the first Court Ball and it was just like last
year, so I shall not describe it again; but it was very brilliant
as always, though fearfully fatiguing as one has to stand up the
whole evening, except for a short time at supper. Alice was
presented to Princess Eitel Fritz, the wife of the Kaiser's second
son, and had a pleasant chat with her. The Emperor and Empress came around the room and spoke to all the Ambassadors,
Ministers and their wives in turn, the Embassy ladies standing
behind their Ambassadresses and the secretaries behind their
chiefs. The most interesting thing about these balls is the
various old court dances, minuets, etc., which are danced beautifully by a large number of the ladies, together with the royal
princesses, and the officers of the various regiments in Berlin,
each having its own particular uniform; the Kaiser and Kaiserin
sit on the throne and beam on the crowd and seem to enjoy
it all hugely.

partment of State, *Register of the Department of State, December 28, 1909*
(Washington: Government Printing Office, 1909), pp. 107–8. "Every new Executive Order of the kind recently issued," Mr. Grew wrote his father-in-law on
December 16, 1909, "will make it just so much harder for a new administration
to overturn things and reclothe the Service in its former character of a Congressional plum orchard. This is very gratifying."

    5 The Executive Order of November 26, 1909, also stated that transfers should
not occur from one branch of the Service to another without examination.

The gala opera was no less splendid an affair. The Emperor and Empress sit in the Imperial box with all the different kings, grand dukes and princes of the various German states gathered around them, and the other boxes, galleries and stalls filled with the guests of the evening. Such a collection of brilliant uniforms, beautiful dresses and magnificent jewels would be hard to find anywhere else. After the royalties had come in and everyone had bowed and curtseyed in response to the Kaiser's greeting, the orchestra played Wagner's "Kaiser March," and then the curtain went up for the 2nd act of *Rienzi*. Afterwards the Kaiser and the various princesses held a "cercle" in the foyer.

I am very glad to see that at all these functions the Kaiser singles out Dr. Hill and talks to him longer than to anyone else, sometimes for half an hour at a time. . . . It is a great big tribute to Dr. Hill that he should have been able to secure the Kaiser's liking and confidence as he has, after such an in-auspicious beginning,[6] but there is no doubt about it that he has done so fully and is making a great success of his mission to Germany. . . .

To my mother, April 24, 1910

. . . It seems hardly necessary to tell you anything about Mr. Roosevelt's plans for Berlin as you must see it all in the paper.[7] What a triumphal march he is making through Europe. People in society here are generally very facetious on the subject; I think the aristocratic element resent having a mere untitled citizen shown so much honor, especially in being asked to stay at the Schloss itself. Of course they are usually careful what

6 In the latter half of March, 1908, the rumor reached print that the appointment of Dr. David Jayne Hill to succeed Charlemagne Tower as Ambassador to Germany was unacceptable to the German Government. Doubts had been evidenced in German official quarters that Dr. Hill had enough money to carry out the social responsibilities of the office to the satisfaction of the German Government. On March 29, an official withdrawal of any objection by the Kaiser to Dr. Hill's appointment was made. *New York Times*, March 26, 1908, p. 1; March 30, 1908, p. 1.

7 Theodore Roosevelt sailed from the United States on March 23, 1909, to hunt big game in Africa, to travel, and to fulfill speaking obligations in Europe.

they say in our presence, but in one or two cases they have spoken plainly. The Russian conseiller, Nicholas de Shebeko, sat next to Alice the other night at a dinner and spent the whole time criticizing Roosevelt, though she gave him as good as she got. He was really exceedingly rude and it must have been on his conscience, for the next day he sent her an enormous basket of azaleas — the biggest I have ever seen — asking if she would accept it as an olive branch. She got in one or two good digs at him at that dinner; on her other side was the Rumanian Minister, Dr. Alexander Beldiman, and they were both saying how absurd it was that a private citizen like Roosevelt should visit every capital in Europe like a monarch, to which A. sweetly replied that she hadn't heard that he was taking the trouble to visit either Russia or Rumania. After that they were pensively silent for several minutes.

At the Ambassador's suggestion I asked Kermit to stay with us while in Berlin, for the Embassy will be pretty full and we should have some good hunting talks together. I received a nice but funny letter from him yesterday in which he accepted our invitation and then went on to describe his father's wonderful reception in Budapest with pride radiating from every word. . . . Besides Professor Carl Schillings for our luncheon I have now got ahold of another German big-game hunter, Herr Paul Niedieck, whom Mr. Roosevelt wrote me he especially wanted to meet. . . . It has now been definitely decided that I shall go over to Sweden to meet Mr. Roosevelt and welcome him for the Embassy; I shall probably spend the day in Copenhagen and get on the train at Trelleborg that night. . . .

To my mother, May 7, 1910

It is just our luck that King Edward should die just as Mr. Roosevelt is about to arrive, and spoil all the fun.[8] It would have been very considerate of him to have waited a week longer. But this is hardly a reverent attitude to the memory of a great sovereign, so we shall try to be philosophical. We re-

8 The mother of Kaiser William II was Victoria, Princess Royal of Great Britain, sister of King Edward VII.

ceived the news this morning and as yet nobody knows just what alterations will have to be made in the program for Mr. Roosevelt's reception. The Ambassador said smilingly this morning that he fully expected to receive a telegram from him in the course of the day, saying "Will King Edward's death affect Grew's luncheon?" for he has spoken of it in every single letter which he has written the Ambassador thus far as the event which he was looking forward to most of all in Berlin.[9] We think now, from what we have learned from the Foreign Office today, that the Emperor will receive Mr. Roosevelt after all, though in a quieter way; but whether the Emperor will dine at the Embassy and whether we shall dine at the castle is very doubtful. It was to have been a very interesting week and it is hard to have it changed. . . .

To my mother, May 15, 1910

This whirlwind week is over at last and we lie back with sighs of satisfaction, for delightful and interesting as it has been to have the Roosevelts here, their visit has certainly meant for us a strenuous existence. I suppose it will interest you to hear of it in detail, so I shall try to give you a satisfactory account, although you have very likely already read in the papers of the main events of the week.

[9] Mr. Grew had written to Mr. Roosevelt at his camp on the White Nile in Africa asking whether, during his visit to Berlin, he would care to meet some of the German big-game hunters at luncheon at the Grews' apartment. Mr. Roosevelt replied that he particularly wanted to meet these hunters, and that the pleasantest way of doing it would be at such a luncheon. He added: "We'll all come."

The Ambassador, who was not interested in the luncheon, told Mr. Grew that Mr. Roosevelt was going to be extremely busy during his week's stay in Berlin. When the Ambassador sent the program to Mr. Roosevelt in Cairo, the luncheon was omitted. Mr. Roosevelt promptly telegraphed to Dr. Hill: "Program approved but please include Grew's lunch." Then King Edward died; the German Court went into mourning; and the Roosevelt visit was reduced to three days. The Ambassador said to Mr. Grew: "Now, of course, your luncheon will have to go overboard." "Of course," said Mr. Grew. But when the revised program was telegraphed to Rome, back came Roosevelt's reply: "Revised program approved but don't forget Grew's lunch."

Mr. Grew observed that at that point his relations with his chief had become "extremely tenuous"!

Before beginning I must say that Mr. Roosevelt and his entire family have made an excellent impression in Berlin and
the press has almost universally shown itself favorable and
appreciative. Both Alice and I were charmed with them all
and Alice, who has always been a little prejudiced against Mr.
Roosevelt on political grounds, cannot now say enough in his
favor for he endeared himself by his frank cordial manner and
entire lack of pedantry or conceit. Kermit stayed with us all
the time and he is one of the nicest young fellows in every sense
of the word we have ever known. . . . Alice and Miss Roosevelt
shopped together and Kermit and I devoted hours to hunting
chats and literary discussions, in which the ladies sometimes
joined; they are both well read beyond their years and have a
really extraordinary knowledge of English poetry, which was a
delight to us as one seldom finds this among one's friends
abroad. It is indeed a satisfaction to know that Europeans are
finding out, in this visit, that even in America, politics and
culture sometimes go together and, in the case of Mr. Roosevelt, that the qualities of a statesman and a littérateur exist in
a high degree in the same man.

To begin at the beginning of the week, I went to Copenhagen last Sunday night, saw Dr. Egan [Maurice Francis Egan,
American Minister to Denmark] there, who spoke most kindly
and appreciatively of you and asked me to send you his best
remembrances, lunched with William Wallace, the Secretary,
took tea with the von Radowitzes, the German Chargé
d'Affaires who were great friends of ours in Berlin and whose
wedding we had recently attended, and crossed the straits to
Malmö, Sweden, at 5 o'clock. The Roosevelt private train arrived from Stockholm at 9.45 P.M. There was a great crowd on
the platform and speaking no Swedish I had a difficult time to
explain who I was and to get through the line of police; but a
newspaper correspondent finally rescued me and I was on hand
as the train pulled in. A large band then played the "Star
Spangled Banner" while the crowd cheered its welcome, and
while the Burgomaster made a speech and Mr. Roosevelt replied from the back platform of his car, and a chorus of young

men and women sang Swedish songs, I boarded the train and went at once to the Roosevelts' private saloon, where, after the train pulled out, he welcomed me most cordially. I welcomed him in the name of the Ambassador and then gave him full information regarding the program for his Berlin visit, after which he went through the large package of correspondence I had brought him, examining carefully even postcards from admiring small boys in America, requests for autographs, letters from crazy men, and rubbish of all descriptions. He was very hoarse from much public speaking and could talk only in a whisper, but he was most pleasant to me and I did not leave him till nearly midnight, when he finally got through with his mail. We had by that time arrived at Trelleborg, where the train is placed on a large 5000-ton steamer and is ferried 60 miles across to Sassnitz in Germany, the trip occupying four hours. It was blowing great guns, but the ship was so large and so steady that we felt hardly any motion. The captain came below, took some of us through the engine room, and then with him, Kermit, Mr. Lawrence Abbott of the *Outlook,* Mr. Roosevelt's private secretary, and several of the dozen or so correspondents who were on the train and had been with the party since leaving Khartoum, went on the bridge and saw the start, after which we had a genial supper in the saloon and finally retired, Kermit and I occupying the same double compartment which had been reserved for me in Stockholm.

The train reached Berlin at 9.08 in the morning; the Emperor had sent his great regrets that on account of the court mourning he could not be at the station as he had intended; but the Ambassador should have been there, the Emperor's representative Baron von Reishak, and several state carriages from the palace. But unluckily somebody had telephoned from the station that the train would be a half-hour late and the only officials present were Baron Wilhelm von Schoen, Minister for Foreign Affairs, and the Staff of our Embassy, including Alice, who had fortunately not received the erroneous message. Dr. Hill felt very badly about it, but fortunately arrived at the station a moment later and was able to get back to the Embassy

to greet the party there. As the state carriages had not arrived
we bundled the party into our various automobiles and drove
through the packed streets while the crowd cheered at the top
of its lungs and showed Mr. Roosevelt that his arrival was not
wholly overlooked. Kermit came at once to our apartment,
where Alice had fitted up the little room next to ours most
cosily for him, while Mr. and Mrs. Roosevelt and Ethel stayed
at the Embassy. At noon the whole Roosevelt family went to
Potsdam and lunched with the Emperor and the whole Imperial family, including all the princes and princesses, together
with the Hills and Laughlin [Irwin B. Laughlin, First Secretary of the American Embassy at Berlin]; Belknap [Reginald R.
Belknap, Naval Attaché of the American Embassy at Berlin]
and Shartle [Samuel G. Shartle, Military Attaché of the American Embassy at Berlin]. Unfortunately the 2nd and 3rd Secretaries do not come in for festivities of this kind, though if King
Edward had not died and if the reception had been in the
Berlin Schloss, the affair would have been less private in character and we would surely have all been invited. You know
that it was the Emperor's intention to have Mr. and Mrs.
Roosevelt as his house guests in Berlin for three days; but all
this had to be given up on account of the court mourning. I
heard afterwards that the meeting between Mr. R. and the
Kaiser was exceedingly cordial and that after lunch they moved
to a far corner of the room and talked to their hearts' content
waving their arms in the air and banging their fists on the
table, doubtless while discussing plans for universal peace. It
was a memorable meeting. After lunch they went through the
Sans Souci park and did not return till evening. At 6 o'clock
the staff of the Embassy went to the Hills' for tea but Mr.
Roosevelt was very tired and did not appear.

   The next morning, Wednesday the 11th, Mr. Roosevelt was
the Emperor's guest at Döberitz, where maneuvers were held,
both Mr. R. and Kermit being mounted and the former taking
his place beside the Kaiser while the troops marched past, an
honor reserved only for foreign sovereigns. At the close of the
review the Emperor turned to Mr. Roosevelt and in the hear-

ing of the officers said, "My dear Roosevelt, you are the first civilian who has ever reviewed the troops of Prussia," a pleasant and gratifying remark and one which pleased T.R. immensely.

That day, Mr. Lawrence Abbott, of *The Outlook* and private secretary to Mr. R., lunched with us, and in the evening we went to a big dinner at the Embassy, the Imperial Chancellor [von Bethmann-Hollweg], the Minister for Foreign Affairs, and other prominent German officials being present. The Kaiser was to have been there, but unfortunately the court mourning prevented his coming. Instead he sent Mr. Roosevelt a number of splendid colored engravings, depicting the different Prussian war flags and uniforms, and several books as gifts; these were laid out on the table in the drawing room and we found them there after dinner. In each book the Kaiser had written "To Mr. Roosevelt from William I.R." with a dozen or so lines of remarks about each volume. Two books were on the life of Jesus, and in one of them which I saw he wrote: "Our Lord possessed one of the strongest personalities in history; whoever follows in His footsteps cannot fail also to develop marked personality." In almost every inscription he made some allusion to "personality" or "character" and in a sense very complimentary to Mr. Roosevelt. When the gentlemen adjourned to the smoking room Mr. Roosevelt went at once to his bedroom, for he was very tired and his voice was completely worn out, and I was the only guest who had a chat with him; he asked me to come into his bedroom and we sat on the two arms of a chair and talked for quite a while, he telling me all about his impressions of the Emperor, whom he considers a wonderfully virile and thoroughly good man. I was a good deal pleased when he picked up a copy of my book, *Sport and Travel in the Far East,* from his bed and said that he had taken refuge from the Chancellor and all the other guests in order to read it alone, but I guess there was more politeness than truth in his remark. I suppose the Ambassador, to whom I had given a copy, had shown it to him. He also said not only to me, but three or four times to the Ambassador, that he was looking forward to our

The Author's bungalow in Cairo, 1904

The Author and Mrs. Grew on their honeymoon
in the Maine woods, 1905

Mrs. Grew in Cairo, 1905

A diplomatic reception in Mexico, 1906. The American Ambassador, David Thompson, is in the center. Fenton McCreery,
First Secretary of the Embassy, is second from left, Paxton Hibben, Second Secretary, with black beard, to the right, the Author,
Third Secretary, is second from right

E. Bieber, Berlin

Mrs. Grew in Berlin, 1909

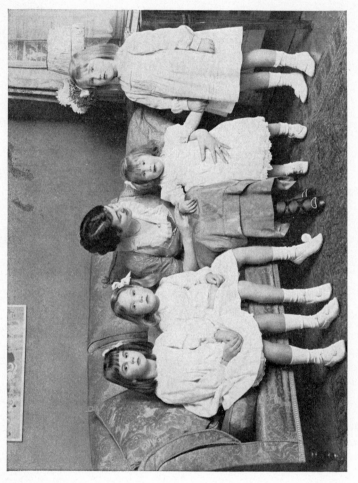

Edith, Lilla, Mrs. Grew, Elsie and Anita, in Berlin about 1913

K. u. k. Ministerium des kaiserl. und königl. Hauses und des Äußern

Nr. 23491/1.

1 Beilage.

Wien, am 8. April 1917.

Nachdem die Vereinigten Staaten von Amerika erklärt haben, daß zwischen ihnen und der kaiserlich deutschen Regierung der Kriegszustand besteht, hat Oesterreich-Ungarn als Verbündeter des Deutschen Reiches beschlossen, die diplomatischen Beziehungen zu den Vereinigten Staaten abzubrechen und ist die k.u.k. Botschaft in Washington beauftragt worden, das Staatsdepartement hievon in Kenntnis zu setzen. ./.

Indem der Unterzeichnete bedauert, unter diesen Umständen auch die persönlichen

Seiner Hochwohlgeboren

Herrn Joseph Clark Grew,

Geschäftsträger der Vereinigten Staaten von

Amerika.

Beziehungen, welche er mit dem Herrn Geschäftsträger der Vereinigten Staaten von Amerika zu unterhalten die Ehre hatte, ein Ende nehmen zu sehen, verfehlt er nicht, Demselben hierneben den Paß für seine und der übrigen Mitglieder der Botschaft Abreise aus Oesterreich-Ungarn zur Verfügung zu stellen.

Gleichzeitig benützt der Unterzeichnete diesen Anlaß, um den Herrn Geschäftsträger den Ausdruck seiner vollkommensten Hochachtung zu erneuern.

Czernin

Note from
Count Czernin,
Austro-Hungarian
Foreign Minister,
breaking diplomatic
relations with the
United States,
April 8, 1917

Note from Colonel House to the Author regarding the terms of
the Armistice of November 11, 1918

F. H. Jullien, Geneva

Signing of American-Turkish Treaty, Lausanne, 1923. Facing the camera,
left to right, Mustafa Cherif Bey, Riza Nour Bey, Ismet Pasha (Standing),
Munir Bey, Hassan Bey. The Author (in profile) faces Ismet Pasha

Reception of the Non-Stop American flyers by Kemal Atatürk in Turkey, 1931. Front row (left to right): the Author, Boardman, the Gazi, Polando, Tewfik Rushdi Bey

Kemal Atatürk, his adopted daughter and the Author at the
Gazi's farm in Ankara

luncheon more than to all the rest of his stay in Berlin put together. There has been a good deal of adverse feeling in the American colony here about it, for he has had to refuse all sorts of invitations, from the American Chamber of Commerce, the Consul General and many other more important people than ourselves, who wished to give receptions or dinners for him, and thought he ought to give up coming to so humble a house as that of the 2nd Secretary of the Embassy, but nothing would induce him to cancel his acceptance of our invitation and indeed, he had the time of his life.

On Thursday, the 12th, Mr. Roosevelt delivered his lecture in the Aula of the University, after which the degree of Doctor of Laws was conferred on him.[10] He was first introduced by His Magnificence Dr. Eric Schmidt, the Rector of the University, in an excellent speech, and then he ascended the platform and spoke for nearly two hours on the world development of culture, tracing it up from the earliest times and ending with an exposition of his various doctrines — peace only with honor, clean home life, lots of children, etc., etc. It was a good lecture and made a good impression: he spoke in English and his voice became husky only towards the end, though nobody thought it would hold out. Ethel and Kermit both said that it was not so good as some of his other lectures and that he did not hold his audience as he usually does, but it seemed to me that it was excellent. It must be considered too that he was speaking to the foremost savants of Germany, who had probably never before heard a mere statesman or politician, or however they regarded him, lecture to them, and though there was no outward sign of it, I imagine they must have felt a certain amount of condescension. The Emperor and Empress and most of the Imperial family sat in the front row and the Emperor's head nodded continually in sign of approval and appreciation. In one place Mr. Roosevelt smilingly quoted Frederick the Great as saying (while on the subject of the

[10] The lecture given at the University of Berlin was called "The World Movement." Theodore Roosevelt, *Presidential Addresses and State Papers and European Addresses* (New York: The Review of Reviews Co., 1910), pp. 2223–56.

necessity of preserving armies and the fighting spirit) that the greatest punishment he could wish his country would be to be ruled over by philosophers — a good dig at the wise professors present in large numbers — and the Kaiser shook all over with merriment. . . .

Saturday, the 14th of May, finally arrived, the day of our own luncheon and for us quite naturally the climax of the week. Alice had done wonders to make everything go off well; the apartment was neat and clean as a whistle and prettily arranged with flowers in all the vases . . . and the table, a round one, was exceedingly pretty. I took Mrs. Roosevelt in on my arm and Alice followed with the ex-President; then came Mr. Henry White with Mrs. Hill, who sat on my left, and the Ambassador, who sat on Alice's left, with Mrs. White; Professor Schillings, who sat next to Mr. Roosevelt at his request, took in Ethel, and Kermit and Herr Niedieck brought up the rear. Alice had a first-rate and most delicious luncheon: caviar, scrambled eggs cooked with tomatoes and truffles, sweetbreads with mushrooms, ducks with salad, asparagus, whipped cream and strawberries, and for wine I had a light but very good Moselle, which caused Harry White to smack his lips and ask me where I found such a delicious wine, a good Bordeaux and finally champagne with small strawberries in it. I noticed that Mr. Roosevelt, who takes little wine, indulged in several glasses of the last named. It was a thoroughly pleasant luncheon, even if the host does say so himself — for there is nobody else to tell you, and if, in my letters, I should draw the veil of modesty over all we do and think and hear, you would I am afraid not find them quite satisfactory from your indulgent point of view. The doorbell began ringing at frequent intervals before we had left the table and when we had finished, a considerable number of after-luncheon guests had gathered in the library. There was Count von Götzen, the German Minister at Hamburg, who had come at Mr. Roosevelt's request, Herr Karl Goerz, the inventor of the world-famous Goerz lens, Dr. Berger, author and sportsman . . . Count Seherr-Thoss, Mr. White's son-in-law, Herr von Prittwitz, formerly of the German Embassy in Washington and a friend of Miss Roosevelt's, the entire staff of our own Embassy with their wives, Henry Fletcher, who has done such excellent work as Chargé d'Affaires at Peking and is now going as Minister to Chile, Willard Straight, representative in China of the American Group of financiers, Dick Derby,[11] Warwick Greene, Harvard '01, and Peter Bowditch, Harvard '03, the last-mentioned five having arrived that morning from the Far East and we having met them at the station, and a number of others. Schillings then presented Mr. Roosevelt with a fine camera for big-game work and several of his best pictures in a long frame, mounted with a dedication on a silver plate, and then we had coffee, liqueurs and cigars, while Mr. Roosevelt talked hunting and game photography to his heart's content with one after another of our guests. Then the three children came in and were good as gold, though Anita, who is teething, finally began to cry and had to leave. Edith and Lilla were not a bit shy; they played with Mrs. Roosevelt, who sat on the floor with them, and then examined Mr. Roosevelt's watch and other interesting contents of his pockets with delightful unconcern and friendliness. He beamed all over and I'm sure was mentally remarking "No evidences of race-suicide in the Grew family."

Meanwhile Schillings had arranged his stereopticon and white curtain in the dining room and after a half-hour or so we all went in and after a short address of eulogy Schillings showed us all his best colored game photographs, explaining and describing each. Mr. Roosevelt, who sat in the front row with Alice, simply loved it and especially the last slide which was a letter written to himself by various representative beasts of the African jungle, saying, "You greatest of naturalists and hunters, who hold so much influence not only over men but over animals as well, please do your best to preserve us from extermination." It was signed by the lion, the rhinoceros, the elephant, the hyena, the leopard, and the antelope, each with its Swahili name, which Mr. R. read off with evident delight,

11 Richard Derby, who met Miss Ethel Roosevelt at the Grews' luncheon, not long afterwards married her.

and nothing pleased him so much in the whole entertainment. This lasted about three-quarters of an hour and when it was over we telephoned to the Director of the Zoölogical Gardens and the Secret Police that we should start for the Zoo in ten minutes. Kermit took his father back to show him his room and finally at about four the party broke up, Mr. Roosevelt telling Alice with apparent sincerity that he had enjoyed this luncheon more than any other single entertainment he had been given during his whole trip through Europe. On his way to the Zoo, the Ambassador, Schillings and I being in his automobile with him, he talked continually of how much he had enjoyed it and said that he wanted the letter from the beasts given to the press both in America and Germany, so you will doubtless already have read it. At the Zoo he was welcomed by the Director, Dr. Ludwig Heck, to whom I introduced him, and then went through the whole thing, walking at a terrific pace, which quickly left the ladies gasping behind, so that they gave up trying to follow and went home. The most extraordinary thing of all was Missy, the Chimpanzee, whom Schillings himself brought from the African jungle; she used to adore him and always showed her affection, but one day she saw him there with a lady, and ever since then her whole manner towards him has changed; she still follows him continually with her eyes from the cage, but if he comes near, she barks angrily and he says if he went in she would tear him limb from limb. During the walk through the gardens a terrific hailstorm came on and we all got soaked, but nobody minded and the ex-President enjoyed every minute of his visit.

That's about all to tell you — surely it is enough; I did not realize that I had rambled on for twelve verbose pages of description. So I shall quickly finish. . . . This morning the Roosevelts left at 11.40 for London, everybody being down at the station to see them off and giving cheer after cheer as the train pulled out. It has been a memorable week. Familiarity has bred nothing but greater respect for Mr. Roosevelt and his charming family. May he be our next President.

To R. S. Reynolds Hitt, May 27, 1910

. . . We have been having an amusing spring here for all sorts of people from home have been dropping in and keeping things fairly lively. The Roosevelt week was pretty strenuous, but all went off well and we found the whole family charming. It was a great treat to see T.R. and the Kaiser chatting together — waving their arms in the air, banging their fists on the table and showing pretty clearly that they would preserve universal peace even if it had to be done with a gun and a hammer. During his lecture at the University Mr. Roosevelt would bring down the house with merriment in the most serious parts by banging the sacred eagle-supported lectern with his fist till one expected to see it fly into bits of kindling wood.

It sounds disgraceful but we are actually going home on the "bandwagon" June 9th; this was partly due to Ethel and Kermit who desired a renewal of the fun we had had together in Berlin and partly because after three years away from home we thought it about time to have a look at the old country again.[12] We shall be there till August 16 and if by any chance you take leave before then be sure to let me know at Manchester, Mass., so that we can connect.

Perry Belden, our new 3rd, has just arrived and seems anxious to do his share; but as neither he nor Laughlin speak one word of German, Scholle is going to be sadly missed. Willing Spencer [Third Secretary of the American Embassy at St. Petersburg] is here for a day or two on his way to St. P. and we play tennis daily; he speaks German fluently and why they didn't send him here instead of Belden, I can't make out. . . .

To John Van A. MacMurray, United States Embassy, St. Petersburg, Russia, June 11, 1909

. . . A letter which I recently received from a friend of mine prominent in official circles in Washington and a great personal friend of Mr. Knox told me things about the Service

12 The Roosevelts and the Grews sailed together on the *Kaiserin Augusta Victoria* for the United States. Mr. Grew returned to his post in Berlin on August 25, 1910.

which were good hearing. Although Mr. Taft has been obliged to put in a good many rank outsiders as chiefs of mission, they are all determined in Washington to keep on the efficient secretaries, promote them duly and make them chiefs of mission when the time comes. But it's heraus mit the loafers. Thus, my son, we are tempted to trust that the little busy bees will be permitted to buzz merrily along the diplomatic highway, gleaning their honey from the choicest blossoms of the proverbial plum tree, while the SLOTH and the CATERPILLAR and the WORM will be brushed aside onto the dry and prickly branches of the desert shrub, there to cling till thirst compels them to abandon their tenacious hold and sink forever into oblivion. Let us therefore improve each shining hour. . . .

To John Van A. MacMurray, September 4, 1910

I was awfully sorry that we could not meet in America; there was so much to do and so many people to see after being away from home for over three years that I found it difficult to go down to Washington till half way through my leave.

Your delicious letter, however, went far to make up for my disappointment at not seeing you yourself. . . . When the next Democratic administration comes in and you and I are turned out to pasture (which Heaven forbid) I will collaborate with you in composing a very readable volume entitled "Secretaries we have met." On the hypothesis that truth is stranger than fiction, it ought to make nice reading.

I have no news — anyway certainly none from Washington, if you except the stray bits of diplomatic gossip picked up when I found time to drop in for a chat with the Secretary of State, and during the odd moments I was able to give to Huntington Wilson during my very busy stay in Washington. You know yourself how hard it is to find time to see as much of those officials as one would like.

All humor aside, after a week at the Department, had I strolled out on the desert and met the Sphinx, I would have welcomed her with shouts of joy at finding something really human again. Everyone's face in that ancient and honorable institution, from the Mail Clerk up, seems to wear a continual expression of "Hush! the very walls have ears!" I found one or two very nice fellows there, though; Evan Young [Chief of the Division of Near Eastern Affairs] seemed to me one of the best. And that wild Indian, Hugh Gibson [Private Secretary to the Assistant Secretary of State] is a crackerjack; you should have seen him on Saturday afternoon, after Wilson had left, playing chimes on *all* the bell buttons, which called *all* the chiefs of bureaus to the Secretary of State's room, and then fleeing down the corridor of that sedate old Department like an Apache on the war trail. . . .

To my mother, October 2, 1910

. . . I have been working lately on the case of the four English and American journalists who were assaulted by the police a few nights ago while watching the strike troubles in Moabit, a quarter of Berlin.[13] The assault was entirely unprovoked and an outrageous affair. The four men, all of whom I know intimately, were standing by the sidewalk in an automobile, at a spot in the strike district to which they had been advised to go by a police lieutenant himself; six policemen had been driving some strikers through a park and the street at that point was quite clear and quiet. Suddenly a man on the sidewalk, whom the journalists believe to have been a detective in plain clothes, shouted to the six policemen: "Attack these fellows in the auto — beat them up!" The policemen immediately came at them with drawn swords and, in spite of the fact that they shouted out their identity and showed their red press cards, proceeded to cut and beat them in the most brutal manner. . . .

The strike riots in Moabit, which is only about ten minutes from our house and the quarter where I keep my motors, have been very serious this last week. Hundreds of people have been

13 Workmen backed by the Transport Workmen's League struck against the coal merchants of the Moabit. The Coal Merchant's League, however, refused to negotiate with the worker's organization and hired strikebreakers. On September 26, a series of riots began against the property of the merchants and the police guarding it. *The Times* (London), September 28, 1910, p. 5; September 29, 1910, p. 5.

wounded every night by the police and many policemen seriously hurt by the strikers. It may be held that the journalists took their lives in their hands when they went there, but this is a weak argument, as they were standing in a quiet spot at the time, with no mob about them to justify a mistake on the part of the police, and at a spot to which they were actually advised to go by a police lieutenant and permitted to pass through the police lines; and they were, of course, making no disturbance of any kind or doing anything which could be interpreted as incentive to disturbance.

We moved our chancery to Rauchstrasse this week and for the last three days have been working in the midst of the most awful confusion you ever saw. Plumbers, masons, carpenters, tapissiers and electricians all hammering and banging around us, and the air filled with brickdust, mortar and sawdust. All our furniture is heaped in clumps and piles in the middle of the various rooms, while the workmen work at the walls, and we have somehow set up our desks in the midst of this confusion and try to compose diplomatic Notes and Despatches as on a battlefield amidst the "trump of war." I fear it will be a month or six weeks before we are settled; the old porcelain stoves have to be pulled down, steam-heating apparatus put in, the walls papered, the floors painted and carpeted, and then the chancery furniture arranged before we can begin to work in peaceful surroundings once more. The Ambassador and his family will not move in until November 1st, but the chancery had no alternative as we had to vacate our former quarters on the last day of September. . . .

To Paxton Hibben, October 8, 1910

Kak vui pojevaetye? I have been meaning to send you a line for a long time in answer to the postcard you sent me, but I fear my good intentions are better than my execution. Perry Belden came back with glowing accounts of your hospitality at The Hague and it seems that you showed him a pretty fair time. I thought for a few moments yesterday that I should come over there myself for we received a telegram from the

Department which stated that I had been appointed to attend
and cast the vote of the United States at the Venezuelan Arbitration Court! I saw beautiful visions of myself stepping up on
the Bench and voting with my judicial colleagues, not at all
fazed by the fact that I didn't know beans about the case in
hand. It was quite clear that the American judge had been
taken with collywobbles and that I, with my acute insight into
matters of international law, was to replace him. However,
after a little deliberation it occurred to us that something was
twisted with that telegram, so we shook up the letters of the
cipher groups a bit and finally found that my distinguished appointment was only as delegate to a confounded medical congress in Berlin. Better luck next time.

I hope you like The Hague; it ought to be a fine post I
should think and a mighty interesting one. Do you still recall
our days together in the balmy (?) South [Mexico] and the
many happy hours we passed proofreading the Ambassador's
choice and artistically worded despatches, to say nothing of the
valuable time spent in planning out a wonderful future for the
United States Diplomatic Service while we sipped a certain
nectar brewed somewhere on the Calle San Francisco? It was
rather curious that I should have gone to Russia at once after
leaving Mexico, considering all you had told me about it.
You will remember how keen I was then to get the 3rd
secretaryship in Berlin which remained tantalizingly open for
several months.

On the whole the Service has taken big strides in the right
direction and I think it has a great future. . . .

To Charles B. Curtis, Secretary of Legation, Christiania, Norway, October 26, 1910

. . . I was interested to see a despatch of yours in the Information Series, regarding the question of blockade in Nicaragua.[14] These series are a great institution and most interest-

14 As part of the reorganization of the Department under Knox and Wilson
a new agency was created called the Division of Information. This Division had
the responsibility of publishing a pamphlet entitled the *Information Series*, a

ing to study, but they make one feel that the Department sets much more store by Latin American and Far Eastern affairs than it does by European. However, we are conducting negotiations in the Embassy here just at present which are about as ticklesome as one wants and which may have far-reaching consequences, so we are not without excitement and an opportunity for learning diplomacy. . . .

digest of information on affairs of the United States in various parts of the world. Stuart, *op. cit.*, p. 217.

VI

Vienna

1911 – 1912

Mr. Grew was appointed First Secretary of the Embassy at Vienna on January 27, 1911, at a salary of $3000. He served in this position under Ambassador Richard C. Kerens, who had been a railroad builder and Republican politician in the United States. In Vienna, Mr. Grew started, for the first time, to keep a diary of his experiences in the Foreign Service.

Friday, February 3 [1911]

. . . I reached Vienna at 7.21 and went to the Bristol . . . where I met Nelson O'Shaughnessy [Second Secretary of the American Embassy at Vienna] at 10 and we went together to the Embassy, Heugasse 26. It is a splendid big house, having been built for young Oscar Rothschild who shot himself because his parents would not let him marry the girl he wanted to, and well and attractively furnished. Mr. Kerens, the Ambassador, received me cordially and a letter which I presented to him from Dr. Hill seemed to smooth over the first formalities of our acquaintance and to secure me his confidence at once. He is a fine-looking man with snow-white hair, moustache and beard, a good eye and a pleasant voice, though he speaks with a carelessness of grammar and laxness in pronunciation which might call forth censure from the fastidious. He is dignified, simple and above all kindly in his address and manners. He began at once and continued during our subsequent walks in the Schwarzenberg Gardens to tell me of the state of affairs in Vienna, namely that he had come last spring without experience or knowledge of diplomatic usage of any kind. . . .

There are very many reforms to be made in the Embassy at Vienna if it is to be made an up-to-date office; a very brief examination of the chancery showed me that the system was hopelessly antiquated and that much useless labor is expended. My suggestions must come slowly and by degrees, but the few which I ventured to take up with the Ambassador at once were met by him in the most friendly manner possible and I hope eventually to have the place running as it should. . . .

Sunday, February 5 [1911]

. . . I, in Vienna, lunched at the Embassy, the other guests being the Batchellers [1] and the singer Yvonne de Tréville and her mother. One speaker held forth at length on international peace, getting so excited with his own arguments and rhetoric that nobody else was able to say a word for or against the subject under discussion, and forgetting that the luncheon table was not a lecture platform he conclusively put a stop to all conversation. Mrs. Kerens seems intelligent and amiable and certainly knows her own mind about things. . . . It is said that she personally takes the stump for her husband during his campaigns in Missouri; he was a candidate for Senator and his adversaries, in order to get him out of the way, insisted on the President's appointing him to some federal position. It was expected that he would be made Secretary of Commerce and Labor when the present Cabinet was formed, but this was found to be impossible and he was given the ambassadorship to Austria instead, much to the astonishment and misgivings of even his adversaries. Mrs. K. was exceedingly cordial to me and I think that Alice will get along well with her. . . .

Thursday, February 23 [1911]

. . . I arrived at Budapest at 9.40 A.M. after a most comfortable night's journey and went to the Bristol. . . .

[1] Francis Batcheller was an American businessman, and his wife, Tryphosa Bates Batcheller, was a singer and author.

I found Mr. Kerens just going in to breakfast with Major
William Allaire, the Military Attaché, and joined them. Later,
after a cleanup and change, the Ambassador, Allaire, Mr.
Batcheller (Tryphosa is of course on hand) and I went out in
the automobile to see the city. We first ascended the hill on the
Pest side of the river where stands the magnificent Schloss and
from there had a splendid view of the whole city, both of them
in fact, Buda on one side and Pest on the other and the "beautiful blue Danube" (though it was at the time a muddy gray)
running between them. I don't think there is a more beautiful
city in the world. . . .

In the evening the court ball.[2] They say it is the most
brilliant court function in Europe and I think rightly. The
costumes of the Magyars, trimmed with fur and studded with
enormous jewels, are picturesque and lend a medieval aspect
which one sees nowhere else. The hall itself, and indeed the
whole palace, is a marvel of architectural splendor. The Ambassador and Mrs. K. took me in their auto, and as we had an
outrider we had little delay in arriving, though the zigzagging
road up the hill was packed three rows deep with carriages
slowly crawling along. The diplomats met in an antechamber
where I was presented to the Master of Ceremonies and to
Count Aloys Lexa von Aehrenthal, the Prime Minister, and
subsequently to most of the Diplomatic Corps present. In the
ballroom the diplomats take their places to the left of the
throne and the Archduchesses to the right, the reverse of the
custom in Berlin. The Emperor soon arrived and passed
down the line of diplomats, followed by the Archduchess
Annunziata who was taken from a convent to act as the "first
lady of the land." I was shocked at the old man's appearance,

2 By the Compromise of 1867 the Hapsburg empire received a dual structure
as the Austro-Hungarian empire. Each of the two kingdoms was to have its own
constitution, parliament, and administration, making it in effect a separate state.
They were to be united under the Hapsburg monarch, with common departments of foreign affairs, war, and finances. Delegations made up of equal
numbers of delegates from both the Austrian and Hungarian parliaments were
to meet to discuss these common services.

for from his pictures one gets the idea of a tall straight fine-looking sovereign. But when one stops to think that he is 82 years old,[3] one is hardly surprised to see a rather pathetic little figure with bent head and deeply lined face walking with short, almost feeble steps. He has, however, a kindly eye and a still more kindly voice. When he came to us he shook the Ambassador's hand, but there was no conversation for he speaks no English and the Ambassador no French or German. To Mrs. K. he said a few words, to which she could only answer, "Oui, oui, oui." I was then presented and he talked to me most pleasantly in French, asking if I had just come and if from America, and he seemed interested when I told him that I was fresh from Berlin. Then, after a few casual remarks, he said in the kindliest manner, "J'espère que vous serez très content à Vienne," after which he passed on. The Archduchess Annunziata is tall and handsome, but with nothing but sadness in her face; she speaks English and the conversation when I was presented to her was much the same as with the Kaiser. During the evening I was introduced to the various Ambassadors and such Ambassadresses as were present and they were all, without exception, cordial and friendly. The Spaniards, Marquis and Marquise d'Herrera, the French, Monsieur Philippe Crozier, the Russian, Count de Giers (just from Brussels) and the German, Count Heinrich Tschirschky, impressed me especially pleasantly. The British Ambassador, Sir Fairfax Leighton Cartwright, has some trouble with his eyesight which gives him the appearance of being half-paralyzed and he is very difficult to talk to, but they say he is nice. The Ambassador did his best to present me to everyone; to those who spoke only French or German I had to act as interpreter which shocked me and made me realize the handicap which Mr. K. is under in his diplomatic relations. During the evening many old Magyar dances were danced and after supper a cotillon was held. The

[3] The Emperor Francis Joseph I was born on August 18, 1830. The Emperor was eighty years old at the time of Mr. Grew's writing.

ball began at 7 and was over punctually at 11.30, the Kaiser
leaving at that hour with Archduchess Annunziata on his
arm. . . .

Vienna, Tuesday, March 7 [1911]

. . . I was at the chancery from 9.30 till 6; it will need a
good deal of work to get things straightened out. I found
the accounts in a very much muddled condition, and discovered errors in simple addition . . . after five minutes examination; also cleaned out the safe which had apparently not been
orderly arranged for many years as there were important documents there which nobody in the Embassy knew existed. Mixed
up with sundry other papers was an envelope containing railroad shares which some poor woman had temporarily deposited
at the Embassy long ago and had doubtless failed to discover
them when called for; only her name was on the envelope. The
only worse case of this kind which has come to my notice was
a few weeks ago when [a member of the staff's] failure to
read a letter — because it was in German — kept a wretched
American in prison a week longer than was necessary. When
the letter came he apparently saw the word "militär" in the
first few lines and assuming that it was an ordinary military
case, with which I usually have to do, he put it in my basket to
await my return from Oberhof a week or so later. On my return a glance showed that an American citizen was being held
in prison in Germany merely until he could produce his cer-
tificate of American naturalization, which paper he had lost.
It was necessary only to tell him to cable to the court in which
the paper was issued and they would at once send him an
authenticated copy — but he had to wait a week longer than
was necessary for this simple piece of information. . . .

Wednesday, March 8 [1911]

. . . In the evening I went alone to a soirée at Archduke
Frederic's and Archduchess Isabelle's, parents of the charming
Princess Salm-Salm in Berlin. Alice was too tired to come.

O'Shaughnessy took me in and introduced me to several aides-de-camp and other minor officials as we passed through one room after another in apparent endless succession; in one of these rooms a very nervous-looking elderly person was standing, to whom O'Shaughnessy presented me and who made a few remarks punctuated with hysterical giggles which made it difficult to refrain from laughing back at him. After we had moved on I learned that this was the Archduke himself and that his nervousness was due to the fact that the Archduchess Annunziata, who ranks officially as the Empress, was coming upstairs just behind me and he had come forward through some of the antechambers to meet her and was evidently afraid that I was going to retard her progress. Fortunately I moved on in plenty of time, but the old man's giggles amused me so that I might well have remained for a pleasant and extended chat with him and effectually clogged the wheels of the court's procedure.

Subsequently I was presented to the Archduchess, a fine-looking woman of ample proportions (euphemism for "very fat") and covered with the biggest jewels I have ever seen outside the royal collection at Constantinople. She turned on the usual questions, "How long have you been here?" "Where did you come from?" and "How do you like Vienna?" with such astounding rapidity that my efforts betweentimes to tell her that I had the honor of knowing her daughter and her son-in-law, the latter very well, were quite in vain. Perhaps no explanation of her intense eagerness to bring the conversation to a close is really necessary, but in this case it appeared to be the arrival of the Duke and Duchess of Cumberland, she a sister of the Queen Dowager of England. I don't know exactly what rank they have in the *Almanach de Gotha* . . . but in Austria he is recognized as King of Hanover and given the rank of a reigning sovereign, Prussia's assimilation of that state being officially disregarded. He looks like a carpenter and has a perfectly bald head shaped like an egg — a very low collar, a very long gawky neck and old iron-rimmed "specs" — probably the most unkingly-looking king that ever existed. She is less handsome than Queen Alexandra, but wears her snow-white hair piled high on her head and is tall and rather imposing.

O'Shaughnessy very kindly introduced me to a great many people, but it was a great bore; the room was packed and frightfully hot and I was heartily glad that Alice had not come. . . .

Sunday, March 12 [1911]

A telephone message from the Embassy said vaguely that the Ambassador would call for me at 10.40. I supposed that he wanted to take me out for a drive and was prepared to say that Alice and I had already planned an outing and that I could not leave her. At 10.55 he drove up in his motor and I went out to see what he wanted. My surprise was great to find him with Major Allaire and Philip Hoefele [private secretary to the Ambassador] all in full rig and begging me to hurry. I happened by chance to have on a morning cutaway coat and silk hat, so put on an overcoat and got in. I was then for the first time informed that we were going to a big mass to cele-brate the 90th birthday of the Prince Regent of Bavaria and that the Emperor and all the Grand Dukes as well as the Diplomatic Corps were to be present! We were fifteen minutes late and reached the church immediately before the Emperor and went up the aisle just before him; Allaire pushed in ahead of me, though he is my junior in rank, and tried to wedge himself into the front pew next to Mr. Kerens and the other Ambassadors who occupied the first two rows, but he was immediately shown out by an usher and obliged to move back several rows. I do not relate this from any personal annoyance, but merely to show how our Embassy here makes itself the laughingstock of the place. The Ambassador and I should have been in full evening dress, no matter how unplea-sant that may seem; it is the only possible substitute we have for a uniform, and the frock coat, which is regarded by all Europeans as less formal, is on such occasions incorrect and frequently gives offense as showing a lack of due courtesy. Hoe-fele had no possible right to be there at all as he is not officially accredited and does not appear in the diplomatic list. Thus much for the savoir faire of the Embassy.

The mass was truly magnificent; the old Emperor came up the aisle followed by the Archdukes to the music of the Austrian national hymn, sung by a splendid choir; the service was impressive and the music grand. . . .

Thursday, April 20 [1911]

. . . Alas, my efforts to make Mrs. Kerens give dinners have been to no purpose! She has given up the idea entirely and decided instead to give merely a big soirée and ask everybody at once — a thing that people *hate* and in no way a fit return of hospitality received. A day or two ago Mrs. Kerens decided, as was proper, to give her first dinner for the Duke and Duchess of Cumberland and I wrote a personal note to Count Germand Grote, their Hofmarschall, asking for an audience for the Kerenses in order that they might personally request them to come to dine, the correct method of procedure. Grote replied that Their Highnesses regretted that they were leaving town almost immediately and would not be able to accept this year. That settled Mrs. K. and she informed me today that she would wait till next winter before beginning. It is not through stinginess on her part, but only her dread of making some mistake and also her desire to get her best tablecloths, etc., out from America! I protested again, hard, and told her frankly what people were saying, but all to no purpose. She is now absolutely immovable. She is afraid of not being able to get through with all the Ambassadors, of whom one can ask only two to each dinner, before the end of the season, and so will not risk it. But it would be so easy to give six dinners a week if necessary to finish them up rather than have people regard the American Embassy as nonexistent and a receiver but not a renderer of hospitality. I am disgusted and discouraged too. The Nicolas de Gierses [Russian Ambassador to Austria-Hun-

gary] came long after the Kerenses, but they have already had
everyone in official Vienna at their Embassy. . . .

Thursday, March 31 [1911]

Am still very busy at the Embassy — a very different life
from Berlin where my hours were 10.30 till 1.30. Here I am
at the office soon after 9 and stay till 1, returning after lunch at
2 or 2.30 and working usually till 5 or 6. One night this week
I had a note to translate at home which took from 8 till 12
without intermission, for the technical expressions in it were
very difficult. I had wondered how [some other members of
the staff], who were not much given to consecutive work, managed to get through this translating which the Ambassador
says they used to do. This point was cleared up the other day
when a young Austrian lady asked to see me at the Embassy
and told me confidentially that both . . . had been in the
habit of giving her all their translating work to do, paying her
out of their own pockets at the rate of 3 kronen per 100 words.
As some of the notes we receive from the Foreign Office must
amount to over 1000 words, this must have been somewhat
expensive. The Ambassador was quite unaware of this arrangement, but had wondered why they never translated a note the
same day he gave it to them.

It is to be hoped that M. Marshall Langhorne [newly appointed Second Secretary of the American Embassy at Vienna]
will be able both to translate from German into English and
to typewrite. In this Embassy, for instance, where there is no
clerk to fall back upon, [another secretary I know] would be
able to do absolutely nothing, since he neither typewrites nor
translates. Hoefele, the clerk here, is also the Ambassador's
private secretary and the greater part of his time is taken up
with the Ambassador's personal and private correspondence.
He is a thoroughly nice fellow and a very hard worker and
quite willing to take on as much as he can of the work. But
it does not seem to me right that the Embassy clerk, who is
paid by the Government at the rate of $1800 a year to do

Embassy work, should combine with those duties the functions of a private secretary, doubtless receiving extra salary therefor, and thus being only half at the Embassy's disposal. It throws a much larger part of the routine work onto the shoulders of the Embassy secretaries than should be theirs by rights. . . .

To return to the affairs of the Embassy, it seems to me somewhat out of proportion that the Embassy in Berlin should receive a contingent allowance of $15,000 a year and two clerks at $1800 each, while we here have to scrimp along on a mere $5000 and only one clerk. The $15,000 arrangement was made when Elihu Root was Secretary of State to help Dr. Hill meet his rent and to buy furniture. . . .

Mr. Kerens wrote to the Department the other day, asking for an increase of the contingent allowance to $7000; even this seems to me out of proportion. When one considers what has to be paid for out of that amount — the rent of the Embassy offices, the heating and cleaning of same, the salary of the two messengers and porter, all postage and incidental expenses, subscriptions to papers, electric light, stationery and a hundred other items — it does not go far, and not a red cent is left at the end of the fiscal year to buy furniture with. When Rives left he took nearly all the furniture from the First Secretary's room, as it belonged to him personally, and now my spacious office is decorated only by a rickety desk, two chairs and a couple of deal-board tables — besides the three bookcases kindly lent by the Ambassador. . . .

Tuesday, May 2 [1911]

. . . I was busy with prima donnas from the Opera (which the Ambassador rightfully observes are harder to deal with than an armful of wildcats) arranging for music at the big soirée which the Kerenses are giving on the 11th. All our efforts to persuade Mrs. K. (who exclusively runs the social affairs of the Embassy) to dispense with music at this enormous rout and to give a small and select musicale later, which would be far more appreciated and which would to a certain extent make up for the dinners that have not been given, have failed;

she is obstinate beyond belief and arguments are of no avail once she has made up her mind; I have never met a person so difficult to discuss things with for she simply refuses to listen and talks steadily without permitting a word to be said on the other side of the question — a discouraging trait when one is trying one's best to assist her. Today Mrs. K. requested me to see Madame Cahier, an American by birth and the best contralto at the Opera — a woman with a really superb voice and great musical feeling — to ask her to sing. I went out to her house on the outskirts of the city and was received by her and her husband, a Norwegian. As soon as she had heard the circumstances she said that it would be quite impossible to sing at so large a rout, for people could not be kept quiet (Mrs. K. has invited her entire calling list — in other words, the entire society of Vienna, the Diplomatic Corps and resident Americans). Both Mme. Cahier and her husband said that it would be infinitely better and wiser to have an orchestra play than to have singing on this occasion and I, agreeing heartily, returned to tell Mrs. K. After she had listened (in this case) to Mme. Cahier's answer and my own advice, she said sweetly: "Now that Cahier has refused we will ask Kurtz." Frau Selma Kurtz is the best soprano at the Opera . . . difficult to deal with and quite a different type from Mme. Cahier. . . . I went at once to Kurtz's apartment and was received; she said at once that she would be glad to sing and then came the difficult proposition of arranging the fee. Kurtz said immediately that she never received less than 4000 kronen; I replied that the Ambassador did not wish to pay so large a sum and after a few pleasant remarks on various subjects, got up to go. Then the negotiations really began and were conducted, as is usual in such cases, on the threshold with my hand practically on the doorknob. They resulted in Frau Kurtz finally agreeing to sing for 3000 kronen, though she said it was "sehr peinlich" and that she had never done such a thing before and that it must be kept quite confidential. I returned to the Embassy, there was a council of war in the Ambassador's room (the only time in my experience that Mrs. K. has consulted Mr. K. about any matter whatsoever — in fact she has sometimes forbidden me to speak to him about certain things which I felt should certainly be submitted to his judgment) and the consent of the holder of the family check book was secured; I promptly tracked Kurtz to her modiste's and the deal was closed. . . .

Thursday, May 11 [1911]

. . . Embassy soirée in the evening at 9. About 300 out of the 800 invited guests came. Kurtz sang charmingly (five songs at 600 kronen apiece!) and in spite of the Cahiers' fears there was absolute silence during the singing. I am glad that Mr. Cahier was there and heard it. At the end of the fourth song I was obliged, at Mrs. Kerens's request, to battle through the crowd in order to present the prima donna with a bunch of orchids. Mrs. K. thought that this touching tribute would impress the lady favorably and induce her to sing more than the customary five songs, but when I later requested her to do so, she quite firmly declined. The story is told of her here, and I have every reason to believe in its veracity, that once when her host made such a request, she replied that she would do so but must receive her fee for every extra song given. She had been invited to remain for supper afterwards and was somewhat surprised when supper was announced to find her host giving her his arm and conducting her downstairs with the remark that her carriage was waiting. She was however enlightened when, on protesting, the gentleman politely said: "Madame, business is business."

In spite of all our fears, the soirée was a decided success; many people stayed till twelve and all seemed to have a good time. It was marred only by two young American girl-tourists, or students — appearing in enormous hats, which they did not have the sense to remove throughout the evening. . . .

To Henry Sturgis Grew, May 19, 1911

. . . One of the pleasantest things in being stationed at posts like Berlin and Vienna is the music one has the opportunity

to hear. Alice and I have both developed a love of Wagner
which takes us regularly to the Opera whenever anything of
his is given — though it is only the *Ring* and *Tristan* that
fully satisfy us. *Tristan* is now, to me, the acme of pleasure.
We heard it again a few nights ago and have been walking
on air ever since. But the voices here are, I fear, far behind
what you hear in America. . . .

We have a vague hope of running over to the old country this
fall, perhaps in October, but no plans can be sure at present
since I am absolutely dependent on those of my chief; I expect
to be Chargé d'Affaires all summer and have no idea when he
will return after his vacation. In any case, I have my eye very
firmly fixed on our decennial next June [at Harvard] and hope
surely to be able to be on hand for those very tempting festivities.

It may interest you to know that we are very well satisfied
with our new post and that I have now got the chancery running entirely to my liking. At first the old man used to handle
the despatches, notes and letters which I wrote much as a lawn
mower treats the verdant herb of the greensward, but things
have gradually changed and the climax of my satisfaction was
reached the other day, I think, when he signed eight consecutive notes to the Foreign Office, which I had written, without
altering a word. This is what I have been aiming at, and I
now have the reins fairly well in my own grip. The Ambassador is a fine old gentleman of the American business school
and one has to get up pretty early to beat him at poker —
which is analogous to diplomacy. There is more bluffing in the
game than ever took place at a card table. I have now had good
opportunity to compare the scholar and the businessman as
diplomatists, and the more I see of the latter type, the more
I am convinced that it wins out in these days of trade and
commerce. . . .

Thursday, June 1 [1911]

. . . In the P.M. I went to the Foreign Office and saw Consul

General Josef Hempel about some military cases, one man, Tanenbaum, having been imprisoned somewhere in Austria and having telegraphed wildly to the Embassy to get him out as he was protected by our naturalization treaty. The officials in the small towns, especially in Hungary, have a way of arresting all naturalized Americans on their return to their native country and keeping them in prison until their military records can be examined; they say that they cannot read American passports as they are in English! I protested vigorously in this case and the man was released by telegraph the same day. He wrote us at once saying that he would include us in his daily prayers for all future time. . . .

Sunday, June 18 [1911]

A fine warm day and doubly appreciated by me as a break in this "dinner pail" existence. We breakfasted on the terrace and sat under the trees all the morning, basking in the delicious country sunshine. . . . I worked — all day long — on Embassy business. The very day of the Ambassador's departure a pouch came in with more new work than we have had for many months — three or four puzzling new cases which I shall have to study up in detail.[4] On top of all this Hoefele informed me that he would like to go on leave in July! I suppose the Embassy servant will apply for leave next and leave me to sweep the floor together with the rest of the job. Needless to say, the Department has not appointed another 2nd Secretary. However, Hoefele was good enough to say that he would not leave me alone in any case, and I wrote the Ambassador asking him to cable again from London urging the absolute necessity of another secretary at once. The Department refused the Ambassador's request for an increase in the contingent allowance from $5000 to $7000 (even though Berlin received $15,000), so there is no money to employ extra assistance with. However, the Ambassador authorized me to do so

[4] Ambassador Kerens left Vienna on June 17, for a four-month visit to the United States. During this period Mr. Grew acted as Chargé d'Affaires.

if I wished and he will pay it out of his own pocket; if much translation work comes in, this will be absolutely necessary. . . .

To my mother, September 18, 1911

. . . Lately I have been even busier than before, seldom getting out before dinner time, and having several long reports to prepare and get off to Washington. In the last few weeks I have sent in reports on 132 different newspapers in Austria-Hungary, called for by the Department, giving their circulation, politics, influence, name of owner, editor, etc., and full details regarding each one. Then last week came an instruction calling for a full description of the parcel-post system in Austria for the use of the Committee on Post Offices and Post Roads in the Senate and after a hard week's work I got off a 30-page report on Saturday — and now I know everything there is to know about the subject, which at least is interesting. . . .

Yesterday there was a great public socialist demonstration in Vienna; much damage was done and many people injured by charging troops; the Government has been acting disgracefully in keeping up the high price of food and keeping out foreign meat from the country and I expect that this will make them change their policy to some extent. . . .[5]

Sunday, January 7 [1912]

. . . I find that I neglected to mention a call on Archduke Franz Ferdinand, the heir to the throne, which the Ambassador and I made on December 31. When the Ambassador went to see the Burgomaster of Vienna last fall with regard

[5] The difficult economic situation in Austria and the food riots were covered in a series of despatches to the Department of State, produced by the sweat of my brow throughout that summer. When visiting Washington on a leave of absence, I called on the Chief of the Division of Near Eastern Affairs, which dealt with Austria-Hungary, fully expecting something in the nature of an accolade. Alas, for such unsubstantial dreams. The Chief, who was not a Foreign Service Officer, had his feet on a clean-swept desk and was reading the baseball news. He hadn't read or even seen my economic reports. They were probably in the files, he suggested. That was another shattered dream for me! — J. C. G.

to possible city-owned sites for a new Embassy building, the latter told him that the best plot was one on the Karlsplatz, just behind the French Embassy; I had learned this myself from the Vice Burgomaster last summer and had reported fully to Washington, as instructed, regarding the cost thereof, but the Ambassador seemed to think it necessary to do this again. The Burgomaster, Dr. Josef Neumayer, told the Ambassador that Franz Ferdinand was interested in the architecture of the Karlsplatz and that he would have to pass on any building which it was intended to erect there, so although we had received no instructions of any kind to open negotiations nor any intimation from the Department that it intended to acquire a site here within the next few years, what did the Ambassador do but request a private audience with F. F. in order to discuss the matter with him. The Archduke politely replied that he was particularly busy at that moment, but would send the Court landscape architect, Count Karl Lanckoronski, who could give the Ambassador full information. Lanckoronski came and had a pleasant hour's conference with the Ambassador, both talking at once and neither hearing nor paying any attention to what the other was saying. Finally he took us around to the Karlsplatz and showed us the site which was for sale, pointing out to Mr. Kerens the various splendid views of the two-century-old Karlskirche, the pride of Vienna and of his own heart (he has written a work on the past and future of the Karlsplatz) to which the latter replied: "Yes, here would be the entrance to the kitchen and there we could place the garage," etc. I was never so much entertained in my life.

 This all leads up to the call on Franz Ferdinand, which I set out to describe. One day a few weeks later, Baron Karl Rumerskirch, the Archduke's Hofmarschall, came to see me and said that the Archduke had now returned from the country and if the Ambassador still desired some information which Lanckoronski had not been able to give him, he would be glad to receive him at 11.30 on the 31st of December. The Ambassador accepted like a shot and at the appointed time we were at the palace, I in the capacity of interpreter, as the Archduke does not speak English. Franz Ferdinand is a fine-looking man, tall, well-built, with light hair, blue eyes and a thoroughly pleasant expression; he received us cordially and then the Ambassador proceeded to talk for twenty minutes, all of which I translated into French, wishing him first all the good wishes for the New Year which he could think of and then telling the Archduke all about the law for the acquisition of embassy buildings which had been passed by Congress, even down to the specific amounts of money appropriated! Finally he had me open the plan of Vienna which we had brought and proceeded to show the Archduke all the possible sites in the city which might be used for an Embassy. Not a question did he ask nor did he allow the Archduke to do any talking, and at the close of the interview, we went away without having obtained from the Archduke a single piece of information, to secure which was the whole ostensible purpose of the audience. But, as the Ambassador remarked to me as we drove away, "we got near the Archduke, and that won't be so easy once he is Emperor."

To Lilla Cabot Perry [Mrs. Grew's mother],
January 10, 1912

A typewritten letter seems at first sight a poor return for your delightful and most interesting one of December 17th, but as you know that I wield that weighty machine myself I am sure you feel that the result is quite as personal as my ill-formed and painful caligraphy. Someday we shall all come to it and shall carry around our pocket typewriters instead of our leaky fountain pens, but for the present the pioneers must go forward apologetically. You probably know that the present Prince Regent of Bavaria insists on having all type-written documents copied into longhand before he will consider them, and a regular staff of clerks is employed for that particular purpose. I wonder that he consents to read the printed newspapers — or books.

Your letter gave me much pleasure and all you said about Mr. Lowell's ambassadorship was very interesting.[6] I quake lest they now break the long line of able men our Government has sent to London by putting in some political boss — and then place us under him. Alice and I have had five posts and *not once* have we been under a chief and chéfesse who could teach us how to do things right — as Bellamy Storer, Bob Bacon or Henry White could have done [7] — and when we become a Minister, if we ever do, we shall lack just that training which can be had only from one's own chief. Mr. Lowell's record in England is something we all ought to be proud of. . . .

I am making more time for reading this winter, fortunately, as we seldom go out in the evenings as yet, and am actually going through Thackeray and Dickens with the greatest delight. What I read of them was years ago before I could half appreciate their style and now I welcome the end of the day which lets me get back to our library and turn from dry despatches and Foreign Office notes to the delights of those volumes. . . .

Saturday, February 17 [1912]

. . . Baroness F. told me that Count Aehrenthal was in his last moments and at 9.45 P.M. Robert Atter, of the A.P., called me up and said that the Emperor had finally accepted his resignation and appointed Count Leopold Berchtold in his place as Minister for Foreign Affairs. At 10.45 Atter again called me up to say that Aehrenthal had died at 9.45. We felt profoundly moved at the passing of this great statesman. There has been a good deal of comment at the Emperor's action in thus accepting a deathbed resignation and bestowing upon the dying man the brilliants for his Grand Cross of the Order of St. Stephan which, together with the Emperor's "Hand-

[6] James Russell Lowell was Minister to Great Britain from 1880 to 1885.

[7] Bellamy Storer had been Minister to Belgium, Minister to Spain, and Ambassador to Austria-Hungary. Robert Bacon had held the posts of Assistant Secretary of State, Secretary of State, and Ambassador to France. In addition to various career posts below the rank of Ambassador, Henry White had been Ambassador to Italy and to France, and Special Ambassador to Chile.

schrift," appear to have reached him after he had finally lost consciousness. But it is probable that this was done to let Aehrenthal know that the man of his choice had been selected as his successor, before he died, which perhaps was even better than permitting him to die in harness. Count Aehrenthal had twice in the last few months tendered his resignation, but it had not been accepted, and it is felt that the worry of holding the burden of office when so ill and the bitter attacks made on him by the war party in Austria, headed by the Archduke Franz Ferdinand, materially hastened his end. His had been a policy of peace, the upholding of the Triple Alliance and the maintenance of good relations with Italy at any cost. The war party, always eager to regain the provinces once torn from Austria by Italy,[8] desire the strengthening of the garrisons on the Italian border and the increase of the army at the expense of the people, at a time when they can badly afford added burdens of taxation. The war element, represented by the Christian Socialist Party, caused the downfall of General von Schönaich, Minister of War, and his Chief of General Staff, Baron Conrad von Hötzendorf, last fall, and then proceeded to direct their attacks on Count Aehrenthal.

Count Berchtold, although practically pledged to carry on the general policy of his former chief and friend, is nevertheless liked by Franz Ferdinand, as well as the Emperor; is popular in Hungary as being a Hungarian by naturalization and a member of the Hungarian House of Magnates, and would in every respect appear to be starting upon his new duties under exceptionally favorable auspices. . . .

Thursday, February 22 [1912]

Count Aehrenthal's funeral at 2.30. The music was magnificent. Afterwards we marched behind the coffin from the church to the Schwarzenbergplatz, but as most of the Diplo-

---

8 Sardinia-Piedmont, the leading Italian state of the nineteenth century, received Lombardy as the result of victory in the War of 1859 with Austria. At the end of the Seven Weeks' War of 1866 against Prussia, Austria had been forced to cede Venetia to the newly created kingdom of Italy, the ally of Prussia.

matic Corps got out of the church long after the coffin, those who marched were far behind the procession and did not come in sight of it until it had reached its destination. On the Schwarzenbergplatz the officers, Foreign Office officials and diplomats who had marched behind took leave of the coffin and it proceeded up the Heugasse past our house to the Staatsbahnhof where it was taken to Bohemia for burial. The court-hearse was used and it was a magnificent sight with its outriders, candle bearers and trappings.[9]

[9] Count Leopold Berchtold, his charming wife, Nadine, and his sons became close friends of ours, and our visits to his old family castle, Buchlau, in Moravia, were among the pleasantest we made.

When I had official business to transact with him, we sometimes asked him to dinner in our home and did the business in an informal atmosphere there. One interesting case involved two men who had broken into a jewelry store in Boston, escaping with a big haul of diamonds to Austria, where they were convicted of some minor crime and sentenced to a few months of imprisonment in the provinces. The Boston police learned about this and sent two detectives over to Vienna to extradite the criminals on their release.

I confidently applied to the Foreign Office to arrange this extradition, only to be told that our extradition treaty failed to include the crime of breaking and entering with which the criminals were charged. Appeals to the Minister failed to solve the impasse, although the detectives sat optimistically in my study at the Embassy day after day for a month or more. My argument that it was to Austria's interest to have these criminals punished fell on deaf ears.

On the eve of the release from the Austrian jail of the two men, I asked Count Berchtold to dinner and made a last plea with all the force at my command. The next day he telephoned and asked when the detectives were returning to America. "As soon as they can, I suppose," I replied. "Well," he said, "you might tell them that there is a very good ship, the *Martha Washington*, sailing from Trieste to New York tomorrow, and that I can recommend that vessel." The detectives took the hint, and just before the gangplank of the *Martha Washington* was drawn up the two criminals were delivered to them, handcuffed on board. Not a word had passed in writing. No extradition papers were ever prepared.

A year or so later I visited Boston. The Boston police took me on a visit to the State Prison. "You see those two men over in that corner?" my escort asked. "You had better not let them know who you are or your life might not be very safe. They are the two men you helped deliver to us, put away for terms of twelve and fifteen years." Thus diplomacy! — J. C. G.

VII

Return to Berlin

1912 – 1914

On September 12, 1912, Mr. Grew was appointed First Secretary of the Embassy in Berlin, a post he was to hold until the United States broke relations with Germany in 1917. Mr. Grew's new appointment occurred during the heated presidential campaign of William H. Taft, Woodrow Wilson, and Theodore Roosevelt backed by the new Progressive party. The election of Woodrow Wilson brought the Democrats back into the Presidency for the first time since 1897. The resulting clamor for political positions by "deserving Democrats" was immense. The President and his Secretary of State, William Jennings Bryan, were overwhelmed with requests from thousands of officeseekers for State Department positions. Mr. Bryan was more sympathetic to these requests than the President. Although Alvey Adee, Second Assistant Secretary, who had been in the Department for thirty-six years, was retained, most of the administrative posts in Washington were changed. In the Foreign Service, the President took direct charge of selecting a number of able men for the most important posts. Walter Hines Page, editor of The World's Work, *was appointed to London; James W. Gerard, New York lawyer and judge, to Berlin; Thomas Nelson Page, the author, to Rome; Professor Henry Van Dyke of Princeton to the Netherlands; and Brand Whitlock, Mayor of Toledo, to Belgium.*

During the first six months of the new Administration twenty-nine out of some forty-odd diplomatic chiefs of missions were changed. Many of those who lost their positions had worked their way up through the Service. The changes involved Ambassadors and Ministers, although Mr. Grew's letters

*and diary expressed concern, at first, that the secretaries might
be changed as well.*

*Secretary Bryan's attitude toward diplomatic appointments
was widely criticized, particularly after the publication of a
letter written to the Receiver General of Customs at Santo
Domingo in which Bryan stated: "Now that you have arrived
and acquainted yourself with the situation, can you let me
know what positions you have at your disposal with which to
reward deserving democrats? . . . You know . . . how difficult
it is to find suitable rewards for the deserving."*

To Perry Belden, American Legation, Honduras,
November 28, 1912

. . . Our transfer to Berlin came, I think, after you wrote me.
We were absolutely delighted, for I always liked this place and
the work in Vienna never quite filled my soul. It is also a
great satisfaction to work under a diplomat like Mr. Leishman,
for one learns. Someday I shall have to write a book on "Chiefs
I have Met," for mine have been varied: Riddle the society
man; Hill the scholar; Kerens the businessman; and now, at
last, a real diplomat.[1]

We have taken an apartment here in a new house on the
corner of Rauch and Friedrich Wilhelmstrasse, where your
successor [Albert B. Ruddock, Third Secretary of the American
Embassy at Berlin] and his wife are so far the only other inhabitants. I don't know if you know him; he is a splendid
worker and very valuable acquisition to the Service. Willing
Spencer you know already. Heaven only knows where we shall
all be this time next year, but the general opinion seems to be
that President Wilson will stand firm for maintaining the
Foreign Service on a Civil Service footing and will make few
changes among the secretaries. I believe his intention is to
put the whole Service, including chiefs of mission, on this basis
eventually — probably after it has been carefully filled with

[1] John G. A. Leishman was appointed Ambassador to Germany on August 12,
1911. Since 1897 he had held various diplomatic posts in Switzerland, Turkey,
and Italy. Before entering the Foreign Service, he had been president of the
Carnegie Steel Company.

Democrats! Of course there will be tremendous pressure brought to bear, but Wilson is undoubtedly a strong man and an honest one, besides being intelligent, and the combination of those qualities ought to bring good results. Of course you know him well yourself and I hope you are strong with him. I myself, though I do not know him, admire him greatly and believe that the country is in safe hands. . . .

To Norman Armour,[2] Princeton University, December 21, 1912

. . . My wife and I are now comfortably installed in Berlin and are very happy here; I like it infinitely better than Vienna for ever so many reasons; in fact, from my point of view, there is no post like it in the Service; one has good sport, good music, nice people and above all most interesting Embassy work. The only sad thing is that prospect of walking the plank next March. You perhaps know that the Senate has refused to confirm Mr. Taft's recess nominations, among which ours to Berlin is included, which means that we automatically lose our job at the end of the present session of Congress. Whether Dr. Wilson will reappoint us to the same post seems very uncertain, even if he retains most of those already in. After the expense which we have been put to in this recent move and in fitting out another apartment here, I could not and would not accept any other post of equal or lower grade, both on account of my wife's health and the expense involved. This is a somewhat sad outlook after eight interesting years of work in the Service, which, as a Service, has been very close to my heart. I may come home in February and see if we can

2 Norman Armour and a young Princeton classmate named Berry came to Vienna on a European tour in the summer of 1911 or 1912, visiting us at Semmering with letters of introduction. After sizing the boys up I told them that I badly needed help at the Embassy, and that if they would stay with me that summer I would make them private secretaries, and that they would thus learn much more about European politics than by touring with a Baedeker and camera. They stayed, and thus Armour became the first of many private secretaries who worked with me at different posts. Fortunately he eventually entered our Foreign Service at my advice and ultimately became one of our outstanding ambassadors. — J. C. G.

do anything to get reappointed, but I have no connecting links with Mr. Wilson whatever and I'm afraid that nothing we could do would be of any use. . . .

To John Leishman,[3] December 27, 1912

I received your letter of the 25th instant this morning and immediately made an appointment with Herr Arthur Zimmermann [Under Secretary of State] whom I saw at 1 o'clock. . . .

Now as to the Balkans and Vienna. Herr Zimmermann had very little to tell me, beyond the fact that they were urging — that is, the German Government was urging — Turkey to give in on the question of the retention of Adrianople, Janina and Scutari.[4] He thought that Turkey would take this advice, though it was a bitter pill to swallow. He mentioned the fact of the Turkish lack of money, supplies and Generals as absolutely precluding the possibility of further resistance, though there were plenty of good soldiers to fight if the organization were not entirely depleted. As for Vienna, he said that while Serbia had not yet definitely announced her agreement with the proposals made, he thought that she would make a favorable announcement shortly. I talked with him a little about Count Berchtold and he agreed that his position was at present a little embarrassing owing to the false news given out regarding the Prochaska incident; [5] he also spoke with regret of the

3 The Ambassador was in Paris, and Mr. Grew was acting as Chargé d'Affaires.

4 On October 8, 1912, Montenegro had opened hostilities against the Turks. She was soon joined by Serbia, Bulgaria, and Greece. The Balkan states captured every piece of territory for which they had hoped with the exception of the three fortresses of Scutari, Janina, and Adrianople. On December 3, an armistice was signed providing for peace negotiations to take place in London, and pressure was brought to bear upon Turkey by the Great Powers to surrender these three fortresses. Ernest C. Helmreich, *The Diplomacy of the Balkan Wars 1912–1913* (Cambridge: Harvard University Press, 1938), pp. 125–45, 193–280.

5 An Austrian consul, Oscar Prochaska, had been accused by the Serbians in November, 1912, of aiding the Turks and Albanians against the Serbians in fighting around Prizren. Many rumors circulated in Austria-Hungary about the indignities and violence to which Prochaska had been subjected by the Serbs. No official denial by Austria of these baseless reports was issued until December 17, 1912. The government was severely criticized for not having made such

great economic losses which Austria had sustained. These crumbs are, I'm afraid, of little originality or interest. . . .

Wednesday, January 29 [1913]

. . . I have to go a good deal to the Foreign Office as several difficult questions are pending, chiefly those of the Chinese Loan and troubles in Liberia over which we spread our protecting wing.[6] My relations at the Foreign Office are particularly pleasant, since most of our work is carried on with the Under Secretary of State, Zimmermann, or with Count Adolf Montgelas, both of whom are friendly and agreeable to deal with. The Ambassador now leaves the greater part of the work to me; I go through all the mail and show him only the most important things; the habit of dictating communications to our stenographer comes easily and saves an enormous amount of time. . . .

Tuesday, February 4 [1913]

. . . All Germany has recently been laughing at the Strassburg hoax. . . . Some wag sent a telegram to himself, erased the address and contents and substituted a message to the Governor of Strassburg signed "Wilhelm I. R." ordering the entire garrison of the town to be alarmed and to parade immediately, as he, the Emperor, would arrive in an hour by automobile. The perpetrator of the joke then disguised himself as a telegraph boy and delivered the message at the Governor's house. The whole garrison, including the Governor,

a statement earlier, which would have averted the war scare. *Ibid.*, pp. 213–15, 227–30.

6 Because of lack of funds the new republican government of China had negotiated for foreign loans with a six-power consortium, an international banking agency composed of banking groups from England, France, Germany, Japan, Russia, and the United States. Although the American banking group withdrew when President Wilson took away official government support, the Reorganization Loan Agreement was completed on April 26, 1913. Paul Hibbert Clyde, *The Far East* (New York: Prentice Hall, Inc., 1948), pp. 368–70. The United States had offered to co-operate with Germany and Liberia to settle difficulties arising between the latter two countries when German citizens and property in Liberia had been attacked. U.S. Department of State, *Papers Relating to the Foreign Relations of the United States, 1913* (Washington: Government Printing Office, 1920), pp. 655–80.

the commanding General and several other important person-
ages, including the Kaiser's own son, Prince Joachim, did parade without delay and stood there in the chief square of the
city until someone thought of ascertaining, three hours later,
whether the telegram was authentic. Meanwhile, as anyone
would have known who read the papers, the Kaiser was at exactly the other end of the Empire, holding a review there.
They say that the poor old General who commands the forces
at Strassburg is in for it; anyway, he has been summoned to
Berlin to report. The wag was caught and will probably have
ample time to cogitate on the success of his joke alone for the
next several years. . . .

To Franklin D. Roosevelt, February 25, 1913

Randolph [Mr. Grew's brother] sent me your letter to him
of February 1st and I want to send you a line or two to tell
you how much I appreciate your interest and promised assistance towards my remaining in the Diplomatic Service. You
must not embarrass yourself in any way in taking the matter
up with the new Administration, but you may be sure that I
shall be exceedingly appreciative and deeply indebted to you
for any word of recommendation that you may be able to
say. I have found this old Service intensely interesting in the
last nine years and should be sorry to leave it if that could
be avoided.

I do not think I have ever had an occasion to congratulate
you on your political success but we are all very proud of you
and hope to see you higher up still before long.[7]

To my mother, March 13, 1913

. . . You say that I seem to have several strings to my bow
and this is true, for I have made a point of getting as many
endorsements sent in to the new Administration as possible.[8]

[7] Mr. Roosevelt had been elected to the New York State Senate in 1910 and
had been an early supporter of Mr. Wilson for the Democratic nomination in
1912. President Wilson appointed Mr. Roosevelt Assistant Secretary of the Navy.
Roosevelt and Mr. Grew had been friends at Groton and Harvard.

[8] Mr. Grew's appointment as First Secretary of the Berlin Embassy — a recess
appointment — was confirmed by the Senate on March 1, 1913.

If there is any question of overturning the Service they will come in useful. I know of at least five separate influential Democrats who have put in a word for us. I don't like to blow my own trumpet, but have no objection to others doing it for me at this critical period, and if we should be turned out while others were kept in, I should always regret having left any stones unturned. . . .

To my mother, May 27, 1913

. . . Berlin began to fill up for the wedding of the Emperor's daughter, Princess Victoria Louise, to Prince Ernst August of Brunswick and Luneburg, the son of the Duke of Cumberland on May 26. This was entirely a love match and a very interesting one. When Prince George [oldest son of the Duke of Cumberland] was killed in a motor accident last year on his way to the funeral of the King of Denmark — we knew him well in Vienna and he had been going to dine with us when he was killed — the Kaiser showed some mark of condolence and later the younger brother, Ernst August, who was in a Bavarian regiment, came to Berlin to express his father's thanks to the Kaiser. It was then that he met the little Princess and they promptly fell in love with one another. The Grand Duke of Baden saw what was up and asked young Ernst if he would let him go ahead and arrange the match. Ernst said that it was the one great hope of his life, etc., etc., but that it was useless to ask his father's permission as he would never consent, owing to the permanent grudge he bore the Kaiser over the Hanoverian succession. The Duke of Cumberland, as rightful King of Hanover, has never waived the question of his succession and sovereignty since Prussia assimilated the kingdom and the two families had previously not been on speaking terms at all.[9] As things turned out, the Grand Duke of Baden managed to fix it up, the Duke gave in and the young couple and their parents met at Carlsruhe and were formally engaged.

9 By the Prussian decree of September 20, 1866, Hanover had been incorporated as a province of Prussia. This annexation followed Hanover's participation in the war of 1866 between Prussia and Austria, in which Hanover had sided with the latter.

The wedding, which took place yesterday, was quite the most splendid affair we have ever seen and I don't suppose we shall ever be present at a more brilliant and interesting gathering than met in the chapel in the Schloss last evening.[10] Besides the young couple, the Kaiser and Kaiserin, the Duke and Duchess of Cumberland, the Tsar of Russia and the King and Queen of England, there were present many of the reigning princes and grand dukes from all over Germany, besides the entire Court of Berlin in double-barreled gala array. The "Fürstlichkeiten" had been arriving in Berlin for several days and the Emperor had been very busy going to and from the station to meet people like the Cumberlands, the Tsar and the King and Queen of England. Night before last we were asked to the gala opera, when the 1st act of *Lohengrin* was given at the little Princess' request. It was exceedingly well done, as they had relegated most of the lamentably deficient regular cast to the background and imported singers . . . for the occasion and the scenery and costumes were entirely new and most brilliant (I'm afraid I'm overworking that word!). The house was simply smothered in flowers and the invited ladies had done themselves proud in matters of costume and jewels. At 8 the young couple appeared in the big royal box, followed by the Kaiser and the Duchess of Cumberland, the Kaiserin and the Tsar, the Queen of England with somebody else, and the King with the Crown Princess, and then all the rest of the assembled royalty. Alice was near the royal box upstairs, with the wives of the 1st Secretaries of Embassy and Naval and Military Attachés, who alone were invited, besides the *chefs de mission,* to the gala opera and to the wedding itself, and I was downstairs in the parquet with the men. After the Vorstellung, there was a "cercle" in the foyer, where the royalties wander through the crowd and speak to whom they please. We had met the King and Queen of England in Cairo only eight years ago, when as Prince and Princess of Wales they came to tea at our Agency, and I was an old friend of the Tsar from St. Petersburg, but they totally failed to

[10] This was the last general gathering of European royalty before the outbreak of the First World War.

recognize us, which was very careless on their parts! However, the little Cumberland princess, Olga, did recognize us both and she had a pleasant chat with Alice. . . .

Yesterday Alice got into her court dress and train and I into my uniform, which is the most uncomfortable thing you can imagine with its choking collar and tight Duke of Wellington boots, but is better than a dress suit on such occasions, at 3.30 and at 4.30 we were at the Schloss and took our places in the chapel. At 5 punctually, for they are absolutely punctual at court, the young couple entered, followed by the rest of the royalty in the usual order, with the Kaiser, Kaiserin and the Cumberlands first, the Tsar and the Queen of England next, and the King of England and Crown Princess third, preceded by heralds in marvelous costume and each group of royalty escorted by an assortment of chamberlains, ladies-in-waiting and pages. The pages were in pink costume with white lace bibs and tuckers and they stood in a great circle around the chapel, with the royalties in the center and the rest of the guests around the walls on raised platforms so that we could see well. Nobody was seated. The Prince and Princess stood on a dais before the altar and were married by the principal court clergyman in a short and simple service, interspersed with truly magnificent music by choir and orchestra and organ. After the service they each kissed their respective parents in turn and then the procession went out in the same order in which it had entered, very slowly, each group of royalty and its attendants separately.

After that the royalties took their places in the Weisser Saal in a long row, the Princess looking quite charming with her little crown of diamonds and red plush and the Prince, a fine-looking youth in Hussar uniform, in the center and we all filed past for our congratulatory curtsey or bow to the newly married couple. This was followed by supper, a really excellent supper and well served, the diplomats being together, and then, at 8, came the "Fackeltanz" which is a regular custom at German royal weddings. Preceded by the Hofmarschall and about twenty pages bearing large candles, the Princess takes a man on either hand and the Prince two ladies and they walk once round the room, changing their escort each time around until every royalty present has done a lap. It was especially amusing when, the second time around, the Princess was escorted by the King of England and the Tsar, for I had always thought they looked exactly alike but was now able, by actual comparison, to dispel this illusion. They do resemble one another, but there would be no possibility of mistaking one for the other. The Tsar is fuller and squarer, much more hairy about the face and even the neck, where his beard seems to grow almost around behind and he has that square Slav expression about the forehead and eyes, quite different from the King's. The King is slimmer, balder and thinner of face. Queen Mary is really very pretty and attractive-looking. As for the old Duke of Cumberland, with his totally bald head polished like a shiny white billiard ball and his iron-rimmed specs, he is the funniest-looking old character imaginable.

So that ends the entertainment. After the dividing of the bride's garter by Countess Brockdorff, the Mistress of the Robes, the royal procession, still in its exact order as before, again forms, the bride again kisses her parents and they leave the hall to the strains of sweet music, preparatory to going to the station to see the young couple off for the St. Hubertus hunting lodge where they are to pass their honeymoon, the Tsar at the same time departing for Russia. I don't know whom they took us for, but Alice and I were cheered all the way home by the tremendous crowds that lined the streets, which we gracefully acknowledged by repeated bows to right and left, which caused the cheers to redouble! It was quite a wonderful sight to see the dense crowd which surrounded the Schloss, from the palace windows, and in the twilight just before dark, with the palace all ablaze with light, it made an extraordinary picture. Every time one of us appeared at a window, a tremendous cheer went up. . . .

When we got home I could not believe that we had seen a real live wedding. Everything had been done so absolutely according to rote, even to the kissing of the parents at the

proper time, in the proper way and in their proper order, and
the costumes and setting of every scene had been so unusual,
that one felt much more that one had been to the opera and
had beheld a stage wedding with an all-star cast of actors. It
was certainly worthwhile having seen it and I am glad we were
invited. The happiest thing about it is that it is a love match
and not one of the many which are brought about purely for
political reasons, though the political advantages of this one
cannot well be overrated. . . .

P.S. There were 57 royalties present at the wedding; doesn't
this remind you of Heinz's 57 "different varieties" of
pickles! . . .

To Willing Spencer, June 26, 1913

I have a great piece of news for you. . . . A telegram came
this morning from the Dept., beginning, "To be deciphered
by the Ambassador." Indeed I haven't the slightest objection
to his deciphering it and promptly forwarded it to him as
received, as he has the code. But if you think that my New
England conscience prevented me from deciphering it too,
you may have one more think. I guessed pretty well what it
contained and needed any possible information which might
help me to make my plans for leave. Unfortunately that has
gone up in smoke, but the name of our new chief consoled me
for any personal inconvenience. The Amb. is instructed to
obtain immediately the Emperor's agrément to the appointment of Justice James W. Gerard, of the Supreme Court of
New York, a distinguished scholar and citizen. He is also
instructed to leave Berlin a fortnight before his successor's
arrival or at once on leave, as he pleases, and to inform the
Dept. which plan he adopts. That looks as if our new chief
would be here before long. . . .

To my mother, September 16, 1913

. . . I am still in charge and I am not at all sure that Mr.
Leishman will return at all, for the Emperor is away and it
may not be possible for him to have a farewell audience; he

may however return to pack up. We have had a few dinners lately . . . I don't know if I wrote you that we gave a dinner for Count Bernstorff [German Ambassador to the United States]; he told me a lot of interesting things confidentially which were of great value to me. My chargéship has been particularly interesting this time, for there have been important questions on hand. I had one great satisfaction, namely the withdrawal by Congress of the clause in the new tariff bill placing a duty of 15 per cent on German books, after I had cabled the State Department that the passage of the clause would cause great irritation in Germany and would distinctly hurt the good relations of the two countries. They appear to have acted immediately. Everyone was furious about it here and the newspapers were appearing with headlines "American Tax on Culture." It was a useless provision, bringing in little revenue and simply calculated to restrict German sentiment and learning in the United States. I have also been working very hard to get the German Government to reconsider its decision not to participate in the Panama Exposition in 1915.[11] The outlook is not now very hopeful, but there will in any case be a large unofficial exhibit, and I still have hopes of getting some kind of a Government exhibit, if it is only an educational and not an industrial one. . . .

To the Managing Editor of the Harvard *Crimson,*
November 12, 1913

Will you kindly extend to me, as a former editor of the *Crimson,* the courtesy of your columns for the inclusion of the following comment with regard to the editorial entitled "Consular Service" which appeared in your issue of October 30, 1913?

You state therein that more college men would enter the

[11] A proclamation of President Taft, February 2, 1912, invited other nations of the world to participate in the Panama-Pacific International Exposition at San Francisco in 1915 with exhibits illustrating their resources, their industries, and progress in civilization. U.S. Department of State, *Papers Relating to the Foreign Relations of the United States, 1912* (Washington: Government Printing Office, 1919), pp. 4–5.

Diplomatic and Consular Services were not those branches of the public service largely given over to the spoils system. In view of the fact that an organization has recently been instituted at Harvard with the object of interesting men in this subject, an innovation which deserves the warmest support, it would seem important that the present status of the Diplomatic and Consular Services under the Government of the United States be clearly explained for the benefit of those members of the University who may consider eventually entering them.

The application of Civil Service provisions was extended to the Consular Service by the Executive Order of June 27, 1906. This means that entrance to the Service is dependent upon examination and that transfer and promotion are regulated solely by the merit system and by seniority. Far from being subject to the spoils system, the Consular Service has been rigorously governed by this Executive Order throughout the last two presidential administrations and it has been intimated by the present Administration and already indicated by such transfers and promotions as have occurred since March 4, 1913, that Civil Service principles with regard to the Consular Service will scrupulously be observed. In view of this attitude of both Republican and Democratic administrations, it is hardly conceivable that, even in the absence of legislation by Congress, any future administration will presume to oppose the unequivocal sentiment of the businessmen of the country by giving the Service over once more to the spoils system, ousting those officials who by long and careful training possess the expert qualifications necessary to fulfill the difficult requirements of the work, and thus destroy the permanency of the career.

With regard to the Diplomatic Service, all secretaries of embassy and legation are likewise protected under Civil Service provisions by the Executive Order of November 26, 1909, and in this case also it has been intimated by the present Administration that the Order is to be respected. Examinations are held in Washington annually, or oftener as occasion may require; candidates who pass the examination are admitted only to the lower grades of the Service as vacancies occur, without regard to their political affiliations, and transfer and promotion are governed by seniority and merit.

It is unfortunately true that the positions of ambassador and minister are still regarded as excepted from these Civil Service principles, but it must be remembered that the great progress already made in the permanency of both the Diplomatic and Consular Services has been effected within the last few years, after over a century of the spoils system, and that perfection cannot be expected overnight. Taking into consideration the present sentiment of the country in regard to the entire question, there seems to be every indication that the offices of ambassador and minister will eventually be in part if not largely filled by succeeding administrations by men who have proved efficient in the lower grades of the Service, thus affording an incentive to enter the diplomatic career as a permanent profession.

I trust that this statement will serve to correct any false impressions which may exist in the University regarding these two important branches of our public service and that an increasingly large number of Harvard men may become interested from year to year and may go up for the examinations in Washington with the intention of adopting one or the other of the services as their life's work.

To Thomas Sergeant Perry, November 12, 1913

. . . My new chief [Gerard] is most agreeable both in the office and out of it: he began by trying to do things himself without consulting me and answering communications without showing me his replies, but speedily got into hot water. . . . But I have to suffer for his original faux pas, of which there were a-plenty, for other people take it for granted that a new Ambassador consults his secretary, who has been on the job before. For instance, the American colony here is furious with me for letting him accept an invitation to attend the Thanksgiving Dinner in Hamburg, where there are but a handful of Americans, when, from time immemorial, the American

Ambassador has been the feature of the Thanksgiving Dinner
in Berlin. He never consulted me about it, but nobody knows
that. . . . He must now realize the disadvantages of his mistake. As a matter of fact, he is very agreeable . . . and perfectly willing to accept a reasonable proposition when it is
put to him, which is all I ask from any chief. The thing I like
best about him is that he is perfectly square and aboveboard.
Leishman regarded life as one big poker game and never
by any chance showed his hand or let one know what he was
thinking, which made our relations with him extremely difficult . . . and as the first requisite of teamwork in an Embassy is
perfect confidence between a chief and his secretary, there were
many hitches in the day's work. The only thing that made
working under him possible was that his subterfuges were so
perfectly transparent that we all saw through them and were
able to act accordingly. He never gave a direct and explicit
instruction, but always veiled them in generalities. . . . You
can imagine that I am pleased with the new régime. . . .

Friday, December 12 [1913]
    . . . As I expect to shoot also at the Max von Wogaus' next
week, a little narrative concerning him may be of interest.
Last year he was insulted by a man in the club in Karlsruhe
and was hit in the face, but did not retaliate. The next day
the man apologized. Von Wogau went to Count August Bismarck, who lives nearby, for advice, as he, Wogau, was formerly
a Russian before he became a German subject and having
lived in Baden but a short time was uncertain as to the definite code of honor to be followed. Bismarck told him that
as the man had apologized, he need do nothing further. This
was generally acknowledged as bad advice for it is a definite
rule that if a blow takes place, apology is insufficient and a
duel must take place. The result was that the commanding
officers of the regiments in Karlsruhe forbade their officers to
go to Wogau's house and his social position was thus ruined.
Negotiations then were reopened and the matter finally arranged; a duel was fought in the Black Forest two days ago,

two shots were exchanged on each side at 30 paces and neither man hit. Wogau is thus thoroughly reinstated and his happiness . . . was evident. Ruprecht Böcklin told me a good deal about the German system of dueling, apropos of this. If one man insults another and apologizes without a blow being struck, the matter is settled, but if a single blow be struck, a duel must follow, the conditions depending on the nature of the insult. Generally they are confined to one or two shots apiece, but last year a duel was arranged near Baden in which each man had to shoot until one was seriously wounded; 32 shots were exchanged and then one man was killed. Punishment for dueling is comparatively light — generally a few weeks' imprisonment in a fortress for mere dueling without result, and from one to two years in a fortress when one man is killed. Wogau will have to undergo about six weeks' imprisonment in a fortress, but he can choose the time most convenient to him, can have all the books he wants, can receive visitors, and, if the commander of the fortress is a good sort, can take daily walks outside and even get occasional leave of absence! The original sentence is also generally shortened by the Government. Böcklin himself has a pistol range and practices with a dueling pistol daily in case of future need! . . .

Tuesday, January 27 [1914]

. . . In the evening a gala opera on the Emperor's Birthday, to which we were as usual invited. The first act of *Afrikanerin* was given, the stupidest music I have ever heard, though the scene and costumes were good; I don't know whether the Emperor consults his own taste or that of his guests in choosing the pieces for his gala entertainments, but they are generally stronger in point of scenery than of music. Germany is without doubt the most musical country in the world, yet it is almost entirely the second-class people who have the real musical sense; at the opera and at concerts we seldom see more than three or four people whom one meets in society. The audiences are for the most part composed of good old beer-drinking Fritz Schmidt und Frau, a plentiful sprinkling of

learned and bespectacled Herr Professor Drs, and a very plentiful sprinkling of Isaac Isaacsohns or Jakob Jakobsohns, all
accompanied by their placid, benevolent and very corpulent
Frau Gemahlins.

Alice as usual sat up in the first tier of boxes with the Ministers' wives, the Botschaftsrätins and the wives of the Military
and Naval Attachés, while the men were down in the parquet.
Afterwards there was the usual meeting in the foyer, where the
Emperor and Empress, their sons and daughters and all the
visiting royalty, who have come for the Kaiser's birthday, wander around and speak to the people they know. The Emperor
spoke a word or two to Alice and Eitel Fritz [the Kaiser's
second son] talked to her for a long time, while I had a pleasant
chat with Friedrich Karl [cousin of the Kaiser] about athletics,
in which he takes an active part; he is already training for
the Olympic Games in 1916! . . .

Sunday, February 1 [1914]

. . . In the morning Prince August Wilhelm, the Emperor's
fourth son, telephoned to me asking if he and his wife and
sister-in-law, Princess May of Schleswig-Holstein, might come
to our dance which he had heard we were giving that evening.
We had arranged a dance together with the Ruddocks and
had asked about 80 people, the dancing to take place in our
apartment and the supper in the Ruddocks', just across the
hall.

At 8 I went to a stereopticon lecture given by Paul Niedieck
at the Bristol, about his travels in the Bering Sea and Alaska;
it lasted less than an hour and was very interesting; there were
a lot of interesting people there, and Alice and I had been
asked to supper afterwards, but she was resting for our dance
and I had no time to stay. I was home at 9.30 and soon after
ten the August Wilhelms came and I at once opened the dance
with the Princess. Our friends are good enough to tell us
. . . that it was the best dance of the winter; certainly it had
a lot of go and merriment and everyone seemed, at least, to
enjoy himself. Our principal guests were, besides the August

Wilhelms, Duchess d'Arenberg, Princess Baby Hohenlohe with her daughter Elrica, Prince and Princess Max Thurn and Taxis, Prince Serge Belosselsky — passing through Berlin on a special mission from the Tsar. . . .

For a moment at the beginning I feared it was going to be a total failure, for our middle room quickly crowded up and our guests were packed like sardines in a box and the hubbub was frightful, but soon people scattered, some dancing, some playing bridge and others sitting out in the smoking room, and from then on it went with a bang. At 12.15 supper was served at tables in the Ruddocks' apartment, I taking out the Princess, Ruddock the sister, and August giving his arm to Alice. After supper we had a delightful cotillion with flowers for favors, and then we again adjourned to the buffet at the Ruddocks' where the Princess put away at least a dozen caviar sandwiches one after the other and followed that up with a plentiful amount of chicken, fruit salad, etc. All doubts as to the success of the dance were removed when the August Wilhelms asked us to keep the dance going and it went steadily till nearly 4. The Prince danced with Alice six times and was as gay as a boy out of school, although there was no undignified romping so long as they stayed. When they finally left they said it had been the best dance of the winter and that they had never had so good a time before; I hope this was sincere; they also asked us to their dance on the 5th. I escorted the Princess downstairs to the door of the house, where we had an awning running out to the carriages, and then returned where I found our other guests turned loose in a one-step orgy, half of them officers in uniform who had been forbidden by the Kaiser to dance it anywhere; they all informed me that they were blind and couldn't see and that I was totally mistaken in assuming that anything but the waltz was being played or danced; so we let it go and had a bully time. . . .

To Thomas Sergeant Perry, March 9, 1914

Your letter of February 23rd reached me in spite of your doubts as to whether you had posted it, and I have given the

most careful consideration to all you say regarding the future
of the Diplomatic Service and of ourselves. This is a matter
which I have not unnaturally thought over a great deal, especially during the last year, and I appreciate the suggestions
you make in regard thereto.

To be perfectly frank, I think you are misinformed as to the
probability of Wilson's turning out the members of the Diplomatic Service below the grade of Minister. It is not alone a
natural optimism, but impressions founded on actual information from Washington — from various people in touch with
the Administration — that makes me feel practically certain
that none of the secretaries will be touched during the present
régime. The President has let it be known, and I think has
actually announced, that he regards the secretaries as protected
by Civil Service principles. . . .

The Democrats came in last year after having been out of
power for 16 years; they were accordingly more hungry than
usual and promptly ate up most of the ambassadorial and ministerial posts, thus undoing the good work of forming a permanent Service started by the Republicans.[12] There has however, so far as I am aware, never before been such a row in
the press all over the country over this looting of the Service.
Formerly it was taken for granted that every single official
would be changed; now it is spoken of as a scandal that those
ministers who have worked their way up from the ranks should
be turned out, although the entire Consular Service and all
the secretaries have been left alone. Chambers of Commerce
and other organizations all over the country have protested
and continual articles have been written in the press.

It seems to me, and to many others with whom I have talked,
that this is a very material sign of the views of the country,
and that while the advocates of a permanent Diplomatic Service may still be far in the minority, they are rapidly increas-

12 Graham Stuart says that twenty-nine of the approximately forty diplomatic
chiefs of mission were changed within six months of Wilson's inauguration.
Only in a few instances were career diplomats retained as chiefs. Stuart, *op. cit.*,
pp. 226–29.

ing and may well have to be reckoned with at the next change of administration. I have enough friends among the Republicans and Progressives to be fairly certain of favorable consideration if either of those parties come into power. As for the Democrats, they have seen how the country feels about the question, and it is not beyond the bounds of possibility that at the next election they themselves will come forward with a plank in their platform for the permanent reorganization of the Department of State, the inviolability of the Consular Service, and the certainty of a permanent career for those secretaries in the Diplomatic Service who have made good. Even then there will always remain a very fair percentage of ambassadorships and ministerships for purposes of political patronage.

I think the fact that President Wilson has just appointed Billy Phillips, a well-known Republican, to the important post of Third Assistant Secretary of State — the official who is supposed to have charge of the personnel of the Diplomatic Service — is a sign that the President is not wholly hidebound with politics. Bryan contested this appointment with all his force, but was overriden. . . .

To Thomas Sergeant Perry, April 6, 1914

. . . Lansing's appointment to succeed John Bassett Moore is highly gratifying and I don't attach much importance to the newspaper tirades about his exorbitant commission in the Chinese indemnity matter.[13] Every public official in the United States is a fair mark for foul insinuations. I am inclined to think that President Wilson's gravest mistake during his first

---

[13] While his nomination was pending as Counselor for the Department of State, Robert Lansing and his father-in-law, John W. Foster, were accused of having gotten a very large fee from the Chinese Boxer indemnity. Lansing and Foster had acted as attorneys for the heirs of General Frederick T. Ward who had organized an army which had helped to put down the Taiping rebellion in China in the middle of the nineteenth century. Thus the Ward claim did not legitimately grow out of the Boxer troubles, but with the consent of the Chinese Government, the United States had used the Boxer funds to settle the claim.

year of office has been his wrong perspective of foreign vis-à-vis domestic affairs. In his naturally exuberant desire to put through the tariff and currency bills, he has let foreign affairs go temporarily; Diplomatic Service patronage meant senatorial friends, or perhaps his fault was merely negative and with his interest concentrated on home matters, he left Bryan with free rein as regards appointments. Anyway, whether negative or positive, I think he now sees his error; he has had extraordinary and unprecedented success with his domestic measures and now he is turning his attention to foreign questions and perhaps beginning to realize that his appreciation of their importance has been temporarily obscured. His advocacy of the repeal of the Panama Tolls Bill was the action of an honest man and a courageous one too;[14] nothing has pleased me so much or raised him in my own humble opinion so highly since he took office, just as Taft went down in my estimation when he signed the bill. Now he has appointed two Republicans to important positions in the State Department on the ground of fitness and efficiency. I suppose he had to appease Bryan for this by letting him give the solicitorship to a Texan politician. . . . At any rate, from every present indication, I shall be very much surprised if before the end of Wilson's Administration none of us secretaries is promoted to be minister somewhere or other, and I still optimistically feel that within the next ten years, the Diplomatic Service will be established on a permanent basis which no succeeding administration will dare tamper with. The element of hazardous uncertainty adds to the interest of every activity in life, whether it be tiger-shooting or diplomacy, and I find myself all the more in love with the latter from the fact that it is not yet a cut-and-dried proposition but is in the making, with the outlook for the future a thousand times brighter than it was a year ago. . . .

[14] The Hay-Pauncefote Treaty of 1901 between the United States and Great Britain had stipulated that all nations using the projected Panama Canal would pay the same rates. In 1912 Congress incorporated in an act concerning operation of the Canal a provision exempting American coastwise shipping from paying tolls. President Wilson, considering our national honor was at stake, urged repeal of this act. Repeal passed the Senate on June 11, 1914.

Tuesday, April 14 [1914]

. . . Prince Eitel always travels incognito as Count Tecklen-
burg and unless somebody recognizes him, there is nothing to
give him away except the big crowns which take the place of
the usual police numbers on the back of his cars, and most
people in the small places do not know what they signify.[15]
When visiting the castles and other places of interest en route
he never tells who he is and always awaits his turn when other
parties are ahead of him and pays the usual entrance fees,
though many of them belong to his family. In Quedlinburg
he was annoyed because the policeman on duty in the square
opposite the hotel recognized him, having once served in his
regiment, and when we started in the morning the whole
square was packed with people waiting to see him. The whole
town must have been assembled there. The Prince started in
the first car, which he was driving, with the Princess, Alice and
Hohenzollern [the Hereditary Prince of Hohenzollern] and
was apparently taken for the chauffeur, as nobody paid any
attention to him, but when I followed in the second car . . .
a shout went up which must have kindled patriotism in the
heart of the most blasé prince on earth. I hadn't the brazen-
ness to acknowledge the cheers by saluting, but was sorry that
the Prince, for whom I was taken, must have appeared so cold
and unresponsive to the cordiality and enthusiasm of the
crowd. . . .

Wednesday, April 15 [1914]

. . . One cannot help wishing that Prince Eitel, with his
simplicity, modest bearing and intelligent outlook on life, were
the Emperor's eldest son. The character of the Crown Prince
does not seem to be so stable and his nature is far different.
He is a great poseur, inclined to go off at a tangent when he
gets a chance and anything but discreet regarding public affairs.
Recently at the tennis club he remarked to Rattigan [W. Frank
Rattigan, Second Secretary of the British Embassy at Berlin],

[15] The Grews accompanied the Prince and Princess Eitel Friedrich of Prussia
on an automobile trip through the Harz Mountains.

Harvey [Roland B. Harvey, Second Secretary of the American Embassy at Berlin] and others who were standing near him, "There goes that old fox of a Russian Ambassador [S. N. de Sverbéew]; he is the biggest liar in Berlin and I wouldn't trust a word he said." Perhaps, but it doesn't sound well as coming from a future Emperor. Some of his remarks would lead one to believe that he were a veritable firebrand, an exponent of the most radical pan-Germanism and anything but an element for the future peace of Germany. He said frankly at the tennis club the other day that Germany would fight Russia soon. Let us hope that he will mellow with age. . . .

To Albert Ruddock, United States Embassy, Berlin,
June 2, 1914 [16]

. . . I came away from Washington with a very optimistic opinion as to the future of the Service. Phillips has infused new blood into the Department and although Mr. Bryan was originally against his appointment, it appears that they get on exceedingly well and that Phillips now has the personnel of the Service practically entirely under his charge. He has induced Mr. Bryan to give his full approval to a bill, already introduced into Congress which I believe has already been favorably reported from the Committee, for the appointment of secretaries and consular officers to grades rather than to posts. The original bill contained a clause for the examination of candidates, but Mr. Bryan finally struck it out, not because he disapproved of it, but because he was afraid it would injure the chances of the bill passing at all.[17] Of course this is a tremendous step forward. . . .

I saw Mr. Bryan, who wanted to know if we could buy our present Embassy building in Berlin. Also had a pleasant chat with the President who impressed me pleasantly and favorably. I heard Theodore Roosevelt's lecture in Washington — 3000

16 Mr. Grew wrote this letter in the United States. He left Germany on May 2 and arrived back in Berlin sometime between July 24 and 27.

17 This act for the improvement of the Foreign Service was approved February 5, 1915.

people gathered in one hall on a sweltering hot night — and am sorry to say it was very poor; involved, unconvincing and redundant, and his voice carried so poorly that few could hear him at all. But there is plenty of enthusiasm in his favor over here — outside of the business world — and he will be a strong candidate in 1916 without any doubt. . . .

PART TWO

Berlin, Washington, Paris: In War and Peace
1914–1919

*A*LTHOUGH *the years prior to 1914 seemed to be peaceful and stable, beneath the surface of events developments were taking place that brought about the explosion in 1914.*

In the turbulent Balkans, for instance, the interests of several powers clashed. As Turkish power in Europe declined, Austria and Russia sought to extend their influence over the small Balkan states, and to checkmate by diplomatic and military means the advance of each other. France and Great Britain, meanwhile, strove to keep the Turkish Empire alive as a block to further Russian expansion into the Mediterranean area.

In the last decade of the nineteenth century, Germany under Kaiser William II came into conflict with the imperial interests of France, Britain, and Russia. Although Britain had been anti-Russian and anti-French in the past, faced with Germany's rising power, Britain, France, and Russia formed a series of alliances. This three-power-alliance arrangement was opposed by the older Triple Alliance of Germany, Austria-Hungary, and Italy.

Military expenditures of the Great Powers more than doubled from 1900 to 1914. War was averted, however, in the Morocco crisis of 1905, the Bosnian crisis of 1908, and the Agadir crisis of 1911. The Great Powers, too, avoided an international war at the time of the Tripolitan War of 1911, the First Balkan War of 1912, and the Second Balkan War of 1913.

In 1914, however, neither Germany nor France checked the

125

actions of Austria and Russia over the crisis caused by the assassination of Archduke Francis Ferdinand. As the situation developed, control passed from the diplomats into the hands of military groups like the German General Staff, and war became unpreventable.

Under the German constitution, the Kaiser wielded great authority. He also enjoyed military pomp and power. The American dislike of German militarism and autocracy made American entrance into the war on the German side impossible. In 1914, however, it was also felt to be inconceivable that the United States would join the Allies, although there was little doubt of the American desire for an Allied victory.

President Wilson from 1914 to 1917 felt that his first duty was to maintain peace, and that his second duty was to preserve the neutral rights of the United States. These two concepts, of course, could be contradictory. On January 31, 1916, Mr. Wilson recognized this when he said: " . . . there may at any moment come a time when I cannot preserve both the honor and the peace of the United States. Do not exact of me an impossible and contradictory thing."

Soon after Germany resumed her policy of unrestricted submarine warfare in 1917, the President asked for a declaration of war. Although he based American entrance into the conflict on the issue of protecting rights jeopardized by submarine warfare, there were other leaders who felt that a German victory would be a threat to American security. America, therefore, in their opinion should have entered the war even earlier to check the German threat to the world balance of power.

The price of peace for the United States in 1917 was a submission to the German conception of warfare and the resulting death of neutral citizens traveling on merchant ships torpedoed without warning. Such a submission, requiring a surrender of national honor, also might well have meant a German victory over the Allies. The peace treaty that Germany forced on Soviet Russia at Brest-Litovsk in 1918 furnished evidence that a German peace might have been far more punitive than the peace the Allies drafted in Paris. If the Allies had had to surrender then, the United States alone would have had to face the German military colossus.

The tragedy was not that the United States went to war, but that the world failed to secure a stable peace settlement after November 11, 1918. President Wilson returned from Paris in the summer of 1919 with a compromise peace, which might have worked had the United States not refused to join with the Allied Powers in maintaining world peace through the League of Nations and the Versailles settlement.

VIII

The Outbreak of War

1914

On June 28, 1914, an agent for the Serbian nationalists assassinated Archduke Francis Ferdinand at Sarajevo. A week later the German Kaiser assured Austria-Hungary that it could count on German support "in this case also." On July 18, however, the Russian Foreign Minister warned the Austro-Hungarian Ambassador in St. Petersburg that Russia would not be indifferent to any attempt to humiliate Serbia. A few days later, on a state visit to St. Petersburg, Raymond Poincaré, President of the French Republic, announced that the Russian Foreign Minister "must be firm, and we will support him."

On July 23, Austria-Hungary delivered an ultimatum to the Serbian Government demanding the suppression of all anti-Austrian propaganda and conspirative societies in that country, dismissal of Serbian officials suspected of complicity in the assassination, and the collaboration of Austrian representatives in investigations to be conducted by the Serbian police. The Serbs were given forty-eight hours to accept this ultimatum unconditionally.

The day following the despatch of the ultimatum, Germany sent notes to Russia, France, and Great Britain asserting that Austria was demanding no more than was "equitable and just" and urged a localization of the crisis. On July 25, the Serbian Government mobilized, although it accepted the ultimatum except for one or two points considered crucial by the Austrians. The next day Austria-Hungary ordered partial mobilization. At this point Sir Edward Grey, British Secretary of State for Foreign Affairs, recommended that France, Germany,

129

Great Britain, and Italy hold a conference and all active military operations be suspended pending the outcome of their meeting. Germany, however, refused to attend such a conference contending that the basic dispute concerned only Austria-Hungary and Serbia. Austria naturally refused also.

On July 28, Austria-Hungary declared war on Serbia. Two days later the Tsar ordered general mobilization. The following day, Germany presented a twelve-hour ultimatum to Russia demanding cessation of preparations on the German frontier. A German inquiry to France the same day demanded to know the French attitude in the event of hostilities between Russia and Germany.

On August 1, Germany ordered general mobilization and declared war on Russia, while France ordered general mobilization. The same day Turkey signed a secret treaty with Germany promising to aid her against Russia. The next day German troops invaded Luxembourg, and Germany demanded that Belgium allow German troops to cross the country to the French frontier. Belgium refused this ultimatum and appealed to Great Britain for aid.

On August 3, Germany declared war on France. The following day, Great Britain sent an ultimatum to Germany demanding to know whether Germany would respect her treaty guarantees to Belgium. When Germany that same day violated her treaty by invading Belgium, Great Britain declared war. On August 7, Montenegro joined Serbia against Austria-Hungary, and on August 23, Japan declared war on Germany.

The outbreak of war came unexpectedly as far as the Department of State was concerned. No specific warnings had come from any of the diplomats in Europe except one report from a vice consul in Budapest. Not until July 28, when Ambassador to France, Myron T. Herrick, urged President Wilson to mediate, did Secretary of State Bryan realize the gravity of the situation.

Mr. Grew was in the United States from mid-May until July 7, when he sailed for Great Britain. After approximately two weeks in Britain, he returned to Berlin sometime between July

*24 and 27. Many years later, in 1929, when reminiscing about
the outbreak of the war, he made the following statement:*

I turn to the beginning of the war, which so effectually put
an end to those old days of diplomatic serenity — a fool's para-
dise. Fate is supposed to announce her dreadful purposes with
a knell, or a series of knells. The first knell struck for me on the
golf course at Manchester-by-the-Sea in America. I met an old
Austrian friend whom I had not seen for years and asked him
to dinner. "I'm sorry," he said, "I can't come; we've just had
bad news," and then as an afterthought he added: "Our Archduke Franz Ferdinand has been murdered in Bosnia." I expressed my condolences and departed, but the news did not then
convey to me its full significance. I wonder to how many it did.

The second knell struck in a lovely old English country house.
It was my first visit to the English countryside; I was immensely
impressed by the marvelous stretches of smooth lawn and the
mighty oaks that studded it. Pointing out one especially magnificent tree I remarked on it to my hostess, Lady Ampthill.
"Yes," she replied, "it's a lovely old tree — and an interesting
one too, because it was beneath the branches of that tree that
Henry VIII asked Anne Boleyn to be his wife." A little farther
on we came to a hill with a cross on its top. I inquired if the
monument commemorated some event. "Not an event," said
my hostess, "but a dwelling. Catherine of Aragon had her castle
there, but it later burned down." In the evening, to my lasting
and profound regret, my hostess asked me to play the piano and
I audaciously embarked upon Liszt's "Liebestod" from Tristan
and Isolde. When I had fumbled disgracefully through it, my
hostess said reminiscently: "It's nice to hear that old piece again.
The last time I heard it, it was played by Liszt himself on this
same piano. You know that Wagner and Liszt gave me that
piano!" My hostess had been the British Ambassadress in Berlin
during the War of 1870. I longed for nothing so much as a trap
door through which I might disappear and cover my utter confusion.

But to return to the war. Colonel Alexander Russell, who
had invited me down to visit his mother, was British Military
Attaché in Berlin at the time and had just come home on leave
of absence. At dinner he received a telegram, read it and uttered

something that sounded remarkably like "Damn." Afterwards he said to me: "Our War Department is too arbitrary and inconsiderate altogether. They have canceled my leave and have ordered me to return to Berlin immediately." That was the second knell. It reverberated in my mind and led me to hasten my own return to my post in Berlin.

The third knell occurred on the channel boat. I met one of the Austrian archdukes — Franz Salvator — on board, an old acquaintance of Vienna days, and asked him where he was going. "Back to Vienna," he said; "they have called me back urgently."

From then until the fatal 31st of July events moved with dreadful precision.

Berlin, July 31, 1914

War practically certain. Germany has given Russia twelve hours to stop mobilizing and recall the order, and France the same time to declare her intentions. Crowds marching through the streets and cheering. Issued 35 passports to Americans. *Imperator* did not sail. I hear that the *Cecilie* will be sent back to New York if they can reach her by wireless today.[1] No further provisions can be exported. Streets white with extra Blätter of newspapers giving latest news. . . . Worked till midnight. Just passed through cheering crowd in front of Italian Embassy. Hugh Gurney [Second Secretary] of the British Embassy has laid in no provisions — significant. . . .

August 1, 1914

An exciting day. Russia has asked for two hours more but

---

1 Mrs. Grew sailed from New York on the *Kronprinzessin Cecilie* of the North German Lloyd to rejoin me in Berlin. The ship was said to be laden with gold. When war broke out when she was more than halfway across the Atlantic, the ship was chased by the British cruiser *Essex,* and had to turn back. The passengers were not told of these developments and recognized the change of course only because a passenger, while walking around the ship's deck, noticed with surprise that the moon had followed him around to the other side! The *Cecilie* finally landed in Bar Harbor where one passenger on looking out of his porthole found the ship anchored directly off his own home which he had left but a few days earlier. Mrs. Grew, after a delay of some six weeks, finally sailed on the Dutch liner *Nieuw Amsterdam,* but our four daughters remained in the United States throughout the war. — J. C. G.

has apparently not been heard from further. Crowds marching through the streets cheering and singing "Die Wacht am Rhein." Chancellor von Bethmann-Hollweg made a speech from his window. Worked at chancery from 9 A.M. till midnight with only a moment for dinner; issued nearly 200 passports; the Embassy literally packed with Americans asking for advice. Much hardship owing to inability to get checks cashed. Boylston Beal, Attaché, worked like a Trojan all day with us. Many Americans leaving tonight for Holland at our advice. Ambassador has wired Washington for ships and gold. Francez [of the French Embassy] and Leon de Lens, French Attaché, whom I met on the walk home expect to leave tomorrow or Monday. De Lens said that all countries were responsible for the war except France. Radowitz [of the German Foreign Office] showed how Germany alone had no responsibility for it! De Lens said he hoped to be riding up the Linden within a few weeks and would see me then! [2] At midnight the streets were still crowded with cheering, singing crowds. Enthusiasm quite different from three days ago when the first certainty of war had a sobering effect. No autos allowed to leave Germany; many Americans thus stuck. Russian and French Embassies to be in charge of Spanish. A few tired diplomats at dinner at the Bristol . . . Ambassador issued passports himself today also, so great was the pressure. Mobilization order out, to begin tomorrow, lasts six days. All telegrams must be in German and are censored. No foreign papers or mail arrived. Food prices gone up. No gold or small change to be had. . . .

August 2, 1914

Another day with the atmosphere charged with electricity. This is the first day of the mobilization, of which there are six. All departing trains are now full of officers and departing tourists. Issued over 200 passports; at Embassy from 9 till 11 P.M. Lunched at Embassy; dined at Ruddocks' — they are most hospitable souls to us all. Gave last letters to an American

2 Francez was among the first French officers killed in the war. — J. C. G.

at the station to post in Holland. Rumor that cables have been
cut and that Washington has sent two ships with gold. Clash
between patrols near Russian frontier. Luxembourg taken
by Germans. No foreign papers or mail arrived. Very sad at
station to see officers' wives seeing them off and weeping.
Streets still full of cheering, singing crowds. Enthusiasm for
the war is tremendous. Princess Belosselsky turned back at
Russian frontier; will leave with the Russian Ambassador tomorrow. In the evening came the news that the Landsturm —
militia forces — had been called out in many districts — a radical step. The Embassy porter, the Ruddocks' chauffeur and
several of the Embassy servants must go. Wilhelm's porter
buried his wife today and must go to the front tomorrow,
leaving four small motherless children behind. The Guards
leave tomorrow, Ruli Kleist [German friend of the Grews]
among them. Bob Beal worked at Embassy with us all day,
issuing passports. Laurence H. Hoile [clerk of the Embassy]
returned from his wedding trip; we are now a full staff, thank
heaven, for the work is enormous. The Embassy hall is packed.
German affairs in Russia and France placed in American
hands. We shall probably have charge of British affairs here
if England joins the war. Not yet involved. Saw Eitel Fritz
and his wife who waved cordially.

August 3, 1914

We issued 418 passports today; worked at steam heat. . . .
Lunched at Embassy, dined at Ruddocks', which is to be the
regular régime from now on, thanks to our kind hostesses. All
very tired tonight — I have lost over four pounds in three
days. Russian Embassy left today in the midst of a howling
mob outside the Embassy, who shouted, "Mörder, Spitzbuben,
Pfui," etc., and tried to beat them as they passed out in autos.
I saw Princess Belosselsky as far as the Russian Embassy and
got her baggage there. Impossible to get taxis or even horse
droshkys today; such as are left are reserved for officers. Troops
moving all day long amid the cheers of the crowds who follow
them. All foreigners forbidden to leave Germany today until

after the mobilization; those who left last night were probably stopped at the frontier; I wonder if our letters got through. Several letters have already been returned. Telephoning allowed only in German; I tried to speak with the Spanish Ambassador tonight in French and English, as he speaks no German, and we were immediately cut off after a warning. I finally got José de Landecho [Second Secretary of the Spanish Embassy at Berlin] at his house — the Russian Chargé d'Affaires at Darmstadt wanted to be met at the station and thought we were in charge of Russian interests. No news yet as to what England will do. Papers declare that France has crossed the frontier and begun war; fighting with Russians in East Prussia but meager details. Bomb said to have been dropped by French airship on Nuremberg; I have my doubts; news is being manufactured at the F.O. these days I imagine. German cruiser said to have shelled Libau, which is said to be in flames. Two American ministers arrested at Baden-Baden for taking photos; suspected of spying; cannot be released till after investigation owing to great number of alleged Russian and French spies in Germany; many have been shot already. Seymour Conger [Director of the Berlin Bureau of the Associated Press] arrested in East Prussia on his way to St. Petersburg; suspected of spying as he was with the French correspondent of the *Temps*. Mrs. Gerard and Mrs. Ruddock opened charity offices in the ballroom and are dealing with all cases of destitution and of excitable persons. Some people cannot speak without crying and we have not time to attend to them. . . . Former Ambassador Henry White came to Embassy for passport today. Also Louis Frothingham, Boston attorney, who is with Clayton Johns, the American composer. No telegrams from Washington or home received. Only one telegram from Dept. since beginning of war. We are rapidly being cut off from outside communication.

August 4, 1914

Events have moved quickly today. We have been at the chancery from 9 this morning until after 1 tonight. Grafton

Minot and Charlie Russell came up from Dresden to help us
and have been made Attachés. There were also several others
who helped us issuing passports. Jules M. Cambon [French
Ambassador to Germany] and his Embassy left tonight; Count
Gustave de Manneville [Counselor of the French Embassy]
came in to say good-bye; the Germans are sending them to
Vienna and thence they will get to France via Switzerland!
Sir Edward Goschen [British Ambassador to Germany] asked
for his passports today also, as England has declared war. The
feeling against the English here is at boiling point. All the
windows in the British Embassy were broken tonight and a
big and hostile crowd has been in front of it all the evening.
When the Ambassador and Harvey went to arrange our taking
over the Embassy, Harvey was assaulted as they took them for
English and the Ambassador was spat at; he jumped out of
the automobile and went for the man, who apologized. About
ten this evening Karl von Wiegand [correspondent for the
New York World] ran into our Embassy and told us that Frederic Wile [Berlin correspondent for the London *Daily Mail*], S.
Miles Bouton [Berlin correspondent of the Associated Press]
had just been arrested at the Adlon; Wile had been at the
Embassy ten minutes before. The police had entered and
taken them away with great roughness and they had been
beaten by the crowd. I immediately took the Ambassador's
car and Fritz, the chasseur, as the Ambassador was not there,
and went to the Adlon with Bob and Harvey; the crowd at
the entrance said, "Hier sind Engländer," and would have
assaulted us had not Fritz gone ahead and cleared a path, saying that we were Americans, whereat the crowd simply growled.
We found an excited crowd in the Adlon and I verified the
report; the men had been taken out by the police with drawn
sabers. I then immediately went to the Foreign Office, asked
for Herr Zimmermann, the Under Secretary of State, and told
him of the occurrence, adding that if the Germans took this
tack, they would lose the best friends they had. He was profoundly apologetic, said it must have been a mistake and promised to get them out at once. I then motored to the Mittel-

strasse police station where they had first been taken and then
to the Polizei Präsidium, where I found them just being released and they almost embraced me; they returned to the
Embassy with me in the motor, hardly half an hour after their
arrest, with stories of rough treatment by the police who said
"Hang them" and "Shoot them" when they had them at the
station, though at the Präsidium they were treated well. It
appears that they had been using a taxi all day, going often
to the telegraph office and speaking English in the auto, and
the chauffeur thought they were English spies. Everybody
has been warned not to speak a word of English on the street.
A great number of Russians have been caught in Berlin and
shot as spies today; we saw a crowd of them being taken to
their death; two were disguised as nursemaids, trying to escape
that way, and Mrs. Ruddock saw them in the Tiergarten just
before they were arrested, her nurse commenting on their
big feet. Every Russian in Berlin has been arrested and it will
be the same with the English tomorrow I fear. . . . Tower
came to the Embassy about midnight and asked us to take him
to the Adlon as he did not dare go alone; he had been badly
beaten over the head; Major George Langhorne [Military Attaché of the American Embassy at Berlin], Lanier Winslow
[private secretary to Mr. Gerard] and H. Rivington Pyne [At-
taché of the American Embassy at Berlin] motored him there
and I think he got in safely, though there was still a crowd
before the entrance as we passed at 1. We had an exciting time
ourselves getting out of the Adlon tonight and through the
double cordon of mounted police drawn up before the British
Embassy.

Stories have come to us tonight of Russians having been
literally torn to pieces by the crowd in various parts of Germany. Having seen the temper of the mob tonight, I can
quite believe this. Berlin is no longer a civilized city; the inherent barbarity of the German race never showed itself so
strongly.

The Kaiser opened the Reichstag today, which voted the
war fund absolutely without opposition, even the socialists

cheering the Chancellor's speech, an unprecedented event. Troops are still steadily moving through the streets to the front. Taxis are impossible to get any more; if one has not his private motor, he must walk. Every horse in Berlin has been taken for the war and nearly all the taxis; even private autos can be taken. Benzine cannot be had, but fortunately the Ambassador laid in a store of 2500 kilos last week for the Embassy. I have stocked up with provisions, oil, candles, etc., to last for several months if the worst comes, as we all have. Gold is absolutely unobtainable, even the Reichsbank, and many storekeepers refuse to accept bills, though they are required to do so by law.

Telegrams come in every minute from Americans in different parts of Germany asking for help, some of them hysterical. The Ruddocks' chauffeur's wife has husband, four brothers, father and brother-in-law going to the front, and the wife of their new chauffeur has seven brothers all going. I shall try to get this out by the British diplomats.

Italy is remaining neutral! Germany is furious and the crowd, which a day or two ago was wildly cheering Riccardo Bollati [Italian Ambassador to Germany] are now making hostile demonstrations before his Embassy. He says he has not slept for eight nights, poor man. This has been a long day for us — 9 A.M. till 2.30 A.M.

August 5, 1914

Spent most of the afternoon at the British Embassy sealing up their archives with Sir Horace Rumbold [Counselor of the British Embassy] and Gurney and taking over charge. The insults which have been heaped upon Englishmen here are past belief; the hotels will not keep them, they are spat on in the street and arrested whenever found by the police. We all wear small American flags in our buttonholes now, merely for safety, for no Englishman is safe. There seems to be little animosity against France; she is regarded as coming into the war against her will and nothing but pity is felt for her; all the German venom is vented on Russia and England. We hear

that the German Embassy in St. Petersburg has been totally
wrecked by the mob, which broke in and ruined all Count
Pourtalès' [German Ambassador to Russia] beautiful things,
and threw the bronze horses on the roof into the Moika
Canal. . . .

August 6, 1914

There is not much go left in Little Willy tonight, so the account of the day will have to be short and sweet — as possible.
Was up at 5.15 A.M. and it is now 12.30 A.M., and there have
been no breathing spells. I took Wile from our Embassy, where
he had spent the night, at 6.15 to the British Embassy and
from there to the Lehrter Bahnhof; the British Ambassador
and the staff of the Embassy left for Holland at 8.16 in a special
train supplied by the Government and Wile went with them.
The F.O. has declined to guarantee his safety and he was
afraid of being taken from the train at the last minute, so I
waited till it steamed out. I sincerely hope he got through.
The train was to reach Hanover at 7 P.M. (11 hours against the
usual 3 hours!) and the Dutch frontier at 8 tomorrow morning.
Mr. Grant Duff, the British Minister at Dresden, and his wife
had their windows broken by the mob and on coming to Berlin
by special train (which by the way took 9 hours) had to keep
the curtains down all the way and were not allowed to light
the lights — and were told that if they stood up or showed
themselves at all they would probably be shot! It was a thoroughly unpleasant journey for them. However, they treated
the British Embassy better on their departure, apparently to
make amends for the disgraceful behavior of the crowd previously, and Count Botho Wedel [official of the German Foreign Office] was at the station to see them off. Poor Sir Edward
— what a way to end his long career. He said sadly to me:
"I am too old a man for all this." The Belgians went also,
of course. Several British newspaper correspondents were also
with the party; most of them had not been allowed to take a
single thing from their rooms — even a handkerchief. One of
them had been arrested the evening before and most of his

things, including pearl studs, etc., stolen while he was away. All Englishmen were turned out of the hotels — even Conger had to leave the Adlon as they were afraid of the mob. And all were openly insulted. . . . Tonight we held a meeting of the Embassy staff and divided the work into four divisions, with one of us at the head of each and responsible for its running — I take general correspondence with Hoile to help me; Harvey has Berlin passports, with Winslow, Minot and Russell; Ruddock takes outgoing passports with Charles B. Dyar [clerk] as well as deciphering and enciphering; and Boylston takes the British division with Pyne. We also have a great deal of help from stenographers and others who have volunteered to help; there are at least four men and four girls helping us daily, and we divide them as the work necessitates. . . .

The papers today published long and prominent appeals to the crowd not to mistake Americans for English people, as there were many Americans in Berlin and they were friendly disposed toward Germany. It is however unsafe to speak English on the street. In a German conversation which I held on the telephone today the words "Englische Botschaft" came into the conversation and we were immediately cut off. I complained and the girl was furious and said that such a conversation was not "statthaft." This is about the limit. There are amusing elements to this too: Major George Langhorne tried last night to give Mrs. Gherardi an important message over the telephone and he speaks German so badly she could not understand it at all.

We heard from Washington today that the *Tennessee* is coming with gold and 24 officers, under Mr. Breckinridge, Assistant Secretary of War, to supervise the transportation of Americans in Europe to America by ships which are to be chartered and sent over. Ruddock has placed 10,000 Marks at the disposal of our charity department — organized by Mrs. Gerard and Mrs. Ruddock — and has telegraphed to his grandfather for $100,000 for the same purpose. There are many sad cases of want and they will increase daily, for it is impossible to cash a check anywhere. Every gold coin that falls into my hands — and there are precious few — I store up; they will come in handy later.

We have recently noticed that a policeman is standing on our corner day and night and on asking him today we found that he was placed there especially to guard our house; Ruddock has had double locks put on his doors and hired an extra porter to stand at the back entrance. . . .

August 7, 1914

News comes tonight that Liège has fallen to the Germans this morning at 8 o'clock. This is a very important victory, if true, for it is the stronghold of Belgium and an advantageous base for the Germans. There was great rejoicing in the streets tonight and the church bells were ringing to celebrate the first victory of the war. I fear, however, that we are going to get very little news here and that what we get will be carefully colored. The Ambassador had a glimpse of an English newspaper today which somebody had got through the lines and it told of lots of things that we did not know about — for instance, that the *Königin Luise* (the old *Deutschland*) had been sunk, on August 5, 1914, by the English off the mouth of the Thames, loaded with mines; that the *Vaterland* had sailed from New York, full of coal and armed, and that she was shortly followed by the *Lusitania*. I wonder how much of this is true.

Otherwise there is little news today; we receive daily an enormous mail (all from Germany of course) — at least 50 telegrams alone, I should say — and it means hard swimming to keep one's head above water. I bought a tea set today and had tea served to all the members of the staff at 5, which made it much easier to work till dinner; lately I have been pretty hungry at 5 and working till 8 on an empty stomach was no fun. Came home at 11 tonight as my head was too addled to answer another communication intelligently. . . .

We were lent a multiplying machine today — every American in town seems to want to help us, bless them — and can now turn out 1000 copies of any paper in fifteen minutes.

Thus, after this, we shall issue general information in bulletins which will obviate much private correspondence. The *Lokal Anzeiger* is going to publish them also.

The State Department keeps cabling instructions to pay so and so $1000 which has been deposited in Washington, but where on earth the *cash* is to come from they do not seem to consider. A draft or check here now is not worth the paper it is printed on so far as the possibility of cashing it goes. When the *Tennessee* arrives with gold, she will find many a destitute American who at home can draw perfectly good checks for mostly any sum he pleases.

Everyone is still cursing England for coming into the war; they refer to the Chancellor's speech before the Reichstag on August 4, in which he gave Germany's word of honor that she was occupying Belgium merely for strategical purposes and would leave immediately when the war was over, and they say that England's shortsighted policy will forever prevent friendship in future between the two nations. They realize fully that they are in a critical situation and that their fleet must be sacrificed, but they count on so weakening England that she will be powerless for many years on the sea, while Germany's army will carry all before it. The spirit and enthusiasm here are tremendous. All the soldiers and recruits moving to the front look happy; they sing continually and wave to the crowd, and nobody could imagine that bloody battles lay before them.

Germany is now beginning to worry about American friendship; they know that England is coloring the reports against her and that she has no chance to show her own side in the American press, and much space is given in the papers to the necessity of showing the greatest friendship to Americans in Germany now. The Ruddocks, as well as the Ambassador, have large American flags on their cars and the crowd wave genially to us as we pass. Last night an American was thrown out of a café, having been taken for English, but as soon as they found that he was an American they had him back in a minute and up on the shoulders of the crowd being lustily acclaimed with hurrahs.

August 8, 1914

Another very long day, steady telegrams to be answered, letters by the hundred, passport applications by the thousand, inquiries by the million. The Kaiser saw the Ruddocks' car today and stopped and turned to salute the American flag as it passed; the papers are full of one theme now — American friendship must be cherished. Indeed they need it. This war is not the result of any one event; the murder of Franz Ferdinand supplied the match, but the fuel was all there, piled up during the last generation of German success and prosperity. She could expand no further and something had to give. Add to this the inherent hostility of Slav to Teuton and Teuton to Latin, which has existed through all ages, and the net result is no surprise.

Germany is ready for this war, but I do not believe, from all I have seen, that she brought it on. Jealousy of her success on the part of other nations is the key factor. I have been told on good authority and from three different sources that the Russian Prime Minister and the Minister of War went to the Tsar when he was trying to smooth things over and said that they could not guarantee his life for twenty-four hours if he gave the order to demobilize. Tonight I saw an entry in Gherardi's diary, dated Kiel, about July 20th — "There are two English war ships here; the Germans are most friendly and are doing everything to fraternize, but the English seem jealous and suspicious, and are inwardly hostile." The English knew what was coming very soon after July 20th, if not before, for when I was at the Ampthills', Alexander Russell received a telegram from Rumbold, which he opened in my presence, directing him to return to Berlin immediately. . . . I suppose I have already related the incident about a member of the British Embassy staff. I was talking with him soon after my return to Berlin and told him that I had laid in a large supply of provisions and said I supposed that he had done the same. "No," he said, "I don't think I shall need them." "That's just what I wanted to find out," I replied. He went red as a beet and seemed much embarrassed. This was before the Germans or any of us thought that England was coming in. The next day he appeared at our Embassy with an obviously manufactured excuse and in the course of conversation said — "It's nice that things are looking so much brighter." I said that this was very good news, but that we all thought that things could not well be darker than they were just then. "Oh," he said, "I mean our relations with Germany." It was too evident that he had come around to try to patch up his break of the day before. In other words, England knew that she was coming in all the time; she would have come in whether Germany had occupied Belgium or not. We all believe here that this war was carefully cooked up by Russia, England and France — which is doubtless at variance with the views of the American press, which now gets its information from English and French sources. And we, of course, have to take the German point of view with a grain of salt. However it may be, history alone will show.[3]

In any case, Germany is wonderfully well prepared for war. I saw yesterday one of the cards which every man in Germany liable for military service constantly has with him. This one read: "On the 2nd day of mobilization you will report at 6.30 P.M. at the military bureau at Potsdamerstrasse 56" — or whatever address it was. At the beginning of mobilization, every bulletin post in Berlin has red placards telling exactly at what hours the mobilization trains would start — and they have never been a minute late in their schedule. Most countries require a "période préparatoire" of a week or so before mobilization begins in order to arrange these schedules. Germany's "période préparatoire" began on July 31st, 1871, and has been going ever since. Everything has moved like clockwork. The best brains of a generation have been working in the old Generalstab building on the Moltkestrasse — where

---

[3] As I have already noted in the Foreword: "It shocks me profoundly to remember that on the outbreak of war in 1914 most of us in the Embassy in Berlin accepted the German point of view, hook, bait and sinker, for in those dramatic days we were unused to war and war propaganda, and we were, for a time at least, cut off from all other points of view." — J. C. G.

Field Marshal Moltke's spirit appeared an hour after he had died and spoke to the soldier on duty at the entrance, so that he actually saluted, and where for years afterwards he was seen walking through the offices, examining papers and maps — and now, in wartime, police with rifles stand at every street in its vicinity to prevent anyone approaching anywhere near it, for the brains are still at work, but now putting into execution what through a generation they have planned. Every move is a secret in this big game of chess, and nobody outside the Generalstab will know of the moves until they have been carried out and have succeeded or failed. Germany is fighting for her life and she knows it. But powerful and ready as she is, I can't see how she can win with the tremendous forces out against her.

August 9, 1914. Sunday

. . . The great question that we all think of now is, will the British and German fleets meet in force, and where and when, and what will be the result? The Germans fully expect to lose their fleet, but they also expect and intend to sink at least one British ship for every one they lose, and thus to cripple England on the sea for another generation.[4] The United States, they all say, will in another month be the first naval power of the world.

We are planning as best we may how to get the Americans out of Germany and home. The United States Government will send ships, but can they get to any northern port with

[4] At the outbreak of war the Allies had preponderant naval strength. German merchantmen had been driven from the seas by the end of the first month of war, and the Battle of Falkland, December 8, 1914, put an end to any effective German cruiser warfare. With the exception of a few German cruiser raids in the North Sea and the Battle of Jutland, May 31, 1916, the German Navy did not attempt to break from home base. When the British and German fleets did meet at Jutland, the result was indecisive. The British losses were six cruisers, eight destroyers, and 6000 men, and those of the Germans, five cruisers, five destroyers, one battleship, and about 2500 men. The German fleet finally surrendered bloodlessly two and one-half years later. Captain B. H. Liddell Hart, *A History of the World War, 1914–1918* (Boston: Little, Brown & Co., 1935), pp. 103–6, 357–82.

every one of them strewn with mines? Yesterday the F.O. told
us that they could come to Rotterdam, but today we receive
hints on good authority that by the time they arrive, Rotterdam will no longer be a neutral port! What does that mean
but that Germany is about to occupy Holland? Herr Arthur
von Gwinner [Director of the Deutsche Bank] came to us tonight and recommended that all Americans be sent to Genoa.
Perhaps he is right. We shall see what the next few days bring
forth. Pathetic letters come in by the score from destitute Americans begging for help and transport home; our relief department, composed of Mrs. Gerard, Mrs. Ruddock, Mrs. Gherardi
and Miss Kerr (the English girl), work as hard and long as
we do, 9 till midnight daily. The ballroom is flooded daily
and they say they now allow applicants to cry for ten minutes
and then put them out. But people say that our system and
organization is excellent, while the Spanish Embassy, with its
Russian and French protégés, has no system at all, and that
the Regentenstrasse is a seething mass of hysterical weeping
women. At our Embassy every person, as he or she arrives,
is given a number and the numbers are called out in order
by the faithful tireless Hall, who stands at the barricade halfway down the corridor and lets them through three or four
at a time; they are then directed to the division which they
seek — the passport department, the relief department, the
information department or the British department. Each department runs like clockwork, carefully superintended by its
chief and carried on by his subordinates. The corridor of the
Embassy looks like an advertisement board, with its mass of
bulletins of information and placards tacked up on every
available bit of wall. We get out bulletins daily and these are
published in the *Lokal Anzeiger* and sent to all Consuls and to
the individuals whose names and addresses we have. Ruddock
works like a Trojan, getting out passports and forms by thousands, literally, every day. The Ambassador began by signing
about a thousand passports daily, but now we have had a stamp
made with his signature to save him from writer's cramp. His

signature has now developed or deteriorated to a mere wavy line.

Every French or English sign or advertisement on the Friedrichstrasse has been painted out; this alone shows the intense feeling of hostility which pervades the masses. . . .

August 10, 1914

The Ambassador was called to the Emperor today at ten minutes' notice, as he had a message from President Wilson, offering his services for mediation if the opportunity should ever come, to deliver. The Emperor was sitting at a table in the garden of the palace and personally wrote out a long five-page statement of the events just before the war, calculated to show how he had tried his best to avoid it. It is an interesting document and will be still more interesting in the future when the history of the war of 1914 comes to be written. . . .[5]

As usual we worked till well after midnight. Otto Gunther Wesendonck has been given us by the F.O. to attend to German affairs in Russia, France and England, which considerably helps us in answering that class of correspondence. The Embassy staff and assistants now number nearly 30 persons! . . .

August 11, 1914

. . . An American, Mr. King, also arrived from Holland today and brought a sad story of conditions along the railroad. He said that those Americans who had tried to get out of Germany by the scheduled trains, which have now begun to run again, were frequently ejected when soldiers wanted transportation, and were obliged to wait at small stations without food until another train happened to come along, which might mean a day or more. Unaccompanied women and children were among them and their condition was pitiful. This is what led me to telegraph Alice not to come at present until conditions are more settled; it is too risky now, to my great regret. We are

[5] The document is printed in U.S. Department of State, *Papers Relating to the Foreign Relations of the United States, 1914, Supplement, The World War* (Washington: Government Printing Office, 1928), pp. 60–61.

sending out a special train to Holland tomorrow, chartered by the Embassy, but whether such trains will come *from* the frontier for a long time is unfortunately a different matter and very unlikely.

There was a meeting of important officials in the Rathaus today to emphasize Germany's friendship for the United States and many warm speeches were made; the papers every day are full of articles on this subject, aiming to show the great sympathy existing between the two countries and urging the people to show Americans in Germany every possible sign of hospitality. They are suing for our friendship in no uncertain terms. Tomorrow there will be a meeting of Americans at the Adlon to reciprocate the compliment. The Ambassador made an excellent speech today.

Today we accepted applications for transportation to America from Americans whose names begin with the letters A, B or C, and this will continue daily. The Ambassador personally supervises this work, with a large staff of assistants, who keep a card catalogue of all applications, in three categories: 1. Persons with children under 13; 2. Unaccompanied women; 3. All others. Winslow has charge of the special train and has opened a ticket office in the waiting room to sell tickets. I still have charge of the correspondence, having moved into Harvey's room for more quiet, with Russell and a stenographer as assistants; but even there I am interrupted almost every minute, and with telegrams pouring in at the rate of about 40 or 50 a day, it is almost discouraging trying to keep my head above water. However, our organization is perfect and all are in good spirits, so that things hum and it is a pleasure to be in the midst of it. The Embassy resembles a large business house, with many typewriters clicking in every room, people swarming outside, far into the street, and held back by the faithful porter, and hurrying about inside on one job or another; at least six women are steadily at work making card catalogues of different subjects — passports issued (many thousands already), American registrations, British registrations, inquiries, requests for financial assistance, arrests, applications for transportation to America, etc., etc. Our staff of helpers increases daily as necessity requires, for there are plenty of volunteers. . . .

The real strain of the work is the mental gymnastics one has to accomplish: in the midst of writing an important memorandum or note or telegram, the telephone rings and a Foreign Office official delivers some piece of information or makes an inquiry, and before one has time to jot it down or look it up, a visiting card from some high official is handed in and one has to listen to him at once; then somebody rushes in to say that the Ambassador wants me immediately, and when I get back to my room with three separate and perhaps complicated things to remember, it is already full of people waiting to see me. All this time my desk is piled literally high with unanswered telegrams — most of them unopened even — and almost every one of them is from some poor American in distress — in prison, or without money, or begging hysterically to know what to do to get out of the country and home. It is indeed an exhilarating job. The human element that it brings out is the best of it and we all agree that in a crisis of this kind, the average American shows up in a first-rate light; he is generally patient and philosophical, shows his appreciation of the strain we are laboring under and that mountains cannot be removed in a minute, and almost always tries to take up as little time as possible in stating his case — though there are occasionally startling exceptions. . . .

August 16, 1914, Sunday

The last few days have been a great strain on us — steady work all day and a good deal of the night without any letup, and we are all beginning to show the effects. The Ambassador almost broke down the other night and had to leave the office early and go to bed. Harvey looks like a skeleton and whenever he gets a chance he throws himself on the sofa in the chancery, thoroughly exhausted. Minot and Russell, who are now helping me with the correspondence and have desks in my room, are about the only ones who still seem fresh, though they work as long as any of us, but they are only 21 and 22.

The number of telegrams and letters increases daily and I cannot possibly cope with them; there is now a pile of at least a hundred on my desk, unanswered and many of them unopened. Tomorrow I am going to organize another bureau, outside of the Embassy, for dealing with inquiries about and requests to send messages to friends; I am hoping that the North German Lloyd, who now have no business, will place their office at our disposal for this purpose. Such a bureau would deal with at least 50 per cent of our correspondence.

Today we have had an almost complete rest, for the Ambassador decreed that no one should return to the office after lunch — though as a matter of fact we worked till 4 — and then the whole Embassy en masse motored out to the Grunewald and played tennis for two hours — a perfect delight. Last night I gave a dinner at home, as Madame Gadski had offered to come and sing and we all needed the distraction. . . .

Today, while we were playing tennis, one train after another steamed slowly past carrying soldiers to the front; they were all of freight cars, covered with green boughs — the sign that they were going to the war — and from the doors of the cars the soldiers leaned out and cheered continually and waved to us. After the cars with the troops came flatcars with the mounted guns, transport wagons and an occasional automobile full of officers, to be used on the scene of action. I fear that few of them will return alive, for we hear reports of terribly bloody battles and great losses. The strain of what we are going through is not entirely the work and long hours themselves; the sad cases that continually come to our attention cannot fail to leave their effect. Today I saw the little Princess Ratibor with her parents at the Bristol; she has just taken the plaster and bandages off her neck where she was shot by a soldier near Berlin for not stopping in her automobile when called upon — a mighty narrow escape, judging from the location of the wound, which fortunately was slight. Any number of people have been killed during the last two weeks in this way — even a German general! The people are hysterical just because, at the beginning of the war, the General Staff warned them

through the press to be on the lookout for two Russian automobiles full of gold which were trying to get through into
Russia. Both have been captured and the papers now every day
state in large type that not another hostile auto exists in Germany, but the "Auto Jagd" still continues. . . .

Yesterday a woman came to the Embassy with the London
Daily Telegraph of August 10 and 11; how she got them
through we could not imagine and she would not tell. But it
was a revelation to us to see how the English accounts of the
fighting differed from the German. According to their story,
the forts at Liège had not yet been taken by the Germans, who
had been badly repulsed; that the French troops had been
victorious at Muhlhausen and around Belfort and that in general the Germans were getting decidedly the worst of it! . . .[6]

August 23, 1914, Sunday

Last night at 11 my head was literally addled and I could
not have answered another letter or telegram if a man's life
had depended on it, so when Fabritz came in this morning at
7.45 as usual, I turned over with the happy prospect, it being
Sunday, of being able to sleep for another hour. But no luck.
He announced that Winslow, who had just returned from
Holland, was on the telephone and the latter told me that he
was at the Adlon with the Assistant Secretary of War, Mr.
Breckinridge, and the seventeen officers and others who had

---

[6] The German invasion of France had been skillfully planned by Schlieffen, the
German Chief of Staff until 1907, who projected an outflanking movement
around the French fortification system, involving the invasion of Belgium and
Luxembourg, and entry into France across the less protected northern frontier.
In execution of this plan the German army invaded Belgium on August 4,
meeting with rather effective resistance from the Belgians in the early weeks of
the war. Although the town of Liège was entered on August 7 by German
troops, the last fort at Liège did not fall until August 16. By August 20, however, Belgian troops had fallen back to Antwerp, German troops had entered
Brussels and reached Namur, the last fort between their armies and the Meuse
route into France. In Lorraine "see-saw" military encounters were occurring
between the German and French troops. Here the main thrust of the French
had been defeated at the battle of Morhange-Sarrebourg on August 20, but not
decisively. The French offensive into Upper Alsace, begun on August 7, had
also been halted but was renewed on the 19th. Liddell Hart, *op. cit.*, pp. 78–83.

come over with the *Tennessee*. So I had to get up as usual and was soon at the Adlon, where I met Mr. Breckinridge, a pleasant young man of 28 years and other members of his party, and we went together to the Embassy, where the whole morning was occupied in a general conference regarding measures to be taken for getting Americans out of Germany. At 12 the Japanese Chargé d'Affaires, Dr. Funakoshi, called and informed us that the Foreign Office had given no answer to their ultimatum [7] and that they were leaving tomorrow morning and wished to turn over their Embassy to us, together with the care of Japanese subjects in Germany, for which they gave us a large sum of money; they had paid the rent of their Embassy for a year ahead, as well as the wages of all their German servants, rather different from the British Embassy's provisions. Their passports had been handed them today. I lunched at the Bristol with Harvey and Percival Dodge, of the State Department [Special Agent in Charge of American refugees in France] and afterwards went with Harvey and Minot to the Japanese Embassy, where we carefully attached our respective seals to 34 cases of archives, a rather long job, and I took them over in the name of the United States Government. We then took leave of the Chargé d'Affaires and his staff, who were anxious to get to work on a big Japanese "Festmahl" which we saw being laid upstairs and wishing them good luck, departed.

August 24, 1914

The correspondence that came in today was positively overwhelming: as soon as we got through a bunch of fifty or a hundred telegrams and letters, another batch of equal size came in. Every incoming communication is placed on my desk and I have to distribute them to the various departments and every answer to telegrams or letters is placed in my personal basket so that I may pass on it before it goes out and correct mistakes. Thus the responsibility for the whole work of the Embassy falls on me and I am accountable for any error that

7 Japan sent an ultimatum to Germany on August 17 to vacate Tsingtau, China, before the twenty-third.

may be made. With several hundred communications to pass upon every day, besides the great number I have to answer myself, the mental energy expended is great; and I regret to say there are very few members of the staff I can absolutely trust to get things correct the first time. I insist on every letter written being initialed, so that I can immediately trace an error, but with a dozen or more stenographers and secretaries at work, it is most difficult to see that this is done and I often have to search through the chancery for someone who has made a mistake and failed to initial the letter in question. Yet our system is running admirably and each department is carrying out its special duties in most satisfactory style. I have 18 separate baskets on my desk, which alone shows the complication of the system. In these I have to place the various letters and telegrams as they come in. There is the Ambassador's basket, in which I throw everything which must be taken to him to pass upon; Harvey's basket, for all communications regarding passports and citizenship; Ruddock's basket, for all questions of consular passports, circulars, stationery, etc.; Dyar's basket for all ciphering and deciphering and consular exequaturs; Russell's basket for all private telegrams; Minot's basket for all inquiries about relatives and friends; Winslow's basket for all questions regarding transportation by train; Captain Enoch's basket for questions about steamship transportation; Pyne's basket for questions relating to British subjects; Mrs. Gerard's basket for questions of financial relief; then there is the urgent basket, the pending basket, the basket for communications that can be answered by circular, the Foreign Office basket, the outgoing basket for Hoile, in which all letters and telegrams which I have passed upon are placed for final sending, and still the basket for letters to America, incoming letters, etc., etc. It would be bewildering were not our organization complete, but each chief of department comes in from time to time, empties his own basket and takes appropriate action on the contents thereof, placing his replies in my personal basket for examination before sending. Thus matters are sure of immediate attention and the total result seems to be satisfactory. . . .

In the evening Count Oppersdorff [member of the Reichstag] gave a very large dinner at the Automobile Club, comprising the whole Special Commission and the whole Embassy, besides many prominent Germans.[8] I sat between Max Taxis [Prince Maximilian of Thurn and Taxis, Captain in the Prussian Cavalry] and Admiral Rampold and had a pleasant time. Afterwards I went up to Breckinridge's room at the Adlon and talked to him for almost an hour alone about the general situation in Germany, tracing the developments from the beginning and trying to show him to the best of my ability that in spite of certain unfortunate incidents, Germany was laying herself out to cherish the friendship of the United States; in fact, this was the purpose of the dinner, for Count Oppersdorff, I suspect, was appointed by the Reichstag for this particular job. This was also why he wanted to bring four German naval officers to my party last night. The duty of the Embassy is to propagate friendly relations between the two countries, and I am most anxious to do what I can to offset the prejudiced statements which are naturally appearing in the American press, as they are all coming from England. Mr. Breckinridge seemed impressed and I think that he will go home with properly balanced sentiments. My party last night seems to have accomplished a good deal in that direction for Oppersdorff and the German officers present made a good impression on the American Commission. Madame Gadski's singing fortunately relieved the evening of the official character which it would otherwise have assumed; it was thoroughly "gemütlich." . . . Oppersdorff and the German officers thanked me in such cordial tones tonight that I was greatly pleased at their having been able to get in their work in just the way they wanted.

After the dinner I returned to the chancery, worked till very late — and it is now, after writing the foregoing, so late that I

[8] The *Tennessee* had brought Assistant Secretary of War, Breckinridge, and other army and navy officers to Germany with gold to expedite American financial transactions in Germany. Army officers who arrived with Breckinridge took over affairs regarding the repatriation of Americans. This commission, housed in the hotel Kaiserhof, was headed by Majors J. A. Ryan, J. H. Ford, and G. W. Martin.

shall have time for only a snooze before Fabritz comes to tell
me that the fatal hour of 7.45 has arrived.

August 25–September 1 [1914]

I have not kept up writing this week simply because there
has been no go left at the end of the day's work. It has been a
steady grind, all day and every day, and now Russell is leaving
for London with despatches and I must hurry this up to date
and send it along for what it is worth.

The German successes have been simply astounding, if we
can believe the reports published here, and I am convinced that
they are approximately correct and that it is the English press
that has been lying. We have seen various English papers and
they are full of German defeats and French and Belgian victories. On August 25th the taking of Namur by the Germans
was announced, as well as the five surrounding forts, while four
other forts were said to be on the point of falling. On the 27th
we heard of the terrible affair of Louvain, that historic and
picturesque Belgian town. The German troops, according to
the report here, were suddenly shot upon by the inhabitants of
the town after they were in apparently peaceful possession for
several days, a sortie from Antwerp having taken many of them
away. Many were killed and then the Germans rallied and a
24-hour battle began between the inhabitants and the troops
and when the latter were victorious the commanding officer
gave orders for the complete destruction of the town, which
was carried out and it was literally razed to the ground. Up till
then there had been rumors that things had not been going
well for the Germans on the Russian frontier and it looked as
if troops were to be rushed across Germany from the western
frontier to support the other armies against Russia, for our
special trains for Americans were canceled and all available
transportation was requisitioned for the sending of troops and
the moving of wounded and prisoners. Then on the 29th came
the news that five Russian army corps had been defeated and
that the English army had been completely broken up and
routed near St. Quentin. On the 30th the papers published the

news of the sinking of the German cruiser *Ariadne* and the torpedo boat *V-187* near Heligoland. It was said that they had been enticed out by small British ships, in thick weather, right into a bunch of large battleships and had been destroyed immediately with a few shots. The *Mainz* was also sunk, young von Tirpitz, my tennis friend, and the brother of our kitchen maid being among the saved. On the 31st we heard that 60,000 Russian prisoners had been taken in East Prussia and that the old *Kaiser Wilhelm der Grosse,* now used as a scout cruiser, had been sunk by the British ship *Highflyer* in the neutral Spanish colony of Rio de Oro. Of course the Germans made much of this breach of neutrality, but the *Kaiser* had already done a lot of damage to Allied merchantmen and international law has gone by the board long ago. Today we learn that the Russian prisoners total 70,000 and 300 officers, besides many guns. Also that the German troops in France are at Compiègne, hardly 80 kilometers from Paris! [9]

9 On August 23, the retreat began of the Allied forces to the Marne. The pursuit of the Germans was slowed by the British stand at Le Cateau on August 26, and that of the French at Guise on August 29. Moltke's detachment of forces to join the armies in East Prussia and to invest various Belgian cities hampered the effectiveness of the German army. The Germans were also outmarching their artillery and supplies and often were out of communication with headquarters. Encouraged by the retreat of the French and British and anticipating that another Sedan could soon be achieved, Kluck, the German First Army Commander, wheeled in toward Paris, leaving the German right flank exposed. Thus the way was prepared for the first Battle of the Marne, September 6 through 10, a tactical and "psychological" defeat for the Germans. In East Prussia, the German armies under Hindenburg and Ludendorff had decisively defeated Samsonov's army at the Battle of Tannenberg, which lasted from August 23 to 31, 1914. Liddell Hart, *op. cit.,* pp. 83–86, 133–45.

IX

Viewing the War from Berlin
1914

On August 19, 1914, President Wilson issued a proclamation calling upon the American people to be neutral in action, as well as in thought. The majority of the American people, however, after they had recovered from the initial impact of war, were sympathetic to the Allied cause. The United States and Great Britain were bound by ties of language, literature, law, and custom. Political leaders like Woodrow Wilson, Theodore Roosevelt, William H. Taft, and many others were much closer to British traditions and ideas than to German. With France, American relations were not only sentimentally cordial, but the functioning French democracy was closer to American ideals than the German and Austro-Hungarian monarchies.

Most American newspapers, in 1914, received their European news from London. Few American newspapers maintained European staffs, and, from the outset of war, the majority of American papers were pro-Ally. In spite of Tsarist Russia's participation on the Allied side, the New York Times, *for instance, on August 2, 1914, viewed the war as a crusade for "the crushing out of the imperial idea, the end, once for all times, in those three empires of absolute rule and the substitution for all-powerful sovereigns and their titled advisors of an executive with power to carry out only the will of the people."*

Mr. Grew at this time was still First Secretary of Embassy in Berlin. He served there as Second Secretary from 1908 to 1911 and as First Secretary from 1912 to 1917.

To my family, October 21, 1914

. . . I will sometime endeavor to find a moment to comment

on your comments about the war. Much of what you say is justified but a great deal is not. You have sent me many clippings from the American press, the statements contained in which have subsequently been totally disproved. We now see the English and French papers regularly and are able to see both sides of every question. But realize that while you, in no uncertain terms, are implying our easy gullibility over here, you yourselves from the first have received your news and impressions from one country and one country only. Every single cablegram to America, whether from hostile, neutral or friendly countries, passes through England and there they are so carefully censored that you are absolutely in the dark as to the *other* side of the question. There is another side and gradually you will become aware of this, though I gather from the tone of your letters that just at present you would not be willing even to listen to it.

I do not want, at present, to go into the question of the atrocities that have been committed. These will be dealt with by experts after the war, unhampered by a biased public opinion. They have been grave, barbaric, horrible, and the responsibility for them will surely be fixed sooner or later. According to you, one side is alone to blame. Perhaps you are right. Anyway we shall someday see.[1]

I must however comment on the news you receive and accept as trustworthy. Let us leave out the mention of the fall of Antwerp unfortunately included in one of my letters long ago, as that never appeared in the press here and is not a cri-

---

[1] The Schlieffen Plan had envisioned a speedy and effective overthrow of Belgian resistance to the German armies pressing toward France. Given this end, the German military leaders were prepared to sanction severe methods to gain it. The outrages committed by the German army against individuals and both public and private property in Belgium seemed to many to be greater than those usually attendant on military invasion. The heavy bombardment of some Belgian cities, the damage done to Aerschot, Alost, Reims, Dinant, the firing of Louvain with the destruction of the library, university, and Church of St. Pierre combined with well-substantiated stories of crimes against civilians to arouse a feeling of revulsion against such "atrocities." For communications to the United States Government about these methods of warfare, see *Foreign Relations, 1914, Supplement*, pp. 791–809.

terion of the news published. The telephone operator, when I called for a number that night, imparted this false piece of news gratuitously and being sleepy and careless at that late hour, I included it in my diary without waiting to verify it. Nothing further was of course heard of it. But take as an example the clipping which you covered with exclamation marks, announcing General von Hindenburg's victory [2] over the Russians in East Prussia. You covered it with exclamation marks because it was repeated as showing the way false news was given out in the German press and you thought the Russians were daily approaching Berlin. Now every Russian has been driven out of Germany and far back across the border. The German news was absolutely correct. The Russians may not *stay* out, but they are certainly out now. The broom has swept clean.

Take again the English report of the German submarine victory over three English cruisers. The English press reported that the cruisers were assailed by a whole fleet of submarines, of which they sank two. This was quite incorrect. There was but one submarine engaged or in the vicinity.[3] Lost submarines cannot be kept secret; the news leaks out if it is not published, for the families must soon know of their lost relatives, and when more than one ship is engaged in a successful fight, the commanders of all must be given public credit. Otherwise the spirit and incentive on which the Navy is founded would soon fail. In this case there was but one submarine engaged and the Germans gave the credit to Commander Weddigen for a great action. Again the English and American press announced that the Reims Cathedral had been totally destroyed and was a heap of ruins. This was false. The

---

2 The Battle of Tannenberg, August 23 through 31, 1914.

3 On September 22, the English cruisers *Cressy*, *Aboukir*, and *Hogue* were sunk with losses of about 60 officers and nearly 1,400 men. At first it was believed that five or six German submarines had taken part in the attack, because six torpedoes were fired in about an hour's time. As the investigation proceeded there seemed little reason to question the German assertion that the sinking of the three ships had been accomplished by one German submarine, the *U-9*. Julian S. Corbett, *A History of the Great War . . . Naval Operations* (London: Longmans, Green & Co., 1920), I, 175–77.

edifice is still standing; it has been gutted and there are holes and a few windows partially broken, but it is not a heap of ruins and it can be repaired.

Again the English press described the bombardment of Antwerp as raging inferno, the air thick with shells, the city a seething mass of flames. Conger, of the Associated Press, returned to Berlin after examining Antwerp from end to end when it was all over. He reports practically no damage. Here a house has been hit by a shell and burned and then one drives a mile or a mile and a half before coming to another. The Cathedral has one hole in the roof, but the shell did no damage inside. The German batteries were instructed to drop a shell as near as possible to the Palace and another to the Town Hall without damaging them. They landed on the sidewalk as intended and did no harm. Conger reports 80 shells fired in all; the English press reports 800.

Well, enough of this. I must sound very pro-German. But I am not. My position is an absolutely neutral one. I speak as I do only through an inherent and natural love of argument and perhaps also of common fairness. You have shown us emphatically your side — that is, the news and impressions you receive on your side. I have only wanted to show you this side. After all, history will show who was right and who wrong — probably both. And the world will eventually sit in judgment on many things which we have no right, either of us, to judge now, in the heat and horror of the moment and influenced only by incomplete evidence and information. . . .

To Emil Ahlborn, Ouchy-Lausanne, November 13, 1914

. . . I quite agree with you about the prejudiced news which is received and published in America and I have myself done my best in an unofficial way to counteract this. I think on the whole that lately the news received has been less one-sided than at the beginning though there are still gross exaggerations and much misapprehension. My position is, of course, an absolutely neutral one and in all my letters I have carefully avoided touching on the moral, ethical or political side of the war, and confined myself merely to the question of distorted news and information. It will be time to take up the other side of the question when the war is over and the world can look at the matter from a calmer standpoint, though I fear prejudices are now being formed which can never entirely be dissipated. . . .

To my mother, November 15, 1914

I am sorry that my letters are so few and far between, but it is the most difficult thing in the world to find free moments for writing any personal letters at all. I get to the chancery an hour earlier than most of the others and from then until late at night have to work at steam heat in order not to let one day's work lap over to the next, which would be fatal. The Ambassador has broken down completely and has gone away with Dr. Karl Ohnesorg [Assistant to the Naval Attaché of the American Embassy at Berlin] to look after him for an indefinite stay. Lately he has lost all the forcefulness and quickness of decision with which he handled the early part of the crisis and he has several times told me that he thinks he is going to die. The strain of the last few months has been enormous. This leaves still more work for me, as I have now to receive all the visitors as well and this consumes a lot of valuable time, often uselessly. Lately the correspondence has been increasing and we now receive and send more telegrams daily than even at the beginning of the war. I wish I could go into all the interesting questions that arise in this letter, but that would not now be possible.

On November 2nd old Wilhelm Knoth completed his fortieth year of service in the Embassy and we presented him with a silver dish, inscribed with all our names and the dedication "From the Ambassador and the Staff of the American Embassy in Berlin to WILHELM KNOTH upon his completion of forty years of faithful service, November 2, 1914," as well as 1000 marks, to which we all contributed. We held a little ceremony and the Ambassador made a speech of presentation. Had he done this service under the German Government, he would have received a pension of 1765 marks a year, but I did my best in Washington last summer to get something for him and had no success. The best I could do for him was to get him a decoration from the German Government. . . .

Our only dissipation lately has been an occasional concert. There was a magnificent philharmonic under Fiedler last week, at which they gave the Unfinished Symphony and the 9th with full chorus — truly magnificent. We have been to two Nikisch concerts and one by Leo Slezak. The other day Fritz Kreisler came to the Embassy to get a passport for his wife's maid and I asked him to dinner. He is perfectly charming — quite modest and very gentle, the antithesis of his wife, who is lively, very amusing and distinctly clever as a conversationalist. Edith Kleist [American-born wife of Baron Kleist] was also there, as well as a little Miss Walker, who is helping us at the Embassy — a pupil of Kreisler — and Grafton and Charlie Russell. Kreisler still hobbles about on a stick, the result of a wound received from a Cossack in a night attack in Galicia; he was ridden down and lanced, but fortunately, save for a bruise from the horse's hoof, his arm was not hurt. He is now invalided from the Austrian Army and sailed the next day for America where he will give a concert tour in January. You will see him in Boston. Why not go to his concert and write him to come to dinner — you would enjoy meeting him, I am sure. . . .

The Ambassador was, as you know, beaten for the Senate, though he ran 100,000 votes ahead of his ticket, which I think can be regarded as a great personal victory.[4] He had not solic-

4 Campaign headquarters for Ambassador Gerard for the post of Senator from New York were opened on October 3, 1914, with the announcement of an unusual campaign in which the candidate was to be 4000 miles away and no funds were to be solicited. While Gerard had indicated his desire to win, he refused to leave his post in Berlin at such a time of crisis. As the Democratic candidate Gerard had the support of many of the national leaders, President Wilson's letter endorsing him being made public on October 18. The election resulted, however, in what the *New York Times* called a "landslide" for the Republican ticket in New York. Although the Democratic Party still retained a plurality in Congress, the eastern states of New York, Pennsylvania, and Connecticut evidenced a decided swing away from the party in power nationally. Gerard re-

ited the nomination, but I think he is very much disappointed. We are very congenial in the work here and I am glad that we are not to lose him, although I suppose, speaking quite selfishly, it would have been better for us personally had he been elected as he told me that he would enter office with absolutely no political obligations and would have secured us a good post. . . .

To Boylston Beal, November 17, 1914
. . . There have been many interesting cases since you left, but it would be impossible to go into them now. When we meet I shall have much to tell you. One case, however, has just had its denouement. A German named Lody recently was arrested in England as a spy, though he had an American passport made out for a man named Inglis.[5] We issued this passport to Inglis early in August on good documentary evidence of his citizenship. Lody said in his trial that he was given his choice of three American passports at the German Foreign Office and chose Inglis' as his signature was the easiest to copy. It was probably one of those we sent over to be stamped and did not come back before Inglis departed. Anyway, Lody was convicted and shot in the Tower ditch on November 5th. I hardly think the blame rests with us.

They are making very stringent regulations against the English remaining here. All men between 17 and 55 have been interned at Ruhleben; all the English women have to report at their police offices twice a day and cannot go out after 8 P.M. It is said that they will soon be expelled from Germany. This is in retaliation for the arrest of Germans in England. They

ceived about one hundred thousand more votes for the senatorial post than did the Democratic candidate for Governor. *New York Times*, October 3, 1914, p. 6; October 18, 1914, II, p. 9; November 4, 1914, pp. 1, 3.

[5] Carl Hans Lody, a German naval reserve officer, was arrested in England on October 2, 1914, and charged with attempting to convey to Germany information about the movements and the losses of the British fleet. Entering England with the passport of an American, Charles Inglis, Lody had traveled about the country gathering data on defenses and troop movements which he had tried to relay to Germany in letters. He was tried and sentence was passed on November 3. *The Times* (London), November 2, 1914, p. 4; November 3, 1914, p. 4.

are frightfully angry here. There are lots of difficulties for us and it is immensely hard to negotiate at all, the feeling is so strong. Admiral Reginald Neeld [retired British naval officer] and the other aged invalids at Bad Nauheim are still held — they will make absolutely no exceptions in the case of retired officers. . . .

To Lilla Cabot Perry, December 6, 1914

. . . I have striven from the beginning to avoid any comment whatever on the moral or political side of the war, confining myself entirely to the question of news, but I see that to try to show certain sides of the German point of view by discussing certain false elements in the news which has reached America is to give the impression that I personally am heart and soul on the side I am arguing for. This is far from the case, but when you write letters taunting us with our easy gullibility, you must expect to receive replies dealing with the other side of the question, for I have enough of the lawyer in me — added to a sufficient sprinkling of the cussedness of human nature — to welcome the challenge to an argument. If Tom has really stopped his subscription to the *Transcript* because it is publishing *one* article a week on the other side of the question, I shall not presume to discuss the matter any more and make him wish that he could stop his subscription to my letters too!

But please let me say just one thing more before I leave this painful subject. We have had and are having a very difficult road to travel here, and it is steadily becoming more so, for whatever we feel and think personally, it is our particular job to maintain the strictest sort of neutrality in word and deed. It is therefore very discouraging to learn from various sources that the report is being spread in Boston that we are radically pro-German. To tell two people is to tell a hundred — and the returns are beginning to come in to me. This does not accord with the strictly neutral attitude which we have since the beginning of the war striven to maintain; still less does it tally with the radically anti-German reputation which, in spite of all our efforts, our Embassy is credited with here. Now until this dreadful war is over, I am not going to depart from this neutral attitude in any letter that I write; you have given us a pro-German reputation because we ventured to discuss false press reports and did not violently attack the German cause. Here we have been given an anti-German reputation because we have been kind to the English prisoners. What's a poor man to do? You know that Alice and I are human; you know that we are just as much horrified and disgusted as you at the dropping of bombs on defenseless cities, the killing of innocent people, the shooting of noncombatants, the violation of the Red Cross, the maiming of the wounded; you also know that we are honorable people and therefore regard the breaking of a word of honor — whether oral or written — in just as black a light as you do. But from your letters one would not suspect it.

Perhaps you have led me to say more than I intended — perhaps I would say much more if I could. But at any rate, please do not regard us as either pro or anti anything at present; a politician straddling the fence is open to scorn — but a diplomatist representing a neutral country during a great war fails to fulfill his duty if he does anything else!

Here endeth the first chapter. . . .

To Thomas Sergeant Perry, December 6, 1914

. . . Whatever may be our sympathy for individual Germans and our admiration for the great fighting machine they have built up and for those of their military and naval exploits which have been clean and aboveboard and in accordance with the provisions of international law, we are, at heart, entirely pro-Ally. We are opposed to the German cause, and all it stands for, the origin of the war, the method of conducting it. The dropping of bombs on defenseless cities, killing innocent people, the shooting of noncombatants, the violation of the Red Cross, the maiming of the wounded — all these things have horrified and disgusted us as much as they have you — so far as they are true, and certainly some of them are true, though we are convinced — with our many sources of information — that of every ten such reports published and told in the United States, nine are exaggerated or false. We believe that a German victory would be a step backward in civilization and a misfortune to mankind, and we realize that if militarism is not now killed once and forever, the progress of the world will be retarded for many generations to come. You have made me put this on paper by the tone of your letters and I hope you will appreciate its confidential character. We have a hard road to follow here, as I have said, but we are doing it to the best of our ability. In our actions we are neutral and are heartily doing as much for Germans as we are for others, for human want, sorrow or suffering know no creeds.

To my mother, December 7, 1914

. . . Last week the Empress visited our American Kitchen, where members of the American colony serve 200 poor people every day. Alice served as a waitress one whole week and greatly enjoyed it. As the Ambassador was away I had to meet the Empress at her automobile and escort her in to the Kitchen, which is a large well-lighted house away off near the Schlesischer Bahnhof. She stayed there for almost three-quarters of an hour, inspecting everything and chatting with the ladies of the Embassy, the American women helping and the poor people themselves. I am glad that an official mark of approval was thus placed on it, as everything is of use that can serve to counteract the unfortunate anti-German reputation which we all have here.

This reputation is caused partially by the reflection of American public opinion at home and partially by the efficient manner in which we have looked after British interests and British prisoners of war in Germany. It should not be considered unneutral to fulfill such a job to the best of one's ability, but the Spanish Ambassador [Polo de Bernabé], who has charge of French, Russian and Belgian interests here, will do practically nothing for them as he is so afraid of being considered anti-German. The American Chargé d'Affaires in St. Petersburg during the first few months of the war seems to be

equally conservative and when the Russian mob began to storm
the German Embassy there, he is said merely to have telephoned
to an under official at the Foreign Office.[6] The least he should
have done would have been to get into touch with the Minister
of Foreign Affairs himself and demand an immediate and sufficient force of police or troops to protect the building, but I
think that if he had had any warning at all as to what was
going to happen, he should have nailed the American flag
to the door of the Embassy — as the property was under the
protection of the United States Government — and have done
what little he personally could until the troops came. In reply
to a recent request we made to him to deliver a message to a
German prisoner, he said, "You will of course understand that
I can hold no communication whatever with Germans in Russia" — yet we are corresponding and communicating personally every day with British prisoners in Germany, looking after
their wants, supplying them with clothes and money and endeavoring, when possible, to get them freed. You doubtless
know that all English civilians in Germany were placed in a
concentration camp at Ruhleben, outside of Berlin, several
weeks ago, as retaliation for the imprisonment of Germans in
England, although the circumstances were not at all analogous.
I have myself been out there two or three times and talked
with many of the men, once going with Chandler Anderson —
legal adviser to American embassies and legations in Europe —
when he officially inspected the camp.[7] There is a good deal
of hardship and lack of comfort, but the authorities seem to
be doing their best to improve matters. At Torgau, where the
British officers who are prisoners of war are interned, they
are in most sympathetic relations with the German commander;
he lets them censor their own letters and every possible way
tries to make life easy for them. Alice has sent a great quantity
of books down to them and has received most appreciative

[6] *Foreign Relations, 1914, Supplement,* pp. 733–34.

[7] A memorandum written by Anderson about conditions in German camps
appears in U.S. Department of State, *Papers Relating to the Foreign Relations
of the United States, 1915, Supplement, The World War* (Washington: Government Printing Office, 1928), pp. 997–1002.

letters from Colonel Gordon, the senior British officer, and I am getting together a large quantity of hymnals, Bibles, etc., for their chaplain. . . .

This is a wonderful time for public service; opportunities to do untold good come to one's attention every day and that is what makes this diplomatic work a joyful one, even in the midst of the sorrow and suffering which also continually come to one's notice. It is a shame that it should be hampered and limited by red tape, formalities and official hindrances. Yet that is what we see every day. At the very beginning of the war I saw that very soon we should be flooded with inquiries about captured or wounded relatives and accordingly organized a separate bureau in the Embassy, under Charlie Russell, to deal with this business exclusively. He has handled it admirably and has built up a card catalogue recording every bit of information that comes to us and the name and address of every inquirer, and no inquiry goes unanswered, even though we may not be able to find out anything. We also have different colored printed forms to be filled out by Germans desiring information about relatives or friends in any other country and these we send on to our respective Embassies to attend to and return to us. But our channels of information are sadly unsatisfactory! The Spanish Embassy simply throw in the waste-paper basket the inquiries they receive, so it is useless to turn to them for information about French or Russian prisoners. The Foreign Office refers us to the War Office and the War Office sends us on to their information bureau — which apparently does nothing. The Red Cross at Geneva lumbers along but seems to accomplish little. And all this time wives and mothers are anxiously awaiting news of their sons or husbands, which could so easily be given them if organization and efficiency would take the place of red tape and departmental delay. Not long ago, through a *clerical error*, the Spanish Embassy sent the list of French prisoners which they had received from the German Government to Russia, and the Russian list to France, thus causing a delay of over two weeks. What must those two weeks have meant to many anxious families. And the worst of it was that the French Government, being annoyed at the supposed delay on the part of the German Government in sending forward their list, refused temporarily to send forward any further German lists and there was delay all along the line. Recently the German Government sent us a list of their hospital ships, which under the Hague Convention are inviolable, for communication to the various belligerent countries. I drafted and sent the telegram myself, as I do in all these cases, with the greatest care, going over it again and again to see that nothing was missing. Through a *clerical error* — I will not mention where it occurred — the name of the hospital ship *Ophelia* was omitted from the list as finally communicated to the belligerent governments. A naval action took place at an expected point and the *Ophelia* was to have been there to pick up the wounded. But not having been announced to the British Government as a hospital ship, she was previously captured and taken to an English port, and no hospital ship attended at the battle. This "clerical error" cost many lives.

If anyone accuses us of being unneutral in our care of British interests, we can only say that we do everything in our power to help Germans when cases are brought to us. I have made a particular point of this, in some cases even directly disobeying the Department of State's instructions in order to help somebody out. Recently a German lady came to me and pleaded with me to send a telegram to Peking to find out whether her brother had been killed at Tsingtao. We had been instructed to send no more private telegrams of any kind and at first I had to refuse, but then it occurred to me that it might be done unofficially and I wrote to Peter Jay at Rome to ask if he could get a personal telegram through for me to our Legation at Peking. He did it and within four days I received a reply that the brother was well and unwounded and a prisoner of war in Japan. The cry of joy which she gave when I telephoned the news to her and the letter she wrote me afterwards were full recompense. She told me that she had used every

possible influence with various departments of the Government
and could hardly believe that the news should have reached
her first through us.

Our life is full of dramatic incidents and happenings. It is
not particularly dramatic to have women weeping on your
shoulder in the chancery, which they have a way of doing and
which led our Relief Committee — of which Alice is a member
— to make a rule that weeping was allowed for ten minutes
by the clock and then — heraus! But it is dramatic to inform
Frau Brandt that her husband, who had been condemned to
be shot in Morocco, had been reprieved; to rush off another
telegram without a moment's delay to try to save the life of
another poor wretch and later to learn that our telegram had
arrived just too late; to read to the Foreign Office the telegram
from Captain von Müller of the *Emden* containing his report
of her destruction, November 9, and the long list of killed and
to transmit to him in return the information that he had been
given the 1st and 2nd classes of the Iron Cross and made a
"free citizen" of the city of Emden . . . to take part in a race
down the streets of Berlin to capture a man who had forged
the Ambassador's name to a check; to dine one night with two
Englishmen who had assisted us in our English Bureau and
the next day to learn that they had both been arrested as spies
— all this is the dramatic side of our work and the element increases daily.

As regards the two Englishmen, Spottiswoode and Weston,
our conscience is clear — only we made the mistake of not
asking the Foreign Office in writing whether they had any objection to our employing them, instead of merely verbally, as
the Ambassador had done. The Foreign Office swore that they
had nothing whatever to do with the arrest, but we found out
— by the "underground" — that it was they who had given
the order. They simply thought that the men were being
given too many advantages for corresponding with England
through our Embassy, and the poor fellows — as well as the
German lady to whom Spottiswoode is engaged — and her
sister! — because they might have participated in the spying

— have been in solitary confinement for nearly two months. It is outrageous, but there is nothing whatever that we can do for them as they are "subjects of an enemy country." We protested, of course, but the Foreign Office simply replied that "similar unpleasantnesses" could be avoided in future if we would always first ask their permission before employing "alien enemies." Yet there are several Germans employed in our Embassy in London!

The suspicion under which we in the Embassy have fallen was never more clearly marked than by a recent episode. A few days ago Princess Ella Radziwill arrived in Berlin with her sister, Princess Blücher, from their place at Krieblowitz, en route to London. Princess Blücher is German by marriage and had fixed up the matter of her entry into England through myself and John Gregory of the British Foreign Office, with whom I had been in correspondence. Princess Ella is a Russian, although her family are scattered throughout Europe and are of all nationalities and she has many highly placed relatives in Berlin, such as her aunt Duchess Paul of Mecklenburg, her cousin Duchess Marie Antoinette of Mecklenburg, another aunt, the old Princess Radziwill, Countess Mocenigo, etc. Well, Princess Ella came to see me at the Embassy the day before her prospective departure for England and asked me if she had to do anything with her passport before leaving. I was astonished as I had supposed that everything had already been arranged and I had to tell her that there might be serious difficulty about it and that she certainly in any case could not get off for two or three days, as the Kommandantur always required at least that length of time to examine and stamp passports. I sent Charlie Russell around to the Kommandantur with her in order to see Falkenstein, an officer whom I personally know there, and he said that he would do what he could but that there might be some delay. As I fully expected, he later telephoned to say that she could not possibly leave at present, and I well knew what that meant: she had been living down in the country without reporting herself to the police as a Russian — as she didn't know it was necessary — and now she was under suspicion as a Russian spy. Princess Blücher therefore left for England without her, as she had to go then or never according to the arrangement with Gregory, and as Alice had asked Princess Ella to come and stay with us in case she should ever be in Berlin alone. She lunched that day with her cousin, Countess Oppersdorff, and was there told that the American Embassy was under the gravest suspicion of being anti-German, that we had let Englishmen escape from the country with American passports, etc., etc., and that we were all being *carefully watched* and our mail regularly opened. (Fortunately this will go by a means by which it can't be opened!) And that it would therefore compromise her to come and stay with us. Almost at the same time the Counselor of the Austrian Embassy, who has his ear pretty close to the ground, telephoned to me — and in my absence spoke to Alice — to say that as a friend and colleague he would strongly advise us not to take Princess Ella in as we would be seriously compromised by so doing. By this time we were both mad, thoroughly mad, and we told Ella that we should naturally stick by her and that even though she would not, under the circumstances, come to stay, she must take her meals with us whenever she wished and she has done so regularly for the last five days, during which a glimpse of life in the dark ages has been revealed to me. The police follow her most carefully and Fabritz, our German servant, has told us that he has been instructed to give any information that he may learn at our house and thought it his duty to warn us — good old man that he is. I called on —— and gave him a piece of my mind for not standing up for a woman whose position in Vienna he well knew and whom he had known personally all his life and was now disclaiming. The Spanish Embassy would of course, as usual, do nothing. She wrote a letter to Countess Parr in Vienna to get the Austrian Emperor to intercede for her personally and while waiting for a reply to this, we feared daily that she would be taken off to prison as a spy. Then something happened which changed everything. The chief reason why she was under suspicion was on account of her brother,

Prince Nicholas Radziwill, who is a dashing officer in the Russian Army and an A.D.C. to General Paul Rennenkampf. On the day that war was declared he was coming through from England to Russia on the Nord Express, but just after crossing the Belgian frontier into Germany he heard on the train that it was just going to be searched for foreigners — in fact he was personally told so by the guard who did not know him — and he quietly dropped off behind without his luggage and footed it back into Belgium, getting from there to England and so to Russia via Sweden. It turned out that the authorities had heard that he was on the train and knowing that he was an important officer with knowledge of Germany, they gave orders for his arrest and they searched the train all the way to the Russian border without success and could never understand how he escaped! Princess Ella told me all this. I occasionally got news of him for his sisters; he was wounded, recovered and returned to the front — and two days ago came a telegram to me from Princess Gagarine in Rome saying that he had fallen. Alice and Countess Oppersdorff had to break the news to her and it was terrible; he was devoted to her and she to him and she was to have gone to live with him when the war broke out, as he had quarreled with his wife. To make matters worse, if possible, she had given him most of her money for an investment and she never took a receipt, and now both her brother and the only other man who knew of the transaction are both dead, and her sister-in-law not on speaking terms with her. Her future is indeed black. Well, the news of her brother's death caused the German military authorities to give her permission to return to Russia; she has just dined with us and is about to start tomorrow, but she has not yet received her passport back from the Kommandantur and I still have fears that this may be a mere blind and that she still may be imprisoned as a spy. It has been a sad case. Alice has been with her continually and she has taken most of her meals with us and the authorities can be damned. I suppose we are now more under suspicion than ever.

This is a long yarn I am spinning, but free Sunday evenings

come seldom and it may be as well to bring this "Contemporary Comment on the War of 1914" up to date for future reference and the present boring of our respective families. . . .

The feeling in Germany against America and Americans is steadily growing more bitter. They now fully realize the sentiment in America and they are still more annoyed by our exportation of arms and ammunition to England, though we are perfectly within our rights according to international law. Two days ago a member of our Embassy was sitting in a tramcar next to two Germans and overheard their conversation, which he immediately reported to me. One of them said he was "second-in-command at one of the Ministries." I think, from the description given, that I know who he is. They were discussing the above subject and speaking of Americans in a nasty sneering way. Finally the high official, becoming very hot, said: "They will all, including the members of the Embassy, find themselves at Ruhleben one of these days!"

Just one word more before I end this all too long effusion. We are pitied at home for our lack of authentic news; we are regarded as groping in the dark and totally without reliable information upon which to base intelligent opinions; I gather from letters that Boylston Beal has given that impression, but things have changed vastly since he left us. When I say that we regularly read the London *Times* (daily edition), London *Daily Mail* and the *New York Times,* besides the German papers, and that we have at our daily disposal the French press and the *Corriere della Sera;* that I continually, in fact daily, talk with people fresh from England, France, Belgium and Russia, chiefly American travelers; that I am in close touch with my colleagues at other posts both by personal and official correspondence, and that I have access to important documents from many countries, of which the public knows nothing, it can hardly be said that we are ill informed, whatever deficiencies may exist in our powers of discernment and deduction. I therefore feel justified in repeating what I have said before, that although the intense anti-German character of American public opinion is *based* on certain perfectly solid facts, it has been inflamed and prejudiced by false and garbled reports of many kinds. This statement is in no way a criterion of my own views for or against Germany, any more than the statements contained in any of my letters have been, but it does represent my disgust that the American press should have run riot in the way it has done since the beginning of the war.

I will not continue to give samples of these false reports, though we in the Embassy have evidence of many such and the evidence does not come from German sources. It is a diplomatist's first duty to be well informed. Let me, however, for your interest mention simply one, which is a good sample of many others. A friend, in one of her recent letters, spoke of the danger to neutral commerce caused by floating German mines, used contrary to the provisions of the Hague agreement, and the bitter tone of her comment showed that this was at least one of the factors which has inflamed anti-German feeling at home. Now listen to this. Commander Gherardi, our Naval Attaché, who is also Naval Attaché at The Hague, recently had an interview with the Dutch Minister of Marine, in which the Minister stated in confidence — and I repeat it in confidence — that approximately 100 unexploded mines had recently been washed up on the Dutch coast, that he had personally examined them, and that *every one of them was English.* As the Dutch Government is neutral with strong pro-English leanings (only the Queen being pro-German) there is no reason to suppose that the Minister lied. I don't mean for a moment that these were free floating mines, for I do not think that any country is foolish enough to use free floating mines which are as dangerous to themselves as to the enemy, but I do mean that these English mines were not strongly enough anchored to withstand the gales and that the Minister's statement is highly indicative that many of the accidents to innocent shipping, gratuitously credited to the Germans, have undoubtedly been caused by English mines dragging about in this way.

But I have already seen that to try to show *anything* in favor of Germany is to give the impression that we are heart and soul pro-German, so I will endeavor to abandon the habit lest we still further become outcasts from the family circle and lest we continue to augment a reputation at home which would ensure our being torn limb from limb should we ever dare show our faces in Boston. Whatever our personal feelings may be, in our actions we are neutral and are heartily doing what we can for both Allies and Germans. . . .

X

Crisis With Germany

1915

With the outbreak of war, Great Britain proclaimed a blockade of the Central Powers and drew up a list of articles as contraband of war. Direct American trade with Germany was shut off by the blockade and indirect trade through the Netherlands and Scandinavia was largely checked. President Wilson protested these violations of neutral rights many times, but war with Great Britain over this question was unthinkable, since the United States wanted an Allied victory and the dispute only involved property rights.

Whenever American disputes with Great Britain over the question of neutral trade in wartime reached an intense point, Germany usually diverted American attention by her policy of unrestricted submarine warfare. In December, 1914, for instance, Germany announced that the waters around the British Isles were a war zone and that all commerce with the Allies found in that area would be destroyed. Germany justified her policy of violating international law on the ground that it was necessary in order to counteract the equally lawless Allied blockade. American public opinion, however, recognized a difference between Allied and German violations of neutral rights. German violations entailed the loss of life, while Allied violations resulted in property losses for which return might be made at the close of the war.

President Wilson warned Germany on February 10, 1915, that the United States would "hold the Imperial German Government to a strict accountability for property endangered or lives lost." The torpedoing of the British liner Lusitania *on May 7, 1915, with the loss of over eleven hundred lives includ-*

ing one hundred and twenty-eight Americans, brought to a head the question of holding Germany to a "strict account-ability."

Although there was some clamor for war, President Wilson felt that the country was not ready. He despatched a note on May 13 demanding that Germany disavow the sinking, make reparations, and take steps to prevent a recurrence. When the German reply was unsatisfactory, he despatched a second note on June 9. The President stated that the United States was contending for the rights of humanity; that the nation would not admit that American citizens could not travel on merchant ships of belligerent powers; and that the country would not admit the right of Germany to sink a ship without warning and without taking precautions for the safety of the passengers.

Secretary of State Bryan thought that this note meant war, and he resigned rather than sign it. He was replaced by Robert Lansing. It was Bryan's belief that the United States should renounce responsibility for Americans who traveled on belli-gerent ships. The President, however, had already made clear his belief that "once accept a single abatement of right, and many other humiliations would certainly follow."

In August, while tension over the Lusitania *was still acute, the British liner* Arabic *was torpedoed with the loss of two American lives. A break with Germany now seemed unavoid-able. The German Ambassador to the United States, Count Bernstorff, however, described to his Government the dangerous tone of American opinion, and Germany on September 22 agreed to stop sinking liners without warning and without taking precautions for the safety of the lives of noncombatants. The crisis over the submarine then abated until Germany, in February, 1916, once more resorted to unrestricted U-boat warfare.*

Thursday, February 26 [1915]

. . . Muriel Seherr [Countess Seherr-Thoss, Henry White's daughter], who sat next me at lunch, told me in confidence that when Lanier Winslow [newly appointed as Third Secretary of the American Embassy at Berlin] returned to Berlin with his newly wedded wife . . . the military authorities in the Ministry of War came to her husband and told him that he must warn the Ambassador unofficially that Winslow would have to leave Berlin as he had been so outspokenly anti-German and was so much under suspicion that they could not have him here. Manni Seherr told them that they did not understand Americans, who sometimes talked more than they meant, and that he was aware that Winslow was far from being anti-German as they supposed. So the matter was dropped. This trouble apparently originated during the first part of the war when various members of our Embassy discussed matters and expressed their opinions much too openly. They used to talk far too freely at the Adlon bar, often in the presence of Germans and always in the presence of the German bartender, until I asked the Ambassador to forbid any member of the Embassy staff to go there at all. . . . The Ambassador has also unfortunately shared this anti-German reputation and not long ago they were on the point of starting a press campaign against him with the object of having him recalled, but some of his friends found out about this in time and managed to have it stopped. . . . But I think the press has been slightly more friendly lately and the press is absolutely controlled by the Government.

In the evening dined with the Seherr-Thosses at the Esplanade with Major Hans von Herwarth. . . . Afterwards Herwarth, now working on the General Staff, who is almost fanatic in his ideas, talked to me for a long time, expressing the most bitter hate against England "which all Germans will cherish till death and afterwards." He said that England fully intended to keep Calais, the entire Channel coast and most of Normandy after the war, that she had gotten the French fleet bottled up in the Mediterranean with this end in view and that when the German army was obliged to retreat from Paris in September the Allies could have driven them much farther back if England had not refused to move her troops farther south out of Normandy, simply because she was holding Normandy for her own use in future. He then went on to tell me many stories of the kindness and chivalry of the German troops, which are apparently his stock-in-trade, as he had told me nearly all of them before. His pet story is about two Belgian officers, who held a Belgian fort until all their men were killed and then refused to surrender. When finally taken, the German commanding officer allowed them to keep their arms and gave them a letter addressed to all German military authorities in Belgium asking that these brave men be allowed to proceed to Brussels and then to rejoin their own army to fight again against the Germans. Herwarth was in the Governor's House when their cards were brought in; he noticed with surprise that they had their swords and revolvers and asked smilingly if they had come to destroy the German army. When they showed him their letter, however, he asked them what they would have to drink and said he was ready to comply with any request they might make. They asked to be allowed to spend three days with their relatives, so he had them conducted to their families and at the end of the three days they were taken by a German guard to the German outposts before Antwerp and here allowed to return to their own lines to continue to fight.

Hugh Gibson, our Secretary of Legation in Brussels, who recently spent a few days with us, had something to say on the other side of the story, however. The military régime is terribly strict. One cannot move anywhere even in the city without a special pass for the particular purpose for which he sets out. If he gets a pass to proceed by a certain tramcar, he is liable to arrest if he takes any other car or goes in any other direction. Recently a German officer in the Government was told various stories regarding the brutal way in which American members of the Relief Commission and others were treated on crossing the frontier, and not believing them he said he would investigate himself. So he put on civilian clothes and proceeded to the frontier. There he was taken out of the train by a German soldier and when he protested and tried to show his papers he was set upon by the soldiers and the station official and beaten almost into insensibility; his nose was broken and both eyes blackened. He returned to Brussels with this firsthand information, for which he had set out, and the officials who attacked him are now undergoing court-martial and will probably be given long terms of imprisonment. It is to be hoped that this will have a salutory effect on the future treatment of innocent travelers. . . .

Friday, March 5 [1915]

. . . I am on very close terms with the Ambassador and always tell him frankly everything I hear, even at the risk of hurting his feelings, for it is the wiser course. Occasionally the Ambassador, not liking to be under criticism all alone, gets back at me, and the other day he said, "I suppose you know that you yourself are not free from criticism," and he related to me how at lunch one day a German had remarked: "I can understand how the Gerards are anti-German, because they have not been here long enough to understand and to sympathize with the country, but I can't understand how the Grews, who have been here so long and have accepted so much German hospitality, can be anti-German." . . .

Sunday, March 7 [1915]

. . . No bread is served any more in the hotels or restaurants without tickets, which are issued daily allowing a limited amount to each person and the same applies to each household. The amount allowed will probably soon be cut down. We have no white bread any more; it is brown and the flour is mixed with a specified percentage of potatoes, but it is not bad. Various other signs of economy are to be observed now. After March 15th no automobiles for pleasure purposes or for ordinary transit will be allowed; new permits must be secured and these will be issued only for good reasons, such as to drays for business firms, Red Cross cars, etc. The taxicabs will also be cut down by about half and there are precious few now and often they are impossible to find when one wants them. This is to save benzine and rubber. We have put in applications

for our Embassy cars but don't know if they will be granted.
We have not had our own car for nearly a month now. My
chauffeur, who was excellent, was taken for military service.
I asked if I could not retain him and my request was granted,
but the permission came two hours too late, after he had left
Berlin, and once with his regiment they would not let him go;
it was very hard luck. His only brother has already been killed
and his mother is absolutely dependent on him — but this is
war.

Monday, March 8 [1915]

. . . The Greek situation has been the chief topic of interest
lately. Everyone thought that Greece was coming in surely, so
much so that the Theotokys [1] had actually packed, until the
King put his foot down solidly, dismissed Prime Minister
Venizelos and started to form a new Cabinet under former
Prime Minister Zaimis. Theotoky's father, formerly Minister
President, was one of the few who strongly supported the King.
The only doubt now is whether the people, who are generally
in favor of war and devoted to Venizelos, will have their way.
They want to have a share of the prize at Constantinople when
the Dardanelles are finally forced. But the general opinion
here is that the crisis is safely passed.[2] It is also said that Italy's
neutrality has finally been secured definitely, Austria having
met all her demands and probably agreed to cede the Trentino
in the Tirol, though it must have been a bitter pill, forced
upon her by Germany. If this is all true, the atmosphere for
Germany is considerably clearer than it was a few days ago.
For if Italy, Greece and Rumania remain neutral and German

1 Theotoky, Greek Chargé in Germany, who was later Minister of War in the
Greek Cabinet, was lined up against a wall in Athens with the Cabinet and
shot by a successor government. — J. C. G.

2 The Allies wanted Greek co-operation and aid in their attack on the
Dardanelles in 1915. Venizelos urged King Constantine to participate in the
war, but the King refused because he considered the chances of success and the
gains for Greece too small. Venizelos resigned on March 5, the subsequent
political crisis ending on March 10, 1915, when Gounaris took office to carry
out Constantine's policy of neutrality. *The Times* (London), March 8, 1915,
p. 8; March 10, 1915, p. 10.

successes in Russia continue, the prospects of peace would seem to be within measurable distance. This is the general view here. I personally, however, have never thought and do not still think that Germany can win, though I believe I am the only one in the Embassy with this opinion. It is going to depend on bigger things than battles and campaigns, and the biggest of all is starvation. I have little faith in the reports that one hears on all sides of abundance of food and more than plenty to tide over till the next crop. There are already districts where the pinch is being felt, but this is kept very dark and one hears nothing but optimism and boundless self-confidence. . . .

Sunday, March 14 [1915]

. . . We Americans are bitterly hated here, almost as much as the English, certainly far more than the French for whom there is no hatred, only pity. (I wonder who will be the pitier in the end!) This hatred has been steadily increasing since the beginning of the war, started by the intense anti-German feeling in the United States but fanned into open flame by our delivery of arms and ammunition to the Allies. There is no use arguing, no use even discussing the subject with them; I have clearly, concisely and unanswerably submitted our position time and again but without making the slightest impression. There is no use in pointing out that Article 7 of the Hague Convention both for land and sea warfare expressly provides that a neutral government may not prevent its private firms from delivering arms and ammunition to belligerents; [3] that at the time of the discussion of this article at The Hague it was the United States who opposed it and Germany who insisted upon its inclusion in the Convention; that Germany herself delivered arms and ammunition exclusively to Spain in our Spanish-American War and to Russia in the Russo-Japanese War, as well as to the Balkan States in the Balkan War; that Count Bernstorff on December 15th last wrote an official Note

[3] Article 7 of the Hague Convention XIII of 1907 concerning the rights and duties of neutral powers in naval war stated that a neutral power was not "bound to prevent" exportation of arms and ammunitions to belligerents.

to our Government stating precisely and clearly that his Government acknowledged the right of American firms to export arms and ammunition to either or both of the belligerents (a copy of which Note we have in our archives); [4] that it is not the fault of the United States that England is in a position to prevent our delivering such munitions of war to Germany and that our firms would be only too glad to do so if they could. All these arguments fall flat against the inevitable reply of the Germans — that the war would already be over if American supplies had not enabled the French to continue the combat. The German Government, moreover, do their best to inflame this hatred through the press. When the Ambassador protested to Herr von Jagow [German Secretary of State for Foreign Affairs] the other day, he replied that the Government could not control the press. Rot! They have the entire press of the country in the hollow of their hand. The very next day after this interview, the official daily bulletin of the Oberheeresleitung, published in every paper in Germany, called attention to the fact that many of the shells picked up which had come from the French side were of American make. Nothing could be more official than that and it was only one of the digs which we are being given daily. The Government say that they cannot control the press, but they were able to prevent the press from publishing Congressman Bartholdt's letter in which he said that in the event of war, every American of German extraction would rally to the flag of the United States against England, against Germany, against the world. [5] They had good

4 For the text see Count Bernstorff, *My Three Years in America* (New York: Charles Scribner's Sons, 1920), pp. 73–75.

5 Congressman Richard Bartholdt from Missouri was one of the voices of the German-American element which placed its sympathies with Germany, decried the "misrepresentation" of German aims, people, and institutions in the press of the United States, and hoped to change what they thought of as the pro-Ally arms policy of the United States. In Bartholdt's farewell address before the House, however, he emphasized the "steadfast devotion of all citizens of German blood to American ideals and the flag." In case of our involvement in war "the Germans of this country would again as loyally rally around the Stars and Stripes as they did against our enemies in every crisis of the past . . . the Germans are for America against England, for America against Germany,

reason for not wanting that to be published for it is commonly believed here that if war should break out between the United States and Germany, the Germans in America would rise and easily overpower the Government. Zimmermann himself told this to the Ambassador with apparent conviction.[6] Meanwhile the feeling against us grows steadily and it would take a very small match to fire it into war. But if another American ship is sunk, perhaps the match will be applied on the other side of the water. . . .[7]

Saturday, March 20 [1915]

Alice went to a ladies' luncheon. . . . One or two of the ladies protested at Alice's speaking English and one of them said in Edith Kleist's hearing that she deplored Germans marrying foreigners! It is evident that the Germans want to make things as uncomfortable as possible for Americans and Alice and I have agreed to go out as little as possible. I lunched at the Bristol with Russell and Lithgow Osborne, one of our Attachés.

In the evening we gave a very successful dinner for Colonel and Mrs. House, our other guests at table being the Ambassador, Montgelas, the Gherardis and Muriel Seherr-Thoss. Afterwards came many people and we had three tables of bridge as well as poker in my smoking room. Mrs. House is

for America against the world! They will never waver for one second in their allegiance to the land of their choice and adoption." U.S. Congress, *Congressional Record*, 63d Cong., 3d Sess., vol. LII, pt. IV (Washington: Government Printing Office, 1915), pp. 4124–27.

6 According to James Gerard in *My First Eighty-three Years in America* (Garden City: Doubleday & Co., 1951), p. 203, when Zimmermann told him that five thousand trained German reservists would rise, if the United States Government attempted any action against the German Government, Gerard replied: "That may be, but we have in America five hundred thousand and one lamp-posts, and that is where the reservists will find themselves hanging the morning after they try to rise!"

7 The American ship, the *William P. Frye,* carrying wheat from Seattle to Queenstown, had been sunk by the German auxiliary cruiser, *Prinz Eitel Friedrich,* on January 28, 1915. Other American ships such as the *Carib,* carrying supplies to Germany, had been blown up by German mines. *Foreign Relations, 1915, Supplement,* pp. 339–41, 344–45, 826.

very pretty and charming and the Colonel is one of the most
interesting men I have ever met; he is up to date on practically
every subject. He is here as the President's personal representative, feeling the pulse of the various nations for the first signs
of a desire for peace, but they are not yet ready. He has taken
me into his confidence, but I can't go into this very interesting
subject on paper, much as I would like to do so. . . .[8]

*On April 14, the Grews left for a month's leave in Switzerland,
Italy, and Austria. When he arrived at Basel, Mr. Grew wrote
in his diary: "It was a blessed relief to get into a neutral
country, to be able to talk English at the top of our lungs and
to throw off the depressing atmosphere in which we have been
enveloped during the last eight months." In a letter to a friend
on April 7, Mr. Grew had pointed out that some Germans
were refusing to dine in public with Americans, and he added:
"If you won't tell a soul I will confide to you that we are just
about as much loved here as a Russian flea is loved by a Japanese poodle."*

Friday, April 16 [1915]
 Arrived in Rome at 9.30 A.M., where Peter Jay [First Secre-

---

[8] In writing of his impressions to President Wilson, Colonel House said that
his "visit in Berlin was exceedingly trying and disagreeable in many ways. I
met there no one of either high or low degree who did not immediately corner
me, and begin to discuss our shipment of munitions to the Allies, and sometimes
their manner was almost offensive.

"Upon the streets one hesitated to speak in English, for fear of being insulted. . . .

"I feel, however, that with the Government and with the influential people
with whom I talked, a better understanding of our purposes was brought
about; and I hope this feeling will sooner or later reach the people at large."

As to the prospects for making peace at that moment the Colonel felt "that
the people in both Germany and England have been led to expect much more
than is possible of realization. Neither government can fulfill these expectations.
If they attempted to make peace upon a different basis from that which the
people have been led to believe will ultimately come about, there is a possibility
that the Governments would be overthrown. . . .

"I am somewhat at a loss as to what to do next, for it is plain at the moment
that some serious reverse will have to be encountered by one or other of the
belligerents before any Government will dare propose parleys." Edward M.
House, *The Intimate Papers of Colonel House,* ed. Charles Seymour (Boston:
Houghton Mifflin Co., 1926), I, 401–2, 413–14.

tary of the American Embassy at Rome] very kindly met us at the station and took us to the Grand Hotel. . . . After a bath and a change of clothes and breakfast I went to the chancery which is just across the square from the hotel, and there met the various members of the Embassy staff. . . . There seems to be very little work going on, but they expect the usual deluge if Italy comes into the war, as America would probably have charge of German and Austrian interests. The Ambassador, Thomas Nelson Page, asked me to give them some idea of the organization of our Embassy in Berlin, so I spent the morning writing out on the typewriter a long memorandum covering every possible point on this subject, which seems to have pleased them so much that they have asked me to remain and help organize the Embassy here, should Italy join the war during my stay. . . .

Saturday, April 17 [1915] Rome

. . . There are signs of imminent war on all sides and everyone talks of it, but nobody seems to know just when it will begin. Today, for instance, another military class has been called out and two transatlantic liners to America, scheduled to sail in early May, have postponed their sailings. There is also continual movement of troops. But after long talks with the Ambassador and Jay, I am convinced that nobody knows what is going to happen. Italy is bound to get what she requires — the provinces taken from her by Austria — but she is playing the political game for all it is worth and if she has to fight at all will try to come in as late as possible. She could not stand the expense of a long war. But if she does not get what she requires, the people will want to know what she has to show for the expense of mobilization and there will surely be a revolution. Her mobilization and preparation are now practically complete. The Ambassador says that Prince Bülow [German Ambassador to Italy] has been showing the greatest cheeriness and high spirits lately, but it is to his advantage to do so and perhaps he is a good actor. The other day Sonnino, the Minister for Foreign Affairs, told Mr. Page that Baron Karl Macchio, the Austrian Ambassador, had rushed in to see him and had exclaimed "I hear that you are going to mobilize on the 20th!" "Is that so," replied Sonnino, "I haven't heard it myself." The air is full of rumors and counter-rumors daily. I have talked fully with both English and German diplomats here and both are equally in the dark as to what is going to happen and when. . . .

Wednesday, April 28 [1915]

Left Florence at 10.45 A.M., arriving in Venice at 7.10 P.M., where we took a gondola to the Regina Hotel. . . .

Imagine Venice at this the most perfect time of year, with not a single American tourist and perhaps no tourists of any other country, with the hotels literally empty, most of them closed and with only a few sad gondoliers waiting at the stages in vain for employment; no singers passing up and down the Grand Canal before the hotels in the evening and little traffic save for the busy little vaporetto and an occasional private gondola with its smart sailor-dressed gondoliers and its owner sitting luxuriously among the cushions; the Lido hotels closed and several black ominous-looking warships anchored in the lagoon; and in spite of this absence of tourist life, the same lovely Venice with a sunny cloudless sky smiling on the rippling or motionless waters, warm summer weather, a full moon at night and a private terrace from which we look down upon the scene and feel as if it were ours alone.

Every day since we have been here one or two more torpedo boats have come in and they now lie, six or more of them, just at the mouth of the Grand Canal. Farther down towards the Lido are anchored the *Carlo Alberto,* the *Etruria* and the *Montebello.* One night, just as we were about to turn in, I saw what at first looked like a comet in the sky but what proved to be an airship with the searchlights playing on it. It circled three times around the Giudecca, each time lower and each time passing directly over the warships. For the moment I could not help wondering if war had been declared and if this was not an Austrian airship come over from Trieste to drop bombs on the ships; but it soon sailed away inland. . . .

Monday, May 3 [1915], Venice

. . . I went to the Austrian Consulate to have our passports visaed; it is near the Rialto and a pleasant walk, and as well has a most pleasant Consul. I wondered how long he would remain and I suppose he was wondering too, but there was no occasion to enter into a political discussion with him, though I enjoyed hearing the soft Austrian-German spoken again, so much more graceful and agreeable than the pure but raucous Prussian Aussprache. . . .

The probability of war now seems so great and imminent that I do not dare tarry here longer. At any moment the railways could be closed to passenger travel and devoted exclusively to mobilization and the risk of getting caught is too great to run. Italy's mobilization must be practically complete, for if she is coming into the war she has had long enough to prepare for it. Every station through which we passed en route from Florence to Venice was full of troops and trains of them were continually moving. Every shopkeeper, head waiter, hotel manager, guide, with whom you talk tells you that war is absolutely certain; I have not heard a single contrary voice. In Florence the buildings along the Lungarno were chalked with bellicose inscriptions, "Evviva la Guerra!" "A basso Austria" — or whatever the correct Italian is — and here and there a crude picture of Francis Joseph hanging from a gallows. Apparently no steps were taken by the police to erase them, for they continued there during our stay. On one statue the inscription had been written in acid. So, in spite of the fact that Peter Jay telephoned to the Ambassador today and was told that everything was quiet and that there was absolutely no reason to hurry back, we have both agreed that the situation appears too tense for us to dally longer. In any case, during the last few days I have had a perfectly clear presentiment that big events are pending and my whole instinct is to get back towards Berlin.[9] Our decision is somewhat hastened by the

[9] On May 24, 1915, Italy declared war against Austria and diplomatic relations were broken with Germany. The Italian declaration of war against Germany did not take place until August 27, 1916.

news published today that King Victor Emmanuel has given up his prospective visit to Quarto for the Garibaldi celebration and the statement that there is trouble with the Turks in Tripoli. . . .[10]

Saturday, May 8 [1915], Vienna

After breakfast this morning I bought a *Freie Presse* and went into the sitting room off the hall with Alice to read it at leisure and there we saw the terrible headlines LUSITANIA TORPEDIERT UND IST GESUNKEN! The dreadfulness of the calamity struck us with full force at once and I immediately went to the Schlafwagengesellschaft and reserved berths on the night train to Berlin. Knowing the situation in Berlin when I left it, it did not seem to me at the moment that this could mean anything but an early severance of diplomatic relations. I saw our Ambassador, Penfield, at once at the Embassy and even before I could tell him of our changed plans he said, "I have just telephoned Mrs. Penfield that you and your wife will not be lunching with us tomorrow." Then Alice and I talked it over and tried to adjust our thoughts to this new and terrible development. If Washington had been stirred by the attacks on the *Frye* on January 28, 1915, the *Falaba* on March 28, 1915, the *Gulflight* on May 1, 1915 and the *Cushing* on April 29, 1915, what must be the feeling which would be engendered by the practically certain loss of American lives on the *Lusitania*. . . .

Sunday, May 9 [1915]

Arrived in Berlin at 10.25 and found an appalling amount of mail awaiting me to answer. . . . It is amusing to note that a copy of every telegram addressed to the Embassy is furnished to the Foreign Office by the telegraph office and sent to the ap-

---

[10] In April, 1915, Italian troops guarding the harvesting of the barley crops in Tripoli had been attacked by rebels. Later in the month another Italian column suffered losses in an engagement with the rebel forces. Reports were current that the rebels had been led by Turkish officers. *New York Times,* May 8, 1915, p. 11.

propriate bureau. Thus the other day Lithgow Osborne, when calling on Dr. Schüler [of the Foreign Office] saw on his desk a copy of a telegram from the Department of State to the Embassy on the very subject about which he had come to talk to him and which we had received only that morning. A good many communications which we make to the Foreign Office under instructions are quite superfluous, for the Foreign Office knows about them quite as soon as we do. . . .

The Ambassador feels certain that diplomatic relations will be broken off. We received today a telegram from the Department instructing us to secure and cable as soon as possible the report of the German Government on the sinking of the *Lusitania* and saying that the latest reports in the United States estimated the loss of life at more than one thousand, many of them being Americans. . . . The Ambassador jumped at conclusions somewhat hastily and yesterday cabled the Department suggesting that in case of trouble he be instructed now to whom to turn over British, Japanese and American interests and what should be done about the Embassy building, for which he pays the rent and which contains the archives, etc. He suggested Argentina, Brazil or Chile and said that if there were a prospect of strained relations we might not be able to communicate. . . .

Monday, May 10 [1915]

. . . Yesterday, the 9th, we sent a telegram to the Department saying that Gherardi, our Naval Attaché, had called on Admiral Behncke, Chief of the Staff of the Admiralty, and had asked for a report on the sinking of the *Lusitania;* Behncke said they knew nothing more than they had seen in the papers but that he would send a report later. The Foreign Office issued a circular statement to neutrals regarding attacks on neutral vessels, stating that Germany had no intention of attacking such vessels and had issued instructions to its submarine commanders to that effect; reparation would be made for accidents when the German Government was convinced that the attacks had been actually made by German submarines. . . .

After long efforts and many conferences we have finally succeeded in having conditions at Ruhleben, the camp for British
civil prisoners, very materially improved. . . . I have been in
some of the lofts over the barracks where the smell was over-
powering, practically no light, dirty clothes hanging from the
rafters so thickly that one could not move without touching
them and the filthy mattresses — no beds — packed like sardines. In one of these lofts there were two lunatics and several
men suffering from tuberculosis and other worse diseases and
among the inmates were English gentlemen, whom I knew
well. . . . Men had been allowed to die because the young and
disagreeable doctor (responsible for the health of 5000 men)
would not come when called; he said, "Bring him to my office
tomorrow" — but on the morrow he was too weak to go to the
doctor's office and simply died in pain for lack of help except
what he could get from his fellow prisoners. Now all that has
been done away with; we have had over a hundred invalids removed to a good sanitarium outside Berlin; there are better
doctors at the camp; the barracks have been improved; the
latrines removed from the center of the camp where they
previously were; the large racecourse given over to the prisoners for exercise and sports; the commissary department has
been taken out of the hands of a grafting contractor and is now
managed by the prisoners themselves. This has been done by
endless conferences with the commanders of the camp and the
authorities higher up. At first the Commandant of the camp
could do nothing; all his recommendations to the Kriegsministerium were met by the order "Be stricter; no kindnesses; show
these swines of Englishmen what they get by having brought
on this war!" But the Ambassador plugged away at it, took a
firm stand, charged the higher officers with lack of humanity
and finally secured absolute freedom of action for the Com-
mandants of the camp, Count Schwerin and Baron von Taube,
both sympathetic and humanitarian men. All this has come
slowly and after much suffering and some of the Englishmen
who have been exchanged on grounds of ill health (we have
arranged many such exchanges) have written bitter reports on
their return to London. . . .

But the Germans are difficult people to deal with; many of them are kind and human, but they are so often overruled by the officers higher up, bureaucrats without a vestige of human sympathy, their one ambition to carry out the motto, "Gott strafe England." Even the cigars I bought in Austria had bands wrapped around them with this motto printed on them. The evidence of brutality which continually comes to us in the Embassy is incontrovertible — often even in the case of American women travelers — and we are powerless to do more than enter formal protests. . . .

The worst story of all which has come to us — and we have it on absolutely reliable evidence — is of a party of British prisoners brought into Germany after their capture. They were crammed into a cattle car, officers and men together so jammed that they could not sit down or move; the floor was several inches deep with fresh manure, which nearly asphyxiated them as there was not a crack to let air in. They were kept here for three days and nights without food or water; some of them were wounded. Finally, when they were near suffocation their blows on the side of the car were heard and small holes were bored to let in the air. At the various stations where they stopped, the Red Cross people were not allowed to give them either water or the coffee which is prepared at every station for the German soldiers, though the French prisoners in the same train were regularly fed; the German officers stood by and saw that the British were allowed nothing. Major Vandeleur, who escaped from Crefeld and wrote a full report in England, describes this himself without heat or emotion and simply says, "It was what I have imagined the Black Hole of Calcutta must have been, only much worse." Well, enough of this. It is only one of many such incidents, for which someone must be held responsible after the war.

The Ambassador had an interview with von Jagow today and the latter handed him a memorandum saying that Germany had been forced into retaliatory measures on account of the English plan of starving the German civil population and refusing to let foodstuffs through. The Ambassador said that if this was the only complaint and if Germany would stop her submarine warfare if England consented to let foodstuffs through, he thought he could arrange the matter within 24 hours. Then von Jagow found himself in a hole and he quickly altered the memorandum to include not only foodstuffs but raw materials — namely copper, rubber, cotton, etc. — as well. When von Jagow submitted his original memorandum to the Ambassador, Mr. Gerard said, "Is that actually and exactly what you mean?" and von Jagow had to reply, "Not exactly." "Very well," said the Ambassador, "give me a memorandum saying exactly what you do mean and I will cable it to Washington." So the memorandum was sent back to Count Montgelas who wrote between the lines in red ink "Including raw materials" and thus it was cabled.[11] It was another attempt of Germany to pose as the injured one. Of course Great Britain will never accept a compromise which includes raw materials out of which arms and accessories can be manufactured.

Jagow expressed the deepest sympathy for the loss of American lives on the *Lusitania,* but said that the responsibility rested with the British Government; that the British merchant vessels were armed and frequently tried to ram the submarines (How could they act so ruthlessly?); that the *Lusitania* was armed and carried 5400 cases of ammunition besides much other contraband; and finally that he could not but regret that Americans felt more inclined to trust to English promises rather than to pay attention to warnings from the German side. . . .

On May 13, the Embassy received word from Washington that President Wilson's note on the sinking of the Lusitania *was en route to Berlin via Rome. The day before, a Department cable instructed the Embassy to ascertain as promptly as possible and in strict confidence the number of Americans in Germany and their location. "The situation began to look serious," Mr. Grew noted in his diary on May 13.*

Friday, May 14 [1915]

At 10 P.M. Alice and I were about preparing to go to bed

11 For the text see *Foreign Relations, 1915, Supplement,* p. 389.

when Winslow telephoned from the Embassy that the note had arrived — 31 pages of cipher! So we hurriedly dressed and a little later the whole staff and their wives met at the chancery and we worked in relays till after 1 A.M., deciphering it. It was a thoroughly thrilling evening and the consensus of opinion was that it was a good Note if our Government intended to live up to it.[12] That we shall have to wait to see.

Saturday, May 15 [1915]

. . . The Ambassador presented the *Lusitania* note to von Jagow at 10.30 this morning. Although he was instructed to read it to von Jagow himself, the latter asked that he might read it as he understands written better than spoken English. While reading it he laughed and said, "Right of free travel on the seas; why not right of free travel on land in war territory?" In confidential conversation he said he was sure that Germany would not give up her submarine warfare. The Ambassador cabled, "I am myself positive that Germany will continue this method of war and that it is only a question of short time before other American ships or lives are destroyed and if that happens you say that the United States will not omit any act necessary to maintain the rights which you have claimed for the United States and its citizens. Your cables take two or more

[12] The note sent from Washington on May 13, 1915, affirmed the rights of American citizens to travel on merchant ships of belligerent nationality and American shipowners to take their ships anywhere on the high seas that legitimate errands called them. In assuming this position the Government of the United States "must hold the Imperial German Government to a strict accountability for any infringement of those rights, intentional or incidental . . . non-combatants, whether they be of neutral citizenship or citizens of one of the nations at war, can not lawfully or rightfully be put in jeopardy by the capture or destruction of an unarmed merchantman. . . .

"The Government of the United States, therefore, desires to call the attention of the Imperial German Government with the utmost earnestness to the fact that the objection to their present method of attack against the trade of their enemies lies in the practical impossibility of employing submarines in the destruction of commerce without disregarding those rules of fairness, reason, justice, and humanity, which all modern opinion regards as imperative." The note expressed the expectation that the German Government would disavow these acts, make reparation for the injuries, and take action to prevent recurrence. *Ibid.*, pp. 393–96.

days to reach Germany and therefore in view of your Note and what I take to be the inevitable consequences I hope you will cable me full instructions as to all possible contingencies." [13] The Ambassador is advising all Americans to leave Germany. Of course he puts it on the ground that he has been giving the same advice ever since the war began, but now he makes no effort to conceal his pessimism as to the eventual outcome. I cannot help feeling that he is anticipating events and that it is a mistake for him to play the alarmist just at present. Washington has informed us that there will be plenty of time to warn all Americans before anything happens, and should things be patched up temporarily through some compromise or understanding the Ambassador's present attitude and advice cannot fail to hurt him personally. . . .

Monday, May 17 [1915]

The Ambassador cabled, "German press states that German reply to Washington will make it plain to Mr. Wilson in a form alike polite and clear that we are obliged to carry on the battle as we are carrying it on and that we can carry it on with a clear conscience." [14] This is the tenor of the entire German press. The Foreign Office is much too busy with the Italian situation just now to give much attention to our note, but there is a tendency there to try to smooth things over if possible. The Admiralty, however, which has the upper hand, is evidently inclined not to budge an inch. . . .

Wednesday, May 19 [1915]

. . . The Cologne *Gazette* (*Kölnische Zeitung*), semi-official organ of the Government, writes that the American Note will receive the answer it deserves: It is merely a continuation of the unneutral attitude assumed in an increasing degree by the American Government towards Germany. The Note is therefore assured of the approval of the Allies but that will be its sole success. We take it that the German military establish-

---

13 For the full text see *ibid.*, p. 396.
14 *Ibid.*, p. 398.

ment will not permit it to cause a swerving of one inch from the course recognized as necessary by the German Government after mature deliberation. The Note pretends to plead the sacred freedom of the seas. But does not America know that England was the first to repudiate this principle by the tearing up of the Declaration of London, an instrument that the civilized nations had drawn up to safeguard this very freedom of the seas? Has America forgotten how England trampled upon this principle by closing the North Sea to neutral trade, or the many infringements of the principle recited in the long note to England last December to which no satisfaction was given? Was it not England's infamous starvation warfare which even America's power did not suffice to check, as the case of the *Wilhelmina* showed, that drove Germany to take up submarine warfare in retaliation? Germany offered to hold back if America could enforce the freedom of the seas, but in vain; the cargo of the *Wilhelmina* was seized and the United States resigned itself to the fact. By its acquiescence in all these violations of the freedom of the seas, which it would seem that America has omitted to mention, she has forfeited all right to plead for the freedom of the seas. We shall enforce this principle with our own swords and if our blows strike neutrals who will not keep out of the way, then they have themselves to blame. Let us take for the moment the position of the American Government; England prevents food from entering Germany and Germany foregoes the use of her submarines; England carries on her ships not only food but all kinds of munitions of war destined to destroy thousands of German soldiers. Could a more unreasonable demand be made? Certainly not if one stands on the ground of neutrality, justice and equity, but only when one has made the cause of our enemies one's own cause. For this reason the American note will fail of all effect on the German people. Its threats do not frighten us, for, as an English paper writes, America cannot be of more assistance to the Allies than she is now. The complaints and moral phraseology of the note do not move us for we know what are behind them. We shall put the Note with the rest of them and go steadily on our way.

I give this article in full as it represents the tone and arguments adopted by nearly the entire press. It is needless to point out the big flaw in these arguments — that it is not simply the ban on foodstuffs that has caused Germany to resort to submarine warfare on merchant ships, but the ban on *raw materials,* from which arms and ammunition can be made. That point, as I have already explained, we have thrashed out officially. Germany is very glib in finding arguments to justify whatever action she sees fit to take, whether in accord with international law or not, but in these cases she always suppresses the main point. In blaming us for selling arms and ammunition to the Allies, the press never by any chance mentions the Hague Convention of 1907, Article 7, or acknowledges that we should be distinctly unneutral if we did refuse to allow our firms to do it; they never mention the selling by Germany of munitions to Spain in our war, to the Boers in the Boer war, to Russia in the Japanese War and to various of the Balkan States in the Balkan War; nor do they mention that when a year and a half ago our Ambassador to Austria asked Count Berchtold if he could not prevent the shipment of arms and ammunition to Mexico, the latter replied that he had no right to interfere with the lawful functions of private Austrian firms.

As for the food question, it seems hardly consistent that while posing as a martyr under England's plan of starving the women and children of Germany, the press should continually dwell on the inexhaustible food supply of the country. But we have had no rain for some six weeks now and if the drought continues, it will raise havoc with the crops on which Germany is pinning so much faith. I long ago predicted in this diary that the ultimate pressure on Germany would come about through lack of supplies, both food and material, and if the war continues long enough, it seems to me that this will be the inevitable result. But I think that a great deal will also depend on the action of the Balkan States; Italy is causing grave concern, though of course the press makes out that her action will not in any way influence the final outcome; and the press is daily dwelling on the assured neutrality of Rumania, Bulgaria and Greece, which shows that all is not well there.[15] The assured neutrality of Denmark is also finding plenty of space in the newspapers, and an occasional word is also seen regarding Holland and Switzerland. . . .

The Ambassador today cabled Washington that he was sure that Germany would not abandon her present method of submarine warfare; that the newspapers and all classes were unanimous in declaring that enemy ships carrying munitions of war should not be made immune from attack by the fact that they carried American passengers; that the prospect of war with America was contemplated with equanimity; that it is said that in the case of war, American ships carrying munitions could be destroyed and that the delivery of such munitions to the Allies would be diminished because more munitions would be required in the United States; that if our Government did not desire to go to extremities it would perhaps be possible to arrange for British ships carrying American passengers to be inspected at American ports before sailing; that the American Government should then guarantee both that the ships were unarmed and carried no contraband and that such ships would carry distinguishing flags and other marks and would of course be subjected to the usual rules of visit and search, capture and destruction by enemy vessels, but not to be torpedoed without notice. This suggestion did not however emanate from the German Government. He continued "If you authorize me to negotiate on some such basis, perhaps an arrangement can be made, but haste is essential. Germans of position here, bankers, editors, officials have told me that America has not enforced her right to trade with Germany but has acquiesced in England's holding cotton destined for Germany, although there is no effective blockade of the German coast. They also refer to fact that Americans were told by American Government that they remained in Mexico at their own risk and they cannot

15 Rumania declared war on Austria-Hungary on August 27, 1916. Bulgaria entered the war against Serbia on October 12, 1915, and Greece became one of the Allied Powers on July 2, 1917.

see why the American Government should enforce the protection of cargoes of munitions of war by the presence of American passengers in British ships, who can travel abroad on American ships in perfect safety and without causing complications. Germany has had great success in the East, is perfectly prepared to fight Italy with Austria and is quite ready for war with the United States." [16]

The same evening he cabled that an article in the *Vorwärts*, the leading German socialist paper, commenting on the sinking of the *Lusitania* warns the German Government against a continuation of retaliatory measures, a practice in its nature unreasonable and bound to lead to new political complications. They can never decide the war but only make its wounds deeper and the future more difficult. This article is severely commented on in the other papers.

I forgot to say that on May 17th the Ambassador cabled that his impression, amounting almost to certainty, was that Germany would refuse to abandon her present method of submarine warfare, although she would reply to our Note in polite terms, and suggesting that he be authorized to advise Americans to leave and be given directions for all contingencies. The Department replied that inasmuch as there would be time if necessary to give advice to Americans residing in Germany after the receipt of the German reply to our Note, the Department did not desire to take any initiative now. The Ambassador might as a precaution, however, advise the Consuls confidentially to keep closely in touch with the Americans in their respective districts so that communication might be the more prompt if it should be found necessary to give any instructions.[17]

We also received a confidential telegram from Colonel House in London saying that it was of momentous importance that the Ambassador get the German Government to delay its answer to our Note until he should receive a letter which Colonel House was sending by messenger today. Soon afterwards

[16] See *Foreign Relations, 1915, Supplement*, p. 402.
[17] *Ibid.*, pp. 398–99.

came a second telegram saying that he had decided to telegraph instead of waiting for his letter to arrive; his proposition was simply that the German Government be asked to give up submarine warfare and the use of poisonous gas in return for England's permitting the passage of foodstuffs into Germany. The Ambassador replied simply that this proposition had already been put up to Germany and that she had declined it, as raw materials were not mentioned. . . .

Saturday, May 22 [1915]

. . . The Ambassador cabled to Secretary of State Bryan today at noon, "Prominent German acquaintance of mine, head of a large German concern, was called to the Foreign Office and cross-examined for an hour and a half about the possibility of German-Americans rising in arms against our Government. Zimmermann told me yesterday that Dumba, the Austro-Hungarian Ambassador in Washington, had cabled you that you had told him that the *Lusitania* Note was not meant in earnest and was only a sop to public opinion. German Defense Union met May 20th and passed resolutions calling on the Chancellor to prevent by force the export of arms from America. The newspapers this morning print a note of the Emperor dated May 19th to the widow of Lt.-Commander Otto Weddigen of submarine fame authorizing her to keep the orders given her husband and saying that the whole Fatherland mourns with her for her husband who was a shining example. Italian Ambassador still here." [18] Later he cabled, "Tomorrow's papers will publish official thanks of the Kaiser to Germans in foreign countries for standing by Germany."

I think that Zimmermann was rather indiscreet to tell of Dumba's telegram about his conversation with Bryan. It seems to me quite possible that Bryan did give Dumba that impression, but now that it has come out it will put both Bryan and Dumba in a hole and each will have to deny everything publicly.[19] Zimmermann told of this . . . at lunch at the Embassy

[18] *Ibid.,* p. 407.
[19] Bryan made it clear in a cable to Ambassador Gerard on May 24, that there

and said quite frankly that he knew that the United States would not back up her threats! . . .

Saturday, May 29 [1915]

. . . We cabled at 11 A.M. that we had just received from the Foreign Office the reply to our *Lusitania* note from the Foreign Office and that it would be sent off as soon as translated and coded. It states that the German Government will not take its final position regarding our demands concerning submarine warfare until an answer shall have been received from our Government to the alleged facts set forth regarding the arming of the *Lusitania* etc. The note itself was cabled to Washington at 7 P.M. . . . [20]

Wednesday, June 9 [1915]

Lunched at Esplanade with Mrs. Jackson [wife of John Jackson, in charge of the British Bureau at the American Embassy] and Baroness Speck v. Sternburg [wife of the former German Ambassador to the United States]. The latter, who has many friends in high circles including the Emperor, is

was no justification for Dumba's interpretation of his remarks. Bryan also sent to Gerard a memorandum of the conversation and urged Gerard to explain to the German Foreign Office that "it would be a great mistake to minimize the earnestness of this protest." *Ibid.*, pp. 407–9, contains the full texts.

[20] The German note was constructed around the idea "that certain important facts most directly connected with the sinking of the *Lusitania* may have escaped the attention of the Government of the United States." It then went on to point out that the *Lusitania* had been constructed with British government funds as an auxiliary cruiser and was undoubtedly armed. The *Lusitania* was carrying both troops and munitions at the time she was sunk. The British had encouraged merchant ships to ram German submarines, thus making the ordinary methods of capture impossible for submarine commanders. In view of these facts the "Imperial Government begs to reserve a final statement of its position with regard to the demands made in connection with the sinking of the *Lusitania* until a reply is received from the American Government, and believes that it should recall here that it took note with satisfaction of the proposals of good offices submitted by the American Government in Berlin and London with a view to paving the way for a *modus vivendi* for the conduct of maritime war between Germany and Great Britain. The Imperial Government furnished at that time ample evidence of its good will by its willingness to consider these proposals." *Ibid.*, pp. 419–21.

doing her best to influence the relations between Germany and the United States towards a mutual understanding and from time to time she reports to me what she learns; for instance, she was at the Bethmann-Hollweg's the other day and the following night she dined with Prince Bülow. There is no doubt that the Chancellor is in favor of satisfying the United States in the submarine question, as he does not want war with us, and in this attitude he is at one with the Foreign Office and the Kriegsministerium, but when the time comes for the final decision of policy they will have to deal with Admiral von Tirpitz [Secretary of State for Naval Affairs] and the Admiralty and the latter will not give in an inch if they can help it. I do not know what the Kaiser's personal view of the matter is, but it looks as if he might be the Court of last resort. . . .

Monday, June 14 [1915]

An article appeared in *Der Montag* by Eugen Zimmermann, a well-known correspondent who is in close touch with the Foreign Office, acknowledging the absolute right of the United States in the arms and ammunition question and saying that it was Germany herself who insisted on the inclusion of Art. 7 in the Hague Convention for Land and Sea Warfare. This is the first time that our point of view and the correctness of our position has been allowed to appear in the press and it augurs well, as the F.O. wants to do everything possible to prevent a break. But the result of the publication of the article was unfortunate, for every other newspaper in Germany came down on it like a load of bricks, saying that this sort of thing was weakening the unity of the Fatherland! Zimmermann has been practically ostracized by his fellow correspondents.

Tuesday, June 15 [1915]

. . . One of our chief duties at present is transmitting German protests at conditions in French and Russian prison camps; they come in almost daily and we simply send them on to Washington, whence they are relayed to Paris or Petrograd. The other day came a German note regarding the prisoners at

Toulouse — food not only insufficient but said to consist of horse and mule meat and decayed fish; water bad and many cases of typhoid fever; packages addressed to prisoners not delivered and if so part of contents removed. Also complaints about camps in Russia, where there is much typhus, much vermin and no chance to wash. We have inspected nearly all the camps in Germany now and they are uniformly good. I think only one was found radically bad and this was at Würzburg where only four British officers are confined; they were being kept practically in disciplinary confinement and had hardly any chance to exercise at all. Mr. Jackson and the rest of the camp inspectors of our Embassy are now on such good terms with the military authorities that a word from them will insure an immediate improvement. The other camps are really excellent. Ruhleben is a different place from formerly; Döberitz is almost perfection. Mr. Jackson went out to see a play given by the prisoners the other night; it was the Commandant's birthday and the prison band went to his house and serenaded him and he was so pleased that he canceled a sentence of four days' imprisonment which he had just passed on a British soldier who had been disrespectful. The British Government is publishing all the reports of our Embassy on prison camps as separate white books, so they may be ordered and read by anyone. . . .

Tuesday, June 22 [1915]

. . . The *Tageszeitung*, the paper to which Count Reventlow contributes his naval and anti-American articles, was today suppressed as it contained an attack on the Chancellor for his alleged weak policy towards the United States. This is taken as a sign of strength on the part of the Chancellor and the Government, but the suppression of the paper is widely criticized in Germany on the ground that it tends to destroy freedom of speech! There is a bitter fight on between v. Bethmann-Hollweg and v. Tirpitz and the latter is frequently spoken of as the next Chancellor. . . .

Saturday, June 26 [1915]

. . . Yesterday the Ambassador telegraphed to Washington that the German *Lusitania* Note, as at present drafted, would offer security to ships which were usually and especially engaged in passenger traffic and that there was a fight on between the peace and war parties, headed respectively by v. Bethmann-Hollweg and v. Tirpitz, as to whether this offer should be unconditional — simply expressing a hope that arms and ammunition would not be sent on those ships — or whether it should be conditional on the ships not carrying such arms and ammunition. The Ambassador suggested that the feeling between the two countries would be helped if the President would come out with a statement that he would endeavor to secure such nonshipment of munitions of war on these passenger ships. . . . He also cabled that a friend in the Foreign Office had suggested that the President send the Ambassador a message for the Kaiser personally; the Kaiser would then have to see him, which the friend thought would help, as the Kaiser is now entirely surrounded by the military and hears only war talk.[21]

The suspension of the *Tageszeitung* for criticizing the Chancellor has been severely criticized by the rest of the press and public and it is now permitted to appear again. The attempt to gag the press is resented everywhere. The clerical and conservative papers side with the *Tageszeitung* and deprecate the publication of evidently inspired articles like that in the *Lokal Anzeiger* (*Der Montag*) of June 14th, maintaining that this is a falsification of public opinion in Germany, which does not want war with America but will not approve of any understanding with America at the cost of any concession which would impair the efficiency of the submarine. The impression seems to prevail that the conciliatory articles — such as Eugen Zimmermann's in *Der Montag* — originated in official quarters and it is feared that they will weaken the position of the German negotiators. But precious few conciliatory articles have appeared; most of them are mere "Hetzerei."

21 *Ibid.*, p. 453.

The Consul General at Hamburg [Henry H. Morgan] reports that it is an open secret that large quantities of goods have been imported into Germany through Sweden, Holland, Denmark and Switzerland, as the export figures to these countries from the United States show that they have suddenly become large consumers and the inference is that the increased exports have entered Germany. It is believed that Germany has received practically all the lubricating oil, copper and rubber needed for military operations. From reliable sources it is learned that millions of bushels of wheat have actually been imported into Germany from Russia, but no actual proof of the truth of these statements can be obtained.

To Edward Bell, July 6, 1915

. . . We know absolutely nothing here about the Balkans, but my own impression all along has been that the whole bunch will eventually come in with the Allies and this impression has not been altered. Rumor is always rife, but I don't think that any of the Scandinavian countries will do anything; Sweden is a little restive against England, but Norway is a lot more restive against Germany, just as is Denmark. The most important dope I have received lately, however, is that public opinion in Holland has completely swung round in favor of Germany; this was not merely rumor but straight from the inside. It is not on the whole surprising in view of the havoc that England is playing with her commerce, but she certainly cannot afford to come into the war with the sure loss of her colonies staring her in the face if she does so.

The most hated people in Germany at present are we Americans. It is not at all a pleasant position for any of us here. We are taking up passports right and left of so-called Americans who slander the President in public, but that is all we can do.[22] On July 4th some German-American laid a wreath at the foot of the statue of Frederick the Great, draped with an American

[22] Ambassador Gerard describes the cases of some of the Americans whose passports were taken up in his book, *My Four Years in Germany* (New York: George H. Doran Co., 1917), pp. 310–11.

flag with a band of mourning on it and at the 4th of July reception given by the Consul General several people asked openly and facetiously of their host whether he had secured England's permission to give the party. The answer of the German Government to our last *Lusitania* Note is going to suggest several compromises, but it is absolutely unsatisfactory if the President maintains the exact position he adopted.[23] The F.O. and von Tirpitz have had a big fight about it, the former wanting to give in and the latter not. The Germans don't want war with us under any circumstances and I think the whole thing will be smoothed over somehow, but another spark might well set things alight again and then it would sure be bang. . . .

The third Lusitania *note from Washington arrived at the Embassy on July 22 and 23. The note stated that "rights of neutrals in time of war are based upon principle, not upon expediency, and the principles are immutable." Thus the Government of the United States refused to accept the German argument that the naval policies of Great Britain made German retaliation through ruthless submarine warfare acceptable. The United States again demanded that Germany disavow the action of its navy in the sinking of the* Lusitania *and make*

[23] After restating the desire of the German Government to act in accord with the principles of humanity, the second note concerning the sinking of the *Lusitania* went on to point out that Germany had merely followed the precedent of Great Britain in declaring the high seas to be a war zone. Losses incurred by neutrals in the war at sea could not be considered differently from those suffered on land, when neutrals ventured into dangerous areas in spite of warning. The ammunition and troops on board the *Lusitania* had made it a fair target of war. Its sinking without warning was necessary to save the German submarine from destruction. Several suggestions were offered by the German Government to circumvent future controversies. American passenger steamers would be given "free and safe passage" by German submarines, if such steamers were marked in a special way and sufficient notice was given of their sailing. To increase facilities for travel for Americans, a number of neutral steamers, or as many as four enemy passenger ships taken under the American flag, would be allowed safe passage under the same conditions. The German Government also affirmed its willingness to use the good offices of the President to suggest to Great Britain proposals for altering the method of maritime warfare. *Foreign Relations, 1915, Supplement,* pp. 463–66.

reparation for losses. The German proposals that certain ships be designated as free upon the seas were rejected, but the United States invited the German Government to "practical co-operation" to attain freedom of the seas for ships and commerce of all nations. Persistence of activity of German naval vessels in violation of the principles upon which the rights of neutrals are based would be regarded as "deliberately unfriendly."

Friday, July 23 [1915]

The rest of the note had arrived in the early morning and was soon deciphered. It is thoroughly polite but as definite and strong this time as one could wish — any more illegal submarine business will be regarded as a "deliberately unfriendly act."

The Ambassador telegraphed . . . that although he had advocated making concessions to preserve peace, he was convinced that no concessions on the part of the U.S. short of actually joining Germany in the war would satisfy the extreme party which seems at present to be in control. The hate campaign against America continues with unabated violence, backed by v. Tirpitz, Reventlow, etc., who seem to desire war with America. . . .

Wednesday, July 28 [1915]

The Department today sent the following enlightening telegram, which I quote in full as it is of particular interest and as it was communicated to the Foreign Office verbatim:

> The Department of State is informed concerning the case of one Robert Rosenthal, arrested in England on a charge of espionage, as follows — He bore passport No. 48545 issued by the Department January 26, 1915, upon a false application made at the American Embassy at Berlin, and had previously obtained two emergency passports from the Embassy upon false applications in which he alleged that he was born in New York City. Rosenthal has confessed that he was a native German, that the statements in his passport applications were false, that he had

been offered a counterfeit passport by Captain Prieger of the German Admiralty, who had on his desk a number of blank counterfeit American passports and a replica of the seal of this Department and who had shown him how well the watermark in the paper had been counterfeited. He said that Prieger had informed him that he had a rubber stamp similar to those used by this Department in preparing passports, and that he told Prieger that he preferred to use the passport which he had fraudulently obtained through the American Embassy. . . .

The Government of the United States is loath to believe that officials of the Imperial German Government have, with the knowledge and acquiescence of that Government, deliberately printed and issued counterfeits of an American passport. Passports are certificates of citizenship issued, signed and sealed with extreme care and solemnity by the highest officials of a nation and are protected from misuse by stringent laws imposing heavy penalties. It is needless to dwell at length on the injury inflicted indirectly upon American citizens traveling abroad by the issuance of forged American passports. As a result of the case here mentioned and of the Lody case, already brought to the German Government's attention, all American passports are objects of suspicion in countries at war with Germany. The United States cannot but view these indications of the fabrications of such documents by German authorities, which if true would constitute an offense against the honor and dignity of the United States, otherwise than as calling for the most thorough and searching investigation on the part of the Imperial Government and the immediate adoption of measures to stop the practice, if found to exist, as well as the recall of any fraudulent passports which have been issued.

Please orally impress upon the Minister for Foreign Affairs the serious view which this Government takes of this affair and urge upon him the necessity of prompt action. . . .

Friday, July 30 [1915]

. . . An extraordinarily interesting "find" came our way today in the shape of a young American sailor from Seattle, who after a voyage of 142 days on a sailing ship and when within 5 hours of their port, had his ship sunk by the Germans and was taken on board the German submarine where he spent *eleven* days and watched them torpedo other vessels and dodge British warships until their ammunition gave out and they returned to port at Heligoland. Apparently they thought he was a German for they let him go and after visiting some relatives he came to the Embassy to get sent home. You can imagine that we examined him by the hour, Gherardi found him intelligent from a technical point of view and we learned more about the interior and working of a German submarine than has probably ever before been learned by any Naval Attaché or other foreigner. We are sending him home for further examination by our Navy Dept. His was the submarine which attacked the *Anglo-Californian,* while he was on board, too, killing the Captain on the bridge by shell fire and several of the crew, though she ultimately escaped. He confirmed what we suspected but did not know before, namely that the submarine did not torpedo the *Anglo-Californian* simply because she had no torpedoes left when she met her. She had already been out for three weeks, torpedoing vessels continually. While the boy, Carl List by name, was on her, she had several narrow escapes from being sunk by British destroyers and sometimes just managed to sink in time, while the shells were peppering all around her. He said that she could totally submerge in less than a minute and a half. Gherardi tested him on many technical points and satisfied himself definitely that he was telling the truth in all respects. One night the submarine went to the bottom of the ocean and remained there to give the crew a sound night's sleep. List said that the air was smelly but that breathing was quite comfortable. He was kindly treated and fairly well fed; when a vessel was torpedoed, the whole crew, including List, were allowed on deck to see her sink, and during the fights he could tell what was going on as the gunner at the forward periscope would report to the others from time to time. He said that the commander never once sank a vessel without warning her first. We had List in my room for the greater part of a morning and kept him talking steadily; he is a bright and distinctly intelligent boy of about 16 or 17; he had kept his eyes open on board and was able to answer Gherardi's questions, even down to details such as gun mountings, etc. On the other hand, if he didn't know something, he said so frankly and never guessed; the steering gear aft, for instance, he had never seen as he was never allowed to go aft.

To Edward Bell, August 30, 1915

. . . The Admiralty and the Foreign Office are, as you doubtless know, just at this moment at daggers drawn over the *Arabic* incident.[24] The Foreign Office had demanded that instructions be given that no more British passenger ships should be torpedoed without warning. Von Tirpitz had apparently given instructions absolutely to the contrary.[25] Incidentally I may observe that Bethmann-Hollweg and von Tirpitz both beat it to the Emperor in Silesia with the speed of the bounding gazelle when the *Arabic* was sunk and from all reports a fight is now on which makes the war itself look like spring potatoes. Which side will win out, we cannot yet even guess with any assurance, but the sinking of the *Arabic* has stirred up a most serious domestic crisis in Germany quite apart from any interest which the Government of the United States has in the matter.

It is absolutely impossible yet to tell what is going to happen as a result of the sinking of the *Arabic*. I rather think the Germans will try to smooth the crisis over by a skillful use of words; they may, very likely will, express regret and make

24 The British passenger ship, *Arabic,* was sunk by a German submarine on August 19, with the loss of two American lives.

25 On September 8, 1915, the German Ambassador, Bernstorff, wrote Mr. Lansing: "With regard to the *Arabic* incident I am authorized to inform you confidentially that since several months the commanders of our submarines had orders not to attack the large ocean liners without warning and safety for noncombatants. Therefore, if the *Arabic* was attacked without warning, this would have been done contrary to the instructions given to the commanders of the submarines. These orders have now been modified, so as to comprise all liners. These instructions are and will remain in force pending the negotiations with the Government of the United States, which as we hope will in the end lead to a complete understanding on all questions of maritime warfare." *Foreign Relations, 1915, Supplement,* p. 540.

reparation, but I don't now think that they will give satisfactory guarantees which will prevent the same thing happening in the future. The Foreign Office and the Chancellor cut a very small figure here at present and von Tirpitz is very strong. I feel sure, and in fact have very good grounds for believing, that the German program is to take Calais sooner or later and then, after clearing the straits of Dover, to send out an enormous number of submarines and try to crush England eventually in this manner. That is why they have no intention of tying their hands for the future by giving permanent and definite guarantees which would restrict this mode of warfare. Whether they can ever carry out this program or not is another question which neither you nor I can answer now, though we may have views on the subject. I said above that von Tirpitz had probably given definite instructions to his submarine commanders contrary to those demanded by the Foreign Office, but this is probably exaggerated. It is more likely that they have been told to avoid torpedoing passenger ships and that the submarine commander in the *Arabic* case took her for a transport — since she was very far south of Ireland and the usual transatlantic course of liners — though well knowing that he would not suffer for a mistake of this kind anyway. If a submarine commander knew that he would be disgraced for such an error, he would be far too careful in his operations to please v. Tirpitz, and this is why I do not think that absolutely satisfactory guarantees will ever be given, though the general instructions may direct that passenger ships be left alone. . . .

Now, as things stand, I think that the whole question as to the final results of the *Arabic* incident depend entirely on the form of the pill which Washington will send; they will do their best to swallow it here if they can, for they don't want a break with us for financial reasons, if they can avoid it and still not sacrifice their submarine program. But if the pill is hairy and means a definite abandonment of submarine warfare, you and I shall be drinking each other's healths in person before many moons are out.

All this dope is for your own interest and represents the opinions of Gherardi and myself, after a careful study of the field. The Ambassador, who at every previous submarine incident has told us that we might just as well pack our trunks at once, has this time swung round to a boundless optimism and thinks that everything will work out satisfactorily. I fail to reach his conclusions.

I hope you will give me some dope from your end from time to time, particularly as regards the Balkans and the Dardanelles. Is not the latter a pretty discouraging proposition? [26] I think they feel here that the final attitude of the Balkans will be considerably influenced by what the United States does and this is at least one element which may make them pause in Germany to consider.

To Ulysses Grant-Smith, Secretary of the American
Embassy at Vienna, September 10, 1915

. . . The German Government in reporting to us the facts regarding the sinking of the *Arabic* states that the vessel altered her course, as she approached the submarine, in such a manner that the commander of the submarine became convinced that the steamer had the intention of attacking and ramming him. In order to anticipate this attack, he gave orders for the submarine to dive and fired a torpedo at the steamer. After firing he convinced himself that the people on board were being rescued in fifteen boats. According to his instructions the commander was not allowed to attack the *Arabic* without warning and without saving lives, unless the ship attempted to escape or offered resistance. He was forced, however, to conclude from the attendant circumstances that the *Arabic* planned a violent attack on the submarine. This conclusion was all the

26 The British campaign at the Dardanelles, begun March 18, 1915, had proved a failure. A stagnation had set in following the British landings, for the British lacked the men, artillery, ammunition, and position to facilitate an advance beyond their landing places. An attempt was made in August by the British to break through the opposing Turkish forces, but it met with no success. British troops were withdrawn in December, 1915, and January, 1916. Liddell Hart, *op. cit.,* pp. 211–42.

more obvious as he had a few days before been fired upon by a liner at a great distance in the Irish Sea.

The German Government deeply regrets that lives were lost through the action of the commander, and particularly expresses this regret to the Government of the United States on account of the death of American citizens. The German Government is unable, however, to acknowledge any obligation to grant indemnity in the matter, even if the commander should have been mistaken as to the aggressive intentions of the *Arabic.*

If the two Governments are unable to reach a harmonious opinion on this point, the German Government will be prepared to submit the difference of opinion to the Hague Tribunal of Arbitration; but in so doing it assumes that as a matter of course the arbitral decision shall not be admitted to have the importance of a general decision on the permissibility or the converse under international law of German submarine warfare. . . . [27]

To my mother, September 14, 1915

Just a week ago today we received the report of the German Government regarding the sinking of the *Arabic,* which you will already have seen published in the press. If they wanted to precipitate a break with us, they could not well have worded this note in a manner better calculated to bring this about, for both its contents and tone were deliberately impertinent. A day or two later when the Ambassador asked von Jagow for a report about the sinking of the *Hesperian* [on September 4, 1915], he replied that so long as no American lives were lost he did not see what business of ours it was and that unless it were shown that there had been loss of American life, he would give no such report.

The curious thing is that we are convinced here that they do not want a break with us. The Chief of the Admiralty Staff resigned because they were being obliged to restrict their sub-

[27] For the full text of the German note, see *Foreign Relations, 1915, Supplement,* pp. 539–40.

marine warfare on our account and there is no doubt that still more explicit instructions have been sent out to the submarine commanders to avoid passenger ships. And yet in spite of this, when disavowals and assurances from headquarters would smooth everything over, they write us an absolutely tactless note giving an entirely contrary impression. I cannot see how our Government can fail to take action under the circumstances. They say that the commander of the submarine thought that the *Arabic* was going to ram him, but that even if he was mistaken, no reparation can be made. That is like saying, "I was right in shooting that man because I thought he was going to hit me, but even if he wasn't going to hit me, I was right anyway."

The whole question still resolves itself into a big controversy between the Admiralty and the Foreign Office. The Foreign Office are furious and were as much dismayed by the sinking of the *Arabic* as we were. But Tirpitz is the strong man at present and it is difficult to can him. The Emperor is easily swayed and listens to the last man who gets at him; Bethmann-Hollweg is not a scrapper; Tirpitz is. Hence all the trouble. I suppose that in a few days we shall know where we stand, but it is nervous waiting.[28] The country must be considerably stirred up at home if the newspapers up to August 26th, which I read last night, are any criterion. . . .

Saturday, September 25 [1915]

Very early at the chancery as Saturday is a busy day up to 1.30. Among our daily batch of telegrams from Washington I found one stamped "Abschrift für A.A. Original befördert." [29] In other words, the telegraph office had made a mistake and sent us the Auswärtiges Amt copy instead of the original. We always knew that copies of our telegrams were sent to the Foreign Office, but this confirms it. . . .

28 Mr. Grew recorded in his diary on September 22, that "Gherardi had a talk with Holtzendorff, the new Chief of the Admiralty Staff, in which the latter said that the Admiralty was now in complete accord with the Foreign Office and that there would be no more torpedoing of liners without warning."

29 "Copy for the Foreign Office. Original has been forwarded."

To my mother, November 9, 1915

... The war may last a long time yet. Prices are soaring here and food is scarce; on two days in the week one can get no meat whatever — the hotels serve fish and eggs — and on other days one can have only boiled meat or some other specified kind. We now have milk and butter as well as bread cards. There are many riots throughout the country owing to high prices, but these are promptly put down and the press of course says nothing about them. ...

XI

Another Crisis With Germany—Temporarily Solved

FEBRUARY – MAY, 1916

The President's personal envoy, Colonel E. M. House, visited Germany in January, 1916, in an attempt, which proved to be futile, to persuade Germany that the time was ripe for a peace conference. A month later, he made an agreement with Sir Edward Grey in London that President Wilson would propose a peace conference when France and Great Britain informed him that the time was opportune. The agreement also stated that if Germany refused to participate, the United States would probably *enter the war against Germany. If such a conference met, Colonel House expressed the belief that it would secure peace terms not unfavorable to the Allies. If the conference failed, the United States would leave the conference as a belligerent on the Allied side, if Germany were unreasonable.*

When the President saw the agreement, he inserted the word probably *before the statement that the United States would leave the conference as a belligerent on the Allied side if Germany were unreasonable.[1] After the House-Grey agreement, Wilson waited for word from Great Britain, but the Allies were not victorious in 1916 and were afraid that a peace conference might leave their war aims unobtained.*

Meanwhile Germany precipitated another crisis with the United States by resuming unrestricted submarine warfare late in February, 1916. During the next few weeks, the United States kept a careful record of merchant ships sunk and American lives lost. Then, on April 18, Washington sent the Ger-

---

[1] Edward M. House, *The Intimate Papers of Colonel House*, ed. by Charles Seymour (Boston: Houghton Mifflin Co., 1926), II, 201–2; Sir Edward Grey, *Twenty-Five Years, 1892–1916* (New York: Frederick A. Stokes Co., 1925), pp. 127–28.

man Government a despatch stating: "If it is still the purpose of the Imperial Government to prosecute relentless and indiscriminate warfare against vessels of commerce by the use of submarines without regard to what the Government of the United States must consider the sacred and indisputable rules of international law and the universally recognized dictates of humanity, the Government of the United States is at last forced to the conclusion that there is but one course it can pursue. Unless the Imperial Government should now immediately declare and effect an abandonment of its present methods of submarine warfare against passenger and freight-carrying vessels, the Government of the United States can have no choice but to sever diplomatic relations with the German Empire altogether." [2]

To William Phillips, Third Assistant Secretary of State, February 22, 1916

Charlie Russell [Attaché] has just returned from America and I am glad to learn that he saw you in Washington. He has told me of his conversation with you and I hasten to take up one or two of the points which were touched upon. In fact I am very glad that your conversation with Russell gives me an opportunity to do so.

First, the question of the general information received by the Department from our Embassy. I gather from Russell that the Department is not over-satisfied with the amount and nature of the material turned in and this is a cause of great regret to me. I must try to explain one or two things to you and ask you to let me do so confidentially.

So far as the Embassy as a whole is concerned, the great difficulty is that I myself and the rest of the staff are quite unaware as to the amount and character of the general information turned in by the Ambassador. He has adopted the method of reporting what he gathers and what he himself thinks, in pri-

2 U.S. Department of State, *Papers Relating to the Foreign Relations of the United States, 1916, Supplement, The World War* (Washington: Government Printing Office, 1929), p. 234.

vate and confidential personal letters written weekly to Mr. Lansing and to Colonel House, the latter for eventual perusal by the President. Copies of these letters are not kept on file in the Embassy and he does not show them to or discuss them with any of us, nor does he invite advice or suggestions in preparing them. Of course I do not for a minute question the propriety of this method of communication with our Government, which is doubtless approved by Mr. Lansing. The only difficulty is that I and the other members of the staff do not know just what ground has been covered by the Ambassador and we are therefore inclined to leave all such general reports to him.

This is of course as it should be, for it is the Ambassador alone who assumes the responsibility for the running of the Embassy and he is well in a position to keep the Department intelligently informed as to the general situation, the character and influence of officials, etc. He often talks with the higher officials at the Foreign Office, meets and keeps in touch with other influential persons, discusses affairs with bankers, politicians and officials and, in general, keeps his hand on the pulse of governmental and public opinion. He continually has prominent persons at his table and he spends the entire morning and part of the afternoon receiving visitors, which should keep him well in touch with affairs which I presume he reports upon fully.

Of course I am not saying all this with the slightest feeling of resentment against the Ambassador. We are indeed all fortunate in being personally on the friendliest terms with him and it is not our business to question to what extent he shall take us into his confidence. The only manner in which his method of privately rather than officially communicating information to the Department could affect the Embassy unfavorably would be in case he should at any time go away and leave a secretary in charge, in which event the secretary would not have had the benefit of the information which the Ambassador had acquired through the advantages of his position and would enter upon his chargéship under a handicap. But this contingency has not yet arisen. . . .

One thing more. Russell said that you had inquired as to
the influence of Zimmermann, Under Secretary of State at
the Foreign Office. I think that Zimmermann may be regarded
as a coming man and that he will rise high. He has been handicapped by not being of noble birth, a handicap which in Germany is difficult to overcome, but his personal ability and character have already brought him a great deal of influence. Von
Jagow is more or less of a figurehead at the Foreign Office and
carries much less weight than Zimmermann, who will probably
eventually succeed him. I know Zimmermann well personally
and it is always a pleasure to take things up with him at the
Foreign Office. He is a great big blond-haired giant with a
charming and cordial manner and a sunny smile which goes
a long way in gaining one's confidence; he speaks English well,
works like a cart horse and shows a keen interest in everything
which is taken up with him and a genuine desire to carry out
one's requests — quite the contrary to some of his colleagues
who seem to look for red tape and reasons why a thing can't
be done. It has even been hinted that Zimmermann might
eventually be Chancellor and from what I know of him I do
not think this impossible or even improbable in the future,
but, as I have said, his lowly birth would be a great handicap
in that particular direction. It will depend upon what he
accomplishes in his next step, which will probably be Secretary
of State for Foreign Affairs.

The person at the Foreign Office next in importance to
Zimmermann is von Stumm, now chief of the Political Department, the position previously held by Zimmermann himself.
He is a man of about 55, of long diplomatic experience (Zimmermann began in the consular service), reticent, conservative
but with lots of brains. He is generally spoken of as the next
Ambassador to Great Britain. Incidentally I might mention
that he has just become engaged to a girl of some twenty summers, a Countess Plathen, who will make a beautiful and charming if youthful Ambassadress. Zimmermann is unmarried.

The person we have most to do with at the F.O. below von
Jagow and Zimmermann is Count Adolf Montgelas, who is

in charge of their American Bureau. He is one of my best friends and married to an American girl, formerly a Miss Hazeltine of Grand Rapids, and I have a very high opinion of him. He has been in Washington, speaks English perfectly and might well be a future Ambassador to the United States. I believe that it was he who drafted the replies to our *Lusitania* Notes, but all such things are done after a conference of the various powers that be. From all appearances, both Zimmermann and Montgelas are distinctly friendly to the United States — or have been so. . . .

Visit with the Ambassador to the Grosses Hauptquartier at Charleville, France, to Confer with the Emperor Regarding the Submarine Warfare Issue, April 27–May 2, 1916 [3]

The first phase of the submarine issue centered about the sinking of the *Lusitania, Arabic* and *Hesperian;* the second about the *Persia* and *Ancona,* and the third about the *Sussex, Englishman, Manchester Engineer, Eagle Point* and *Berwindvale,* following upon the German manifesto of February 8, 1916, to the effect that owing to England's having armed her merchant ships and instructed them to fire on submarines at sight, the German submarines would hereafter attack such ships without warning.

On April 19 we received the American note summing up the circumstances of the whole submarine controversy and stating that should the German Government not now immediately declare and effect an abandonment of her present methods of submarine warfare, the Government of the United States would to its regret be obliged to break off diplomatic relations altogether. The first of the eight sections of the note arrived at about 11 o'clock, just as I was about to turn in; I went at once to the Embassy and deciphered the telegram with Winslow and Van Houten [clerk] finishing six of the sections at about

[3] James Gerard's *My Four Years in Germany,* pp. 324–46, presents his record of this visit.

3.30 A.M. Sections 4 and 8 did not come in until the next morning. The kernel of the matter was contained in section 7, which I was deciphering and I remember no more exciting moment of my life than the hour between 2 and 3 A.M. as the impressive and fateful words of that historic telegram took shape — especially the words "immediately declare and effect an abandonment of her present methods of submarine warfare." [4] This constituted an unequivocal ultimatum and for the moment it seemed to us that a severance of diplomatic relations could not possibly be avoided.

The entire next day was spent deciphering the last two sections, correcting errors and typewriting the telegram in the form of a note to Herr von Jagow, which the Ambassador delivered personally to him at 7.40 P.M. After reading it, von Jagow said that he thought it meant a break as Germany could not give up torpedoing freight ships in the war zone. The following day the Chancellor came up from the Grosses Hauptquartier and asked to see Mr. Gerard. He gave the Ambassador the impression that he wished to avoid a break if possible, but that he would have to confer with the Emperor and with various prominent persons and that in view of the Easter holidays, an answer could not be expected for several days. Meanwhile the press had as a whole received the note with more moderate comment than we had been led to expect; in fact, its strong and definite terms had the effect of quieting the previous blustering of the press.

The Chancellor was to have returned immediately to see the Emperor at the Grosses Hauptquartier, but he remained another day and saw Mr. Gerard again, telling him that he regretted that the matter had been taken up in a formal note and given to the public instead of trying to settle the matter by personal discussion. The Ambassador told the Chancellor that he had received no information beyond the note itself and the President's speech to Congress,[5] but said that he would ask for fuller instructions regarding the distinction between

4 For the complete text see *Foreign Relations, 1916, Supplement,* pp. 232–34.
5 Delivered before Congress on April 19, 1916.

armed and unarmed mechantmen and regarding the nature of the reparation which our Government would require for the *Sussex*. (The German Government had already denied that it had had anything to do with the sinking of that ship.)

The Ambassador then sent off a telegram to that effect, but I told him that I thought I could write out the nature of our Government's reply without waiting for it — namely that the matter was one which did not admit of further negotiation and that the German Government was already fully aware of the nature of our demands, that submarine warfare should be carried out in accordance with the accepted and precise principles of international law. I urged him strongly to tell the Chancellor this and not let him get the impression that the matter could be further negotiated or a compromise effected, as this would cloud the main issue and assuredly lead to a break. It is evident to me that the Chancellor is trying to quibble over technicalities and thus gain time, which seems highly dangerous in view of the forceful expression "immediately declare and effect" contained in our Government's note. The Ambassador's clear duty is to show the Chancellor clearly the attitude of the President and the temper of Congress and the people, which admit of no delay, quibbling or further discussion. Unless he can grasp this, a break seems absolutely unavoidable.

On the 26th we received a telegram from Washington instructing the Ambassador to report the exact words used by von Jagow when he said that he thought our note meant a break. On the 27th, von Jagow came over to the Embassy to say that the Emperor wished to see Mr. Gerard at the Grosses Hauptquartier in Charleville and that he could leave Berlin the same evening. He decided to take me with him and we left on the 9.53 train in a private saloon car, accompanied by von Prittwitz [Friedrich von Prittwitz und Gaffron, Special Aide to von Jagow] of the Foreign Office, an old friend of mine, and Fritz, the Jäger, as guests of the Government. Before starting I arranged to have some one at the Embassy most of the night to decipher any telegrams that might arrive from Washington and also arranged with Count Montgelas and Geheimer Hofrat Propp, chief of the cipher bureau at the Foreign Office, to forward such telegrams to us immediately at any hour of the day or night, either to reach us en route at Frankfort or Metz or at the Grosses Hauptquartier.

Immediately after crossing into France, soon after leaving Metz, the ravages of war became painfully visible. In the larger towns, such as Longuyon, whole blocks of houses were completely gutted and their walls full of shell holes. In the open country, some of the smaller villages and separate farms seemed not to have been touched, others completely ruined. We saw some soldiers' graves and here and there old trenches and barbed wire. Every town swarmed with German soldiers and the old French signs on the stations were mostly covered with German military directions; there were also large numbers of Russian prisoners working and a few French peasants, but I saw very few of the latter. I noticed no French rolling stock whatever. A great number of bridges were completely destroyed; Prittwitz said the French knew how to do it thoroughly, but the Russians did not and thus the Russian bridges were comparatively easy to mend. We traveled very slowly as the expresses cannot move faster than the troop and hospital trains; we passed a continual stream of the latter, with freshly wounded soldiers lying in their hammocks, bound for Germany.

Just outside of Sedan Prittwitz showed us the small white cottage where Bismarck received the Emperor Napoleon and discussed the French surrender in 1870. They fought over the same ground in this war.

Arriving at Charleville, the Grosses Hauptquartier, just across the Meuse from Mézières, at 7, we were met by Count Zech, the Chancellor's A.D.C., the Commandant and other officials and driven in the Chancellor's automobile — with two guns placed conspicuously beside each seat, according to regulations in case of attack — to a pretty little private French villa which the Emperor had placed at the Ambassador's disposal. It is generally used for guests and the King of Saxony was the first guest to use it, since when it has been known as the Villa Saxe. The French *bonne à tout faire* is still with the house and proved herself to be an excellent cook.

We found a cipher telegram from the Embassy waiting for us and I barely had time to decipher it and dress in time to dine at the Chancellor's at 8. There were only eight at dinner, the Ambassador on the Chancellor's right, I on his left and Stumm, Zech, Prittwitz, Grünau and Dr. Riezler — of the Foreign Office. Von Bethmann-Hollweg seemed in excellent spirits; he greeted us warmly and when the Ambassador remarked that Charleville looked like a town in Friedenszeit, he said with a laugh that he hoped the Ambassador had brought peace in his valise. We stayed till about 11 and then returned to our villa, where I found another cipher telegram answering one I had sent to the Embassy after dinner, to the effect that the Foreign Office was expecting two telegrams from Count Bernstorff and that they should be delivered with the greatest urgency. Evidently Lanier Winslow spent the night at the Embassy, for we received one telegram dated 2.30 A.M. and one 6.30 A.M. Stumm remarked during the evening to me that a good many people had been surprised at his marriage, but no one so surprised as himself.

After breakfast on the 29th Prittwitz called and took us for a long walk through the town and along the bank of the Meuse into the country; a perfect day, though windy. The life of the town seems to be going on pretty much as usual; the shops and markets are wide open and do a thriving trade with the soldiers, either French or German money being accepted. French money is issued especially for the different communes, each commune having its particular notes. French police are on duty in the town, but they wear civilian clothes with a distinctive armband. At every few rods one sees an orange-colored shingle hung out conspicuously bearing the words "Schutz von Fliegerbomben" and behind it the entrance to the cellar where refuge may be taken. The soldiers call them "Heldenkeller" — hero cellars! French aviators, it is said, do not come over very often nowadays, for there are powerful guns all about the town, but the day before we arrived two planes came over and dropped three or four bombs, killing six people within a few yards of our villa, where the hole and shattered window panes are still visible. They were all in one of the "Helden-kellers" but were stupidly peeking out and the bomb fell just beside it. One of the men killed was the Emperor's locomotive driver. Rupi Böcklin was within sixty yards of it.

Rupi Böcklin turned up and asked me to lunch, but as we were starting out on an auto trip immediately afterwards, I stayed and lunched alone with the chief. At 2 we started off in three cars, the Ambassador and General von Zöllner, Quarter-master General for the occupied portion of France, Prittwitz and Count Wengersky, formerly Agent in London for the Hamburg-American Line, now in charge of the "ravitaille-ment" of the French civil population, and Böcklin and I. The Chancellor had applied to General von Falkenhayn, Chief of Staff, to see if we could go to the front, which is only about 50 kilometers away, but after telephoning to all the command-ing Generals in the neighborhood — as he said — von Falken-hayn announced that the French were dropping shells behind the German lines in all directions and that he could not take the responsibility of our approaching the front at all. So to our infinite regret, this had to be given up. Of course they had no intention of letting us do it anyway. Instead, they decided to show us the working of the system of the distribution of the supplies furnished by the American Commission for Relief in Belgium, which applies also to this portion of France, namely the Ardennes.

The supplies, which consist of meal, cornmeal, coffee, car-rot seed, condensed milk, wooden shoes, lard, etc., are brought from Belgium over the waterways to certain distributing cen-ters, from which they are sent out to various subcenters, all of which they showed us marked on the map. We began with the distributing center in Charleville, which, as all of them are, was under the control of a Frenchman, a Monsieur Pillot [Agent-General at Charleville for the Comité d'Alimentation du Nord de la France], in times of peace a merchant, now the right-hand man of Count Wengersky. He showed us with considerable pride through his storehouse, where the sacks were piled high awaiting distribution, and it was evident from the cordiality and consideration with which all the German officers, from the General down, treated him, that his relations with them were excellent. They made him pass ahead of them, made him keep his hat on in their presence, greeted him warmly, even affectionately, and finally took him with us on our subsequent tour in the automobiles. I thought that this might perhaps be put on in order to impress the Ambassador, but when an opportunity later occurred to speak with him alone, I asked him about the relations of the French civilians with the Germans and he, told me frankly that while they were excellent in this particular district and that the French civilians in the Grosses Hauptquartier were allowed special privileges, it was not the same everywhere. He said that the Ardennes was the only Department in France which was completely under German occupation.

From Charleville we drove at a terrifying pace to Viviers, the next distributing center, and pulled up at a factory, which in times of peace turned out automobile accessories, whose owner, a cheerful red-bearded Frenchman, was now in charge of the relief work for that district. Fortunately it was the one day in the week, Saturday, on which the supplies were given out and we were thus able to see its operation. The civil population of each district are divided into three categories, those who are able to pay cash for supplies, those who are unable to pay now but whose circumstances will enable them to pay after the war, and those who are unable to pay at all. Each family receives a card with a particular number, giving the name of the family, the number of its members and the category in which it falls. One of the family presents the card at a desk in the factory; if they are in the first category, they pay at once; if in the second, the amount bought is charged to them; if in the third, the supplies are given gratis. They then pass along to various counters, where Frenchmen — formerly mechanics or workmen in the factory — give out the supplies, superintended by the owner. The French Government pays the American Commission for all supplies distributed in France — to two and one half million people; the cash actually paid by the people is refunded to the French Government through the American Commission in London; the amounts charged in the second category, mentioned above, are booked up until the end of the war, for the French Government to collect in due time. So carefully do the overseers undertake that nothing thus supplied shall ever be used by the Germans, that they actually destroy the very tins in which the lard is delivered — the British authorities having expressed the fear that they might serve the Germans for hand grenades! We saw a heap of the tin bottoms of these cans, thus conscientiously destroyed. In this center, also, the French superintendent seemed to work in perfect accord with the Germans. On leaving, General von Zöllner passed through the factory and commented with regret on the now idle machinery. The owner shrugged his shoulders, as only a Frenchman knows how to shrug, to which the German General replied genially, "Il faut attendre; toujours la belle patience, mon ami."

I should add that while the French civilians are fed by the American Commission, whatever they themselves cultivate goes to the German Army.

Thence like a whirlwind to Sedan, passing many a ruined shell-deluged house on the way, through the very country where the War of 1870 was decided, direct to the Mairie and up to a little office where the Maire sat stolidly behind his desk, the rest of us — our party having now been increased by several other German officers — ranged ourselves in chairs in a circle and a little wizened member of the town council talked so fast for twenty minutes on the whole system of "ravitaillement" that I for one could not understand one word he said and I doubt if the others caught much of it. We then visited another distributing office, where the little town councillor, now dragging his overcoat in the flour on the floor and trying simultaneously to talk with his hands and hold on to an enormously fat dossier, elucidated the perfection of each department to our entire satisfaction. When I had an opportunity I asked him also about the German end of the relief work, but his "les Allemands ont considérablement facilité l'organization" was not quite so wholehearted as the verdict of Monsieur Pillot.

Then came the really interesting experience of a visit to the little white house, outside of Sedan, where Bismarck received the surrender of the Emperor Napoleon after the Battle of Sedan in 1870. This part of the country had been much shot up in 1914, during the first few days of the war when the French were rapidly retreating from the frontier; whole rows of houses were gutted by fire and shell bursts, here and there a grave by the roadside with a rough wooden cross, bridges with the sand bags used to defend them still in evidence. The little house itself was scarred with rifle bullets, of 1914 not 1870, and inside, the steel jacket of a bullet was still sticking out of a hole which had been made in a china vase on the mantelpiece after the bullet had come through the window. Madame Fournier, who had received Count Bismarck in 1870 — she still calls him "Count" — apologized for having had to mend the hole through the windowpane — but it had been a cold winter. She took us up a tiny dark winding staircase to a very tiny room upstairs and showed us the two chairs in which Bismarck and Napoleon had sat facing each other across a round table — while she stood in the next room because her husband would not let her disturb them! Napoleon's chair has been broken — I suppose by tourists having sat in it too often — but Bismarck's is as hale and hearty as it was on that historic day 46 years ago. In a case on the table are the four gold louis which the Emperor Napoleon gave her as a tip and surrounding them are similar gold tips, mostly 20-mark pieces, from Emperor William II, Prince Henry, Prince August Wilhelm, Prince Oskar, the King of Saxony, a Turkish prince or two and I think a couple of other kings. When Madame Fournier had shown them with pride to the Ambassador he pulled from his pocket and presented to her a perfectly good American gold eagle; she took it with delight and asked him to write

a card to add to her collection, and as he had no card, I gave
him one of mine and he wrote on the back, "James W. Gerard,
Ambassadeur d'Amérique, le 29 Avril, 1916." How have the
humble risen in greatness! The card will take its place in the
glass sanctuary on the historic table with the ten-dollar gold
piece attached and my descendants, when they visit the old
house in future, will find — upside down, it is true, but still
there — the name of their ancestor, a lowly Conseiller d'Am-
bassade, enshrined among the names of two Emperors, a couple
of Kings, six Princes of the Blood — and one Ambassador!
Heaven help me to bear the honor modestly.

We visited one more distribution office on the way home and,
at the Ambassador's request, were shown also one of the Etap-
pen storehouses for the German troops; there were Russian
prisoners working there and I tried a little of my fast-failing
Russian on one genial giant from Riga, who grinned sympa-
thetically at hearing at least an attempt at his mother tongue
once more.

At various places on the way I noticed groups of young
women and girls working in the fields, each group under the
eye of a German soldier. One or two of them waved or saluted
genially as we passed, but most of them looked downcast and
weary. This was explained later, as will be seen.

We reached our villa at 5 and were then informed that as
a surprise to the Ambassador — the Germans have certainly
put themselves out to entertain him royally — a special train
had been arranged to bring seven American members of the
Relief Commission from Brussels to meet Mr. Gerard at Count
Wengersky's at tea. We went there at 6.30 and found the
Americans already there, a William B. Poland [a Director in
Brussels of the Commission for Relief in Belgium] being the
leader. At the tea table Poland suddenly cleared his throat
and addressing General von Zöllner, began a serious criticism
of the German method of haling young women and girls from
their families in Lille and other cities to make them work
in the fields in various parts of the occupied territory. This
explained the groups we had seen. He said that an order would

be given from headquarters to gather say 200 girls from one city within a few hours; the noncommissioned officer, to whom the order would be handed down, would have to make good his quota immediately and the result was that he would go from house to house, taking girls indiscriminately, girls of good family together with their own servant girls, factory and shop girls and any others he could lay his hands on. They were torn from their families by force and sometimes a husband would return from work to find his young wife taken in this brutal manner, without knowing where she was to be sent or how long she would be away — probably for months. Thus young women who had never done a stroke of manual labor in their lives, would be obliged to leave their comfortable homes at a moment's notice with a few garments done up in a towel and go to another part of the country to live in tents and work all day at forced labor under guard of a German soldier. . . . The discussion became acrid, but General von Zöllner was visibly impressed and promised to look into the matter immediately and arrange that the system be carried out in future with greater discrimination. I think he was sincere and it is possible that our visit will have served at least to rectify a very grave fault in administration.

We dined again with the Chancellor, at what will always be to me the most interesting dinner I ever had the fortune to attend. The guests were the same as last night, with the addition of Carl von Treutler [Prussian Minister to Bavaria], the Emperor's right-hand diplomat, who always accompanies him on his travels. The Chancellor had asked me to try to punctuate the telegram which had been received about our Government's attitude towards armed merchant ships, as the sense was far from clear. This took about half an hour after dinner and then we sat in a circle, the Chancellor, tonight looking very weary and worn, the Ambassador, von Treutler, von Stumm, Prittwitz, Zech, Grünau and Riezler and discussed the whole submarine issue through and through. The Ambassador and I, in turn, explained our Government's position precisely. Then the Chancellor became very angry and said that we had no right to dictate what should be and what should not be international law. The Ambassador, with perfect calm, said that we were not trying to make new international law, but to uphold what had already been made; that international approval of merchantmen arming themselves originally came about through the necessity of resisting pirates; that pirates now no longer existed, but that the Treaty of Paris [Declaration of Paris, April 16, 1856], although it abrogated many other obsolete rules, neglected to forbid such an armament and that therefore the principle still existed in international law today, which we were bound to uphold. I spoke about the absolute impossibility of a submarine distinguishing between an armed and an unarmed merchantman while submerged and until fire had been opened and submitted that the German theory could not be carried out in practice without mistakes becoming certain. The Ambassador then showed up admirably. He said that it would be ridiculous for Germany to go to war with America; that if we put a barbed wire around our country, we could live happily and independent of any other country on our own produce indefinitely. Stumm observed that at least we could not get dye stuffs, to which the Ambassador replied that we could produce plenty of dye stuffs and that the only reason why we turned to Germany for them was that chemists were paid but 4000 marks a year here, which was what we paid a policeman at home. He then said that practically every implement of war used by Germany today originated in the United States — the telegraph, the telephone, the submarine, the rifle, the electric light — and I added the aeroplane and the locomotive. The Chancellor said nothing more throughout the evening, but sat silent and heavy-eyed; then the Ambassador, who had talked calmly and intelligently, observed that the former was tired, and got up to go, the Chancellor taking him by the arm almost affectionately. He hinted that the Emperor would probably receive Mr. Gerard the next day. Tonight I could not tell to save my life which way the die is going to fall.

Sunday, April 30, 1916

An ideal day, blue sky with fleecy clouds, summer-warm and not a breath of wind. Prittwitz and Grünau called for us at 10 and motored us out into the country, where we took a long walk along the bank of the Meuse, between wooded hills as on the Neckar at Heidelberg, with the fruit trees in full blossom, the meadows bright with wild flowers and the song birds filling the air with music, among them a nightingale — ideal conditions in which to forget the strife of nations. Ending up at a small French château in the woods high up above the Meuse, where Grünau and his friends occasionally dine on a summer evening, we sat for a moment on the terrace — drinking in and trying to store up a little of the fragrance and peacefulness of our surroundings — and then back to town, where we learned that we were to lunch with the Chancellor. There is still no sign of the Ambassador's being received by the Emperor, but I gathered the distinct impression from Grünau that the German answer to our note would be satisfactory. In the course of discussion he said, "What will be your next step?" and when I asked, "Do you mean in the event of the present controversy being settled satisfactorily?" he answered "Yes." It was significant that he said "will" not "would."

On returning from our walk, I went out with Fritz to see the place where the French bomb fell the day before we came. It fell in the middle of the street in the square in front of the railway station and broke all the windowpanes in a wide radius besides indenting the adjacent houses with flying fragments. The interstices between the cobblestones are still filled with very small pieces of glass in all directions. The bomb did not make a deep hole but burst horizontally and thus killed the six men on the sidewalk who had just left the "Heldenkeller," besides wounding two, who are now in the lazaret.

On our morning's walk I discussed with Grünau, of the law department of the Foreign Office, all the many points of dissension between our two countries and he put the German side of the case in a more impressive light than the average press-fed individual with whom one talks in Berlin. He could see our point of view in the arms and ammunition controversy, but took the position that while we were technically absolutely correct — an admission which precious few Germans will make — because international law did not oblige us to place an embargo on arms and ammunition, it nevertheless did not oblige us to refrain from doing it and that therefore practical, not theoretical, neutrality could have been maintained only by our doing so.[6] I disagreed with him and spoke at length on the various considerations which had dictated our policy, so admirably expressed in our Government's note to Austria-Hungary, commenting also on the fact that it was the German delegates who had prevented the adoption of a rule at the Hague Conference requiring the signatory governments to forbid the exportation of arms and ammunition by the private firms of their respective countries. But we argued without heat or rancor — a blessing seldom given in these days of international animosity. The submarine issue was also fully discussed along the same lines, but there also we could not meet. However, I feel that every word we are saying down here will carry weight. Our conversations with the members of the Chancellor's staff will be reported to the Chancellor himself and he will in turn report them to the Emperor. Seldom have two men, Gerard and I, been placed in a position where their words may so easily sway an issue between peace and war and thus influence history. I say this with all due reserve, but it seems to me a fact. I believe that the Ambassador was called to Headquarters in order to enable the Chancellor, and thus the Emperor, to ascertain whether there can be any possibility of further temporizing. They themselves are in a difficult position vis-à-vis the people. They have let the people believe that the war can be won by the prosecution of their submarine warfare; now

---

6 There was some discussion in the United States during the war of applying an embargo on the export of arms and ammunition to all warring powers. Among the reasons why the Administration opposed such an embargo were that Wilson knew how Jefferson's embargo of 1807 had failed to persuade the belligerents to respect American rights, that the American people wanted the Allies to win, and that an embargo would have seriously threatened American prosperity.

they must reap the result. The people will believe that the United States has put the spoke in their wheel which may wrest victory from them and their animosity against us will assuredly develop into a bitter hatred. They will also regard their own Government as weak. All this is a result of their press system and the fact that they have permitted and encouraged the press to incite animosity against us almost since the beginning of the war. In the Government itself, the issue lies between the Army and the Navy on the one side and the Chancellor and the Foreign Office on the other, with the Emperor as referee. It is our business while here to influence the Emperor's decision with force and determination, and this the Ambassador is doing with all his outspoken directness and energy.

I would have far more respect for the views and opinion of the average German if he would master his subject before trying to discuss it; but the average German assumes from the start that we have taken up each position purely out of hostility to Germany and friendship for the Allies, without rhyme or reason to justify us, and logical discussion is therefore impossible. Each of the questions of dissension between Germany and the United States has its well-founded grounds for argument — as did the questions at issue in the Civil War; [7] I believe that Germany will give in in the present case, not because she thinks she is in the wrong, but because of the fatal policy of adding another powerful enemy to her list of adversaries.

[7] During the Civil War, Confederate commerce destroyers had been constructed in British shipyards. These ships practically drove the merchant marine of the North from the high seas. Building of such ships seemed to violate Great Britain's neutral position and the intention of her statutes which prohibited the building of war vessels for belligerents. Protests by the North and the fears of Britain that her own action might set a precedent, which would be used against her in some future war, led the British Government to seize one warship being built for the Confederacy, although the legality of such action was later denied in a British court. This, however, was too late to prevent the damage already done to northern shipping. The claims of the United States against Great Britain for the damage done by the *Alabama*, the most famous of the commerce destroyers, were settled in 1872, when the United States was awarded $15,500,000.

Böcklin is difficult to argue with, because he is one of the "press-fed." He said yesterday that France, Russia and England would find it hard to make peace because each of those governments had made certain definite promises to the people of territorial gains in order to justify their fighting; [8] Germany, on the other hand, had made no such promises because it was well known that she was fighting a purely "defensive" war! The various Allied governments did not dare to stop the war because they knew it would mean their immediate downfall and no government liked to contemplate such a contingency even if it meant the welfare of their country. This was the argument on which he based his belief that the war would last at least another year. Incidentally he stated that the French population of the occupied territory acknowledged that they had never been governed so well and so honestly under their own government as under the German occupation.

We lunched at the Chancellor's with the same officials as usual, took a walk in the garden and had coffee under a magnificent copper beech and later in the afternoon Prittwitz and Grünau called with the Chancellor's car and took us for a long drive through the Argonnenwald, stopping at the historic fortified old town of Rocroi — where the Ambassador gathered some French schoolboys and quizzed them on French history, on which they were unfortunately very weak — and then drove on over the hills and along the winding course of the Meuse for several hours through charming scenery.

The Emperor is still cogitating and talking with his military and naval advisers, who are the stumbling blocks in the way of a settlement with us, and still has not received the Ambassador. When the Ambassador asked the Chancellor this morning if he had been to church, he replied, "No, but I have been doing a lot of talking with a lot of people." I should not have put that in quotation marks, for the Chancellor speaks to us

[8] The Allied Powers had signed agreements promising territorial gains with Italy, Japan, and Rumania to bring these nations into the war on the Allied side. The new Soviet Government of Russia published some of these agreements in November, 1917.

practically always in German and that is the language used at meals, though he speaks English fairly well. Each day the Chancellor has hinted that the Emperor would receive the Ambassador the next day, but each day it is put off.

The Ambassador asked the Chancellor today how he had slept and the Chancellor replied that he had finally learned the secret of routing care at night. If he allowed himself to drift from one subject of thought to another or if he tried to think of nothing, he would lie awake all night, but if he fixed his mind on one particular subject and kept it there, he would soon become drowsy and drop off to sleep.

This noon the Chancellor picked up a paper and called the Ambassador's attention to the fact that a German submarine had allowed a merchant ship to pass unmolested because she was 120 miles from land and because it would have been impossible to ensure the safety of the crew at that distance from land. We later saw the same paper and noticed that the ship was not British but Norwegian!

Dinner at the Chancellor's again; it begins to feel quite homelike there, for there is always just his personal staff present and no formality whatever. If all German officers were like those we meet at the Chancellor's table, Germany would have a quite different reputation in the world than she has. The Ambassador spends each evening "explaining" America; tonight it was our taxation system and he did it well. After dinner they brought forth some extraordinary mechanical musical toys, belonging to the owner of the house . . . and after that the Chancellor insisted on my playing the piano. I say insisted because I have forgotten nearly everything I ever knew and tried to get out of it. However, it went somehow, the instrument was decidedly good, and I managed to get through the "Liebestod" from *Tristan and Isolde* and one or two other things. The Chancellor plays himself and is particularly fond of Brahms, but I wonder how his enormous hands can find their way over the keys. He was most agreeable tonight, genial, kindly and sympathetic, but never in my life have I seen a face that showed the cares of state so much as his does. He

receives an occasional telegram while we are there and if it is
press news he reads it to us.

May 1, 1916

The clock went forward an hour at midnight in accordance
with the new daylight-saving law; thus the events of the
day actually occur one hour earlier than usual, an excellent
arrangement for summer. Stumm called early to say that we
were both to lunch with the Emperor at 1, after which the
Ambassador and I eluded our usual escort and took a long
walk through the city and out into the country. The Chancellor called for the Ambassador at 12.40 and Stumm for me at
12.50 and we motored to the villa now occupied by the Emperor in a big garden on top of a hill outside of the city. As
Stumm and I came into the courtyard, von Treutler and General von Falkenhayn, the Chief of Staff, were standing deep in
conversation and after a handshake we passed on, entered the
villa and were shown into a sunny drawing room, absolutely
full of flowers, which the Emperor loves, giving onto the
garden and park. I was somewhat bewildered by the crowd of
officers there, all of course in Feldgrau uniform, but did the
necessary, according to German custom, of going up and introducing myself and then passing on to the next. The only ones
I knew were the Prince of Pless, General von Plessen, General
von Gontard and General von Chelius, but there were eight
or ten others. Although luncheon was to have been at 1 o'clock
it was well after 1.30 before the Emperor, the Chancellor and
the Ambassador appeared below in the Garden, walking slowly
towards the house, the Emperor still talking volubly and forcibly as his gestures showed. When they reached the house, the
Emperor entered the drawing room from a smaller room next
it and greeted me pleasantly, chatting for a few minutes about
the Towers [Charlemagne Tower, American Ambassador to
Germany, 1902–8] in Philadelphia and asking me several questions about them. Then he spoke to Prince Pless and some
of the other members of his staff, until luncheon was announced
and the Kaiser walked in ahead of everybody. The Ambas-

sador sat on his right, I on his left and the Chancellor opposite. On the Ambassador's right was Pless and on my left von Treutler. The Emperor's chair is separated from his neighbors' chairs by a little more space than the spaces between the other guests. He has his own carafe of red wine in front of him and a big golden handbell, which he rings after each course to summon the servants who do not remain in the room. For dessert he has merely a little saucer of plain chocolates. He was dressed in cavalry uniform with riding breeches and leather Gamaschen. He looks extremely well, has a cheerful expression and is tanned to a good healthy color, but his hair and upturned moustache are much grayer than when I last saw him. His left arm, which was next me, is only about half as long as the other and quite useless, but the size and power of his right hand (the mailed fist!) appears to have developed all the more to make up for his loss of the use of the other — I don't mean "loss," for he was born with it so. After luncheon, which was simple but good, we adjourned to the drawing room again and chatted in groups for a half-hour or more, the Emperor, the Chancellor and the Ambassador remaining apart in the little anteroom. As he got up from table, the Kaiser shook my hand and asked if I had learned to say "Mahlzeit"! Then the Emperor said good-bye to the Ambassador and myself, bowed to his staff and went upstairs, after which we returned to our villa. We there found a telegram from the Embassy, saying that a memorandum had arrived from the Department and would be telegraphed as soon as recoded. I called Harvey up on the telephone and asked him to hurry it along in sections, as it was most important that we should receive it before our departure this evening. The telephone connection with Berlin was excellent. . . .

At 8.15 we again dined with the Chancellor, with his usual staff and Karl Helfferich, the Secretary of the Treasury, who is a coming man in Germany and may rise to the Chancellorship some day. I took our code along and left it on a table in the dining room during dinner, and as the telegram from the Embassy, in two sections, was handed to us as we got up from table, I was able to decode it in Stumm's office without delay.

Its purport was that our Government was getting restive at the delay in receiving the German answer and giving a further statement about our attitude towards armed merchantmen in case further inquiry should be made.[9] The Ambassador, as soon as I had handed it to him, asked the Chancellor whether he wished to hear it, but the latter replied in the negative, and asked that it be given to Stumm, which indicated that the German decision had already been arrived at and the note in course of preparation. We are to receive it in a day or two. Thus the die has been cast, but we do not yet know exactly what the note will contain, except that it will in all probability be satisfactory. I cannot give the conversation which the Emperor had with the Ambassador as we are pledged to secrecy.[10] The Chancellor was busy, continually going out of the room and returning for a few moments, only to be called away again. Evidently something was up, but we did not know what. However, we left early and after expressing our full appreciation of the excellent hospitality received, left for Berlin at 11.38, in the same private car in which we had come and still accompanied by Prittwitz.

Whatever the result of our visit may be, this much may be said: Mr. Gerard was the right man in the right place at this important juncture. He does not mince his words, he speaks with force and directness — which is sometimes the only method of talk that carries weight here — and once he sees an issue clearly he rams it home straight from the shoulder. Any apologetic tone or sign of weakness would have been fatal. There was no sign of weakness on the Ambassador's part. He spoke admirably throughout our visit. Had he given the least loophole of hope for further temporizing or discussion, the German answer would in all probability have dodged the issue,

[9] In addition to reiterating that submarines must not sink merchant ships without warning and without taking steps for the safety of the persons on board, the note also stressed "that this Government is unwilling and cannot consent to have the illegal conduct of Germany's enemies toward neutrals on the high seas made a subject of discussion in connection with the abandonment of illegal methods of submarine warfare." For the full text see *Foreign Relations, 1916, Supplement*, p. 252.

[10] See Gerard, *Four Years in Germany*, pp. 339–43, for this conversation.

would have been unsatisfactory to our Government and would have resulted in a severance of diplomatic relations, which would almost certainly eventually have led to war. I shall always feel that Mr. Gerard, as the President's spokesman, has swayed the issue between war and peace between the United States and Germany during these four days at Charleville.

One more point. Had the President sent his ultimatum to Germany immediately after the sinking of the *Lusitania,* or in fact at any other time prior to the moment selected, I believe that Germany would have refused our demands. A year ago the German Government was flushed with the successes of its army in Galicia, it had not begun to feel the pinch of internal economic, financial and social conditions and it was in no mood to be dictated to. The President selected the psychological moment for the despatch of a great note and in this he has shown a farsightedness which few statesmen have evinced in history.[11]

[11] On May 4, Ambassador Gerard received the German reply to President Wilson's note of April 18. The Germans agreed to observe international rules of visit and search of merchant ships and to provide for the safety of persons on board destroyed ships. The note then stated: "But neutrals cannot expect that Germany, forced to fight for her existence, shall, for the sake of neutral interest, restrict the use of an effective weapon if her enemy is permitted to continue to apply at will methods of warfare violating the rules of international law. . . .

"Accordingly, the German Government is confident that, in consequence of the new orders issued to its naval forces, the Government of the United States will now also consider all impediments removed which may have been in the way of a mutual cooperation towards the restoration of the freedom of the seas during the war, as suggested in the note of July 23, 1915, and it does not doubt that the Government of the United States will now demand and insist that the British Government shall forthwith observe the rules of international law universally recognized before the war, as they are laid down in the notes presented by the Government of the United States to the British Government on December 28, 1914, and November 5, 1915. Should the steps taken by the Government of the United States not attain the object it desires, to have the laws of humanity followed by all belligerent nations, the German Government would then be facing a new situation in which it must reserve itself complete liberty of decision."

This German note was a victory for the President, but, in view of the above-quoted warning, only so long as Germany was content to wait upon American action against Allied infringements on neutral trade. For the complete text of the German note, consult *Foreign Relations, 1916, Supplement,* pp. 257–60.

XII

Peace Talks

During the period from the end of September to nearly the end of December, 1916, Mr. Grew, in the absence of the Ambassador, acted as Chargé d'Affaires. He was too busy to keep a daily diary. After the break with Germany and Austria-Hungary, while he was on board ship to the United States, he wrote the account that appears in the next two chapters. The material does not appear as a day-by-day description of events but rather an over-all summary of this significant period. He had available for this task not only the freshness of the events themselves but also copies of the despatches to and from Washington and copies of his private correspondence.

DURING the period that the Embassy in Berlin was in my charge from the end of September to nearly the end of December, 1916, our despatches to the Department of State predicted, without exception, that the adoption by Germany of an absolutely ruthless and indiscriminate form of submarine warfare was only a question of time.[1] It was bound to come sooner or later.

There had already been two distinct crises. One was known to the world at the time of the *Sussex* incident. We asked for certain assurances which, after deliberation on the part of the German Government, were definitely given. This crisis has been dealt with in my diary for April and May, 1916.

[1] See, for instance, *Foreign Relations, 1916, Supplement,* pp. 300–305, 314–18. On October 14, Grew cabled Washington: "I wish to repeat that there is no permanent security to be looked for in the situation regarding the submarine issue in view of the attitude of the Navy, the Conservative party and the great mass of public opinion."

Subsequently there was a period of quiet, during which I took my leave in the United States. I was called back to Berlin sooner than expected owing to Harvey's leaving — in mid-June — but there was actually no necessity for my returning so soon, as the Ambassador did not go away for another couple of months. Hugh Wilson, whose assignment to Berlin [as Second Secretary] had been arranged through Billy Phillips' usual considerateness and who returned with me, quickly fell into Harvey's place. He had had sufficient experience to manage the passport bureau without further training and was fully capable of running the whole chancery at that time if it had been necessary.

After our arrival in Berlin on July 6th there was a continued period of quiet, during which I expected that the Ambassador would go on leave. He kept delaying, but finally received so many urgent calls from Democrats to come home and campaign for Mr. Wilson that he applied for leave in September. Mrs. Gerard took passage towards the end of September and the Ambassador went to Copenhagen to see her off, although his leave had not been granted up to that time. Just after he had left Berlin, a telegram came asking that he postpone his leave. Then, within 24 hours, came another telegram saying that the President felt that he could be of great service in the campaign and asking him to come home. So he sailed with Mrs. Gerard on September 28.

The next crisis between the United States and Germany, which fortunately did not develop into more than a domestic political crisis at that time, arose the very day after the Ambassador had sailed. The first I knew of it was when Conger, the Associated Press correspondent, called me up on the telephone and said: "You have a pretty scandal on your hands already." It appeared that Sergeant Kiffen Rockwell, an American aviator in the French Army, had been killed and that this item of news was about to be used by the German press for a virulent attack on the neutrality of the United States. Practically every newspaper in Germany came out with hostile editorials. I knew that this presaged trouble in the impending session of the Reichstag, but went immediately to the Foreign Office and told them that these attacks on the United States must cease, as the Government was fully able to control the press when it wished. The Foreign Office had for a long time been able to suppress all articles in the press tending to inflame public opinion against the United States and it appears that this outburst was forced past the Foreign Office censor by the military representative at the daily press conference, who gave out the material regarding Rockwell and the corps of American aviators in the French Army and permitted it to be published before the Foreign Office could interfere.[2] It seems probable that the whole incident was a carefully timed political move on the part of the adversaries of the Chancellor, just before the meeting of the Reichstag, in order to stir up public opinion against the United States and thus to weaken the Chancellor in dealing with the submarine issue in the coming deliberations of the legislative body. There is no doubt that the Chancellor and the Foreign Office were greatly perturbed over the incident and that my representations had effect, for they took immediate steps to suppress all further comment in the press, and after the first squall, nothing further appeared to the detriment of America. I am aware that the Chancellor referred the matter to the Emperor himself.

At about the same time we received information from various confidential sources that the Admiralty Staff were hastening their preparations for a resumption of the ruthless submarine warfare, for they hoped and apparently expected that the political situation would develop in a way to permit them to carry out their plans in this direction, and in fact all my information, which came from various confidential sources in close touch with the Government and the Reichstag, indicated that another crisis over the submarine question was impending. I informed the Department of State that a grave political

---

[2] It was obvious that this press attack had been artificially trumped up. American citizens had, on their own private initiative, been fighting in every belligerent army and there was nothing new whatever in the Rockwell case. — J. C. G.

crisis was at hand, which might possibly result in the resignation of the Chancellor and the resumption of the ruthless submarine warfare in violation of neutral rights on the high seas
and the promises made to the United States.

The situation did not however develop as was expected by
the Admiralty. After the Chancellor's opening speech in the
Reichstag on September 28th, twelve days were spent by the
Budget Committee in secret session, for the purpose of considering foreign affairs, and it was during these sessions that
the Chancellor succeeded in coming at least to a temporary
agreement with the leaders of the various political parties, his
hand being so strengthened by various speeches by his supporters that he was able to prevent the question being brought
up in the plenary sitting.

I now know that my sources of information during the term
of my turbulent chargéship were trustworthy. They enabled
me to report fully and correctly to our Government on everything that was devolving and developing beneath the surface,
even to following the general trend of the secret sessions of
the Budget Committee. During this crisis I sent confidential
telegraphic reports to the Department almost daily.[3]

The meetings of the Budget Committee were strictly secret,
members of the Reichstag not belonging to the Committee being
excluded. The principal witnesses before the committee were
the Chancellor (von Bethmann-Hollweg), the Secretary of
State for the Navy (von Capelle), and the Secretary of State for
Foreign Affairs (von Jagow). The principal topic of discussion
was the submarine issue and whether to take up the submarine
warfare in its extreme form, thereby involving neutrals in the
war, or not. The opponents of such action were the Chancellor,
supported by the Emperor, Helfferich (Minister of the Interior), von Hindenburg (Chief of the General staff),[4] Ludendorff (Hindenburg's Chief of Staff), the Foreign Office, and

3 See *ibid.*, pp. 58–65.

4 On August 29, 1916, Falkenhayn had been dismissed as Chief of the General
Staff, and Hindenburg had taken his place, Ludendorff becoming Quartermaster-
General. As early as August 30, Ludendorff and Hindenburg discussed the ques-

what appeared to be the majority of the Reichstag, including the Socialists, the Peoples' Progressive Party, a few of the National Liberals, and most of the Center Party. Its advocates were the Navy in its entirety, including of course von Tirpitz, the former Secretary of State for the Navy, now engaged in active propaganda, a large percentage of the Army, the Conservatives, and most of the National Liberal Party in the Reichstag, and above all, the majority of public opinion, which had been carefully educated by the press to regard the ruthless submarine warfare as a sure means of causing England's downfall.

At certain phases of the discussion the leaders of the various parties in the Reichstag were called before the Budget Committee and allowed to state the views of their respective parties in regard to the matter.

One of the strongest speeches in support of the Chancellor appears to have been made by Helfferich, who elaborated the importance of avoiding a break with the United States, first on account of the necessity of retaining American financial co-operation after the war; second, on account of the effective closing of the frontiers of the neutral countries contiguous to Germany which would result from the combined pressure of England and the United States, thus putting an end to the importation of supplies which still entered Germany in certain

tion of unrestricted submarine warfare, deciding against resumption, because it might lead to war with Denmark and Holland. As the seriousness of the German military position became apparent to Ludendorff, and it seemed to him that if "the war lasted our defeat seemed inevitable," the quick victory which the navy assured would follow the resumption of submarine warfare became essential. Ludendorff decided that unrestricted sea war could not begin again until the campaign in Rumania had been successfully completed, and until it was seen "whether any success would be achieved by any intervention by President Wilson, along the lines indicated by our Government in September, or by our own offer of peace. . . . The result of our efforts for peace would be sure to be known by the end of December or early in January, and this, too, seemed to point to the beginning of February as the date for opening the unrestricted campaign." With Hindenburg and Ludendorff as strong supporters, the actual decision to begin unrestricted submarine warfare was taken on January 9, 1917. Erich von Ludendorff, *Ludendorff's Own Story* (New York: Harper & Bros., 1919), I, 288, 365, 369–78.

quantities across those frontiers. Helfferich's speech, in fact, may be regarded as the turning point of the political crisis.

During these secret sessions it was announced in the press that a confidential memorandum, written by the Admiralty Staff and submitted to the Chancellor on the subject of the economic effects which an indiscriminate submarine warfare would have on England's commerce, had been surreptitiously distributed to the political leaders, in order to influence them in demanding by resolution in the Reichstag that the ruthless submarine warfare be adopted. An official statement was later published to the effect that this memorandum was simply a work on England's political economy as affected by submarine warfare, sent by the Admiralty to the Chancellor in February last, marked "confidential, not for publication," and described as a purely economic memorandum prepared for the use of the Admiralty.

The arguments used by the Chancellor in the secret sessions of the Budget Committee I shall recur to later. At any rate, he won out in the Committee by a vote of 24 to 4, and when the open session of the Reichstag came, what had promised to be a debate of great acrimony, with the possible result of a vote of lack of confidence in the Chancellor, was reduced to a few mild speeches by the leaders of the Conservative and of the Socialist Labor parties, that is, the extreme right and the extreme left, who had refused to accede to the resolution of the Budget Committee and who spoke on the submarine issue, but without effect. Count Westarp, the leader of the Conservatives, said that while his party regarded a resumption of the indiscriminate submarine warfare as absolutely essential, he would refrain, in the public interest, from stating their reasons therefor. The general sentiment of the Reichstag was that the decision should be left in the hands of the highest military authorities, namely the Emperor and von Hindenburg.[5] It was

[5] For instance, a declaration drawn up by the Center on October 16 stated that in "taking his decisions the Imperial Chancellor must rely upon the views of the Supreme Command. If it is decided to initiate a ruthless submarine campaign, the Imperial Chancellor can be certain of the agreement of the Reichstag." See Arthur Rosenberg, *The Birth of the German Republic* (London: Oxford University Press, 1931), p. 146.

them generally felt that confidence in the Government had been restored as a result of the proceedings in the Reichstag and that the political atmosphere had for the moment been cleared.

In this connection it may be interesting to quote an extract from a letter from Admiral Scheer to the Emperor, which came into my hands through our "underground" service. Admiral von Scheer, since the battle off the Skagerrak — the Battle of Jutland, May 31 – June 1, 1916 — had been the dominating personality on the active list of the Navy and was of course a strong supporter of the ruthless submarine warfare.

. . . It is true that if operations to be inaugurated take a favorable turn, the enemy may be considerably injured, yet there cannot be the slightest doubt that even the most fortunate result of a high-sea battle cannot force England in this war to peace; the disadvantages of our military-geographic situation as compared with that of the island Power and the great material superiority of the enemy will not allow us to overcome England or the blockade directed against us, even if the U-boats are all available for military purposes. A victorious ending within a foreseen time can only be achieved by destroying the English economic life, i.e. by using the German U-boats against the English commerce.

I am constrained according to my conviction and duty to counsel Your Majesty against employing any weaker method, not only because it does not correspond to the character of the weapon and the risk to the U-boats, which is in no proportion to the gain to be achieved, but because in spite of the great conscientiousness on the part of the captains of the U-boats, it is not possible for them to avoid incidents in English waters, in which waters American interests are active, incidents which are liable to humiliate us and would force us to recede, if we cannot hold through to the fullest extent. . . .[6]

At about this time, the German submarine *U-53* appeared off the Atlantic coast of the United States and took on supplies in Newport harbor — on October 7, torpedoing several [9] merchant ships soon after her departure. This was about

[6] *Foreign Relations, 1916, Supplement,* p. 296.

October 10th. On the 12th a statement appeared in the *Nord Deutsche Allgemeine Zeitung*, the semiofficial organ of the German Government, which, while not labeled official, had all the earmarks of emanating from the Admiralty Staff. It said that the operations of the *U-53* were being carried out in strict accordance with the German Prize Rules, that there was no question of a blockade of American ports, since only ships carrying contraband of war were being held up, and that "in strong contrast to the complaints of the American Government regarding the operations of the *U-53* stands the fact that since the beginning of the war, English cruisers have been standing guard before American ports, New York for instance, which approach the coast so closely that they may be seen with the naked eye from the roofs of high buildings."

The records of two of my visits to the Foreign Office at this period are as follows:

Berlin, October 6, 1916

Saw Zimmermann and told him I feared that my Government might become disquieted over the rumors of a possible resumption of the indiscriminate submarine warfare which were appearing in the press. He assured me that the Chancellor had the situation well in hand and that there was no danger at present and that I might inform my Government to that effect. He added, however, that the submarine issue would never be finally laid away until the United States should take steps to force England to give up the blockade and said that any such steps would materially aid the Chancellor in dealing with his political opponents here. He said he did not think that the submarine issue would be brought up for discussion in the plenary sittings of the Reichstag, as they hoped to arrange the matter in the secret committee sessions.[7]

Berlin, October 11, 1916

Saw von Jagow and told him that although I had had no instructions from Washington, I feared that my Government, judging from the press reports, was disturbed over the operations of

7 *Ibid.*, pp. 294–95.

a German submarine or submarines off the Atlantic coast of the United States, and I asked him informally and unofficially whether he had any information to give me on the subject which might reassure the Government at Washington. He asked me to formulate any question I wished to ask. I said: "Can you authorize me to inform my Government that you have given me assurances that the Imperial Government has no intention of altering its present submarine policy or of departing from the assurances given us last spring?" He replied in the affirmative. He then went on to say — speaking, as he said, without obligation (unverbindlich) — that he presumed the raid of the German submarines was for the purpose of proving that Great Britain did not control the seas. He alluded to the fact that British cruisers had been stationed off our coast for the purpose of intercepting German commerce. I said I understood from the press reports that they had been withdrawn at the request of our Government. He replied that in that case, our Government should properly have informed the German Government of the steps taken, as they knew nothing about it. He then went on to say that the German submarines could not take their prizes into American ports, owing to the *Appam* decision.[8]

The interview ended with a repetition on my part that I was not acting under instructions in coming to him and that the interview was merely an unofficial "conversation," to which he agreed, giving me renewed assurances on his part that the German Government contemplated no alteration of policy in regard to the conduct of submarine warfare.[9]

---

[8] The *Appam,* a British-owned ship, was captured by a German vessel on its run between West Africa and Liverpool. A German prize crew was placed aboard, and the ship was brought in as a prize to a United States port. A libel was filed against the vessel in a United States District Court by her owners, the British and African Steamship and Navigation Company. The court ruled on July 29, 1916, that "the manner of bringing the *Appam* into the waters of the United States, as well as her presence in those waters, constitutes a violation of the neutrality of the United States; . . . that she, as between her captors and owners, to all practical intents and purposes, must be treated as abandoned and stranded upon our shores; and that her owners are entitled to restitution of their property." The United States Supreme Court delivered an opinion on March 6, 1917, upholding the decision of the lower court. *Ibid.,* pp. 722–45.

[9] *Ibid.,* p. 774.

I now return to the arguments advanced by the Chancellor before the Budget Committee of the Reichstag in opposing the ruthless submarine warfare. Germany had one card left to play before she staked her last — namely, the proposition of immediate peace.

Von Jagow had intimated to the Ambassador before his departure that Germany would be glad to consider terms of peace without further delay. This intimation was regarded as so confidential that it was cabled to the Department in our special secret code, Winslow and I being the only members of the Embassy in the secret.[10] It was said that if the intimation should leak out, Germany would immediately disavow any connection with it. Therefore I knew, and cabled Washington to that effect, that the Chancellor had secured a stay in the declaration of a ruthless submarine warfare (ruthless seems the best translation of "rücksichtslos") in order to give the President an opportunity to act on this intimation, if he so intended, without embarrassing him by such a declaration. At that time I was confidentially informed that the limit of the delay would be November 20th, a reasonable interval after the presidential election. But subsequent events prolonged the interval.

The development of this peace "motif" in the symphony — or more correctly cacophony — of the history of 1916 has been fully elaborated in a confidential report made to the Department on December 21st, the last day of my chargéship.[11] The world first knew of it on December 12th, when the Chancellor

10 On August 18 and September 2, Bethmann-Hollweg had instructed the German Ambassador in Washington to encourage a mediation effort by Wilson. On September 25, Gerard cabled Wilson that Germany hoped Wilson would initiate peace negotiations. The President's campaign for re-election, however, made a peace overture on his part impossible. In a speech on September 30, Wilson said: "From this time until the 7th of November it is going to be practically impossible for the present Administration to handle any critical matter concerning our foreign relations, because all foreign statesmen are waiting to see which way the election goes, and in the meantime they know that settlements will be inconclusive." See Harley Notter, *The Origins of the Foreign Policy of Woodrow Wilson* (Baltimore: The Johns Hopkins Press, 1937), pp. 554–60; Bernstorff, *op. cit.*, pp. 285–87.

11 *Foreign Relations, 1916, Supplement*, pp. 129–38.

sent for the Spanish Ambassador, the Swiss Minister and myself, and handed us formally the first peace proposition of the war, subsequently informing the Reichstag of his action. But much was happening before then.

On November 17th, I directed the Department's attention to the importance of an interview with the Chancellor which William Bayard Hale, the Berlin correspondent of the Hearst newspapers, was about to cable to the New York *American*.[12] There had been during the last few weeks in Berlin a marked increase of peace talk and sentiment, which, so far as I could observe, extended practically to all parties and classes, and when I learned of the Hale interview and was informed that it was in the nature of an informal suggestion to the President, whose response was awaited with interest, there seemed every reason to attach weight to it, particularly as Hale's relations with the German Government were closer than those of most of the other American correspondents, and as the Chancellor would not be likely to give an interview at this time without some particular purpose.

The Hale interview was however unexpectedly delayed, after he had understood that it had been approved and passed, and had expected it to be published in New York on the morning of November 18th or 19th. I reported this to the Department and was informed in reply that Count Bernstorff was trying to stop the publication of the interview in the United States,[13] and that it might now be held up by the German censor, and I was instructed to endeavor to obtain a copy of it and cable it to the Department. No intimation was given me, however, as to whether the Department itself considered the publication of the interview as advisable or not.

This was one of those cases where American diplomacy is handicapped beyond the diplomacy of other nations by the failure of the Government at Washington to keep its diplomatic officials in intimate touch with the sentiment, policy and intentions of the Administration. In reading the life of Lord

12 *Ibid.*, pp. 64–65.
13 *Ibid.*, p. 67.

Lyons [14] and other foreign diplomatists and observing how closely their Governments kept them informed of the trend of the policy at home, one cannot help feeling that American diplomacy suffers in comparison. The American diplomatic representatives are too generally treated as office boys and directed to transmit certain communications to the Governments to which they are accredited or to take certain action, without being told in confidence the underlying reasons for the communications or action or the general purpose in view. One is often tempted to believe that our Government is feeling its way in the dark, leaving its policy to be formulated by events, not prevision. In this particular case, of the Hale interview, I would have been in a better position to act intelligently had the Department informed me whether it considered the publication of the interview in the United States at this time as desirable or undesirable. I was told only that Count Bernstorff was trying to stop its publication, not that our Government wanted it stopped. Had I known this definitely, I could probably have prevailed upon Hale to delay cabling it. But looking at the matter from every point of view, I could not foresee whether the publication of the interview would embarrass or assist the President in any action which he might be contemplating.

On November 25th, I informed the Department that the Chancellor, in view of recent developments such as the death — November 21, 1916 — of the Austro-Hungarian Emperor, the changes in the personnel of the Foreign Office (von Jagow had retired and Zimmermann had succeeded him as Secretary of State), and the establishment of the Government Auxiliary Service,[15] had now decided that it would be preferable to base

14 Thomas Newton, *Lord Lyons* (London: E. Arnold, 1913).

15 On December 2, 1916, the Reichstag ratified a draft of a law creating a National Auxiliary Service. The Service was to be made up of all male Germans from 18 to 60 who had not been called into the armed forces. Those persons employed in war industries or organizations, in agriculture, nursing, official institutions, or other professions or enterprises which were of importance, directly or indirectly, in carrying on the war or supplying the people, were to be considered as engaged in the Auxiliary Service. Persons not so employed

the interview primarily on these developments and thus to avoid approaching the subject of peace directly, while bringing it into the interview incidentally. I had however managed to obtain a copy of the original interview, and although it had now been withdrawn and could not be regarded as authorized by the Chancellor himself, I cabled various excerpts in order to indicate its general nature and the tendency of the Chancellor's thoughts.[16]

On November 28th, Hale gave me a copy of the interview as finally approved and passed, after it had been revised five separate times, and in accordance with the Department's instructions I cabled it in full, though it must have cost nearly $1000 to do so. The great amount of padding in the interview and the fact that, so far as I was aware, it would be published in the United States, made me hesitate to cable it in full, but the Department had asked for the text and I feared that to omit any portion of it would be to confuse the relative importance of the subjects mentioned.[17]

Meanwhile, on November 22nd, my first interview with the Chancellor regarding the Belgian deportations gave him an opportunity to turn to the subject of peace and to elaborate the theme at considerable length, knowing that what he said would be brought directly to the President's attention — we two were alone. He approached the matter directly and definitely and left no doubt as to his intentions in bringing up the subject. As soon as the Belgian matter had been discussed, he settled back in his chair and began to speak slowly and distinctly in German, giving me the impression that he had carefully considered his words in advance. He said that these difficulties in Belgium would never have arisen if his suggestions that Germany desired peace, which he had expressed in the Reichstag last December, almost a year ago, and subsequently

could be drawn into the Service at any time. This amounted to a threat, wrote Mr. Grew in his diary, to "volunteer in some profession which is of importance directly or indirectly to the carrying on of the war or the supplying of the people, or else be conscripted."

[16] *Foreign Relations, 1916, Supplement,* pp. 69–70.

[17] *Ibid.,* pp. 71–74.

to Mr. Gerard and to Colonel House [18] and in other speeches and interviews, had been acted upon abroad. England and France, he said, had replied that this was no time to talk of peace. It had been said in those countries that he had made conditions (Bedingungen); this was not true; he had made no conditions. If his intimations that Germany was ready for peace should be continually ignored, Germany would be forced in self-defense to adopt hard measures, but this would not be Germany's fault. Germany's readiness for peace absolved her from the guilt of this continued slaughter. It was utter craziness (Wahnsinn) to continue this useless and futile taking of human life. This he repeated several times in different words. "What do these difficulties in Belgium matter," he said, "compared to the hecatomb of lives which have been lost on the Somme since last July?"

This interview was impressive beyond description and I can only remember the man as he seemed to me that day, Busstag, the German day of penitence, sitting at his desk, speaking slowly, deliberately and sadly of the horrors of the war. He seemed to me like a man broken in spirit, his face deeply furrowed, his manner sad beyond words. Perhaps it was his role to act this part; if so, he is a great actor. Possibly the fact that this was Busstag reminded him of the deaths of his wife and son since the beginning of the war. His terms of peace were not touched upon. He did not ask me to say anything to my Government, but simply talked as if in personal confidence. I left with a few words of hope that peace would soon be at hand.

Immediately after this interview, which had lasted the greater part of an hour, I returned to the Embassy and sent off

[18] Bernstorff forwarded to Colonel House on October 18 a memorandum from the Kaiser in which the Kaiser referred to a statement by Mr. Gerard in April, 1916, that "President Wilson possibly would try towards the end of the summer to offer his good services to the belligerents." The Kaiser added that "the constellation of war has taken such a form that the German Government foresees the time at which it will be forced to regain the freedom of action that it has reserved to itself in the note of May 4th last and thus the President's steps may be jeopardized." Mr. House sent this memorandum to the President on October 20. House, *op. cit.*, II, 335–36.

a long confidential telegram to the Department,[19] stating, as I could not fail to state under the circumstances, that the whole impression made upon me by the Chancellor was one of great weariness and sadness and discouragement at the failure of his peace suggestions to bear fruit. I said that quite apart from any consideration of mood or manner, the Chancellor had given me the distinct *impression,* although not directly expressed, that he was disappointed that the United States had not taken steps looking toward peace.

On December 1st, I communicated to the Department my impressions of the general situation in Germany regarding the issue of peace.[20] I stated that with the exception of a certain element in the Army and the Navy and certain politicians of the Reventlow type, Germany as a whole was ready to welcome peace overtures, as there was a general weariness of war and as the food situation, while not critical, was becoming more and more difficult from day to day. As it was not generally believed, however, that peace could yet be brought about, owing to the growing doubt of the possibility of inducing Russia to conclude a separate peace and owing to the irreconcilable attitude of England, the German Empire was gathering all of its potential resources with a view to meeting and if possible to exceeding the enemy's output of trained soldiers, guns and ammunition. Three principal steps were being taken in this significant and large-scale movement, namely, the organizing of the National Auxiliary Service, the impressment of laborers in Belgium, and the same or similar action in Poland. These steps would undoubtedly release a very large number of men to the front (it has been said a million and a half) and would effect a great increase in the number of available munition workers. It was hoped that by this method Germany would be in a position to conduct a successful offensive against Russia in the spring or sooner (probably a movement into Bessarabia and towards Odessa) and to check a similar offensive on the part of the Allies in the West. For this reason, the Army

---

[19] *Foreign Relations, 1916, Supplement,* pp. 68–69.
[20] *Ibid.,* pp. 77–78.

leaders appeared to believe that they could secure more favorable terms after their spring offensive than now and were therefore probably averse to steps looking toward peace at the present moment. The attitude of the Navy was well known to the Department from my previous reports: the Navy would never feel that its trump card had been played until the ruthless and indiscriminate submarine warfare had been reopened and England starved out by the cutting off of all commerce approaching her shores.

The Chancellor, on the other hand, I said, was to all appearances sincerely and heartily in favor of an early peace, and I believed these sentiments to be shared by Zimmermann who, although a stronger and more determined man than von Jagow, was in agreement with the Chancellor that the war could now only result in a draw, that the continued loss of life was and would be futile, and that although Germany would be able to maintain her present position indefinitely, if not to advance, humanity called for an end.

It was not impossible that the Chancellor might encounter a certain amount of opposition from the German public should his repeated peace suggestions be acted upon, but so far as I was able to gauge the situation, any such opposition or criticism would be based upon the fear of a confession of weakness rather than upon any lack of desire for peace among the people, officials and politicians of Germany as a whole.

This telegram was sent only after repeated conferences with the various members of the Embassy staff, and it was altered until it met with the full approval of the Military Attaché, Colonel (now General) Joseph Kuhn, and represented the consensus of opinion of the staff as a whole. The Naval Attaché, Commander Gherardi, would not agree that there was any sentiment in Germany for peace based upon terms which would even be considered by the Allies. The rest of us disagreed with him, and I still think we were in the right, judging from remarks made to me by Zimmermann not long after.

In this connection, I may say that I never sent an important political telegram involving personal judgment or opinion, without first consulting with my various colleagues on our staff. We did not always agree and I did not always take their advice, but their point of view always helped me to form mine. The men upon whom I could best rely for sane and unprejudiced judgments were Hugh Wilson and Alexander Kirk [Second Secretary of the American Embassy at Berlin]. Gherardi, being radically pro-Ally, and John B. Jackson radically pro-German, furnished opinions the mean of which was valuable, but their views taken separately were generally distorted by prejudice.

The result of my interview with the Chancellor was an early reply from the President,[21] touching first upon the Belgian deportations and directing me, after making a textual protest against the Belgian deportations on behalf of the Government of the United States, to represent to the Chancellor in confidence and with great earnestness the very serious unfavorable reaction which the Belgian deportations were exerting upon public opinion in the United States at a time when that opinion was more nearly approaching a balance of judgment as to the issues of the war than ever before. I was also, and more particularly, to point out the great embarrassment which the President had been caused by that reaction in regard to taking steps looking towards peace. I was authorized to say that the whole situation was being watched by the President with the utmost solicitude, as it was his wish and definite purpose to be of service at the earliest possible moment in that great aim and that it had repeatedly distressed him to find his hopes frustrated and his occasion destroyed by such unfortunate incidents as the Belgian deportations and the sinking of the *Arabia* — on November 6, 1916 — and the *Marina* — on October 28, 1916. Furthermore, authorization was given me to say that my report, cabled on November 22nd, of the evident distress and disappointment of the Chancellor that nothing had come of his intimations regarding peace, had been noted by the President with the deepest interest and that what the President now earnestly desired was the creation of a favorable opportunity for some affirmative action by him in the interest

21 *Ibid.*, pp. 70–71.

of an early restoration of peace, this opportunity to be brought
about through practical co-operation on the part of the German authorities.

This telegram was received at the Embassy on December
2nd. Between this receipt of the President's message and my
next interview with the Chancellor on December 5th, I passed
through a very uncomfortable time. My telegram had distinctly said that I had drawn the *impression* that the Chancellor was disappointed that the President had taken no steps
looking toward peace, not that the Chancellor had openly said
so. But the President, in his reply, had assumed that the Chancellor *had* said so. There was no time to discuss this point
further with Washington; I had to act at once. There were
two possibilities of ruin for me: first, I might have mistaken
the Chancellor's intentions in speaking to me as he did; perhaps he had merely wished to tell me that he personally hoped
for peace overtures from the belligerents themselves, not that
he had any intention whatever of asking the President to intercede; he might resent the President's message as uncalled-for.
Second, even if he had wished the President to intercede, he
might resent the tone of the latter's message, which was distinctly sharp in wording. He might make a scapegoat of me
and say: "Who asked the President to intercede, anyway?
Young man, you must have misunderstood me." I would have
to report his reply, of course, and then it would be all over
with me, disgraced for having led the President into an impasse, a rebuff to his overtures and an indignity to the United
States. Agreeable prospects.

On receiving the Department's telegram containing the
President's message on December 2nd, I immediately applied
for an interview with the Chancellor. First it was set for the
morning of the 4th, but this was postponed until evening
owing to the funeral service for the Austro-Hungarian Emperor — which the Chancellor had for the moment forgotten!
At 6 I presented myself at the Chancellor's palace and was met
by Count Zech, his adjutant, who told me most apologetically
that the Chancellor had been detained by an unexpectedly

long sitting of a Reichstag committee and had to put me off until the next morning at 10. Another night of waiting.

But one is fresher for battle in the morning. Von Bethmann-Hollweg received me cordially at 10 with many apologies for the postponements. I approached the matter warily, first going over his previous conversation in full, repeating, so far as I could remember them, the Chancellor's exact words, in German, receiving confirmation after every few sentences. Then I said that I had gathered from His Excellency's remarks that he was disappointed that no steps had been taken looking toward peace. Von Bethmann-Hollweg immediately interposed: "Yes, disappointed that no steps have been taken in the belligerent countries." For a moment I had "cold feet." He was undoubtedly going to repudiate any intention of soliciting the President's interference. It was suggestions of peace from the belligerents, not the neutrals, that he wanted.

A little quick calculation was necessary. I could still withdraw without delivering the President's message and ignominiously report that I had unfortunately been mistaken in the Chancellor's intentions. Or I could go ahead, trusting to my firm conviction that Germany desired peace above everything, and to the remarks which the Chancellor had previously made to the Ambassador, to Colonel House and in the Reichstag.

I risked it and delivered the message verbatim. It was stiff, very stiff. It practically said: "The naughty boy can't have any candy unless he stops being naughty at once." There was a moment of suspense when I had finished. The Chancellor sat back in his chair and stroked his beard for minutes, and I had no idea whatever what he was going to say. Then he quietly turned to me and said I should receive a reply in a few days after he had discussed the matter with Zimmermann. The interview was at an end and I left. Another sleepless night ensued — literally sleepless, for I was much worried.

In the morning I sought Zimmermann to try to get a line on the Chancellor's attitude towards the President's message. All my forebodings were at once relieved: the Chancellor's reply, he said, would be favorable and friendly. So they had determined to accept the President's sharp message and not make a scapegoat of me after all. They might easily have done so. But Germany was too anxious for peace.

On the evening of December 7th, the Chancellor sent for me and said that while the answer of the German Government to our representations regarding the Belgian deportations would be communicated to me in due course by Zimmermann, he wished to reply immediately himself, before leaving for General Headquarters that night, to the President's message regarding the question of taking steps looking toward peace, and he proceeded to make to me the following confidential oral communication:

> The German Government, desirous of maintaining amicable relations with the United States, has given proof of its willingness to settle incidents arising between the two nations in a friendly spirit by the replies recently transmitted to the American Government in the *Marina* and *Arabia* cases. It is with great satisfaction that I have noted that the President of the United States so earnestly tries to be of service in the restoration of peace. Also my offers to open pourparlers for peace negotiations have so far not met with a favorable response from the other side. I hope the time will come when Germany's enemies will be more willing to lend an ear to the voice of reason. I am extremely grateful to see from the message which you were good enough to deliver to me that in this event I can count on the practical co-operation of the President in the restoration of peace as much as the President can count on the practical co-operation of the German authorities.[22]

Thus a tense situation was at an end.

The next pitfall I had to look out for was the use which the German Government would make of the President's message. It was to her interest, of course, to have the matter published in the United States somehow or other. On the following day, December 8th, Conger, the Associated Press correspondent, mentioned to me in the course of conversation that he was

[22] For the text of this communication see *ibid.*, pp. 81–82.

about to cable an interesting message to America. I displayed no particular interest, but led him on to tell me all about it. To my utter amazement, he knew of the President's message to the Chancellor almost word for word and was going to send his telegram within the hour. The message had been strictly confidential and I had so stated when delivering it.

Endeavoring to look at the matter from every point of view, I could not see that the publication of this interview, so far as it related to peace, could do otherwise than embarrass the President. We did not know at that time that either the Chancellor or the President would shortly come out with a public communication on the subject and it was my opinion, although no intimation of the Department's attitude had been given me, that if the President were contemplating taking action, his way would be rendered more difficult by the unfavorable reaction which the publication of my confidential interview with the Chancellor would have on public opinion in the countries of the Entente. Furthermore, if the President had had no objection to the publication of the interview, the Department would presumably not have characterized the communication to the Chancellor as confidential, as was the case. It did not therefore lie with me to determine the advantages or disadvantages of its publication and it was undoubtedly my duty to call the attention of the Foreign Office to the fact that my communication to the Chancellor had been confidential and that I had so stated when delivering it.

I waited until Conger had disappeared around the corner and then started for the Foreign Office with all sails set and close-hauled, calling immediately on Count Montgelas. I told him that I had delivered a message from the President of the United States to the Chancellor in the strictest confidence and that a newspaper correspondent was about to cable it practically verbatim to America. Montgelas looked flustered and telephoned in my presence to a subordinate, whom he pretended to haul over the coals for having given the material to Conger. (I later learned from Conger, however, that when he was with the subordinate, the subordinate had telephoned in his presence to Montgelas and was told to go ahead and give it out.) I then insisted that Conger's telegram, and all other newspaper telegrams, be purged by the Foreign Office censor of any allusions to the President's message. Montgelas promised me that he would personally examine every such telegram and see that my request was complied with. A few days later Conger came to me and said he had just seen the draft of his original telegram after it had left the censor's hands, and that to his utter disgust all allusions to peace had been cut out. He said it resembled a chicken with the feathers off. I expressed my sympathy.

Before turning to another subject, I appended below, as of interest, the records of my first conversation with William Bayard Hale regarding his peace interview with the Chancellor, and of my conversation with Zimmermann after delivering to von Bethmann-Hollweg the President's message.

Berlin, November 17, 1916

Dr. William Bayard Hale called on me today and informed me that he came on a matter of the greatest possible importance. He said that he had had repeated conferences with the Chancellor regarding the question of peace and that these conferences had resulted in a written interview which he expected to cable to the New York *American* today, as soon as the Chancellor had instructed the censor to release it. He said that the Chancellor might possibly make a few minor corrections, but that the interview as a whole had his approval. He requested me to cable to Mr. Gerard in order that the matter might be given its proper importance in America and he asked me to inform the Department that the interview was in the nature of an informal suggestion to the President, whose response was awaited with the greatest eagerness. He asked me further to say that the interview had the approval of the "highest authority," to whom it had been submitted. I said: "Do you mean the Emperor?" He replied, "Yes, but I would prefer to avoid using his name in the matter."

I told Dr. Hale that I would prefer to delay in cabling to the Department and to Mr. Gerard until I was sure that the interview had actually been released by the censor. He however begged me not to delay, as he said that there was no doubt that it would be released, probably today, and as it would go by wireless, my telegram would arrive after its publication in New York unless sent at once.

Dr. Hale then placed a copy of the interview in my hands at my request. I read it through and asked whether the Chancellor had made his statements in German or English. Dr. Hale replied, "I wrote every word of it myself." I then said, "Can you give me absolute assurances that the Chancellor has seen this text and approved it?" Dr. Hale replied, "The Chancellor has seen the text and approved it in principle; he may make simply a few unimportant alterations and I have every reason to believe that it will be released today."

Dr. Hale then talked at some length on the general subject of peace and told me that he had learned on reliable authority that the recent Austrian deputation to Berlin, headed by Baron Burian, the Minister for Foreign Affairs, had expressed Austria's desire to avoid peace démarches until Rumania should have been defeated, but that the German Government was not in accord with this wish.

Before leaving, Dr. Hale promised to inform me as soon as the interview had been released by the censor.

Berlin, December 6, 1916

Saw Zimmermann and extended Mr. Gerard's, Colonel House's and my own congratulations on his appointment as Secretary of State for Foreign Affairs. He acknowledged the congratulations with thanks, but modestly expressed doubt as to his ability to carry the extra burdens.

After some conversation regarding Colonel House, in which Zimmermann expressed his high appreciation of the former's personality, straightforwardness and sincerity, to all of which I heartily agreed, and in which he said they felt that Colonel House was a man whom they could always trust implicitly, I adverted to the interview which I had had yesterday with the Chancellor, which Zimmermann said the Chancellor had already discussed with him. I repeated to Zimmermann all that the Chancellor had said about peace in my previous interview and in various speeches and conversations, in which he had repeatedly and continually thrown out intimations that while Germany could and would fight on as long as was necessary, Germany was ready and had been ready for a year for a termination of the war. I spoke also of the disappointment which the Chancellor had expressed that these intimations had borne no fruit, to all of which Zimmermann agreed. I then said I hoped most sincerely, that the Chancellor's forthcoming reply to the President's message to him would be favorable and couched in friendly terms and tone, as I felt that this reply would exert great influence on the relations of our two countries, and I asked Zimmermann to use his best influence in molding this reply, in view of its intense importance.

Zimmermann promised me definitely that the reply would be favorable and friendly, that he wished to do everything to promote the good relations of the two countries, and that he would use his best endeavors "to smooth our difficult path." I told him that I had informed the State Department last spring that I regarded him as a warm and true friend of America, to which he cordially agreed.

Having dealt with the submarine issue up to the end of the October crisis, and with the peace theme up to December 8th, I must now turn back to our negotiations regarding the Belgian deportations. These three questions were, in fact, the most important with which I had to deal during the period that the Embassy was in my charge, and more diplomatic work and anxiety were actually crowded into those three months than into any other period during the duration of the war, with the exception of the Ambassador's visit to General Headquarters at the time of the *Sussex* crisis. It was a tremendous relief when the Ambassador returned at the end of December and took over the reins again.

THE BELGIAN DEPORTATIONS

About October 10th, I received a communication from the Minister at Brussels [Brand Whitlock], transmitting copies of letters from the President [M. Ernest Solvay] of the Comité National de Secours et d'Alimentation of Belgium, stating that the German authorities in Belgium had demanded from the

Belgian authorities lists of unemployed civilians, with the object of sending them into Germany for labor. The President of the Comité National referred to certain assurances given by the German Government to Mr. Gerard concerning the freedom of Belgian civilians from forced labor and suggested that the matter be brought to the attention of the German Foreign Office, as it was feared that the British Government, on learning of these new measures, might suppress the further importation of food supplies into Belgium. This information I at once cabled to Washington.

On October 19th the Department informed the Embassy that Mr. Gerard had stated that he had received no assurances from the Foreign Office, with the exception of certain verbal assurances, given him by the Chancellor at General Headquarters last April, to the effect that no more of the civil population of Lille, Roubaix and Tourcoing would be sent to labor in the fields.[23] This was at the time of our visit to Charleroi, when we had noticed groups of young girls working the fields and had learned that they had been taken from their families in the French cities occupied by the Germans, were kept in concentration camps and were forced to labor, against which practice we lodged a protest and were informed that it would cease. The Chancellor appeared at that time to be much annoyed about it, claiming that it was a military measure of which he had been unaware.

At the same time, the Department authorized me, if I deemed it advisable, to draw the reported action of the military authorities in Belgium informally and orally to the attention of the Minister for Foreign Affairs and to remind him of those verbal assurances as to some extent connected with the reported situation in Belgium.

I distinctly did deem action advisable, foreseeing the far-reaching results of these new measures and their ultimate effect on the world's opinion. The record of my first visit to the Foreign Office in this connection is as follows:

[23] *Ibid.*, p. 860.

Berlin, October 21, 1916

Saw Zimmermann and took up with him the question of the action of the German military authorities in sending Belgian workmen, who were receiving aid from the Comité de Secours et d'Alimentation, into Germany as laborers. I pointed out that this was contrary to the assurances given to Mr. Gerard last spring regarding the civil population of Lille, Roubaix and Tourcoing, in spirit if not in letter, and that if the action of the German military authorities were persisted in, the British Government might be led to stop all importations of food into Belgium. Zimmermann promised to investigate the matter at once and to inform me of the result.

On October 23rd I reported to the Department that I had informally and orally brought the question of the Belgian laborers to the attention of the Imperial Under Secretary of State for Foreign Affairs, who had promised to investigate the matter and to inform me of the result.[24] I also informed the Minister at Brussels to this effect.

On October 26th, I requested the Minister at Brussels to keep me fully informed of any developments regarding this question and of the results of any representations which might be made to the Governor General of Belgium — von Bissing — by the neutral diplomatic representatives in Brussels.

Having learned from various sources that the new policy in Belgium was being continued and was resulting in increasing friction in that country and was impressing neutral opinion more and more unfavorably, I sought another interview with Zimmermann on my own initiative and once more pointed out to him informally and orally the unfortunate results of these measures of impressment and deportation, the result of which interview I telegraphed both to the Department and to the Minister at Brussels.[25] Zimmermann, on that occasion, handed me the following memorandum:

Against the unemployed in Belgium who are a burden to public charity, in order to avoid friction arising therefrom, com-

24 *Ibid.*, p. 862.
25 *Ibid.*, pp. 862–63.

pulsory measures are to be adopted to make them work so far as they are not voluntarily inclined to work, in accordance with the regulation issued May 15, 1916, by the Governor General. In order to ascertain such persons the assistance of the municipal authorities is required for the district of the Governor General in Brussels, while in the districts outside of the General Government, i.e., in the provinces of Flanders, lists were demanded from the presidents of the local relief committees containing the names of persons receiving relief. For the sake of establishing uniform procedure the competent authorities have in the meantime been instructed to make the necessary investigations regarding such persons also in Flanders through the municipal authorities; furthermore, presidents of local relief committees who may be detained for having refused to furnish such lists will be released.

I then discussed in detail with Zimmermann the unfortunate impression which this decision would make abroad, reminding him that the measures were in principle contrary to the assurances given to the Ambassador by the Chancellor at General Headquarters last spring and dwelling on the effect which the policy might have on England's attitude towards the relief work in Belgium. I said I understood that the measures had been promulgated solely by the military government in Belgium and that I thought the matter ought at least to be brought to the Chancellor's personal attention in the light of the consequences which the new policy could entail. Zimmermann intimated in reply that the Foreign Office had very little influence with the military authorities and that it was unlikely that the new policy in Belgium could be revoked. He stated, however, in answer to my inquiry, that he would not disapprove of my seeing the Chancellor about the matter.

I may add here that one of the first men to foresee the unfortunate world-wide effects which these measures in Belgium were to have was Raymond Swing, of the *Chicago Daily News*. He came to me at the outset, before the matter had come to the notice of the public, and implored me to use my best efforts to forestall it, drawing a vivid picture of the deplorable hardship on the Belgians which it would entail. But it was already too late to recall the edict.

Under the circumstances of my interview with Zimmermann, I informed the Department that if the matter were regarded as of sufficient importance and if it were felt that, owing to the possible seriousness of the consequences which might result from the new policy in Belgium, further representations could be made with propriety, the only step left would be to consider the advisability of authorizing me to seek an interview with the Chancellor, in order to place the whole matter before him with reference to the principles involved in the assurances given the Ambassador last spring and in the light of international law, foreign opinion and humanity. I stated that I had no reason to believe that such an interview would have any favorable results and was doubtful as to what extent it would be desirable to carry our informal representations, but that I wished the Department to know the circumstances. It was already evident that the matter would eventually assume serious proportions, both in Belgium and in its reaction on public opinion abroad.

Replying to this statement, the Department, on November 2nd,[26] authorized me to request an interview with the Chancellor, in view of the seriousness of the consequences which might result from the proposed policy in Belgium, aside from the humanitarian considerations. The Department left it to my discretion as to the extent to which my informal representations might be carried and stated that they must necessarily be guided by circumstances and upon the Chancellor's general attitude in the matter. I was to point out to him, however, the unfortunate impression which would be created in neutral countries by the proposed policy and especially in the United States, which had the welfare of the civil population of Belgium very closely at heart. It was evident from this noncommittal instruction that public opinion in the United States had not yet begun to exert marked pressure on our Government, as it later did.

26 *Ibid.*, p. 863.

Upon receipt of this instruction, in view of the fact that the Department had left to my discretion the character and extent of the representations to be made, I immediately telegraphed to the Minister at Brussels informing him that I had been authorized to seek an interview with the Chancellor and stating that I would be very glad to receive any suggestions or views which either he or Herbert Hoover, the Chairman of the Commission for Relief in Belgium, might desire to express as to the form in which the matter could most effectively be laid before the Chancellor and to learn whether there were any subordinate concessions to be asked for in case the Chancellor should refuse to consider an alteration of the policy in general. I added that a full statement of the attitude of the Commission for Relief in Belgium would be particularly valuable.

On November 7th Mr. Whitlock telegraphed me that if the German Government felt that the policy must be continued — and they themselves were the best judges of that and had doubtless taken into consideration the effect which the measures would have on public opinion abroad . . . the following suggestions might be worth considering as a means of ameliorating the situation:

1. The measures to be applied only to actual unemployed. These to be ascertained without calling for lists from the Belgian authorities.
2. Married men or heads of families to be exempted.
3. The concentration camps of such deported persons in Germany to be voluntarily opened by the German Government to inspection by representatives of the American Ambassador in Berlin. He suggested American representatives as more confidence would be placed in them abroad than in those of any other country.

At the same time, Mr. Hoover informed me that this forced recruiting of workmen from Belgium and Northern France had created the basis for the most bitter anti-German propaganda which had been seen since the beginning of the war and that it might seriously jeopardize the whole question of relief, as the British Government was only too anxious to find excuses for the latter's suppression. He recommended that if the recruiting were to continue, it should be carried out with more deliberation and careful selection, eliminating the seizure of married men, old men, boys and actually employed workmen and better-class people without notice, and he seconded Mr. Whitlock's suggestion as to neutral inspection of working camps, in order to certify to the nonmilitary character of the employment, living conditions appropriate to free workmen, regular payment of current wages and facilities to correspond with and to remit their wages to their families in Belgium. Mr. Whitlock then quoted to me his confidential telegram of November 6th to the Department and added that he was sending me copies of papers giving details of the foregoing, for my confidential information.

On November 9th, I telegraphed to Mr. Whitlock and, referring to his suggestion for amelioration under Heading 1, requested him to inform me what method of obtaining the names of actual unemployed was suggested as an alternative to the lists which had been demanded from the Belgian authorities.

On November 10th, Mr. Whitlock replied that the German authorities could obtain these lists for themselves by the inspection of factories, farms, business houses, etc., in order to ascertain what men were workers, and that they also had at their disposal the information on file at the Meldeamt or offices where civilians were required to report themselves. They could also take into consideration the sworn statements of employers or employees, supported if necessary by sworn declarations by the Mayors of the various communes. Each case should be treated separately instead of by lists. The German military authorities had asked the Belgians themselves to supply these lists and to designate who should be taken for work, but this they had refused to do as an act of betrayal of their fellow citizens. The German military authorities, according to Mr. Whitlock, appeared so anxious to obtain workers that they were making little or no effort to distinguish between the employed and unemployed, were making the selections in haste and were using the refusal of the lists as a pretext for taking men indiscriminately. The refusal of the lists, however, appeared to be relatively immaterial, as the military authorities had been planning these measures for some time past and had even taken steps to deprive men of work in various artistic trades in order to declare them unemployed. In one province they had forbidden further work on public improvements, which had furnished the entire unemployed population of the province with satisfactory employment since the beginning of the war, greatly to the benefit of both population and state. It appeared that they were even taking members of the Comité National, whose operation had been guaranteed by the Governor General to the patron Ministers in Brussels. Mr. Whitlock added that the Governor General and the German civil authorities were not in sympathy with the present measures, but were powerless before the military party.

On November 11th, Mr. Whitlock telegraphed me that he had just had a long and interesting conference with Baron von der Lancken, the head of the German Political Department in Brussels, who had returned from Berlin, and that the latter had approved highly of the idea of opening the Belgian working camps in Germany to neutral inspection and had telegraphed to Berlin to urge its consideration and adoption. Mr. Whitlock suggested that as Belgian interests in Germany were represented by Spain, it might be indelicate on our part to suggest that the inspection be wholly under American auspices, but that it could be under joint Spanish and American auspices or regarded as an extension of the work of the Commission for Relief in Belgium. Baron von der Lancken informed Mr. Whitlock that he would be glad to correct such injustices as might be brought to his attention.

Finally, after awaiting the arrival of the copies of papers which Mr. Whitlock was sending me from Brussels and which seemed essential in order to understand the situation fully and to have all possible material at hand before seeing the Chancellor, I applied informally for an interview. Almost at the same time, it was announced from some source other than the Embassy — presumably by the Department — that I had been instructed to seek such an interview, and this was published in the foreign and domestic press. I then learned by chance that the Spanish Ambassador [Polo de Bernabé] had likewise applied for an interview with the Chancellor, for the purpose of discussing the same subject, and am under the impression that he was led to this step by the announcement of my own prospective interview, for he had only recently made similar representations to von Jagow at the Foreign Office and had received a formal note in reply, a copy of which he showed me, categorically refusing to make any alteration in the policy in Belgium. Under these circumstances I thought it best, as the Spanish Ambassador was the representative of Belgian interests in Germany, to tell him that my own Government's representations to the Chancellor were to be purely informal and unofficial, but that if he wished to see me in order to talk the matter over, I would be very happy to call on him. This he asked me to do and I had two long and most friendly conferences with him, both before and after he saw the Chancellor. I told him approximately what I intended to say to the Chancellor, which met with his approval, and I believe that he presented the matter in practically the same way and that his own representations added force to the representations of our Government. All of this I reported to the Department in my telegram of November 20th.[27]

The Swiss Minister [Dr. Alfred Claparède] also called on me and inquired as to the nature of the representations which my Government proposed to make; he made a report to his own Government on the matter and I believe he subsequently also had an interview with the Chancellor. I had also informally discussed the question with the Dutch Minister [Baron W. V. F. Gevers] before it had become acute, but met with little sympathy in that quarter, as he seemed wholly in favor of the German authorities doing in Belgium as they themselves saw fit. When I mentioned the possible effect that these meas-

27 *Ibid.*, p. 866.

ures might have on England's permitting the passage of food-stuffs to Belgium, he became angry and said: "If England permits Belgium to starve, it will be England's fault, not Germany's."

Finally, on November 22nd, I was received by the Chancellor and had an interview lasting nearly an hour, the results of which I telegraphed to the Department the same day.[28] Having already learned from the Spanish Ambassador that there was no hope whatever of obtaining a general revocation of the measures of deportation, and in view of the Department's instructions leaving to my discretion the extent to which my informal representations should be carried and informing me that the character of the representations must necessarily be guided by circumstances and upon the Chancellor's general attitude in the matter, it seemed to me that more practical good might be accomplished by endeavoring to obtain certain concessions and points of amelioration in the carrying out of the measures, based on Mr. Whitlock's information and suggestions, than by confining myself to a probably futile protest against the policy as a whole. My representations were to be purely informal and I was not at that time aware of the extent to which the Department would ultimately carry the matter.

In my interview with the Chancellor, I went into the whole matter very fully, taking up the various points brought out in Mr. Whitlock's telegrams and letters and endeavoring to give a clear conception of the unfortunate nature of the policy as a whole and the specific abuses to which it had already led. I first stated that my representations were to be informal and explained the reasons why the Government of the United States could not fail to take a lively interest in Belgium, not only because the problem of Belgium interested the world, but also because of the Commission for Relief in Belgium, the activities of which had been guaranteed by the Governor General to the patron Ministers in Brussels, of whom the American Minister was one.

I then informed the Chancellor that the newly instituted

[28] *Ibid.,* pp. 866–67.

policy of enforced labor and deportations and especially the
manner in which these measures were reported as being carried out were giving my Government cause for concern, in
view of the possibly serious consequences which they might
ultimately entail. It appeared that the selection of workmen
was being made in haste and without due deliberation; that no
distinction was being made between fathers of families, married men, old men and boys, and that men were being taken
from their families without a moment's notice regardless of
whether they were already employed or not, or whether they
were already supporting themselves and their families by useful and profitable labor.

It was reported that considerable friction had been caused
by the Belgian authorities being required to give lists of the
unemployed in their various districts, although the information would appear to be obtainable by the German authorities
at the Meldeamt. The Belgians had refused in many cases to
give such lists as an act of betrayal of their fellow citizens;
they had been imprisoned and the German authorities had apparently used their refusal as a reason for taking men indiscriminately. The refusal of these lists, however, seemed relatively
immaterial, for the military authorities appeared to have begun carrying out these measures several months before the
lists were called for or refused. It was said that they had also
taken steps to deprive men of work of an artistic nature in
order to regard them as unemployed and I was informed that
in one province at least they had prohibited the continuance
of work on public improvement which had greatly benefited
both population and state. They were now taking even members of the communal and provincial committees of the Comité
National, who were obviously employed in furthering the
valuable operations of this organization, and the work of the
Comité National had been specifically guaranteed to the patron
Ministers by the Governor General.

The Chancellor would remember that the question of the
enforced employment of the civilians of Lille, Roubaix and
Tourcoing in the fields in districts away from their homes had

been discussed during the visit of the Ambassador to General Headquarters last spring and that His Excellency, I understood, had given Mr. Gerard assurances that this practice would be stopped. Furthermore, Baron von Huenè, Governor of Antwerp, had given public assurances in 1914 that the Belgian civilians need have no fear that they would be taken to Germany either to be there enrolled in the Army or employed for forced labor. This declaration, written and signed, was publicly announced throughout Belgium and was subsequently confirmed by Baron von der Goltz when he became Governor General of Belgium — August–November, 1914.

My Government feared that the very nature of these new measures and the manner in which they were being carried out would defeat their own objects. Instead of restoring normal conditions in Belgium, they had already created a basis for the most bitter anti-German propaganda that had yet been seen in Belgium and had opened up a vista of renewed disturbance and bitterness which it was feared would offset any good that Germany had done and was doing in Belgium and would make future friendly relations with Belgium after the war more and more difficult. It would seriously jeopardize the whole question of relief, which was now carefully and efficiently organized; would overthrow the balance of the entire organization and very possibly lead England to stop the entire importation of supplies altogether.

His Excellency would realize the unfortunate impression that all this was making in neutral countries, who would believe that these measures were being taken in order to release German workmen to the front, their places to be filled by Belgian workmen. It was said that these measures were being taken in the interest of Belgium; but the Belgians themselves were against them; the Commission for Relief in Belgium was against the new policy; the Belgians on the committees were against it; the Belgian Government was against it. It was a quesion of liberty of domicile, liberty of work, the inviolability of families; a question of the word given by the Governor of Antwerp, later confirmed by the Governor General of Belgium, the immediate representative of the highest authority of the German Empire; a question of the national feeling of Belgium if she were not to be regarded as a subjected and dependent province; a question of the spirit if not the letter of international law; a question of the world's opinion, that of my own Government and country as well as others; and finally a question of humanity.

The points of amelioration which I then suggested as a concession to Belgian national feeling and foreign opinion were as follows:

1. Only actual unemployed to be taken, involving a more deliberate and careful selection.
2. Married men or heads of families not to be taken.
3. Employees of the Comité National not to be taken.
4. The lists of unemployed not to be required of the Belgian authorities, but to be determined by the German authorities themselves, as a concession to Belgian national feeling; and the Belgians, who had already been imprisoned for refusing to supply these lists, released.
5. Deported persons to be permitted to correspond with their families in Belgium.
6. Places of work or concentration camps of deported persons to be voluntarily opened by the German Government to inspection by neutral representatives.

After listening attentively to these informal and oral representations, the Chancellor promised to answer within a few days, and then gave me a general statement of the reasons which had caused the adoption of the policy: namely that there were some six hundred thousand unemployed in Belgium, who were a source of concern to the German authorities and that since England had prevented the importation of raw material into Belgium, there was not now sufficient industry to occupy these unemployed in their own country. He stated that his attitude coincided in principle with that of Governor General von Bissing, as expressed in the latter's interview with the correspondent of the *New York Times* which had lately appeared in the German press. After expressing his appreciation of American relief work in Belgium, he immediately turned the conversation towards the question of peace, which has been mentioned above.

A few days later Count Zech, the Chancellor's adjutant, called on me and communicated to me informally and orally the following replies to the various suggestions which I had made for concessions and points of amelioration:

1. Only actual unemployed were to be taken. The selections would be made in a careful and deliberate manner.
2. Married men or heads of families could not in principle be exempted, but each case would be considered carefully on its own merits.
3. Employees of the Comité National were regarded as actually employed and therefore exempt.
4. It was essential that the Belgian authorities should co-operate with the German authorities in furnishing lists of unemployed, in order to avoid mistakes. Only one Belgian had been imprisoned for refusing to give such lists and orders had now been given for his release.
5. Deported persons would be permitted to correspond with their families in Belgium.
6. Places of work and concentration camps would in principle be open to inspection by Spanish diplomatic representatives. American inspection might also be informally arranged if desired.

Thus, of the six suggestions I had made, four were accepted unreservedly, and a fifth in part. But we have had experience as to how much weight to attach to promises on the part of the German Government; very few of those made to me were actually fulfilled.

I duly communicated the replies of the Chancellor to the Department and the Minister at Brussels.[29] On December 2nd, Mr. Whitlock communicated to me the text of a telegram which he had sent to the Department on November 28th, stating that he had been encouraged by the report of the results of my in-

29 *Ibid.*, p. 867.

terview with the Chancellor, but that it would appear that the orders had not yet been put into effect as the recruitment of Belgian workmen was continuing without distinction between employed and unemployed; that the selections were being made with great rapidity and allowing no time for examination; that in the Province of Namur, where a mayor had given a list of unemployed as directed by the Germans, practically none of the persons so indicated were taken, while hundreds of employed workmen were taken from the same district; that the Germans apparently based their choice only on physical fitness and the skill of the workmen; that iron workers and blacksmiths were greatly in demand; that employees of the Comité National were still being taken; and finally that conditions in certain places of deportation were very bad, the men being given no food for 83 hours and being without blankets, apparently in order to force them to work.

On November 29th, the Department, apparently influenced by the ever-growing resentment of public opinion at home at the Belgian deportations, instructed me to seek a further interview with the Chancellor and to read to him verbatim a formal protest on the part of the United States. I received the telegram on December 2nd and immediately applied for an interview, which was accorded me on December 5th, when I read to the Chancellor the following communication:

The Government of the United States has learned with the greatest concern and regret of the policy of the German Government to deport from Belgium a portion of the civilian population by order of forcing them to labor in Germany and is constrained to protest in a friendly spirit but most solemnly against this action, which is in contravention of all precedents and those humane principles of international practice which have long been accepted and followed by civilized nations in their treatment of noncombatants in conquered territory. Furthermore the Government of the United States is convinced that the effect of this policy if pursued will in all probability be fatal to the Belgian relief work, so humanely planned and so successfully carried out, a result which would be generally deplored and which, it is assumed, would seriously embarrass the German Government.

Subsequently, in informal conversation, I brought out the points mentioned in Mr. Whitlock's telegram of December 2nd. The Chancellor stated that a reply to the formal representations of the United States Government would shortly be communicated to me by the Foreign Office.[30]

On December 11th, Zimmermann handed to me the following reply of the German Government:

The Government of the United States has protested against the deportation of the Belgian laborers to Germany and against their being compelled to work, proceeding from the view that these measures are incompatible with the principles of humanity and international practice as to the treatment of the population of occupied territory. The German Government believes that the Government of the United States of America is not correctly informed as to the reason for these measures and the manner in which they are being carried out, and therefore considers it appropriate first of all to explain the true state of affairs.

In Belgium unemployment has been spreading for sometime among the industrial laborers in an alarming manner. This great increase in the unemployed is attributable to the English blockade policy, which has cut off the importation of raw materials for the Belgian industries and the exportation of their manufactures and thus caused the greatest part of the plants to shut down. As a result, nearly half of the Belgian factory laborers, whose total number is about 1,200,000, were completely deprived of occupation and a great many more than half a million Belgians who formerly earned their living by work in industries made dependent on public relief; this number is nearly tripled when the families are added, making approximately one and a half million people. Such a state of affairs made a radical remedy most urgently necessary whether from the point of view of Belgian political economy, for which the unemployed form an insupportable burden, or from the point of view of public order

30 *Ibid.*, p. 868.

and morals, which are gravely imperiled by the general lack of employment and its attendant features. This necessity has long been recognized and emphasized by discerning Belgians also.

In view of this situation, the Governor General at Brussels issued an ordinance on May 15, 1916, whereby persons enjoying public relief who decline without sufficient reason to take up or continue work corresponding to their capacity are threatened with imprisonment or compulsory labor. In consequence of the prostration of the Belgian industries it was not possible to furnish all the unemployed with an opportunity to work or at least some suitable occupation in Belgium itself. There was therefore no choice but to assign them to work in Germany, where a large number of Belgian laborers are voluntarily employed already and feel themselves quite well, the wages being high and personal liberty very extended. Compulsory labor is enforced against those unemployed who do not follow their example.

This measure is completely in accordance with international law. For pursuant to Article 43 of The Hague Land War Ordinance the occupying Power shall take steps to ensure public order and safety in the occupied territory and to this end intervene with supplementary ordinances wherever the laws in force in the country do not suffice. It undoubtedly comes under the head of the maintenance of public order to have those capable of work made to work, if possible, and not permitted to become a burden on public charity and form a national pest on account of their idleness.

In carrying out the measure, hardships have been avoided and all possible consideration has been shown. If isolated mistakes have been made in selecting the persons taken to Germany, and in particular people have been included to whom the conditions of the ordinance of May 15, 1916, do not apply, this is to be connected with the fact that the Belgian authorities frequently refused their aid in drawing up the lists of the unemployed or made false statements. Care has been taken that such mistakes shall be remedied as soon as possible. For the principle that only such persons shall be deported to Germany as received public relief, find no work in Belgium, and refuse the work assigned to them in Germany is adhered to with all possible firmness.

The unemployed deported to Germany are taken from the concentration points established at Altengrabow, Guben, Kassel, Meschede, Münster, Soltau and Wittenberg, to the places of labor where they are employed in agricultural and industrial plants. As a matter of course work which a hostile population cannot by international law be compelled to perform is excluded. If the American Government attaches importance thereto, permission will gladly be granted to a representative of its Embassy here to inform himself by a personal visit as to the conditions in which the people are living.

The German Government regrets exceedingly that the circumstances set forth above have plainly been completely misrepresented in the United States of America through the mendacious press agitation of Germany's enemies. It would greatly deplore it, not the least so in the interest of the Belgian population, if the beneficent work of the Relief Commission should be impaired in any way as a result of these misrepresentations.

In conclusion the German Government cannot refrain from pointing out the fact that the removal of the German population from the parts of Germany occupied by enemy troops and her colonies, in particular the dragging away of women, children and old men from East Prussia to Siberia, did not so far as is known here afford the neutral countries any occasion to take steps with the Governments concerned, similar to those that they have now taken towards Germany. And yet it is not susceptible of any doubt that these latter measures constitute a gross violation of the laws of humanity and the rules of international law, whereas the German measures are quite consonant with those principles according to what has been set forth above.

In the course of informal conversation, after he had handed me this statement, Zimmermann said that steps were being taken to ameliorate so far as possible the conditions and manner of carrying out the deportation measures along the general lines of my informal suggestions to the Chancellor.[31]

I here append, as a matter of record, the account of my second interview with Zimmermann (the one mentioned just above was the third) on this subject:

[31] *Ibid.*, pp. 868–70.

Berlin, October 27, 1916

Saw Zimmermann and inquired whether he could give me any information regarding the question of the enforced employment of Belgian laborers about which I had spoken to him on the 21st. He handed me a memorandum showing that the decision of the military authorities was definite and that the matter was now being carried out. I told him that I understood that the matter had already been given out by the press bureau of the Foreign Office and that at least one correspondent had cabled it to America and that his despatch had been passed by the censor; also pointed out the fact that it would undoubtedly make a very bad impression abroad as it involved a definite breach of international law, that it would probably put a stop to any peace sentiment in England, would result in England's refusing to let further supplies through to Belgium and would bring about the eventual withdrawal of the American Commission for Relief in Belgium, besides helping to prolong the war. Besides this, the principle was contrary to the assurances given to the Ambassador by the Chancellor at General Headquarters last spring, to the effect that the civil population of Lille, Roubaix and Tourcoing would not be forced to labor or evacuation. I said I felt that the Emperor would veto the measure if he knew of it and that I would very much like to have it at least brought to the Chancellor's personal attention, as it had probably been promulgated purely by the military authorities in Belgium.

Zimmermann in reply said that he approved of any measures which would help Germany to win the war *regardless of international law;* that he was not aware of any peace sentiment in England, although Germany had shown her readiness to consider peace terms; that if any hope of peace were held out, the measures taken in Belgium might be revoked, but that they were military measures and the Foreign Office had very little influence with the military authorities. He asked me exactly what my instructions were; I told him that I had simply been instructed to take up the matter informally and orally with the Secretary of State for Foreign Affairs. I asked him if he would approve of my seeing the Chancellor if authorized by my Government, to which he replied in the affirmative. He asked me not to state that the decision of the military authorities was irrevocable as "accidents might still happen." I took this to mean that if peace propositions were forthcoming from the Allies, the measures in Belgium might be revoked.

The net result of the representations of our Government, I informed the Department in my report of December 12th, both informal and formal, appeared to be that the attention of the Chancellor and other high German authorities had been drawn to the world's opinion of what constituted one of the most flagrant violations of international ethics and one of the most inhumane departures of German policy and administration which had been seen since the war began. The measures, as they were reported as being carried out — and there seemed to be no reason to doubt the accuracy of the reports — were nothing more nor less than a method of securing more workmen for German industries in order to release a corresponding number of German employees to serve in the fighting line. The measures were synchronous and in direct relation with the new policy in Poland and the establishment of the Government Auxiliary Service, all tending to increase the fighting force of Germany. They were in my opinion purely military measures and in all probability planned and executed directly by the General Staff. I doubted if the Chancellor himself was aware of their exact nature until they had been brought to his attention by the comments in the foreign press and by the representations of the neutral diplomatic representatives in Berlin. In fact I was aware that only recently a prominent official in the Foreign Office had stated in conversation that if the German Government had ever realized the criticism which these measures would evoke abroad, the policy would never have been entered upon, but that they were now too far committed to withdraw.

I believe that our Government took the initiative, first in making informal representations and then in formally protesting. In any case, several of the other neutral diplomatic representatives subsequently sought similar interviews with the Chancellor or took the matter up with the Foreign Office, and there was no doubt in the minds of the German authorities as

to the unfavorable impression made abroad and the high disapproval of neutral opinion. It seemed unlikely that the general policy of impressment and deportation would be altered
and the measures revoked, but the pressure of foreign opinion,
so clearly indicated, would perhaps eventually result in an
amelioration of the conditions and methods of carrying out the
measures. If even this much were accomplished, the steps
taken would not have been futile.

I added to the Department that in my conversations with
the Chancellor and the Foreign Office in regard to this subject, I had carefully avoided mentioning Mr. Whitlock or the
Legation at Brussels or the Commission for Relief in Belgium
in connection with the information and reports which they
had so kindly sent me and which had been of the greatest value
in dealing with the matter.

For a long time, all the reports which reached us indicated
that the measures of impressment and deportation were still
being carried out with a total lack of discrimination between
the employed and unemployed and that the Chancellor's promises to me had been worthless. Our Legation at Brussels was
obliged to open a separate office to deal solely with the complaints resulting from the German practice. Only in April,
1917, when I met Mr. Whitlock and Albert Ruddock [Second
Secretary of the United States Legation at Brussels] in Paris,
just after they had left Belgium and were on their way to
Havre, the seat of the Belgian Government, did I learn that
the deportations had in a large measure ceased and that many
of the deported persons had been returned to their homes.
Whether this was a direct result of our work in Berlin or merely
expediency from the German point of view, I am unable to
say. At any rate, nothing was left undone that could have
been done by our Embassy on behalf of the suffering Belgians.

I now return to the submarine issue which, as I have said,
fell into temporary abeyance after the weathering of the political crisis in October. But it very soon cropped out again, for
in a few weeks we began to hear of merchant ships and liners
torpedoed with or without warning in all directions, their

crews forced to the boats and left adrift in stormy weather, occasionally, as in the case of the *Rowanmore,* being shelled — on October 26, 1916 — even after they had left their vessels. Loss of life naturally resulted, and several Americans were among those killed, especially on the *Marina.* The *Rowanmore* and *Marina* were the first and most serious cases to come to public attention, and they were soon followed by the equally serious case of the *Arabia,* a P. and O. liner in the Mediterranean. Within a period of a few weeks I presented ten separate notes to the German Foreign Office, based on instructions from Washington, requesting "an immediate investigation and report" in cases of sinking, by German submarines, of peaceable merchant vessels. These ten ships were the American ship *Lanao* — on October 28, 1916, the *Marina, Rowanmore, Arabia, Columbian* — on November 7, 1916, *Eagle Point* — on March 28, 1916, *Berwindvale* — on March 16, 1916, *Barbara* — on October 20, 1916, *Lokken* — on November 11, 1916, and *Strathtay* — September 6, 1916.

The record of my talk with Zimmermann regarding the *Rowanmore* and *Marina* cases is as follows. It was the first and only instance in which I saw Zimmermann lose his temper and become as angry as a petulant child; generally he is all smiles, polite and cordial; on this occasion he was quite the reverse.

Berlin, November 2, 1916

7 P.M.

Telephoned to the Foreign Office to ask if von Jagow would receive me, but was informed that he was absent. Accordingly saw Zimmermann and presented the two notes on the *Rowanmore* and *Marina* cases. I told him first that I had asked to see von Jagow, but that he was not there and that I must therefore trouble him, Zimmermann. As the reports on these two cases were of a very serious nature, involving the loss of lives of American citizens, I entered the room with a serious expression, which typified my own feelings under the circumstances. I said I feared I came with bad news and let him read the notes. After he had done so, I asked him if he had any information on either of

these cases, to which he replied in the negative. I then said that
while I supposed it would not be possible for the German Government to give an immediate reply to our inquiry, owing to
the absence of the submarines in question, I desired to urge that
the investigations be made and the results communicated to me
at the earliest possible moment. Zimmermann understood me to
say that I *did* suppose he could give me an immediate reply, and
he immediately lost his temper, banging his fist on the table and
exhibiting the utmost petulance and nervousness. He said, approximately, "Do you dare to come to me, Herr Grew, believing
these damnable Reuter reports which are aimed simply to stir
up trouble between our Governments, and to tell me that you
expect an immediate reply?" He continued to storm for some
moments while I remained silent, and when he had somewhat
calmed down, I told him that he had quite misunderstood me;
I had said I supposed it would *not* be possible for him to give
me an immediate reply until reports had been received from the
submarine commanders, but that I simply desired to urge all
possible haste in conducting the investigations. He then at once
broke into smiles and said he had been somewhat upset by my
"funereal face" when I came in. I told him that I also had been
upset by the seriousness of the reports, which I sincerely hoped
might prove to be untrue.

I indicated that I had resented Zimmermann's manner to
me by avoiding him for some time and by handing all of the
other submarine notes to Montgelas, who was after all directly
charged with the investigation of these cases. When next I
saw Zimmermann, he was more cordial than ever and apparently somewhat ashamed of his outburst. Montgelas subsequently told me that Zimmermann had been disturbed by
something else just before I saw him and that this accounted
for his state of mind. It is a fact, however, which I have observed in very many cases, that the average German official
will generally take refuge in anger when finding himself in a
weak position. I have frequently seen von Jagow angry; the
Chancellor indulged in a childish outburst of fury with Mr.
Gerard at General Headquarters last spring when discussing
the question of armed merchantmen; and there is the historic

case of Laughlin's interview with von Kiderlen-Waechter [German Foreign Secretary, 1910–12] regarding the lease of the Galapagos Islands to Germany, when the latter gave his hand away completely by breaking into anger at the crucial point of the discussion. Laughlin said: "I thank Your Excellency for having told me exactly what I wanted to know," and left the room.

The German Government replied in due course to our various notes about the torpedoings, giving denials here and excuses there, and they were simply placed on the ever-mounting dossier in Washington concerning our strained relations with Germany, until such time as the strain could endure no longer.

Before adverting once more to the question of peace, I will mention one or two of the other diplomatic cases with which we had to deal during the period that the Embassy was in my charge.[32]

ATTACKS ON GERARD

One development which caused me considerable concern during my chargéship was a well-marked propaganda against Mr. Gerard, with a view to having him recalled from the ambassadorship. He had a certain number of enemies in Berlin, chiefly hyphenates whom he had called down for criticizing the President or for anti-American utterances. Among these was the so-called League of Truth, which was organized and run by a German-American named William F. Marten.[33] Marten had published various attacks on the Ambassador and one day when the latter was out walking with Conger, he called at the offices of the League of Truth and told Marten that if he didn't stop his propaganda, he would burn down the building. Marten revenged himself by publishing an open letter attacking Mr. Gerard in virulent terms, which was cir-

[32] Nine typewritten pages of material covering the Embassy's handling of the affairs of foreign belligerents, the inspection of prison camps, and the administrative structure of the Embassy have been deleted, since the subjects have been covered in earlier chapters.

[33] See Gerard, *op. cit.*, pp. 311 ff., for further material on this.

culated shortly after he had gone to the United States. It was sent to all the foreign Embassies and Legations, members of the Reichstag and prominent German officials. I spoke to Zimmermann about it on October 21st and he said that he also had received a copy and had written to the League of Truth, expressing his profound indignation and condemnation, and that he would take steps to have the letter suppressed. He incidentally remarked smilingly that this was nothing to what Count Bernstorff had to go through in Washington.

Also when the Ambassador left for the United States, the press was full of rumors that he had been permanently recalled and that this was preparatory to a break of relations. I gave out an official statement to the press, which was published in Switzerland but barely noticed in the German press, to the effect that there was no political significance whatever in Mr. Gerard's departure. The Department approved this action.

At about this time, the letters of D. Thomas Curtin, a newspaper correspondent who had spent several months in Germany, began to appear in the London *Times*. His action in publishing in England information which he had obtained in Germany through the courtesy of the German Government was generally disapproved by his newspaper colleagues, who I believe refused to attend a luncheon given in his honor by the American Luncheon Club in London. The Germans were of course furious and all sorts of insinuations were made, and apparently given out from the Foreign Office, that Curtin had been officially introduced in Berlin by Mr. Gerard and that he had been able to pass from England to Germany at Lord Northcliffe's — owner of *The Times* — instigation through our Embassy in London having issued him a passport "irregularly" for that purpose. Insinuations were also circulated that Mr. Gerard had taken across the frontier, when he went on leave, a suitcase containing manuscripts written by Herbert Bayard Swope, of the New York *World,* while in Berlin. The German authorities knew of the existence of the suitcase and had telegraphed to the frontier officials at Warnemünde to stop it, but it was not found with Swope's baggage; hence sus-

picion fastened on Mr. Gerard, with whom Swope was traveling. I am not at all certain that Swope . . . did not manage on
his own initiative to get the suitcase conveniently mixed up
with the ambassadorial baggage when it crossed the frontier. . . .

At any rate, these rumors and insinuations, which I was able
to trace directly to the Press Bureau of the Foreign Office,
made me believe that there was a well-formed movement going
on with a view to discrediting Mr. Gerard and having him
recalled, and that unless this was nipped in the bud, serious
trouble might ensue. The expulsion of Boy-Ed and von Papen
from the United States still rankled in Germany and was probably the basis of this propaganda against the Ambassador. . . .[34]

Berlin, October 24, 1916

Called on Count Montgelas and told him I had heard that the
Press Bureau of the Foreign Office had given out to certain newspaper correspondents the fact that Curtin had been introduced
to Baron von Mumm, of the Press Bureau, by a card from Mr.
Gerard, and also that a rumor seemed to have emanated from
the Foreign Office to the effect that Curtin had been enabled
to come to Germany through our Embassy in London having
issued him a passport "irregularly" for that purpose. I spoke of
the impossibility of such a thing happening and described our
passport regulations, which forbade the issuance of passports
to enable a person to pass from one belligerent country to an
enemy country. These regulations must have been followed by
our Embassy in London.

Count Montgelas said that the only rumor he had heard was
to the effect that Walter Hines Page, being interested in *The
World's Work*, which Curtin represented, had probably influenced the State Department to give him a passport to come
to Germany when he had already been in England, although

---

[34] On December 1, 1915, Secretary Lansing had in conversation with Bernstorff asked for the recall of Captain Karl Boy-Ed, Naval Attaché, and Captain
Franz von Papen, Military Attaché, of the German Embassy. A former member
of the Austrian consular service had charged Boy-Ed and von Papen with being
the leaders in the United States of a ring of 3000 Teutonic spies. The Department of Justice felt it had conclusive, if less dramatic, evidence, to substantiate the claim that the two had been engaged in activities which involved
violations of American laws.

this was contrary to the Department's custom as he understood it. I said that this hypothesis was absurd and that the Department would use its own discretion in the issuance of passports, according to the regulations in force. I then went on to say that it seemed to me a great pity that the Press Bureau of the Foreign Office should give out material of this kind; that if these things were cabled to America and appeared in the American press, the Department of State could deal with them, but that it was my business to prevent their appearing here if possible, since such material in the press only served to cause further friction between the two countries through its influence on public opinion, and that the Foreign Office ought to see to it that all propaganda against the Ambassador was stopped.

Count Montgelas said he agreed with me and that he would speak to the Press Bureau and try to stop such material being given out. He also promised to take steps to prevent the publication in the German papers of Mr. Gerard's name in connection with Curtin.

He then went on to say that Zimmermann had spoken to him about my conversation regarding the open letter from the League of Truth attacking the President and Mr. Gerard and that steps had been taken to prevent its publication in Germany. Three or four papers had applied for permission to publish it, but had been refused. Zimmermann had also written a letter to a friend of Marten, the author of the letter, expressing his indignation and condemnation of it. As regards prosecution, the German Government could not prosecute Marten for his attack on the President, since Paragraph 103 of the Strafgesetzbuch applied only to attacks on "sovereigns"; but, according to Paragraph 104, they could prosecute him for his attack on the Ambassador if Mr. Gerard should apply for such prosecution within three months from the date of his learning of the "Beleidigung." I told Montgelas that I did not believe that Mr. Gerard would care to make such an application, but that I would submit the matter to him by letter.

To return to the Curtin matter, I referred to the fact that Curtin had come to Germany highly recommended by Prof. Hugo Münsterberg [Professor of Psychology at Harvard] and that in any case Mr. Gerard could hardly be held responsible for Curtin's actions simply because he had given him a personal card of introduction to Baron von Mumm. This was something which every well-known correspondent would expect of his Embassy as a matter of routine. Count Montgelas said that Dr. Charles Drechsler, of the Amerika Institut, to whom Curtin had come from Prof. Münsterberg, was of the opinion that Curtin's arrangement with Lord Northcliffe was made after his visit to Germany and not before, and that his statement in the London *Times* that he had come here purposely to write for the English papers was fabricated for the purpose of making a good story.

Count Montgelas further said that a press despatch had today been received from a Dutch paper — and suppressed in Germany — to the effect that Curtin had stated at a meeting of the American Luncheon Club in London that Mr. Gerard was a spy and also that the United States would long ago have come in on the side of the Entente if our Government had not been afraid of an uprising of the German element in America.

Count Montgelas then turned the subject to the *Lusitania* case and said that the Chancellor had received two telegrams from the New York *Sun,* the first asking for the text of the German *Lusitania* note of February 16, 1916, which our Government had never published, and the second inquiring whether the German Government regarded the case as settled by that note. As the Foreign Office understood from Count Bernstorff that the Government of the United States did not consider it desirable to publish the note at this particular time, and as he, Count Montgelas, believed that the aim of the *Sun* was simply to make political capital and to embarrass the Administration, no replies had been sent to these telegrams. I expressed my appreciation of this attitude of the Foreign Office. (This expression of appreciation was subsequently confirmed by the Department.)

Count Montgelas then asked me whether I had heard if the *Lusitania* negotiations had been reopened between Count Bernstorff and the Department, to which I replied in the negative.

I inquired whether anything was known at the Foreign Office regarding the reported sinking of the Cunard liner *Alaunia* [on October 19, 1916] with 183 passengers on board, but he said he had no information on the subject.

As a result of these representations, nothing further to the detriment of the Ambassador appeared in the German press.

I have the following further record of a visit to the Foreign Office not long before Mr. Gerard's return to Berlin after his leave of absence:

Berlin, December 11, 1916

. . . Zimmermann spoke pleasantly of the Ambassador's return and said that he and Mr. Gerard were intimate friends and understood each other perfectly, and that it was only necessary to speak out clearly in order to avoid misunderstandings. He wished, however, that the Ambassador would not lose his temper in discussions as it sometimes made negotiation difficult. He also alluded pleasantly to a report in the French press that Mr. Gerard was bringing with him large quantities of food, whereas Mrs. Sharp, wife of the American Ambassador to France, on her return from America, had brought nothing but flowers.

He said he hoped to attend the dinner of the Association of Commerce and Trade on December 27th to meet the Ambassador, but could not say definitely as he might have to go to a wedding.

Said also that he had spoken to Ludendorff at General Headquarters about getting Steinbach, the Ambassador's butler, freed from military service, and that Ludendorff had agreed with him that such exceptions ought to be made, but that it was the Kriegsministerium that made the difficulties. I said I hoped that Steinbach could be here before the Ambassador's and Mrs. Gerard's return.

Peace Talks

I now return to the development of the peace issue. . . . A few days after my confidential conversations with the Chancellor on this subject, we learned that the Reichstag had suddenly been called to convene on December 12th. The wildest rumors were circulating as to the purpose of the meeting: some said that the ruthless submarine warfare was about to be declared, others that a new Balkan kingdom was to be established, and still others that definite terms of peace were to be announced. It was impossible to sift the well-founded rumors from mere gossip and I telegraphed the Department with considerable reserve. The Chancellor and Zimmermann had just been to General Headquarters with the Emperor and von Hindenburg. Even on the 11th, nobody seemed to know what was going to happen and even the confidential lines which I had out failed me, although they had fathomed the secrets of secret committee meetings before. Generally, in fact, my "secret service" had beaten the Germans at their own game. In this case, the Reichstag itself did not seem to know what was coming.

On the evening of the 11th I received an "Einladung" to call on the Chancellor the following morning at 11.30. He received the Spanish Ambassador at 11, the Swiss Minister at 11.15 and myself at 11.30. None of us had any idea what was going to happen. The Spanish Ambassador, Polo de Bernabé, who was a warm friend of mine, called on me afterwards and told me that he had been equally in the dark and that when invited to the Chancellor, he had thought it not unlikely that the latter was about to announce a resumption of the ruthless submarine warfare. The very first intimation I had of a definite nature was when the Swiss Minister, Claparède, met me as he came out from the Chancellor's study just as I was going in, and whispered in my ear, "Friedensantrag" — peace offer.

I was admitted at once, the Chancellor seated me with him at a small table in the corner of his room and immediately proceeded to read to me his note asking the Government of the United States to convey to the Governments of Great Britain, France, Russia, Serbia, Japan and Rumania (where we were charged with the protection of German interests) the first formal offer of peace since the beginning of the war. Spain was asked to do the same to Belgium and Portugal, and Switzerland to Italy. Then the Chancellor read me a supplementary memorandum for the President, owing to the latter's previous offer of intercession. (I have not this with me, but its text is on file in the Department, as cabled by the Embassy.) [35]

I immediately returned to the Embassy and left the note to be translated into English and encoded for telegraphing. The

[35] *Foreign Relations, 1916, Supplement,* p. 87.

note was accompanied by an official French translation. The English translation of the note, the official French translation (en claire), the Chancellor's supplementary memorandum, an account of the proceedings in the Reichstag, the press comments on the note, and two messages reporting conversations with the Spanish Ambassador and the Danish Minister [Count Carl Moltke], which I shall shortly describe, were all cabled to Washington within 24 hours, the English translation being sent to the telegraph office at about 6 P.M. The next day I received a telegram from the Department saying: "Press reports German peace note; cannot you hasten its transmission by cable? Vienna already reported receipt of note." I wonder if the Department thought I was going to send it by mail! What actually happened was that the press in the United States received it by wireless two days before our telegrams, relayed at Copenhagen, could reach Washington. It was not strictly true that Vienna had reported the receipt of the note first, as I later verified from the files of the Embassy in Vienna. Baron Stephen Burian, the Minister for Foreign Affairs, had received Mr. Penfield on the 11th and had told him in confidence what was going to happen, but my text reached Washington before Vienna's did, and Sofia's and Constantinople's straggled in some days later. The telegram from Berlin reached Washington on the night of the 13th.

After leaving the note at the Embassy to be translated, I went with Alice to the Reichstag, which was to assemble at about 1 o'clock. It was a great scene. The diplomatic box, as well as the galleries and every other spot in the Reichstag, was packed, so that I could with difficulty find standing room. The bells rang at 1.45, the Chancellor immediately entered and, surrounded by all the Ministers, began without a single word of prelude to read his speech.[36] There was no great enthusiasm called forth by the speech, which was quietly delivered, although his remarks were frequently punctuated by "Bravos" from the floor of the house. When it was ended, the leaders of the Central, Conservative and Socialist parties spoke, but at no

[36] For the Chancellor's speech see *ibid.*, pp. 87–89.

great length. The representative of the Party of the Center moved to adjourn, leaving it to the discretion of the President to fix the day of the next meeting. Herr Ernst Bassermann of the National Liberal Party took the position that a measure of such moment as the peace proposal required dignified discussion by the Reichstag and moved that such discussion be entered upon immediately. Count Westarp, of the Conservatives, and Ledebour, of the Socialist Labor Wing supported Bassermann's motion for open discussion by the Reichstag. Upon vote being taken, the motion to adjourn was passed by a large majority.

In the afternoon, the Spanish Ambassador called on me and said he had been taken completely by surprise by the peace note. When summoned to the Chancellor he had expected a declaration of ruthless submarine warfare and he felt that if the peace proposals failed, as they probably would, the submarine warfare would then commence without restriction. On the following day Count Moltke came to see me and said approximately the same. His remark on leaving was: "If these peace proposals fail, we shall have to look out for our ships."

During the next week Berlin was all agog as to the way in which the Allies would take the peace note. There was little optimism to be found: a few people hoped against hope that some arrangement would be forthcoming as a result of the German initiative, but the majority shook their heads mournfully. I had one talk with Zimmermann, on the 19th, in which he said that the peace terms of the Central Powers would be reasonable — far more reasonable, he said, than would satisfy the German people — but Germany could not divulge her terms at once, first on account of the demoralizing effect which this would have on the troops in the trenches and the people at large, who would believe that there was no further purpose in fighting, and second because one party to a negotiation could not give its hand away at the start.

Then, on December 21st, came the President's peace note of the 18th.[37] Ambassador Gerard had reached Copenhagen on

[37] *Ibid.,* pp. 97–99.

his return from America and, in the ordinary course of events, would have arrived in Berlin on the 20th in time to deliver the note himself over his own signature. But the German Minister in Copenhagen [Count Ulrich Brockdorff-Rantzau] invited him to lunch and he waited over one day. The telegram containing the note arrived on the morning of the 21st; I had it decoded and typewritten immediately, and read it to Zimmermann at about 5 P.M., just four hours before Mr. Gerard's arrival. Incidentally I may remark that the next morning, the Ambassador cross-questioned me as to the exact hour of the arrival and presentation of the note, evidently annoyed that he had not been able to present it himself, but I had signed it before he ever crossed the frontier and had been entirely correct in my procedure, so he could say nothing.

The form in which to present it was a good deal of a puzzle. The instruction from the President simply said: "You will read the foregoing to the Minister for Foreign Affairs and leave with him a copy of this *paper*." Technically it should have been an *aide-mémoire,* the form ordinarily used when a communication has been made verbally and the writing is merely to confirm the conversation. But it seemed too important a document for an ordinary *aide-mémoire* and my personal inclination was to make it a signed *Note.* So I put it in that form, beginning "Your Excellency," and signed it as Chargé d'Affaires. I seem to have been the only one to do this: Mr. Page in London, doubtless influenced by the precise Laughlin, labeled his written communication quite simply "Paper" and left it unsigned. Mr. Penfield in Vienna likewise presented an unsigned *aide-mémoire,* and I believe Paris did the same. I was somewhat pleased, on coming to Vienna, to find that Mr. Penfield, that long-trained diplomatist, was disappointed that he too had not delivered a signed Note, having been influenced to the contrary by his Second Secretary, Rutherfurd Bingham. This no doubt seems like making a mountain out of a molehill, but as a matter of fact the Germans regarded the signing of such a note as of considerable importance, as the following incident shows, though I relate it as an amusing anecdote

rather than as a weighty matter. A day or two after my chargéship was over, a prominent German called on me and said he
had been entrusted by a high official of the German Government to say that the Government regretted it could not, owing
to the regulations of the American Diplomatic Service, give me
a decoration for the part I had been permitted to play in the
peace overtures, but that they felt that the highest decoration
that could be conferred was the honor of signing this note, and
that this honor had devolved upon me instead of the Ambassador through the German Minister at Copenhagen having
invited Mr. Gerard to luncheon in Copenhagen on the 20th!
Rather farfetched, but I accepted the compliment with full appreciation.

To return to the delivery of the note. I presented the matter
to Zimmermann with the utmost earnestness, as directed, and
clearly conveyed the impression that it would be very hard for
the Government of the United States to understand a negative
reply. Zimmermann listened to the reading of the communication, a copy of which I left with him, with earnest attention
and expressed great satisfaction at and appreciation of the
President's "wise and high-minded action." He said he would
have to discuss the matter with the Emperor and the Chancellor before replying and that in any case he did not think an
answer could be given or action taken until the Entente Powers
had replied to the Chancellor's note of December 12th. He
said he felt quite sure that Germany's peace terms would be
more moderate than those of the Entente, but repeated that
Germany could not be the first to divulge her terms. I remarked that if Germany could not be the first to divulge her
terms, and if, as was probable, the Entente Powers would be
similarly reticent, the process of elimination would leave a
mutual and simultaneous statement of terms as the only alternative, and I asked him if he would not authorize me to cable
to Washington that such a proposition would be satisfactory to
Germany. Zimmermann seemed pleased at the idea and the
formula, thought for several minutes and then said that such a
proposition might be considered, but that he must first discuss

it with the Chancellor. In referring to the note, he said that the word "soundings" struck him as peculiarly appropriate and he believed that in any case the action of the President was a step nearer towards peace and that favorable results might possibly be expected.[38]

I had some further conversation with Zimmermann before taking leave of him as Chargé d'Affaires. He said that we must all work for peace. . . .

In summing up the situation in my report to the Department, I stated that in my opinion this peace propaganda was a direct outcome of the food situation in Germany, which was steadily becoming more difficult. The German masses were suffering from undernourishment, which was already affecting adults, but particularly young children, and there would probably be several months to come before the next crop was ripe, when the supply of food available for rationing human beings and animals would be sensibly less than at present. If it became necessary to go through this period in a state of war, it might be expected that it could be done, but with great and widespread hardship. The fighting could then be prolonged for a considerable period, but under these circumstances, even if victorious in a military sense, Germany would probably be so far exhausted as to render a victory barren of results. It was, therefore, necessary for Germany to make sacrifices at the present time in order to try to secure a peace. The attempts to detach Russia from the Alliance having proved abortive, the sacrifices to be offered appeared at present to be directed towards France and England.

As a basis for discussion, I said that something of the following nature was talked about among well-informed Germans: Belgium and Northern France to be given up; France to be compensated with a part of Alsace and Lorraine; England to be compensated with certain colonial possessions. On the other hand, Germany to be allowed to follow her development of the Bagdad road and Mesopotamia; to have an influential position in the Balkans; and the independent kingdom of Poland to be

[38] *Ibid.*, pp. 110–11.

continued as a buffer state. It is significant that in 1915 it would not have been possible to find a German voice to speak of the ceding of a square foot of Alsace-Lorraine.

I continued:

The morale of the masses is low. The successes in Rumania and the peace propaganda have given them new spirit for the moment and the Chancellor's action on December 12th was received with unconcealed joy. But this frame of mind cannot be expected to last if the peace offer fails.

The year 1916 has seen a definite step in the growth of liberal ideas in Germany. The ideas so freely expressed by the ruling classes at the beginning of the war and throughout 1915, that Germany by virtue of her leadership in the arts of civilization and the moral superiority of her people must spread her power and methods throughout the world, are now generally relegated to obscurity.

Nevertheless the full regeneration of the country can only come from within. When it is brought home to the people that the building up of vast armaments for conquest and expansion and the fostering of that spirit of force which is militarism has led them to failure and suffering, the time will be ripe for new forms of government in Germany and for a stable condition in Europe.

It would appear from the statements made in the countries at war with Germany that they recognize this condition and are not prepared to accept terms unless they impose upon Germany definite losses and hardships which will bring home to her people the futility of future wars of expansion.[39]

The Ambassador returned at 10 P.M. on the 21st of December. He was most agreeable, but I very soon gathered that he had no confidential information from the Administration whatsoever. The President had apparently told him only two things: first, that he must be friendly and "jolly the Germans"; second, that he must support the President's view that armed merchant ships must not be fired on without warning. When he said that he would do so, the President banged his fist

[39] *Ibid.*, pp. 129–38.

on the desk and said: "I don't want you merely to support my view; I want you to *agree* with it." The Ambassador was very pessimistic as regards the outlook for the Diplomatic Service. He said that there would be few changes in missions during the coming Administration and that those would be filled by deserving Democrats and that I must "pull the wires" if I wished to get on. He hinted that I was regarded as a Republican in Washington.

There was not much diplomatic excitement during the next few weeks. The various peace notes and their answers filled the public mind. . . . The peace proposals fizzled out.

XIII

The Final Break
JANUARY – APRIL, 1917

Early in December, 1916, President Wilson decided to move for peace independently of the belligerent powers. The peace note was submitted to Secretary of State Lansing on December 9 or 10. After Lansing had approved it, the President delayed sending it to the warring powers. The German peace move on December 12, then, placed Wilson in an embarrassing position. He feared that his own move would appear to be in collaboration with the Germans. On the other hand to delay his note might mean missing an opportunity to stop hostilities. Mr. Grew had advised Washington on December 13, that rejection of the German offer would probably be followed by unrestricted submarine warfare. On December 18, Wilson issued his note asking for a statement of views as to "the terms upon which the war might be concluded and the arrangements which would be deemed satisfactory as a guaranty against its renewal." He added that the "objects which the statesmen . . . on both sides have in mind in this war are virtually the same, as stated in general terms to their own people and to the world." After listing what these objects were, he said that he was not offering mediation or proposing peace, but "merely proposing that soundings be taken in order that we may learn, the neutral nations with the belligerent, how near the haven of peace may be."

The answers to Wilson's note were unsatisfactory. Germany, on December 26, reiterated its suggestion of a peace conference but refused to state terms. Germany's allies sent the same type of reply. The answer of the Allies to the German offer of December 12 was sent to Wilson on December 29. It declared that the German proposal was insincere and that no peace was possible "as long as the reparation of violated rights and liberties, the acknowledgment of the principle of nationalities and of the free existence of small states shall not be assured," and as long as there was no assurance of a suppression of German militarism. Not until January 11, 1917, did the Allied reply to Wilson's note of December 18 reach Washington. It restated the Allied indictment of the Central Powers for beginning the war and set forth their terms which included the restoration of Belgium, Serbia, and Montenegro, with indemnity; the evacuation of the invaded parts of France, Russia, and Rumania, with reparation; the expulsion of Turkey from Europe; and, the liberation of Italians, Slavs, Rumanians, and Czecho-Slovaks from foreign domination.

Meanwhile Wilson had prepared a major speech to Congress designed to reach the people of Europe and evoke a peace demand which the belligerents could not resist. On January 22, President Wilson delivered his speech to the Senate suggesting a League of Nations and warning the belligerents that only a "peace without victory" could last.

By this time, however, Germany had decided to revert to unrestricted submarine warfare. On January 16, Bernstorff was informed that the decision had been made and unrestricted submarine warfare would start on February 1.

As indicated in the preceding chapter, this account was written by Mr. Grew on board ship to the United States after the break of relations.

. . . We learned that the Chancellor and Zimmermann had gone to meet the Emperor at General Headquarters and we knew that something was brewing. On pouch day, January 30th, the Ambassador had a talk with Zimmermann and on returning to the chancery he advised us to take out of the pouch any confidential letters we might have written as our bags would probably never get through, for Germany was about to declare for unrestricted submarine warfare.[1] We did not know

[1] U.S. Department of State, *Papers Relating to the Foreign Relations of the*

then just how radical the declaration was to be. But the next day, January 31st, Zimmermann sent for the Ambassador at 6 o'clock and handed him the German memorandum, prescribing a "Sperrgebiet" around England and in the Mediterranean and announcing that all ships entering it would be torpedoed without warning, with certain exceptions for the American Line and an extension of time for ships that were then in British ports. This was to begin the next day, on February 1st.

After our telegram reached Washington we had but one telegram, saying that the Department realized our difficult position and would inform us at the earliest possible moment as to the decision of the Administration, which would be taken shortly. On Sunday, February 4th, about 10 A.M. von Nimptsch [German banker] telephoned me that Herbert Gutmann, of the Dresdner Bank, had a report that diplomatic relations had been broken. Soon other telephone messages arrived, and at noon the *B.Z. am Mittag* announced in large headlines that diplomatic relations between the United States and Germany had been broken. The excitement in the Embassy was of course tremendous; we were of course all gathered there and people and telephone calls kept coming in every few moments. We lunched at the Embassy with Fanny Montgelas [American-born wife of Count Adolf Montgelas] and von Bülow of the Foreign Office, Ellis Dresel [Special Assistant in charge of the Embassy's British Civilian Bureau] and Lithgow Osborne [Third Secretary]. Fanny broke down and wept in the middle of lunch and it was rather a sorrowful affair, although the Ambassador joked as usual.

That evening we dined at the Alexander Kirks' [Second Secretary of the American Embassy at Berlin] with Baby Friedlaender [Mrs. Friedlaender-Fuld-Mitford] and after dinner a telephone message from the Embassy announced that a cipher telegram had come, so I hurried down there. It was the

United States, 1917, Supplement 1, The World War (Washington: Government Printing Office, 1931), p. 97. Hereinafter cited as *Foreign Relations, 1917, Supplement 1.*

last telegram we received from Washington, as our telegrams were stopped by the Germans from then on, and it announced the break of relations and instructed Mr. Gerard to ask for his passports. The telegram simply quoted President Wilson's address to the Senate.[2]

We did not leave Berlin until the following Saturday, February 10th, and that week was a hectic one, packing and winding up our affairs. On Tuesday the Embassy telephone was cut off, and as this was a usual channel of business, we were thus greatly handicapped. When the Foreign Office found that it could not talk with us over the telephone (Montgelas and I had been continually calling each other up on Monday and thus transacting urgent business without delay), it was very angry with the military or police authorities who had cut us off and its protest resulted in the telephone being restored to us a day or two before our departure, but too late to be of much use. All our telegrams from Washington were held up and never delivered and local telegrams from our consuls and others were delivered in bunches after they had accumulated for two or three days. No letters at all were delivered to us. Thus we were almost completely cut off from the outside world. Our outgoing telegrams had to be submitted to the Foreign Office for censorship and could not be in cipher and only some of them were passed. Three or four very urgent and important telegraphic circulars to our consuls throughout Germany, instructing them what to do, were held up and only some of them were finally forwarded to some of the consuls. Thus many of our consuls were kept completely in the dark, being able neither to telegraph nor telephone to us, and few of them knew what to do with their archives, offices, seals, etc., or whom to hand them over to. The Spanish Embassy, to whom we were entrusting our affairs, had Spanish consuls only in certain places and much confusion thus resulted. As to their departure from Germany, what actually happened was this: those who came to Berlin before our departure came with us

2 President Wilson's address announcing the breaking of diplomatic relations was given on February 3, 1917.

and the others later assembled in Munich and left for Switzerland on a special train, except those who had been assigned to Holland or Denmark or the Scandinavian countries. The only ones who left with us were Henry von Struve from Erfurt, Harry Seltzer from Breslau and one or two vice consuls.

All the work of arranging for our departure and that of the consuls devolved upon one person in the Embassy and that was Fräulein Frentzel, a young German woman who had formerly been Winslow's stenographer and had later, on his departure on vacation, taken full charge of our so-called Commercial Bureau, which included all arrangements for our diplomatic couriers, etc. She came up to the scratch beautifully and worked until she was practically a wreck, acting as our go-between with the Foreign Office and getting everybody's papers in order for departure. As our list had to be altered a dozen times a day, it was nervous work for her.

My wish was to get every American citizen who had any possible claim to special recognition on our special train, as there was no telling when the others would be allowed to depart. Our treaty of 1798 with Prussia provided that the citizens of each country would, in case of war, be permitted to remain for nine months in the country of their residence and then to leave with all their goods, but when it came to the question of confirming this treaty, the Foreign Office tried to add a clause providing that the ships of each nation would be free to leave the other country whenever they pleased, but must not be forced to leave.[3] As Germany had some 400,000 tons of shipping in our ports and we not a single ship in a German port, this clause was somewhat one-sided, and the Ambassador naturally refused to have anything to do with it. He even refused to cable the German proposal to Washington, saying that he

[3] The Treaty of Amity and Commerce, negotiated with Prussia on July 11, 1799, by John Quincy Adams, provided in Article XXIII that "merchants" of either country would in event of war between the two countries be given nine months to collect their debts and settle affairs and then would be allowed to depart freely with their goods. Hunter Miller (ed.), *Treaties and Other International Acts of the United States of America* (Washington: Government Printing Office, 1931), II. 450.

would communicate with our Government on the subject only from Switzerland after we had been released.[4] We thought then that they were holding us in order to force Gerard to sign this protocol, but I think they only wanted to be treated properly; the German is suspicious by nature and they were not going to give us the benefit of any doubt. The German watchword is "reciprocity" — but the other nation must always do the good act first.

To return to the making up of the list for the special train. First of all, of course, was our official staff and servants. Second, our American clerks — at least those who wanted to go. Several were remaining at my suggestion, to carry on the work under the supervision of the Dutch Legation for British interests and the Spanish Embassy for all the others, namely American, Rumanian, Serbian and Japanese. Miss Frances Mackintosh [clerk] remained in the British bureau, Miss Schneider in the passport bureau, Miss Sadie Walker in the file room, etc. After the official and unofficial staff came the newspaper correspondents: Carl Ackermann of the United Press, Philip M. Powers and William Dreher of the Associated Press, Oscar King Davis of the *New York Times*, Raymond Swing of the *Chicago Daily News*, with their respective families. Then came C. L. Marcus of the Hebrew Sheltering and Immigrant Aid Society; Reginald Foster, of the Rockefeller Foundation; an American Red Cross doctor or two; the consular officers who were ready to go, and Hartwig Devison and his wife, treasurer of the American Benevolent Association. I also persuaded the Ambassador to include two American dentists, Dr. Abbott and his wife (she a daughter of Richard Olney — Secretary of State, 1895–97), and Dr. and Mrs. Elliot, the latter wishing to get home quickly to see her sick father, simply because they were the first and only ones who asked me to try to include them. I never in my life have seen such gratitude as they expressed. . . .

On Saturday the 10th I went to the Foreign Office to say good-bye personally to the people I had known well there. I

[4] *Foreign Relations, 1917, Supplement,* pp. 588–91.

had previously asked Montgelas if he thought it advisable and he answered that he himself would always be glad to see me, but that he could not answer for the others. However, I decided to do it even at the risk of rebuffs. Fortunately there were no rebuffs. Of the eight men I saw, seven were warmly cordial and the eighth was merely tactless, insisting on showing me where we were wrong and Germany right. I said that whatever happened, my personal feeling for my friends in Germany would not change towards them individually; he immediately interposed an expression of doubt as to his side of this and said that if certain things happened he could not be sure of his personal feelings even towards individuals. He then launched into a long political tirade, to which I listened without putting in a word — as it was not the place or time to argue, either for him or me — and then quietly withdrew, with little of the personal feeling, which I had long had for him, left. This man was Geheimer Legationsrat Schüler, and the others were Zimmermann, Stumm, Baron Bussche-Haddenhausen, Montgelas, Zahn, Dr. Friedrich von Keller and Prittwitz. Stumm, Under Secretary of State, was more cordial and expansive than I had ever seen him in my life; Bussche equally so, and the others no less cordial, and regretful at our departure. Zimmermann talked to me for a long time; he went into the whole subject of the submarine warfare and said that Germany actually could not avoid the step, but his tone was rather explanatory than ranting. Finally he said good-bye in the warmest way possible. The duty of a diplomat is to cultivate friendly relations with the officials and people of the country to which he is accredited; I had cultivated those personal relations and could not suddenly break them, in the case of individuals, whatever political events had intervened.[5] Zimmermann has always shown himself friendly, and whether, as some say, he wanted the unrestricted submarine warfare, or not, I am convinced that he was profoundly sorry to break with the United States. I am also convinced that our action came as a surprise to him and to many other Germans, who thought that we would swallow the

[5] After all, we were not yet enemies. — J. C. G.

pill without a word, or at least with a note or two, as we had
done before. Z. told the Amb. that they had been forced to the
step as Germany could not last a year on her present food
supply.

The last day was a very hectic one, with so many final affairs
to wind up. I sealed up our old archives with Gil Delgado
[Minister Resident] of the Spanish Embassy; our current
archives we were to leave open, under the charge of Mrs.
Michaelis and her staff, so that the Spanish Embassy and the
Dutch Legation, who were going to keep our chancery open,
could carry on the work with greater facility, with previous
correspondence to refer to. All our cipher codes and every
original cipher telegram received or sent since the beginning of
the war were carted to the cellar and burned in the furnace, as
well as all confidential documents and correspondence; it was
a great scene — Wilson, Gherardi and several other secretaries
stoking the furnace like firemen with the papers upon which we
had labored so hard during the last two and a half years. The
Ambassador was convinced that sooner or later the Germans
would break into the safe and he didn't want anything of a
confidential nature to fall into their hands.

On the last day, all the clerks and stenographers gave me a
silk pocketbook with a pleasantly worded "testimonial" signed
by all. I imagine I could get another job on the strength of
that alone! Some of them wept and all were moved at saying
good-bye. I took my last look at the old chancery at about six
o'clock, dined at the Esplanade with Dresel and Foster, and
went to the Anhalter Bahnhof soon after seven to superintend
the arrangements in the train, which left at 8.10. There was a
large crowd down to see us off and the station platform was so
packed that it was difficult to find the various people who were
going with us and show them their places. Some did not know
until the last moment if they could join us, but fortunately I
was able to find places for everyone to whom I had held out
any hope. Among those who came to see us off were Montgelas,
Polo de Bernabé, the Landechos, Alfred Horstmann of the German Foreign Office, Prittwitz, Bülow, Bernardo Rolland,

Third Secretary of the Spanish Embassy, Alfonso Fiscowich, Second Secretary of the Spanish Embassy, Gil Delgado, Carlos Arcos, Attaché of the Spanish Embassy, the Gevers, etc. Two German officers, Baron Wernher Ow-Wachendorf from the Foreign Office and another man, Major von der Hagen from the General Staff, accompanied us on the special train. There was one saloon car, containing the Gerards, the Jacksons and ourselves, two sleepers and two day coaches, besides two large baggage vans for as many trunks as we wanted to take. The Gerards alone had 65. Also a dining car. There were 120 persons in our suite.

We reached Gottmadingen at about 4.30 the following afternoon, the German frontier, and there the two German officers who had accompanied us said good-bye and left. They had been most courteous and friendly throughout. I had supposed that there would be at least some sort of formalities at the German frontier — examination of passports, etc. — and our surprise was great when a few minutes later we pulled up in another station and found ourselves in Schaffhausen, with a guard of Swiss soldiers drawn up at the salute. . . . Otherwise there was no indication that we had left Germany and were now on neutral soil. Some wine was opened in the saloon car and healths were duly exchanged with the Swiss officers.

A few minutes later we passed the Falls of the Rhine, which I had last seen in 1887, just 30 years ago, and at about 6 arrived in Zurich. Here we changed trains and came to Berne at about 9.30 that night. . . .

The following morning, February 12th, I went early to the Legation, which was as busy as a beehive with the new arrivals, and found a telegram saying: "Grew may be assigned to Vienna temporarily; await instructions; Lansing." For a moment this was a tremendous shock, as we had been looking forward so long to returning to the children.[6] I told Mr. Gerard and he said he wanted me to come at least to Paris with them in order to help with the special train. He said he thought that a break with Austria was a question of hours and that I would surely in

<hr>

[6] Mr. and Mrs. Grew had left their children in the United States in 1914.

the end sail with them from Spain. All that day I was very busy arranging for the assortment of our baggage; we had been the guests of the German Government as far as the German frontier, even including our baggage and the champagne consumed on the train (thorough hospitality, that),[7] but the baggage had to be paid for from the Swiss frontier to Berne, and it was a tremendous job getting it sorted and paid for by each owner. In the evening there was a very hot and dull soirée at our Legation. Alice was tired and stayed in bed, I having dined with her in our room.

The following day, February 13th, I had a mass of work to attend to at the Legation, sending various telegrams to arrange for the steamship passages of the Ambassador and staff, etc. In the afternoon Pleasant Stovall [American Minister to Switzerland] took the Ambassador and myself to call on the President of the Confederation, Edmund Schulthess, and Arthur Hoffmann, Chief of the Political Department. The President talked for an hour about Swiss affairs, which was intensely interesting. He went into the question of their water power — "la houille blanche" — in detail, and also into the question of defense in case of war. In the case of war with Germany, he said, the Swiss troops would immediately have to give up a considerable portion of territory, as the country around Basel had no defenses. The conversation in both cases was entirely in French and poor Mr. Stovall, our Minister, had to preserve unbroken silence as he spoke not a word of that language. . . .

That evening — February 14th — we left for Paris, a large crowd being at the station to see us off, including all the Ministers whom we had met in Berne and many others. Left

---

[7] Later in the year when I was directing the Western European Division in the Department of State, the Swiss Chargé d'Affaires, representing German interests in the United States, came to me with his customary long list of problems. When he came to the end of the list he said that there was one more problem which he did not propose to present. I asked him what it was. He said it was a bill from the German Government, and he asked if I remembered our railroad journey from Berlin to the Swiss frontier at the time of the break. I said: "Don't tell me that the bill is itemized." He replied: "Yes, it is itemized down to the last bottle of beer." The bill was never paid. — J. C. G.

Berne at 7.30 and arrived at Pontarlier, the French frontier, at
about 9.30. . . .

We were informed that we should have a special train to
Paris, with two sleepers and two day coaches. The porters of
the two sleepers came up, both very intoxicated, to obtain a
list of names for their respective cars, and while the rest of the
party dined in the station restaurant, I found a seat apart at
one of the tables and proceeded to apportion the Embassy staff
and their families to the various berths, 16 in each car. We
then had our passports stamped and attended to the passing of
our luggage, which was attended with considerable confusion.

It was decided that our official and unofficial staff should go
by the special train, and that the other Americans who were accompanying us would follow on another train immediately the
same night. . . .

*The American group reached Paris on February 15, and the
next morning Mr. Grew received instructions to proceed to
Vienna at once to serve under Ambassador Frederic C. Penfield. Mr. Penfield had held diplomatic posts under Cleveland
as Vice Consul General at London and Diplomatic Agent and
Consul General in Egypt, and had written articles on economic
and political subjects.*

*The German newspapers announced Mr. Grew's appoint-
ment with the comment that he was a brother-in-law of
J. Pierpont Morgan. Mr. Grew actually was Mr. Morgan's
cousin by marriage. The German papers described Mr.
Morgan as the furnisher of arms and ammunition to the Allies
and said that it was evident that President Wilson was trans-
ferring his "nest of spies" from Berlin to Vienna. Mr. Grew
soon received a postcard from "an ex-American" living in
Germany, which stated:*

> Hello Mr. Grew
> Now Vienna's in view
> Be sure they don't want there such fellows
> They'll soon kick you out
> They'll put you to rout
> And for chance you adorn there the gallows.

A Morgan paid spy
of Entente the Ally
To appoint as a Sec. to the U.S.
Sheer imprudence mean
Of that hypocrite dean
Who neutrality daily abuses.

Well times will appear
When open and clear
Truth verily rules as the victors
When Wilson & Co.
In opinion sink low
And the peoples act as their lictors.

Such men as you,
Joseph C. Grew
Are thrown into Dante's damnation
Hot tar be your fate
With Morgan your mate
And never to hope for salvation.

Git up and git
Spare us your wit
We despise your dirty profession
Return to the slum
Wherefrom you come
Thus, Germany shows her Depression!

*On March 16 Mr. Grew wrote the following letter to his
mother about conditions in Vienna:*

... The atmosphere here is quite different from Berlin. The
Austrians don't know how to hate anybody. Count Czernin,
the Minister for Foreign Affairs, told me himself the other day
that there was no real hard feeling between the Austrians and
the English or the Austrians and the Russians. They come as
near hating the Italians as anybody, because they consider that
they acted treacherously.[8] As far as we are concerned, every-

8 Italy, which had been linked with Germany and Austria since 1882 in the
Triple Alliance, refused to join the other two powers in war, declaring its
neutrality on August 3, 1914. On May 24, 1915, Italy entered the war on the

body is delightful, cordial and our old friends gave us a very warm welcome. The papers had my return to Vienna in headlines! We discuss the political situation quite openly with the Austrians, which we never for a moment dared to do with any German; they always express the hope that we are going to stay, but shake their heads doubtfully.

There has been some important diplomatic work going on and the Ambassador has taken me to his conferences with Count Czernin, which have been intensely interesting. In fact, in arranging for the last conference, Count Czernin sent word that he particularly wanted me to be present, which was very gratifying. It appears that I somehow managed to establish a diplomatic reputation while in charge in Berlin, but heaven knows how. Even that conservative sheet the Paris *Temps* recently referred to your son as a diplomat "de haute valeur"! You mustn't tell people this; I am positively ashamed to repeat it even to you.

At Countess Czernin's diplomatic reception the other day, Alice and I went punctually at 5, hoping to avoid the German Embassy, as the reception was from 5 till 7 — but as luck would have it, the whole crowd trouped in five minutes after our arrival, Ambassador, Ambassadress and staff. Countess Czernin was very tactful and led them to another corner of the room from where we were sitting, so we only had to bow formally from a distance. The whole situation is ridiculously funny to me, for the Ambassador, Botho Wedel, is an old friend of ours, as are also Prince Wilhelm Stolberg, the Counselor, and his wife, and young Count Albrecht Bernstorff — and Philip Hoffman, of the Bavarian Legation, is one of our really intimate friends. We grin at each other whenever we meet. Walter Mumm, a German officer, comes up to our room every few days. But in official society, etiquette forbids anything but the most formal and distant bows. If we go to war with Germany, even these bows will have to be dispensed with. One may despise and detest a nation as a whole, but why should one's

side of the Allies. One of the most important considerations leading to this decision for war on the Allied side was Italy's desire to profit at Austrian expense.

feeling towards personal friends alter? There has been far too much personal hatred in this war, often directed against old friends who had nothing to do with bringing it on and who perhaps, in their heart of hearts, were dead against it.

But there have been some amusing episodes to offset all this — as, for instance, when the British Military Attaché, staying at the Hotel Bellevue in Berne, recently invited to an official function, sent round to Lt. vom Rath [Assistant to the Military Attaché], of the German Legation, who was living in the same hotel, and asked if he would lend him his sword for the evening! Vom Rath told me this and thought it a huge joke. He wanted to do it but did not dare to.

But as a rule, the various belligerents in the Hotel Bellevue simply glare at each other. When Alice was there recently, she was sitting between the Serbian Minister [Dr. Slavko Gruyich] and the Russian Chargé d'Affaires [Michel Bibikoff] when one of our acquaintances from the German Legation, a former colleague of ours in Vienna, passed and cut her dead. He later sent word to her through a mutual friend that he was sorry to have to do so, but was afraid that if he bowed to her, the enemies on each side of her might think the bow was intended for them! The real joke is that Alice thought all the time that she was cutting him, as we never could stand him.

This Serbian Minister, by the way, was Gruyich, who was Minister for Foreign Affairs in Belgrade when the war began, and when we were lunching together one day in Berne, with Bibikoff, the Russian Chargé d'Affaires, the latter called attention to the fact that Gruyich was the man who received the first document of the war and Grew the first document of the peace. He referred to the Austrian ultimatum to Serbia, handed to Gruyich,[9] and to Bethmann-Hollweg's peace note, handed to me. . . .

[9] The Austrian ultimatum of July 23, 1914, was handed to M. M. Pachu, Serbian Minister of Finance, the senior member of the Cabinet, in the absence of the Minister for Foreign Affairs who was busy with the domestic elections. Dr. Gruyich, Secretary-General of the Serbian Foreign Office, was present to represent the Foreign Minister.

Tuesday, February 20 [1917]

Vienna is a sea of mud and dirty melting snow, piled along
the streets. There are no laborers to remove it, so it remains
until it melts. The sidewalks are little better than the streets.
In the hotel — I move tonight to the new Bristol, a thoroughly
modern house adjoining the old — the food is considerably
better than in Berlin. One has eggs and sugar, though no
butter, without cards, and there are but two meatless days,
Monday and Friday. On Wednesday one can have only mut-
ton. Every morning a chunk of black bread is left at one's
room, which has to do for the day. People not living at the
hotel cannot have bread there even with cards. Bread is really
the scarcest commodity. . . .

I went to the chancery early — the same apartment which
we took when I was here under Kerens, Wohllebengasse 9,
but with two floors instead of one — and when Mr. Penfield
came, he received me most cordially. . . .

During my short stay in Vienna, from February to April
14th, there was much interesting diplomatic work on hand.
Just before my arrival, our Government had asked the Austro-
Hungarian Government for a statement of its position as regards the German submarine policy.[10] Mr. Penfield was instructed to make the inquiry informally, but he put it in the
form of an *aide-mémoire* and made no reservations as to its
publication, so it was published almost immediately. The
Austro-Hungarian reply was received on March 2nd and as it
was very long, it took seven hours of consecutive work on the
part of Captain Stephen Graham, our Naval Attaché, a good
German scholar, and his clerk Eisenman to translate it, and
thirty hours to encode it, the clerks working in shifts throughout the night and two days. It was a marvelous document,
evidently intended to conceal the disagreeable points under a
mass of agreeable verbiage.[11] Its object was clearly to steer
a middle course between Austria-Hungary's duty to her ally,
Germany, and her desire to remain on friendly terms with the

10 *Foreign Relations, 1917, Supplement 1*, pp. 131–33.
11 *Ibid.*, pp. 161–68.

United States. But our Government was not fooled by the wrapping paper and quickly recognized the salient points, namely that Austria-Hungary was trying to reconcile our demands that warning be given before torpedoings by issuing a general warning to all ships in advance which it regarded as satisfactory as a specific warning in each case; and also that American ships were not likely to be torpedoed by Austro-Hungarian submarines. There were few American ships in the Mediterranean. However, the United States decided to let the matter rest for the present, in order to avoid a break of relations, which would be inevitable in case of an ultimatum. Austria was absolutely obliged to support Germany.

There were two other important diplomatic matters pending. One of them is of so confidential a nature that I cannot mention it even here.[12] It required delicate handling and I think was managed well by the Ambassador. In taking it up with the Ambassador in a telegram in the secret code, marked "to be deciphered by the Ambassador only" — (he turned it over to me as he had not the slightest idea how to use the code) — the Department said that he might tell me if he wished, which pleased me greatly. I attended his conferences with Count Czernin, one at the Ambassador's house and one at the Foreign Office, and translated Czernin's communications from

[12] In March, 1917, Mr. Penfield and Mr. Grew transmitted a note from Secretary of State Lansing proposing peace overtures between Austria-Hungary and the Allies. It was President Wilson's hope to detach Austria-Hungary from Germany and thus so weaken Germany as to force Germany to negotiate for peace on the terms set forth by Wilson in his "peace without victory" speech on January 22. Mr. Grew's translation of Count Czernin's answer revealed that this plan was hopeless: "Austria-Hungary is always ready to end this war because she has always waged a defensive war. She, however, emphasizes the fact that she could only enter into negotiations for peace simultaneously with her allies, that she must receive the guaranty that the Monarchy will remain intact and finally the guaranty necessary to insure the cessation of propaganda on the part of her neighbors, propaganda which led to the assassination at Sarajevo.

"The proposals made by Mr. Penfield, to Count Czernin, as well as those which may be made in future will remain secret; at the same time Count Czernin expects that his reply will remain secret also."

See also *ibid.*, pp. 62–63, 65–66.

French into English, as the latter is more fluent in the former language, while Mr. Penfield does not speak a word of French. Or rather he does speak one word, for he continually talks of reaching an "impassé"! Count Czernin's relations with Mr. Penfield seem to be cordial, although I think the former has to treat him somewhat like a petulant child. When Czernin wanted to see Penfield to inform him of the beginning of the ruthless submarine warfare on February 1st, the latter at first refused point-blank either to receive him or to go to him as he was sulking him because some of his personal letters which came in the open mails had been opened by the censor. This was a minor annoyance which we had to put up with in Berlin continually, contenting ourselves with formal protests, but Mr. Penfield took it as usual as a personal affront, lèse majesté, and insisted on dragging it into the most important diplomatic negotiations. Crosby, who had the room next to the Ambassador's and could hear everything that went on there, has told me that on certain occasions Mr. Penfield has treated Czernin like a pickpocket over this trifling issue.

The other diplomatic matter, which was causing the Ambassador great concern and rightly so, was the question of the reception of Count Adam Tarnowski, the Austro-Hungarian Ambassador-designate, in Washington, by the President. The circumstances connected with Count Tarnowski's appointment occurred before I came to Vienna, so that I have to rely for my facts on the files of the Embassy and what has been told me by the other secretaries who had watched the whole matter from the beginning.

The first development, and what apparently put the matter into Penfield's head, was when Maurice Egan, our Minister in Copenhagen, telegraphed to the Department that he had learned on good authority that the Austro-Hungarian Government would be glad to send an Ambassador to Washington — the post having been open since Dumba's recall[13] — if the United States would send a warship to take him to the United

[13] On September 8, 1915, Secretary Lansing instructed Ambassador Penfield to present a note to the Foreign Office asking that Dumba be recalled.

States. It was evidently Count Dionys Szechenyi, the Austro-Hungarian Minister at Copenhagen, who had broached the matter, as he later suggested it to Mr. Penfield at the coronation of Emperor Charles I at Budapest. An embarrassing error on the part of the Department — unless it was one of those errors committed on purpose — told Penfield what his colleague in Copenhagen was doing and made him very angry as he felt that the latter was trespassing on his own private preserve: the Department sent its reply to Mr. Egan to Vienna instead of to Copenhagen! I do not now recollect the exact nature of the reply, but I think it said that there would be difficulties in the way of sending a warship to fetch an Ambassador. At any rate, Penfield sent a facetious answer to Washington, commenting on the "time-honored methods" of taking up diplomatic matters of this nature, meaning thereby that it was none of Egan's business, and from then on he evidently began to work to secure Tarnowski's appointment. He said openly, in the presence of some of the staff, that he wished to have "a creature of his own making" in Washington. It was evident that he felt his own position would thereby be rendered more secure. It was he who, on his own initiative assured the Austro-Hungarian Government, that a safe-conduct would be granted to Count Tarnowski by the British and French Governments, although he had no guarantees to that effect and there was actually a hitch in the matter until our Government put it in the form of a formal request; and it was he who continually assured Count Czernin that Tarnowski would be received by the President, although he never was.[14] In one instance he said to Czernin verbatim: "On my life I assure you that Tarnowski will be received" (this was overheard by Crosby, Stewart and Allen Dulles [Third Secretary] sitting in Crosby's office next the Ambassador's room), and in another case he said to the Minister in my presence

[14] The Austro-Hungarian Ambassador-designate, Count Adam Tarnowski, arrived in Washington on February 1, 1917. President Wilson refused to receive him, because Austria-Hungary subscribed, in form at least, to the German submarine manifesto of January 31, 1917.

that he would stake his official head that Tarnowski would be received.

Count Czernin repeatedly urged upon Mr. Penfield the importance of having Count Tarnowski formally received by the President. He understood the difficult position of our Government, owing to Austria-Hungary's having subscribed to the German submarine policy, but stated that he was in an equally difficult position, for once having sent Count Tarnowski to Washington, he could not continue to explain to his own Government, people and press the delay in the presentation of his Ambassador's letters of credence. He intimated that the situation could not continue indefinitely.[15]

Mr. Penfield continued to give Count Czernin assurances that it was only a question of time before Count Tarnowski would be received by the President and urged patience.

On March 29th the Department's telegram arrived, recalling Mr. Penfield for immediate conference in Washington and saying that Count T. could not be received.[16] It was telephoned the same evening to Mrs. Penfield, who said that she would not tell the Ambassador until the following morning as he would otherwise not sleep. In the morning Mr. Penfield came to the chancery, after having read the telegram, and informed me that he was leaving Vienna temporarily as the President needed his advice in matters pertaining to the war. He said that he would delay a few days before announcing his departure, which he would do through the press, and would then wait several days longer before informing Count Czernin that the President could not receive Count Tarnowski, as he wished to disassociate the two issues.

I told Mr. Penfield that in my opinion it was the Department's intention not to disassociate the two issues; that the object of his recall was in order to enable Austria-Hungary to preserve her dignity in spite of Count Tarnowski's nonreception by the President, and to endeavor to preserve diplomatic relations by rendering them reciprocal and uniform in the two

15 *Foreign Relations, 1917, Supplement 1*, pp. 143, 169, 177, 186.
16 *Ibid.*, p. 188.

countries. I said I feared that the action of our Government would lose weight and possibly defeat its own purpose unless this were made clear. As he had discussed the whole Tarnowski matter openly with Count Czernin, it would be best now to go to Czernin and explain frankly the meaning of this step, which in any case was obvious. I said that this ought certainly to be done before his announcement appeared in the press.

After repeated representations to the Ambassador, I finally persuaded him to let me go to Count Ferdinand Colloredo, Count Czernin's *chef de cabinet,* to talk the matter over frankly, since he still would not go directly to the Minister, and at the same time to make an appointment for him with Count Czernin to take place as soon as the latter wished. In my interview with Count Colloredo, I said that the Ambassador had sent me to explain the reason of his departure from Vienna, which was to be announced in the press that afternoon, as he wished the Minister to know of it before it actually appeared.

Mr. Penfield's communication to the press gave no hint whatever of the object of his recall. It said that he had been working for four years without a rest and was about to take his first well-earned vacation; that coincidentally the President had need of his counsel in matters pertaining to the war, and that his absence would be only of a temporary nature. It added that one purpose of his trip was to receive a doctor's degree from the University of Pennsylvania, a signal honor.

On the following day occurred just what I had expected. An official communication from the Foreign Office appeared in the press, saying that Count Tarnowski had not been received by the President, that Mr. Penfield was leaving Vienna, and that the diplomatic relations of the two countries would now be uniform and reciprocal with two Chargés d'Affaires. This naturally placed the Ambassador in an undignified position, in the light of his own communication, which could have been avoided if he had gone to see Count Czernin immediately and had let the latter make the original announcement himself. The official communication naturally made no mention of Mr. Penfield's absence from Vienna being of a temporary nature.

Count Czernin saw Mr. Penfield the next day and told him that if the United States should declare war on Germany, Austria-Hungary would sever diplomatic relations immediately. To the Ambassador's inquiry as to what would happen if the declaration were simply to the effect that a state of war existed, Count Czernin replied: "Let matters rest there," giving the impression that such a declaration would not result in a break.

The Department's telegram arrived on a Thursday night, March 29th; Mr. Penfield's communication to the press appeared on Saturday afternoon, the 31st; and the official communication of the Foreign Office was published on Sunday morning, April 1st. Mr. Penfield then planned to leave Vienna either the following Thursday or Saturday night. I urged him to leave as soon as possible, intimating that if Congress should act before he left, he would risk being handed his passports instead of being able to leave voluntarily. I repeated to him on several occasions during the next few days that I regarded the situation as grave, but he merely accused me of overwrought nerves and inquired of some of my colleagues whether I was usually given to excessive nervousness.

Having applied for an audience with the Emperor, which was set for Thursday morning, he decided that he could not leave Vienna before Saturday night, although I again urged him to hasten his departure. It was, in fact, only through the courtesy of the Foreign Office that this delay did not result in his being handed his passports, for the President's proclamation regarding the state of war was officially received in Vienna on Friday [17] and the Government's intention to break with us was already decided. However, they permitted the Ambassador to leave voluntarily on Saturday night and handed me my passports at 2 P.M. the following day.

Throughout the entire week before his departure, the Ambassador continued to all friends and officials to maintain that he was only going on temporary leave and would return in a

[17] On April 2, Wilson asked Congress to recognize the fact that Germany was now waging war on the United States. Four days later Wilson approved a resolution of the House and Senate declaring war.

few months. His private views on the subject altered somewhat, after Captain Graham, the Naval Attaché, myself and
others continued to express our opinions to the contrary, for
he decided a day or two before leaving to give notice on the
lease of his house; but he nevertheless failed to pack up or
remove the private and personal papers which filled the drawers
of his desk at the chancery, which would seem to indicate that
he expected to return.

Towards the end of the week, when radical action by Congress seemed more and more probable, he became frightened
and said he wished he had left on Thursday, but I forebore
to say: "I told you so." He finally left on Saturday night,
April 7th, in a private saloon car placed at his disposal by
the Government, still maintaining that he would be back
soon. . . .

As soon as I found that Mr. Penfield was to leave and that
the Embassy was to be left in my charge, I felt justified in beginning to act on my own initiative and responsibility, with
a view to preserving diplomatic relations if possible. I talked
informally with many people, knowing that what I said would
come directly to the attention of the Foreign Office, suggesting
that a break of relations with the United States at this time
would do Austria-Hungary incalculable harm, while the maintenance of relations even with Chargés d'Affaires instead of
Ambassadors would maintain an important channel of communication and negotiation, which might later be of great value
and service in arranging peace. Certain things drifted back
to me, indicating that these informal conversations had fallen
on good ground and were favorably regarded at the Foreign
Office. I also had a long talk with Colloredo on the same
subject, which he said he would take up directly with the
Minister.

But it was then too late, for I am convinced that the break
was decided upon at the conference between the two Emperors,
Count Czernin and von Bethmann-Hollweg which took place
at Homburg about April 4th [April 3–4]. I am further absolutely convinced that Austria-Hungary did not want to break

with us and that the action was literally forced on her by
Germany. This hypothesis is not founded upon mere guess-
work, but upon many remarks which were made to me by many
well-informed people during the last few days before the rupture. I am aware that just after the break, a secret sitting of
the Hungarian Parliament was called to inquire as to the
reasons for the step, which was totally disapproved in Hungary.
I was told by one well-informed person in close touch with
the Foreign Office that the break could have been avoided had
we been represented in Vienna by a rational Ambassador during the period of the war.

At 1.30 P.M. on Easter Sunday, April 8th, Herr Eugen von
Marsovszky, of the Minister's Cabinet at the Foreign Office,
called me on the telephone and asked in a very polite and
courteous manner if he could come to see me. He came at 2.15
and handed me my passports, very politely together with a note
from Count Czernin, informing me that diplomatic relations
had been broken. He said that the Government desired to
meet my views and wishes entirely as to the time and method
of our departure and that he had been assigned to make all
our arrangements. We finally selected Saturday, April 14th, as
the day of departure and handed in a list of unofficial Americans whom we desired to have accompany us, which was accepted in its entirety. A special train was placed at our disposal to Buchs, across the Swiss frontier, to which point we
were the guests of the Government. The baggage of the Embassy staff was not examined and that of the consular officers
and the unofficial Americans was examined in a purely per-
functory manner. There were approximately 90 persons on
the train, about half of whom were diplomatic and consular
officials.

On the day of our departure I called at the Foreign Office
and said good-bye to Colloredo, Josef Hempel, Leo di Pauli,
Ladislaus Gömörry-Laiml and Marsovszky, all of whom were
most cordial. I presented Marsovszky with a gold cigarette
case, inscribed with his monogram, in appreciation of the work
he had done on our behalf. There was no sign of hostility

or unfriendliness in any quarter, and a very considerable number of people came to the station to see us off, including Walter
von Mumm in full German uniform, although we were at
war with his country! I hope he did not get into trouble for
it. . . .

We arrived at Zurich late in the afternoon, where we were
met by the Consul General, Francis Keene, and although
there was not time to have our baggage transferred, we proceeded at once to Berne, reaching there in the evening in
time for dinner. I found there that the telegram which I had
asked Charles Campbell [Second Secretary of the American
Legation at Berne] to send to Madrid requesting the Embassy
to reserve accommodations for us on the first steamer sailing
for America on or about April 26th, had been altered by the
Legation to on or before April 26th, so they had fixed us up
for the *Alfonso XIII,* sailing from La Coruña for Havana
on April 21st, and as the passages had already been paid for,
we had to try to make it, although we would have liked to
have a few days for a trip through Spain. . . . We sailed at
6 P.M. on April 21st, passed the Azores about three days out,
sighted the Bahamas on May 2nd and arrived in Havana early
in the morning of May 3rd. . . .

XIV

Pre-Armistice Negotiations

OCTOBER – NOVEMBER 11, 1918

During the year and a half of war, Mr. Grew worked at various tasks in the Department of State, including direction of the Western European Division, and he, also, went on a speaking tour of Midwest farm areas for the Food Administration. Of this activity, he wrote to a friend on February 8, 1918: "I never undertook anything so strenuous before — traveling almost every night and speaking from two to six times a day, sometimes to as many as 20,000 people in one day . . . [I] try to rub it in that every individual in the country must bear a piece of the war on his own shoulders and that the job ahead of us is no easy one."

Mr. Grew kept no diary of his activities from April, 1917, to October, 1918. The two letters that are at the beginning of this chapter do, however, reveal the nature of his work in the Department. In October, 1918, Colonel E. M. House asked Mr. Grew to serve as one of his private secretaries on a mission to discuss, with the Allied nations, armistice terms to the enemy powers. Colonel House had been greatly impressed with Mr. Grew's work in Germany. Mr. Grew had written to his mother on January 31, 1916, while Colonel House was in Berlin: "The Colonel had one or two talks with me and they were most satisfactory and left me with high hopes for the future. He said that our Embassy and the Embassy in Paris had the best records of all and rather implied that we were the better of the two."

Mr. Grew's diary, covering the activities of the American Commission attending the pre-armistice negotiations, adds considerable information to the account in the fourth volume of The Intimate Papers of Colonel House.

To Ellis Dresel and Hugh Wilson in Berne, July 5, 1917

You must be cursing me out for a rotten correspondent, but blame the Department, not me. My first week here I loafed around and complained that there wasn't enough to do, but everyone laughed at me and said WAIT. That first week is all part of the initiation; then the avalanche falls and you never get head and shoulders above ground again. Once in a great while in Berlin we used to go home . . . with the comfortable feeling that our baskets were empty, our desks clean and the pouch gone. Good old days of yore. That feeling is unknown here. . . .

I will tell you a little about my job, so that you will see how keenly interested I am personally in everything that you are doing. In the first place, I have to digest all the information about the Central Powers which reaches us from every possible source and prepare a weekly report based on that information, which goes to the President, the Secretary, Colonel House and all the principal bureaus of the Department, as well as to Naval Intelligence. I will enclose one or two to show you what they are. You can see how eagerly I scan the telegrams from Berne, as well as from The Hague, Copenhagen, Stockholm and Christiania, for those are the posts from which we get most of our intelligence. You can't possibly send us too much, whether by telegram, despatch or personal letters.

Then I have all questions relating to Jewish, Polish, Armenian and Syrian relief and it is a positively awful job, receiving deputations of Jews from New York and elsewhere and trying to explain to them why we can't allow unlimited sums to go abroad until we can effectively control their distribution. . . . Of course a certain amount of all these relief sums will directly or indirectly give "aid or comfort" to the enemy, but we want to reduce that aid or comfort to the least possible amount.

Then I have all questions relating to German prisoners of war and detained or interned civilians in the United States, which is daily becoming a bigger job. We have a couple of thousand of them already, mostly sailors and officers from the

German ships, and I have to see the Swiss diplomats almost daily and wrangle out various questions with War, Navy, Labor and Justice. It is bewildering to find out who has charge of what. For instance, before drawing up an ordinance for prisoners' correspondence and the censoring thereof, I must have a conference with War, Labor, Justice and Post Office!

Grant-Smith and I are together handling questions of Americans and American prisoners of war in Germany. I suppose you noticed the telegram I sent asking the Spanish Embassy in Berlin to communicate only with you on that subject; it may give you more work but it will avoid a lot of confusion, and you, Ellis, are the one man to handle that question, with your wide experience of it. It is grand having you there. I hope you will make recommendations on every case which you submit to us, especially applications from Americans in Germany who want funds from America. They ought not to have any unless they have a mighty good reason for staying there.

Besides these subjects, I have to receive diplomats for Billy Phillips [Assistant Secretary of State] on every subject in the almanac; read every telegram which comes to the Department from all over the world — and that in itself is some job, believe me — and every despatch or report or newspaper clipping which has to do with Teutonic affairs. The telegrams arrive every hour or so in pink envelopes and pile up on one's desk by the dozen until one has a chance to get at them. They used to be typewritten on impossibly thin flimsies and very hard to read, but now we have persuaded the powers to spend about $30 a day and have them decently printed on a machine; I enclose one or two copies to show you the form in which your messages reach us.

I am lucky to have a big splendid room next to Billy Phillips and a very congenial crowd to work with. As it is much more satisfactory to know just what happens to your telegrams and reports, I will try to describe the process here. When I was in the field, I always regarded the Department as a big mysterious machine or secret society and would have been glad to know more about it.

Your telegrams, as I have said, are printed and distributed to all the different bureaus, whether interested or not. There are three grades: ordinary, confidential and very confidential. The first category go to everyone; the second only to certain interested bureaus; the third only to Secretary Lansing and Frank Polk [Counselor for the Department]. I get the first two categories. The original telegram, on a yellow sheet, is first indexed and then marked for the interested bureaus or officials. For instance, a telegram on political conditions in Germany would be marked for the Secretary, the Counselor, the Assistant Secretary, Western European (Fred Sterling), Intelligence (Hugh Gibson and Phil Patchin), Secret Service (Leland Harrison and Lanier Winslow) and myself, each with his special hieroglyphic. Each man passes it on to the next, often appending a slip with some comment, and when it comes to the most interested party, he acts on it — if he is able to spot it as his property. But this is difficult, as nobody seems to know just what is his property. The general tendency here is to pass the buck. Sometimes a telegram will go the rounds without being acted on at all and then it has to begin all over again. Supposing it is unquestionably mine; if lucky, I may get it after it has been in the Department about three days. I call for back correspondence, which takes three or four days more, or else I get a reply that there is no back correspondence, although the telegram itself shows that there is. Then I have to send my stenographer down to Indexes to look it up personally. She returns and says that the correspondence was tallied up to Western European last March; Western European searches its files and finds they referred it to Intelligence last April. Intelligence swears it never saw the correspondence, but if it did, Mr. Phillips' private secretary Jones must have it. Jones swears equally volubly that he hasn't got it, but I slip into his room at night and find it hidden under a three-foot pile of back correspondence underneath the radiator. Having acquired the back correspondence, I then proceed to make a note how it is to be answered, and send it up to the Diplomatic Bureau. The draft, if lucky, returns to me in three

days. I take it in to Mr. Phillips, who initials it. Then it goes
to Alvey Adee [Assistant Secretary of State] who changes two
words and a comma and sends it back. It is again written and
returns to Mr. Adee, who initials it and probably passes it
on to the Secretary. The Secretary signs it and it reaches the
coding bureau ten days after the original was received at the
Department. What happens then, heaven only knows. This
is a little exaggerated, but not much. It probably explains much
to you. As a curio, I enclose a memorandum of the peregrina-
tions of a telegram which required action by me and took 15
days to reach me after its arrival at the Department. This is
not at all exceptional. . . .

To Thomas Sergeant Perry, August 24, 1917
Confidential

Can you help me out on the following proposition? Recently the Secretary held secret conclave with three of us and
said he wanted us to prepare memoranda for use at the peace
conference, whenever that may come. This doesn't mean that
a peace conference is impending in the immediate future:
there is not the slightest intention of our Government, so far
as any of us can see, of accepting the olive branch now. But
the war must stop sometime, in a few months or a few years,
and the end must be preceded by a peace conference between
the belligerents. I think the Secretary simply wants to be prepared against that day. His instructions were broad, but we
held a meeting and decided that the first phase of the subject
we would deal with would be "the aims and desires of the
present belligerents." This phase of the subject is in itself
broad, but I understand that it is not intended to be historical:
we are only to trace the development of these aims and desires
during the period of the war. . . . My share of this seemingly
colossal task includes Germany, Austria-Hungary, England,
France, Belgium and Portugal. We have been given no time
limit, but I gather, from insinuations, that we should turn in
our work "sometime soon." . . .

I greatly enjoyed your last letter. There are many things

about our democracy which disgust me as much as or more than they disgust you. Every day I see pettiness, arbitrariness and selfishness in administration which tend to discourage one with our whole system of government. But there is a hopeful streak running through the whole and in certain respects we have accomplished far more, since the outbreak of our war, than England and other countries accomplished in the same time. If we aimed at nothing but efficiency in administration, we should by all means adopt the autocracy of the German Empire forthwith. One's disgust with American politics is tempered by one's admiration of the spirit and patriotism of countless men who have given up their own work to turn a hand to anything down here, regardless of salary or distinction. Washington is flooded with men begging to serve in any capacity. . . .

Aboard Ship, Friday, October 18 [1918]

A great piece of good fortune has come my way, for Colonel House has asked me to accompany him to the Supreme War Council in Paris and, if things work out as we now hope and expect, to the final Peace Conference of the war. I had hardly dared let myself hope for this, but now that it has come it is agreeable to think how trivial everything else in the world seems. We measure things by bigger standards now than five years ago; great events have come so thick and fast that it is sometimes difficult to see them in their true perspective and to gauge their relative importance; yet through it all we have looked forward to the Peace Conference as the greatest event of all. It will indeed be the great event of this age or of any age, just as this war has been the greatest war in history, and so Dame Fortune is smiling kindly on those who are to be in at the death. But the army of officials who will attend the final Peace Conference have not yet set out, have not indeed yet been chosen except in the minds of the two men, the President and Colonel House, in whose hands their selection will lie. This little group which now starts for France are the trail blazers, the pioneers who go forward to see if the road can be cleared towards peace, and their leader, Colonel House, is the confidential adviser and official representative of the man who now, above all others, is directing and will direct the destiny of the world. Big words, these, but true. I carried in my valise from Washington the President's signed commission accrediting Colonel House as the official representative of the Government of the United States of America and empowering him to act as such "in all matters pertaining to the war." *Carte blanche*. The Colonel is the Head Pioneer.

When Alice and I passed Admiral William Benson [Chief of Naval Operations] on the Chevy Chase Bridge on Sunday, October 13th, I little thought that I was so soon to start on this trip with him. But that same afternoon Gordon Auchincloss [Assistant to Counselor Polk] told me the news. The German Government had just answered the President's three questions:[1]

1. Were they ready to conform to the conditions laid down in the President's various addresses, particularly that of January 8, 1918 (which I had heard him deliver in the House of Representatives amidst great enthusiasm)? [2]
2. Were they prepared to evacuate all occupied territory?
3. For whom was the Chancellor speaking?

[1] Generals Ludendorff and Hindenburg, facing military defeat in the late autumn of 1918, persuaded the new Chancellor of Germany, Prince Max of Baden, to send an appeal for an armistice to President Wilson on October 3. President Wilson replied on October 8 asking the three questions listed by Mr. Grew. See U.S. Department of State, *Papers Relating to the Foreign Relations of the United States, 1918, Supplement 1, The World War* (Washington: Government Printing Office, 1933), I, 343; Charles Seymour, *American Diplomacy during the World War* (Baltimore: The Johns Hopkins Press, 1934), pp. 305–13.

[2] This speech included President Wilson's Fourteen Points which were, in summary:
1. Frank and open diplomacy in the peace discussions and after.
2. Freedom of the seas in peace and war.
3. The removal of economic barriers among nations and the establishment of equality of trade conditions.
4. A reduction of national armaments.
5. A reasonable adjustment of all colonial claims.
6. The settlement of questions concerning Russia.
7. The evacuation and restoration of Belgium.

The replies to the first two questions were in the affirmative, although the German Government held that the terms of the armistice must be drawn up by a mixed commission. As for the third, Prince Max of Baden, the Chancellor [appointed October 3, 1918] stated that he had been chosen by the great majority of the Reichstag and therefore was speaking for the German Government and the German people.

Tuesday the 15th was one of the most electric days I have ever lived through. The country from coast to coast was afraid the President would take the German bait, that he would let himself be drawn into the quibble of words, a repetition of the *Lusitania* notes, that the war would end in an inconclusive peace and that all our sacrifices were in danger of going for nothing. The country was unable to fathom the President's purpose in asking the German Government questions when it felt that there was only one answer to give to the original peace offer — a perfectly straightforward "complete surrender or nothing." The country, and certainly the Allies, have failed from the beginning to comprehend the President's policy of playing to the German people rather than to the German Government; they have not understood or cared to understand the psychology of the German people; the President has and does; it is the campaign within the German Empire that the President has rightly regarded as of no less importance than the campaigns in the field, the policy of disrupting Germany and Austria from within, which is now bearing fruit. The President's reply to the Chancellor's answers to his three questions was issued at 5.30 on the 15th: it said in effect that he

8. The return to France of all her invaded territory and the matter of Alsace-Lorraine "righted."
9. The redrawing of the frontiers of Italy along lines of nationality.
10. The opportunity for the autonomous development for the peoples of Austria-Hungary.
11. The evacuation of Rumania, Montenegro, and Serbia with free access to the sea for the latter.
12. Protection for the minorities under Turkish rule and the permanent opening of the Dardanelles.
13. The erection of an independent Poland.
14. The formation of a "general association of nations."

could not recommend an armistice to the Allies while Germany was still engaged in inhumane and barbarous practices on land and sea.[3] I read it with Colonel House, Frank Polk, Billy Phillips and Gordon Auchincloss in the Department and the Colonel's face was wreathed in smiles. It was a masterpiece; the country endorsed it completely and sank back with a sigh of relief and contentment.

I went to New York at 1 o'clock on Wednesday the 16th, dining with Henry Perry who had traveled around the world with me, spending the night at the Harvard Club and lunching with Mr. Gerard at the Bankers' Club downtown the next day. New York was making a whirlwind finish for the Fourth Liberty Loan; Fifth Avenue was a solid mass of flags and it is well called "The Avenue of the Allies." Every taxicab, almost every private automobile, every van and dray and delivery wagon, every shop window, every hoarding carries its posters — "Buy," "Lend," "Buy more." The traffic signals which the policemen turn at the street crossings say: "Go, buy bonds" or "Stop, buy bonds." The shop windows are filled with paintings of Belgian atrocities, horribly realistic pictures, with such inscriptions as "Save the world from this by buying bonds." The streets themselves are filled with people selling bonds, even policemen and firemen taking a hand. Downtown a troop of mounted police were carrying bedraggled effigies of the Kaiser, the Crown Prince and von Hindenburg — one

3 The President's note, also, rejected the German suggestion of a mixed commission to negotiate the terms of evacuation of occupied territory and the conditions of an armistice. These terms Wilson wrote "must be left to the judgment and advice of the military advisers of the Government of the United States and the Allied Governments . . . no arrangement can be accepted by the Government of the United States which does not provide absolutely satisfactory safeguards and guarantees of the maintenance of the present military supremacy of the armies of the United States and of the Allies in the field." Furthermore, there could be no armistice as long as German submarines continued to sink passenger ships and the retreating armies committed wanton destruction. The note closed by referring to Wilson's July 4, 1918, speech which demanded the "destruction of every arbitrary power anywhere that can separately, secretly, and of its single choice disturb the peace of the world." Wilson added that "the power which has hitherto controlled the German Nation is of the sort here described." *Foreign Relations, 1918, Supplement 1,* I, 358–59.

effigy between each pair of troopers — and they were followed
by a solid platoon of police all singing. Douglas Fairbanks was
speaking from the steps of the Treasury to an enormous throng,
where Mr. Gerard is to speak tomorrow, and later in the day
I saw the former still selling bonds from a wagon on Fifth
Avenue. The enthusiasm and spirit are tremendous and make
one proud to be an American.

On the evening of the 17th I went down to Pier A at the
Battery and spent half an hour in the office of Dock Commissioner Murray Hulbert, who talked interestingly of prospective
improvements in New York harbor, until Colonel House's
party arrived and at about 9.30 we went on the Police Boat
down to the Narrows and there boarded the U.S.S. *Northern
Pacific* upon which we are to cross. She is a good-sized boat,
of some 14,000 tons, 525 feet long and very narrow, and good
for 20 to 21 knots; she used to ply up and down the Pacific
coast. Captain Preston, U.S.N., commands her. She is carrying about 500 troops and a number of army and navy officers,
but no passengers beside ourselves. Our party is composed of
Colonel and Mrs. House, Miss Frances Denton, the Colonel's
confidential secretary, and Miss Tomlinson, his assistant secretary, Admiral Benson and his two aides, Commander Andrew
Carter and Lieut. Commander Dick Russell of Boston, Frank
Cobb of the *New York World,* Dr. McLean as medical adviser,
Gordon Auchincloss and myself. Our cabins are simple and
with no drawers or cupboards of any kind and narrow uncomfortable berths, but I am a thousand times happy to be at sea
again.

We were to have sailed at 11 P.M. but it was somewhat foggy
and Admiral Benson seemed nervous; fog, he said, was the one
thing he feared; so we postponed getting under way until 4 A.M.
on the 18th when the fog finally lifted. Two destroyers, the
Waters and the *Rathburne,* carefully camouflaged in white,
black and blue zigzag stripes, accompany us, one on either side.

Life on shipboard in wartime is very different from what
we have been accustomed to. The *Northern Pacific* has, of
course, like other merchant ships, been taken over by the Navy

and is run strictly according to navy regulations with full naval crew, her former captain being on board in the subordinate capacity of navigating officer. I cannot with discretion go into all the measures and precautions that are taken against submarines, but they are as thorough as seems physically possible. The ship is well-armed with big guns, a separate crew for each, and at least thirty men, sailors and soldiers, are continually on the lookout in various parts of the ship, especially constructed for the purpose, each man being assigned a small sector of the ocean to cover with powerful glasses. It is difficult to see how a periscope or torpedo could approach in any but the roughest weather or in the dark without being seen and promptly reported to the bridge. At sundown every light on the ship goes out and stays out, except in the dining saloon and smoking room which are hermetically sealed so that not a ray of light can escape nor a breath of air enter. One has to grope through the passages, down the stairs and into one's cabin in darkness and undress in pitch blackness, for not even a match may be struck — and woe to the thoughtless passenger who has forgotten where he put his pyjamas! Not even a pipe or cigar may be smoked on deck, which seemed rather absurd the first few nights as the whole ship was lit up by a full moon. The course is a zigzag all the way over, at irregular intervals, so that a submarine ahead or abeam could not calculate on the ship's passing any certain spot at a certain moment. No wireless messages are sent out unless vitally urgent, for that also would give a clue to our position, but the regular messages from Sayville and Nauen are received daily and published in bulletins and we have thus received the recent exchange of notes between Germany and the United States. The sides of the ship and the upper deck are thickly hung and covered with life rafts, each with its pair of paddles, and to each passenger is issued, as well as to officers, soldiers and members of the crew, a life jacket with water flask filled and an emergency ration which must be worn or kept nearby at all times. Every day the order "Abandon ship" is practiced and at the alarm everyone goes to the particular lifeboat to which he is assigned and remains there until "Retreat" is sounded.

The ship is prepared for a large number of troops but we are carrying only 500 as the others were not ready when we sailed at such short notice. . . .

In the afternoon of the day of sailing, before we had had a decent chance to acquire our sea legs (and stomachs) it came on to blow and for three days we had a steady northeast gale and for three days I (and others) were very, very ill. The good doctor filled us up with every known medicine in vain: I struggled for a day or so and attended all meals with great difficulty and pain, only to lose them immediately afterwards, and then weakly succumbed. It was not agreeable for our staterooms and the dining saloon were, as I have said, hermetically sealed and, as Tom Cobb aptly remarked, they smelled "like a nestful of puppies." The strongest stomach would cave in under such conditions, I think. The destroyers were having such a beastly time of it, bucking into the tremendous seas, that on Sunday Admiral Benson sent the *Rathburne* back to pick up a convoy coming out of Halifax and on Monday, the *Waters* having signaled that she must slow down or bust (we were making a good 21 knots), she also was instructed to beat it for home and we proceeded without convoy. On Tuesday it ceased to blow and became very warm, as we were in the Gulf Stream. Gordon Auchincloss solved the problem of ventilation by taking up our pillows and blankets and sleeping in the smoking room with the doors open after lights went out, although they would leave them open only one night. We should probably never have thought of it if a mouse had not run over Gordon in the dark in his own cabin and caused him to seek safety in flight — or, in the terms to which we have recently become accustomed, "to retire to previously arranged positions according to prearranged plans."

On Wednesday we expected to be met by an escort of destroyers from the other side, as ordered, but they did not turn up and for two days and nights we were without any escort whatever, much to the Admiral's annoyance and concern. We had received warnings of submarines within 100 miles or less of us and the weather was absolutely perfect for an attack.

Wednesday night we did not undress and slept in the smoking room with life jackets handy, but early on Thursday morning I went up on the bridge and there approaching us, spread out at intervals like a fan, were six fine American destroyers rushing up to convoy us in — *Stringham, Cushing, McDougal, Cummings, Warrington* and *O'Brien.* They swung into line beside and in front of us and after signaling the point we were to make for dashed along, they and we zigzagging regardless of the others. If the submarines could get us through that escort they could get anything.

On Monday we received by wireless direct from Nauen the English translation of the German answer to the President's last note and on Tuesday came the German text which I checked up with the translation for Colonel House and found only a few minor inaccuracies.[4] Colonel House was greatly pleased with its tone and thinks they could not have gone farther than they did. It is significant that the Germans agree to leave the terms of the armistice to the military advisers, which, if taken in connection with the President's note, means the Allied military advisers. I know something of what those terms are to be and they are very, very stiff. On Wednesday we received the speech of the German Chancellor before the Reichstag — very long and windy and clearly aiming to prepare the people for what is coming — and on Thursday came the President's reply to the German note of the 20th.[5] As for other news, such as the situation on the fronts, etc., we have received hardly a word.

---

[4] On October 20, the German Government sent a note accepting Wilson's conditions. The note pointed out that an amendment to the Constitution had been introduced into the Reichstag providing that the decisions of war and peace rested with the representatives of the people. Furthermore, in the future "no government can take or continue in office without possessing the confidence of the majority of the Reichstag." *Ibid.*, pp. 380–81.

[5] On October 23, President Wilson informed the German Government that he had communicated his correspondence with Germany about peace to the Allied Powers "with the suggestion that, if those Governments are disposed to effect peace upon the terms and principles indicated, their military advisers and the military advisers of the United States be asked to submit to the Governments associated against Germany the necessary terms of such an armistice as will fully protect the interests of the peoples involved." *Ibid.*, pp. 381–83.

We shall land in Brest on Friday morning and probably go to Paris Friday night, where I shall continue this diary.

Confidential [No date]

Colonel House feels that the Germans are finished and know it and that they will have to accept our terms; if things break right at the Inter-Ally Council [6] he sees no reason why the military leaders of both sides should not meet at once, perhaps next week, to arrange for the armistice and this might lead into the Peace Conference early in December. But he foresees difficulties in the Council; Lloyd George, Clemenceau and Orlando do not like the President; they feel that he takes the lead too much without consulting them and will probably now feel so more than ever. They are frankly jealous of the President's role. The Colonel suggested that the President might have consulted them somewhat more than he did.[7] He said that they will try their best to place all responsibility on the President. But America can fight for two more years while they cannot, so they cannot play the game alone. Lloyd George is the difficult one to deal with; he does not always live up to his promises; Balfour [British Foreign Minister] and Grey [former British Foreign Minister] never promised more than they carried out. . . . The Colonel said that if Clemenceau co-operated with him as well as he did last time, all would go smoothly. Yet his own position is not an easy one in view of the general attitude towards the President. The Colonel is ready for the fray; he rested and read cheap novels the first three days on board for he was very tired having been under a steady strain continually; he said he had no protection in America but that abroad he was able to see only those whom he wished. . . .

[6] In November, 1918, the Supreme War Council was created. It was composed of the principal Ministers of the Allies and, in addition, various military representatives. The group, which was to sit at Versailles, was designed to bring better co-ordination of Allied efforts and a more unified command.

[7] The President's exchange of notes with Germany was purely personal. He warned Germany in the October 23d note that armistice negotiations were dependent upon the provision that the Allies deemed "such an armistice possible from the military point of view." *Foreign Relations, 1918, Supplement 1*, I, 382.

Saturday, October 26 [1918, Paris]

I went to the Hotel Crillon at 9 in an army automobile detailed for my own particular use and soon found myself acting as a barrier between the Colonel and numbers of visitors, telephone calls, letters, etc. The Colonel told me to open and read every letter that might come for him, no matter how confidential, and when the question arose as to organizing his intelligence work he said he would need me for much more intimate work than that, which is decidedly pleasing. There is not to be any routine about this job fortunately. . . .

At 11.30 Colonel House went to the British Admiralty office to telephone to Sir William Wiseman [British Chief of Secret Service] in London over their direct wire and learned that Lloyd George and Balfour would arrive in Paris on Monday. Sonnino [Italian Foreign Minister] is expected at about the same time from Rome. Sir Douglas Haig [Commander in Chief of British Expeditionary Forces in France], Lord Milner [British Secretary of War] and Admiral Benson lunched with the Colonel in his salon; they are also stopping at the Crillon. It is decidedly interesting to meet these men about whom one has heard and read so much. I lunched with Arthur Frazier [Counselor of the American Embassy at Paris] at his apartment and in the afternoon went with Colonel House and Admiral Benson to call on Ambassador William Sharp [American Ambassador to France] at the chancery where I saw Fred Sterling, Hugh Gibson and Philander Cable [Secretaries of the American Embassy at Paris]. The state of affairs in the Embassy, which I shall discuss later, is not a happy one. Afterwards we moved to 78 rue de l'Université; three or four young naval ensigns, several yeomen stenographers and two telephone girls were assigned to us; army officers came in and started work on a telephone switchboard, bringing American telephones to place in every room, and we were soon in working order. A staff of sailors act as doorkeepers and messengers. Four army automobiles await at the door at our disposal. Surely the American Army and Navy are on the job!

I had an interesting talk with Colonel House this afternoon.

He said it was his intention, before sitting down at the conference table at Versailles on Tuesday, to know exactly what every other man was thinking and what he would say; he had already learned the minds of Haig and Milner and had docketed the information and filed it away in the pigeonholes of his mind for further use. The others he would learn before Tuesday, one by one. This, I think, is the secret of his success in political life and it will mean his success at this conference. He said he never worried in advance but did his best and let it go at that; but he is under a strain and looks very tired; he is trying to avoid seeing unnecessary people and to keep his mind clear for the big event. Pershing wanted him to come to General Headquarters but he says Pershing must come to him.

After a long and very tiring day I dined with Fred Sterling . . . and then at 9.30 I went back to 78 rue de l'Université on the chance that Colonel House might need me. It was fortunate that I did so as he had been trying to find me ever since he saw Clemenceau late in the afternoon; he asked if Frazier had found me or if I had come on my own initiative and seemed pleased when I said that the latter was the case. He took me aside alone, drew the doors of the salon together and said that he had received from Clemenceau what was actually the most important document in the world today and that nobody had seen it except Marshal Foch, Clemenceau and himself — not even President Poincaré. It was Foch's statement to Clemenceau of the terms upon which he, after consultation with the other Allied commanders in chief, felt that an armistice with Germany could safely be agreed upon. Colonel House said that Miss Denton was copying it upstairs, but that as she did not know French, he wanted me to help her and then to translate it into English; he had to return the document to Clemenceau in the morning. I found that Miss Denton had got through the better part of the copying so I started in on the translation and had it finished in about two hours. I will not state its contents here; they will doubtless be adopted by the Allies and will soon be known to the world.[8] The Colonel

[8] See *ibid.*, pp. 463–68, for Colonel House's telegram of November 4, 1918, including the terms of the armistice agreed upon.

had gone to bed when I had finished, but he took the document and placed it under his pillow, and he had an American sailor stationed at each door of his bedroom throughout the night. The successive lines of evacuation had been sketched by Foch on a map which Clemenceau had also handed to Colonel House; he asked me if I thought we ought to copy them and I told him that while we had no similar map in the house I could trace them later by taking down a list of the principal towns through which they passed; so he gave me the map and I spread it out on the floor and made a rapid list of the towns and cities which we cabled to the President the next day. Then I sat on the edge of the Colonel's bed and we discussed the terms proposed by Foch; he asked me my opinion and I said I thought they were as just and reasonable as was compatible with military safety. He seemed very much pleased at his talk with Clemenceau who had apparently taken him entirely into his confidence. I said good night and returned to Frazier's apartment about midnight.

I should add that we were shown today, by the British, a copy of a telegram sent by Lloyd George to Clemenceau in which Lloyd George said that he did not want to have Clemenceau go ahead and draw up the terms of armistice on his own initiative but that he should accept President Wilson's points as stated.

It is interesting to note that Foch's letter paper is headed "Commander in Chief of the Allied Armies." [9]

General Clarence Edwards told me tonight that the Germans were fighting like the devil and giving us a fearfully tough job.

Paris is, of course, crowded with khaki and it seems to me that a very large percentage is American; certainly a very large number of American army automobiles, trucks, ambulances, etc. are in evidence. The Place de la Concorde and a good part of the Champs Elysées are lined with captured German guns of all sizes and the Tuilleries, fronting on the Place de la Concorde, is lined with German airplanes of different makes. The statue of Alsace-Lorraine is of course completely covered with

[9] Foch was made Commander in Chief of the Allied Forces in France on April 14, 1918.

the flags of the Allies and with flowers. The streets are still darkened at night, but the Place de la Concorde and the Champs Elysées are lighted once again as there have been no air raids for a long time.

October 27 [1918]

. . . Venizelos [Greek Premier] also came in and wanted to know whether he should go to America to see the President and give him a lot of data about the Balkan situation. The Colonel told him that he had had this same data for many months. This seemed to surprise Venizelos a good deal. . . .

Told newspapermen that they must work for unity of political action among the Allies with Wilson in command. Great body of people in the world recognize Wilson as the political leader of the Allies but that those in control of the Allied Governments were reluctant that he should occupy that position and were doing their best to take the direction of affairs out of his hands and to put them in their own hands. The Colonel will have a very difficult job to force Great Britain and France to accept our leadership when it comes down to real business. . . .

Difficult position for Colonel is this — can the President force the Allies to permit him to control the kind of peace that is to be made? The Allies individually and collectively are making strenuous efforts to take the leadership away from the President.

October 28 [1918]

A very hectic day at the "chancery," for that is what the lower floor of 78 rue de l'Université has developed into. We have finally sent the corps of yeomen stenographers upstairs, banished the telephone girl to somewhere behind the scenes, installed telephones in every room with a central exchange and established a waiting room and two offices for Gordon and myself. Mine has a garden on one side, into which one can step at will through a large door window, and a Roman tiled bath on the other — which looks positively indecent in an office. The entire day was spent amidst incoming telegrams, messages, telephone calls, visitors, pressmen and rumors of all kinds. The rumor that Austria-Hungary had agreed to unconditional surrender was confirmed late in the afternoon and I had the satisfaction of translating the text of the note to Colonel House when it arrived and hearing him say: "Well, that ends it; we shall stay." [10] Lloyd Griscom [who had held several posts as Ambassador and Minister] and I were sitting beside his bed, for he had an attack of indigestion, and he reminded me of his prophecy on the steamer that the peace conference would take place about December 11th. Germany can hardly refuse any terms now.

In the afternoon Colonel House went to call on the President of the Republic and when he returned I asked him his impressions. He said that M. Poincaré was a very intelligent man but a "bitter-ender." I said that I also was a bitter-ender so far as results were concerned but that I wanted those results to take place as soon as possible and that if Germany was ready now there was no use in sacrificing further lives and treasure for the mere satisfaction of beating her into a jelly and letting loose all the evils of bolshevism which would certainly come back on the rest of the world like a boomerang.[11] I thought the armistice pill should be made as palatable as was compatible with complete military and naval assurance that she could not take up arms again if the peace conference should fail. The important thing was that Germany should swallow the pill and swallow it now. He said he agreed with me and that he was inclined to be magnanimous. I said that the step we were about to take would go down into history as a great event and that it was up to us to make a record of which we need not be ashamed in the future. I am not sure of the use of the word "magnanimous" but I am sure that wisdom and expediency are

[10] The armistice with Austria-Hungary was signed on November 3, 1918.

[11] On November 7, 1917, the Bolsheviks in Russia had overthrown the Kerensky Government, and a month later Russia signed an armistice with Germany. At the Versailles Peace Conference, Allied leaders were fearful of the spread of communism to other nations.

against turning Germany over to Bolshevism if we can accomplish our rightful and necessary ends now. I had another talk with Colonel House at his bedside before he got up this morning; he asked me what I thought of demanding as terms of armistice that Germany immediately lay down all arms and demobilize, as this would save the Allies a hundred million dollars a day in the manufacture of arms and ammunition and would enable Germany to get food immediately as the blockade could then be raised at once. I said I doubted if the carrying out of these terms in good faith could be controlled by the Allies but he said that this could be done. "Then," I said, "why not give Germany her choice of these terms and the terms of Foch and thereby show her that we desire to do what we can to make the way easy for her." He said he thought that a good suggestion and I think he may propose it at the Supreme War Council which has now been postponed till Wednesday. What I emphatically feel is this: if we can offer the terms of armistice in such a form that they will effectually guarantee the impossibility of Germany's again taking up arms and enable us to impose our complete will at the peace conference and at the same time in such a form that Germany can and will accept them, it would be a crime against humanity to make them impossible of acceptance in order that the carnage may be continued, the lust of revenge satisfied and the destruction of Germany completed. Yet this, I fear, is what some of the so-called "bitter-enders" desire. I am profoundly glad that Colonel House holds the opinions he does; I think Clemenceau agrees with him, however jealous he may be of President Wilson; but Lloyd George is uncertain. They say he does not know his own mind in advance and may be influenced by a bad night or a fit of indigestion as to which way he will turn. . . .

October 29 [1918]

Lloyd George and Lord Reading [Lord Chief Justice of England] came to the house at 12 and stayed to luncheon, being joined later by Balfour and Sonnino.[12] Conference at the Quai

---

[12] See *Foreign Relations, 1918, Supplement 1,* I, 421–23, for Colonel House's telegram about this meeting.

d'Orsay at 3. I went to General Pershing's headquarters at
73 rue de Varennes to get a copy of a telegram from Newton D.
Baker [Secretary of War] to Pershing which Colonel House
wished to have at the Conference, having been instructed by
the President to read it. Colonel Carl Boyd, General Pershing's
aide, would not give me the original but insisted on keeping
me waiting for nearly an hour while a copy could be made. I
protested, saying that it was an urgent and most important
matter that the Colonel, who was the President's direct representative, should have it without delay and that as the conference of the Prime Ministers was now going on, the delay
might be serious. He replied that General Pershing, who was
still ill upstairs, refused to let the original go out of his possession; I said that the General must then assume all responsibility. So I whiled away the time looking out at the beautiful
garden which lies behind the General's house. When the copy
had been made I took it to the Conference, returned to the
house, found another urgent letter for the Colonel and took
that to the Conference too.

At the informal meeting at the house this morning,[13] it was
decided that the armistice could not be discussed separate from
the peace terms since that would appear as if all the Allies had
accepted the President's Fourteen Points, which was not the
case. At the Conference in the afternoon Clemenceau and
Lloyd George stated that President Wilson had never asked
their opinion of his statements and that they had never expressed any opinion. Lloyd George found difficulty with some
of the President's Fourteen Points, particularly with Point 1
(secret diplomacy) until its intention was satisfactorily explained, after which he withdrew his objection. Point 2 (freedom of the seas) Lloyd George said England could never ac-

[13] Throughout these pre-armistice negotiations, the significant decisions were
made at morning meetings at Colonel House's residence, attended by Clemenceau, Lloyd George, Orlando, House, and certain advisers. This was done to
avoid endless debates with other delegates on less important issues. At the
afternoon sessions of the Supreme War Council, the decisions of the steering
committee were ratified, and little time was lost in debate. Seymour, *op. cit.*,
pp. 340–41.

cept. Colonel House then sprung a bombshell by stating that if the Allies refused to accept the President's Fourteen Points, the United States would then have to consider whether to continue to fight for the aims of the Allies or to conclude a separate peace. This naturally caused great excitement. Colonel House asked if he should withdraw to allow them to discuss the matter alone, but Balfour said that they had no secrets from the United States. He suggested that the Allies draw up a reply to President Wilson's suggestion for an armistice, showing where they disagreed.

Much time is lost at these conferences, particularly by Sonnino who rambles off on tangents, so tomorrow Colonel House, Lloyd George and Clemenceau will meet alone in the morning at the Ministry of War and discuss things in advance.

After the meeting today the Colonel called his entire staff together — that is, General Tasker Bliss [American Military Representative on the Supreme War Council], Admiral Benson, Frank Cobb, Gordon Auchincloss and myself, and Ambassador Sharp — told us just what had taken place at the conference, said that we were his advisers and asked our opinions.

Colonel House seemed a little worried tonight as to how things were coming out — whether Lloyd George and Clemenceau were going to repudiate the President's Fourteen Points. He told me that he had advised the President as long ago as last summer to clinch them with the Allies but that he had delayed too long. He asked me how long I thought it would be necessary to prepare for the Peace Conference; I said I thought it could be started in two weeks after the Germans had carried out the terms of the armistice, or sooner. It would only be necessary to cable for Mr. Lansing (accompanied by Leland Harrison [Secretary assigned for duty in the State Department] and Richard Crane [private secretary to Mr. Lansing]) and the rest of the American delegation to start immediately. Lloyd George had said two or three weeks for the preliminaries and one week for the Conference itself. . . .

SUPPLEMENTARY NOTES TO DIARY

October 29 [1918]

The general opinion of all American correspondents in Paris is that the one definite policy of the Allies at this time is to take the control of the peace negotiations out of the hands of President Wilson. The same opinion is expressed by correspondents who have just returned to Paris from London. That also is the tone of a large section of the French papers.

October 30 [1918]

Lloyd George, Clemenceau and Colonel House met for forty-five minutes this morning alone at the Office of the Minister of War.[14] Just before they entered Clemenceau's office, Lloyd George handed Colonel House a proposed answer to the President which the British authorities had drafted, as follows:

The Allied Governments have given careful consideration to the correspondence which has passed between the President of the U.S. and the German Govt. Subject to qualifications which follow they declare their willingness to make peace with the Govt. of Germany on the terms of peace laid down in the President's address to Congress of January 8, 1918, and the principles of settlement enunciated in his subsequent addresses. They must point out, however, that clause two, relating to what is usually described as the Freedom of the Seas, is open to various interpretations, some of which they could not accept. They must therefore reserve to themselves complete freedom on this subject when they enter the Peace Conference.

Further, in the conditions of peace laid down in his Address to Congress of January 8, 1918, the President declared that invaded territories must be restored as well as evacuated and freed. The Allied Govts. feel that no doubt ought to be allowed to exist as to what this provision implies. By it they understand that compensation will be made by Germany for all damage done to the civilian population of the Allies, and their property (by the forces of Germany?), by land, by sea, and from the air.

14 See *Foreign Relations, 1918, Supplement 1,* I, 425–27.

Colonel House told Lloyd George that he was afraid his attitude at yesterday's meeting had opened the floodgates and that Clemenceau and Sonnino would have elaborate memoranda to submit containing their objections to the President's Fourteen Points and that he doubted whether Clemenceau would accept the answer as drafted by the British which was in marked contrast to the position taken by Lloyd George yesterday.[15] It at once developed at the Conference that Clemenceau was having prepared an elaborate brief setting forth France's objections to the President's Fourteen Points. Colonel House promptly pointed out to Clemenceau that undoubtedly Sonnino was preparing a similar memorandum and that if the Allied Govts. felt constrained to submit an elaborate answer to the President containing many objections to his program it would doubtless be necessary for the President to go to Congress and to place before that body exactly what Italy, France and Great Britain were fighting for and to place the responsibility upon Congress for the further continuation of the war by the United States in behalf of the aims of the Allies.[16] As soon as Colonel House said this, Lloyd George and Clemenceau looked at each other significantly. Clemenceau at once abandoned his idea of submitting an elaborate memorandum concerning the President's Fourteen Points and apparently accepted the proposed answer drafted by the British. Colonel House suggested that the word "illegal" be placed before the

[15] Since the meeting the day before, Lloyd George's attitude toward Wilson's Fourteen Points had become more conciliatory. On the whole, the British were less unsympathetic to Wilson's program than the French and the Italians.

[16] Writing in his diary on February 6, 1929, after having read Volume IV of *The Intimate Papers of Colonel House*, Mr. Grew observed: " . . . I well remember the day that the Colonel came down and told me of the inspiration which had come to him at 3 o'clock in the morning . . . to the effect that if the Allies refused to accept Wilson's Fourteen Points as the basis of the peace, he would advise the President to go before Congress and ask whether the United States should continue to fight for the aims of the Allies or make a separate peace. He was happy as a schoolboy over it and, indeed, it proved to be a completely effective method of bringing the Allies into line, probably the only one. But this is only of academic interest now, for once the Peace Conference got to work there was little that remained of the Fourteen Points."

words "damage done to the civilian population of the Allies" in the last sentence of the draft of the proposed answer. George accepted this suggestion but Clemenceau stated he preferred that the draft should be left as it was. Colonel House believes that the suggestion would be accepted by all if the President saw fit to insist upon it but was not yet entirely clear that this was necessary.

Colonel House ascertained that George and Clemenceau believed that the terms of the armistice, both naval and military, were too severe and that they should be modified.[17] George stated that he thought it might be unwise to insist on the occupation of the west bank of the Rhine. Clemenceau stated that he could not maintain himself in the Chamber of Deputies unless this was made a part of the armistice to be submitted to the Germans and that the French army would also insist on this as their due after the long occupation of French soil by the Germans but he gave us his word of honor that France would withdraw after the peace conditions had been fulfilled. Colonel House was inclined to sympathize with the position taken by Clemenceau. He pointed out the danger of bringing about a state of bolshevism in Germany if the terms of the armistice were made too stiff and the consequent danger to England, France and Italy. Clemenceau refused to recognize that there was any danger of bolshevism in France. George admitted it was possible to create such a state of affairs in England, and both agreed that anything might happen in Italy. Colonel House asked Clemenceau where he thought it would be wise to hold the Peace Conference. He answered Versailles but, however, did not argue with the others when George stated that he and Colonel House had agreed on Geneva. Colonel House stated that he thought this matter should be discussed later. Upon leaving the Conference George and Colonel House again agreed that the Conference had better be held in neutral territory than in a belligerent country and the Colonel still has in mind to urge Lausanne. It was agreed that this afternoon

17 After long discussion, Marshal Foch's military terms were finally approved and incorporated with minor changes in the armistice.

they would discuss, first, the terms of the armistice with Austria; second, the terms of the armistice with Turkey (with which Colonel House explained we had nothing to do); [18] three, the terms of the armistice with Germany. It was agreed that there should be a meeting at Colonel House's headquarters tomorrow morning of Clemenceau, Lloyd George, Orlando, Marshal Foch and Colonel House, with Sir Eric Geddes [British First Lord of the Admiralty] at hand to advise concerning naval questions. Of course Colonel House is in constant consultation with our military and naval authorities. In the event that the answer drafted by the British and quoted above is adopted by the Allies as their answer to the President's communication, Colonel House strongly recommended the President's accepting it without alteration. . . .

October 31 [1918]

. . . Attended Supreme War Council at Versailles at 3, where the terms of the Austrian armistice, military and naval, were discussed point by point. It was a great scene; I cannot help comparing it to the gathering at the Palace in Berlin at the wedding of Princess Victoria Louise [daughter of the Kaiser] a few years ago, where the Kaiser and Kaiserin, the Tsar of Russia, the King of England and all the royalty of Germany were assembled. Now kaiserism and tsarism are dead and today the representatives of democracy met to decree their death knell. There was Clemenceau, presiding, Lloyd George, Balfour, Sir Henry Wilson [British Military Representative on the Supreme War Council] and Sir Henry Rawlinson [Commander of the Fourth Army], Sir Eric Geddes, Orlando, Sonnino, Colonel House, General Bliss, Admiral Benson, Venizelos, Vesnitch [Head of the Serbian Mission], Marshal Foch and many other military and naval celebrities. They were at one big table in the conference hall and we secretaries were at small tables directly behind our respective delegations. I will not discuss the conversations; record of them is kept; Sonnino

18 The United States broke diplomatic relations but never went to war with Turkey.

and Vesnitch afforded most of the by-play; the others, particularly Lloyd George, Colonel House, in his quiet manner, and Geddes spoke directly and to the point. When the discussion tended to ramble, Clemenceau would stop it by a few well-placed words. The French spoke French and the English and Americans English and an exceedingly capable interpreter, Professor Paul Mantoux, translated each remark or speech into the other language, quickly and exactly, as soon as the speaker had ceased talking. I will chronicle only the impressions received — of Clemenceau, in his gray cotton gloves which he never took off, rapping with a paper cutter to maintain silence, his high cheekbones, his frequent gleams of humor, as when he said: "The only thing we aren't taking from Germany are the Kaiser's pants," and Lloyd George's trite remark, when they were wrangling as to who should receive the surrender of Turkey — "Why the only French troops fighting in Turkey were the Negroes sent to see that the British didn't rob the Holy Sepulchre"; Balfour, tall and kindly, speaking in his gentle, courteous manner, walking about the table to hear the speaker better; Colonel House, speaking in a whisper and the fewest possible number of words, pointing with his finger at the person he was addressing to emphasize his points; Orlando, always speaking with southern heat and waving his hands as he spoke; Vesnitch, always inclined to take offense, as when Balfour remarked, "We have not recognized the Yugo-Slavs as an independent state," V. hotly inquired: "Don't you recognize Serbia, then?" And whenever an acrid discussion occurred, Clemenceau's arms and shoulders waved continually. It was a most amusing sight to watch if not to hear. We American secretaries had two small tables, with Frazier, Auchincloss, General P. D. Lochridge, Colonel William Wallace, Commander Carter, Lieut. Commander Russell and myself. These meetings, indeed, surpass in importance anything that has ever occurred or will occur again. The Conference lasted from 3 till about 5.30 and we then adjourned and motored back to Paris. I had much work to do, then hurriedly dressed, dined with Mrs. Whitelaw Reid [widow of the American diplomat and journalist] at the Ritz . . . and then I left immediately after dinner and worked till midnight. . . .

November 3 [1918]

The three Prime Ministers met this afternoon at Col. House's headquarters to discuss the 14 points. As a matter of fact, Clemenceau and Orlando will accept anything that the English will agree to concerning Article 2. Col. H. has spent almost every minute outside his conferences discussing this article with the British. He is insisting that they must recognize the principle that it is a subject for discussion at the Peace Conference or before, and he is having the greatest difficulty in getting them to admit even that much.

He has contended that they might as well refuse to accept the principle that laws governing war upon land were not a subject for discussion. He believes if he could get the matter postponed until the President comes that some satisfactory solution might be arrived at.

Austrian armistice signed; to be published in America in the afternoon papers November fourth; in Europe on the morning of the fifth.

It was clear that the Conference held at the house this afternoon was to be a critical one and Colonel House was prepared to exert strong pressure in order to secure from the Allies an acceptance of the President's Fourteen Points, set forth in his speech of January 8, 1918, and in his subsequent addresses. Lloyd George, Clemenceau, Orlando and Paul Hymans [Belgian Minister of Foreign Affairs] were there. George opened the discussion by stating that he was prepared to stand by the proposed answer mentioned above. Col. H. pointed out that the following phrase of this answer was not satisfactory to the President inasmuch as it was not clear that the Allies accepted the principle of the freedom of the seas: "They must therefore reserve to themselves complete freedom on this subject when they enter the Peace Conference." Col. H. then read to the Conference a paraphrase of the President's tele-gram to him dated October 31st.[19] Clemenceau then stated: "We accept the principle of the freedom of the seas" and turn-ing to George he said: "You do also, do you not?" George an-swered: "No. It is impossible for any British Prime Minister to do this." [20]

On November 4, the Supreme War Council agreed to the terms of armistice and also to accept the Fourteen Points as the basis of the peace with a single reservation and a single ex-planatory statement:

" . . . The Allied Governments have given careful considera-tion to correspondence which has passed between the President of the United States and the German Government. Subject to the qualifications which follow they declare their willing-ness to make peace with the Government of Germany on the terms of peace laid down in the President's address to Congress of January 1918, and the principles of settlement enunciated in his subsequent addresses. They must point out, however, that clause 2, relating to what is usually described as the free-dom of the seas, is open to various interpretations, some of which they could not accept. They must therefore reserve to themselves complete freedom on this subject when they enter the peace conference.

"Further, in the conditions of peace laid down in his address to Congress of January 8, 1918, the President declared that invaded territories must be restored as well as evacuated and freed; the Allied Governments feel that no doubt ought to be allowed to exist as to what this provision implies. By it they understand that compensation will be made by Germany for all damage done to the civilian population of the Allies and

[19] The President's cable made it clear that he could not recede from the principle of the freedom of the seas. *Foreign Relations, 1918, Supplement 1,* I, 427–28.

[20] At the November 3d meeting, Lloyd George finally went on record with the statement: "We are quite willing to discuss the Freedom of the Seas and its application." With this compromise the matter was left for the Peace Con-ference. Seymour, *op. cit.,* pp. 386–89.

their property (by the forces of Germany) [sic] *by the aggression of Germany by land, by sea and from the air. . . ."* [21]

Charles Seymour comments in American Diplomacy During the World War, *p. 394: "Colonel House had forced the acceptance of Wilson's principles by the Allied leaders, in the face of a hostile and influential group in the United States and the distinctly unsympathetic personnel constituting the Allied Governments."*

[No date]

The week from November 4th to 11th was comparatively quiet after the exciting and strenuous days through which we had passed. One evening Colonel House called us together in his salon and said he was going to recommend to the Department that a man be sent immediately into the new States of Austria-Hungary to organize our political and economic intelligence work there and to report conditions in those countries as they actually were; [22] he said that this official would have all the prerogatives and qualifications of an Ambassador and would take with him a large staff including military and naval attachés, and that it must be a man who knew German and was familiar with men and affairs in Germany and Austria. Then, to my utter astonishment, he pointed to me and said: "I don't want to spare you but all fingers point at you as the man to go." That evening he sent a cablegram to the President making the recommendation and I began immediately with the provisional plans in case I should have to start at a moment's notice; the men I thought of taking were Captain Gherardi as Naval Attaché, General Frank McCoy as Military Attaché, Hugh Wilson, Hugh Gibson, Walter Lippmann, Voska — who spoke Czech — and a few others, including experts on food, transportation, finance, etc. I prepared a schedule of what I thought the nature of our work should be and how we should go at it and was ready to start on this most in-

21 *Foreign Relations, 1918, Supplement 1,* I, 461.
22 On November 11, the Austrian Emperor relinquished his throne, the old empire dissolved, and new states like Czechoslovakia were formed.

teresting journey, which would have included German-Austria, Czechoslovakia, Yugoslavia, Rumania, Hungary, Poland and Ukraine, when a telegram came from Washington, crossing ours, and announcing that Herbert Hoover was about to sail with a staff in order to investigate the economic needs of those countries and presumably to organize a new Commission for Relief in Belgium. We were still uncertain whether the Department would want me to go ahead on this mission either alone or with Hoover, but after waiting for several days for an answer Colonel House again cabled recommending that I be placed in charge of the entire political intelligence organization for the peace conference, with headquarters at Paris. The Department approved of this in due course, but in the meantime came a cablegram, dated November 13th, saying that after consultation with the President I had been selected to act as Secretary of the United States Commission to the Peace Conference and that my Assistant Secretaries would be Harrison and Philip Patchin [Assistant to the Counselor of the Department of State]. They asked me to cable at once any suggestions which I might have as to needs. This of course put an end to any question of my going to Austria and the other new central states, and gave me a very big job to attend to here, for I shall now be responsible for the question of sleeping and office accommodations for the entire American Commission, as well as for the organization of the Commission's work, the taking of minutes at the Peace Conference and the political intelligence work besides. With the help of Major Willard Straight [former American diplomat, attached to General Headquarters] a plan was drawn up for the detailed organization of the work, committed to paper in the form of a sketch and submitted to Colonel House. He said it was the best and in fact the only practical one he had yet seen, although he had copies of the British and of one prepared by Dr. Mezes' Committee.[23] Just as Willard Straight, Walter Lippmann and I

23 The Inquiry, directed by Dr. Sidney Mezes, President of the College of the City of New York, was composed of students of history, politics, economics, and other fields, who studied the relation of these disciplines to the problems

were starting to put this plan into execution, we all three came down with influenza.

In the meantime the armistice negotiations were being carried on, some delay being encountered owing to the German Delegation having difficulty in getting back to their own lines after receiving the terms. Even before they had received the terms, the rumor reached Paris that the armistice had been signed and so authentic did the source of the story appear that Major Barclay Warburton, the Military Attaché of the Embassy, cabled it to Washington as official, which resulted in a premature celebration throughout the United States — and subsequent angry demands for investigation on the part of the War Department. As a matter of fact the armistice was signed at about 5.30 on the morning of the 11th, hostilities to cease at 11 A.M. on that day. Officers subsequently returning from the front told me that an attack by our troops was ordered and carried out *after* the armistice had been signed and before hostilities ceased and that many officers and men lost their lives in those last few moments of the war. How unnecessary that seems! The returning officers said that they did not wish to criticize their orders but they were angry none the less.

Monday, November 11, 1918, was the greatest day I have seen or ever shall see. Little by little during the morning the news that the armistice had been signed spread through the city; at 11 guns announced the cessation of battle and the gun on the submarine lying moored near the Quai d'Orsay bridge banged away as fast as it could fire. All offices closed — indeed there was no point in keeping them open when all their employees had joined the crowds in the streets — and Paris gave herself over to complete and joyous celebration. Flags and bunting appeared from every side, great motor lorries were taken possession of by cheering, singing soldiers and girls, lines of midinettes went dancing down the boulevards, kissing everything in khaki they met and the captured German guns in

of the peace. Because the members were drawn largely from the staffs of universities, they were dubbed "Colonel House's troupe of performing professors."

the Place de la Concorde were one after another appropriated by bands of students and carried off in triumph without a word from the police to stop them. In all this celebration, which lasted about three days, there was a note of restraint which seems to have made police intervention unnecessary. The French people have suffered too acutely to give themselves over to abandoned joy; the end has come so fast, when once started, that it is not easy to realize that the war is over, and there were too many widow's tears among the smiling throngs to make the joy complete.

At 4 o'clock Clemenceau read the terms of the armistice in the Chamber of Deputies. I had not thought of trying to get in but Mrs. McCombs [wife of William McCombs, American lawyer], with whom I was lunching with Fred Sterling, Mildred Bliss [Mrs. Robert Woods Bliss] and others, wanted to make an attempt, so we worked our way through the dense crowds and when we got to the entrance I managed to push in my card with "Counselor of Embassy — Attached to Colonel House" on it and in a few minutes we were inside the lobby and being announced as "Monsieur le Délégué du Président Wilson et Madame." The net result was that just as Clemenceau entered and the crowds in the galleries rose from their seats, thus making more room, Mrs. McCombs, Madame Foch, myself and a few celebrities were ushered into nooks and crannies inside the Chamber. It was tremendously impressive and the enthusiasm as the principal terms of the armistice were read out by Clemenceau was glorious to hear. I suppose I am the only person who heard Bethmann-Hollweg present his first peace note in the Reichstag in Berlin on December 12, 1916; President Wilson deliver his Fourteen Points in the House of Representatives in Washington on January 8, 1918; and Clemenceau read the terms of armistice in the Chamber of Deputies in Paris on November 11, 1918.[24] It is a well-rounded picture. And through it all, Alice and I have maintained that this war would end in revolution in Germany and that the end when

24 On November 10, the Kaiser, deposed by action of the Chancellor, crossed the Dutch frontier.

it came, would come with surprising suddenness. I have always, when my opinion has been asked, mentioned the figure of the snowball rolling downhill; once really started on its course it would go like lightning, and it has surely done so, Mr. Gerard and many others to the contrary notwithstanding. . . .

Clemenceau sent the following typical note to Colonel House today:

Le Président du Conseil,
Ministre de la Guerre.

Paris 11 Nov. 1918.

Mon bien cher ami,

En ce moment solennel d'une grande histoire où votre noble pays et son digne chef auront joué un si beau rôle, je ne puis retenir l'envie de vous ouvrir les bras et de vous presser sur mon coeur.

à vous toujours
G. CLEMENCEAU. . . .

XV

The American Commission to Negotiate Peace
NOVEMBER, 1918 – DECEMBER, 1919

The Paris Peace Conference opened on January 12, 1919. Until May 7, 1919, when the conditions of peace were handed to the German delegation, the conference was simply a meeting of the victorious nations.

Representatives of the United States, Great Britain, France, Italy, and Japan organized the conference. Two representatives of each of these five powers composed the Supreme Peace Council, or Council of Ten. This Council decided what should and what should not be discussed at the plenary sessions where the small powers also were present. The five principal powers, in addition, had membership on every commission or committee that was appointed.

On May 7, 1919, the conditions of peace were handed to the German delegation, and the treaty was signed on June 28. The Austrian delegation received the conditions of peace on July 20, and the treaty was signed at St. Germain-en-Laye on September 10, 1919. The Bulgarian delegation received the conditions of peace on September 19, 1919, and the treaty was signed at Neuilly-sur-Seine on November 27. The Hungarian conditions of peace were not ready until January 15, 1920, and the treaty was not signed until June 4, 1920, at Versailles. The conditions of peace for Turkey were transmitted to the Turkish representatives on May 11, 1920, and the treaty was signed at Sèvres on August 10, 1920. The treaty, however, did not go into operation, and a new conference was called for at Lausanne in 1922–23.

President Wilson headed the American delegation at the conference. Although the President returned to the United

States after the signing of the treaty of peace with Germany, the American Commission to Negotiate Peace continued its activities through the conclusion of the treaties of peace with Austria and Bulgaria. The Commission returned to the United States on December 10, 1919.

After this date, the American Ambassador to France was empowered to sit on the Supreme Council in behalf of the United States "as an observer and not as a participant." By this time, the United States Senate had refused to ratify the Versailles Treaty. In 1921, the United States signed separate peace treaties with Germany, Austria, and Hungary.

President Wilson took to the Paris Conference Secretary of State Lansing, former Ambassador to France, Henry White, General Tasker H. Bliss, and Colonel House, as well as many experts to help on the various detailed issues.

The President's Fourteen Points occupied an important position in the peace negotiations, but there was considerable opposition among some of the Allies to many of the points. Wilson's primary purpose at the conference was to write the Covenant of the League of Nations into the treaty. Although the treaty as finally drafted did not completely satisfy Wilson, he believed that the League would compensate. The central structure of the peace agreements was the League, and postwar stability hinged on the League being effective. Wilson, although agreeing to a number of compromises, also forced a number of concessions on the Allies. "While the results fell short of public expectations," Colonel House later wrote in What Really Happened at Paris, "yet it is doubtful whether more could have been done, considering the conditions existing after the signing of the armistice."

Mr. Grew served as Secretary-General of the American Commission to Negotiate Peace, with the rank of Minister Plenipotentiary, and he, also, was the American Secretary on the International Secretariat of the Peace Conference. "I never before have been in such a strenuous life or had such a difficult job to tackle," he wrote his mother on February 17, 1919. "It will be a wonderful relief when the whole business is over. I feel

*as if I wanted to do nothing but grow potatoes for the rest
of my life." The positions Mr. Grew held required so much
time on administrative details that he was unable to keep a
diary for most of the conference. Many of the letters that
he wrote, however, as well as the diary he was able to keep,
add some new material to available accounts of the conference
by other Americans such as* What Really Happened at Paris,
edited by E. M. House *and* Charles Seymour; At the Paris
Peace Conference, *by* James T. Shotwell; The Intimate Papers
of Colonel House; My Diary at the Conference of Paris, *by*
D. H. Miller; What Wilson Did at Paris, *and* Woodrow Wilson
and World Settlement, *by* R. S. Baker; *and* The Peace Negotiations, *by* Robert Lansing.

December 19, 1918

On Thursday, December 12th, at ten o'clock in the evening,
General Pershing and General Bliss, with their respective staffs,
and Gordon Auchincloss and I left Paris for Brest on a special
train to meet the Presidential party. The train was very long
and luxuriously fitted out, with all sorts of special cars, for
the President and his party; and we were accompanied by such
celebrities as M. Stéphane Pichon, the Minister of Foreign
Affairs, the Minister of Marine, André Tardieu, who will probably be one of the French Commissioners at the Peace Conference, M. Franklin Bouillon, Chairman of the Foreign Relations Committee of the Chamber of Deputies, and several high
French officers.

Arrived at Brest at 12.30 on Friday, the 13th. We embarked
on a launch, where we were joined by Admiral Benson, Admiral William Sims [Commander of Naval Forces in European
waters], and Admiral Wilson [Commander of Naval Forces,
France], and went out into the harbor just as the *George
Washington* appeared far away in the mist, and soon the guns
began to boom out to welcome the first President of the United
States who had ever set foot on foreign soil while in office. It
was a splendid and most moving picture. The fleet of American battleships which had gone out to meet the *George Wash-*

ington had already preceded her into port and anchored, and the *Pennsylvania,* which had escorted her across the Atlantic, as well as a large number of destroyers, came in ahead of her and took their places to right and left, so that she steamed in between a solid line of French and American warships which, one after another, saluted the President. She came up very slowly, and it was well over an hour that we were on the launch before she anchored; and we went out into the outer harbor in a somewhat choppy sea and finally went on board. I saw Alice and Mrs. Lansing by the rail, some distance away, and waved to them before we came along side.

The President held a reception in his room of the high officials who had gone out to welcome him, and I, meanwhile, was very busy greeting Alice and the members of the Commission as well as the Jules Jusserands and the Count V. Macchi di Celleres, the French and Italian Ambassadors in Washington, with their wives. The day had been very misty, bordering on rain; but just as the *George Washington* dropped anchor and we came along side, the sun streamed out through the clouds, making a magnificent picture and an appropriate welcome to the President.

After some time, the President and Mrs. Wilson, followed by the high officials who had come to meet them, and a few of the rest of us — including Mr. and Mrs. Auchincloss and ourselves — went on board a larger tender which had come out, and amid tremendous cheers from the crew of the *George Washington* she steamed slowly ashore.

On landing, we entered a long line of automobiles, the President at the head of the procession, and went up through the streets of the town lined with American troops and, I think, thousands and thousands of school children, each waving an American flag and shouting himself hoarse, while behind these stood the townspeople; and the windows of every house were packed with onlookers. The road led up through the old fortress, now used by American troops and soldiers, who gave an even more vociferous welcome to the President; and then along the esplanade overlooking the harbor, and so to the station, where an address of welcome was delivered by the Mayor of Brest.

At four o'clock we entered again the special train which had brought us down; but the welcome to the President did not stop with Brest, for at every station on the way crowds of people had assembled and cheered the President as he passed. This, in fact, kept up all through the night, and even at two or three in the morning we heard cheers at various stations through which we passed, the people having assembled merely to see the train go by in the darkness. Whenever an opportunity occurred, the President would appear on the platform and shake a few of the hands outstretched towards him.

On the journey, I showed Mr. Lansing and Mr. White the chart of our organization which we had drawn up, and explained briefly what had been done to prepare for the Commission. The rest of the personnel of the Commission came in a second train, which left two hours later, but arrived in Paris two hours before us, as our train stopped three hours for dinner so that the Presidential party could eat in peace. We all sat down to specially seated tables.

Punctually at ten o'clock on the 14th, the train steamed into the Champs Elysées station, where the President was greeted by the President of the French Republic, Raymond Poincaré and other French officials; and then the cortege started over the same route by which the King of England and the King of Belgium had come on the preceding two weeks. The Auchinclosses and ourselves jumped into an automobile and took a roundabout way in order to reach the Place de la Concorde before the procession, and as good luck would have it we followed behind the car of the French Minister of Marine, whose chauffeur knew the way, and enabled us to reach the Place de la Concorde about five minutes before the President arrived there. As it was impossible to get across the rue Royale to our offices, from which we had hoped to see the procession, we followed the Minister of Marine into his Ministry, dashed upstairs uninvited, and finally found a window overlooking the Place de la Concorde from which we had a wonderful view of the whole magnificent scene. I had previously seen the arrival of the King of England and the King of the Belgians, but neither could be compared to the tremendous ovation given the President by the French people. It was a scene which I shall never forget; and it showed us very clearly that, whatever opposition the Government might have to the President's partaking in the Peace Conference, the people of France, as a whole, stood solidly behind him and regarded him as the great chief who is coming to found the League of Nations and put an end to wars forever. . . .

Then we went to the Crillon, where I showed Alice our rooms, and left her to prepare, as quickly as she could, for the luncheon at the Elysée Palace at 12.30. It was a great scurry, but we managed to do it in time, and arrived at the Palace soon after the hour set, while a long line of automobiles was still coming with the many guests. There must have been at least 250 people at the luncheon, all seated at one enormous table in the great banquet hall, which surely must have surpassed in size any other existing one. President Poincaré came in with Mrs. Wilson and President Wilson with Madame Poincaré, and when they had taken their places at the head of the table, we all sat down to a marvelous luncheon. Alice sat between M. Ribot, former Prime Minister, and M. Klotz, the Minister of Finance, while I sat next to M. Millies-Lacroix, former Minister of the Colonies. I gathered from George Creel [Chairman of the Committee on Public Information], who was sitting opposite me, that he was having a hard time, as neither of the ladies next him appeared to speak any English, while he knew no French. At the end of the luncheon, toasts were exchanged, and President Wilson's speech was translated aloud into French by Bob Bliss. The rest of the day was a great scurry, getting the Commission settled in its quarters. . . .

The next few days were a nightmare of confusion, for many members of the Commission were dissatisfied with their rooms and offices, and a hundred different problems presented themselves, which almost turned my hair gray. I managed to see Colonel House for a few moments every day to learn how things were going from the point of view of the President and of the Commissioners, and as he takes me into his confidence on all subjects I received some startling sidelights on the situation. It appears that several things have been done in preparing for the conference upon which the President had not been consulted and about which he was very angry. Leland Harrison and Phil Patchin, the two assistant secretaries, had both got in wrong; Harrison on account of unsatisfactory assignments on the boat to the Professors of Dr. Mezes' Committee, and Patchin through earlier difficulties in the Department of State; and the President vowed to the Colonel that he was going to send them both home. The Colonel asked me to recommend two men to replace them, but I went to him the next morning and begged him to tell the President that, in my opinion, they were indispensable to the Commission and the best men who could possibly have been picked, and that it would be a calamity, not only to their own reputations, but to the work of the Commission, to have them sent home at this juncture. The Colonel told me that evening that the President had forgotten all about it, although he took the handling of the press away from Patchin and gave it to Ray Stannard Baker [American editor, Director of the Press Bureau for the American Commission], which was a great relief both to Patchin and myself as it took all the responsibility off our shoulders. I knew at the start that the press would be the most dangerous element which we should have to handle, as there were some 300 American press representatives in town.

I will not go into all the various problems which presented themselves within the next few days, but they were many and difficult ones, and it required a great deal of oil poured on the wheels of the organization to get things satisfactorily adjusted to all. There was not only the difficulty in arranging for the proper assignment of rooms and offices to deal with, but a steady fight against the Army, especially General William Harts, the Commanding General in Paris, to prevent their taking the whole control of the organization out of our hands, as they clearly wished and intended to do. Fortunately, I had the backing of Mr. Lansing and Colonel House, and also of the President, in this respect. We had built up our organization very largely by drawing on the Army for personnel, but we had taken principally officers who were formerly in civil life and who understood that when they were assigned to us they discarded all question of Army rank and were directly under the authority of the civil officers of the Commission. There was also some difficulty with the Navy in regard to the work of naval communication, which they had first agreed to handle, but later tried to get out of, owing to the fact that the Department of State desired to handle the Washington end and the Navy did not want divided authority; but this was finally obviated by a little diplomacy. . . .

On Thursday, we lunched at Marquis de Chambrun's, where I sat next to Briand, the former Prime Minister, who talked most interestingly on the subject of the League of Nations, which, he said, he himself had been the first to propose in 1915. He said he considered the only solution to be a foundation for the League, composed of the United States, France and Great Britain, as it would result in hopeless confusion to invite all the small new states to become members at the start.

Our job during these first few days has been chiefly one of smoothing out the various difficulties which were bound to rise in such a heterogeneous organization, even between the Commissioners themselves, and this meant continual conferences with Mr. Lansing, Colonel House, Mr. White and General Bliss. There has unfortunately been continual electricity in the air, but at this moment of writing, Thursday, December 19th, we seem to be almost coming out of the woods, and I was much pleased tonight to have Major James Brown Scott [American lawyer and educator, Adviser on Legal Questions to the American Commission] say to me that the American preparations for this conference had been far ahead of those which had been made for the Hague Peace Conference — in 1907 — which he had attended as a delegate. The President visited the Crillon yesterday, and held his first meeting with the Commissioners, and afterwards interviewed the press. He was to have inspected our offices also, but did not have time, and I believe intends to do so soon; I hope by that time to have the assignment of rooms so straightened out that everybody will be satisfied, and that it will meet with his approval.

King Victor Emmanuel III of Italy made his State Entry into Paris today, but it was a somewhat pathetic anticlimax after the arrival of the President, and the enthusiasm of the crowd was pitifully tame. Fortunately, however, the rain which had poured off and on during the morning, stopped shortly before his arrival and the sun came out, so that the picture on the Place de la Concorde was no less magnificent than on the arrival of the other three chiefs of state.

To William Phillips, Assistant Secretary of State,
January 1, 1919

This is the first letter of the New Year — in fact the first personal letter I have written for many weeks — and one is certainly long overdue to you. I will try to make it short, for I well know how unwelcome long letters are in these strenuous days.

First of all I want to thank you very sincerely for this wonderful appointment. I have felt ever since it came that it was due to you, just as I am convinced that you have had a hand in every good thing that has come our way in the last few years.

Then I want to tell you a little about our organization. Your very friendly telegram of caution about taking on socially prominent men was fully appreciated, but it did not disturb me as I know that the criticisms which came to you were not justified and I hope that my reply convinced you also of that fact. Whatever course we steered there was bound to be criticism and I was fully prepared for it. I entered on this job with the definite assumption that a Congressional investigation would some day take place and have continually held that assumption in view. I believe that our organization is bulletproof.

When my appointment as Secretary of the Commission came, Colonel House told me to go ahead and build up an organization, drawing on the Army and Navy as might be necessary, which would be prepared to meet the requirements of the Commissioners when they should arrive. We had no precedent or experience to guide us and had to try to foresee as well as we could what would be needed. The very first day I asked Willard Straight to be our general executive officer and together we drew up a provisional chart of the proposed organization and started work. We fell ill the same day; I was up in a week and he, who could so hardly be spared, died a fortnight later.[1] I shall always be grateful for those two or three days of work with him.

Lieutenant Reggie Foster — attached to Artillery Headquarters — took on the work while I was ill and accomplished wonders; it was he who conducted the negotiations for requisitioning the Hotel Crillon and finally got it. Then we began to organize our various bureaus or divisions. We picked a first-class man to head the Executive Department — Captain Richard C. Patterson, formerly a civilian on Mayor John Mitchel's staff of New York City — and he has made good in every respect. Under him come the various offices of the business organization, the management of the hotel, personnel, room and office assignment, courier service, repair and construction, requisitions, automobiles, post office, etc., etc.

I asked Charles Moorfield Storey to head the political intelligence work provisionally, Captain Henry Whitehouse the Ceremonial Office, Lieut. Col. Dick Williams [former American tennis champion] the Liaison Office, each of these divisions being essential to the Commission. They have built up their offices in fine form and are filling the bill to perfection. I need not say that I consulted certain high officers and others before picking these men and I think all are agreed that no mistake was made.[2]

Of course, when the Commission arrived, many adjustments had to be made; our Political Intelligence Department was

[1] Willard Straight died from the terrible influenza that was then sweeping Europe. — J. C. G.

[2] William Delano and J. Hopkins Smith were also among our most helpful assistants. — J. C. G.

combined with the "Inquiry," and is now a single division
called the "Political, Territorial and Economic Intelligence
Section," under Dr. Mezes, and there have been various other
alterations.

I regret to say that there has been a very marked attempt
on the part of certain military authorities over here to mili-
tarize the Commission, and this I have fought against from the
beginning, realizing that we were purely a civilian and diplomatic organization, and should preserve our status as such.
I had received various intimations of this attitude of the military authorities, and received definite corroboration of it when
General Marlborough Churchill — General Military Liaison
and Co-ordinating Officer for the American Commission, soon
after his arrival, came to me and said that he ought to be
given charge of the military personnel within our organization
as, according to the way things were going now, we were heading straight for the rocks. General Churchill was not given
charge of our military personnel; but knowing him to be an intelligent and reasonable man, I asked him to make a complete
survey of the organization and report to me on the necessity
and capability of every officer now assigned to us. It is a somewhat significant fact that in spite of his original prejudice,
doubtless received from outside sources, his first report, which
was submitted to the Commissioners a few days ago, indicates
that we are not overstaffed, and that with only two or three
exceptions every officer assigned to us is performing duties
essential to the efficiency of the organization. He is now examining the capabilities of the individual men, as I wished to
disprove the charge that we had chosen men of meager ability,
and while his second report is not yet completed, he has informed me personally that we have secured an exceptionally
efficient lot of men, and that so far he has discovered few, if
any, flaws. I think we can have no better answer to our critics
than those reports, prepared by a regular Army Officer, who
started completely prejudiced against us, on a group of men
about ninety per cent of whom are civilians in uniform merely
for the period of the war. We have taken men from all walks

of life — chiefly businessmen who recognize clearly that they have lost their military status while with us and that rank does not count, and in some cases Majors are working under Lieutenants. They come from all over the country, and I knew very few of them before. Those who might be called socially prominent are almost exclusively in the Liaison and Ceremonial offices, and were selected because they spoke French and had the affiliations in France necessary for that particular work.

Before the arrival of the Commissioners, I held a meeting in my office every morning of the heads of the various sections to discuss progress and co-operation, and every day we tried to detect flaws and to rectify them. Now the Commissioners themselves have a meeting daily, at which I am present, and important administrative questions are put up to them. Yesterday I took up 21 different questions! That is an indication of the size of the work.

I am enclosing the provisional chart of the organization as we had it ready for the Commissioners on their arrival, but it had many defects, and a revised chart is now being prepared and will soon be ready. I knew very little about the functions of the men who came with the Commission, and it was quite impossible to get them in their right places before their arrival, but these defects were very soon rectified.

One thing more and then I will cease this chatter. You must have been surprised at the telegram proposing to designate me as "Supervising Director" of the Commission with the rank of Minister, and probably you questioned the purpose of this ponderous title. I need not assure you that it was not my proposal. . . . Colonel House and General Bliss seemed to think that my rank ought to be nearer that of the corresponding British official, Lord Charles Hardinge, who is a "Superintending Ambassador," and also that it would make my relations somewhat easier with some of the military officials here who seem to have misunderstood the prerogatives of a mere Secretary. The Colonel, in the kindness of his heart, wanted me to be an Ambassador on the spot, but it was pointed out that this might make my rank equal with that of the Commissioners! So the matter was put up to the President and he approved of the rank of Minister with the designation "Supervising Director." I personally think that there is nothing more dignified than the title of Secretary of the Commission, and I propose to keep it and call the office "Secretary and Supervising Director," since the inclusion of the latter term is desired by the Commissioners.

I have thought very often of the old Department and have wished sincerely that you and Frank Polk were with us. . . .

To William Phillips, February 10, 1919
Personal and Confidential

. . . You ask for the gossip which comes in advance of information. There is so much gossip flying around that it fairly bewilders one to try to pick the wheat from the chaff, although there are several well-defined currents of opinion which I will tell you about. Within the Commission itself it is difficult to obtain expressions of views or purpose, for with the President on hand there is a general tendency to leave matters to him and there has been little concerted working out of policies by the other Commissioners. It is a situation which paralyzes initiative but I am by no means prepared to say that it is not the best and most effective solution. The President is clearly getting results and these results, so far as I can see, are good. If he can return to America with the League of Nations constitution in his pocket, it will be a tremendous achievement. The only thing we might wish is that the actual peace treaty might be hastened and the various problems at issue between the Allies discussed subsequently. All this delay is in Germany's interest and her propaganda is growing more insidious and effective. I shall touch upon its influence on our troops of occupation. . . .

As someone has aptly remarked, the honeymoon between America and France is over and they are entering upon the unromantic stage of adjusting themselves to their new relationship. The enthusiasm of the people on the President's arrival, which was unquestionably genuine and deep, is rapidly being discounted by the French press which has launched a well-defined campaign against the President and the United States. Although outwardly everything appears to be smooth between the French and American statesmen, one has the feeling that the former are using every opportunity to lessen our prestige, with the press as their principal weapon. I trust Tardieu less than any of them and believe that he is at the bottom of most of the propaganda. We have seen it indicated in little ways. For instance, it is now well understood with the International Secretariat that no procès verbaux or statements of the proceedings either in the plenary sessions of the Peace Conference or in the sittings of the Council of Ten or in the various sub-committees shall be given out until the French and English versions have been compared and agreed upon by the secretaries of the Great Powers and that they shall then be given out by the International Secretariat simultaneously. Yet at the first meeting of the Committee for Responsibility for the War the other day, Tardieu had his opening speech circulated in French together with an incomplete version of Mr. Lansing's speech, and when the secretaries had drawn up their joint version after the meeting, it had lost its value as news, having been already published, and the papers would not use it. This was simply Tardieu propaganda. Mr. Lansing formally protested before the Council of Ten.

The present situation is undoubtedly one of considerable friction. The French press is complaining that we came into the war at the last moment (forgetting entirely that we saved them from defeat) and now want to boss the whole show and rob them of their fruits of victory by helping Germany. The papers are doing everything possible to discredit the President. A great deal is made of the President's failure to visit the devastated regions and this has an undoubted effect on the people. After long delay, he merely spent one day going to Reims which did not satisfy the people. Furthermore the papers say that our only interest is to establish a League of Nations, impose our ideas on the Allies and then go home, leaving them to bear the brunt and shoulder the responsibility if anything goes wrong. They are suspicious of the effectiveness of the League of Nations and only want effective guarantees which will release them permanently from the fear of German aggression. They express the fear that the United States is going to rob them of these guarantees.

I am simply giving you the general trend of the French press and French public opinion as one hears it expressed every day. The picture is not agreeable, but there is worse to come and that is the very unfortunate ill-feeling existing between the French and American armies. There is friction between Pershing and Foch and this is carried all the way down to the ranks. The other day I saw Foch, who was talking to a French senator, keep Pershing waiting five minutes at his elbow before he turned to include him in the conversation; this may have been simply bad manners but I think it was studied bad manners. The French have incensed the Americans by various high-handed acts in arranging the zones of occupation and the apportionment of the bridgeheads to suit themselves, and still more by the high prices they are charging the American soldiers for everything. The Americans, on the other hand, have angered the French by their friendly attitude towards the Germans in the occupied territory. This is a just criticism. We have, I understand, sent regiments into Germany which are composed largely of men of German origin; the Germans, with carefully prepared propaganda as always, have turned themselves inside out to be agreeable to the Americans and have kept their prices down to the lowest possible limit. The Americans compare the neatness of the German towns, their cleanliness, their love of music, their morality, their sense of system to the disfavor of the French; they forget the former atrocities and barbarities and wonder why we ever went to war with them. All this is not mere gossip but well-substantiated fact. . . .

As for the British, they are watching with much amusement our increasing friction with the French. They express themselves as satisfied with the progress made in forming the League of Nations, have very little to say on the freedom of the seas, are considerably stirred up by our naval program and are, of course, very much worried by the strike situation at home. Mr. Balfour says that the strikes are very serious [3] and by no means over. The volunteer army formation, with additional pay, was regarded as a wise move, and much progress has been made in financial matters since the armistice, thanks to Bonar Law [Leader of the Conservatives in the House of Commons, British Delegate to the Peace Conference]. Undoubtedly a good deal of old-fashioned diplomacy is going on beneath the surface and a good deal of dickering. . . .

To sum up, the French attitude towards us is one of suspicion and fear that we shall rob her of the fruits of victory. The British attitude is not unfriendly, but they have a very definite feeling that the United States must assume her share of the White Man's Burden and that it will not be possible for her to withdraw without leaving a stake in the game; members of the British Peace Commission state this openly. The attitude of the American Army is one of open hostility to the French. And there is hostility from all sides to our policy of relaxing the blockade and building up German industry. I shall try to write you more fully on this subject anon.

This is not a pretty picture and the dove of peace does not seem to be much in evidence above the Quai d'Orsay. Mr. Balfour hit the nail on the head when he recently remarked: "Five years ago we entered upon this war in order to end war, and now we are entering upon this peace in order to end peace."

---

[3] Labor grievances which had been temporarily quiescent during the war again became serious soon after the armistice. In January, 1919, the miners put forward demands for wage increases, hour reductions, and full wages from state funds for former miners not yet absorbed back into the industry from the armed forces. This marked the beginning of numerous strikes and strike threats. A police strike to gain union recognition was narrowly averted. To support the demands of the engineering and shipbuilding trades for shorter hours, the gas and electricity of the city of Belfast were turned off, and only Government intervention prevented the same thing from happening in London. Subway services in London were suspended by a strike on February 3. Although success was met in the early part of February in settling some of these disputes, this period marked the beginning of protracted disputes between labor and industry. See *The Annual Register . . . 1919* (London: Longmans, Green, & Co., 1920), pp. 5–11.

I have tried in this letter to tell you something about the undercurrents of public opinion. Later I want to write you more about the organization of our own Commission; there have been many difficulties to contend with and the job is anything but an agreeable one. It makes one long for the Maine Woods! . . .

February 7, 1919

Prince Michael Gagarine [former member of the Russian diplomatic service] our old Russian friend and colleague of Vienna days, came in to see me and we had a short talk on the usual subject of bolshevism. Gagarine said more or less the same thing Baron Schilling [former member of the Russian Foreign Office] had said the other day; namely, that a great percentage of the Bolshevik forces in Russia had joined them only through necessity and that if any military aid was sent in by the Allies many of these would immediately go over to them. He said there was no use in trying to do anything from Archangel, where the country is sparsely populated; but that if one regiment were sent in through Libau it would immediately be joined by a very great number of so-called Bolsheviks.

Things are going swimmingly for us at the Peace Conference just at present, as we are in a fair way to put through our proposition for sending food into Germany; Clemenceau having withdrawn his objections and asked only for a few days delay in order to prepare French public opinion.

Today at the Council of Ten, Hoover [Chief of the Food Administration, Adviser on Food and Relief Questions] put through his proposal that he should be given a mandate over all the railways and rolling stock of the former Austro-Hungarian Monarchy, including those portions occupied by Italy, and that credits should be arranged by which he could send food into Austria immediately. The Italians had done their best to oppose this, but found England, France and the United States against them, and they finally came to terms with only a few minor changes in the resolution — chiefly that Hoover should work through the Economic Council. When

Hoover's resolution had been introduced, Foch got up and said that as peace had not yet been signed he was in supreme command of all enemy railways and rolling stock and that if he surrendered this authority to Hoover he would have no control in case of further hostilities. Hoover immediately got up and said that he was only going to use twenty per cent of the railways and that, in any case, Austria was hardly now in a position to resume hostilities; to which Foch had nothing further to say. . . .

Monday, February 17 [1919]

. . . Attended meeting of the Commissioners this morning, at which Captain Walter Gherardi reported on his work in Germany. The principal idea that he brought out was that Germany was preparing to work for everything possible that could be got out of the Peace Conference and to show the danger of bolshevism as the reason for her demands. It was difficult to make the Germans see that the questions of boundaries and frontiers had no connection whatever with that subject. The wearing of uniforms is a handicap rather than an advantage and leaves our officers open to actual danger; in fact, a well-substantiated plot against Gherardi's life was discovered. An American woman married to a German overheard some men talking in a café and heard them say that they intended to kill Gherardi in the same way in which the German Ambassador was killed in Moscow.[4] They would go to the Hotel Adlon, find Gherardi's room, and kill him there. The woman followed the men to two other cafés, where they were joined by others, one of whom was obviously a sailor though in civilian clothes and one a Russian. Gherardi thought it might possibly be a personal matter resulting from enmities which he had made when he was in Berlin as Naval Attaché, but it seems more than probable that it was a Bolshevist plot (which would seem to be substantiated by the presence of the Russian), and that their intention was to discredit the present Government in

[4] Count Mirbach, the German Ambassador to Russia, was assassinated by the Social Revolutionaries in Moscow on July 6, 1918.

that way. The Commissioners decided to accept Gherardi's advice to withdraw our officers gradually from Germany, leaving only one or two civilians and secretariat at Berlin. . . .

A stormy interview with General Bliss this evening. I went to see him after dinner with regard to General Mason Patrick's [Chief of Air Service of the American Expeditionary Forces] recommendation that we appoint representatives from our Peace Mission to the Inter-Allied Aviation Committee. General Bliss emphatically said that he considered that this matter had no pertinency to the Peace Conference; and he felt that every man we were putting on committees or sending into the field, and that every dollar spent which did not directly contribute to the signing of peace, was nothing short of a crime. This led him to launch out on the whole subject, and he expressed himself very forcibly on the shilly-shallying and criminal delay of the Conference in not signing peace at once. He said that every day's delay brought the United States nearer to another war with Germany. Before this afternoon's conference at the Quai d'Orsay, at which the Russian problem was to be discussed, General Bliss had drawn up a memorandum [5] . . . to the effect that the problem of bolshevism could not be effectively dealt with or fully appreciated in the United States until peace was signed and the people of Europe shown the frontiers to which they were to confine themselves; at present, to the people of America, bolshevism was but one of many blots on the map of Europe. Mr. Lansing and Colonel House had both approved of this memorandum and promised to read it at this afternoon's session; but when the appropriate moment came, as General Bliss expressed it, "they lost their sand." He expressed great disgust with the lack of initiative of the other Commissioners, and said that he was sick of the whole thing and would like to go home. I later talked with Leland Harrison and found that the Russian question had been referred to the military leaders for a report and that when this report was returned our Commissioners would have another chance to read General Bliss's memorandum. . . .

5 For the text of this memorandum see Frederick Palmer, *Bliss, Peacemaker* (New York: Dodd, Mead & Co., 1934), p. 369.

Thursday, March 6 [1919]

Lunched at Madame Marie Louise de Sincay's with several interesting people, including Count Orloff, who had come to Paris to talk Russia — and for whom I had brought Fred Dolbeare [Adviser on Political and Diplomatic Questions, our Russian expert] and also Baron Schilling, who was formerly Sazonoff's Chef du Cabinet in the Russian Foreign Office, and later Senator. He had been imprisoned by the Bolsheviks and only recently escaped. I had a long and most interesting talk with him about conditions in Russia generally. He emphasized the fact that a very great number of the so-called Bolsheviks had become so only through necessity and would immediately desert if actively supported by the Allies. He said that the Hotel Metropole in Moscow was used as an internment place for the wives and children of Russian officers who had joined the Bolshevik army, and that if one of these officers showed in any way that he was not in sympathy with the Bolsheviks his family was immediately taken out and shot. All Russian officers, prisoners of war in Germany, who were released were met at the frontier and asked whether they would join the Bolsheviks or not. If they refused, they were immediately shot without trial. He said that in the prisons in Moscow men would become completely lost through the lack of system. A prisoner, for instance, would be sent from one prison to another and a receipt given for "one man" without any name; and thus there was nothing on the records to show what had happened to the prisoner in question and he could not be found even if desired. He said that soldiers and sailors would frequently come to the prisons and demand 30 or 40 prisoners, who would be delivered to them indiscriminately and who would be taken out and shot. He said that once when he was being taken from one prison to another by two guards, he insisted on one of the guards walking behind him and one in front, so that the one behind could not shoot him in the back without shooting his comrade also. These guards, when they had to take prisoners for some distance, would often avoid the trouble by simply shooting the prisoner and saying that he had tried to escape. In this particular case, he got into conversation with one of the guards, who told him that he had joined the Red Guards simply because he was at the verge of starvation and had no employment, and he begged Schilling to try to get him a job as locksmith, which was his profession. Schilling was imprisoned in a very small room that contained 5 other prisoners and only one chair between them. Some of them were left there for months. . . .

Monday, March 10 [1919]

Had a long talk this morning with Dr. James Brown Scott, with whom I had been discussing the question of the final form of the Peace Treaty and the languages to be used therein and had helped me in drafting a letter to M. P. Dutasta [Secretary General of the Peace Conference] on the subject. He told me that the Americans had won out on every point in the Committee on the Responsibility for the War, with the exception of the question of trying the Kaiser before a tribunal, which the British insisted upon, evidently owing to election pledges given by Lloyd George in England.[6] I asked Dr. Scott if our delegates would be content with submitting a minority report, but he said, on the contrary, that we should refuse to have anything to do with it, and that if the Kaiser is to be tried it will have to be done by England herself. The American proposition is simply to draw up a statement of the charges against the Kaiser and place them before the world and history. Dr. Scott said that we fully expected to have our way in the Committee on Cables, as we had a card to play which England would never dare allow; namely, a public statement showing that England had grabbed all of the cables to the United States, having attached the German cables to her shores so that she could control every word passing between Europe and the United States. . . .

[6] Before going to the Peace Conference Lloyd George called for elections in December, 1918, to determine whether his Government still held the confidence of a majority of the people. He won a sweeping victory with the aid of campaign slogans like "Hang the Kaiser," "Make Germany Pay," and "Shilling for Shilling and Ton for Ton."

Persuaded Mr. Lansing today to send Hugh Gibson to Prague as Diplomatic Agent with the personal rank of Minister Plenipotentiary, and he will leave shortly. We are always at least one step behind the other powers, and in this case England, France and Italy have all had experts at Prague for some time, while we, to whom they most look for help in creating their new State, have up till now not even sent a consul, and we are represented only by a young lieutenant, Freddy King, a member of Archie Coolidge's field mission. . . .[7]

To William Phillips, March 18, 1919

. . . Since I last wrote you there has been, as you are aware, a great change in the attitude of the French press towards the United States and the President particularly. The hostile press campaign, of which I wrote you, was promptly stopped when the President let it be known informally that if it continued he would recommend that the Peace Conference be transferred to a neutral country. I think there is no doubt that the greater part of the French press has been controlled all through the Conference by a newspaper hierarchy, culminating at the top in Tardieu, who holds the wires in his hands and pulls them as he sees fit. The very generous, and in some cases enthusiastic, comment of the newspapers on the President's return,[8] as well as Marshal Foch's unstinted praise of the accomplishments of General Pershing and the American Army in his speech at the dinner given to the American Commission by the

[7] In November 1918, Colonel House, disappointed by the misinformation coming into Paris concerning conditions in Central Europe, had cabled Washington suggesting that a special group of agents be sent to these countries under Mr. Grew to study and report the actual situation. *Supra*, p. 355. Mr. Grew was unable to go, and Professor Archibald Coolidge of Harvard, who had been a member of The Inquiry, was chosen to head the group. His commission from Mr. Lansing stated that he was "assigned to the American Commission to Negotiate Peace for the purpose of proceeding to Austria for that Commission to observe political conditions in Austria-Hungary and neighborhood countries." Coolidge and his subordinates left Paris for Vienna on December 27. Harold J. Coolidge and Robert H. Lord, *Archibald Cary Coolidge* (Boston: Houghton Mifflin Co., 1932), pp. 194–96.

[8] President Wilson left Paris for the United States on February 14. He returned one month later on March 14.

Inter-Allied Press Club, was significant of this change of policy. I do not think, however, that this change of policy signifies any change of heart, and I feel from all that can be gathered in personal conversation with French people of all classes that there still exists a very deep feeling that the President is approaching the peace terms from a detached point of view, that he does not sympathize with or understand what France has suffered during the war and that the United States is not sufficiently interested in obtaining from Germany the complete reparation and safeguards for the future which France feels she deserves.

In spite of all this we have made good progress and have overcome many obstacles, such for example as arranging finally for the feeding of Austria and Germany to prevent the anarchy which would overwhelm those countries if these arrangements had not been made without further delay.

There are, however, far more serious obstacles still to overcome. The French have practically given an ultimatum that they will not support the League of Nations unless some separate arrangement is made with the United States and Great Britain which will specifically guarantee France against German aggression in the future.[9] Such an agreement would, of course, compromise the whole structure of the League of Nations and would be entirely contrary to the principles for which we entered the war. It would, in effect, be reverting to the days of the Triple Alliance. Unless we can overcome this attitude of the French, I really do not see that we can do anything but withdraw from the Conference and conclude a separate peace.

The other great obstacle which looms up is the reported certainty that Germany will refuse to sign the treaty in the form in which it is now proposed to submit it. I think there is no

9 On June 28, 1919, when the Treaty of Versailles was signed, two supplementary guarantee treaties, one Franco-British and the other Franco-American, were also drawn up. These treaties guaranteed to France that the two other Powers would support France against German aggression. The United States Senate, however, refused to approve the Treaty, and thereupon the one with Britain, although already ratified, became void. Its acceptance had been made "contingent upon the United States Government undertaking the same obligation."

doubt that the German Government will do its best to delay matters in order to save its face, but I am optimist enough to believe that it will eventually go through, since the Germans must realize that it is either that or anarchy for them.

As regards Bullitt's mission,[10] of which you are no doubt fully informed, the whole thing was arranged, so far as I am aware, by Colonel House, and I do not think that the plan was ever discussed with the other Commissioners. I have no idea of the action, if any, it is proposed to take with reference to the suggested agreement with the Soviets, and I do not think that Mr. Lansing, Mr. White, or General Bliss have any idea themselves. The whole thing seems to me to be pretty full of dynamite.

So far as the routine work of the Commission is concerned, I think things are going pretty well. Some time ago we decided that it was essential to separate the current correspondence work from the Intelligence Section (Dr. Mezes' Committee), and I asked Ellis Dresel to head a new department called the Section of Current Diplomatic and Political Correspondence, composed of such men as Jordan Stabler [Chief of the Division of Latin American Affairs] for Latin America, E. T. Williams [Chief of the Division of Far Eastern Affairs] for the Far East, Allen Dulles for Austria-Hungary, Frederic Dolbeare for Russia, and others for various subjects. Each one of these men is responsible for keeping the Department fully informed in regard to his particular subject and I think you are receiving everything of value that comes to us. We have been cutting

10 In an effort to facilitate a solution of the Russian problem, William Bullitt had been sent to Russia to investigate political and economic conditions. His mission was kept secret from all other delegations excepting the British. Bullitt arrived in Petrograd on March 8, and a week later returned with the terms of peace which the Soviet Government was willing to accept. In a report to President Wilson he said that no "government save a socialist government can be set up in Russia to-day except by foreign bayonets, and any governments so set up will fall the moment such support is withdrawn. . . . This proposal of the Soviet Government presents an opportunity to make peace with the revolution on a just and reasonable basis — perhaps a unique opportunity." William C. Bullitt, *The Bullitt Mission to Russia* (New York: B. W. Huebsch, 1919), p. 54.

down somewhat on our military staff, but we have not one single diplomatic officer too many. Many of them, such as Dulles, Alexander Kirk and Christian Herter are serving on some of the territorial commissions of the Peace Conference, and they are all one hundred per cent busy. I fear you feel that we have depleted many of the Legations, but I do not see how it would have been possible to carry on the work of the Commission unless we had had these men. . . .

To William Phillips, April 13, 1919

I have no news of interest for you. As a matter of fact, the Commission itself knows very little as to just what is going on; all important questions are now discussed and decided by the Council of Four (President Wilson, Lloyd George, Clemenceau and Orlando) and as no secretaries or stenographers are present at their meetings and no notes are taken we hear little of the results achieved. Two days ago my Italian colleague asked me for the names of the American appointees to a new Commission which he said the Big Four had decided upon although he was somewhat uncertain as to its purpose; not one of the four Commissioners knows anything about it and I have as yet been unable to ascertain a word of information. This is simply an illustration of how things are being done — or not done. Our right hand does not know what the left is doing. Colonel House never attends the daily meetings of the other Commissioners and his office frequently takes action unknown to them and often disapproved by them when they finally learn of it. Our only link with the President is Arthur Hugh Frazier [member of the Secretariat] and he has become more sphinx-like than the Sphinx. He recently called John G. d'Arcy Paul, who was going to The Hague, to his office, shut all the doors, told him that he had a very secret and important message for him to take which could not be consigned to writing — and then whispered in his ear: "Tell John W. Garrett [American Minister to the Netherlands] that we have reason to believe that the birth rate in Germany is declining." This story, I am told by Paul, is not exaggerated. It describes to perfection the atmosphere in which we are working. . . .

As regards the Russian matter, I had the Bullitt reports prepared to cable to the Department but the Secretary stopped
them and they were only sent considerably later. The Commission and the personnel thereof has been considerably torn
with dissension on this subject. I am personally in entire accord with the food proposition: Bolshevism thrives on hunger
and armed opposition; if you fight it with arms it will grow;
if you fight it with food it will die a natural death. . . .

To Butler Wright, Counselor of the American
Embassy at London, April 24, 1919
Personal and Confidential
    . . . Your point that a great many Americans returning to
the United States would be glad to endorse the Service if their
attention were called to the importance of doing so, is well
taken. Very often, when a man leaves our office with expressions of appreciation for courtesies shown him, we feel like saying: "You can show your appreciation in a material manner if
you will simply talk about it when you get home"; but a sense
of modesty, or good taste, or something, generally prevents our
doing so. However, I think, for the good of the Service, we
ought to take every opportunity to get people of that kind
interested and simply *make* them go home and talk.
    I am afraid I can't agree with your feeling that it would be
the rankest sort of desertion for us to leave the Service during
the period of reconstruction. This reconstruction will go on
for a good many years, and there are a good many reasons why
some of us in Class I will not, and ought not to, remain indefinitely in that position. If it were a question of patriotism we
would, of course, put aside the element that makes a man feel,
when he has put 15 or 20 years of service behind him, that he
does not want to remain permanently a subordinate with his
colleagues of other nations going ahead of him and with the
fair chance always existing that he may be placed under a chief
who will regard him as an office boy and with suspicion into
the bargain. That element, can, of course, be put aside if it is
for the good of the Service; but I think, as a matter of fact, it
is most important for the Service that there should be con-

tinual motion upwards through the various classes with new blood continually coming in at the bottom, and if vacancies are not to be created by promotion, then I think they should be created by resignations. I think there will undoubtedly be a good many resignations as soon as the new Legations which are to be created as a result of the war are filled mainly by out-siders, as I fear is to be the case. I have recently had one or two talks with Mr. Lansing of a very discouraging nature. I suggested that even if only 30 or 40 per cent of the Legations could be given to Service men, it would be sufficient to stimu-late the whole Service from top to bottom; but he said he did not feel that even that percentage would be possible; that the Administration had lost the friendship of several Democratic Senators as a result of the appointments of Republicans such as William Phillips, Henry Fletcher [American Ambassador to Mexico], Lester Woolsey [Solicitor of the Department of State] and others, and that they could not afford to antagonize them in that way. He also said that, in his opinion, long service abroad as Secretary of Embassy or Legation did not, as a rule, fit a man to be a Minister or Ambassador, as it tended to nar-row his point of view and render him bureaucratic. There is undoubtedly some truth in this; but there are still a great many good men in the Service who have broadened rather than nar-rowed during their experience abroad, and it is only those men who need be considered for promotion to important posts. . . .

All this is for your ear alone. It sounds very pessimistic, and I can't say that I am in any other frame of mind at present. The Administration depends on the Senators and it will take a long time to persuade the latter that the Diplomatic Service is not a fair stamping-ground for patronage. It can be done only by influencing public opinion at home and that can be done only by the method suggested in your letter. I am heartily in accord with you and shall take every possible opportunity to sow seed in the right quarters.

To my mother, May 8, 1919

. . . Yesterday was one of the most impressive days I have ever lived through, for it was the day on which the peace treaty was handed to the Germans at Versailles: and being the anniversary of the sinking of the *Lusitania* it was a particularly appropriate date. All the delegates of the Allied and Associated Powers who had declared war on Germany were assembled in the Trianon Palace Hotel, in a large room near the one where the Armistice conferences took place last November; and two secretaries from each delegation were also admitted. The tables were arranged in a big square, with Mr. Clemenceau, President Wilson and Lloyd George sitting at the head and places reserved for the German delegates opposite them at the foot. At three o'clock everyone sat down, and a few minutes later the officer announced in a loud voice "Messieurs les Plénipotentiaires Allemands." They filed in, with Brockdorff-Rantzau [head of the German delegation to the Peace Conference] leading, and after the usual stiff German bows sat down. As they came in there was a momentary pause and then all of the Allied delegates stood up until the Germans were seated. Clemenceau immediately arose, declared the meeting open and then, trembling with emotion, made a short and very dignified address, of which I will enclose you a copy. He ended with the words "This second treaty of Versailles has cost us too much not to take on our side all the necessary precautions and guarantees that that peace shall be a lasting one." This was translated into German by the interpreter, and a copy of the treaty handed by Mr. Dutasta, the Secretary General, to Brockdorff-Rantzau.

To the surprise and disgust of everyone, Brockdorff-Rantzau remained seated while making his reply. Some people said his legs were trembling so from nervousness that he could not stand, but I rather doubt the validity of such an excuse, as he could at least have risen to begin and then sat down afterward. He made his speech in German, and it was interpreted sentence by sentence first into French and then into English. It was about the only thing he could have said, but there were a good many raisings of eyebrows among the Allies while he was talking. President Wilson, as he went out, said to me "What abominable manners." As soon as Rantzau had finished speaking Clemenceau declared the meeting closed and the Germans filed out, the Allies waiting until they had entirely disappeared before moving. It was a great event and I am happy to have seen it.

You ask me about my work and the people we are seeing. It would be impossible to tell you all the different jobs that fall to my lot daily; in general I have to direct the whole organization of the American Commission so that one part of my work is like that of a department-store manager, a hotel manager and a transportation director combined. If anyone wants a room in the hotel, or another office or an automobile from the pool or a passage home, they come to my office. The other day someone sent around for a razor strop! Whenever anyone wants to bring a piece of information or a request or an inquiry to the attention of the President or the Commissioners, it passes through my office. The Commissioners hold a daily meeting to consider matters presented to them and I have every such communication transcribed on a printed form and taken up at meeting by Chris Herter who acts as secretary; he enters the comment or decision of the Commissioners on the foot of the form and it comes back to me to advise the interested party. Besides that, I am responsible for all the diplomatic and political correspondence that comes to the Commission and I have a section of some ten or a dozen men, under Ellis Dresel, to deal with various subjects, such as Stabler for Latin America, Prof. Williams for the Far East, Allen Dulles for Austria, Sheldon Whitehouse for Russia, Dresel for Germany, Leon Dominian for Turkey, etc., etc. Everything they write comes to me for signature. We also have a large corps of technical experts for various territorial questions, chiefly well-known college professors, with whom I am in continual consultation. And then there are the Technical Advisers, including such men as Hoover, Vance McCormick, Bernard Baruch, Norman Davis, Edward Hurley, Samuel Gompers, James Brown Scott, David Hunter Miller, Tom Lamont, Bradley Palmer, Admiral Benson, etc., and I am also consulting with these men continually on one subject or another. The Administrative Offices, which are running the business end of the show, require a good deal of supervision, as well as the disbursing officer who can take no step without my authority. And finally I am the American secretary of the Supreme Council of the Allies, so that I have to be responsible for editing all the minutes, protocols etc., of the meetings, although Leland Harrison, Colonel Ulysses Grant and Lieut. Chester Burden generally do the actual secretarial work for me. . . .

To my mother, June 26, 1919

. . . I have written little about the Peace Conference for two reasons: first because I would prefer to look at it from the perspective of a few years hence rather than under the confused impressions of the present, and second because I could not write about it without showing up a great deal of dissatisfaction, errors of judgment and policy and disagreements within the Commission itself. I am far from satisfied with the treaty with Germany, still less so with the treaty with Austria; both unquestionably contain the seeds for future wars. But no one will ever know all the difficulties the President and the Commission have had to contend with; if we could have imposed our own will in every question, all would have been well; but there have had to be compromises. On the whole the President has fought a great fight and this Peace Conference has been as great a fight as was the war that led to it. All we can do now is to put our trust in the League of Nations; it is the only solution for the future; the cornerstone has been laid and the name of the President will always be great for laying it; the structure has yet to be built. . . .

To my mother, July 2, 1919

At 6.45 on the 23rd the guns at the Invalides announced that the Germans had agreed to sign the Treaty and all Paris gave itself over to celebration; flags appeared on every house, the streets were full of cheering people and Montmartre, to which we later repaired, was a seething mass of enthusiastic humanity.

On the 24th Hugh Gibson and Reggie Foster turned up from Warsaw and I spent most of the day going over the Jewish situation in Poland with Hugh and particularly Louis Marshall's attack on him in the *New York Times;* also discussed the proposed commission of investigation into the alleged Jewish pogroms, the chairmanship of which I am trying to persuade Henry Morgenthau to accept. . . .[11] [On the evening of June 26] the Poincarés gave a big farewell banquet to the Wilsons at the Elysée — about 250 people. The President had absolutely refused to accept at first and Ambassador Hugh Wallace [American Ambassador to France from February, 1919] was tearing his hair as it would have been a bad error and would have bitterly offended the French, just as they were offended by the President's refusal to go to the front to see the devastated regions; but some pressure must have been brought to bear as he was led to change his mind — as an exception — and accepted. It was a very beautiful dinner, splendid floral decorations, soft music by the band of the Garde Républicaine and all the usual paraphernalia; the two Presidents exchanged toasts at the end. . . .

After dinner, while everyone was standing around drinking coffee, President Wilson sent for me and gave me his seal ring for sealing the treaty on the day following; he explained which side should be up and said that the hieroglyphic on it was his name in shorthand. Then, to my embarrassment, because there were a lot of high statesmen waiting to talk to him, he started to chat with me — something he had never done before — and kept me in conversation for ten or fifteen minutes.

---

11 Reports of the wholesale slaughter of Jews in Poland had been circulated in 1919. These stories were met with denial by the Polish Government. Gibson's report to the State Department seemed to substantiate the validity of this denial. Louis Marshall, a prominent Jewish lawyer, attacked Gibson in the *New York Times,* June 17, 1919, for his report which came, Marshall said, "out of the fullness of his [Gibson's] ignorance." In June, 1919, Paderewski, the Polish President, asked President Wilson to appoint an American Commission to investigate the situation. On July 10, 1919, this mission headed by Henry Morgenthau and General Edgar Jadwin was sent to Poland. Arthur Goodhart, counsel to the group, described the investigation in *Poland and the Minority Races,* New York, 1920.

He said he had learned shorthand to help in jotting down his lectures and speeches and that he then copied them himself on his Corona typewriter; I asked him if anyone else could read his shorthand but he said not; he had to transcribe it himself. He said many people, particularly Congress, failed to understand why he did such unconventional things; he, for instance, was the first President to set foot outside of the United States during his term of office, except Taft who had once straddled the Mexican frontier. Then he had broken all precedents by delivering his own addresses to Congress in person;[12] he said he felt a speech carried infinitely more weight when delivered personally as one could really get at the people one was addressing. Then he talked about the dinner and said (all too loudly) that he hated dinners of that kind and that it was an awful bore; President Poincaré was standing almost at his elbow — I hope he didn't hear. He kept on in a chatty vein for some time and I was never so much impressed by the charm and cordiality of his manner and particularly his smile — quite different from the serious, almost severe, face I had so often watched in the sessions of the Peace Conference. I took the first possible opportunity to break away as this was a French party and not just the time for him to be monopolized by Americans.[13]

On the 27th . . . Leland Harrison and I went to the Quai d'Orsay to affix the seals of our Commissioners to the Peace Treaty. The French intended to make it a very solemn ceremony: the sacred treaty, bound in white vellum and printed on Japanese paper, was carried in by the Chef du Protocol, William Martin, and laid on the central table in the Salle d'Horloge, and the seals of all the different delegates were arranged on the table ready for use in turn. Then, when all was ready, the machine for melting the sealing wax was produced and it was found that it had to be attached by a wire to an electric applique in the wall — but to the consternation of

12 John Adams had been the last President to deliver his messages to Congress in person.

13 I have no doubt that the President did this on purpose in order not to have to talk to the French. — J. C. G.

everybody no applique was to be found in the Salle d'Horloge. So to the evident disgust of the Chef du Protocol the treaty had to be transferred to a small room adjoining where an applique was found, the wax was duly melted and then, with infinite care and solemnity, the seal of each delegate was affixed in turn, beginning with President Wilson and the other Americans. It was indeed a breathless moment when the first drop of melted wax was allowed to drop beside the place reserved for President Wilson's signature; it might have run, it might have burnt a hole in the treaty! But it didn't — it came out just right and everyone gave a sigh of relief.[14]

After that I returned to my desk and remained there till 4.30 A.M. preparing the list of Americans who should receive tickets to the signing of peace at Versailles; we had 11 tickets for the secretaries, 67 for invited guests to the Salle des Glaces and 75 to the terraces outside. We had forced the last possible ticket out of the Secretariat-General, having camped on their trail most of the afternoon, and now it was simply a question of deciding who had prior claim to those 67 tickets and making lifelong enemies of those who thought they ought to get in but didn't. We had a list of nearly 200 to boil down to 67. It was a horrible night, for after we had gone through the list time and again and thought we had it complete, Admiral Cary Grayson [physician to President Wilson] sent down for 6 more tickets for the President (he had 6 already) and General Pershing asked for 4 tickets for some American Generals and we had to give them and cut 10 people off our list, already pared to the quick. Leland Harrison and I got to bed at about 5 and had to be up early on the 28th for the big day.

All the morning of the 28th — the fifth anniversary of the assassination of the Archduke Franz Ferdinand, by the way — I was hounded by people who had not received tickets, many of whom blustered and threatened. The one ray of sunlight in a dark atmosphere was Hoover who said he had never expected to be included and expressed surprise and gratification at receiving a card. A great man with a child's modesty is to be ap-

14 I affixed his seal. — J. C. G.

preciated, yea much. . . . The signing was to be at 3. We started at 1.15 and arrived at the Château at Versailles at 2, so that we had a solid hour before the beginning of the ceremony.

The approaches to Versailles were carefully guarded by troops and only those cars which had tricolor affiches on their windshields were allowed through the lines. As we came up the broad avenue to the Château a truly magnificent sight awaited us: the Garde Républicaine in full uniform and mounted lined both sides of the road. Once inside the Château at the entrance to the Salle des Glaces I did a little jockeying with Alice's and my tickets and managed to get Madame Arnavon [wife of the Chief of Cabinet of the Secretary General] through as well as ourselves, to say nothing of Mrs. Kirk [Alexander Kirk's mother]; the Secretaries at the door were flustered and I don't think they quite knew what was happening. Arnavon, when he saw his wife inside, was officially furious and personally delighted. There was a full hour or more before the signature, during which time I obtained the signatures of most of the principal delegates on the cover of my peace treaty, including President Wilson, Clemenceau, Lloyd George, etc. In fact everyone was obtaining signatures and the only person who appeared to object to it was Clemenceau who snorted as each request was made, but signed all the same. . . .

Finally the meeting was called to order and the two German delegates appeared, Dr. Herman Müller [Foreign Minister] and Dr. Johannes Bell [Colonial Minister], escorted by Allied officers and one or two German secretaries, and took their places at the foot of the long table. I have seldom seen two such wretched specimens of humanity: one tall and thin, the other short and black and peering through his heavy glasses like a lost owl. Clemenceau arose, stated that the treaty on the table was identical with the one the Germans had seen, and invited the Germans to sign. They did so, the secretary handing Dr. Bell a special fountain pen with a low bow and a large flourish. Immortal pen! Then the Allies signed in turn, 13 documents altogether. My seat was directly beside the signing table, the first of the secretaries. Pershing also sat on our bench. The signing lasted about an hour, Clemenceau declared that the treaty was signed and adjourned the meeting. The Germans bowed and left immediately. The whole ceremony was simply carried out but the historical background, remembering what happened in that same room nearly fifty years ago,[15] robbed it of any banality and made it impressive beyond description. . . .

October 1, 1919

Now that the work of the Peace Conference has relaxed a little I hope to find a few minutes in the day for renewing the old diary which has been sadly neglected during the last strenuous months. The brunt of the strain is over, although we are still comfortably occupied, but I fail to see how the Conference can continue indefinitely. The Bulgarian Treaty has been handed to the Bulgarians and there will be nothing further to do on that until they come back with their reply, for which they have been given 25 days and will probably ask for an extension, so that we shall not get it in any case before November 1st. The Hungarian Treaty is as nearly finished as it can be at present and only awaits the formation of a stable government in Hungary in order to present it. The Turkish Treaty cannot be prepared until it is known whether the United States will accept any mandates or not.[16] Meanwhile, the Council of the Heads of Delegations continues to meet daily and to consider odds and ends, of which there seem to be still a considerable number. Lloyd George did his best to break up the Conference, but Mr. Polk[17] and Clemenceau

---

[15] In 1871 the King of Prussia had been proclaimed German Emperor in this room after the defeat of France in the Franco-Prussian War.

[16] The unfavorable reaction of the United States Senate to the peace treaties made it clear that President Wilson could assume no mandated territories in the former Turkish Empire.

[17] Under Secretary of State Frank Polk was appointed a Commissioner to Negotiate Peace on July 17, 1919, and made head of the American delegation on July 28.

persuaded him not to do so and he finally compromised by taking home practically his whole delegation and leaving Sir Eyre Crowe [Assistant Undersecretary of State for Foreign Affairs, Adviser on Political and Diplomatic Questions to the British Commission] to represent Great Britain alone. . . .

I have been out driving and walking with Colonel House twice recently and we have discussed the affairs of the nations. He feels as strongly about Bullitt's action as the rest of us do. . . . The original draft of the League of Nations bearing the penciled words: "To W. C. Bullitt, as a mark of appreciation of his help in an hour of need. From E. M. House," which Bullitt submitted to the Foreign Relations Committee of the Senate in order to show the confidence placed in him by the Commissioners was given to him in this wise: The President sent the draft down to the Crillon late one night with the request that it be printed before the following morning. Colonel House tried to find Harrison, myself and others but we were all out at the time. As he happened to meet Bullitt in the hallway he asked him if he would take on the job of getting it printed over night. Bullitt stayed up all night and had the job ready by breakfast time. Colonel House told Bullitt that the President would be very much pleased and it was simply because he had stayed up all night that the Colonel gave him the document as a memento. The Colonel said that in slamming Lansing, Bullitt had injured his best friend for it was Lansing who had finally approved of his going to Russia and had given him his credentials. Dr. Manley Hudson [Adviser on Legal Questions to the American Commission], who has just returned from Washington, saw Bullitt himself and says that he seems now a little ashamed of having told what Lansing had said to him in confidence. Some people in Washington seem to think that the information was wormed out of Bullitt by the Senate Committee, but Hudson has studied the minutes of the meeting and it is quite evident that he freely volunteered all the remarks and that the Committee was particularly careful not to press him on any point, in fact they actually declined to hear some confidential remarks made by Colonel House which Bullitt was going to repeat to them.[18]

18 On May 17, Bullitt sent his letter of resignation as an assistant in the Department of State to Mr. Lansing. In a letter of explanation to President Wilson he indicated that this was in protest against the terms of the treaty of peace. "Russia, 'the acid test of good will,' for me as for you, has not even been understood. Unjust decisions of the conference in regard to Shantung, the Tyrol, Thrace, Hungary, East Prussia, Danzig, the Saar Valley, and the abandonment of the principle of the freedom of the seas make new international conflicts certain. It is my conviction that the present league of nations will be powerless to prevent these wars. . . . Therefore the duty of the Government of the United States to its own people and to mankind is to refuse to sign or ratify this unjust treaty. . . ." On August 23, Bullitt was summoned to give testimony before the Senate Committee on Foreign Relations. The hearing took place on September 12, 1919, with Henry Cabot Lodge as chairman.

Bullitt testified at length on the various plans for a league of nations considered at Paris, Wilson's attitude toward these plans, and on his own mission to Russia. The part of his testimony, however, which was most damaging to the case for the United States entering the League was that in which he reported his conversations with some of the most important Americans at the Conference. In answer to Senator Lodge's question of whether the members of the United States delegation had expressed any opinions on the general character of the Treaty, Mr. Bullitt said:

"Well, Mr. Lansing, Col. House, Gen. Bliss, and Mr. White had all expressed to me very vigorously their opinions on the subject.

"THE CHAIRMAN. Were they enthusiastically in favor of it?

"MR. BULLITT. I regret to say, not. . . . It is no secret that Mr. Lansing, Gen. Bliss, and Mr. Henry White objected very vigorously to the numerous provisions of the treaty.

"THE CHAIRMAN. It is known that they objected to Shantung. That, I think, is public information. I do not know that it is public information that they objected to anything else.

"MR. BULLITT. I do not think that Secretary Lansing is at all enthusiastic about the league of nations as it stands at present. I have a note of a conversation with him on the subject. . . .

"This was a conversation with the Secretary of State at 2.30 on May 19. The Secretary sent for me. It was a long conversation, and Mr. Lansing in the course of it said:

" 'Mr. Lansing then said that he personally would have strengthened greatly the judicial clauses of the league of nations covenant, making arbitration compulsory. He also said that he was absolutely opposed to the United States taking a mandate in either Armenia or Constantinople; that he thought that Constantinople should be placed under a local government, the chief members of which were appointed by an international committee. . . . Mr. Lansing then said that he, too, considered many parts of the treaty thoroughly bad, particularly those dealing with Shantung and the league of nations. He said:

October 2, 1919

. . . I have taken over all questions pertaining to Russia and there are two particularly which are engaging our attention at present; first, the question of policy involved in continuing to send supplies to the Estonians who are reported to be negotiating for peace with the Bolsheviks, and second, the question

"I consider that the league of nations at present is entirely useless. The great powers have simply gone ahead and arranged the world to suit themselves. England and France in particular have gotten out of the treaty everything that they wanted, and the league of nations can do nothing to alter any of the unjust clauses of the treaty except by unanimous consent of the members of the league, and the great powers will never give their consent to changes in the interests of weaker peoples."

" 'We then talked about the possibility of ratification by the Senate. Mr. Lansing said: "I believe that if the Senate could only understand what this treaty means, and if the American people could really understand, it would unquestionably be defeated, but I wonder if they will ever understand what it lets them in for." . . . ' " U.S. Congress, Senate, *Treaty of Peace with Germany,* Hearings before the Committee on Foreign Relations, U.S. Senate, 66th Cong., 1st Sess. (Washington: Government Printing Office, 1919), pp. 1273, 1276–77.

Fifteen years later when Bullitt, then Ambassador to the Soviet Union, visited Mr. Grew in Tokyo, the two of them discussed the 1919 episode, and Mr. Grew wrote in his diary for November 12, 1934: "As there were no events today I will take this occasion to give a brief summary of Bill Bullitt's account to me of the real story — from his point of view — of the incidents at the Peace Conference which led to his testimony before the Senate and his resultant ostracization by the public, the press and his own friends. . . .

"Wilson and Lloyd George sent him to Russia during the Peace Conference to report on the probable stability of the Soviet regime and the conditions of recognition. In Moscow he conferred constantly with Lenin, Tchitcherin [Commissar for Foreign Affairs] and Litvinoff [Assistant Commissar for Foreign Affairs] and finally came away with an agreement in his pocket, signed and sealed, providing for immediate demobilization and the complete independence and autonomy of the Ukraine, Siberia, Poland and all outlying provinces in return for Allied recognition. Bullitt called immediately on Colonel House who congratulated him warmly on his success and telephoned to Wilson who asked Colonel House to convey his own congratulations. Wilson was at that time ill with influenza and could not see Bullitt at once, so, in reply to an invitation, he had breakfast at the Majestic with Lloyd George and Philip Kerr (now Lord Lothian). Lloyd George was much impressed by his report but said that he could not possibly consider recognizing Soviet Russia as Lord Northcliffe, the *Daily Mail* and his other political enemies would 'tear me limb from limb.' When President Wilson recovered and came down to the Crillon he met Bullitt and cut him dead, the inference being that he was angry at Bullitt's having first reported to Lloyd George. Subsequently Admiral

of turning over to Nikolai Yudenich [Commander of anti-
Bolshevik forces] the supplies now in Germany which were
taken from the Russians during the war. In regard to the first
question, it is very difficult to ascertain just how serious these
peace negotiations of the Estonians with the Bolsheviks are.
While Consul Thornwell Haynes, our representative at Hel-

Kolchak began his advance towards Moscow, and although it failed of success,
all question of dealing directly with the Soviets died in the meantime.

"Meanwhile the Peace Conference was getting deeper and deeper into the
mire of political intrigue, totally disregarding the Fourteen Points on the
basis of which Germany had capitulated, and a treaty was being formulated
which not only was hypocritical and contrary to all the ideals set forth on
its convocation but which contained the seeds of future wars. . . . Bullitt
resigned in May, 1919, in accordance with his convictions. He left the Crillon
(where he and I had been working together as we had formerly worked at the
same desk in the State Department) and took up quarters elsewhere. Only
when the Commission was about to return to the United States did he call on
the Commissioners to say good-bye, and it was during that call that Mr. Lansing openly inveighed against the Peace Treaty, calling it thoroughly bad and
characterizing the proposed League of Nations as useless.

"Presumably Bullitt divulged this talk in conversation because, when he
returned to the United States, he heard that the Republican senators who
wanted to defeat the Treaty of Versailles were going to call on him to testify
before the Committee on Foreign Relations. He did not tell me how the
news of the conversation reached the senators and I am unable to say whether
he did that deliberately or not. But he did tell me that at about the time
of the Senate hearings he took a long canoeing and camping trip in the Maine
Woods with his first wife, Ernesta, hoping thus to avoid being called. However, on emerging from the woods at Fort Kent he was met by the sheriff
with a subpoena from the Senate.

"At this point Bullitt tends to dramatize the story. He said he wrestled
with himself all day at Fort Kent and by evening he had decided to tell the
Senate the whole truth. According to his tale he said to his wife that as a
result of his testimony he would become a social pariah for the next fifteen
years and that she would have to share the brickbats with him. He also,
according to his story, told her that the Soviet Union would be recognized
by the United States within the next 'fourteen years' and that then his proph-
ecies would be found correct and he would be reinstated in public estimation. He pointed out to me that his guess had been accurate within one
year. . . .

"This testimony of course carried great influence in the defeat of the Treaty
of Versailles by the American Senate, and Bullitt was branded throughout
the country by the press, the public and his friends as disloyal to his former
chief. . . . He told me of his subsequent wanderings abroad during the time
he was practically a social outcast. I asked him if any of his former friends

singfors, reports that they are sure to make peace, we hear from other sources that this is highly improbable. On the one hand, if we continue to send supplies into Estonia, the Bolsheviks would profit by them if peace were made, but on the other hand, if we stop these supplies that action might in itself drive the Estonians into the arms of the Bolsheviks as indicating that the Allies were withdrawing their support. As regards sending to Yudenich the supplies in Germany, it is possible that this might be accomplished under the provisions of Articles 169 and 116 of the Treaty with Germany.[19] The first article provides that all these supplies taken from the Russian Army shall be turned over to the Allies for destruction within two months after the Treaty goes into force, and Article 116 provides for restitution and reparation to Russia based on the principles of the Treaty itself. Mr. Polk does not wish to take up Russian questions at present as he holds that they are not directly concerned with the work of the Commission in preparing the various peace treaties and that it is a subject for the Department of State and the Embassy to handle, but we cannot get away from the fact that some of these questions are

had stood by him, to which he replied that Colonel House had done so through thick and thin.

"Bullitt's action raises a nice point of ethics. In the light of our present knowledge, doubly reinforced by Harold Nicolson's recent book *Peacemaking* — published in London, 1933 — giving the inside story of the Peace Conference, Bullitt was profoundly right in regarding the Treaty of Versailles as a disaster, and if he felt — as he did feel — that it ought not to be ratified by the United States, the question arises whether his loyalty to his political ideals and to what he considered to be the best interests of our country was not superior to his loyalty to his former chief, the Secretary of State. At any rate, he had the courage of his convictions — (he had no respect whatever for Mr. Lansing for not resigning as Secretary of State owing to the latter's attitude towards the treaty) — and he apparently foresaw what the penalty for telling the truth would be and accepted it with open eyes. . . . One would have to get into Bullitt's own mind as it worked at that time to know whether to condemn him still for disloyalty or to admire him for extraordinary courage. From his own story, one is inclined to choose the latter course. I put all this down as an interesting historical cliché."

19 See U.S. Department of State, *The Treaty of Versailles and After. Annotations of the Text of the Treaty* (Washington: Government Printing Office, 1947), pp. 272–74, 324–28.

inseparably bound up with the Treaty with Germany and the interpretation of it, and I am hoping to persuade him to bring up this Yudenich matter to the Supreme Council. . . .

Yesterday Prince Lieven came to see me and threw some optimistic light on the general situation. He recently commanded an army in the Baltic Provinces, was shot through the abdomen by the Bolsheviks, but continued to direct the operations for three weeks, being carried from place to place on a litter. He is still in a bad way, looks as if he had suffered terribly and hobbles around on two canes. He told me that he thought it was extremely doubtful if the Estonians would sacrifice the support of the Allies by making peace with the Bolsheviks, and he also told me that he thought that bolshevism was on the wane, that public opinion in Russia was becoming more and more antagonistic to it and that it was only a question of time before it would die out in the face of the offensive of Anton Denikin [White Russian General in South Russia], Yudenich and Alexander Kolchak [Commander of anti-Bolshevik forces in Russia] and also in the face of starvation which threatened on account of lack of transportation and the fact that Deniken held most of the coal and oil lands and richest agricultural districts. . . .

October 16, 1919

. . . In the late afternoon I went down to the station with Allen Dulles to see Paderewski and Mme. Paderewska off to Warsaw and delivered to Paderewski a letter written him by Mr. Polk stating what a great work he had done in Paris for his country.[20] Paderewski is going to have a very difficult time on his return, owing to his failure to obtain Eastern Galicia outright for Poland and we may possibly permit him to publish

20 In 1921, Colonel House wrote of Paderewski at the Peace Conference: "He came as the spokesman of an ancient people whose wrongs and sorrows had stirred the sympathies of an entire world. . . . His fervored eloquence brought about the renascence of Poland, and added new lustre to a famous name." Edward M. House and Charles Seymour (eds.), *What Really Happened at Paris* (New York: Charles Scribner's Sons, 1921), p. viii.

the letter from Mr. Polk in case it can help him at home. I had a long talk in the afternoon with Prince Casimir Lubomirski, the new Polish Minister to Washington who is just about to leave for his post, and told him that if I had my way Eastern Galicia would go to Poland without any strings attached to it. The proposal to leave the question to the League of Nations will not be satisfactory to the Polish people and a plebiscite in the future would be even more distasteful to them. Paderewski's opponents feel that he has been too docile at the Peace Conference and that although this has increased his personal prestige in Paris it has not helped the Polish interests and that he would have got more if he had taken a firmer stand and fought the way the Czecho-Slovaks and others have done. There have certainly been inconsistencies in some of the decisions of the Supreme Council and other countries have been given territory to which they had far less claims than Poland to Eastern Galicia. The British have been the main stumbling block in this particular question and Paderewski, I think, feels it is mainly due to Phillip Kerr, Lloyd George's secretary who has much influence with the Prime Minister and who is himself an idealist. Although the Poles are numerically in the minority in Eastern Galicia, they nevertheless represent the intelligent classes and it seems a pity that Poland cannot be given at least an opportunity to do what she can with that country, free of all reservations and if she fails, its future can be decided by the League of Nations. . . . [21]

December 9, 1919

The American Commission to Negotiate Peace went out of business tonight — a full year less five days since it began its difficult labors, on December 14, 1918. I have been extremely

[21] In December, 1919, the Supreme Council granted East Galicia autonomy under a Polish protectorate for twenty-five years, after which the League of Nations was to decide its future. Poland, however, treated East Galicia as an integral part of Poland, and this was recognized as such by the Council of Ambassadors on March 14, 1923.

busy arranging for the closing up of the Hotel Crillon and the transfer of many of its offices to the Embassy to which Harrison and I have been assigned, together with some twenty-five of the Peace Commission personnel. . . .[22]

Mr. Polk, Mr. White and General Bliss with all of the members of the Commission who are not remaining in Paris left for Brest tonight at 8.40 to sail on the *America* tomorrow. Clemenceau, Maréchal Foch, and the other members of the Supreme Council were at the station to see them off, and I believe they were sincerely sorry to have them go. The old General, just before he stepped on the train, actually kissed Foch, on his own initiative — I saw Foch turn the other cheek, but the General apparently thought that one was enough. . . .

Frank Polk before his departure gave out the following message to the French people:

At a moment when we are about to leave this historic Crillon building, where we have worked with all our hearts for a whole year, I wish to declare, in the name of us all, our deep regret in leaving France and our sincere joy in having been associated with France so closely in Peace efforts, as well as her supreme efforts in war.

Personally my grief is soothed by the happy satisfaction that I feel in seeing the last clouds which once menaced our common work float away. There is no doubt at all today that Germany will submit to the just demands of the Allies. Moreover, Rumania will, in a friendly spirit, append the signature which we have not yet had the joy of seeing on the Treaty of Saint-Germain.

Finally, the treaty with Hungary is ready in every detail. The laborious building up of the world's peace is thus being completed.

I shall never forget the welcome I received here. I loved and admired France before I arrived. I leave loving and admiring France more than ever before. May France know that only one

[22] Mr. Grew became Counselor of the Embassy at Paris. Ambassador Wallace as early as June, 1919, had asked him to take this post.

sentiment exists in America for her — and that is affection. And that affection is unanimous and eternal!

We have all of us greatly admired both the Polks and have been very proud of having such representatives over here. From what I have heard, he has been equally liked and admired on the Supreme Council, for although obliged frequently to fight one-sided battles against the other representatives, sometimes with very weak arguments to support his position, he has always done so in a gentlemanly and graceful manner. . . .

PART THREE

Diplomacy in an Age of "Normalcy"

1920–1927

DURING *the postwar decade, an exaggerated nationalism and a wave of uncritical reaction swept the United States. Attention was focused on "100 per cent Americanism," closing the doors to immigrants, and a general revulsion set in toward facing pressing domestic and world problems.*

The United States, with its immense economic and naval strength, might well have been expected to play a bold and statesmanlike role in world politics in the post-Versailles world. The desire of the American people to return to "normalcy" during the Harding-Coolidge years, however, prevented any dramatic leadership from the new power in the western hemisphere, except perhaps with regard to the Far East.

The United States did not exactly stand aloof from international conferences nor did it fail to send observers to the League of Nations. American diplomats were more active than in the past, but the nation was wary of commitments to assist in keeping the peace. American diplomacy was based on the idea that peace was a matter of good will and of promises like the Kellogg Pact of 1928. This proposal to outlaw war reflected the American belief that it was possible to have peace without bothering to maintain it by physical force.

By refusing to ratify the Treaty of Versailles, the United States Senate had withdrawn the nation from the grand alliance that had won the war. This alliance continued to disintegrate as Great Britain, France, and Italy pursued separate policies. The alliance suffered severe strain when France occupied the

Ruhr in 1923, and the three powers were unable to present a united front to Turkey at the Lausanne Conference.

Serving first as Minister to Denmark and then as Minister to Switzerland, Mr. Grew was in a key position to witness the disintegration of the grand alliance. At the Lausanne Conference, particularly, he was to see the diplomacy of the Allied world crippled by indecision and suspicion, and, finally, defeated by a bitter split between Great Britain and France.

From 1924 to 1927, Mr. Grew was to serve as Under Secretary of State and to receive entirely new experiences from service at home. Instead of executing American foreign policy in a post overseas, he was now to be in a position to help formulate policy for all portions of the world. The Department of State, however, was trying to formulate policy for a people little concerned with world events. The collapse of Wilsonian idealism, an ingrown piety, and a glorification of the one hundred per cent American all relegated diplomacy to, at least, a secondary position in the "age of wonderful nonsense."

XVI

Paris and Copenhagen
1920 – 1921

January 10–31 [1920, Paris]

. . . The Embassy work has not been heavy — just enough to keep one pleasantly occupied — a very great relief after the strain of the past year. I practice the piano for an hour or an hour and a half in the morning, get to the Chancery at about 10.30 and leave generally between 6 and 7. On January 14th I called on Baron Kurt von Lersner, the President of the German Delegation, and informed him, by instructions, that the United States regarded the armistice between the United States and Germany as being still in full force and effect in spite of the deposit of ratifications of the Versailles Treaty by other Powers. I think von Lersner was afraid that I might not shake hands with him for while I was waiting in the anteroom he suddenly shot in with his hand outstretched as if he wanted to surprise me into taking it. I had, however, no intention of not doing so. After the deposit of ratifications and the signing of the protocol which actually brought peace between Germany and the other Powers, Clemenceau saluted von Lersner but did not shake hands.

On the 15th I saw Claude-Louis Hermite at the Foreign Office to urge early and favorable action on the question of the exhumation and transport to the United States of the bodies of the American dead buried in France in the zone of armies. . . .

On the 24th I went with the Ambassador [Hugh Wallace] to his first interview with Alexandre Millerand [Prime Minister and Foreign Minister]. The latter impresses me as straightforward, thorough and determined and he gave the impression

407

of wanting to do everything to help the good relations of France and the United States. He speaks no English — in fact all conversations at the Foreign Office have to be carried on in French (and I have had some trouble in getting familiar with the technical language necessary to discuss complicated political questions, having to bone up very carefully in advance) — so, as the Ambassador speaks no French, I read him a long statement of the matter which we had come to discuss, namely the exhumation and return of the American dead in France. They have already permitted the removal of the bodies buried outside the war zone but the last Government definitely refused to apply this to the 60,000 or more American bodies buried in the zone of armies until similar permission could be given to the French families to remove their dead. We pressed the matter very emphatically and Millerand, while pointing out the difficulties involved, finally said he thought he could agree in principle and that the details could then gradually be arranged, but hinted that there would have to be some delay. On the whole we were well satisfied with the result of the interview and the progress made. The question has become a very serious one in America and is likely to cause a lot of friction unless we can get the French to give in. However one cannot help recognizing the justice of their own attitude; the Government is deluged with petitions from French families for the recovery of their own dead and it will place the Government in an embarrassing position when they allow us to remove ours. The question of transportation is going to be difficult; France can hardly afford to spare the means at present when every car in the country is needed for economic reconstruction. Personally, I think the idea of removing the dead is all wrong; they should be left where they have fought and died, in well-cared-for military cemeteries. Nothing could be more venerable and impressive than the American Cemetery at Belleau Woods. . . . However, legislation is pending in Congress to demand the return of the dead, nation-wide societies are being formed and the pressure is so great that we have had instructions of the most emphatic character, intimating that the good relations of the two countries would suffer unless the French Government came across. We have carried out these instructions to the letter and every one of our conversations at the Foreign Office and the wording of our repeated notes has been of a most emphatic nature.

To Butler Wright, January 18, 1920

I feel a good deal of remorse at the very casual replies which you have received from me to your various letters about the Foreign Service. Your letters have all been interesting and extremely valuable and my answers have by no means expressed my appreciation of what you are doing for the Service. You will never have any comprehension of what the work of the Peace Commission has been. To me, as I look back upon it, it has been the worst nightmare I have ever been through. One never had time even to think clearly and it was not congenial work; an officer in the Diplomatic Service ought never to be called upon to become a department-store manager, a director of traffic and a sweeper-out-in-chief of the Hotel Crillon as I was, and as for the purely diplomatic side of it, who can be satisfied at the results? So you may gather that having got down to normal diplomacy again, I feel a new lease of life and a joy in work and living that I have not experienced for over a year; in fact I feel gathered once again in the arms of my father and mother, the Service.

Now as to your letter to Billy Phillips of November 24th — this is what I think. It was extremely useful as an expression of fact and opinion to the Department. Certainly many men in the Service will resign unless some hope can be held out of higher salaries or better allowances; the Department knows this and, as Bill Phillips wrote you, we can count on the Department's support. But the Department is not the primary factor that we have to consider, nor, in fact, is Congress. The Department is dependent on Congress and Congress is dependent on American public opinion and it is to public opinion that we must turn. What can influence it? Not appeals for better pay; that is putting the cart before the horse. The public

has hitherto believed that the Diplomatic Service was instituted
for the purpose of permitting the gilded youth of the country
to shine in foreign society and to afford comfortable berths
for undesirable or decayed politicians. It must first learn what
the Diplomatic Service stands for and what it can, if properly
supported, accomplish in their interest. Once the public is
educated, the question of pay will take care of itself; we shall
be supported to the limit. You and I and half of our colleagues
may resign either from necessity or by way of protest but the
public, until educated, will be wholly unimpressed. More
vacancies at the trough, that's all.

What will influence public opinion? Not just exactly what
Hugh Gibson [American Minister to Poland] said in his admirable memorandum which he sent you with his letter of
December 2nd. That material was bully for the Department
and for a few wise men at home but not for the public. The
public doesn't care about the political situation in Silesia or
what is happening on the Lithuanian frontier or the Danzig
question. The only element of the Foreign Service that appeals
to the public is the ability of the Service to ensure business,
better business, bigger business. We must get it out of the
mind of the public that the Consular Service is the only one
that looks after that side. Rather, the Diplomatic Service, in
its commercial activities, paves the way for the Consular Service to function at all. Here is a case in point. The Alsatian
potash mines are falling down on their American contracts
because the French Government won't supply enough railway cars and coal. The German potash mines, supported by the
German Government, are rushing their output into the American markets and filling their contracts completely. Where are
the American buyers going to turn in future? Certainly not to
France, who will lose the American market opened to them
through the war, unless we can show them the error of their
ways. Now who is to persuade the French that those American
contracts must be filled somehow or other? Not the Consular
Service because it hasn't the affiliations with the high Government officials who alone can turn the trick. The Diplomatic

Service steps in, talks like a father to the Minister for Foreign Affairs, the Minister of Reconstruction, the Minister of Commerce, the High Commissioner of Alsace and Lorraine, and the American contracts are filled in spite of all handicaps — or should be shortly. This sort of thing, if properly presented, would show the American public just what the Diplomatic Service is for.

Of course there are other elements. The American public doesn't like to see the country made ridiculous abroad by its representatives. Even the man in the street dislikes that. He could be shown that just at present about 50 per cent of our diplomatic posts abroad have been deserted by their incumbents — Rome, The Hague, Copenhagen, Berne, Peking, Bangkok, and a raft of them in Latin America. They have deserted the ship. Much can also be said about the knowledge of foreign languages; it has not been given its due importance among the many arguments for a better Service. What firm would send an agent who did not speak a word of Spanish to Latin America to negotiate a complicated and delicate million-dollar business deal? Yet hardly one in twenty of our chiefs of mission abroad speaks a word of any foreign language. How can they conduct a negotiation? Answer: through their trained and experienced Counselors of Embassy who often conduct the negotiations alone in their name. And yet these trained and experienced Counselors of Embassy, paid after ten, fifteen or twenty years of service at the rate of $3000 per annum, have nothing to look forward to but the scrap heap or a $15,000 job with some private firm when they leave the Government. Is this economy or democracy or business from the point of view of the American public and taxpayer? . . .

To Colonel E. M. House, May 4, 1920

Ever since my appointment as Minister to Denmark [1] was announced I have been intending to send you a line to thank

[1] On March 17, Mr. Grew received a telegram from the Department of State offering him the post of Minister to Denmark. His commission was dated as of April 7.

you most sincerely and heartily for what you yourself have done towards bringing about this promotion. There is no Legation we would rather have, not even Berne, and we would much rather have it now than when the matter was mentioned two years ago, for in that case I should have missed being with you at the Armistice negotiations and also the Peace Conference itself, and while God knows we didn't love the Peace Conference, no one wanted to miss it.

Judging from the letters that have come since the appointment was announced, it is going to have a marked effect on the morale of the men in the Service and encourage a good many to stay on who were becoming restive and were on the point of resigning. Peter Jay's appointment [as American Minister to Salvador] will help and the whole outlook is promising.

I fully realize what a friend you have been to me and am grateful for the interest you have taken. . . .

The Grews left Paris by automobile on May 22 and arrived in Copenhagen on May 31. Mr. Grew wrote in his diary: "The old Cadillac is well 'besetzt'; it contains Alice, Elsie and myself in front, Nurse Gibson, Edith, Lilla and Anita on the back seat and Chief Machinist's Mate Cunningham on one of the little seats, while the rest of the car is filled to the brim with petrol cans, oil cans, golf clubs, spare tires and coats. Two large petrol cans are strapped to one running board, a smaller feed-can and two spare tires to the other, while three large tires are fixed behind. But the pièce de résistance and real joy of the outfit is the little remorque or trailer which is hooked on behind and runs gracefully along exactly like a colt behind its mother. It is on two wheels and does not look big but the amount of baggage it holds is extraordinary; first, a large wooden case holding a multitude of things from spare clothes to rugs, food and cameras; then seven suitcases, one for each of us, a gun case, two hatboxes, a traveling bag, two typewriters and a big black hatbox belonging to Alice, two tins of biscuits, a large tire and over all a tarpaulin. . . . Of course with the trailer and the petrol cans strapped like torpedo tubes to the footboards we look like a first-class battleship. . . .

"From 67 Avenue Victor Hugo to the Hotel d'Angleterre, Copenhagen, is a far cry and none of the several discoverers of the North Pole could have been prouder of their sledge teams than we were of the old Cadillac and the graceful little trailer. They both did their jobs successfully and the incredulous looks of the people who watched us piling our heavy baggage into the latter in front of our house on the Avenue Victor Hugo just nine days ago would surely have changed could they have seen it bob into Copenhagen today, undaunted."

June 1, 1920

Came to the Legation, Amaliegade 12, at 10 o'clock but found very few signs of life. When the staff gradually turned up they seemed somewhat surprised to find the new Minister already installed at his desk. On my desk was a charming bunch of pinks with a card "To wish you a hearty welcome from the Staff of the American Legation." I first discussed with Arthur Schoenfeld, the Chargé d'Affaires, the question of taking over the Legation as far as the Department of State is concerned. Of course a new Minister has no official relations with the Government to which he is accredited until he presents his letters of credence to the Chief of State but there was some doubt in my mind as to whether I should not begin at once to function vis-à-vis our own Government. Schoenfeld however said that he had had several precedents at other Legations for the Chargé d'Affaires to continue to sign telegrams and despatches to the Department until the Minister had been received by the Chief of State . . . so I only too gladly agreed to postpone shouldering the responsibility until presenting my credentials to King Christian X.

Captain Kenneth Castleman, the Naval Attaché, Norman L. Anderson, the Commercial Attaché, Maurice Dunlap, the Consul, Hal O'Flaherty of the Chicago *Daily News* and Viggo Cavling of the *Politiken* called during the morning one after the other. Anderson told me that Leonid Krassin [President of the Soviet delegation to negotiate a trade agreement with Britain] was already in London to negotiate the opening up of trade with Russia but that H. N. Andersen, the big Danish shipping man, was also in London to fight it and he doubted if anything would be accomplished. The Russians will evidently have to give some guarantees for the payment of their foreign debts before any agreement can take place. It was originally stipulated that they were to deposit a sum not to exceed five million pounds in a Danish bank as a basis for starting the trade but Schoenfeld does not think that this has yet been done.

Cavling talked interestingly about the seamen's strike which is still hampering Danish shipping although many ships are running with volunteer crews and it is expected that the strike will soon be over. The strike is aimed first at the repeal of the Danish law governing the rights and duties of seamen which is antiquated and second to enforce their demand that each ship have a Union representative on board in order to register complaints. The first condition involves delay as the repeal of the law requires ponderous political machinery; the second condition cannot well be granted as the shipowners are naturally against divided authority on shipboard. A strike of waiters began this morning, so that we had to serve ourselves at the hotel at lunch. . . .

June 2 [1920]

Rainy. The first thing that greeted me in the morning was a long "interview" with me published in the *Politiken,* the radical paper. I had especially asked Cavling yesterday not to publish an interview or to quote me and he assured me that I might always rely on him with perfect confidence and that he would simply say something about our arrival. Was at the Legation at 9.30 and when signs of life appeared after 10 I had the article read to me. Fortunately it is innocuous and says very little at great length but I strongly dislike to fly into print immediately on arriving. Incidentally it quotes me as making several statements which I did not make at all, but no harm done. It is decidedly complimentary, speaks of the custom of American diplomats not to draw a thick veil between themselves and the representatives of the press and quotes me as saying that I could make no political statement until I had become familiar with conditions in Denmark — quite correct. But it will be a very long time before any political statement will issue from this quarter. The only thing I can object to is his quoting me as speaking of the socialistic unrest in France — better left unsaid. He very kindly puts into my mouth some highly complimentary remarks on the "excellent Danish harbors" — mythical but all to the good. . . .

Wednesday, June 9 [1920]

Still cold but clear. The staff assembled at the Legation at 10.30 in full dress and shortly before 11 a Chamberlain of the Court arrived with the gala coach and two other coaches to escort us to the Palace named for Christian VII for the audience of the King and Queen. Were met at the head of the stairs by the Grand Marshal of the Court, Mr. William Rothe, all dolled up and with a big, heavy and dangerous-looking staff in his hand and presented to the various court officials drawn up in line, equally resplendent in gold and silver. The Marshal then announced me to the King and I was ushered into the throne room, the doors were shut behind me and I was left caged with the monarch. He was big, very big — 6 feet 2 inches he works out at, I believe — but not at all terrifying; he has pleasant eyes and an agreeable expression. I made an appropriate bow at the threshold and fortunately having no sword to trip over reached the royal presence in the center of the room without mishap, grasped the proffered hand and launched immediately into my formal address. The King looked at me sort of pityingly as much as to say, "Poor chap, what rot he is talking," but he was very patient until he had finished learning all about the good relations of the two countries which had so long and happily existed, etc. and how I was to spend all my time from now on seeing that they kept good, and then replied in a few well-chosen words to the effect that he would back me up through thick and thin. I handed him my letter of credence and my distinguished predecessor's letter of recall . . . and then he settled right down to friendly conversation. He speaks English moderately well but gets involved now and then and it was not always clear just what he was driving at. He started on the upset state of the world just at present which he said was due to "the bad behavior of Europe," whereat I remarked, "Part of Europe, Your Majesty," and he grinned. He then talked of the importance of international co-operation in the work of reconstruction and from that got onto the President's health, asking me if I had seen him lately. I said I had not seen him since he left Paris but that all was going along well and that the President was making steady progress and had received several of the new diplomats in Washington.[2] He then spoke of our trip from Paris by automobile, asked about the children and was interested at hearing that we had moored them at Hornbaek, and finally said he had heard that we were thinking of taking the Raben house which would be very nice as we should be right next door to him. I said that would be fine. After about ten minutes of chat he asked me to present my staff, they were ushered in and I introduced them in turn: Captain Castleman, Naval Attaché; Mr. Schoenfeld, First Secretary; Lieut. Col. William Colvin, Military Attaché; Mr. Anderson, Commercial Attaché, and Stokeley Morgan, 2nd Secretary. He talked for a few moments with them and then signified that the audience was finished, at which we backed out in good order. The Marshal immediately took me to the Queen's apartments and ushered me in. I bowed low at the threshold, advanced, kissed the lady's hand with another bow and was about to settle down to good homely talk when the Marshal pulled me by the arm and indicated that I was to proceed further. This was not my idea of an audience at all but the Marshal was firm and I had to follow. He then whispered that he would now announce me to the Queen and I gradually tumbled to the fact that the last lady was only the Mistress of the Robes, Mlle. Louise de Grevenkop-Castenskiold. If I ever start a Court I shall have each personage carefully placarded for the information of arriving diplomats, thus:

2 On September 26, 1919, President Wilson had to give up his tour of the United States to win popular support for the treaty with Germany. He returned to Washington, where he suffered a physical collapse.

"Marshal," "Mistress of the Robes," "King," "Queen." This would avoid such embarrassing mistakes as my own. Queen Alexandrine, when I finally got there, was most agreeable but not an easy talker; she tried out several topics, each of which had possibilities, but didn't get fairly started on any of them, so that I could only listen politely and answer a few questions. She also said she hoped we would take the Raben house. She has not the good looks of her sister, the German Crown Princess Cecilie. This time I asked her if I could introduce my staff and when that ceremony was over we retired with the satisfied feeling of having gone through the whole ordeal without making the old American eagle blush.

Alice had her audience with the Queen in another of the four palaces around the Amalienborg Square a few minutes after mine. She went in hat and street dress and the Queen made her sit down and had a really cosy talk. Incidentally the Queen told her the story of how when President Deschanel [of France] fell out of the window of the train, arrived at the next station in pyjamas and announced himself to the stationmaster as the President of the Republic, that worthy had replied: "Oui, oui, mon vieux; et moi je suis Clemenceau." . . .

June 22–29 [1920]

. . . With regard to the Bolshevik gold which was to be deposited here as a basis for opening trade between Denmark and Russia, the following is the situation: On June 12th the Department cabled asking me if the report were true that the Danish Government had sent a representative to Russia to get the gold. I replied on June 14th . . . that the Foreign Office was not aware of any gold shipment coming here from Russia and that no Government representative had been sent to receive such a shipment. My informant had said that it was doubtful if any gold deposit would be made in Copenhagen since it would almost certainly be attached by Russia's creditors. The only negotiations which had been carried on were those between Krassin and Sir Martin Abrahamson [head of the Clearing House]. The Danish Government does not consider itself able to prevent trade between private Danish merchants and Russia should it be found possible to finance such trade, but up to the present time it has been practically negligible.

In spite of this information, however, the gold arrived in Copenhagen a few days later and on June 19th . . . I reported that two million rubles had been received by a new concern called The International Clearing House, Ltd., and deposited in the National Bank in Copenhagen. The Foreign Office informed me that it had no official connection with the matter which was entirely in the hands of private individuals. This Clearing House is started with a share capital of two million Danish crowns (announced on June 19th), the capital being one third British and two thirds Danish and to be increased later in accordance with and in proportion to the support the Company will be able to give to the resumption of trade with Russia.

On June 25th . . . I reported further particulars regarding the renewal of Danish and Russian trade. The two million rubles deposit is to be used only as security and will be returned to Russia when the transactions are over. The amount of the deposit can be increased when necessary but a larger sum is not wanted at the present time as the plan is still in its elementary stage. No shipment of supplies is supposed to have gone forward to Russia as preliminary negotiations concerning prices, commodities to be exchanged and means of transportation will first take place, probably at Reval, between the Soviet Agents and representatives of the Clearing House. Several Danish companies now have men at Reval. The first shipments will probably consist of goods from the free harbor [3] which have been stored there for a long time, having been imported for speculative purposes but never reshipped owing to the fall of currencies in the neighboring countries, particularly

[3] The Free Port was established in the Port of Copenhagen in 1894. Here goods could be received, stored, manufactured, and reshipped without being subject to customs duties. The Free Port was the most modern and largest part of the Port of Copenhagen and received extensive use from shippers of goods not for Danish consumption.

Germany and the Baltic Provinces. These goods are said to be practically unsalable except in Russian markets and consist of foodstuffs, leather and low-grade textiles. The difficulties of obtaining return shipments from Russia constitute the greatest weakness in the plan. It is barely possible that some payments may be made in national currencies other than rubles. The Transatlantic Company, a powerful Danish organization which was said to be recently in financial difficulties but which I am now informed is on a firm footing, built up the Clearing House and provided the Danish capital while it is believed that the British capital was provided by the United Baltic Corporation.

My sources of information are so far not numerous but they are sufficient for us to check up the various statements: the Foreign Office, Fin Lund (representative of the National City Bank of New York), Løve (representative of Grace and Co.), Col. Tryggve Siqueland (formerly American Military Attaché), etc.

On June 25th a document came into my hands which purports to be an accurate account of a meeting which took place in Moscow in May between the Soviet Government and representatives of the communist movement in India, Persia, Armenia, Turkistan, Afghanistan, Azerbaijan, Georgia and other Near Eastern states; also the text of a treaty drawn up and signed by them for mutual co-operation and support in a proposed military and political advance against the Entente countries, especially Great Britain. This I cabled to the Department in telegram no. 8. It sounds genuine.

On June 28th I cabled . . . a report that Fridtjof Nansen was about to start for Moscow to study the condition of prisoners and to negotiate with the Soviet authorities concerning the repatriation especially of German and Austrian prisoners of war. . . .

This is the extent of our cabling up to date and shows how comparatively little important work we have on hand. I should be sending many other telegrams about conditions in Denmark, political and economic, were it not for the fact that the Department, owing to limited funds, has instructed all its foreign missions and consulates to avoid cabling anything not of an urgent nature or information which would be cabled to the American press. Accordingly we simply keep a weekly diary of all developments in Denmark and mail it in the pouch. The war had made all our missions very lavish in cabling and economy of words was never considered until the brakes were put on by the instruction mentioned. It is a wise one and materially reduces superfluous work and expense to the Government. . . .

Wednesday, August 4 [1920]

Colonel and Mrs. Thomas Hollyday and Captain Castleman to lunch. Hollyday was Military Attaché here before our arrival, but was then transferred to Helsingfors and Riga. . . . His opinions regarding Russia seemed . . . to be eminently sound and agreed entirely with my own. I have held from the beginning that the blockade of Russia was a mistaken policy; that all political recognition should be withheld but that the country should be opened up to trade as soon as possible; that bolshevism thrives on starvation and that the greater part of the population is Bolshevik by necessity rather than choice; and that, therefore, when economic stability is secured, bolshevism itself will die a natural death, or, at least, healthy conditions will give the Russian people more force, initiative and energy to combat the present state of internal affairs. The military offensives have also proved to have been mistaken policy, for they have turned bolshevism, at least temporarily, into nationalism. . . .[4]

4 In March, 1918, by the Treaty of Brest-Litovsk, Soviet Russia made her peace with the Central Powers. In the same month British forces landed at Murmansk to prevent the port from falling into German hands and to repossess supplies. In April Japanese troops arrived at Vladivostok to protect Japanese nationals and property in that area. In August British forces landed at Archangel and Vladivostok, and in the latter venture the British were joined by American troops under command of General W. S. Graves. The oil fields of Baku, the port of Batum, and Odessa were occupied by Allied military groups. The Allies in certain areas sponsored anti-Bolshevik governments and contributed substantially in arms and material to the forces fighting bolshevism, particularly those of Kolchak, Denikin, and Yudenich.

Thursday, August 19 [1920]

Went to the F.O. and had a satisfactory talk with the Minister [Harald Scavenius] about Russia. I asked him if he could tell me what the policy of Denmark was in the present Polish–Soviet Russian conflict and towards Russia generally. He said that while no actual position had been formulated, he personally agreed exactly and completely with the attitude of our Government as defined in its recent note to the Italian Embassy in Washington.[5] There would be a conference of the various Ministers of State and of Foreign Affairs of the Scandinavian countries in Copenhagen on August 28th to discuss, among other things, what the attitude of their respective countries would be in case one or more of the Allied Powers should renew the blockade measures against Soviet Russia. We discussed the whole question thoroughly and found that our views were identical in every particular. I also asked him whether any secret treaties or agreements to which Denmark was a party had been published during or since the war, as our Government was making a compilation of such documents, but he said there were none, and the only things he could think of which might be of interest to our Government in that connection were the press reports of the three conferences which had taken place between the Ministers of the various Scandinavian countries during the war. No official record of them had been kept, he said. Scavenius is decidedly warming up and is much easier to talk to than he was at the beginning, although he still weighs his words carefully when speaking. He said that Denmark had never recognized the Baltic States [6] and simply had unofficial representatives exchanged to discuss matters informally, just as we have. No Baltic representatives were carried on the diplomatic list, as O. C. Scavenius [Member of the Foreign Office] had erroneously told me was the case. Curious that the Chief

5 This note of August 10, 1920, is printed in U.S. Department of State, *Papers Relating to the Foreign Relations of the United States, 1920* (Washington: Government Printing Office, 1936), III, 463–68.

6 During 1918 the former Russian Baltic Provinces emerged as independent republics. Estonia and Lithuania proclaimed their independence in February, 1918, followed by the establishment of the Latvian Republic in November, 1918.

of the Political Division of the F.O. should have made such a mistake. . . .

Thursday, August 26 [1920]

John J. O'Brien [of the Philadelphia *Public Ledger*] came to see me in the morning to tell me the results of his conversation yesterday with Maxim Litvinoff, whom he had gone to see at the Cosmopolite Hotel on the ground that he was interested in the question of trade with Russia. Litvinoff, whom he describes as of gentlemanly appearance and speaking perfect English, but with an eye which seems to be taking careful stock of you while he is talking, spent most of the interview damning the present Administration in Washington for refusing to have anything to do with the Soviet Government, and intimating that there would be a change of policy in that direction if the Republicans should come in. O'Brien, at my suggestion, asked about the Americans held in Russia, to which Litvinoff replied that so far as he was aware there was none in prison except Kalamatiano who had confessed to anti-Bolshevik conspiracy and who had been condemned to death but whom they had reprieved out of special consideration for the United States.[7] In fact, he said, even though America had been fighting them on the northern front, they had consistently given Americans in Russia better treatment than the nationals of the other Allies. As for the release of the Americans in Russia in return for the release of Debs and other Bolshevists imprisoned in the United States,[8] he said it was not true that the Soviet

[7] Xenophon Kalamatiano, a naturalized American citizen, who had been employed by DeWitt Poole, United States Consul at Moscow, to obtain routine information about conditions in various parts of Russia was arrested in 1918 as a spy and counterrevolutionary. After lengthy negotiations Kalamatiano was finally released by the Soviet Government in 1921. U.S. Department of State, *Papers Relating to the Foreign Relations of the United States, 1919, Russia* (Washington: Government Printing Office, 1937), pp. 167–71, 173–82, 184–90; U.S. Department of State, *Papers Relating to the Foreign Relations of the United States, 1921* (Washington: Government Printing Office, 1936), II, 800–801.

[8] Eugene Debs, American Socialist leader, was arrested on June 30, 1918, and charged with violating the Espionage Act in a speech at Canton, Ohio. He was sentenced to ten years in prison, although President Harding commuted

Government had made that a *sine qua non;* they only demanded that the American Government should negotiate with them direct and not through the intermediary of British and other people as had been done. Litvinoff said that both the French and British Governments had negotiated with them direct about prisoners, although they were their bitterest enemies, and he could not see why the United States was so fearful of doing so. O'Brien asked him if such direct negotiations would result favorably, to which L. replied: "If this were done, immediate results would ensue." Litvinoff then spoke of me and said he had heard that I was broad-minded and *very* intelligent (!) and had been sent to Copenhagen purely for the purpose of investigating the situation in Russia, but that so far I had, to his surprise, made no effort to get in touch with him, or indeed shown signs of any interest in Russia whatever. He expressed great disappointment. In writing the Department about this I said in my despatch that the broad-minded American Minister was highly gratified by this unconscious testimonial from Litvinoff, who however appeared to be unaware that he was quite satisfactorily being "gotten in touch with" at the very moment of his remark. O'Brien gave me the rough notes he had taken after the conversation. . . .

Friday, September 17 [1920]

I called on Mr. H. N. Andersen, President of the East India Company, called "the uncrowned King of Denmark." He is indeed a remarkable man and made a deep impression on me. He talked for half an hour, in a gentle voice, touching on various world problems with a breadth of view and charm of expression which one meets but seldom. Chiefly he talked about Russia; he believes that the time has not yet come to open up the country, because there is yet no solid foundation

the sentence in 1921. Other labor leaders such as "Big Bill" Haywood, General Secretary-Treasurer of the I.W.W., had been arrested in 1917 on the same charge.

on which to base trade and outside assistance, but he believes that the Soviet Government is killing itself and is bound to fall (he gives it a year more of life), and that then some new structure will rise out of the chaos, with which foreign countries can deal to mutual advantage. Work and production will then gradually rehabilitate the country. In this reconstruction the United States has a great opportunity and a high duty. The world needs a rehabilitated Russia, just as it needs a rehabilitated Germany, for the economic structure of the world cannot be sound if one of its members is economically unsound. He gives Germany 15 years to rehabilitate herself. Turning to the League of Nations he said that he saw nothing practical in it. The spirit of combativeness between nations cannot be overcome by such a body. England and America together should be able to direct the destiny of the world. He said he thought I ought to see the King before going to America. He himself would always be at our service if we wished Denmark's co-operation in any direction. His manner and talk made an exceptionally favorable impression on me.

I then went to see Mr. Hartmann [head of Hjalmar Hartmann and Co., seed exporters] to ascertain whether he had made any further shipments of seeds to Russia or knew of other developments in Russian trade. He said there had been none, that he knew of, with the exception of his shipment of 1,500,000 Kr. of seed in March, a shipment of shoe leather by Ballin [M. J. Ballins Sønner, Ltd.] valued at 1,200,000 Kr. in June, and a 300,000 Kr. shipment of harvesting machines in July. The Danish Government had finally got rid of Litvinoff to Norway, which he thought was a mistake as it made it so much more difficult for Danish firms to trade with Russia; so far as he personally was concerned, the step was in his interest, as his relations with Litvinoff were already formed, while his competitors would find it less easy to commence trade with Litvinoff in Norway. He said that Scavenius had told him that while 2500 cars of merchandise had gone into Russia since trade was started, only 500 had come out. . . .

Monday, December 27 [1920]

The holidays over, I spent a busy day taking stock of the Legation work and called on T. Hart Anderson [Secretary of the American Legation at Copenhagen] for a complete report on all outstanding business.[9] He had it at his fingers' tips and sent over the report within half an hour. We are very nearly up to date and nothing has been allowed to lag. I am having a long report prepared on the subject of the new legislation providing for the partitioning of the large Danish estates. Hereafter the properties will no longer be left to the eldest son, but to all the children equally, and in the case of the larger estates, a considerable proportion of them will revert to the State. Another report I have in view is on the subject of Danish cooperative farming, and we are also working on a report on prominent men, newspapers and correspondents in Denmark. But there is little incentive for initiative just now: the Department seems to take no interest; we never receive comments on our work and many of our questions as to governmental policy remain unanswered. When in Washington, I brought up some of these questions, but nobody seemed to know or care anything about them, and the only constructive criticism I received was: "Don't send in too much stuff." Let us hope that things will be different after March 4th [10] and that we shall have a reorganized Department, thirsting for information, which it will be a pleasure to supply knowing that it will be appreciated, and put to use. . . .

Monday, January 3 [1921]

Had a conference with Dr. L. with whom Gade has placed me in touch and who is going to furnish me with Bolshevik information and the Moscow newspapers, by underground channels, 12 days after their publication in Moscow. He is in close touch and will be a valuable aid. The Department has finally approved my recommendations for obtaining Bolshe-

9 Mr. Grew left for a leave of absence in the United States on September 23, returning to Copenhagen on December 15.
10 Warren Harding was inaugurated as President on March 4, 1921.

vist intelligence and has given me carte blanche for conducting the work in the manner I had planned. Also heard today that the Department, after refusing the recommendations of three of my predecessors on the subject, had finally increased the salary of our clerks $500 each. These are about the first signs from Washington that they know of our existence here and I am feeling quite elated. . . .

In the evening, dinner at Court for all the chiefs of mission and their wives. We were invited for 7.50 but arrived about 7.40, being among the first. After all of us were assembled, the men on one side of the room and the women on the other, the King and Queen came in and shook hands with everyone in turn. When he came to me he said laughingly: "You were giving a feast last night; I saw you." Evidently he looks across from the palace to see what goes on here. Prince Aage [cousin of the King] with whom I was talking later and who lives with his father, Prince Waldemar [uncle of the King] across the street, told me that he had seen Alice filling the children's stockings on Xmas Eve! I suppose they will be commenting on the color of my pyjamas before long. Their Majesties then led the way in to dinner. . . . The King drank no healths and dinner was served quickly. Afterwards we drifted around the ballroom while the King and Queen passed along, talking to everyone in turn. There was little formality and we smoked to our hearts' content. Alice got a good laugh out of the King: when talking with me he asked if we were all comfortably settled and I said that we were still shy a nurse, so when he later reached Alice he said: "Your husband tells me he is still looking for a nurse," to which Alice replied, "Really? What does he need a nurse for?" They all know about the children and that is the usual topic of conversation on the part of both the King and the Queen. The German Minister [Baron Konstantin von Neurath] of course got presented to Alice and after talking to her for some time came over and talked to me. I said: "It is unfortunate that our countries are still at war with each other." He replied, "Yes, but it is only technical; you have a representative in Berlin" — and he might have added, "who is entertaining and being entertained by Germans daily." If he would only keep away from me on official occasions, for the looks of the thing, I would talk with him on informal occasions to his heart's content. . . .

Tuesday, February 22 [1921]

. . . Dinner at the Richelieus' [Vice Admiral Andres du Plessis de Richelieu, Danish industrialist] for the King and Queen. About forty at table. The King drank my health during dinner, at which I stood up and returned it according to custom. Afterwards interesting talk in the smoking room with the King, V. J. Glückstadt [Danish banker], Richelieu, Marling [British Minister to Denmark] and Clan [member of the Foreign Office], on the economic situation in Europe. G. said that the German Government was keeping the value of the mark down artificially so that she could flood foreign markets with her goods. The King said that German patent leather shoes sold in Copenhagen for less than the plain Danish leather ones and were flooding the market; everyone was wearing patent leather shoes now. Richelieu, who lived for thirty years in Siam and organized the Siamese Navy, showed us a piece of quartz with seams of gold in it; he had found it in Siam and dug a mine on the spot at great expense, but the gold only went skin-deep. The King joked with him about it and Marling asked him how many companies he had floated on it. The King spoke of his forthcoming visit to Iceland and Greenland this summer, said he wished he could run across some mines up there and remarked that the Danish people would expect some concrete results from his visit. If they did not occur, the people would say: "Damn the King; what was the use of his trip anyway?" . . .

Friday, February 25 [1921]

. . . I went with Anderson to see Georges Carpentier in an exhibition boxing match. We had seats in the diplomatic box with the Claudels [French Minister to Denmark], Allart [Belgian Minister to Denmark], Beck-Friis [Swedish Minister to Denmark], the Aloisis [Italian Minister to Denmark], etc.

The King sat just below us and when Carpentier appeared in the ring he walked over and shook hands with him, to the great delight of everyone. The King received a tremendous ovation when he arrived. . . . Carpentier, after several minor matches, boxed two rounds with Lenaer, the Belgian, his training partner, and then gave an exhibition of how he knocked out Levinsky. He is a magnificent specimen. Afterwards we were all asked by the *Berlingske Tidende,* which arranged the match, to drink a glass of champagne to Carpentier in the library of the Idraetssal; all the other Ministers departed, it being, I suppose, beneath their dignity, to meet a boxer, but I stayed with the Claudels, who seemed pleased that I had not deserted them too. Claudel introduced Carpentier to me and I had a pleasant chat with him. But I carefully avoided getting into the flashlight pictures which they took of the group. Carpentier received 35,000 crowns for his five-minute appearance in the ring. He has been doing the same in Christiania and Stockholm. It looks a little as if the French were conducting a regular campaign of propaganda in Scandinavia, for following Carpentier's visit, a prominent cast of French actors and actresses from the Vieux Colombier in Paris are coming to give plays from Molière, Racine and Corneille. Among them are Féraudy, and also Pauline Pax who was in the Théatre Michel in Petrograd and finally managed to escape from the Bolsheviks. They are, I believe, also starting a special course of French lectures arranged by Claudel. The French are very popular here and are striking while the iron is hot. Claudel, who has been appointed Ambassador to Japan, is being given a round of farewell dinners by the Danes, especially the literary element. . . .

Wednesday, June 1 [1921]

     . . . Sent two despatches to Department, one recommending that a bulletin be published and distributed throughout the Service, containing information about the Service, such as transfers, promotions, resignations, reorganizations, etc., and the same with regard to other services. We need such a publication to keep up the *esprit de corps* in the Foreign Service and to keep us in closer touch with the Department, of whose present organization we know practically nothing. I suggested that every foreign officer be invited to send in items about other foreign services; they are always of interest and value to anyone making the Service a career. The other despatch was about our reduced clerical assistance; I said that we would get along as best we could with the 50 per cent reduction in staff but that it would cripple the Legation, and incidentally I enclosed a complete list of the various activities of this Mission for the past year, to show where our energies had been spent and how they would have to be curtailed in future. The list is a long one. If every foreign mission did the same, and if these lists were submitted to Congress, it might open the eyes of some of our legislators who think we go abroad to disport ourselves "in the halls of princes" only. During the past year we have reported fully on almost every branch of Danish public life and a great many other subjects. . . .

Monday, July 4 [1921]

Another perfect day, cloudless and warm. At 11 we left Nørlund by motor, arriving at Skjørpning at 11.45, where we took a room at the small hotel and soon afterwards were greeted by Judge N. V. Boeg and his committee, as well as the local committee. A few minutes later the train from Copenhagen arrived and Benjamin Muse [Third Secretary of the American Legation at Copenhagen] joined us, as well as the Minister of War and Marine, Mr. Klaus Berntsen. We attended a formal luncheon at the hotel, given by the committee, Judge Boeg presiding, and there were, as usual, several speeches. I talked extemporaneously for several minutes, answering a toast to Berntsen, Johannes Fønss, the singer, and myself. The chairman then made a very pleasant little speech to Alice and her health was drunk by all standing. We then drove to the Rebild Hills and walked about for an hour before the meeting. It is a pretty spot; the hills, which are steep and close together, are covered with heather, which must be beautiful when in flower in August. People were arriving from every direction, by motor, bicycle, carriage, cart and on foot. When the meeting began there were, it is said, between 15,000 and 20,000 gathered on the sides of the hills around the natural bowl where the speaking and singing took place.

I had realized that this was an excellent opportunity to make an important address on the relations between the United States and Denmark, a subject which, so far as I am aware, has not been approached publicly since Mr. Egan's [American Minister to Denmark, 1907–18] speech at the inauguration of the park in 1912.[11] The time was ripe for something to be said. Little American news appears in the Danish press, and such items as are cabled through the news agencies in England and France are often of an uncomplimentary or derogatory character. Whether by intent or not, the news that comes through Reuter or Havas more often relates to Negro lynchings or other derogatory incidents than to subjects tending to increase the respect and sympathy of the average Dane for the United States. Furthermore, certain unsatisfactory if not fraudulent deliveries of American coal and similar incidents in the business world have worked much harm to the general reputation in this country of America and American business methods, and there is little favorable publicity — American publicity — to offset the unfavorable atmosphere they create. Scavenius was warmly in favor of my making the very complimentary speech I had prepared; he had had it officially trans-

11 On August 5, 1912, the Danish-American National Park in the Rebild Hills was dedicated. Four hundred acres of land in Jutland had been purchased by American citizens of Danish descent to be used as a park, open to the public at all times, with the stipulation that on July 4 of each year it be given over to Americans for celebration of Independence Day. U.S. Department of State, *Papers Relating to the Foreign Relations of the United States, 1912* (Washington: Government Printing Office, 1919), pp. 335–38. At the celebration in 1921, among other things, Mr. Grew praised the contributions made by Danish immigrants to the United States, quoted Theodore Roosevelt that "our only quarrel with Denmark is that she doesn't send us more Danes," described the specific contributions of Danish-Americans like Jacob A. Riis and Gutzon Borglum, and praised the writings of such Danes as Hans Christian Andersen. The full text was printed in the Danish Foreign Office *Journal*, pp. 111–14.

lated into Danish at the F.O. and arranged to have it sent all
over the world. At the suggestion of Alex Gerfalk [of the Associated Press], Boeg and others, I retained much of the speech
made at the Studenterforengingen dinner, with a few additions
and amplifications here and there; the audience was a different
one and the text of the former speech had not been published.

The meeting began at about 3.15. Judge Boeg, presiding,
welcomed the audience and then called for cheers for the King
and the President, after which the two national anthems were
sung. He then introduced the American Minister, who, after
being likewise cheered, mounted the platform to the rostrum
between the American and Danish flags (each of the surrounding hills was likewise crowned with an American or Danish flag)
and let loose. It was not difficult; the hills form a natural
acousticon and by talking fairly loud, the sound seemed to carry
well. I needed no notes and talked for twenty or twenty-five
minutes, the American element in the throng helping greatly
by applauding the important points. The audience was re-
ceptive and keen — even enthusiastic at the end. The Elberg
Society then sang, followed by two fine songs by Johannes
Fønss, and then Klaus Berntsen talked for half an hour on the
subject of the importance of the home to society. He said some
very pleasant things about America and about the Minister
personally which, he said, the Minister would not understand
until he read them in the paper the next morning. But I am
understanding Danish pretty well now and got the pith of all
the speeches. Judge Boeg talked again and another Dane made
a fine speech on the importance of beauty in the home and then
the singers sang the Rebild hymn, after which we dispersed. It
was an impressive gathering. . . .

Tuesday, July 5 [1921]

. . . In the afternoon at 4 I went to see Scavenius. . . . I have
never seen him more cordial and agreeable. Said I was a very
popular man in Denmark as a result of the Rebild meeting.
All the morning papers print the speech in full or with few
omissions and there are several unusually complimentary edi-

torials on it.[12] Frederick Moltke [President of the Madsen
machine-gun manufacturing company] said that no minister
had ever made such a favorable impression before and everybody we met today extended the glad hand. Of course all this
is purely international and not personal: a minister is sent
abroad for the purpose of cementing the good relations between his own country and the country to which he is accredited; it is easy work when an opportunity like the meeting
at Rebild comes his way. . . .

Friday, July 15 [1921]

. . . Louis Fontenay [French Minister to Denmark] came to
return my call of yesterday. Spoke kindly of the "retentisse-
ments" of my Fourth of July speech, which he said he heard
on every side, and that he had telegraphed his Government
that the appointment of a Danish Consul to Chicago, which
happened to be announced a few days later, was the direct result of my activity. It takes a diplomat to work out a conclusion like that! I suppose the decision to send a Consul to
Chicago was taken several weeks before that Rebild speech was
even written. . . .

In the afternoon we had the amusing experience of receiving a girl's school touring Europe. Three of them, whom Muse
described as "peacherinos" came to the chancery in the morning and wanted to see the Minister, so we asked them all to tea.
They were a marvelous crowd; if they hadn't said they were a
school, I should have put them down as the chorus of a Broad-
way review. We took them into the ballroom, turned on the
gramophone and asked them to show us the latest steps from

12 *Politiken's* editorial stated that a "foreigner rarely sets forth the relations
between his country and ours with more depth of understanding and greater
knowledge. We are indebted to Mr. Grew for his appreciative words about the
Danes, the more so as America, after Denmark, shelters more Danes than any
other country." In describing the meeting at Rebild, *Nationaltidende* said
that Mr. Grew had "found words of such wisdom, beauty and sincerity about
our country and his own that he has unquestionably won our hearts." *Køben-
havn* commented that the "American Minister's well-formulated and highly
personal speech was rewarded with enthusiastic applause."

home. They did. After one attempt at "The Camel" and "The Frisco," I considered that they were not compatible with ministerial dignity, and retired to the side lines. . . .

Sunday, August 21 [1921]

. . . I had been invited to lunch at Nimb's by the Danish delegation to the Interparliamentary Congress, to meet the American delegation — returning from the congress in Stockholm . . . and I motored in to Copenhagen straight from Helsingør, having just time to dress at the Legation before going to the luncheon punctually at 1. The American delegation had been met at the station in the morning by Muse and Hans, whom I had instructed to do everything possible for them besides handing them my invitation.[13] We had also reserved rooms for them at the hotel.

On arriving at Nimb's, I found a large crowd of guests gathered, including the Danish and American delegations, several members of the German and English delegations, and many prominent Danes, including Harald and O. C. Scavenius, who came in shortly after me. On being introduced to the Danish chairman, Dr. L. Moltesen, I at once asked to be presented to the American delegates, but his attention was distracted by other arriving guests, so I had to look around for someone else to introduce me, as I did not know the Americans by sight and they were mingled with the crowd. Finally I found someone who introduced me to Representative James Slayden [ex-Congressman from Texas], but he was discussing socialism with two Danish members of parliament, so after a word or two with him, I moved on. Just then George Fuller, our Vice Consul in Malmø, who had come over with the delegation, offered to introduce me to the others, but just after meeting Senator William McKinley [of Illinois], and before I could have any talk with him, Harald Scavenius came up and offered his arm, according to the Danish custom, to take me in

[13] The invitation was to a big spread which I had arranged at considerable expense at our lovely summer place on the Øresund. Incidentally, they did not come and never even answered the invitation. — J. C. G.

to luncheon, where I sat opposite the chairman, between the two Scaveniuses. During luncheon, Moltesen welcomed the guests and Senator McKinley replied for the American delegation, L'Ingénieur Dante Ferraris [Italian industrialist] for the Italian delegation, and an Englishman for the British delegation. I had a speech carefully prepared, but luckily did not have to use it. I consulted O. C. Scavenius, who said it was not necessary for me to reply to the chairman's welcome as the parliamentary delegates were only too glad to have an opportunity to speak. It amused me to see Harald ask the same question of his cousin with regard to himself. McKinley made an excellent speech, but Ferraris, whom I used to see at the Peace Conference, where he was at one time a delegate, was terribly long-winded.

After lunch I tried to meet the other Americans, but had time to get introduced to but two of them before they were hurried off in automobiles to see the town.

As a matter of record I will put down here the subsequent developments attendant upon this historic luncheon; they illustrate the touchiness of the average congressman and his prejudice against diplomatic officers, who are all supposed to be snobs — and therefore, in their opinion, must be. A few days later, Marion Letcher [American Consul General at Copenhagen] received a letter from Fuller, saying that the entire American delegation had been very angry because I had not been introduced to them immediately on entering the room; he said that they had waxed more and more angry through luncheon and had said: "He must be recalled to learn American customs," and "It is fortunate that we have not confirmed him" — thinking no doubt that I had never been confirmed as Minister to Denmark. Fuller evidently had made matters worse — although with perfectly good intentions — by suggesting to them that perhaps I was waiting for them to get introduced to me, according to the Danish custom. This remark simply put more coals on the fire and made them more furious than ever. Still a few days later, Muse, who had accompanied them in the train the next day as far as Hamburg, told me that they were still bitter about the episode and that Representative Fred Britten [Congressman from Illinois] had said: "If Mr. Grew is a product of the diplomatic career, I shall in future oppose all measures in Congress for promoting career men." They were all unanimous and were all for having me recalled immediately. As far as I can gather from Muse's account of the conversation, he put in a rather weak oar for his chief, as he was very busy persuading the Congressmen to have him promoted — the very worst thing he could do in his own interests, as that is the one thing the Department will not stand for, and it always hurts a man more than helps him. Muse said that when he had told the Congressmen that I was really democratic and not a snob, they had replied: "Of course you have to be loyal to your chief." Muse begged me to keep it secret that he had told me what the Congressmen had said about me, as he was afraid it would hurt him with them. In fact, I had to drag the story out of him. I doubt if he would have told me if I had not asked him directly. I am not sure that this was complete loyalty.

I have written the whole story to Henry Fletcher [Under Secretary of State] and have left it in his good hands to take whatever steps he thinks advisable when the delegation returns to America. I also wrote to Letcher, thanking him for having brought Fuller's letter to my attention, and telling him the facts of the case. He sent a copy of my letter to Fuller, accompanied by a very agreeable one of his own. Fuller is going to write to the Congressman who was most bitter about the matter. They will undoubtedly see the President on their return and may say unpleasant things, unless Fletcher sees them first. But my own conscience is clear, and having done everything possible, the matter is now off my chest. If I suffer for it, it will be another instance of the blind prejudice of the average Member of Congress against the Diplomatic Service, and certainly a case of condemning a man on wholly erroneous premises. . . .[14]

14 This incident came very close to wrecking my career. All the Senators and Congressmen on the American delegation wanted to get me out of the

Wednesday, August 31 [1921]

With everything ready for our two-month motor trip in Germany, Switzerland, Italy and France, upon which we were to set out tomorrow morning, a telegram from the Department came today, saying: "The President wishes to transfer you to Switzerland, and in view of your personal letter to the Under Secretary of April 21st it is presumed that this will be agreeable to you. Request agrément for your successor Dr. John Dyneley Prince [of Columbia University]. His biography will be found in *Who's Who*. HUGHES." My letter to Fletcher, referred to, was one in which I said I hoped we should not have to leave Copenhagen, but if we did have to leave, Berne would be our next choice. I replied immediately: "I accept appoint-

Service, and the late Senator Joe Robinson of Arkansas vowed that he would never allow any further appointment of mine to be confirmed by the Senate. When, a few months later, President Harding sent to the Senate my appointment as Minister to Switzerland, my good friend Henry Fletcher, then Under Secretary of State, waited for a day when Robinson went out to play golf and had the nomination quietly confirmed in his absence from the floor. Soon thereafter, when I returned to Washington on leave, Fletcher advised me to make my peace with the senators. Senators McKinley, of Illinois, and Walsh, of Montana, were entirely friendly and admitted that the whole trouble had been based on a pure misunderstanding. But when I sent in my card to Senator Robinson on the floor, he came out to the waiting room, listened for a brief moment to my explanation, turned his back on me and left the room with the remark: "All I can say, Mr. Grew, is that your explanation has not changed my attitude in the slightest. Good day." Later I met Representative Britten at a large and very congenial party. He had been one of the most vociferous advocates of my recall, but when I held out my hand and said, "Why if here isn't my dear old enemy," the hatchet was buried right there.

Of course, at that reception in Copenhagen, after having done everything in my power at considerable personal expense to arrange every detail for our congressional delegation to spend a thoroughly enjoyable day, my whole intent and effort was to meet every member of our delegation immediately. Only the great crowd made this impossible. I think that coals were probably heaped on the fire when the Danish Minister for Foreign Affairs offered me his arm and took me into luncheon where I sat on his right ahead of the Senators. In Washington this would have been unthinkable, but in Copenhagen, where I represented the United States as American Minister, I of course had to be the ranking guest. No opportunity was given me to explain any of this to the Senators. I was judged and convicted *in absentia* and very nearly lost my official head permanently as a result. — J. C. G.

ment as Minister to Switzerland. Have requested agrément to Dr. Prince. It would greatly facilitate my plans for terminating lease contract, etc. if I could learn at once approximately when Department will desire me to proceed to Switzerland." I also cabled Henry Fletcher on September 1st, "Sincerely grateful for all you and Department have done and hope you will express to the President my full appreciation of Administration's continued confidence."

The Department's telegram had been decoded by Andy [T. H. Anderson] and telephoned over to me. . . . I broke the news to Alice who was absolutely delighted. She loves Switzerland, many of her friends are there, and it furthermore solves the question of the children's schooling, for there are no better girls' schools in the world than in Switzerland. As for me, I am sorry to break off here just as our roots were taking a good hold in a congenial soil. But the work in Berne will unquestionably be more interesting and important than here, and in that respect the transfer is a favorable one. What happened, I believe, is this: Dr. Prince originally wanted Copenhagen, but was told he couldn't have it as it was filled by a Service man. They then promised him Stockholm (he particularly wanted one of the Scandinavian countries), but Ira Nelson Morris [American Minister to Sweden] went home, rallied his Senators around him and managed to retain Stockholm, with the result that Prince was thrown back on Copenhagen, dislodging us. On account of Alice and the children I can be nothing but happy over the change. . . .

Made an appointment with the Minister for Foreign Affairs and left a note with him, informing him of my transfer and requesting the agrément for my successor. He was as sphinx-like as usual, but managed to remark that he regretted our departure and referred to the good relations that had always existed between us, etc. It is true, we have never had a fight, simply because no question has arisen which I have had to fight him over. My incumbency has been singularly free from friction of any kind. . . .

Received from the President a very fine picture of himself, inscribed: "To Minister J. C. Grew with appreciation, great confidence and best wishes, from Warren G. Harding."

Altogether, some day. . . .

Monday, September 12 [1921]

. . . At 4 I made my official return of the Admiral's call,[15] and as it is the first occasion on which I have visited an American battleship as Minister, it was very interesting; I had no idea there was so much ceremony attached to it. The Admiral had invited Alice and the children and some other people on board to see the fun, so they left at 3.45. I left the Customs Dock at 4 in a naval launch and in ten minutes we were alongside the *Utah*, which lay far out from the harbor. The usual piping began as I ascended the gangway, and as I reached the deck, the bugles blew the three "ruffles"; here I stopped and took off my silk hat to the flag at the stern and then stood, hat in hand, while the band played a march and the Admiral and other officers stood at attention. At the end of the march, I went forward and shook hands with the Admiral and the Captain, and we all went into his cabin for tea. Leaving the ship, the same ceremony in reverse form had to be gone through, and when the launch was a few yards from the ship, it stopped and the guns let loose like all bedlam, 15 of them for a Minister. Another march was then played and the call was over. It's a great feeling to represent the United States when a ship like that is in port. Alice and the children followed shortly, having been much impressed by the ceremony which is really very moving. It was all cinematographed for the United States. . . .

Saturday, September 17 [1921]

In the morning I presented Admiral Niblack, Captain Frederick Traut, and General Henry T. Allen, commanding

[15] Under the command of Admiral Albert P. Niblack the battleship, *Utah*, accompanied by the *Childs* and the *Sands* arrived at Copenhagen on September 11, 1921.

American Troops in Germany,[16] who had come to visit the Admiral, with his aide, Captain Wilbur B. Sumner, to the King at Amalienborg. To my surprise, the King had me come in alone first and told me how much he regretted our transfer and thanked me very graciously for the hospitality we had shown to the Danes in our house, whose doors, he said, had been thrown wide open. We talked about ten minutes and he described his trip to Greenland to me; I told him of having seen the movies of it. He said he had been terribly seasick. Then he had the officers in and talked with them for another ten minutes — but the Admiral did most of the talking!

In the afternoon we all went to a baseball game which had been staged between the crews of the *Utah* and the *Sands,* the Utahs winning. It was highly amusing and I wondered what impression the slang remarks and base-coaching were making on the Danish audience. Andy umpired, from his experience at Princeton; he had difficult moments, and one American bluejacket was put off the field at the order of Captain Traut for shouting "Kill the Umpire!" through a megaphone. Surely no game of baseball can be played properly without that remark cropping up sooner or later.

Later the Admiral, Captain Traut, General Allen, etc. came to tea and to say good-bye. . . . The officers seemed much pleased with their reception here, both by the Danes and the Legation. In the evening the King's dinner took place on the *Dannebrog,* the royal yacht. I sat next to the Queen, who was most agreeable and talkative. The Admiral, as usual, held the floor and talked across the table to the King steadily; he had us all in roars of laughter. The Crown Prince and his brother, Scavenius and several Danish Admirals and Generals were also there. Afterwards the King showed the American officers the pictures of his trip to Iceland and Greenland and his route on the map. There was nothing stiff about the evening; it was as informal and amusing as in any private house. . . .

16 For General Allen's description of his visit to Copenhagen and his meeting with Mr. Grew and Admiral Niblack, see *My Rhineland Journal* (Boston: Houghton Mifflin Co., 1923), pp. 251–54.

Tuesday, October 11 [1921]

. . . In the evening to dine with the King and Queen at Sorgenfri. Harald Scavenius expressed some surprise when he heard that the King had asked us to a family dinner instead of the usual formal farewell audience and said it was seldom done. There was nobody there except the Crown Prince [Frederik] and his brother [Prince Knud], Mlle. de Castenskiold, the Mistress of the Robes, Rothe, Marshal of the Court, and the military and naval aides. The King talked interestingly through dinner and for two hours afterwards. Said, among other things, that he had greatly admired Theodore Roosevelt and believed that he had sized up the German Kaiser long before anyone else did; the Kaiser did not like Roosevelt because he knew that R. had seen through him. Said that it was his dearest wish to visit the United States, and that it would be proper for him to do so in order to thank the American Government in person for the part our country had taken in restoring Schleswig to Denmark,[17] but that at present he was going through a period of hard work and that he would have to postpone pleasures of this kind until later. Said that he had exchanged telegrams with President Harding after the visit of the *Utah* to Copenhagen. He referred jokingly to the visit of Pirie MacDonald, the photographer who had come to Denmark to take his picture, and pretended that I had committed a great indiscretion in asking for an audience for him. I tried to fasten the responsibility on Mr. Egan, who had sent MacDonald to me, but the King said: "No, you passed him on and you have got to take the responsibility; he talked to me steadily for two hours and made me move all the furniture in the room." Evidently the King thought he was merely a public press photographer intent on getting pictures of all the sovereigns of Europe, but I insisted that he had come all the way to Denmark for the exclusive purpose of taking this king and that he had returned immediately without taking any others. . . .

---

[17] In the Treaty of Versailles Germany agreed to the holding of a plebiscite in Schleswig to determine whether it should be given to Denmark. In 1919 the northern third of Schleswig joined Denmark as the result of such a plebiscite.

Twice during the course of the evening the King said he believed I was being taken away from Copenhagen because I had made too favorable reports on Denmark. He knows, at least, that I am a good friend of the country, but I hardly think that this consideration entered into the question of our transfer.

After dinner, Alice sat down to bridge with the Queen, Mlle. Castenskiold and Rothe, while the King got out his photographs and map of his trip to Iceland and Greenland, took our two chairs away from the others and went over every detail of the voyage; most interesting. Then I sent for my photos of Denmark, which were in the automobile, and showed him those. Finally, when the bridge was finished and the Queen had also seen our photographs, which seemed to interest her, the King asked us to write in his book, and when we had done so, he said with much earnestness that he wanted to thank me for the part I had been able to play in bringing the two countries nearer together, that he realized that I had worked assiduously for that end, and that he wanted to give me a purely personal remembrance of our stay in Denmark in testimony of his appreciation of what I had done — a most pleasantly and courteously worded little speech. He then gave me a signed photograph of himself framed in silver with his monogram and Danish crown in gold. The Queen likewise said that she was going to send Alice one of herself, and asked for one of Alice in return. Finally the King said he would always regard us as true friends of Denmark and held out his hand to say good-bye.

I should really be interested to know whether the King treats all retiring Ministers in so agreeable a manner. It was a simple, cosy and most agreeable evening; not the slightest stiffness or formality of any kind — simply a hospitable family party. I did not have to present my letter of recall, as that will be done by my successor when he presents his letter of credence. . . .

Friday, October 14 [1921] Farewell to Copenhagen
. . . At 10 o'clock or soon afterwards, Prince Aage, Grethe

Hasselbalch and the Andersons came in, and at 10.30 I took my new oath of office as Minister to Switzerland before Andy; Alice and Lilla were also present at the ceremony. Then, as if we still had weeks ahead of us, Alice, Prince Aage, Andy and Norman Anderson sat down to a game of poker, while I hurried to put the finishing touches on things, dictated several final letters, and eventually had to pull Alice away from the poker table by main force.[18] We started at 11.30, everyone in the courtyard to see us off, Hansen driving the Hudson, packed with baggage, and I driving the Cadillac with Alice, Lilla and Elsie with me. . . . The last personal acquaintance we saw in Copenhagen was the German Minister, Baron von Neurath, who took off his hat ceremoniously as we rounded the corner from Amaliegade into Sankt Annae Plads and set sail for Berne. . . .

18 On June 1, 1934, Mr. Grew wrote to T. Hart Anderson, Jr.: "I hope you have not forgotten the old games of poker in the Palace Guard House with Prince Aage and how when the King appeared he used to dash out to give the salute and when he came back would throw his helmet and sword in the corner with the hearty and refreshing comment: 'Damn these kings.' Those were the days."

XVII

Minister to Switzerland
1920 – 1922

*Shortly after the Harding Administration took office, Mr. Grew
was transferred to Switzerland. Harding's Secretary of State,
Charles Evans Hughes, although not too experienced in foreign
relations, had an excellent record as a lawyer, as a Governor,
and as an Associate Justice of the Supreme Court. He surrounded himself with experienced assistants. Henry P. Fletcher,
a career man, was made Under Secretary of State; another
career officer, Fred M. Dearing, was appointed First Assistant
Secretary; and, Alvey Adee, long a valuable support for many
Secretaries of State, continued as Second Assistant Secretary.
A number of the heads of the various administrative divisions
also were career men.*

*In the field, the ambassadorship to Britain went to a political
appointee, Colonel George B. M. Harvey, "the wrong man in
the wrong place at the wrong time." The Italian post went to
Richard Washburn Child, editor of* Collier's Weekly, *and the
German post eventually went to Charles Beecher Warren, a
Detroit lawyer who had had some international juridical experience. Although a few appointments turned out to be unfortunate, according to the historian of the Department of
State, Graham H. Stuart, "the Harding-Hughes regime made
a far better record in diplomatic appointments than the Wil-
son-Bryan administration which preceded it."*

*The career diplomats fared well under Hughes. In addition,
for instance, to the appointment of Mr. Grew, Hugh Gibson
was sent as Minister to Poland; Peter Augustus Jay became
Minister to Rumania; Charles S. Wilson was made Minister to
Bulgaria; and Edwin V. Morgan was retained as Ambassador
to Brazil.*

From the standpoint of Mr. Grew's service in Switzerland, two of Secretary Hughes' policies were of immediate importance. He made no change in the Wilson policy toward Soviet Russia. A trade agreement in 1921 was opposed, because Mr. Hughes stated that the Soviet Government did not yet respect guarantees of life and property, the sanctity of contract, and the rights of free labor. In 1923, the Secretary of State declared that the Soviet Government did not recognize the sanctity of international agreements. Furthermore, there could be no sound basis for relations until Soviet Russia would give adequate compensation for the property of American citizens confiscated as a result of the Revolution, recognize the debts owed to the United States Government, and cease subversive actions aimed at the stability of the United States.

The relations of the United States with the League of Nations was another knotty problem which directly concerned Minister Grew. The Department failed for the first six months of the Harding-Hughes Administration to answer League communications. When Mr. Hughes discovered that these communications had not been answered, he acknowledged them and future communications as well.

Mr. Hughes himself had been one of the thirty-one eminent Republicans who had urged the voters to support Harding in 1920 as a way of getting the United States into the League. In office, however, he had to work with a Senate Foreign Relations Committee dominated by anti-League Senators like Henry Cabot Lodge, W. E. Borah, Frank Brandegee, Hiram Johnson, and George Moses. He also was faced with the fact that a reservation to the American peace treaty with Germany stated that the United States should not be represented nor participate in any body, agency, or commission without the consent of Congress.

Mr. Hughes co-operated with the League to the extent that he thought was politically possible. He sent career officers, for instance, as observers to the International Conference on Customs and Transportation and to the Advisory Committee on the Traffic in Opium, and to the International Narcotics Con-

*ference. He also recommended American membership in the
World Court, but Congress failed to take action.*

*Mr. Grew in Switzerland was placed in an embarrassing posi-
tion on the League question. He had to avoid official contact
with the League but, at the same time, he had to procure information about League activities for the Department in Washington. Mr. Grew himself believed that America's failure to
join the League of Nations was a great misfortune, and he
believed in closer co-operation with League activities than his
instructions allowed.*

Sunday, October 23, 1921 [Berne]

In spite of rumors that a deputation of communists was to
call at the American and Italian Legations yesterday afternoon, to protest against the execution of Sacco and Vanzetti,
condemned for murder in Braintree, Massachusetts, nothing
happened.[1] Four members of the Swiss secret police spent the
day in our garden, but it proved unnecessary. However, we
are receiving a great number of letters from communistic organizations and individuals, some of them of a more or less
threatening nature. The attempt on the life of Ambassador
Myron Herrick in Paris and the bombing affair which took
place in our Consulate-General at Zurich [2] some time ago are
still fresh in people's minds, and Consul Alfred Donegan,
whose life has repeatedly been threatened, has been prevailed
upon to stay away from his post for a while, on leave of absence,

[1] In April, 1920, during the height of the Red Scare in the United States, a
paymaster of a shoe factory in South Braintree, Massachusetts, was murdered.
Two Italians, with anarchistic leanings, Nicola Sacco and Bartolomeo Vanzetti,
were convicted on what to many people seemed weak evidence. Liberals and
radicals all over the world protested and made the case a *cause célèbre*. For
seven years the men remained in jail. In 1927 a committee, appointed by the
Governor to investigate the case, upheld the verdict. Amidst world-wide protest
the men were executed on August 22, 1927.

[2] On October 19, 1921, a package sent through the mail to Ambassador Herrick, but opened by his valet, had exploded, almost killing the valet. Over a
year and a half earlier, on the night of March 3, 1920, a bomb had exploded
before the door of the American consulate in Zurich. *New York Times*, October 20, 1921, p. 1, and March 5, 1920, p. 1.

until the matter blows over. The sooner the proper course
of justice is accomplished at home, the better it will be for
everyone. . . .

Monday, October 24 [1921]
. . . The Walker Smiths [First Secretary] and the Joneses
[Military Attaché] came to tea. W. S. remains Chargé d'Affaires
until I present my credentials to the President of the Confederation. They arrived by pouch today and I immediately
wrote my note No. 1 to the Chief of the Political Department,
Giuseppe Motta, asking for an appointment. Edmund Schulthess is President this year, the same who was President when
I came out of Germany with Gerard; we called on him then,
and I well remember the conversation, which turned on "la
houille blanche" — the water power which runs the factories
of Switzerland. Each of the seven National Councillors serves
as President for a year in rotation.

My staff is composed of William Walker Smith, First Secretary; Herschel Johnson, Third Secretary; Major Ivens Jones,
Military Attaché. . . .

Tuesday, November 1 [1921]
. . . At 11.30, Etienne Lardy, Swiss Secretary of Legation,
called to escort me to the Federal Palace to present my credentials as Minister. We went in one automobile, while my
staff, composed of William Walker Smith, Johnson and Major
Jones, filled another. Large boxes of flowers had been laid out
in front of the palace for the occasion, as well as the customary
red carpet inside, while the huissiers were in their picturesque
red and white cloaks. We sedately mounted the huge staircase,
at the top of which are the three great stone figures representing the founders of Switzerland, and there I was met by one of
the Vice Chancellors, Mr. Robert Kaeslin (who spoke only
German), who led us into the state reception room. Here I was
welcomed by Mr. Schulthess, President of the Confederation,
and Mr. Motta, Chief of the Political Department; I read my
little speech (practically the same that I had made in Copen-

hagen to the King), to which the President replied by reading
his speech in French; I handed him my letter of credence and
Mr. Hampson Gary's letter of recall, and then we sat down in
three chairs in a row and chatted for ten minutes or so. The
conversation was all in French. Schulthess asked me if I had
ever been in Switzerland before, and I told him I had traveled
and resided here frequently since my first visit thirty-four years
ago, and that I had been presented to him when he received
Mr. Gerard on his departure from Germany in February, 1917;
also told him the subject we had discussed at that time — "la
houille blanche" of Switzerland. This seemed to please him.
Both he and Motta said they had already heard of my work
in the Diplomatic Service and both were extraordinarily cordial; the reception was not a bit stiff as I had expected it would
be. The usual pretty phrases were exchanged and then we all
took leave and returned down the great staircase to the entrance, where a crowd had assembled and the inevitable newspapermen and cameras had gathered to snap the new American Minister. Returning to our salon in the hotel, Lardy still
accompanying us, we opened champagne and pledged each
other in various toasts. Later the President and Motta returned
my visit by leaving cards at the Legation. I also left cards on
all the seven Federal Councillors and two or three other officials, notably the Vice Chancellors and Paul Dinichert, Chief
of the Division of Foreign Affairs of the Political Department. . . .

Monday, November 28–Sunday,
December 11 [1921]
   . . . On the sixth I had a busy day . . . I paid my first official
call on the German Minister, Dr. Adolf Müller, who had just
returned to Berne. He is a little bullet-headed man — one
could hardly fail to recognize his nationality — but his address
is not displeasing. He is a socialist (not a radical one) and was
formerly leader of the socialist party in Bavaria; was opposed
to the war and left Germany soon after it broke out, preferring
to live in Switzerland. I had a long talk with him, but found

some difficulty in trotting out my very rusty German, of which I have spoken hardly a word for over four years. However, it was better than his English. He said that there was no question whatever that Germany would eventually be completely democratized but that the process could not take place overnight; that Germany had every wish and intention to live up to her obligations and to carry out the terms of the Treaty of Versailles honorably "so far as it was physically possible to do so." Angels could do no more. Germany would sooner or later struggle up to economic prosperity again, for the German was a hard and conscientious worker. The trouble with the nation was that it had had too much police, too much "Zwang." That was unnecessary for the naturally industrious German, and it killed initiative. When I left he said that he hoped that we, at least, would have no "Streit" between us; I replied that on the contrary I hoped that we should be friends. He is a cultivated man and has written several books on art and other subjects.

Recently, I have neglected to say, I called on Motta and had a long and interesting talk with him at the Political Department. He asked me to tell Mr. Hughes that he and his colleagues on the Federal Council were following the Washington Conference [3] with keen interest and admiration and that they were wholly in sympathy with its aims. He spoke at length on the subject of military disarmament and said that some of the great military establishments of Europe should be reduced as they were causes of suspicion and possible danger at all times. He compared Switzerland and the United States and said that their disinterestedness in international politics was a source of happiness and force to both. He is a very agree-

[3] The Conference for the Limitation of Armaments met in Washington from November, 1921, to February, 1922. The Conference agreed on limitations of naval armaments, and concluded the Nine-Power Treaty by which they agreed to respect the territorial integrity and the political independence of China. The United States, Great Britain, Japan, France, and Italy carried on the naval limitation discussions, and China, Holland, Portugal, and Belgium joined these five Powers in the deliberations on the Pacific and the Far East.

able man, forceful, straightforward in manner, clearheaded and courteous. . . .

The Serbian-Yugoslav Minister, Mr. Yovanovitch
Conversation, November 30, 1921

Miloutine Yovanovitch called at the Legation to return my official visit and in the course of conversation expressed himself very emphatically on the subject of the League of Nations. He said that there was a distinct antipathy to the League throughout all classes in his country and it was felt that the League was so predominated by England that it amounted to nothing more nor less than an English organization. The English Secretary-General — Sir Eric Drummond — exercises great power and was supported by a staff of English officials outnumbering those of other nations. In the Council of Ambassadors England could always count on Japan to support her and in view of Italy's vacillation could generally count on a majority. Every question that came up was regarded by the British purely from the point of view of their business interests and in the Council of the League every member stood out for his own national interests rather than for the interests of the League and what it stands for. The League, in his opinion, would therefore always be a dangerous element in international affairs unless the United States should enter it and act as a balance to England. The United States would furthermore be supported in most questions by the solid bloc of the Latin American nations and would therefore carry great weight in shaping the policy of the League, which, in view of the disinterestedness of the United States, would bring about the very conditions for which the League was established. . . .

Returning to European politics Mr. Yovanovitch said that while during the darkest days of the war he had always been optimistic of the successful outcome and had so expressed himself to the French Ambassador at a time when the latter was most discouraged, he was now distinctly pessimistic with regard to the situation in Europe. No two nations were co-operating and the interests of almost every nation were in direct conflict. The situation between Italy and France, France and England, Italy and Yugoslavia, and many other countries was drifting from bad to worse. He predicted that the next war would be between France and Italy and he told me that when the Italian Military Attaché left Berne a year ago he, the Military Attaché, had made the same prediction. He said that Lloyd George's position in the Albanian question had stirred up great resentment in his country and as for the League of Nations he felt that it would be powerless to prevent war between any of these countries. . . .[4]

With regard to Russia he felt that the outlook for the future was hopeless. All parties were now antagonistic to the Allies, the Bolsheviks naturally, and the Monarchists because they felt that the Allies had deserted them. He pictured the absurdity of a line of independent Russian states stretching from the Black Sea to the Baltic. Russia in her own good time would simply stretch her elbows and scatter them to the winds, League of Nations or no League! . . .

Monday, February 13 [1922]

The question had arisen, as it was sure to do sooner or later, whether the time has come to resume social relations with

[4] The frontiers of Albania had not been permanently fixed in the period immediately following the First World War, and Albania and Yugoslavia had engaged in a protracted territorial dispute. In October, 1921, Yugoslavia resumed military operations to gain her territorial ambitions. The invasion of Albanian territory was generally deplored by the press, political leaders, and the government of Great Britain. On November 7, 1921, Lloyd George sent the following telegram to Sir Eric Drummond at League headquarters in Geneva: "Continued advance of Serb-Croat-Slovene forces into Albania being of nature to disturb international peace, His Majesty's Government desire to call the attention of the Council thereto, and request that you will take immediate steps to summon a meeting of the Council to consider the situation and to agree upon measures to be taken under Article 16 in the event of the Serb-Croat-Slovene Government refusing or delaying to execute their obligations under the Covenant." On November 9, 1921, the Conference of Ambassadors finally announced its decision concerning the placement of the Albanian boundary lines. See J. Swire, Albania, The Rise of a Kingdom (London: Williams & Norgate Ltd., 1929), pp. 327–66.

the Germans. The French, British and Italian missions have all done so. Three years have gone by since the termination of the war. The Müllers, furthermore, represent, personally no less than officially, the new order of things in Germany. So when Müller asked Theo Russell [British Minister to Switzerland] to approach me to see if I would consider an invitation to dinner favorably, I talked it over with Alice and answered in the affirmative. The dinner took place tonight, and although typically German, from the Würstsuppe and Sauerkraut with the Braten, and the Munich beer served throughout the evening, it was an agreeable and interesting evening. The President of Switzerland and Madame Robert Haab, the Russells, the Hungarian Chargé d'Affaires and Madame Parcher de Tarjékfalva, and ourselves were the only guests. The conversation was almost entirely in German, although the Haabs talked French in speaking to Alice. The invitation had come in German, addressed to S. Exc. Minister und Frau Grew, so I replied in English, addressing our reply to H. E. the German Minister and Mrs. Müller! They have evidently cut out French permanently, and recognize it no longer as *la langue diplomatique*. Müller has some extraordinarily fine things in his house in the way of paintings, porcelain, glass, etc., but they are mixed in with such a horrible display of ugly things that the whole impression is unfortunately one of German bad taste at its worst. But he showed us his prize collections with the pride of a connoisseur. After dinner the men sat together in the smoking room and the President told us the story of his political career and gave us many inside glimpses of Swiss politics, which was highly interesting and instructive. I came away feeling that I had crossed the Rubicon but with no regrets at having done so. If a word had been said about the war or anything connected with it, we should have felt differently, but Müller is not that sort. . . .

Wednesday, March 22 [1922]

   . . . I call on the Persian Minister — Emir Zokaed-Dowleh — to congratulate him on the occasion of his national holiday and later to a men's dinner at the Grande Société, where I sit between the President [Mr. de Würstemberger] and Walter de Herrenschwand. The latter, who was in charge up till recently of the Bureau des Etrangers, which decides on the admissibility of foreigners to enter and to reside in Switzerland and who therefore is in close touch with Bolshevist propaganda and the movements of Bolshevik agents abroad, states not as a supposition but as a fact that an attempt is going to be made by the communists in various countries in the immediate future to overturn the existing governments and to gain control, the movement to be started by general strikes and force to be used when the daily life of the countries is dislocated and the governments paralyzed. He said he thought the attempt would be made during the Conference of Genoa; [5] as most of the important statesmen would then be absent from home and their respective governments correspondingly weakened. I asked him upon what facts he based this hypothesis and he said he had talked with various workmen with whom he was in touch and who had told him that whether they wished to do so or not, they would have to take part under the orders of their trade unions or socialist organizations. I do not think the Swiss Government is seriously disturbed over this prospect; similar movements have been announced periodically during the last few years, only to be postponed from time to time, and if trouble should actually break out here, there is the Swiss Civic Union to rely upon, and also the proverbial animosity of the peasant class for the workmen. But there may well be anxiety as to what may happen in the adjoining countries, where disturbances or revolution would seriously react upon Swiss interests. On account of the authority of the source, I reported this conversation in full to

[5] The Conference of Genoa, which met in April and May, 1922, was attended by delegates from twenty-nine European states and from the self-governing Dominions of Great Britain. The Conference dealt with political and economic questions and the important question of the relationship of Russia to the rest of Europe. The Conference ended without a satisfactory solution having been achieved regarding the major points at issue, and its agenda were remitted to a group of experts which met later in the same year in the Netherlands.

Mr. Hughes. We are now directed to report all conversations of interest, touching upon international affairs, in special despatches marked: "Confidential; for the Secretary and the Under Secretary," to be sure of their being given more than routine attention, and it is very satisfactory to feel that one can write on such matters without feeling that one's reports may be pigeonholed by some casual subordinate. I send one or two such reports in almost every pouch, but gather that few of my American colleagues are doing the same, as we not long ago received a second instruction calling our attention to the first one and saying that it was not being generally complied with. . . .

Friday, March 24 [1922]

. . . Alas, another speech rises before me. The "Swiss Friends of the U.S.A." in Zurich had invited me to their annual banquet for March 25, but as we had expected the Orrs [Arthur Orr, colleague of Mr. Grew in the Berlin Embassy in 1908] to visit us on that date, I gave this as a perfectly valid excuse and declined the invitation, although the Orrs later postponed their visit a week. But to my disgust the society, determined on having my blood, went and postponed their banquet too, and have now asked me for April 8. I can't refuse twice and must go. D——n this job! I have written to our Consul General George Murphy asking him how long I must speak, presupposing no such good fortune as a speechless banquet where one can retain one's appetite and really enjoy the occasion. They all know that the relations between Switzerland and the United States are perfectly serene; why should I have to get up and tell them perfectly obvious and well-known facts? I think I shall circularize the members of the society somewhat as follows:

Gentlemen (or Dear Sirs) (or quite simply, My Friends):

You have most kindly asked me to dine with you on April 8. Such an invitation presupposes a desire on your part to extend hospitality, and hospitality is the art of making a guest enjoy himself and feel at home. If I have to make a speech I shall look forward to the evening with dread, shall lose my appetite at the dinner, and shall not enjoy the occasion in any respect. You will therefore not be extending true hospitality. Anything that I may say in a speech will necessarily be banal and obvious, for we are not permitted to do otherwise, and will center about the excellent relations so happily existing between Switzerland and the United States, of which you are, I presume, already aware. Thus, besides having a beastly time myself, I shall bore you too. Permit me therefore to suggest that there be no speeches; that as your guest I be allowed to enjoy myself, to anticipate the event with pleasure, to retain my appetite for the excellent food and drink with which I have no doubt you are going to regale me, to communicate my views on current affairs to you in informal conversation before, at and after dinner, and to carry away with me a pleasant impression of Zurich's hospitality. If any one of you has any doubts about the good relations between our countries, I shall be delighted to set his mind at rest in a personal talk and tell him in a dozen words what it would take me fifteen minutes to say in a speech.

Hopefully yours,
etc., etc., etc.,

Yes, that is clearly the solution. . . . [6]

Tuesday, March 28 [1922]

. . . In the afternoon I go to the General Direction of Customs and have a long discussion with Paul Comte, one of the tariff officials, over the discrimination against American automobiles involved in the gross-weight reckoning of the tariff charges, having been authorized by the Political Department to negotiate direct. At first he said flatly that nothing could be done, but after I had talked for some time and said that I proposed to see Federal Councillor Jean-Marie Musy, Chief of the Department of Finance, on the subject, Comte said that the matter would be "re-examined" and a report submitted to Musy within a fortnight, after which I could see him. Am trying to get them to reduce the "tare" surcharge from 30

[6] Mr. Grew delivered the speech.

per cent to 10 per cent, which would enable American cars to compete with European cars on a fair basis.[7] This is the first big commercial question I have had to deal with here and I hope to pull it off even if it means camping on the doorsteps of the competent Swiss officials until they come around. It was just as well that I started the negotiations on my own initiative, as my first report to the Department crossed a definite instruction from the Department to go to it, and they answered "commending" my action. Commendation from the Department is so rare and beautiful a thing that one's first impulse is to have it framed and hung over the fireplace. . . .

Federal Councillor Schulthess

Conference of Genoa, April 8, 1922

Mr. Schulthess came to see me at my house again tonight at 9.15 P.M. and told me what had happened at the meetings of the neutral delegates and experts of Switzerland, Norway, Denmark, Sweden, Holland and Spain today. They were unanimous that the first prerequisite for the economic and financial restoration of Europe was the raising and stabilizing of the German mark. This depended upon the balancing of the German budget, which in turn depended upon a revision of the reparation clauses of the Treaty of Versailles. It was not for the neutrals to discuss this revision of a treaty in which they had no part, but they intended at Genoa to impress their attitude on the English and Italian and even the French delegations informally, and if this should prove ineffectual they would not leave the conference without expressing their views openly.

With Germany steadily printing more money and dumping her goods in foreign countries, the economic situation in

---

[7] The Swiss tariff computed the charges according to gross weight which included the crates in which automobiles arrived from the United States. European cars could come into Switzerland uncrated and thus enjoyed a much lower tariff rate than American cars. My efforts to have this discrimination removed were successful. — J. C. G.

Europe was impossible. Furthermore, no international loan could be thought of until Germany was rendered solvent.

As for Russia, this question was secondary; one must save the dying before proceeding to reanimate the dead. The logical order of rehabilitation was first Germany and then Russia. Mr. Schulthess agreed that when the Russian question was approached the first essential would be international control of the Russian railways which the Soviet Government would probably not accept.

Mr. Schulthess said that the conference of neutrals had discussed each phase of the Genoa conference in turn, including the financial and economic restoration of Europe, the value of the mark, the budgets, credits, Russia, communications, etc.

He said that the Swiss delegation would warmly welcome any moral support from the United States Government, no matter how conveyed or expressed. All this was told me in the strictest confidence. He would write me if anything should take place at the final meeting tomorrow. . . . [8]

Thursday, May 4 [1922]

After a strenuous few days I get two important despatches off in the pouch to my great relief. One, a long confidential report on Professor Max Huber, the Swiss judge on the Permanent Court of International Justice, who has been named by the President of Switzerland as the third arbitrator in the American-Norwegian dispute. . . . [9] I turned in 11 pages of

[8] There was no doubt of Mr. Hughes' concern over the problem of reparations. In September, 1922, he suggested a solution to France. Then, on December 29, 1922, he delivered a speech to the American Historical Association recommending that outstanding financial experts of the interested countries be appointed to a commission which should recommend a reasonable reparation's settlement. Mr. Hughes added that there could be no economic recovery in Europe until Germany recovered. This speech was the beginning of the Dawes Plan which was adopted in 1924. See Samuel Flagg Bemis (ed.), *The American Secretaries Of State and Their Diplomacy* (New York: Alfred A. Knopf, 1929), X, 374–85.

[9] The United States Shipping Board Emergency Fleet Corporation had requisitioned ships under construction in American yards for certain Norwegian shippers. Under the special agreement of June 30, 1921, the United States and

typewriting and it was an exhaustive report. The other despatch was reporting complete success in the automobile tariff dispute, my first important commercial case here. After the Swiss Government had definitely refused to accede to our request that the duty on automobile cases should be reduced from thirty per cent to ten per cent, to enable American cars to compete with European cars, which are brought into Switzerland without cases, I kept hammering away at them chiefly by personal interviews, until this week they gave in completely and carried out the desired reduction. I have received appreciative letters from the American importers here and the Department ought to appreciate the result also. This furnishes a concrete example which could be used to advantage in showing up the fallacious argument of certain congressmen and others who maintain that the Diplomatic Service is superfluous and that diplomacy could equally well be carried on directly between governments without personal agents, for this case could never have been settled by writing alone. This should mean much to the whole American automobile trade as the Swiss market may now become an important one for us. . . .

Confidential Conversation   May 13, 1922

Mr. Arthur Sweetser

Assistant Director of the Information Section
of the League of Nations

BRITISH MANDATE FOR PALESTINE

Mr. Sweetser called me up from Geneva at 10 A.M. and said that he had conveyed my information of the evening before informally to Lord Balfour and Sir Eric Drummond, and that the matter of the British Mandate for Palestine, so far as the United States was concerned, was now entirely clear and satisfactory.[10] Lord Balfour had received information from London to that effect.

Norway agreed to arbitrate the dispute which had arisen over settlement of the claims of a Norwegian shipping group for losses sustained because of the requisition of their ships. *Foreign Relations, 1921*, II, 571–99.

[10] Although invited by the League to participate in its discussions about the

Lord Balfour, at the meeting of the Council on May 11th, had stated his desire to approve confirmation of the British Mandate before the end of the session, or at least that the Council should go as far as possible towards confirming the Mandate. Marquis Imperiali [of Italy] objected, on the grounds that the subject was not on the agenda for this session of the Council and that he had no instructions. . . .

Mr. Sweetser said that my telephone call last night had arrived at a moment when he was sitting after dinner with Balfour, Imperiali, and several other delegates to the Council, and that they had chuckled over this "subterranean channel between the State Department and the League of Nations." The matter was, however, taken by them in entirely good part.

Mr. Sweetser said that he would mail me today the text of the remarks made by Lord Balfour at the opening meeting on the subject of the British Mandate for Palestine.

[No date]

. . . We sailed on the *Majestic* of the White Star Line, the former *Bismarck*, 56,000 tons, the largest steamer in the world, on June 7th, arriving in New York on the morning of June 13th after a good voyage. . . .[11]

Most of the next two months were spent at Hancock, with week ends at Manchester. . . . I spent a week in Washington, staying with Bill Phillips in the country.[12] Saw President

mandating of former German and Turkish colonies, the United States began negotiating with Great Britain, France, Italy, and Japan, ignoring the League Council. Secretary Hughes undertook lengthy negotiations with Great Britain to ensure the rights of the United States in territories under British mandate. See U.S. Department of State, *Papers Relating to the Foreign Relations of the United States, 1922* (Washington: Government Printing Office, 1938), II, 278–79, for the telegram of Secretary Hughes of May 10, 1922, to Ambassador Harvey embodying the points of agreement which had been reached between Great Britain and the United States regarding the draft mandate for Palestine.

11 Mr. Grew spent most of his three-month leave of absence in the United States. He returned to Berne on September 7, 1922.

12 In 1922 Mr. Phillips, who had been First Assistant Secretary of State and, then, Minister to the Netherlands, was called back to be Under Secretary of State. Henry P. Fletcher was sent to Belgium as Ambassador.

Harding. . . . Told him a little of what the League of Nations was accomplishing, but he made no comment although he listened politely. He asked me to take his best regards to Fletcher in Brussels, whom he is very fond of. Told me how my own appointment to Switzerland had come about.[13] Lunched with Secretary Hughes and Phillips; the former talked for half an hour on the attitude of our Government towards the League. Left to my discretion the question of how far I should go in Geneva. I also called on Senators McKinley, Joseph T. Robinson and Lodge and made my peace with the two former who had taken offense in Copenhagen. They thought I was trying to snub them by not speaking to them because they had refused my invitation to come to our place! I tried to explain that I was not that kind. Lodge told me they had tried to block my confirmation to Switzerland, but he had forced it through in the absence of Robinson from the committee. Lodge said he had wanted Berne for Albert H. Washburn, one of his protégés, but rather than let me fall between two stools he had agreed to send Washburn to Vienna. . . .

To Arthur Bliss Lane, from Hancock, N.H.,
July 19, 1922

. . . I had a long talk with the President and an equally long one with the Secretary. The attitude of the Dept. with regard to the League is to treat it with every courtesy and to answer every communication received. Hughes was under the impression that this had been done. If it is not done in future, we must learn of it and tell the Dept. You may tell Sweetser this if you see him. There is however little hope at present of our joining any of the subsidiary bodies even unofficially, as the Department's hands are tied by the proviso in the Washington treaties to the effect that our Govt. shall be represented on no international body without the consent of the Senate. As for my own attitude in Geneva, the Secretary talked for half an hour on the development of our relations with the League

[13] President Harding said: "I need hardly tell you, Mr. Grew, that there were several other candidates for the post in Switzerland." — J. C. G.

from the beginning up to the present and then said he must leave my own actions entirely to my discretion. This leaves me exactly where I was before. I shall have to maintain the same aloofness as formerly. . . .

To Leland Harrison, Assistant Secretary of State, from Hancock, N.H., August 10, 1922

. . . After my talk with the Secretary I find that my attitude towards the League will have to be exactly the same as before, and that it will not be possible to establish any more open connections than formerly. I had hoped to be authorized to play the role of an unofficial observer, openly . . . but while the Secretary left the matter to my discretion, he emphasized the importance of avoiding publicity, and I cannot therefore run the risk of visiting the League's offices or of openly moving to Geneva during sessions of the Council or other bodies, although this would have enabled me to keep the Department more closely and fully informed. . . .

Berne, Monday, September 11 [1922]

. . . In the course of the morning a pouch came in from Washington containing instructions which necessitated my going to Geneva too, so I took the 2.35 train, arriving at 5.35. Motta was on board and I had good talk with him; he told me much about the Austrian situation. Switzerland regards the possibility of Austria's disappearing from the map as a future danger to herself. It is far safer to be surrounded by four neighbors than by three. . . .

On arriving at Geneva I took a taxi and stopped at the entrance of the League of Nations building to pick up Sweetser to motor out to Genthod together. We had arranged this by telephone as he was too busy to meet me elsewhere. I have always carefully avoided the League premises but it seemed safe enough merely to stop at the entrance to call for somebody. As luck, or ill-luck, would have it, the first person I ran into there was Henry Wales of the *Chicago Tribune*. . . . He said: "Hello, what are *you* doing here! Looking into the Arms

Traffic Commission?" I replied that I was there in a purely personal capacity, was visiting friends in the country and had stopped to see Sweetser, an old friend. I asked him not to say anything about it as there was no news in it and it would embarrass me greatly. . . . When I saw Sweetser he thought the chances were decidedly in favor of Wales making a story of it. . . . I felt pretty uneasy during the next two days, but when the *Chicago Tribune* came from Paris two days later, there was not a word about my presence. . . . The front hall of the League was as busy as a beehive; every one is here for the Assembly, including a regular army of correspondents, and Geneva is positively packed. . . .

Tuesday, September 12 [1922]

Sweetser called for me at 9.30 and motored me in to town and we walked for half an hour on the Quai Mont Blanc, discussing Austria, Mandates, Arms Traffic, Anatolia, etc. He told me much inside information which has not appeared either in the press or the *Journal* of the League, all of which was of value and enabled me to write several despatches on my return to Berne. I gave him some official American statistics for use by the League and took up with him a complaint by the Department that previous statistics had either not been used at all or had been published incorrectly. He will investigate. When Sweetser went to his office I called on the David Jayne Hills at their apartment, 39 Quai Mont Blanc, and had a pleasant talk with my old chief. They asked me to stay for a dinner they were giving for several of the delegates, but I had to decline. Then to the Consulate where I talked with Lewis Haskell and Robert Macatee [Consuls], then took a walk with Markus d'Oldenburg [Danish Minister to Switzerland], who tried to persuade me to stay for a dinner he was giving the same evening for Eduard Beneš, Prime Minister of Czechoslovakia. It would be decidedly interesting if Alice and I could stay openly in Geneva during meetings of the Assembly and the Council and see all these people, but that unfortunately is at present out of the question. . . .

Wednesday, September 27 [1922]

Alice and I went to Geneva at 2.35 for a dinner and dance given by Countess Pourtalès and because I wanted to pick up what was going on. . . . The dinner was highly interesting. There was first of all Mr. Agustín Edwards, Chilean Ambassador to Great Britain and President of the Third Assembly of the League of Nations, now in session, and his wife famed as a beauty . . . Sir Eric and Lady Drummond; Gaston Clauzel, French Minister Plenipotentiary at the Assembly, formerly my colleague in Vienna; Oldenburg, the Danish Minister . . . and a lot of smaller fry. . . . Edwards was particularly cordial, said he had heard much about us and was anxious to talk — "League" of course. He asked Alice and me to lunch alone with him and Madame Edwards in the country on Sunday, but we did not altogether relish the prospect of another trip to Geneva so soon and so begged off. Drummond seemed a little sour, especially over our failure to ratify the Convention of St. Germain prohibiting the traffic in arms.[14] He went so far as to say that the recent massacres in the Near East would not have occurred if the Convention had been ratified and carried out, and it was not difficult to see that he was laying the responsibility at our door. But his statement will not hold water: you can no more prevent the smuggling of arms than you can enforce prohibition. I suppose he had in mind the great amount of war stocks which the French are said to have sold to the Kemalist army.[15] None of the other nations pro-

14 The St. Germain Arms Traffic Control Treaty had been signed in 1919 by American representatives at the Peace Conference. The United States failed to ratify this Convention and even refused to state to the League the reasons for this failure until 1923, when Secretary Hughes addressed an explanatory note to the League. The reasons for withholding ratification, which he stated, were that the Convention provided for no general limitation of armament, that the Convention prohibited the sale of arms to states not signatories of the Convention, and that the Convention required legislation to make it operative with which the United States could not at this time associate itself. Although by October 1, 1922, eleven nations had ratified the Convention, most of them had made their ratification contingent upon the similar action of other Great Powers. It was generally felt that unless the United States adhered, the Convention would be useless.

15 After the Armistice, the landing in and occupation of Turkey by Allied forces, particularly those of Greece, provoked the Turkish Nationalists led by

ducing arms would ratify the Convention unless we did and so
the whole thing fell to the ground.

Thursday, September 28 [1922]

A very full day. First I called on Mr. Edwards at 9.30 by
arrangement for a short talk; then had a short walk with Oldenburg, and a little later Sweetser came and we spent a couple of
hours walking on the Quai Mont Blanc while he brought me
up to date on the League's doings. He told me that the Assembly on the previous day had adopted the report of the
Arms Traffic Commission which contained a provision that
inquiry should be made of the United States Government as
to the reasons for its objection to ratifying the Convention of
St. Germain and whether it had any suggestions to make as to
the sort of convention it could ratify. He said that the form
and method of presenting this resolution would come before
the Council at its next meeting and that they wanted to do it
in a way which would be most likely to elicit some constructive
reply, and he said that if our Government wanted to make
any suggestions "discreetly and confidentially" in Geneva, he
knew that the Council would be largely influenced thereby.
Sweetser then switched over to the Austrian question — a proposed loan — and after sketching the situation up to date he
would go into the League (we were then in front of the building) and get me the latest documents, and he asked me to come
in with him and talk to the man who had the matter in hand.
I told him that he already knew my attitude towards going into
the League, but he blew up then and said unprintable things.
After a somewhat hot exchange of views I said we should have

Mustafa Kemal Pasha. To counteract the successes of the nationalist forces, the
Allies allowed the Greeks to advance beyond the area to which they had been
assigned. France, however, was alienated from the Allied cause by the return
of the pro-German King Constantine to Greece, and thereafter an agreement was
negotiated between France and Turkey in 1921. When the rest of the Allies
failed to reach a settlement with the Turks, the Turkish army began an offensive which completely routed the Greek army. Soon, thereafter, the Nationalists
accepted an invitation of the Allies to discuss the situation. Plans were made
to open the Lausanne Conference on November 20, 1922.

to agree to disagree and left it at that. Later he calmed down and finally acknowledged that I was right and could take no other course. Sir Eric Drummond is reported as saying that I always turn up my coat collar when I meet him in the street!

At 12 I called on Judge John Bassett Moore, of the Permanent Court of International Justice, formerly Assistant Secretary of State, and had a pleasant chat with him. His *International Law Digest* has been my Vade Mecum for 18 years. He would probably have been Secretary of State during the war had he been able to survive Bryan's methods of diplomacy, but he resigned and Lansing took his place. . . .

I stayed over until the 5 o'clock train, called again on Edwards by appointment at 3.15 and had a long talk with him.

Edwards said that in giving me his ideas about the League, he was speaking more as an "American" than as a member of the League. He realized the great importance of solidarity among the various countries on the American continents and felt that if the United States should ever become a member of the League, a solid and disinterested bloc would be formed which would exert a most beneficial influence in world affairs.

The attitude of the United States towards the League, he said, has had a useful influence on the League itself by preventing its developing into a superstate. The League would not exist today if it had followed the lines originally planned in Paris. The present trend is for noncontroversial matters to gravitate towards the League while controversial questions gravitate away from it, as in the Conferences of Washington and Genoa. The Third Assembly has shown this trend of development very clearly. Regional affairs are more than ever worked out directly by the interested parties, and by tacit arrangement the expenses of such cases are paid by the parties themselves and not by the League as a whole.

Article 10 [16] plays no part in the League and, as a matter

---

16 Article 10 of the Covenant of the League of Nations stated that the "Members of the League undertake to respect and preserve as against external aggression the territorial integrity and existing political independence of all

of fact, is so indefinitely worded that almost any interpretation can be placed upon it. An effort has been made to abrogate Article 10 on the ground that this would make it easier for the United States to come into the League should it ever be ready to do so. But his feeling was that no change should be made until the United States had expressed itself on the subject; it would be quickly eliminated from the Covenant if the United States should ever express such a desire.

The whole development of the League, Edwards said, has been along juridical rather than political lines, as emphasized by the Permanent Court of International Justice. If at any time the United States should intimate that it would like to join the Court without becoming a member of the League, some satisfactory arrangement could be made *in a minute* by which we could sit in the Council and Assembly exclusively for the consideration of questions pertaining to the Court, such as (1) election of judges; (2) budget of the Court; (3) amendments to the statutes of the Court, and to have full voting powers. He said that he would be in Washington about the middle of December and would call on Billy Phillips and hoped to meet the Secretary and the President when he would gladly place his knowledge and ideas at their disposal.

He then referred to the Fifth Pan-American Conference, to take place in Santiago next March, and asked me to ascertain informally whether the Government of the United States, as a member of the Conference, would have any objection to accepting an offer which the League had made to lend the Conference its staff of technical experts, as it had done for the Genoa Conference.

Edwards is an attractive personality. He speaks English flawlessly, being of direct English descent, although he has the dark eyes and complexion of the Latin American. He looks and seems young and full of vigor and enthusiasm, and his manner is cordial and open. . . .

Members of the League. In case of any such aggression or in case of any threat or danger of such aggression the Council shall advise upon the means by which this obligation shall be fulfilled."

Friday, September 29 [1922]

Dr. Léo Di Pauli, the Austrian Minister, called on me this morning and said he had been instructed by Dr. Grünberger, the Austrian Minister for Foreign Affairs, at the instance of Mgr. Ignaz Seipel, the Chancellor, now both in Geneva, to request me to propose to my Government that it take part, together with possibly Holland, Belgium, Switzerland, Poland and other states, in guaranteeing the final 20 per cent of the external loan which is to meet the Austrian deficit of 520 million gold crowns, this having been arranged by the League of Nations. Great Britain, France, Italy and Czechoslovakia are each guaranteeing 20 per cent. Di Pauli pointed out that this was an economic rather than a political matter and that it was most desirable for Austria to have the moral support of American participation. I said I would submit the matter informally to Washington, but that I could not hold out any probability of favorable action, for although our Government was sincerely interested in Austria's welfare and eager to see her early financial and economic reconstruction, we had to be guided by our general policy of nonparticipation in European affairs.[17] (Can't say I particularly enjoy representing this policy of ours.) . . .

Wednesday, October 4 [1922]

A perfectly marvelous day — the finest I have yet seen in Berne. The atmosphere was absolutely clear, the mountains superb, especially in the afterglow and later under a full moon. Under such circumstances, Berne is indeed one of the loveliest spots on earth. John Bassett Moore came to lunch and we had most interesting talk. While talking about the arms traffic convention, he told us an amusing anecdote of the Spanish War. He was then Assistant Secretary of State, and one morning a telegram was brought in to him from the Legation at Brussels asking for authority to protest to the Belgian Government against several shiploads of arms which were about to sail from Antwerp under various South American flags. He put

[17] The League Assembly in 1922 worked out a loan for Austria that was guaranteed by the Governments of ten nations but not by the United States.

it aside to act on later in the morning, but inside of an hour an officer rushed in from the Navy Department which h̓ad heard from the Naval Attaché about the telegram and asked if the Department had sent off its reply. Moore replied in the negative. "Then for Heaven's sake, don't do it," said the officer, "Those arms are destined for us!" Worked all day on several different despatches until 6, when Alice and I walked for an hour and reveled in the magnificent view of the mountains.

Mr. Schulthess, Chief of the Division of Public Economy
THE PRESENT ECONOMIC AND FINANCIAL SITUATION IN EUROPE
Confidential Conversation, October 17, 1922

Having heard that I was about to proceed to Berlin to attend an informal conference of my American colleagues, Mr. Schulthess asked me to come to see him and said that he would be particularly glad to tell me briefly of his views as to the present economic and financial situation in Central Europe, which he believed might prove of interest to my colleagues if I should care to bring them up in the conference. I told Mr. Schulthess that the proposed conference was of a very informal nature and was called on the initiative of our Ambassador in Berlin purely for the purpose of bringing a few of us into direct touch with each other and to discuss various administrative questions connected with our Foreign Service, but that I should nevertheless be glad of this opportunity to bring to the attention of my colleagues, in the course of our informal conversations, any views which he might express to me. Mr. Schulthess then made the following remarks:

He referred first to the following statement which he had made in our conversation of May 26th last, reported to the Department in my despatch of May 26, 1922:

The situation appears to me clear enough. The Allies, especially France and Belgium, are lawfully and morally entitled to reparations. For reasons of a material and moral nature, these countries feel the need of realizing part of their claims with the shortest possible delay. That Germany may, for another several months or less time, continue to meet her payment, is of no importance. It is beyond doubt that she will soon exhaust her means if the system followed up to the present time is not modified. Within the near future she will not be able to pay any considerable sums, if the necessary funds are not obtained by means of a loan from abroad. No illusions should be had in this respect. As a neighbor of Germany, Switzerland is in a position to observe the situation at close range. Switzerland is thus enabled to judge and at the same time to measure the entire extent of the danger, particularly from the social point of view, which would be brought about by the collapse of Germany. Order would disappear and the radical parties would acquire possession of power, perhaps according to the Russian example.

Mr. Schulthess then continued:

"The predictions made at that time, especially in so far as Germany's solvency is concerned, unfortunately came to pass in a few months. Will the situation continue to become worse and shall we see the occurrence of that which the last sentence of the above-quoted passage considers possible and even probable when summed up: social collapse, anarchy and the Russian rule? I seriously fear that this may happen, if a *complete sudden change does not take place at the last hour in the method of dealing with the whole reparations problem.*

"The reparations problem is more than ever the one on which depends the fate of Europe and of the world. If it is not solved our continent will go on to ruin and towards the abyss, perhaps more rapidly than it is thought. It is inconceivable how the other countries would not be dragged into the abyss if Germany should be annihilated economically and socially. I have the feeling that many circles are not sufficiently aware of this. It is believed that the collapse of Germany is of concern only to that country, while it would affect not only Europe, but also, although less severely, oversea countries which maintain active relations with the European continent.

"What is to be done today?

"No serious man can question it; Germany is no longer able to pay. In admitting without concealment that this is truly the case, and in deducing the reasonable consequence from this fact, one must admit that the granting of a moratorium is indispensable. This could serve as the starting point of an amelioration and the beginning of the progressive revival of confidence. The inevitable effect of a refusal to grant a moratorium would be to aggravate the situation and completely to annihilate the mark. I see the proof of this in the experiments made during the last few months. If the solution which one has finally been successful in finding had been obtained a few months sooner and without the occurrence of the incidents of which we are aware, the rate of the mark would be far from being as low as it is today and the flight to foreign exchanges, result of fear, would not have assumed the proportion in Germany that we have seen.

"A few months ago the launching of an international loan by Germany could still appear possible of accomplishment before the solution of the reparations problem. Today, this possibility has completely ceased to exist. At the present time it is indispensable to create a clearly defined situation which would permit Germany's credit to recover somewhat. Once this result is achieved, the international loan, designed to procure funds for Germany, *will be the only means of paying the reparations to which* — already pointed out in our preceding statement — *France and Belgium are especially entitled, legally and morally.*

"Measures of coercion are absolutely inoperative. They react against their authors. The total sum of the amount of reparations must be such as to permit Germany to hope that she will be able to effect payment. The struggle against inflation and against the increase of State expenditures is of the greatest necessity in Germany. But it is not sufficient to demand that this struggle be brought about; it is also necessary that it be rendered possible by appropriate measures. Up to the present time, the fall of the mark, its depreciation in Germany itself, or, if it be expressed thus, the tremendous increase in prices expressed in marks, has upset every solution. It does not suffice to prohibit the issuance of notes. The currency must above all look for its support in the re-establishment of confidence.

"In the Allied countries a strong current demands that the question of inter-Allied debts be solved at the same time with that of reparations. Without desiring to express a definite opinion of any kind, I, too, have the conviction that this would be very desirable. If the States continue to protract these debts in their entirety, the rehabilitation and the reconstruction of Europe will be impossible, and the reimbursement, even partial, will become more and more illusory.

"But exclusive of these considerations, it is hoped in Switzerland that the United States of North America will pronounce the liberating word. The United States alone, not only by making a certain sacrifice, but also by all the weight of their moral intervention, can save Europe and render to it, as well as to themselves at the same time, the greatest of services. The most urgent thing, it seems to me, is to do something immediately susceptible of reviving confidence in a small measure. The German people must feel that they can be saved and not that they are marching towards the abyss. If nothing is done in this sense and if one continues to lose time, it is my conviction that partial catastrophes, which will degenerate progressively into a general catastrophe, may be expected. Assuredly, a provisional measure designed to have practical and moral effects and which apparently could alone be in the form of a moratorium, would have to be followed as rapidly as possible by a definite solution which can only be a reasonable determination of the amount of reparations. The situation of Europe cannot be viewed too seriously. The Austrian problem shows the point that can be reached. Often the case of Austria was used to attempt to prove that a State cannot collapse. To-day it is conceded by everyone that, if one did not come to her aid, Austria, in view of the complete depreciation of her currency, would be at the mercy of ruin and that her population would perish from lack of work and food. A thorough study shows how far this process is already advanced and warns against allowing matters to reach such a point elsewhere, especially in Germany.

"It is not necessary to speak of other countries. I confine myself to pointing out that the difficulties of the European countries with high exchange increase, so to speak, every day. The longer matters will develop in this sense, the more difficult it will be, not to say impossible, to begin one's journey to a better future." . . .

Berlin, Friday, October 20 [1922]

Of course the prices in Germany are extraordinary when quoted in marks, but when reckoned in dollars they are not high save in the most expensive shops. I came at just the right moment for purchases, for the mark tumbled overnight from 3200 to 4400 to the dollar and the prices had not yet risen in proportion. For a check of $100 I received 440,000 marks. One gives a tip of 100 marks to one's porter at the station; the taxis charge 80 times the registered fare. A bottle of excellent Rhine wine on the train cost Mks. 138, approximately 3 cents. The German newspapers cost 8 marks. My room at the Adlon cost Mks. 24,000, including the 80 per cent tax for foreigners, without food. I went with Holland, our Consul General, and bought a cinematograph camera and projector; the projector cost 85,000 marks; the next day when I went to the shop again it had risen to 176,000 marks! Also bought very cheaply a camera with a Tessar lens and screen shutter. Hugh Gibson bought a gun at the same time at a proportionately small figure.

We met at the Embassy at 10.30, the Ambassador [Alanson Houghton], General Henry Allen [Commander of American forces in Germany], Gibson, Theodore Brentano [United States Minister to Hungary], Albert Washburn [United States Minister to Austria], Warren Robbins [Counselor of the United States Embassy at Berlin] as secretary, and myself, and of course William Castle [Chief of the Division of Western European Affairs], and each gave a description of the political and economic situation in the country in which he is accredited. The Ambassador, Allen, myself and Washburn spoke in the order named during the morning; Gibson, Brentano and

Castle in the afternoon. It was intensely interesting and gave us a fairly comprehensive picture of Central European affairs. The Ambassador was particularly interesting, for he is in close touch with Hugo Stinnes [German industrialist and member of the Reichstag] and he was with Walter Rathenau [German Foreign Minister] only a few hours before he was murdered on June 24, 1922. I read Schulthess' statement, which impressed them considerably, and told them a little about how Switzerland was suffering from her normal exchange, which caused a good deal of surprise. This is about what I said:

"The relative importance of Switzerland in the problem of Central Europe is perhaps less than that of any of the countries represented here today, for the following reasons: the other countries are all working out new destinies under the new order of things. Their territories and forms of Government have all been altered or newly created as a result of the war, and all have passed through crises or are passing through them now. Switzerland, on the other hand, has undergone no material change in territory or form of government. These are the same as they have been for centuries. But while Switzerland has passed through no great crisis, her position is none the less not an enviable one. Being to a very large extent economically dependent upon her neighbors in Central Europe, she is suffering to almost as great an extent as they. But while their troubles center about depreciated currencies, her difficulties are owing primarily to the fact that her currency is normal and that she therefore cannot compete in trade and commerce and industry with the others. A very brief survey is sufficient to explain this situation.

"The Swiss industries live by importing raw materials and exporting their finished products. These industries cannot compete with other countries manufacturing similar products because of the Swiss wages, which are the highest of those in any European country, and they are paid in currency on a gold basis. They cannot compete with German machinery, nor with Germany, England or the United States in dyes and chemicals.

Their great ribbon trade as well as their trade in spun silk is almost lost.

"Switzerland has no raw products to export save milk and cheese, hence there is nothing to profit on save labor, and labor is dearer in Switzerland than in any other European country, and hence it cannot be employed to advantage. Unless the cost of labor can be lowered, Swiss industry cannot hope to maintain itself in the world's markets.

"Great appropriations for the unemployed and for subsidies to certain industries have increased the taxes to a high degree. This has not offered incentive to work, but has rather aided the workmen in standing out for higher wages than the industries can pay. The laborers are in a sullen mood, as they claim they did not share in the great profits of the war.

"Swiss stocks are in a sadly debased condition. The shares in fifteen prominent Swiss corporations, with a total capitalization of 470 million francs, have declined 923 million francs from the highest market quotations in 1919, up to the end of 1921. Many dividends were passed entirely, or were nominal during 1921 and 1922. Others paid from their reserves. Many small corporations have gone into liquidation, while larger ones are in a state of suspended activity. Almost all are letting out employees as business decreases.

"The proposed remedy of inflating the currency in order to cheapen labor would be doubtful for Switzerland must import half her foodstuffs and most of her raw materials. The high tariff recently enacted in order to shut out foreign competition has not tended to reduce the cost of living, but rather to increase it. The Swiss have gone by thousands into Germany and other countries with a depreciated currency to buy wearing apparel, etc., which has injured the Swiss retail trade. The hotel industry, one of the greatest of the country, has suffered in like proportion from the reduced tourist travel, owing to the high exchange and high prices.

"The banking system is sound. The banks are conservative and money is plentiful and to be had for low rates of interest.

But the Swiss do not want to borrow money. They want trade. As the industries are not operating, capital is not functioning. Laborers are idle, unemployment amounts to 51,000 and has decreased little in the past year. The cost of living is the highest of any European country.

"Switzerland, therefore, has no money difficulties. She is suffering purely from industrial inactivity, and she must await the stabilization of foreign currencies to raise the wages in other countries up to the Swiss standard in order to enable her to compete once more in foreign markets."

After the morning meeting, we all lunched at the Robbins' . . . .

XVIII

The Lausanne Conference

NOVEMBER – DECEMBER, 1922

World War I proved to be a devastating blow to the Ottoman Empire. Turkey had been able to maintain a precarious sovereignty in the decades just prior to 1914 largely as a result of the rivalries of the Great Powers. After the nation cast its lot with the Central Powers, however, the Allies proceeded to sign agreements regarding the disposition of the Ottoman territories.

The defeat of the Central Powers brought an Allied occupation force to Turkey. Then, on August 10, 1920, representatives of Mohammed VI signed the Treaty of Sèvres. Under this treaty, Turkey acknowledged the loss of all her rights in the Sudan, Egypt, Cyprus, Tripolitania, Morocco, and Tunisia, and she renounced all rights over Arabia, Palestine, Mesopotamia, and Syria. Greece received some Turkish islands in the Aegean and a portion of Eastern Thrace, while Smyrna and southwestern Asia Minor were to be temporarily administered by Greece. Italy's possession of Rhodes and the Dodecanese Islands was confirmed, although Italy promised eventually to cede the Dodecanese to Greece.

Turkey, in addition, agreed to recognize Armenia as a free and independent nation with boundaries to be drawn by President Wilson in the area of the vilayets of Erzerum, Trebizond, Van, and Bitlis. Although Kurdistan was to receive autonomy, the boundary could be rectified in favor of Iran. Constantinople and a small part of the European mainland were to remain under Turkish sovereignty, although the zone of the

475

Straits — the Dardanelles, the Sea of Marmora, and the Bosporus — was to be demilitarized and internationalized.[1]

Furthermore, under the mandate system of the League of Nations, France was granted a mandate over Syria and Lebanon, and Great Britain received a mandate over Mesopotamia and Palestine. In addition, on April 24, 1920, France and Great Britain signed the secret San Remo Agreement dealing with Mosul. Before the war, German and British oil prospectors had organized the Turkish Petroleum Company to exploit oil in Mosul. Although no concession had been granted by Turkey, Great Britain, which had absorbed the German shares, claimed a monopoly of Mosul oil on the basis of an unofficial Turkish letter to the German Ambassador in 1914. At the Paris Peace Conference Lloyd George had persuaded Clemenceau to turn Mosul, which had been given to France by a secret agreement, over to Great Britain to be incorporated in the British mandated kingdom of Iraq. In the San Remo Agreement, France was granted a twenty-five per cent share in the Turkish Petroleum Company in return for the right of allowing pipelines to be built from Mosul across Syria.[2]

On the day that Turkey signed the Treaty of Sèvres, France, Italy, and Great Britain also reached a "Tripartite Agreement" calling for the three powers to operate the railroads of Anatolia, and carving out spheres of influence in Anatolia for France and Italy.[3]

The Treaty of Sèvres supplemented by the mandates and the "Tripartite Agreement" represented, in the view of one author, "one of the most punitive peace arrangements and

---

[1] Great Britain, *Treaty of Peace with Turkey, Signed at Sèvres, August 10, 1920*, Cmd. 964, *Accounts and Papers*, vol. 25 (1920) (London: H. M. Stationery Office, 1920); H. W. V. Temperley (ed.), *A History of the Peace Conference of Paris* (London: Hodder & Stoughton, 1924), VI, 1–114.

[2] Great Britain, *Memorandum of Agreement between M. Philippe Berthelot, Directeur des Affaires politiques et commerciales au Ministère des Affaires Etrangères, and Professor Sir John Cadman, K. C. M. G., Director in Charge of His Majesty's Petroleum Department*, Cmd. 675, *Accounts and Papers*, vol. 25 (1920).

[3] Great Britain, *Tripartite Agreement between the British Empire, France and Italy Respecting Anatolia*, Cmd. 963, *Accounts and Papers*, vol. 25 (1920).

one of the most daring and deliberate divisions of war spoils in modern history." [4] *The terms of the Treaty of Sèvres, commented Secretary of State Hughes in 1924, "were severer than those of the European peace treaties, not only depriving the Turks of vast territories but imposing upon them an even greater measure of foreign control than had been the case before the war."* [5]

When the Allies forced Turkey to sign the Treaty of Sèvres, they greatly underestimated the strength of Turkish nationalism. The Allied occupation under the Armistice, and the subsequent attempt at partitioning the country, stimulated the development of the Turkish Nationalist Party under the leadership of Mustafa Kemal Pasha. Kemal had revealed himself as a leading General during the Balkan Wars of 1912 and 1913 and in the defeat of the Allies at Gallipoli in 1915. At Angora in 1919 Kemal began to build a nationalistic military force.

In May, 1919, Great Britain and France, in order to forestall Italian imperialistic enterprises in Anatolia, encouraged Greece to land troops at Smyrna. The resulting pillaging and atrocities fanned Turkish nationalism. Kemal convened two Congresses to unite nationalists throughout the country. These meetings subsequently led to a National Pact issued by the nationalists, which the Sultan's Parliament in Constantinople, containing a majority of nationalists, also adopted in January, 1920. The National Pact proclaimed six principles "which represent the maximum of sacrifice which can be undertaken in order to achieve a just and lasting peace, and that the continued existence of a stable Ottoman sultanate and society is impossible outside of the said principles." The first three principles recognized the freedom of Arab territories and called for plebiscites to determine the destiny of all those areas of the old Empire, under Allied occupation, which still contained

[4] Leland James Gordon, *American Relations with Turkey, 1830–1930; An Economic Interpretation* (Philadelphia: University of Pennsylvania Press, 1932), p. 269.

[5] Charles E. Hughes, "New Phases of American Diplomacy," *Current History,* March, 1924, p. 1059.

a majority of Turks. Article Four asserted the inviolability of Constantinople, and added: "Provided this principle is maintained, whatever decision may be arrived at jointly by us and all other Governments concerned, regarding the opening of the Bosporus, to the commerce and traffic of the world, is valid." Article Five guaranteed the rights of minorities "in reliance on the belief that the Muslim minorities in neighbouring countries also will have the benefit of the same rights." The final article demanded the abolition of the foreign capitulations and all "restrictions inimical to our development in political, judicial, financial, and other matters." "It is a fundamental condition of our life and continued existence," this article declared, "that we, like every country, should enjoy complete independence and liberty in the matter of assuring the means of our development, in order that our national and economic development should be rendered possible and that it should be possible to conduct affairs in the form of a more up-to-date regular administration." [6]

A few weeks later, however, the nationalist movement received a staggering blow when Allied forces — mostly British — seized Constantinople and arrested forty leading nationalists. On April 23, 1920, within a few days of this action, the nationalists at Angora convened a Great National Assembly to "preside over the present and future destiny of Turkey, so long as her Caliph-Sultan and her Eternal City should remain under the dominion and occupation of foreigners." The Great National Assembly also elected Kemal as President as well as commander in chief of the "Nationalist Army."

While the National Assembly was drafting a "law of Fundamental Organization," Kemal repudiated the Treaty of Sèvres and took to the field. In September, 1920, after an agreement with Soviet Russia, Kemal invaded the recently created Armenian Republic of Erivan and reunited the provinces of Kars and Ardahan with Turkey.

Meanwhile fighting with the Greeks had been occurring

[6] The full text can be found in Arnold J. Toynbee and Kenneth P. Kirkwood, *Turkey* (London: Ernest Benn, 1926), pp. 85–86.

since the landing in Smyrna in May, 1919. During 1920, the Greeks, with the support of Great Britain, France, and Italy, conducted a series of successful advances into Turkey. The following year, however, the Allies withdrew their support from the Greeks. On their own, the Greeks tried to capture Angora. The Turks, led by Kemal and Ismet Pasha, resisted fiercely, and on September 16, 1921, a general retreat was ordered by the Greeks. This marked the turn of the tide in the Greek-Turkish War, and, in a sense, demonstrated to the world that the process of carving up Turkey was over.

In addition to these military victories, the world scene also became more favorable for the Turkish Nationalists in 1921. The French, on October 20, 1921, signed a separate agreement with the Kemalist forces — the Franklin-Bouillon Pact — agreeing to a new boundary between Turkey and Syria, withdrawing French occupation forces from Cilicia, and receiving in return various economic concessions. This agreement meant that France recognized the de facto *Nationalist Government at Angora while the British were still supporting the Sultan's Government at Constantinople. The Italians, too, had made overtures to the Nationalists and in March, 1921, had agreed to withdraw their occupation forces from the neighborhood of Adalia.*

Then, in 1922, the Turks completely routed the Greek forces. The Greeks by September had been driven into the sea at Smyrna. Kemal, also, demanded that the Greeks evacuate Eastern Thrace and that this area be returned to Turkey. Nationalist forces moved northward toward the Straits preparatory to crossing over into Thrace to drive out the Greeks. At the Straits, however, British forces blocked the Nationalists. In May, 1921, when the Allies had announced their neutrality in the Greek-Turkish War, they had established a neutral zone on either side of the Straits in which neither belligerent was to enter. Conflict between Britain and the Nationalists seemed imminent. The British, however, could not rely on France and Italy for aid, and public opinion at home opposed a conflict. Finally on October 11, 1922, an armistice was concluded between the Allies and Ismet Pasha, whereby it was agreed to evacuate the Greeks from Eastern Thrace and to restore all Thrace as far as the Maritsa River to Turkey. The Greeks three days later themselves abandoned their claims. The Greek-Turkish War was now over and the Nationalists had secured the territory claimed in their National Pact.

The time had now arrived for a definitive peace. Invitations were issued to Great Britain, France, Italy, Rumania, Yugoslavia, Japan, Greece, Turkey, and the United States to meet at Lausanne. The Soviet Union, although it protested, was invited to participate only in the discussion concerning the Straits.

On November 1, 1922, three weeks before the Lausanne Conference convened, the Grand National Assembly deposed the Sultan. It was not until October 29, 1923, however, that the Assembly proclaimed the nation to be a republic and elected Kemal as the first President.

The Lausanne Conference, which met from November, 1922, to July, 1923, marked the triumph of Turkish nationalism. The Turks led by Ismet Pasha won a series of notable victories. The key questions before the Conference were: the territorial and political problems dealing with the regime of the Straits, Thrace, Mosul, and the Aegean islands; the problem of minorities; and the question of the capitulations.

For centuries the Ottoman Empire had granted financial and judicial concessions to foreigners. In general, the judicial capitulations placed the foreigners outside of Turkish civil law and made them subject to the laws of their respective countries. The financial capitulations made foreign business firms independent of Turkish control and exempted foreigners from taxes.[7] Just before World War I, the Western Powers had contemplated an abrogation of the capitulations. After the war broke out, the Ottoman Government unilaterally abolished the capitulations. The Allies, however, refused to recognize this action, and they sought to reimpose the capitulations in the Treaty of Sèvres. The Turkish National Pact of 1920 had

[7] Nasim Sousa, *The Capitulatory Régime of Turkey. Its History, Origin and Nature* (Baltimore: The Johns Hopkins Press, 1933).

called, however, for their abolition, and this was to be a vital issue at Lausanne.

The Turkish delegation, led by Ismet Pasha, went to Lausanne to fight for the territorial integrity of Turkey and to preserve its sovereignty from infringements through capitulations or through international control of the Straits.[8]

The British delegation, led by Lord Curzon, Secretary of State for Foreign Affairs both in Lloyd George's Government, which had just been defeated, and in the new Conservative Government of Bonar Law, was primarily interested in the freedom of the Straits, disrupting the alliance between Turkey and Russia, and securing Mosul for Iraq.[9] *Curzon, faced with a victorious Turkey at Lausanne, could not depend upon wholehearted support from France and Italy. Although the three powers reached an agreement just before the Conference convened, it was "an alliance only in name . . . Curzon knew that he would have to fight his battle in spite of his allies."* [10] *Curzon's support at home, too, was none too substantial. The Government of Bonar Law was weak, and the fall of the Lloyd George Cabinet had, in part, been attributed to the public's opposition to British policy in Turkey.*

Although the United States had never declared war against Turkey, the Department of State decided to send observers to Lausanne to present the American position on subjects of common concern and to protect American interests in the Near East. An aide-mémoire was sent to the other powers on October 30, 1922, listing the subjects of particular concern to the United States. The American position, as the Conference convened, was:

"(1) Capitulations. — The Department appreciates that the

[8] The Turkish delegation included, among others, Ismet Pasha, Riza Nour Bey, Hassan Bey, Munir Bey, Zekiai Bey, Mustafa Cherif Bey, Veli Bey, Tahir Bey, Mouhtar Bey, Tewfik Bey, and Réchid Safvet Bey.

[9] Some of the other members of the British delegation were Sir Horace Rumbold, Sir William Tyrell, Harold Nicolson, E. G. Forbes Adam, Sir Adam Block, W. K. McClure, Thomas Spring Rice, V. Cavendish Bentinck, and Major General J. T. Burnett-Stuart.

[10] Harold Nicolson, *Curzon: The Last Phase 1919–1925* (New York: Harcourt, Brace & Co., 1939), pp. 283–84.

Turks will in all probability strongly oppose the retention of the capitulations and that the Allies may take divergent views, certain Powers perhaps consenting to barter particular rights under the capitulations for concessions without value for us. It will be difficult, if not impossible, for the United States to maintain the capitulations intact, as would be desirable. It is felt, however, that we should insist upon the retention of the capitulations which are essential to the protection of American citizens. As regards economic capitulations which refer to measures of taxation, customs dues, et cetera, certain concessions might be made provided satisfactory guarantees of another nature to protect American business enterprise could be obtained.

"(2) Protection of American Educational Philanthropic and Religious Institutions. — The list of institutions recognized by the Sublime Porte in 1907 should be brought up to date and Turkey should recognize them collectively and individually, grant rights to hold property in the corporate name of the institution, permit reopening of institutions closed since 1914, the establishment of new schools, the use of the English language, and the enjoyment of privileges of Ottoman institutions as regards taxation and customs exemption.

"(3) Protection of American Commercial Interests. — We should oppose the policy of spheres of influence, exemplified by Tripartite agreement signed at Sèvres August 1920 and maintain the principle of the 'Open Door' and equality of opportunity. Assurances should be secured that discriminatory taxation will not be levied and if capitulatory right of consent to any change in tariff be abandoned satisfactory guarantees for trade and commerce should be obtained.

"(4) Claims for Damages. — Any new arrangement we may make with Turkey should include provision for indemnities for requisitions, loss of life or property resulting from illegal action of Turkish authorities since 1914.

"(5) Protection of Minorities. — American sentiment demands that this Government exert its full influence to protect minorities. As a result, however, of deportations since 1915 it

*is believed that a relatively small number of Christians remain
in Anatolia and it will be difficult to formulate any effective
plan for insuring protection of the scattered remnants of the
Christian population in Asia Minor. The most feasible solution of the problem might possibly be an exchange of Christian
and Moslem minorities in Asia Minor and Greece. The question of the Christian minorities in Europe, particularly in
Constantinople, is one of special interest to this Government
and we shall exert appropriate influence for their protection.*

*"The question of the homeland of the Armenians may be
raised. It is possible that upon the return of more settled conditions in Russia, the Russian Caucasus may offer the best refuge
for Armenians from Turkey.*

*"(6) Freedom of the Straits. — Of the two phases of this ques-
tion relating to the time of peace and the time of war, the
Department is not disposed to become involved in commitments concerning the latter, particularly when Turkey or the
Great Powers of Europe may be the belligerents. It is of distinct interest to this Government, however, to obtain effective
assurances that the Straits would be open in time of peace for
both merchant ships and ships of war to proceed to Constantinople and through the Black Sea. This Sea is a highway of
commerce and should not be under the exclusive control of
Turkey and of Russia.*

*"(7) International Financial Control. — The Commission
controlling the Ottoman Public Debt, some 60 per cent of
which are held in France, 22 per cent in Germany, 14 per cent
in England and Holland, composed before 1914 of French,
British, Italian, German, Austrian and Turkish members, ad-
ministers six important sources of Ottoman revenue and largely
influences trade and commerce. If Turkey should apply to us
for a loan, the possibility of its consolidation with existing
foreign debt would place us in an advantageous position respecting the administration and liquidation of the latter. Both
financial and commercial questions in general should receive
careful consideration.*

"(8) Archeological Research. — American institutions are

particularly interested in securing adequate provision to permit archeological research and study in Turkish territory.

"(9) General Observations. — This Government may further desire to conclude with Turkey naturalization and parcel post conventions.

"To summarize: While it is neither natural nor desirable that we should participate in the peace conference or become involved in the negotiations regarding policies and aims in which we have no share it is essential that the Department should be constantly in command of adequate information, keen for the protection of American interests, ready to throw the full weight of our influence to obtain assurances for the freedom of the Straits and the protection of minorities, candid as to our views and in a position at any suitable time to make the separate agreement which at some time must be made with the Turkish Government recognized by the Powers. No point of advantage should be forfeited, no just influence lost, no injurious commitments made. We should maintain the integrity of our position as an independent power which had not been concerned with the rivalries of other nations which have so often made the Near East the theater of war. . . ." [11]

The American delegates [12] *headed by Richard Washburn Child, Ambassador to Italy, Admiral Mark L. Bristol, American High Commissioner to Turkey, and Mr. Grew received the following instructions from Secretary of State Hughes as to their role at the Conference:*

"The Department considers it important that you should be given an appropriate place in the conference and attend the sessions. You should state the American position if at any time it seems necessary. In view of our direct interests it would expose us to serious criticism were we to keep aloof from the sessions and very likely would put in jeopardy opportunity for complete observation and the use of appropriate influence. The understanding that you are to observe and report, and

[11] U.S. Department of State, *Papers Relating to the Foreign Relations of the United States, 1923* (Washington: Government Printing Office, 1938), II, 887–88.

[12] Other members of the American group at the Conference included Copley Amory, F. Lammot Belin, Harry G. Dwight, Lewis G. Heck, and Julian Gillespie.

not to commit yourself without instructions, will fully safe-
guard your position. You are of course free to affirm the posi-
tion of the American Government as set forth in its aide-mémoire." [13]

To Margaret Perry [Mr. Grew's sister-in-law]
November 13, 1922

. . . I don't quite know what to tell you in the way of news.
So much has been developing and going on here lately that
the Immortal Mémoires have temporarily collapsed. Perhaps
it is as well if they are never resuscitated. Anyway, the swing
of the pendulum has brought us once more into the European
turmoil and has quickly dissipated that somnolent atmosphere
which overhung the Legation, with father peacefully nodding
by the fireside over the last *Wall Street Journal* or the *Political
Science Quarterly.* . . .

To reminisce, I was informed on October 18th that the President desired me to be one of the Observers at the Lausanne
Peace Conference, together with Ambassador Child of Rome
and High Commissioner Admiral Bristol of Constantinople
(good company, that). After all this interesting information
had appeared in the European press as emanating from Washington, I was informed that the Department did not desire any
publicity to be given to the matter until the names of the
American representatives had been officially announced in
Washington. Well, there hadn't been a peep out of me. Then
followed much interesting correspondence as to what we were
to do, which was considerable, and many conflicting reports as
to the date of the meeting of the Conference. I made all arrangements for our delegation to be housed at the Hotel Beau
Rivage at Ouchy-Lausanne, and, in fact, am still at it, for there
are many details to be seen to. We are to have three secretaries
and three or four clerks and are evidently going to do the
thing up brown, Congress or no Congress. Yesterday I was suddenly informed that the Conference would be formally opened
today and there was much scurrying to and fro in diplomatic

[13] *Foreign Relations, 1923,* II, 899.

circles (as the paper says); Lewis Carroll must certainly have had some of my colleagues in mind when he described the White Rabbit in *Alice in Wonderland*. It appeared that the United States had not been included in the list of those who were to be present and the Swiss Government had made no arrangements for us. So up I spoke and said I should be there, seat or no seat. General excitement and more scurrying of diplomats. A few moments later came the news that there would be no meeting today; the Conference was definitely postponed until the 20th, even although the Turks had already arrived at Lausanne. The Allies had important dinner engagements in London, Paris and Rome; they positively could not come; the Turks must be soothed. Apoplexy in the Diplomatic Corps; several Ministers have to be placed in strait jackets, martial law proclaimed, and the future is hopeful. . . .

That's about all the news just at present. Alice and I move to Lausanne on the 17th; heaven knows how long we shall be there. I suppose it will be amusing but rather difficult and complicated work. The Turks are not just in the same position that they were when the Treaty of Sèvres was drawn up; they are coming, not hat in hand, but with a victorious army behind them. That makes a lot of difference. . . .

Lausanne, Sunday, November 19 [1922]

 . . . Took tea with Sir Horace and Lady Rumbold, just arrived from Constantinople . . . Rumbold and I were colleagues in Cairo in 1904 and again in Berlin in 1912, and together we sealed up the British archives when war broke out in 1914. During the war we corresponded steadily, as he was in the British Foreign Office in charge of matters relating to prisoners of war, and I was able to trace many missing British prisoners for him through this informal correspondence. Later he was Minister in Berne and Warsaw and then appointed High Commissioner in Constantinople with the rank of Ambassador, a rapid career.

I had a talk with Rumbold, who seems to be as vague about the procedure of the Conference as everybody else; we discussed the Capitulations, minorities, etc. At 6 he left with Theo Russell to meet Lord Curzon who is arriving from Paris with Poincaré by special train and proceeding directly to Territet to meet Mussolini [14] for an evening conference. They will then all come to Lausanne for the night. Various reasons are given for Mussolini's refusal to come directly to Lausanne and his insistence on meeting the others at Territet, one of which is that Mussolini, in his youth, was arrested in Lausanne as a vagabond and expelled from the city, and that he still resents the incident. But this does not appear to hold water as he is coming here in any case tomorrow. . . . [15]

Monday, November 20 [1922]

The opening day of the Conference. Dick Child who knows Mussolini well, having picked him out as the future leader of Italy long before he came into power and having long been on friendly terms with him, and I were going to Territet this morning to call on him, but Mussolini changed his mind and came to Lausanne to this hotel to meet Poincaré and Lord Curzon at 10 o'clock. At 10.20, after Poincaré and Curzon had fumed for twenty minutes at being kept waiting, they sent a secretary to find out what had happened to him (Bentinck, the secretary who went on this errand, told us about it afterwards). Mussolini, on hearing from Bentinck, said quite casually: "Well, if they're both there I'll come." It was evidently a *beau geste* to show his independence. Child and I went to see Mussolini at 2 o'clock; he was alone in his room over his coffee and received us cordially. I interpreted as Child speaks no French. Mussolini told us the net result of his conversation with Poincaré and Curzon last night and this morning; they

[14] On October 29, 1922, King Victor Emmanuel had appointed Mussolini the Premier of Italy after the Fascist "March on Rome."

[15] According to Nicolson, Poincaré had considered Mussolini's insistence that he and Curzon meet the Italian Premier at Territet an insult to France and Great Britain. On the train to Territet Curzon had sent a message to Poincaré stating that Mussolini wished to avoid Lausanne, because he had been put out of the city by the police on his last visit. This message Poincaré took seriously. Nicolson, *op. cit.*, pp. 288–89.

failed to agree on several points and M. made various reservations. He thinks the Turks are absolutely intransigent and predicts an early breakdown of the Conference. Said he would support the aims of the United States after we had explained that we had no political axe to grind whatever and wished only to protect the commercial interests of our citizens and their humanitarian work in Turkey, as well as minorities. He wished to see close co-operation between the United States and Italy. Told us that the conference would resolve itself into three main committees; (1) territorial affairs, presided over by Great Britain; (2) minorities, presided over by Italy; [16] (3) economic and financial affairs, presided over by France.[17] Subcommittees would be named, to be presided over by other Powers, including Turkey. The presidency of the Conference would rotate between France, Great Britain and Italy as the inviting powers. This denies the rumor we heard today that they were considering asking us to preside. We sent a rush telegram to Washington this morning asking urgent instructions in case the presidency should be offered us. I have little doubt that the answer will be in the negative,[18] although it would give us an added prestige.

Mussolini impressed me as a simple, open, direct, strong man of the people, the patriot rather than the statesman. . . . [19]

[16] The Italian delegation included Marquis Camillo Garroni, Mario Lago, Giulio Montagna, Colonel Umberto Vitale, Mario Arlotta, Bernardino Nogara, Carlo Pugliesi, and Andrea Zanchi, among others.

[17] Some of the members of the French delegation were Camille Barrère, Maurice Bompard, General Maxime Weygand, Jules Laroche, René Massigli, Admiral Lucien Lacaze, and Edouard de Navailles-Labatut.

[18] It was. See *Foreign Relations, 1923*, II, 899.

[19] The story is told that when Claire Sheridan, the authoress and sculptress, turned up at Lausanne, Mussolini jokingly invited her to come to see him in Rome. She promptly accepted his suggestion, traveled by the same train and took rooms in the hotel where he was staying. Mussolini still regarded the matter as a joke until the day after their arrival when several men appeared at his room with many pails of plaster, boards, and nails. He asked what in thunder they were for and was informed that Mrs. Sheridan was about to make a bust of him. Mussolini forcibly put the men to flight and wrote Mrs. Sheridan a letter in which he positively refused to be sculped, adding that busts were only made of dead men and that he himself was still very much alive. — J. C. G.

Opening Session. November 20 [1922], 3.30 P.M.

Met at the Casino de Montbenon. Robert Haab, President of the Swiss Confederation accompanied by Paul Dinichert and Emile Traversini of the Political Department, had come to Lausanne to open the Conference. The President and Dinichert sat on a raised platform facing the delegates who sat in the front row of seats, the delegations arranged alphabetically to the President's right. I had seat No. 1, Child, No. 2, and then came Barrère and Poincaré, France; Rumbold and Lord Curzon, Great Britain; Venizelos and another man, Greece; [20] Garroni and Mussolini, Italy; Hayashi and Otchiai, Japan; [21] two Rumanians; [22] two Serbs; [23] and lastly the Turks, Ismet Pasha and Riza Nour. Stambolisky, the Prime Minister of Bulgaria, looking very like a brigand, sat at the end of the line, with Mlle. Stancioff, the new Secretary of the Bulgarian Legation in Washington.[24] Behind our delegation were Alice and Mrs. Child, Belin and Copley Amory, Vice Consul Fletcher Dexter, Edith and Lilla. The hall was full of members of the various delegations, Swiss officials, the Diplomatic Corps from Berne and some 250 press correspondents. I was the only member of the Diplomatic Corps among the delegations. President Haab opened the meeting with a graceful speech in French, welcoming the delegates to Switzerland, to which Lord Curzon replied. There were to be no other speeches, but Ismet Pasha then arose and made a most tactless address, controversial and threatening in tone; it was not the time or the

[20] The Greek delegation included Eleutherios Venizelos, Demetrius Caclamanos, André Michalakopoulos, Constantin Collas, Jean and Athanase Politis, and General Alexander Mazarakis.

[21] Among the Japanese delegates were Baron Gonsuke Hayashi, Haruichi Nagaoka, Masaaki Hotta, Colonel K. Saigo, Masayuki Tani, and K. Otchiai.

[22] Ion Duca and Constantin Diamandy headed the Rumanian delegation, which also included Toma Dumitresco, Constantin Contzesco, C. A. Constantinesco, and C. Mavrodi.

[23] The delegation from the Kingdom of Serbs, Croats, and Slovenes included Miroslav Spalaikovitch, Milan Rakitch, Milan Antitch, Djordje Djouritch, Vladimir Milanovitch, and Pavlé Georgévitch.

[24] Alexander Stambolisky led the Bulgarian Commission, whose other members were Dimitri Stancioff, Constantin Théodoroff, Constantin Mouravieff, Moustapha Riza Bey, Dimitri Mikoff, and Nadejda Stancioff.

place for that kind of a speech, as the first session was purely ceremonial and if he had to speak at all he should have confined himself to thanking the President for his welcome and for Switzerland's hospitality. It made a very bad impression. Mussolini's face bore an expression of utmost ferocity and he looked as if he wanted to spring at Ismet's throat.[25] M. Camerlynck [of France], the interpreter, translated Lord Curzon's address into French and the President adjourned the meeting. Edith and Lilla were very much thrilled; it was a great experience for them.

After the session I took Child to introduce him to the Swiss President at his room in the Beau Rivage and we had a short talk, the latter commenting on the tactlessness of Ismet's speech. Later I was called on the telephone by Harold Nicolson, of the British Delegation, who said that the secretaries of the three inviting powers were having a meeting and wanted to know how the American delegation wished to be placed. I replied that we expected to be given our proper places at the conference table exactly on a par with the other nations, for we were there in a fully representative capacity even if we were not to negotiate or sign the treaty. He answered: "Hurrah, that simplifies things a lot. We rather feared that as 'observers' you would want to sit away from the conference table and have one all to yourselves — sort of like children coming down from the nursery." He said it so sweetly and seemed so genuinely pleased that we were going to join the others that it was impossible seriously to object to his simile. . . .

Tuesday, November 21 [1922]

Another beautiful day. Switzerland is doing her best to beautify the surroundings and atmosphere of the Conference. At 9.40 Child and I called by appointment on Poincaré and Barrère at the Palace Hotel, where hang the French, Turkish and Japanese flags. Poincaré was more reserved than Mussolini but said that France's interests in the Near East were the same

25 Poincaré and Mussolini did not remain at the Conference after the opening day.

as those of the United States.[26] He spoke of the importance
of a united Allied front but stated emphatically that France
would not send further military forces to clean up a situation
created by the intrigue and errors of another nation and added
the usual formula that France is neither imperialistic nor militaristic. He did not give the impression that zones of influence
would be done away with and intimated that we had no interest in the Ottoman Debt.[27]

Lord Curzon, on whom we called at 10.40, was quite different. He received us very cordially, expressed his pleasure at
our presence and said that we and they ought to co-operate on
every issue, but we had no time to go into details as the plenary
session was about to begin, although he asked us to come to him
whenever we wanted information on any subject. I drew a
favorable impression of him, having been led to expect a pompous and condescending type. On the contrary, his reception
of us was entirely hearty. He talks well, with a beautiful and
precise choice of words and expressions.

1st Plenary Session. November 21 [1922], 11 A.M.

At the Hotel du Château, Ouchy. Lord Curzon presided . . .
with marvelous suavity and overrode the various Turkish objections to the draft of procedure, drawn up by the inviting
powers, with velvet words but steam-roller methods. Ismet
Pasha . . . listened as his secretary whispered to him what was
being said; at the end of each statement he would lean forward

[26] Ambassador Child wrote of this statement of Poincaré's: "His underestimate
of my contempt for this kind of diplomatic clap-trap amused me." *A Diplomat
Looks at Europe* (New York: Duffield & Co., 1925), p. 89.

[27] Under the Ottoman regime, a large foreign debt was incurred. In 1881, as
the result of the failure to meet interest payments, the Ottoman Government
was forced to place control of the payments in a Council of Administration of
the Ottoman Public Debt. Representatives of bondholders in France, Great
Britain, the Netherlands, Austria, Germany, and Italy, and one representative
of the Ottoman Government composed the Council. At Lausanne, the delegates
finally agreed on a figure for the debt and divided it between Turkey and the
succession states of the former empire. Harry Howard. *The Partition of Turkey;
A Diplomatic History 1913–1923* (Norman: University of Oklahoma Press, 1931),
pp. 308–13.

decisively and sign that he wished to reply; then very slowly and emphatically he dictated his replies in Turkish to his secretary who took them down in Turkish (I could see him writing from right to left on the paper) and finally read them in French to the Conference. I sympathized with Ismet's position; he represented a victorious nation but was being regarded as a vanquished enemy and his delegation was being given no consideration whatever in the organization of the Conference. But he made a mistake in objecting to every trifle; he would have done better to pick out important points and stand pat on them. He soon gave the impression of conducting obstructionist tactics. He asked that no countries other than those originally invited be admitted to the Conference. Overruled. He asked for the chairmanship of one of the main committees. Overruled. He asked that a Turk be appointed Assistant Secretary General. Overruled. He asked that the Turks be allowed three instead of two delegates. Overruled. Further objections ad libitum. The only one which Lord Curzon allowed was that Georgia and the Ukraine should be heard when the question of the Straits came up. After each objection Lord Curzon simply passed on to the next point, regardless. . . .

Wednesday, November 22 [1922]

Child's private conversation yesterday with Djémaleddin Arif Bey of the Turkish Delegation brought out some interesting features of their attitude: (1) they desire to get away from mandates and zones of influence; (2) stated categorically and with vigorous expression of honor that no secret clauses are in existence; (3) territorial home for Armenians or other minorities impossible in view of public opinion and sentiment of National Assembly, but expressed willingness to give strongest possible guarantees provided outlook for gradual reduction of minorities should be carried out by emigration over a term of years; (4) in Mosul Oil Fields the Angora Government desires American development equal to or exceeding participation of any other nation; (5) full willingness to protect American philanthropic, educational and religious organizations; (6) capitula-

tions represent a thousand years of grants by corrupt governing groups in return largely for cash; satisfactory arrangements
can be made for protection of foreign citizens, their property
and their trade, but name "capitulations" must be abolished.
The Turkish Delegation is indeed in a difficult position; on
one side is the Angora National Assembly eager for diplomatic
victories and for nourishment to national pride; on the other
their antagonists here who are trying to crush them out with
steam-roller methods. They have no apparent skill or experience of peace conferences, and I must say they have a good deal
of my sympathy. It is not impossible that we may, in the position of friends and advisers, be able to assist in preventing their
making unreasonable demands, which would doubtless break
up the Conference. The more I study those apparently baneful
eyes of Ismet Pasha, the more I believe they are expressive
merely of nervousness, anxiety, ill-ease. . . .

1st Session of First Committee on Territorial and Military Questions, November 22, 11 a.m.

The Conference has resolved itself into a committee of the
whole, the so-called Committee on Territorial and Military
Affairs, including the Regime of the Straits, under the presidency of Lord Curzon.[28] The boundaries of Eastern and Western Thrace were discussed this morning. Ismet Pasha claimed
that the boundaries of Eastern Thrace should be the same as
in the Treaty of Bucharest of 1913 [29] and that there should be
a plebiscite in Western Thrace. Venizelos refuted his claims
on historic and ethnic grounds, insisting that the Maritsa River

28 At Lord Curzon's suggestion, he presided over the First Committee, Garroni presided over the Second Committee to examine the capitulations and
minorities, and, Barrère presided over the Third Committee on financial and
economic matters. The first sixteen meetings of the Conference were held
under the guise of being a Territorial Committee. Barrère's Committee met six
times, and Garroni's met five times. "It was by this technical adjustment that
Curzon from the start obtained control of procedure." Nicolson, *op. cit.,* p.
292.

29 The Treaty of Bucharest ended the Second Balkan War, in which Bulgaria
had fought against Serbia, Greece, Rumania, and Turkey.

should be the boundary. The Serbs advocated a demilitarized zone running from the Black Sea to the Aegean Sea along the northern and western boundaries of Eastern Thrace. The Rumanians supported Venizelos.

Lord Curzon, who spoke in English, presided well. He is a purist and speaks delightfully. . . .

2D SESSION OF COMMITTEE ON TERRITORIAL AND MILITARY QUESTIONS, NOVEMBER 22, 4 P.M.

Stambolisky, the Prime Minister of Bulgaria, was admitted and presented views advocating an autonomous regime for the whole of Thrace. Lord Curzon then presented the British views, insisting (1) that as regards Western Thrace "the Allies have not the slightest intention of permitting any modification of the Treaty of Neuilly; [30] (2) the Maritsa River should be the frontier between Eastern and Western Thrace; (3) a subcommittee should study a plan for a demilitarized zone on each side of the Maritsa River from the Tunza to the sea, providing commercial access to the sea for Bulgaria; (4) the railway from Karagatch to Dedeagatch to be under international control." He added that Greece cannot be asked to cede Western Thrace settled by the Treaty of Neuilly and that the Allied Powers are unable to allow the question to be reopened. Barrère, the 1st French delegate, and Marquis Garroni, the Italian, supported him.

There was one amusing incident today. Ismet Pasha had been giving statistics of the population in Western Thrace which he said were the official Turkish figures for 1914. When he had quite finished, Lord Curzon, in a delightfully dry tone, said that the Conference had listened to these figures with much interest, but how, might he ask, could the Turks have gathered these official figures in 1914 when there happened to be no Turkish officials in Western Thrace at that date (the province having been ceded to Bulgaria in 1913 by the Treaty

---

[30] At the end of the First World War the treaty with Bulgaria had been signed at Neuilly on November 27, 1919.

of Bucharest)? Consternation in the Turkish delegation; much shuffling of papers, raised eyebrows and whispered interpretation to Ismet Pasha. Ismet consults with his technical experts and after some delay he answers that the figures presented were really collected in 1913 although published the following year. A few surreptitious smiles greet this explanation.

The press situation is very troublesome and has brought forth in the Conference formal protests from the Turks. Lord Curzon, at the opening meeting, had enjoined secrecy on all, except for the official communiqué given out daily. But representatives of the press bureaus of the three inviting Powers, France, Great Britain and Italy, are admitted to the sessions, are held to be exempt from the pledge of secrecy and they issue whatever suits the convenience of their own delegations. This results in a complete monopoly of the news by the British, French and Italians and has already resulted in misrepresentation and suppression. One of these was the story intended to indicate that the Turks objected to the presence of the American representatives, whereas the Turks have already informed us that the reverse is true. Edwin L. James, the correspondent of the *New York Times*, tells me the story originated with Poincaré, but I imagine the British had a hand in it. Another case was the appearance of the Venizelos speech textually. We have told Lord Curzon that although we have little to give out and have observed as rigidly as anyone the rule of secrecy, the present arrangement might do harm and that in case of the appearance of any misrepresentation as to our position or as to the attitude of any other nation toward our position, we reserved the right to make corrections by statements to the press, which we could say would not be lacking in vigor. Curzon said he would have to admit this right. . . .

Thursday, November 23 [1922]

The following developed in a confidential talk which Child had with Curzon today: (1) *Open Door.* As long ago as the Tripartite Agreement the British began to abandon any new moves towards zones of influence, concessions and special privileges, and were now ready to support "open door" policy in the Near East. He disclosed that the French and Italians were not in accord on this. He believes that the French will abandon Cilicia, but that both French and Italians desire selected prizes. (2) *United Allied Front.* This front is "tentative." It is to be held until there is a crisis in negotiation with the Turks, and in such an event the most Poincaré has promised to do is to return to Lausanne for further conference. (3) *Mussolini.* Curzon and Poincaré both mystified by him. He creates the usual fears attaching to an unknown factor. He has demanded an equality of all privileges without offering equality of contribution. (4) *Rumania, Yugoslavia and Greece.* They have formed a strong alliance for the purposes of this conference under pressure of fears and this united front has astonished the Turks. (5) *Minorities.* The French and Italians will not support with any zeal a demand for a cession of territory by Turkey as a refuge for minorities. Curzon, however, will take whatever position we take and will appear in person to present his case. (6) *State of Mind.* Curzon is obviously anxious. He asks for our close co-operation. Is fearful of Admiral Bristol's influence on a delicate situation. In his English way he said "You have a — er-er an Admiral Bristol joining you I believe." Child replied: Lord Curzon, we not only have *an* Admiral Bristol joining us; we have *the* Admiral Bristol joining us." Curzon could not help laughing good-naturedly. He has a pleasant laugh and does not at all give me the impression of the pompous and supercilious character I have heard described. We think he has put his cards down face up with us and means to be friendly. . . .

The Conference decided to refer to a subcommission the study of (1) drawing up of demilitarized zone and (2) internationalization of railway from Bulgaria to Dedeagatch and the port of Dedeagatch. I am to be the American representative on this subcommission, with Belin. This subcommission, under the presidency of General Weygand, Foch's chief of staff during the war and said to have been the brains of the French Army, met this afternoon and immediately split up into two sub-subcommissions to study (1) the military and (2) the economic phases of the questions submitted to it.

This is a busy life, almost as busy as Paris during the big Peace Conference. I never get to bed until 1 and often later. All kinds of delegations want to see us continually and take up much time, and there is much correspondence to attend to besides the actual work in conference. But it is mighty interesting.

Friday, November 24 [1922]

Another beautiful day. Lausanne is indeed treating us well so far as weather is concerned, although we have little spare time to profit by it. Began the day by receiving the Swiss-Armenian Delegation. . . . Child tells all these people that the League of Nations, which is interested in the subject, should make representations itself before the Conference, but I know its organization well enough to realize that this is impossible without a direct mandate from the Assembly, which meets only once a year. They all seem to think that at a word from us the Armenian question will immediately be solved. We point out that others must help and that publicity is essential. Next came the Assyrians and Chaldeans — not exactly like wolves on the fold but hat in hand — asking for a home land or some little trifle like that. We turned them over to Copley Amory, and they would have remained all day if he hadn't pleaded another engagement and promised to see them again. Venizelos then called and asked our support for a plea he is prepared to make that an alleged 100,000 males, largely of Greek nationality, now detained by the Turks, should be released on the ground that to solve the general refugee problem, the males must join their families to support the women and children. Venizelos' personality is so attractive and his manner so forceful and convincing that one is always impressed when he talks. He is undoubtedly the outstanding figure in the Conference.

General Weygand's subcommission met this morning and in the afternoon submitted its report to the

4TH SESSION OF THE COMMISSION ON TERRITORIAL AND
MILITARY QUESTIONS, NOVEMBER 24, 4.30 P.M.

The report recommended (1) That a demilitarized zone be established extending thirty kilometers on either side of the frontier between Bulgaria and Eastern Thrace and on either side of the frontier to be set up by the Peace Conference between Eastern and Western Thrace. (2) That in pursuance of obligations to Bulgaria undertaken by the powers which ratified the Treaty of Neuilly a free port be provided at Dedeagatch and that this port and the railway control be placed under an international commission composed of one representative each of certain Powers which signed and ratified the treaty, namely Great Britain, France, Italy, Greece, Rumania, Yugoslavia and Bulgaria, as well as Turkey. (3) That a subcommission of the international control commission be set up to carry out the control and surveillance of the demilitarized zone and to be composed of technical experts, one from each of the countries represented on the main commission.

The afternoon session was lively and brought forth several sparkling repartees and much humor and apparent good feeling. Stambolisky, the Bulgarian Prime Minister, enormous, shock-headed, with lowering brows and brigand-like face, entered with his staff and took his place opposite the chairman, Lord Curzon. Directly behind him sat Mlle. Stancioff, daughter of the Bulgarian Minister in London, who has entered the Diplomatic Service as Secretary of the Bulgarian Legation in Washington, whispering the proceedings into the ear of Stambolisky, who knows only Bulgarian. His replies (they were really hers, not his, for he never said more than a couple of words to her at a time) she translated into perfect English when addressing Lord Curzon or in perfect French when addressing the rest of the Conference, and several times she brought a laugh from the Conference at the quickness of her wit. Her father told me himself that it was she who framed the replies, not Stambolisky. Ismet Pasha agreed to the demilitarized zones but insisted that an international guarantee of the inviolability of these zones must be given by the Powers signing the treaty and he dissented from the plan of a commission of control. Lord Curzon and Venizelos maintained that such a control commission was essential and that the question of the neutralization of the demilitarized zones should be considered later. Ismet Pasha also objected to an international control commission for the railway from Bulgaria to Dedeagatch. His objection was refuted by Curzon. The Bulgarians then made their plea that Dedeagatch should be under Bulgarian sovereignty or else that an autonomous state should be created similar to Danzig. This called forth an impassioned speech from Venizelos in which he showed his power and fire as an orator and every delegate in the room was hanging on his words. The main argument in his speech was that Greece could not be expected to make further concessions to a country which was not a party to the war between Greece and Turkey, the settlement of which was the purpose of the Conference. Mlle. Stancioff replied that poor Bulgaria had only three miserable little ports on the Black Sea, whereas Greece was full of ports, to which Venizelos retorted: "God placed Greece in the middle of the sea; it's not my fault," and everybody, including the Bulgarians, laughed outright. There were one or two further repartees and finally Lord Curzon said: "After this exchange of fraternal embraces the meeting may adjourn." More laughter. Altogether a distinctly merry meeting.

I find the conferences far from tedious. They last from two hours to two hours and a half, and there is not quite so much fresh air as is desirable to the Anglo-Saxon, which tends to make one sleepy in the afternoon sessions. But something of interest is always going on. I miss a good deal of it — many must fail to hear some of the speakers, for people like Barrère . . . and Ismet talk very low, almost in whispers. But I can always hear Lord Curzon and Venizelos, and they are the two most worth listening to. Then many of the speeches are translated by the interpreter, who is easy to hear. Often, when a French speech is going on, Lord Curzon will signal to Camerlynck to take notes, and at the end of the speech the latter immediately translates it into perfect English without a second's hesitation. Lord Curzon is the only delegate who speaks in English, although he understands and speaks French. Ismet Pasha is deaf and his secretary who sits beside him takes down notes while the speeches are going on, Ismet reading them as they are written. When he wishes to reply there is often delay while he thinks or dictates notes.

Saturday, November 25 [1922]

This has been the biggest day of the Conference so far, as we made our first important statement in Conference and, according to the newspapermen, it has had all the effects of a bombshell. It was, in effect, a purely straightforward statement of our traditional "open door" policy, made in this early stage of the Conference before the territorial debates should center about the particular interests of any one nation and thus lay us open to the charge of having directed it against that nation. It was prepared by Child and I approved it after toning down one or two passages which sounded unnecessarily belligerent; the phrase "struggle for special privilege" was altered to "search for special privilege" and one or two other phrases were omitted. He delivered it at the end of the day's session after further discussion of Thrace and the Aegean islands.[31] It created a tremendous commotion. The newspapermen came to see me after the meeting and told me that the statement would have a most unfortunate effect all over the world as tending to "throw a monkey wrench into the works of the Conference," and that it

31 Among other things Child stated: "I am not referring to the specific subject under discussion, but all the various points of negotiation must in the end be considered as a unit. . . . The representatives of the United States are unable, therefore, to hear concluded a discussion of any territorial settlement which, in its turn, may affect other settlements, without drawing the attention of the conference to certain traditional principles of the foreign policy of America. . . . The United States has no intention of seeking for itself or its nationals a position of special privilege, but it desires to protect its rights and to assure the open door." Great Britain, Lausanne Conference on Near Eastern Affairs 1922–1923, Cmd. 1814, Accounts and Papers, vol. 14 (1923), p. 93. This British publication contains a transcript of the various sessions. See also Foreign Relations, 1923, II, 904–8.

would be interpreted as a re-entry of America into European affairs. The other delegations, they said, were astounded and did not know what to make of it. I told them that it meant exactly what it said, no more and no less; that it was a perfectly clear statement of the traditional policy of the United States, and that there was no arrière pensée to be found in it and none was intended. . . . Child and I had a talk in the evening; he seemed somewhat disturbed by the commotion his statement had made but we both agreed that it was wise and justified, and I told him that I stood squarely with him on the issue. We went together to see Garroni; he appeared upset by our allusion to the Tripartite Agreement and said that while that agreement established the respective rights of France, Great Britain and Italy, it did not exclude any other country from participation. We told him what we had told the press, that it was simply a statement of traditional and general policy and had no specific intentions; it was certainly not aimed against Italy as he seemed to think. Curzon told Child after the meeting that he considered the statement both timely and appropriate. I hope he meant it.[32]

To anticipate a little, the Conference buzzed for the next day or two, but then Lord Curzon issued a statement that he was solidly behind our statement and in entire sympathy with it and with the policy of the "open door." This set most of the tongues at rest. The British press accorded it in general a favorable reception, and two days later came a telegram from Mr. Hughes saying: "The President and I heartily approve your statement. It was appropriate and timely." As Child remarked, "They certainly know how to play ball in Washington." . . .

[32] According to Nicolson in *Curzon: The Last Phase 1919–1925*, pp. 296–97, the Conference was embarrassed not because the open door statement was in opposition to secret plans for special privilege, but because Child's remarks, coming after Lord Curzon's dramatic speech to Ismet Pasha on Thrace, "were so foolish and irrelevant." Nicolson writes of Child's diary on Lausanne in *A Diplomat Looks at Europe:* "As a study in American psychology his book is of great value; as a study of the Lausanne Conference it is wholly worthless."

Monday, November 27 [1922]

Ismet Pasha called today. He talks more in the manner of a military man than a diplomat and apparently thinks in the same channel. He emphasized that the rigidness of his instructions from Angora was most extreme as to the points of discussion which touched the independence of Turkey in the control of her own internal affairs. He therefore expected that the subject of the Capitulations would provide great difficulty and requested in advance all possible indulgence of his position which was determined by very strong national feeling at home. He said that Turkey would show that nothing in her laws or legal system could worry foreigners as to their full protection, but he was reminded that practice and administration were as important an element as the law itself. As a result of the talk, Ismet will, we hope, make a reassuring statement in regard to the protection of our religious, philanthropic and educational institutions in Turkey. . . .

Saturday, December 2 [1922]

. . . The first meeting of the Second Commission under the presidency of Marquis Garroni to discuss capitulations took place today. Garroni made his opening speech in Italian and it was translated into French by an interpreter. After that he spoke French. He is old and gentle and will not, I imagine, be able to carry out Lord Curzon's steam-roller methods with much success. Although his commission was originally called the "Commission on Minorities," he suggested that this subject be turned over to Lord Curzon's commission in connection with its handling of the exchange of prisoners of war and populations. Garroni's commission organized itself into three sub-committees: (1) Judicial capitulations; (2) Economic capitulations; (3) Nationalities and antiquities. Ismet read a long statement of the Turkish attitude toward the question of the Capitulations: they must go but appropriate guarantees would be given in their place. Curzon, Barrère, Hayashi and Child all made short statements, the latter stating that in this matter the United States associated itself with the Allies, but that happily both sides had a common interest in the satisfactory solution of the problem and the sooner this common interest was served the better it would be for the Conference. Lord Curzon said to Child after the meeting that he thought his statement "rather wobbly." We smiled sweetly.

Child, Bristol and I all sit in at the meetings of the main commissions, while our assistants . . . follow the work of the subcommissions, make their reports after each session and draft a telegram to the Department. Belin generally takes the minutes of the main commission. A procès verbal is drawn up by the secretariat and circulated to the various delegations, who have 48 hours to make any corrections they wish. These are now being sent daily to Paris to be printed, but owing to the fact that the Turks are hard to please in the matter of the text, there is much delay and no final minutes have yet been received. At the conference table I ceded my place to Admiral Bristol, for although he was named as an associate observer he had the rank of Ambassador and therefore precedes me. We however all three sit at the conference table. . . . [33]

With regard to my colleagues, I have a high opinion of Child's ability and intelligence. He thinks much and says little, and what he does say is generally the result of careful thought and straight to the point. He sizes up a situation well and is able to express it well on paper. Quite rightly he regards this conference as a game of poker, takes no statement on its face value, assumes, in the case of others, that words are a convenient means of disguising their thoughts, and studies the expressions of the other delegates at the conference table in order to read their minds exactly as he would at a game of poker. It is surprising how often this becomes possible. Old world diplomacy is by no means a thing of the past. We are running up against it every day.

The Admiral is quite a different type. No doubt he thinks much, but one cannot say that he talks little. Speech for him is perpetual motion. The running of the brook is but fitful in comparison. Child has expressed it particularly aptly: "When I

[33] I wanted Bristol to have all the prestige we could give him. — J. C. G.

try to milk the Admiral's intellectual capacity," he said, "all four teats run at once." But he is an able man and has a fine record. His knowledge of the Near East is distinctly valuable and an asset to our delegation. . . .

Monday, December 4 [1922]

A highly dramatic meeting, the ninth, of the First Commission on Territorial and Military Questions, under Lord Curzon, to discuss the question of the Straits. The Russian Delegation, with Tchitcherin at their head, with representatives of Georgia and Ukraine,[34] and the Bulgarians were present. Ismet opened with a purely general statement of policy, lacking all details: (1) The Dardanelles and the Bosporus, being in Turkish territory, are of vital importance to Turkey; (2) In conformity with the terms of the National Pact, an arrangement must be made to safeguard Constantinople and the Sea of Marmora for Turkey; (3) The Grand National Assembly desires to have the Straits open to the commercial traffic of the world. Lord Curzon urged Ismet to give further precise details, but he said he was not ready to expound them at this time. Tchitcherin then gave the point of view of Russia, Georgia and Ukraine; (1) Free navigation for merchant ships in time of peace and in time of war without any restrictions whatever; (2) The Straits and the Sea of Marmora to be closed permanently to ships of war, aeroplanes, etc., of all nations save Turkey; (3) Turkey to be at liberty to fortify the Straits in any manner she pleases and to have a navy and air service and any armament she desires to protect these waters. The Rumanian, Duca, followed with a remarkably clear statement of Rumania's point of view — absolute freedom of the Straits of all vessels and the creation of a regime which would insure the

---

34 In addition to Georghy Tchitcherin the Russian delegation included Chrétien Racovski, Commissar for Foreign Affairs for the Ukraine, Polycarpe Mdivani, Commissar for Foreign Affairs for Georgia, and Vatzlav Vorovski, Soviet official in Rome. According to Nicolson in *Curzon: The Last Phase 1919–1925*, p. 309, when Tchitcherin spoke at this session his "voice quavered with all the woes that imperialist capitalism had brought upon the holy head of Russia."

realization of this freedom. Mlle. Stancioff then read a statement, first in English then in French, giving Bulgaria's attitude, avoiding all mention of warships.

Lord Curzon then replied in a remarkably clever and amusing summing up. He noted that the Russians had stated that there was present at the mouth of the Straits an armament belonging to outside Powers and that it was desirable that this armament should be removed as soon as possible. Lord Curzon agreed that it was desirable that this force should be removed, but he said with great emphasis, pointing his finger at Tchitcherin, "that force is there and it is a factor in the situation which must not be forgotten." He contrasted the Russian and Rumanian plans for the settlement of the question, showing that they were exactly opposite in their suggestions and that the Bulgarian proposal was different from any of them, and he asked the Turks if they were prepared to state which of the three plans they favored or if they had still a fourth proposal to suggest. Ismet replied that the Russian suggestion corresponded with the Turkish point of view more closely than any of the others but he took the position that the views of the other states should be heard first. Curzon then waxed facetious and said in somewhat scathing terms that Turkey, who was most interested in the question, had been unable to state her point of view while the Russians, to his astonishment, had disguised themselves as Turks and had stated their position for them; if he had shut his eyes he would have believed that Monsieur Tchitcherin had donned a tarboosh and had disguised himself as Ismet. He added that the reply of the Turkish delegation to his request for a statement of their position was trifling and not compatible with the dignity of the Conference and he felt that it would produce a most unfortunate impression on the world at large. Tchitcherin interrupted to say that the Russians desired an expression from Great Britain, France and Italy of their plans for the solution of the Straits problem and insisted that the three Powers should express their point of view. Curzon replied that, as President of the Commission, he had asked for the viewpoints of any of the delegations present, particularly those of the riverain states and Turkey and that he had been endeavoring for half an hour to get a statement from the Turkish delegation without success. He and his colleagues were now going to proceed to consider the suggestions from the delegations that had spoken and at a later day they would present their views to the Conference. The session would now adjourn. . . . [35]

Tchitcherin is anything but prepossessing. He speaks in a thin, high-pitched nasal voice and looks like a bird of prey — indeed like a Bolshevik bird of prey, with malignant eyes and beak nose. Child likens him to one of those mangy roosters one sees in the barnyard with only a few feathers on. He wears a large enameled red flag in the lapel of his coat. The other Russians are not bad-looking men; they are neatly dressed and some have pleasant faces. One, presumably a Georgian, is in native costume with bristling upturned moustaches. . . .

Wednesday, December 6 [1922]

Another highly interesting session, the 10th, of Lord Curzon's commission on the Regime of the Straits. Lord Curzon immediately exposed the Allied plan which, with certain qualifications, comprised demilitarization of the Straits under an international commission of control with one member each of the following powers: England, France, Italy, Japan, Russia, the United States, Bulgaria, Greece, Rumania and Turkey, the Turkish member to be permanent President of the Commission; the Straits to be open to merchant and warships both in time of peace and in time of war.

Child then read the following statement for our delegation, he, Admiral Bristol and I having spent the previous evening going through it with a fine-toothed comb until it met our combined views:

I have listened with interest to the points of view of the various

[35] According to Harold Nicolson, Curzon, by attacking Ismet for allowing Russia to speak for Turkey on the Straits question, inserted a wedge that later resulted in a disruption of the close tie between Russia and Turkey.

delegations on the subject of the Straits, and trust that a statement of the views of the American representatives will not be
unwelcome.

Our position is based upon that policy of our Government
which stands for complete and constant freedom, without special
privilege, for our commerce, and for the commerce of other nations.

The application of this policy to the question of the Straits
is not difficult. We desire, for the good of our own interests, as
well as for the good of all, including those peoples and nations
which border on the Black Sea, that nothing shall be done which
will take from any of them, Bulgaria or Russia, Ukraine or
Turkey, Rumania or Georgia, the guarantee that they shall be
accessible to the commerce of the world. Accessibility to that
commerce is their right. It is equally the right of the commerce
of the world to reach the peoples of this region.

I do not understand that any delegation here would openly
deny that right for times of peace. This is not sufficient. It is in
keeping with the progress of world administration and enlightened international purposes that the commerce of neutral
nations shall not be interrupted during a state of war.

The freedom of the Straits is a term too limited to cover the
field of this discussion. This discussion involves the freedom of
all those nations which border on the Black Sea, and of all those
nations outside the Straits who desire to reach them on their
friendly errands.

We cannot accept the position stated by anyone who has
spoken for the position of the nations on the Black Sea; we
have heard no one speak with the assent of all. We cannot accept the position that the future of commerce in the Black Sea
is the exclusive affair of the States bordering upon it. We assert
that it is the concern of all the nations of the earth. It is untenable that any one nation by the virtue of geographical position
should hold the power of depriving every other nation of these
rights. This would be not only against the interests of our
national policy: it would be against the interest of every nation
on the Black Sea; it would be against the whole historical development of the Freedom of the Black Sea. The unlimited control of the Straits and the Black Sea by any one nation is against
the policy of the world.

I do not understand that any nation here will deny these fundamental principles of the Freedom of the Black Sea. I do not understand that Turkey denies them. I do not even understand that any nation having an eye for extension of territory or seeking to control the policies of Turkey will be heard here to deny them. I assume that these fundamental principles will be established by this Conference and if possible will be guaranteed by this Conference. No other result would satisfy the view of my Government. Without presuming to speak specifically for others, I assume that no other result would satisfy either the nations inside or outside the Straits.

It is our view that the Freedom of the Black Sea is to be gained only by disarmament. More than this, it is our belief that even armament designed to keep the Straits open is in fact a danger to the Freedom of the Black Sea.

If any nation or group of nations representing the interests of all nations accepts the trusteeship of the Freedom of the Black Sea, this trusteeship may be carried out, we believe, with greater guarantee of good faith and constancy, if reliance is placed upon agreements rather than upon force.

It is impossible for me to overlook the proposal made by one delegation here that by such agreements all warships should be excluded from the Black Sea. I would find it equally reasonable to exclude warships from every international body of water. No nation has gone further than the United States in policies of naval disarmament, but no nation would be more ready to uphold the good sense of maintaining sufficient naval force to act as police of the free seas, to protect its citizens and their ships wherever they might be, to suppress piracy and other menaces, and to act at times for the public good and to give relief to suffering, just as ships of war have recently acted in the Near East. Ships of war are not necessarily agents of destruction; on the contrary, they may be agents of preservation and serve good and peaceful ends in the prevention of disorder and the maintenance of peace. We, I believe in common with every commercial nation, wish access to every free body of water in the world and we will not be satisfied if our ships of war may not pursue their peaceful errands wherever our citizens and our ships may go.

Talks with Ismet and Curzon had disclosed that there was some danger of the Turks going over to the Russian position of closing the Straits to all ships of war and fortifying the Straits in the hands of Turkey. This of course would remove all guarantees as to free commerce and leave an opportunity for Russia at some future time to wrest control of the Straits from Turkey. As Child said to Ismet, "You build a fort on the Dardanelles and it's all fine for you as long as you hold it, but what's going to happen to you when someone else takes it? Wouldn't it be better to have no fort at all but an international agreement instead?" It therefore appeared opportune to state our views now in order that Turkey should face our individual position as well as the joint position of the Allies before taking a definite Turkish stand. We think the Turkish Delegation believes that co-operation with Russia has gone far enough and has an increasing fear of the possibility of a Russian menace to Turkey, and we intend to stand pat on our statement and not to debate it.

Ismet Pasha declined to discuss the question until he had studied the Allied plan. Tchitcherin then indulged in a tirade against England. He said it was all very well for Lord Curzon to allude to Russia having suffered in the past as a result of Turkey's position on the Straits, but as a matter of fact Russia was suffering more at present through England's position in Constantinople since 1919. Formerly one talked of Russia's advance into Asia, but now one spoke of England's advance into Europe. (General smiles around the table with a particularly broad one from Lord Curzon.) Tchitcherin brought out the volte face of the Allies in that during the last century the Powers had accepted the closing of the Straits as a principle of European law but that now, although Russia has supported this view, they insist upon the Straits being free. He further expressed the conciliatory attitude of the new Russia as contrasted with Tsarist Russia and expressed his readiness to enter into any discussion for disarmament which the Powers desired to advance. Lord Curzon, in bringing the meeting to a close, stated that he was glad to hear the Russians express the "inno-

cent intentions" of the Russian Government which if carried
out would lead to the abandonment of the Russian plan for
the solution of the Straits problem.[36]

Thursday, December 7 [1922]

. . . Curzon, Barrère and Ismet have all privately expressed
their gratitude for our statement of principle upon which the
American view of the Straits issue is based, and this afternoon
the Japanese stated their adherence to it in open session. It
now appears that the Russian influence for fortified Straits
and the Black Sea closed to all warcraft has been almost lost on
the Turks who are inclined to be conciliatory. The general
principles, which have been tentatively accepted, are to be
worked out with the Turkish experts. The whole current now
is towards strong limitation of armament, both military and
naval, in the islands near the Straits, the Sea of Marmora, all
water passages and the Black Sea. We believe that this will be
an immense gain for the stability of peace in the Near East. At
the present moment it looks as if we ourselves can avoid being
asked to enter any entanglement whatever in regard to the
question. We regard it as most important for ratifications and
for the future of the naval disarmament program that Russia
should be induced to sign a separate protocol on the Straits and
to make pledges against maintaining large naval forces in the
Black Sea. The whole future of peace in the Near East centers
in a satisfactory solution of this most important question. . . .

Later in the afternoon I called on Adlercreutz [Swedish Minister to Switzerland], Irgens [Norwegian Minister to Switzer-
land], and Oldenburg [Danish Minister to Switzerland], returning their calls on us. Oldenburg told me that the neutrals
had all presented their views on the capitulations at this morning's session of the subcommittee and that they had all made

36 All these speeches are in Great Britain, *Lausanne Conference on Near
Eastern Affairs 1922–1923*, Cmd. 1814 (1923), pp. 138–50. The discussion of the
Straits continued throughout the Conference. The meetings on December 4
and 6 were decisive, however, in that the Russo-Turkish alliance was split, and
led by Curzon, Allied unity prevented the Black Sea from being made a
Russian lake.

somewhat general and noncontroversial statements except
Francisco Reynoso [Spanish Minister to Switzerland], the
Spaniard, who did not mince his words and said that His Catholic Majesty the King of Spain would not hear of the abolish-
ment of the capitulations in any form. The others were of the
opinion that Reynoso had gone further than was wise and that
he did not appear to have a very good grasp of the situation,
since an attitude of that kind could only do harm by getting the
Turks' backs up and making them more intransigent than
ever. Everyone knew that the capitulations had to go, and the
emphasis should be laid not on retaining them as such but on
securing satisfactory guarantees to replace them. That, indeed,
is exactly the situation. . . .

Friday, December 8 [1922]
[After a discussion of the Straits question] Lord Curzon, in
a solemn tone, then brought forward the demand that there
should be Allied ownership of the Allied cemeteries in Turkey,
as this was a question of profound national sentiment. Ismet
asked what precedent there was for such ceding of actual territory and immediately Curzon replied that the house and place
in which the great Napoleon had lived and died on the island
of St. Helena had been deeded by the British Government to
France and that the French flag now flew there perpetually.
Indeed, Curzon is never at a loss at the conference table. I
saw Venizelos, who sat in the next seat to me, moving restively
and thought he was going to speak of the Greek graves in
Turkey, but he evidently thought better of it and held his
peace. He however did provoke one dramatic incident when
Tchitcherin said he hoped Rumania would be careful and
not allow herself to get into the position of Greece, or words
to that effect. Venizelos immediately challenged him, saying
that it was not customary at such international conferences to
make cryptic remarks of that nature and that he demanded
an explanation. Tchitcherin shuffled his papers, consulted his
experts and made a rather lame reply that he was referring only
in general terms to the international situation, at which Veni-

zelos shrugged his shoulders and said he would not press the point as he did not wish to delay the procedure. Whether we sympathize with him or not, we all listen when Venizelos speaks; he is a man who would command attention in any situation, and his free, self-confident, clear delivery is a blessed relief after the halting, indistinct speech of such delegates as Ismet, Barrère, Hayashi and others. Venizelos is always clear and immensely forcible; Curzon equally clear, never at a loss for the right word and expression, always certain to complete what he has to say in perfect form and well-rounded sentences, direct, precise and sure; Barrère whispers; Garroni never says anything worth listening to anyway but "tags along"; Ismet speaks bad French haltingly and with the indistinct enunciation of a deaf man, frequently searching for his words or consulting his notes; Hayashi speaks English with a bad accent, three or four words at a time and then trying to express his next thought with his hands until the words come, laboriously; Tchitcherin sounds like a slate pencil; . . . Spalaikovitch and Duca speak clearly and well, always without notes; Child sounds as if he were reciting a lesson at school when he reads his written declarations. Thus the cynic who, if he had to speak himself, would of course make the walls ring with his resounding eloquence.

At the end of the meeting chronicled above, the various points still in dispute were referred to the Allied and Turkish experts for discussion. Tchitcherin insisted that the Russians should join these discussions, as they had been invited to take part in all deliberations on the question of the Straits, but Lord Curzon overruled him, on the ground that the points at issue concerned only Turkey and the Allies. There was a somewhat prolonged argument before Tchitcherin remained silent long enough to enable Curzon to adjourn the meeting. . . .

A most welcome telegram received from Mr. Hughes saying that he was much gratified by the way we had presented the Government's views regarding the Straits.[37] All clear up to date; it is a profound satisfaction.

One incident at the meeting today I have neglected to men-

37 *Foreign Relations, 1923,* II, 915.

tion. Tchitcherin, in the course of his remarks about the discussions with the military experts, said he thought the most important thing was to get on with the drafting of a treaty. Lord Curzon's reply was delightful; he said that the Conference had hardly yet reached a stage where the final clauses for a treaty could be drafted, but if Monsieur Tchitcherin would shut himself up in a room all by himself and apply himself solely to that task, he felt sure that he would turn out something which would be of greatest interest to the Conference. . . .

Sunday, December 10–Thursday, December 21
[1922]

The progress of peace conferences is not easy to size up from day to day. Here at Lausanne the commissions and subcommissions continue to meet and to discuss the various questions before them, but the end of each session seems to leave innumerable points still unsettled. Only one subcommission has as yet reported back to its main commission — and it is in the subcommissions that the detailed negotiations are worked out. And yet they talk of submitting a preliminary draft treaty to the Turks on December 23rd. One thing is certain and that is that from now on, the important work of the Conference will be carried on in the private rooms of the various delegates and not across the conference table. There is to be no Christmas vacation, for neither the Allies nor the Turks want a break in the proceedings. Meetings will continue to be held in the conference room as a gesture, but the dickering and bartering will go on in the rooms of the two hotels. I shall not attempt any further in this diary to record the work of the conference sessions, for it would be merely a list of proposals and counter-proposals. The interest lies rather in the personal conversations which we have with various people. Child conducts most of these conversations, but the Admiral and I also do a good deal of talking and listening too, bring information to our daily conferences, and make suggestions with regard to our general policy and the method of carrying it out, receive delegations, run the chancery and a good many other things. We all three meet in my office, often several times a day, and almost always in the evening, to discuss developments and to decide on action when action is necessary. Above all, we have to keep always before us the fact that we are not here to negotiate a treaty, and while watching out for American interests and declaring our general policy from time to time at the conference table, as well as talking privately with the various delegations, we must carefully avoid "throwing monkey wrenches into the works" and taking action which might embarrass the Allies and the Turks in arriving at peace.

This consideration has arisen especially with regard to the International Commission of Control for the Straits. We believe that such a commission is not only superfluous and that the neutrality of the Straits can better be safeguarded by treaty rights and obligations, but that it will merely offer opportunity for future intrigue. But both Allies and Turks appear to have agreed upon it and we therefore decided not to protest against it in open conference as that might afford a stumbling block for all the negotiations on the Straits. We therefore drew up a statement of our position and handed it to Lord Curzon as President of the Commission at the beginning of the session where the matter was to be discussed. It thus becomes a matter of record for future reference if need be, but without airing it at the conference table.

> The Representatives of the United States, on behalf of their Government, take the position that the full freedom of the Straits to all nations of the world, without discrimination, would be served best by reliance on treaty rights and agreements rather than upon a joint or international commission of the Straits. This view has been made known already to the delegations which have desired to know our attitude.[38]

Admiral Lacaze of the French Delegation told me that all the military and naval experts of the Allied delegations were

38 *Ibid.*, p. 928.

opposed to an international commission of control and that
the only person who believed in it was Lord Curzon himself.
The Japanese have told us that they are against it too. But
the Turks have accepted it in principle and it now looks as
if it would be adopted.

In the session of December 19th, after numerous drafts and
counterdrafts of a proposed agreement on the Straits had been
submitted by the Allies, the Turks and the Russians, Lord
Curzon took a highhanded stand and gave what was practically
an ultimatum, although the word itself was carefully avoided.
He said that the Allies had made their last concession and
would go no further, but they would give the Turks one more
chance to answer, if they wished, the following day. Curzon
said to Child afterwards that he, Curzon, was taking big chances
and he gave an amusing description of himself from an objec-
tive point of view — talking to the Turks in a facetious and
derisive tone as if they were a defeated enemy haled before
their captors to hear the terms of peace. As Lord Curzon
said, Ismet could have made a defiant reply and put the Allies
completely in a hole. The rest of that day and the morning
of the 20th, the hotel corridors buzzed; no one seemed to know
what was going to happen. Duca, the Rumanian Minister
for Foreign Affairs, said to Alice just before lunch, in a particularly choice metaphor: "The abscess is going to break today,
but we don't know whether the result will be good or bad."

The crucial meeting took place at 4 o'clock on the 20th,
Curzon opening the session with the simple remark: "La parole
est à la Délégation Turque." Ismet then read his reply to
Curzon's remarks of yesterday. It was moderate and conciliatory in tone even although Ismet still stood out on several
important points. Curzon replied that he believed matters
could now be adjusted to their mutual satisfaction outside of
the conference room. The Russians, to everybody's surprise,
made no remarks at all. Tchitcherin wore a facetious smile.
They must realize that they have lost the Turks as allies and
that their work at Lausanne has been as much a failure as it

was at Genoa.[39] The Japanese, Hayashi, made a singularly tactless speech to the effect that after he had heard the "ultimatum" yesterday he had feared a rupture and was glad that it had been avoided. Sir William Tyrell, who dined with us that evening, told me that a shiver had run down his spine when he heard Hayashi used that word "ultimatum" which everybody else had so carefully avoided.

I should like to have been in Ismet's place at one stage in the proceedings of that dramatic session, for he had a wonderful chance to score. They had been talking about the stationnaires[40] in Constantinople which Ismet said must go. Curzon remarked that these stationnaires were really only means of conveyance and of getting from place to place, like cabs and taxis, and he said that Constantinople being on the sea was in quite a different position in this respect from capitals like Paris and Berlin which were inland. If Ismet had only spoken up and said: "Then I assume Your Excellency will have no objection to our maintaining a Turkish stationnaire in London, which is a port," what a hit he would have made. But he is very deaf and is dependent upon his secretary's notes to follow what is going on and has little opportunity for repartee, of which Curzon himself is a past master.

After Curzon's remarks today, in which he dwelt upon the attributes and obligations of sovereignty, Child wrote out a short statement along the same lines which he wanted to make immediately as being helpful to all concerned. He passed it to the Admiral, who concurred, but when they passed it to me I objected on the ground that, made at this juncture, it would undoubtedly give the Turks the impression that we were supporting the position of the Allies, which is just what we most wish to avoid. We conducted quite a hot argument at the conference table, all in writing on the sheet on which Child

39 The Conference of Genoa, which had met April 10 through May 19, 1922, had discussed relations between Soviet Russia and other European governments.

40 Stationnaires are naval ships permanently moored in a foreign port presumably to afford protection and, when necessary, a means of escape for diplomatic and other official representatives in case of an uprising or other trouble. They were sometimes kept in foreign ports where conditions were unstable. — J. C. G.

had written his proposed statement. Finally, after the other two had come back at me three times and I had met each of their arguments with counterarguments, the Admiral came over to my position and Child, seeing that he had now become a minority, folded up the sheet which was scribbled over from top to bottom, wrote on the outside "The Kitten is dead" and passed it back to us! Our colleagues at the table wondered what we were laughing at. I feel very strongly that as we are not a party to the negotiations, the less we say at the conference table, the better. If we speak but seldom and only on important issues and at important junctures, our declarations will carry their full weight. That weight will be lessened if we "butt in" when it is not absolutely necessary. The "helpful" work can better be done outside the conference room and that we are doing every day. But while doing it — and this I am impressing upon my colleagues — we must never sacrifice or impair the good will of the Turks towards us or give them the impression that we are lined up with the Allies. For some day we shall negotiate a treaty with them ourselves and we must never lose sight of it, no matter how much we may wish to hasten the present negotiations on to a successful termination. Our aim should be, and is, to counsel moderation and conciliation upon the Turks in every issue, but at the same time to make them feel that we are doing it in their own interests exactly as much as in the interests of the Allies.

In filing with the Conference the statement as to our position with regard to the International Commission of the Straits, the Allies felt that we were strengthening the position of the Turks — Barrère told Child this. The correspondents of the anti-Administration papers, especially James of the *New York Times* which is habitually hostile to us, also took this view and hinted that it was seriously interfering with the Allies in their negotiations and had greatly strengthened Ismet's back. We told them all that we had issued the statement with the least possible noise, handing it in to the President without making it at the table, and that it was absolutely essential for us to place our attitude on record for the future. We

handed in the statement before the negotiations began, and
we were really forced into it by the fact that the Allied draft
contained a clause providing for United States membership
on the Commission if we should adhere to the convention —
this in spite of the fact that we had repeatedly told Curzon
that we would have nothing to do with it and were against it
on principle. It was very stupid of Curzon to put that clause
in at all. Child, foreseeing the attitude of the press and the
public at home, which might accuse us of blocking the negotiations, was at first doubtful about the wisdom of making
our statement at all, but I was insistent and he and the Admiral
finally agreed, although adopting the most unobtrusive method
of doing it. We did not even know that it would get to the
ears of the pressmen, but the Secretary-General circulated it
among the delegations, as he was in fact bound to do, and of
course the Turks promptly gave it out. Our objection is really
based more on the fact that we don't like the principle of the
commission itself, as leaving the regime of the Straits open
to all sorts of political intrigue in future, than on the fact that
the Senate would not let us participate in it if it were formed.
It looks now as if there would be a commission, but with
limited powers, competent only to control the number of warships passing through the Straits. This was Ismet's final proposal and it will probably be accepted. As things have turned
out, I am exceedingly glad that we took a position on the issue
and am not sorry if we did strengthen Ismet's hand. It may
save the world much trouble in future. Child was intensely
worried for a day or two and did little sleeping, for it undeni-
ably offered both the Turks and the Russians an opportunity to
quote our attitude on the floor of the conference and then,
if a break had occurred, as did not seem impossible on the 20th,
the Allies could have fastened the responsibility for the break
on us. But all turned out well, and all three of us, Child, the
Admiral and I, were in rare spirits on the evening of the 21st
when the uncertainty was over. I imagine that Curzon will
think twice in future before introducing the name of the
United States into a clause of the treaty without consulting

us in advance. We saw the newspapermen and explained our attitude and reasons clearly and emphatically.

The American press is, of course, impossible to handle. While the foreign press correspondents will accept any point of view their respective delegations wish them to elaborate, for the purpose of national propaganda, there is not the slightest use in our asking our own correspondents to do likewise. The anti-Administration correspondents will always try to put us in a hole, and all of them, whether anti- or pro-Administration, will write sensational stories on any pretext. If fact is dull, they will write fiction. Charley Smith of the A.P. is about the only man we can put faith in. He came up to the offices full of a story about our Straits declaration, but when Child explained the matter to him, he threw up his hands in mock disappointment, said: "Confound you, you've spoiled my story" and went out good-humoredly slamming the door behind him. I wish they were all like him.

Indeed, there is sensation enough at some of the conferences if the newspapermen were there to see it. At a meeting of the subcommission on Minorities on the 21st, Venizelos, out of a clear sky, suddenly began a tirade against the Turks, on the ground that while they had chased hundreds of thousands of Greeks out of the country, they would not now allow the few who remained to go of their own free will. He became so violent that Montagna, the Chairman, begged him to be tranquil. Venizelos, becoming more and more frenzied and waving his arms above his head, bellowed: "I am tranquil, I am tranquil!" [41] Riza Nour Bey, the Turk, then turned the solo into a duet and proceeded to shout at Venizelos across the table. Montagna pounded on the table with both fists trying to restore order, but finding it impossible he declared the meeting adjourned. This, however, had no effect on Venizelos who had worked himself into a perfect frenzy. At these subcommittee meetings he often gets out of hand and sometimes appears to lose grasp of the proceedings as he brings up irrelevant points.

41 As I was seated next him at the conference table, this was not always conducive to my personal comfort. — J. C. G.

or clauses which have already been settled satisfactorily to both
sides. Montagna is an excellent Chairman, stating the case with
the utmost tactfulness to both sides and often bringing them
together by his adroit way of handling an issue. Laroche, for
the French, is also good, but Rumbold and Ryan, for the
British, are weak and lack forcefulness.

To turn to other subjects, I had an interesting dinner with
Tchitcherin on the 14th. Irgens, the Norwegian Minister,
asked me if I would meet the former in an entirely private
way, together with Adlercreutz, the Swede, and Oldenburg,
the Dane, at dinner in a private room at the Savoy Hotel. My
first inclination was to refuse — in fact I had already written
a letter declining the invitation, in which the Admiral concurred. But Child, when he heard of it, urged me strongly to
accept, so I yielded. We have been authorized by the Department to meet the Russians in our discretion, and I told Irgens
frankly that I should come to listen, not to talk. Tchitcherin,
it appears, had asked Irgens to arrange it; both Adlercreutz and
Oldenburg told me afterwards that they were profoundly relieved when they heard I had accepted, as they themselves were
not at all sure of the advisability of the meeting. Norway has
a commercial treaty with Russia and has an unofficial representative at Moscow, but Sweden and Denmark are in the same
position in regard to Soviet Russia as ourselves.

The dinner was highly interesting. We sat around a small
table, the five of us, at an excellent dinner beginning with
caviar and vodka, which furnished the initial topic for conversation, and there was no hitch or embarrassment throughout the evening which lasted from 8.30 until nearly midnight.
Tchitcherin, although far from an attractive personality, talked
well on a multitude of subjects, painting, literature, government, etc., asked no questions and embarked on no controversial themes. He described at length the system of elections and
also of schools under the Soviet regime, and then we discussed
fascism and other national movements. Tchitcherin said:
"Mussolini has a passion, not a program." Once, in speaking
of the Conference, he turned to me and said: "Every rebuke

that Lord Curzon addresses to me across the conference table strengthens me just so much with the Soviet Government and strengthens the Soviet Government proportionately." In reply to my inquiry as to whether developments were taking place in Russia tending towards a more moderate and less radical regime, he said: "Yes, but don't tell the people so. The people must not be allowed to suspect what is going on in this direction. If they were openly aware of it, further development would become impossible" — or words to that effect. This was when we were sitting together after dinner and had a short talk alone. Hoping to draw him out on the question of the Straits I briefly outlined our attitude as already stated at the Conference, but he would not draw, merely replying that the United States was too far away to understand some of these questions. I had expected that his purpose in asking to meet me was to approach me on the subject of an American commercial mission to Russia, which we have heard from other sources he is anxious to secure; but he did not allude to the matter, and in fact he made no remark during the evening which bore the marks of any kind of propaganda or ulterior purpose. The conversation was that of any small gathering of cultivated men, meeting on a purely social basis. I imagine he merely wanted to establish a contact for future use. In any case, I should have refused to be led into any discussion of an American commercial mission, or any other kind of mission whatever.

The inevitable official dinners are beginning, and while some of them are useful and interesting as providing contacts with one's colleagues, others are hopelessly dull, a waste of time and a strain on the system with little opportunity for exercise to offset the rich food invariably served. . . .

Thursday, December 21 — Sunday, December 31
[1922]

At the dinner of the Italian Delegation on the 21st I had an agreeable talk with Riza Nour Bey, the second Turkish delegate, which strengthened our belief that the Turks wish to give preference to American participation in concessions but are fearful lest we delay too long. He expressed the opinion that an early treaty would be most desirable and went so far as to say that it would be to our advantage if we could conclude such a treaty before the Allies had signed theirs. When I told him that this was not our present intention he replied that in any case we should find the "open door" whenever we wished to enter, but he distinctly conveyed the impression that the policy of the open door means "first come, first served." Both he and Ismet told us that they welcomed American exploitation because they knew we had no political axe to grind.

However, I do not attach too much importance to what the Turks say after a good dinner. I am told that Ismet, under the warming effects of good champagne, has three times told Lord Curzon that the British could keep Mosul. It is also proverbial at the Conference that on the days following such dinners the Turks are more obstinate than ever and simply say no to everything. Ismet was in rare form at this Italian dinner. He sat next but one to me and when his large champagne glass had been filled to the brim he leaned forward and said: "Mr. Grew, are we on neutral soil?" On my accepting the challenge he tossed it off to the last drop. Considerable mirth was caused by the representatives of the two principal prohibition nations thus pledging one another. . . .

Several of the delegates left Lausanne on Friday the 22nd to spend Christmas elsewhere: Barrère and Bompard, Admiral Bristol and Belin, went to Paris; Garroni to Milan. . . .[42]

The atmosphere at the Conference underwent an extraordinary change during those few days. When we left, there was a general air of optimism. When we returned on the 26th, the clouds had gathered and people were freely predicting an early break on the capitulations. Curzon told Child as much, and on the afternoon of the 27th a meeting was held in Curzon's room of the representatives of the convening Powers and Child, who was invited to attend, at which it was decided to present a united front to the Turks at a session of Garroni's

42 The Grews spent Christmas at Gstaad.

Commission on the following day. It was fairly clear to us that Curzon had found the Turks absolutely obstinate on the question of Mosul, and that rather than risk a break on a question in which Great Britain was the only interested party, Curzon preferred to break on the capitulations, in which he and the others would have the sympathy of the world. . . .

The meeting on the 28th was to be called for the purpose of hearing the report of Sir Horace Rumbold's subcommittee on juridical capitulations which had come to a deadlock. Curzon suggested that Garroni lead off with his opening speech as soon as the session should begin, but Child suggested that as the meeting was to be called for the specific purpose of hearing the report of Rumbold's committee, it would be somewhat more appropriate if Rumbold should read his report first of all. Curzon made a wry face. Afterwards Montagna asked Child why he had made this suggestion. Child replied: "If a break occurs, do you want the meeting to be labelled with Garroni's name or Rumbold's?" Montagna simply grasped Child by the hand and said: "God bless you." . . .

At the meeting Ismet, as prophesied, took a position of complete intransigence as to the capitulations. Curzon, Barrère, Garroni, Hayashi and Bompard each protested in strong terms against Ismet's position in the face of the concessions already made by the Allies toward the abrogation of the capitulations, and then Child made a long statement setting forth our own position which he had repeatedly warned Ismet he would have to make if the Turks maintained their attitude. It was, I think, an excellent statement, the best or one of the best that we have made. Child and I talked it over until almost midnight the night before, and then he set to work and finished it at 2 o'clock. The Admiral and I made a few suggestions and eliminated a few sentences, but it was Child's work. It created a very favorable impression among the Allies, all of whom acknowledged that it was the best of all that were made. . . .[43]

[43] Among other things Mr. Child said: "The position of Turkey towards the juridical status of foreigners and their property in Turkey, as we are now led to understand it, is that Turkey asserts that she possesses a juridical system —

Curzon's speech I thought exceptionally weak, although delivered with his usual force and tone of conviction. In speaking of the complaint of the Turks that their sovereignty would be impaired by the admission of foreign judges to their courts, he said that the exaggerated views of the Turkish delegation on the question of sovereignty were becoming ridiculous. . . . Curzon said that the word "sovereignty" had become an obsession with the Turks, and he wittily compared their state of mind with that of King William who used to say that he had led the charge of the Guards at Waterloo and he talked so much about it that he finally persuaded himself that he had really done it, whereas everybody else knew that he was at least a hundred miles away when the battle took place. The Turks had worked themselves into a state of mind where they believed that every concession they made was impairing their sovereignty, but this strange idea existed in nobody else's mind! Curzon was amusing but not at his best.

At the end of the meeting the Turks asked for time to consider the views expressed and to make their reply in due course.

At the meeting of the subcommittee on minorities on the 30th we handed in our statement regarding a home for the Armenians, [44] as it seemed better to get it on record before it

including not only laws, but their application in her courts — which will satisfy other nations and their nationals. Unfortunately, this satisfaction does not appear at this moment to be the fact. The fact appears to be that other nations and their nationals, no matter how ready they may be for means for co-operation with Turkey, are testifying that Turkey does not offer either the continuance of existing rights or substitution for them of a system which will safeguard foreign persons and property in Turkey. The security may exist in the mind of the Turkish Government, but the vital necessity is that foreigners themselves must feel that it exists." Great Britain, *Lausanne Conference on Near Eastern Affairs 1922–1923*, Cmd. 1814 (1923), p. 494.

[44] Among other things this statement declared: "The proposal for the establishment of an autonomous area to provide refuge for Armenians is one which has engaged the deep and sympathetic interest of large bodies of citizens in the United States. Nor can it be forgotten that the Allied Powers on several occasions have taken the position that a national home for Armenians was a wise provision to give justice and security. . . .

"We have asked the representatives of American societies and organizations for definition as to the territory and area proposed for a national Armenian home; as to guarantees of financing and the methods of equitable distribution should be too late. We had persuaded James Barton, W. W. Peet [both representing the Federal Council of the Protestant Churches of America] and George Montgomery [representing the Armenia-America Society] to state in writing just what they recommended, and as these men represent the principal bodies of public opinion in the United States with respect to that question, it was only necessary to present their views, together with our covering statement, to the conference. I handed it to the newspapermen at 2 o'clock, for release at 5, after the meeting of the subcommittee should begin, as Montagna had begged us not to let it get to the Turks before that hour, feeling that it might stiffen their attitude on other minority questions in the meeting. To my relief the correspondents were evidently so hungry that they hurried off to lunch without asking me a single question when I had expected a cross fire of them. Child had gone to Geneva for the day. . . .

On the 28th, after the spirited meeting on the capitulations, Alice and I dined alone with Curzon in his room. He had apparently thrown off the depressing effects of the last few days and was in good form and a most genial host.[45] But he was openly pessimistic as to the outcome of the conference and made no pretence to the contrary. He described to us some of his talks with Ismet, which must be amusing as he apparently treats him like a naughty school boy. "Ismet," he said, describing one of his conversations, "You remind me of nothing so much as a music box. You play the same old tune day after day until we are all heartily sick of it — sovereignty, sovereignty, sovereignty." To what extent Curzon's cleverness

of financing among the countries interested; as to the protection necessary and how it is proposed that this protection be given to guarantee any new autonomous area from attack or incursion; as to the number of Armenians that would be immediately available for settlers in the proposed area and as to other evidence tending toward a concrete program. And we place in the hands of the chairman of the subcommittee the material submitted to this delegation and ask that it be given full consideration." *Foreign Relations, 1923*, II, 940–41.

45 Never have I enjoyed anything more than the small dinners of three or four which he appeared to love and where, after the table was swept and the port brought on, he would sit hour after hour telling stories, anecdotes, and experiences in a delightful vein seldom seen in present-day society. — J. C. G.

reaches I am in a good deal of doubt. A really clever man would not, I think, have adopted the browbeating tactics which he has followed since the very opening of the Conference. I do not know much about the inherent nature of the Turk, but I believe that a really clever and adaptable man would have used other methods of approach, less derisive, more respectful. But I may be wrong; Curzon may understand the Turks better than we do. In any case, whatever his methods, he appears to have accomplished little. I believe they will soon hand the Turks a draft treaty and tell them to take it or leave it. I asked Curzon if he would give us an advance copy of this draft at the earliest possible moment, in entire confidence, and he promised to do so. He wants to dine with us alone in our room next week and have me play the piano. For the first time, in the course of the evening with him, I saw an indication of his reputed snobbishness, for when I asked him if he knew Boylston Beal in our Embassy in London he replied that of course he saw nobody but the Ambassadors. But I have seen no other indication; he is an agreeable, courteous and amusing man and a delightful host. Possibly with age he is outgrowing the schoolboy rhyme which has dogged him all his life — "George Nathaniel Curzon is a most important person."

Curzon has shown us all of his correspondence with Ismet about Mosul; there has been an exchange of several notes and neither side has budged an inch. Curzon is openly pessimistic as to the outcome of the Conference, Montagna openly optimistic. Perhaps this is policy; who can say? I believe personally that an agreement will be reached, on the principle that neither side wants further war, and when there's a will there's a way. . . .

XIX

The Disruption of the Conference
JANUARY – FEBRUARY, 1923

1923 [Berne, no date]

There are various ways of starting the new year right. One of the most profitable is to appear at the breakfast table in dress suit and high stiff collar, for the comfort of this apparel early in the morning tends to soothe and attune one's temper to the occasion. We thus began 1923 correctly and sallied forth at 10.15, Arthur Lane [First Secretary of the American Legation at Berne] and I . . . to pay our respects to the new President of the Swiss Confederation, Karl Scheurer, in the customary garb — and trying to keep our tempers attuned as best we could. Several of the other Ministers and their staffs were there before us, but each remained with the President but a few moments, so that we had not long to wait. President Scheurer received alone with Traversini of the Political Department, Dinichert being ill. Last year I had prepared a formal speech in French but this year boiled it down to a very few words, and the President replied with equal brevity but with thorough heartiness, and then we chatted about the Lausanne Conference, on which I expressed optimism as to a favorable outcome. These functions are not, indeed, the trying ordeal that they are in some countries. The Swiss are a simple people and like simplicity. They prefer a good straightforward talk to any amount of formality. Scheurer, the new President by rotation, is Chief of the War Department, and Ernest Chuard, the new Vice President, Chief of the Department of the Interior. After the reception we had to run the gauntlet of many curious eyes while descending the great staircase of the Federal Palace, for seats in the galleries are much prized on this occasion and

every available place is taken, and another crowd, held back by
the police, awaits on the pavement outside. But it is soon over
and then begins the inevitable card leaving. As soon as the
diplomatic reception is over, the President drives to the Legation and returns my call without asking if we are at home, and
then my cards are left on all the members of the Federal Council and Political Department, the Directors of the International
Bureaus of Posts, Telegraphs, Railways and Copyright, respectively, and upon all the diplomatic chiefs of mission, but I call
in person on the French Ambassador [Henry Allizé], the
Nuncio [Luigi Maglione] and Edmund Schulthess [Chief of
the Department of Political Economy]. The Nuncio was at
home and I had a pleasant chat with him in which he expressed
great appreciation of what we had done at Lausanne respecting
minorities. . . .

The following day, after a morning at the chancery, we returned to Lausanne. . . .

On the 3rd the Conference began to get to work again. The
air was full of rumors: one, that the Greeks were trying to
bring the Conference on the rocks, believing that if it fails, the
Turks will have to move their troops south and thus leave
Thrace free for the Greeks to enter; another, that the Turks
are preparing several different draft treaties to appeal to various countries and thus to try to get the Allies to split and to
sign separately. But one can put little faith in the many rumors
that pervade these corridors. Curzon, just returned from Paris
and looking very worn and tired, dined with Alice and me
alone in our room. He said he had had a beastly time in Paris
— one conference after another with Bonar Law, Poincaré and
the rest — and two days in the train as he cannot sleep when
traveling.[1] I have never seen him looking so blue and de-

---

[1] Nicolson states that Bonar Law had tried to dissuade the French from occupying the Ruhr. He failed, however, and French troops marched into the
Ruhr early in January, 1923. In view of this pending rupture of the British-
French alliance, Bonar Law desired that the Turkish situation be settled "upon
any terms." Lord Curzon wrote that he "found Bonar Law longing to clear
out of Mosul, the Straits, Constantinople; willing to give up everything and anything rather than have a row; astonished at the responsibility I have assumed at

pressed. But he cheered up after a good dinner, I played the piano for a while and we had good talk until late. He said he proposed to celebrate his birthday on January 11th by submitting a draft treaty to the Turks and that we should all be away by the 20th.[2] This is surely the definition of an optimist.

Nevertheless we do not share the pessimistic conclusions which the press is spreading broadcast and which appear to emanate from the various delegations, particularly the British, Greek and Turkish. This is the propaganda stage of the Conference and we believe that the growling must be discounted. With the possible exception of the Greeks, the interest of all must be for an early peace. The chief obstacles seem to be the capitulations, the financial clauses and Mosul. With regard to the last, the Turks demand the vilayet of Mosul while the British absolutely refuse to yield territory there. The reason given for this refusal is that the British are bound by obligations of honor to the mandate and to the Arabs. The possession of the oil fields is one of the reasons, but the main one is that Mosul is regarded as the military key to Persia and to the unity of the Moslem and eastern peoples. We do not yet know whether Curzon expects to settle the Mosul question here by concessions, or to refuse all concessions, or to negotiate so as to postpone a settlement of the matter.[3] We have little doubt that Venizelos would not be sorry to see the Conference break up and the Turks begin a campaign on their southern border with the possible result that Thrace could be regained by the Greeks. The Greeks have been a most disturbing factor for two weeks and Barrère indicated to Child that the French were irritated that the British, who could influence the Greeks, were failing to do so. Barrère says that so long as he remains

Lausanne and prepared for me to back down everywhere." Harold Nicolson, *Curzon, the Last Phase 1919–1925*, pp. 324–25.

[2] On Curzon's birthday Alice sent him a box of candy which he acknowledged in a charming longhand letter thanking her for the "delectable sweetmeats." — J. C. G.

[3] The question of Mosul was actually postponed by the Lausanne Treaty for later settlement. In 1926 an Anglo-Turkish Treaty returned a small section of the vilayet to Turkey, the revised boundary was accepted as definitive, and Turkey received some royalties from the Mosul oil fields.

the representative of France, he will give the Allies the fullest measure of support and says that he has told the Turks recently that they would make a mistake if they believed that France would be reluctant to go to war if Turkey committed acts of aggression against the Allies. The degree of support he is receiving from his Government is however still doubtful. Various reports of an alarming nature are coming from Angora, but it is our belief that like the emanations of a sensational nature from the less-balanced members of the Turkish delegation here, they are largely theatrical. We realize that the British and Turks are courting danger by competition in badly conceived ultimatums, but that with good fortune the final result will not be affected by these flourishes.

The subcommission on minorities has furnished the chief topic of interest at the Conference during this first week of January. Montagna, its Chairman, after continuous labor and effort, had arranged a settlement with the Turks whereby the Allies would renounce the exemption of Christians from military service in Turkey in return for which the Turks would extend amnesty to all but about 150 Turks, half of whom are out of the country. The lives of the rest would be spared, although they would be obliged to leave the country and their property would be liquidated. This scheme was submitted for approval to Curzon who refused to permit the settlement to be made in the obscurity of a subcommittee, wishing to make it himself in the first commission. Montagna believes that Curzon wishes to get the credit for obtaining an amnesty for the Turks who have aided the British in the Near East, and considers his arbitrary ruling both selfish and unfortunate. It is very hard on Montagna who has done all the hard work, and it will not help the good feeling between the Italian and the British delegations.

A scandal occurred in this subcommittee on minorities on January 6th. Montagna and Rumbold had both spoken in favor of a national Armenian home and Victor Lacroix [of France] had just been given the floor when Riza Nour interrupted and insisted on being heard. He said he realized the Allies had to make such statements as they had incited these people against the Turks and were responsible for their present situation, and that the Turkish delegation refused to listen to any further statements on this subject and must withdraw. Montagna made every effort to persuade Riza Nour to remain, said it was highly unparliamentary procedure and that he would become an outlaw from the Conference. But this had no effect and Riza Nour left the room amid great excitement. Formal protests against the manner of the Turks' withdrawal were read into the minutes, after which Lacroix read his declaration appealing to the absent Turks to be conciliatory in regard to the Armenians. A formal protest and request for an explanation were also addressed to Ismet, who was asked whether he supported Riza Nour's action; he replied evasively and the matter was dropped but left a very bad impression. . . .

Barrère left for Paris on the 6th to confirm the conversations between Poincaré and Curzon. Curzon tells us that adequate assurances were given of continued accord in Lausanne between the Allies regardless of the situation as to German reparations. Two of the experts of the Turkish delegation have left for London; we believe they are going to discuss oil.

As regards the National Armenian Home, the privately expressed views of the Allied representatives are that it is not possible to formulate any concrete plan which will be wise even for the welfare of the Armenians themselves. The creation of these little new segregative areas, autonomous or otherwise, are not regarded favorably, and confidentially Curzon, Barrère and the Italian delegates say so. The entire Turkish delegation appears to hold the opinion that such Armenians as remain in Turkey will be useful where they are, and if not subject to foreign intrigue, will be safe and happy also. As to any plan inducing Armenians to come back to Asia Minor, we believe the Turks would make a flat refusal even if loss of territory or sovereignty were not involved. There is no subject upon which the Turks are more fixed in obstinacy.

Tuesday, January 9 [1923]

The following review of the situation at this date is based on confidential conversations with Curzon, Bompard and Garroni. (1) *General Aspect.* The British do not entertain much hope of signing a peace which will settle all matters discussed but still believe it will be possible to create a peace treaty from which certain specific subjects of the Allied demands may be excluded and in which certain other subjects may be referred to commissions or otherwise held in abeyance. The Italians and French share this view but are somewhat reluctant to refer the question of the capitulations to a commission of jurist representatives of the capitulatory powers and of Turkey because they fear that the welfare and safety of their nationals in Turkey will suffer during any interim before a settlement of their juridical status. It is assumed on all sides that the present exaggerated views of Angora will prevent the conclusion of several questions supposed to affect the sovereignty of Turkey and will tend to an unsatisfactory settlement of others. Under these headings are capitulations, debt control and minorities. These conclusions are becoming crystallized in spite of the well-recognized fact that the Turkish delegation, having learned that the Allies have no inclination to force their claims, is even repudiating some of the decisions already passed. The situation is humiliating to the Allies, jointly and severally, and can only be saved by the fact that the Turks desire to make a treaty and be free to build up their finances and trade. The only three means of Allied pressure upon the Turks are advice, military action and money. The Turks are now wholly disrespectful of the first. None of the Allies is ready to use the second, and the third is the one factor left to bring about a makeshift peace. (2) *Allied Unity.* There is no evidence of any change in this and it is probable that the weakness of the Allies' position will force the three powers to hold together for whatever salvage the situation offers. (3) *Plans for Treaty.* The draft of a treaty is being made and there is considerable perplexity in regard to the policy to be pursued. The inclination now is not toward the submission of any full text but in favor of presenting general outlines for the consideration of the Turks. Secondly, it has not been determined whether it is wise to present only clauses upon which the Allies intend to insist or to include matters such as the National Armenian Home, upon which they will give way. (4) *Mosul.* Curzon says that at first the Turks, in initiating the discussion, asked only for a share in the oil, but that they quickly changed their position and demanded the whole territory. He denies categorically that there has been any negotiation regarding oil but indicates that a situation might arise when the participatory rights of British, French and American interests might have to be scaled down in order to give participatory rights also to the Italians and Turks. . . . (5) *Results of a Possible Rupture.* Curzon and Barrère believe that even if there were a rupture here, war would not result. Both indicated that if war resulted, the initiative would be taken by Turkey. They feel that the Turks would not attack Constantinople while there was a hazard of involving France and Italy, and that the season, snow, discontent in the Turkish Army and other considerations would tend to hold off any Mosul movement for several months. (6) *Russian Influence.* There are strong indications from several good sources that the Turkish delegation is not wholly free from certain Russian agents and of interests looking toward profits in selling war material to Turkey. . . .

It will be observed that three of the four minority points upon which statements have been made by our delegation have now been conceded by the Turks, namely (1) retention of the Greek population in Constantinople, (2) amnesty, and (3) Patriarchate. Leeper told me how the compromise on the question of the Patriarchate was brought about. On the evening before the meeting, Nicolson went up to Riza Nour and talked to him at great length and, he says, won him over. The following morning Ismet came to see Curzon at 10.30, half an hour before the meeting. They talked around in a circle, Ismet refusing to budge an inch or to hear of the Patriarchate being retained under any circumstances whatever. Finally, at 11, Curzon said it was useless to waste further time; that they had come to an impasse and that was all there was to it. They walked over to the meeting together, talking about other things. Just as they reached the entrance and out of a perfectly clear sky Ismet said: "All right, I will yield." This to me, is most significant.[4] It indicates that the Turks will bluff on every issue up to the last possible moment, with a view to getting the maximum advantage out of the Conference. It gives some ground for believing that they will not leave Lausanne without signing. I remarked early in this Conference that it was to be a game of poker. It is.

The foregoing covers approximately the first two weeks of January. . . .

Sunday, January 14 [1923]

. . . I made an appointment with Ismet, called on him at his hotel at 10 P.M. and remained with him for half an hour. The conversation quickly showed him to be in a more intransigent frame of mind than we have seen him before — or else putting up a very firm bluff. He went through the various outstanding questions: Straits — settled except for one or two minor points; Minorities — settled; Capitulations — not settled; Financial Clauses — not settled; Mosul — not settled, and he gave it clearly to be understood that there would be no settlement unless the Turkish positions were accepted. In view of the marked anti-American propaganda now going on at Angora and in the Turkish press — aimed against our various statements at the Conference which they say were aimed at "crushing Turkey" — I went over our attitude at the Conference and pointed out our efforts to be helpful to both sides in reaching a settlement since the beginning of the Conference. Ismet merely remarked that the United States always stood on the side of peace and justice. After some further conversation and in a casual way I referred to Ismet's previous statements to Child, and Riza Nour's to me, that Turkey desired to discuss a

---

[4] See Great Britain, *Lausanne Conference on Near Eastern Affairs 1922–1923*, Cmd. 1814 (1923), p. 327.

treaty of amity and commerce with the United States. Ismet said this attitude had not changed. I asked him when he would like to begin such discussions. He said: "Tomorrow." I pointed out that we should certainly not feel justified in commencing negotiations for a treaty until it was evident that peace was going to be concluded between the Turks and the Allies, but that we should keep the matter in mind. He said it would be an advantage to all concerned to resume diplomatic and consular relations as soon as possible. These points were brought out casually in the course of general conversation and clearly indicated (1) that Ismet is keen to begin negotiations with us and (2) that he will not concede a single further point to the Allies — anyway until the final showdown. We shall then learn just how much of his attitude is bluff. I found Ismet serious and rather stiff tonight; there was no cordial smile and he rapped out his remarks decisively and coldly. It was evidently one of his "off" days — possibly following the Saturday night gaiety, possibly owing to the stiffening of his back by the instructions brought back to him by Hassan Bey from Angora. . . .

Monday, January 15 [1923]

. . . Everybody is blue and depressed at the outlook. Even Barrère seems to have come to the end of his rope and favors at least an adjournment. Montagna, who has been most optimistic of all and always counseling patience and predicting that everything will come out right in the end, meets Child in the hall, who says to him: "Montagna, if this thing keeps on forever and the conference gets nowhere, isn't Mussolini going to be sort of down on you and isn't it going to have its possible effect on your career?" — all very sweetly, of course. Montagna's eyes get big as saucers and a moment later he is seen heading for Curzon's room. Subsequently Curzon sees Child. "What on earth has got into Montagna?" he asks; "He has always been the most calm and optimistic man here, but this morning he rushed into my room with his quills sticking

out like a porcupine and urged me to finish things immediately, cease these useless discussions and fire a draft treaty at
the Turks' heads. I can't think what's got into him."

Curzon sends for Child and says: "Sometime ago you offered
to help if we got into a fix. I want your help now. The Italians
are spineless. The French are doing nothing. What can you
suggest?" Child said he would ask Ismet to come down and the
three would talk together. Curzon suggested that Rumbold sit
in too. Child refused to hear of it. Curzon bridled at thus
being dictated to; he is not used to having his wishes questioned. But Child said the meeting would take place as he himself suggested or not at all, and Curzon gave in with bad grace.
Rumbold, with his pronounced anti-Turkish reputation in
Constantinople, would be the last man to have present at such
a conference.

Child went to see Ismet in the afternoon and suggested that
he come down in the evening to meet Curzon in his, Child's,
room, to see if some solution could not be reached, especially
on the Capitulations. Ismet said: "Am I to be faced with the
same Allied proposal as before?" (foreign judges in the Turkish courts). Child said that he would support no proposal; he
merely wanted to give Ismet an opportunity to make one himself. Ismet agreed and came. Child, Ismet and Curzon talked
throughout the evening — and got nowhere. Child said that
Curzon and Ismet had about as much in common as a lion
tamer and a grower of azaleas. Curzon led off on the juridical
capitulations; no foreigner, he said, could hope to do business
in Turkey as long as the courts of justice, the prisons and the
legal code itself remained as they are. He gave several ex-
amples to prove his argument; one was the case of the wife of
a British major who received a blow in the face from a bunch
of keys by a Turkish policeman. When the husband protested,
both he and his wife were haled to prison; the husband was
charged with assault and battery, and the wife with prostitu-
tion! Ismet quietly replied: "It takes time to adjust these
things." Curzon threw his arms in the air, beat the wall with
his cane and shouted: "That's just exactly what I've been say-

ing!" Ismet said to Child: "You don't exact capitulations from Mexico." "No," said Child, "and we do precious little business there, either, and none at all with Russia." Finally Ismet rose stiffly, bowed and departed without a smile. But I happened to meet him in the hall downstairs as he was leaving; his face was wreathed in smiles and he greeted me most cordially. Sudden transformation. We all still believe that much or part of this attitude is bluff, that he is waiting until the last moment before yielding in order to make the best trade he can, and that he will not leave Lausanne without signing. We shall see. . . .

Wednesday, January 17 [1923]

. . . the Admiral had a long conference with Ismet today. Ismet began by raising the question of Mosul and other matters pertaining directly to the treaty between the Allies and Turkey, but Bristol told him immediately that we did not desire to discuss matters which did not directly affect the interests of the United States, although we were always interested in seeing all questions decided on principles of equity and the "open door." The Admiral concentrated the discussion on the question of the capitulations and urged with emphasis the necessity of establishing some regime in their place if they should be abrogated, using every argument to this end. He pointed out that the main defects in the present Turkish juridical regime were: (1) Lack of confidence in the judges because of their selection and their insufficient salaries; (2) Necessity of recodification of the civil, commercial and penal codes, with the elimination of the effects of the Seriat laws [5] on these various codes; (3) Lack of laws properly governing court procedure and the admission of evidence and weight of evidence; (4) Necessity for laws providing for inviolability of

[5] "Most of the country's legal processes had long been controlled, or at least colored, by the Seriat, the Müslim codes based on the Kuran and the İslâmî Tradition and Interpretations." Donald Everett Webster, *The Turkey of Ata-türk* (Philadelphia: The American Academy of Political and Social Science, 1939), p. 107.

domicile and for habeas corpus proceedings; (5) Need for new prisons and modern prison regulations. The Admiral especially urged that time was necessary in order to establish a juridical regime in Turkey which would inspire foreigners with sufficient confidence to live and do business in Turkey. Ismet did not refute these arguments but he would not admit that reforms in the present juridical regime were necessary for the good of Turkey nor for the benefit of foreigners desiring to do business in the country. He contended that the claims of businessmen were extravagant, and even if they were not willing to take up business immediately, they would later, probably in a year, see that their fears were not realized. As far as benefit to Turkey was concerned, he considered that the advantage of absolute independence by abolishing the capitulations and even without any transitory regime to provide for reform and the establishment of another regime in place of the capitulations was greater than any other consideration. It was the desire of the Turkish people to settle at this time and once for all the question of absolute independence without any outside interference in their internal affairs. Ismet gave every evidence of complete confidence in maintaining his position and willingness, in the face of all the facts, to accept all attendant consequences. Bristol, at the end of the interview, said that as Ismet liked neither the word "capitulations" nor the phrase "Transitory regime," another formula would have to be found to provide for the passage from the capitulations to the new regime in Turkey, by which the United States could resume friendly relations and carry on the various American activities in the country. In all our talks with Ismet — Child, the Admiral or myself — we seem to get nowhere. . . .

Thursday, January 18 [1923]

. . . In the evening the Turks gave their first big dinner at the Palace — about eighty people. Child and I remained till the end and then when we wanted to go, Ismet grasped us each by the hand and refused to let us depart; instead he pulled us into an adjoining room, ordered green chartreuse and proceeded to drink our healths in one glass after another with a speed and regularity which I have never seen equalled. Between glasses he slapped his knee, lay back and laughed most heartily at absolutely nothing and then grasped our hands in both his and remarked what a wonderful life it was. It certainly was. Ismet said he wanted to see America, so we then described in brilliant detail how Child and I would take him to Paris and London and then charter a special train in New York and take him all over the United States and show him Niagara Falls, the Colorado Canyon and the White House. All he had to do was to sign two treaties first, one with the Allies and another with us. Ismet slapped his knee with great gusto and took two more glasses of green chartreuse. He would have signed anything at that moment if we had had it ready. . . .

Monday, January 22 [1923]

Long talk with Child and the Admiral last night. All is now serene. . . . I like the Admiral; he has the best qualities of the sailorman — square, bluff, straightforward. His position here has not been an altogether easy one, but he is playing the game and playing it well. He is very pro-Turk . . . and for that reason, if for no other, his talks with Ismet carry weight.

At 11.30 this morning Child and I went to see Curzon and asked him frankly as to the situation. There was nothing lacking in the frankness of his reply, at least so far as his colleagues were concerned. He said the French had let him down completely; that they were weakening on every issue, especially the capitulations, and that they had disclosed all the conference plans to the Turks. This marked change in the British-French relationship appears to have coincided with Bompard's return from Paris where he saw Poincaré. Curzon described going to see Barrère and finding him in bed — wearing, incidentally, the old-fashioned nightgown — "diplomatically ill and quaking in every limb." Barrère is to leave Lausanne at once, ostensibly under the orders of his physician. But the truth is that he has been let down by his own Government. He has supported the British position all along. but apparently Poincaré will not let him continue to do so. It is a sad ending to a long career.[6] Curzon told us the plans for presenting a draft treaty to the Turks next week. As for Mosul, he said he was going to refer it to arbitration. He said that he proposed to leave Lausanne two days after presenting the treaty to the Turks whether they signed or not.

Until now the French have been asking for more time to deal with the Turks than the more peremptory attitude of Curzon would provide, but today the French indicate that it is better to bring the Conference to issue at once and if the Turks do not wish to conclude a treaty, to wait until the Turks are in a more reasonable mood. Montagna, who heretofore has been optimistic, now believes that under the present weak position of the Allies and with all possible concessions already made, there is little hope of continuing satisfactory negotiations. Both from Montagna and Curzon there come insinuations that the French expect to deal separately with the Turks later and are holding out negotiations for loans as a bait. In fact, the return of Bompard from Paris has not only brought into prominence the flabby position of the Allies, who fail to trust each other, but distinct indications that the French are quite ready to take advantage of any selfish opportunity which the situation may offer.

Curzon told us that when he left Lausanne he would break up the Conference as he didn't want the other Allies "messing up the treaty" during his absence. He would take good care that no one would be left who would have any authority to negotiate.

The situation looks very black, but I still believe that both sides want peace and will find some way out. . . .

---

[6] Barrère had served as French Ambassador to Italy for some twenty-five years. It was said that in his youth he had been a socialist, and that when he presented his letters of credence to King Humbert, the King asked him how it was that such a change had taken place in his political ideals. Barrère is said to have replied: "Sire, a man who is not radical in his youth has no heart, but a man who is not conservative in his age has no head." — J. C. G.

Sunday, January 28 [1923]

... In the evening a long talk with Child in which we went over the whole situation. He feels that he can accomplish something by acting as mediator between the Turks and the Allies and indeed he is doing everything possible to that end by continual conversations with both parties. But the Turks appear absolutely stubborn and it looks, on the face of things, badly. I still firmly believe, however, that the Conference will not break up without a settlement. . . . Later I drafted a long telegram to the Department on the situation, to the effect that we were endeavoring in every practical way to exert our influence for a peaceful settlement and were not without hope that something could be accomplished through informal talks which were now proceeding almost hourly with both Allies and Turks on their initiative. "The result is however problematical and we are unable as yet to report concrete progress." [7] As to the Department's suggestion that we might make a formal statement summarizing the position of the United States towards the important issues of the Conference, we said it might well be desirable to make such a declaration before a final adjournment purely for the purpose of placing the United States on record before the world after the die had been definitely cast, but that such a statement could in no way contribute towards bringing the two factions together and would be useless, even injurious, at the present moment. Only informal talks outside of the conference hall could now influence the eventual result. We said that in view of the flux of the situation from hour to hour and the fact that its ultimate development would probably not be clear until the last moment, we appreciated the Department's desire to leave in our hands the question as to the advisability of making the suggested statement, and we felt that the Department would also wish that its contents, tone and method of delivery be also left to our careful judgment to be determined by circumstances which could not yet be foreseen. "We rate the probability of a peaceful settlement as small but are by no means without hope."

[7] *Foreign Relations, 1923*, II, 961–62.

We received today, from the secretariat, the French text of the draft treaty, comprising 160 articles of 100 mimeographed pages. This includes four conventions regarding (a) regime of foreigners in Turkey, (b) regime of commerce with Turkey, (c) regime of the Straits, and (d) frontiers of Thrace. Also three declarations regarding (1) administration of justice in Turkey, (2) participation of Albania in the Ottoman Public Debt, and (3) amnesty. Also a final instrument.

Monday, January 29 [1923]

. . . Gave an official dinner to the Turks. I had Madame Rouchen Eshref Bey on my right and Mustafa Cherif Bey on my other side. Ismet asked me how I was feeling; I said "Finely, thanks"; he said: "So am I; I am absolutely content" — and he smiled broadly. But he seemed depressed throughout dinner, and as I sat directly opposite I could watch his expression. All of us thought the same. Madame Rouchen Eshref took pains to tell me of their plans for returning to Turkey on Saturday in great detail — just how they were going, etc. But she slipped up later when she and her husband jumped with avidity at a tentative invitation to lunch with us in Berne on Sunday! Later, in a talk with Hassan Bey, he told me that they were all very well content with the attitude which we had taken at the Conference; that our only declaration which had at all offended them was the one about the Armenian National Home, and that they fully understood why we had been obliged to make that one. Ismet had explained all this fully to Angora. I spoke about the anti-American propaganda in the Turkish press, but Hassan said this was due entirely to a misunderstanding of the facts and that all had now been explained satisfactorily. Hassan comes from Trebizond and was formerly Minister of Finance in the Angora Government. . . . Ismet's humor improved as the evening progressed. He watched the dancing for a while and then repaired to the bar where he played billiards with the Italian Delegation and then sat down with Child in the verandah with a bottle of his beloved green chartreuse before him, remaining until after 3 in the morning.

The next day I suggested to Child that he swear off green chartreuse for Lent. He replied: "My God, for life!" . . .

Wednesday, January 31 [1923]

Successive meetings of the first, second and third commissions were held this morning, preceded by a general meeting at which Curzon formally presented to the Turks the draft treaty which they had informally received on Monday.[8] The progress accomplished by the three commissions was outlined and each chairman emphasized the concessions which had been made by the Allies to the Turks during the progress of the Conference. A general meeting was then reconvened, during which statements were made by Child and by the Japanese, Rumanian and Serbian delegates.

Ismet in a brief reply pointed out that the draft treaty contained not only articles that had been agreed upon but also articles that had not been agreed to in committees, and in addition some entirely new proposals which had never been presented or discussed heretofore. He therefore asked for a period of eight days to enable the Turkish delegation to hold conversations with the Allies in an effort to agree upon the terms of peace. Curzon in reply expressed his satisfaction that Ismet had full powers and need not return to Angora.

A recess was then taken during which the Allied delegates withdrew to discuss Ismet's request. Curzon announced that there would be an adjournment of ten minutes, but it lasted just an hour. Something unusual had been going on during the first part of the session, for we saw hurried notes being passed among the British Delegation and Bentinck [Assistant Secretary of the British Delegation] frequently leaving the room and returning. I later learned that he was bringing in the pages, as they were decoded, of a telegram from Paris giving the text of a note which Poincaré had addressed to Lord Robert Crewe, the British Ambassador. Poincaré said, in effect, that France did not consider herself bound not to sign a separate

8 Great Britain, *Lausanne Conference on Near Eastern Affairs 1922–1923*, Cmd. 1814 (1923), pp. 684 ff.

treaty with the Turks, as that agreement applied only to the
Great War and not to the present situation in which peace was
being negotiated with the Government of the Grand National
Assembly, and he maintained that France would reserve all
rights to negotiate and sign a separate treaty after the British
left Lausanne if it were found impossible to sign one en bloc.
. . . Curzon was very much upset by this note, which was aimed
directly at him personally, and when Bompard, Garroni and
he had withdrawn from the conference hall, he taxed Bompard
with having already agreed to leave Lausanne on Friday
whether the Turks signed or not. Bompard denied that he
had made any such agreement and Curzon sent for Crowe and
Rumbold to corroborate him, whereupon Bompard and Garroni promptly arose to leave the room and were only persuaded
to remain after Curzon had climbed down and agreed to further
negotiations with the Turks.

When the session reconvened Curzon stated that although
Ismet's request was eminently reasonable, he was for personal
reasons obliged to return within a few days to London; moreover, as he himself had conducted the negotiations for the
British Delegation he felt that his Government did not wish
to delegate this duty to another person at the final stage of the
negotiations. He was willing, however, to postpone his departure until Sunday night and he asked if Ismet could not
during the interval carry on the necessary conversations. Ismet
replied that he would do his best to meet Curzon's request, and
the meeting finally adjourned with Curzon expressing the hope
that he would be able on Sunday to shake hands with Ismet
on achieving a common victory. . . .

Child's statement seemed to me remarkably good. He said:

> The United States is represented at Lausanne for three pur-
> poses. Our country is represented to protect American interests,
> idealist or commercial, humane or financial, without discrimina-
> tion. It is represented to protect, whenever possible, humani-
> tarian interests regardless of their nationality. It is represented
> to serve in all appropriate ways the cause of peace.
> Our declarations have been free from the seeking of special

privilege or favor. We have declared for the open door in the Near East and our declarations and the spirit of the assent given by the Allied nations in the words of the chief delegate of Great Britain and later in those of the chief delegate of France, speaking for the inviting Powers, constitute an accord creating, we hope, a new understanding, a new régime of international relationship in the Near East not only between Western Powers seeking to aid development there by friendly and fair competition but between the Near East, which desires freedom from political intrigue, and those nations who now have no desire for hazardous and costly experiments in policies of political interference.

We have cast whatever weight our opinion might have in favor of freedom of the Straits and the Black Sea because of our sincere belief that the program was for the good of all.

We have spoken against the expulsion of populations when these appeared to menace human beings with suffering and with injustice. We have asked, in so far as it affected religious liberty, that religious functionaries should be allowed to remain where their people wanted them to be. We have asked for the protection of minorities. We have suggested that the problem of refugees in the Near Eastern regions affecting various peoples could only be effectively administered by some joint action, so that unparalleled suffering should be prevented and relieved, that disease should be checked, so that duplication of effort and waste of resources and loss of economies could be avoided. We reiterate that suggestion, hoping that the matter may be discussed before the Conference ends.

If now, at this important stage, we can assist in bringing about a peace wanted by the whole world and necessary to the whole world, if we can add any contribution to give assurance that the hazards of hostility damaging to all and perhaps wholly destructive of the national vigor of New Turkey may be replaced by agreement, by a stabilized international commerce and the establishment of permanent normal conditions in the Near East, we are ready to give any help in our power.

Perhaps we may be allowed to disclaim the intention to exert any moral influence, if by moral influence it is meant that we set forth our opinions as being more righteous than our neighbor's. We ask only that our opinions shall be received when they are founded upon that justice and good counsel which we are all seeking together. I know of nothing which particularly distinguishes the position of the United States here from that of any other nation unless it is the fact that because we are not at war with Turkey and have not been involved in the ancient and bygone politics of the Near East, we may bring to bear whatever power there may be in detachment and impartiality. If we have been able to be helpful toward peace we have done so because circumstances have saved us from involvement which would have stripped away our ability to maintain that impartiality and convince others of its sincerity. . . . [9]

Friday, February 2 [1923]

This has been an interesting day. The representatives of the three Allied Powers were in solemn conclave all the morning and their legal experts during the afternoon, tinkering with the treaty. They are making certain concessions but we do not yet know what they are. Things have been going on behind the scenes, however, which will have a far greater effect on the ultimate outcome of the Conference. Early this afternoon we learned that there had been a sudden change of attitude in the French delegation, probably due to some diplomatic rearrangement between London and Paris. As a result, Bompard has agreed to support Curzon in presenting an ultimatum to the Turks tomorrow morning; they will be given the revised treaty and will be told that the Allied delegations will be present at the Hotel du Château at 4 P.M. on Sunday in case Ismet wishes to sign; otherwise the Allies will leave Lausanne the same evening. Whether Ismet will sign or not is problematical, but Curzon feels that a continuance of the informal negotiations will only result in the Turks continuing their dilatory tactics. . . . In the meantime we learn in great secrecy that the Italian delegation have received instructions from Mussolini to sign at any price. Garroni did not tell Curzon so. He went to see him and said that as this was Curzon's conference, it was up to him to pull it through. But Curzon is oblivious of the true meaning of this remark. Montagna does

[9] *Foreign Relations, 1923,* II, 962–64, for the full text of Child's statement.

not like that way of doing things. He threw his hands in the air and said to Child: "Oh if I could only have talked to Curzon myself." . . . Anyway, the situation is very complicated tonight and it gives us an insight into old-world politics and diplomacy which makes me personally feel that the United States is well out of these entanglements. Child asked Curzon openly whether there had been any dickering directly between London and Paris with a view to some trade — perhaps the Ruhr against the Near East. Curzon denied this absolutely; he said that he had conducted this Conference on its own merits and without commitments. Child advised him to add some preamble to the treaty with regard to the desire of the Allies to uphold Turkish sovereignty and independence — something which Ismet could take back to Angora to please the public. Curzon said he would consult his drafting experts and try to do it. Child said: "Don't drop this, will you?" Curzon promised that he would take it up immediately. . . .

Saturday, February 3 [1923]

Another interesting day. Everyone asks everyone else how the barometer stands; it varies surprisingly according to the optimistic or pessimistic temperament of the person one is talking to. One person will say that there is no hope, that the two parties cannot possibly reach common ground, that the Allies (or the Turks, as the case may be) have given away their last sou and can make no further concessions, and that Curzon and his delegation will surely leave at 9 P.M. tomorrow. Another will express the opinion that neither the Turks nor the Allies have the slightest intention of leaving Lausanne without a treaty and are merely "carpet dealing" up to the last moment. I personally believe this to be the case. Meanwhile the experts of both factions are working on the clauses. Curzon has told Ismet that the treaty will be on the table for him to sign at 4 o'clock tomorrow afternoon if he wishes and that it will be his last chance. The presentation of the final terms, including certain concessions by the Allies, was made to Ismet this morning in meeting with Curzon, Bompard and

Garroni. It appears that Curzon has been able to hold the French and Italians strictly to their agreement yesterday to support him in stern policy. Montagna, in fact, wrote Child a letter tonight, to be shown to the Turks if Child thought best, saying that the Italian delegation would certainly withdraw from Lausanne with the British and had no intention of pursuing separate negotiations. Among the concessions was a new project for the juridical status of foreigners providing that "the Turkish Government intends continually to engage in its service for such a period as it may deem necessary and which will not be less than five years, legal advisers whom it will choose from a list drawn up by the Permanent Court of International Justice. These legal advisers will depend upon the Ministry of Justice, will participate in the labors of commissions of legislative reforms and their duties will be devoted in particular to the legal jurisdiction of the courts of appeal of Constantinople, Smyrna and of the courts of first instance of Samsoun and Adana. They will be charged in all matters which may be of interest to the international relations of Turkey to follow the functioning of Turkish civil, administrative, commercial, and penal jurisdictions, and to see that actions, appeals, or appeals for reversal of judgment, or revisions be introduced by the Public Ministry against judicial acts or decisions which they may deem contrary to justice, and to receive all complaints which may require either the administration of civil, commercial, administrative or penal justice, or the execution of penalties, or the application of laws with the duty to report thereon to the competent Turkish authorities, with a view to assuring the strict observation of Turkish legislation. . . . In correctional and criminal matters, the release under bond will always have to be granted unless public safety is endangered. All compromises and arbitral clauses in civil or commercial matters are permitted, and the arbitral decisions thus rendered will be enforceable with the assent of the President of the Court of First Instance, who may only refuse his assent in case the decision is contrary to public order."

In compliance with instructions from the Department I drew

up the following letter which was sent to Curzon today over Child's signature, in order to place us on record:

February 1, 1923

Dear Lord Curzon: In view of your statement at the twenty-first meeting of the First Commission on January 23rd to the effect that the British Government, after full examination of the claims of the Turkish Petroleum Company, was convinced and remained convinced of the validity of the concessions given to this company for the oil fields of the Mosul and Bagdad vilayets by the Turkish Government before the war, I believe it may be desirable to call your attention in this informal manner to the note of my Government presented by Ambassador Harvey to the British Government on November 17, 1921, as well as to my statement on this subject on behalf of the American delegation, a copy of which was delivered to you as President at the end of the twenty-second meeting of the First Commission on January 23rd, in which the American attitude towards this question was set forth. I feel sure that my Government's position in regard to the non-validity of the claim of the Turkish Petroleum Company is clearly understood from the full exposition given in the note and statement above mentioned, having particular regard to the suggestion that the claim be determined by a suitable arbitration if it continues to be asserted.[10] Sincerely yours,

RICHARD WASHBURN CHILD

Child has endeavored all day, by repeated conferences with various delegates, to bring about a settlement. He was in the midst of a satisfactory conversation with Nicolson tonight when Sir Eyre Crowe appeared, very angry and saying that there was no use in talking further, that the Allies had made their last concession and would refuse to negotiate further. Child said: "If that is the way you feel about it I shall certainly take no further steps; I wish you good-night" — and he went upstairs.

[10] See *ibid.*, pp. 957–58. American policy was successful in preventing any mention of the Turkish Petroleum Company in the Lausanne Treaty. A final settlement in 1928 permitted American participation in the enterprise. Leland James Gordon, *American Relations with Turkey, 1830–1930;* an Economic Interpretation (Philadelphia: University of Pennsylvania Press, 1932), pp. 276–77.

Sunday, February 4 [1923]

A fateful day. None of us had any idea what it would bring forth. We simply knew that the Allied draft treaty [11] was to be on the conference table at 4 P.M. for the Turks to sign or leave, and that Curzon had sworn to depart at 9 P.M. whatever the result.

At 1.30 while we were all at lunch the first important development occurred. I saw Arlotta hurry into the dining room and hand a document to Garroni who immediately arose and left the room. It proved to be a draft treaty drawn up by the Turkish delegation and handed to the Allies in reply to their draft, containing only those clauses which had been discussed and agreed to by both sides in committee and omitting all others. Ismet accompanied it by a note in which he said that he felt the clauses already agreed to constituted a sufficient basis for peace, and that other subjects still under controversy could be settled later. It was a clever move.

The delegates of the Inviting Powers immediately went into conference in Lord Curzon's room. At 5.30 they summoned Ismet who came down from his hotel with a large group of his experts. At 7 Bentinck called me on the telephone and said that the Turks were probably going to sign in a few moments and suggested that I get our delegates together to be ready to go to Lord Curzon's room to witness the ceremony. I collected Child and Bristol and we went into the hall at the foot of the staircase in the old part of the hotel leading from Curzon's floor. The hall was packed with members of delegations and newspaper correspondents waiting for the final dénouement. The air was full of electricity; hardly anyone talked; we simply listened and waited. The hall upstairs was littered with the packed trunks of the British delegation; in fact when Ismet was calling on Curzon yesterday, the British made a point of bustling about and removing various trunks under Ismet's nose so that he could not fail to be impressed with the definite plans for departure. Thus we waited, expecting any moment to be

[11] Great Britain, *Lausanne Conference on Near Eastern Affairs 1922–1923*, Cmd. 1814 (1923), pp. 832 ff.

summoned to watch the signing of the treaty. Suddenly, at 8 o'clock, the sound of a door opening above; everyone got up and moved toward the staircase. In a moment Ismet appeared, descending the stairs followed by his delegation; he took off his bowler hat, bowed right and left to the crowd in the hall, smiling broadly, and left the hotel. Certainly I shall never forget that scene. The Conference was broken; there would be no signing. After Bentinck's message an hour before we had hardly doubted that a settlement would be made. Child, Bristol and I almost immediately went to Lord Curzon's room. Everyone had left. In a moment Curzon appeared; he burst into the room like an angry bull, glared at us and began to pace up and down waving his fist in the air. He was perspiring and looked about all in. He shouted, "We have been sitting here for four mortal hours and Ismet has replied to everything we have said by the same old banalities — independence and sovereignty. We have all done our best. Even Bompard beat his fist on the table and told Ismet that he was simply stirring up war. Bompard made the strongest speech I ever heard him make." We asked Curzon what Ismet had broken on. Curzon said it was the juridical clauses. (This was only partially correct as it was the economic clauses too.) He said that at the last moment Ismet had withdrawn to another room with his experts and that they had fully expected him to come back and sign. Instead he returned, refused to sign, bowed and left the room. It was all over. Curzon was in a fearful state. We asked him if we could do any good by seeing Ismet. He said that Bompard and Montagna had gone up to see him but that it could do no good. We said we would try and again asked him if the juridical clauses were the real stumbling block. He answered in the affirmative.

Child, Bristol and I then hurried downstairs (where I met Alice just returned from Berne and told her of the rupture), I had the Hudson at the door in a minute and we drove quickly to the Palace Hotel. Bompard and Montagna were with Ismet but we were shown into Hussein's room, where we found Gillespie — of our staff! What he was doing on his own initiative, heaven only knows. The concierge told us that Lord Curzon's train, the Orient Express, was an hour late and would not leave before ten o'clock. This proved to be wrong. Curzon himself had had the train held back for half an hour in order to hear the result of Bompard's talk with Ismet, but as soon as they reported no results the train was released and actually left at 9.25 or thereabouts.

A moment after we were seated Ismet came in, Bompard and Montagna having just left. We were with him approximately an hour. We went over much ground with regard to the juridical clauses, but Ismet told us at once that the economic clauses were no less the cause of the break as they would place Turkey in "financial and industrial slavery." We asked him if he would make further concessions on the juridical clauses provided we should obtain concessions from the Allies on the economic clauses. He asked what we suggested. We said that first of all the foreign judicial advisers should be admitted not only to the courts of Constantinople and Smyrna but to those of Samsoun and Adana as well. The argument continued for about half an hour; Ismet kept rubbing his forehead as if almost dazed. He said in Turkish "My heart is squeezing me" (Gillespie, who remained throughout the conference, told us this afterwards). Finally he got up and went into the adjoining room, stayed there for three minutes, then returned. It was evident that he had gone to consult his experts, but he continued the discussion without a sign that he had seen them. Then quite suddenly he said "All right, I will concede." (He spoke only Turkish, Hussein Bey interpreting.) We said, "Samsoun and Adana?" He replied, "No, only Samsoun." We said: "That is not enough to justify our retaining Lord Curzon." Another twenty minutes of discussion. Again Ismet left the room — for we were pushing him hard — returned and seated himself again. He looked awfully tired. Then after a decent interval, so as not to give us the impression that he had talked with his experts, he said: "All right, I will give you both Samsoun and Adana, but you must give me your word of honor that you will not reveal these concessions to the Allies before you have secured theirs." We agreed, arose, shook hands and said we hoped and believed that this would be a fair basis for renewed negotiations and hurried to the station in the car. We were elated for these concessions that we had obtained were by no means unimportant, Ismet having obstinately stood out on them with the Allies. We felt sure at that moment that Curzon would remain.

At the station I saw Bompard getting into his car and wondered why he was leaving just as Curzon was about to start.[12] Other people appeared to be entering their cars also and I saw some of the Italians coming out of the station. I went up to McClure who was near our car as we got out and asked him how soon Lord Curzon's train was starting. "He's just gone," he said; "the train has just pulled out. They've all gone — the whole delegation." And that's that.

It is idle to speculate upon whether the Conference of Lausanne could have been saved by our arriving five minutes earlier at the station. It is not impossible; in fact I hardly see how Curzon would have dared to leave after what we had to tell him, for it showed that the Turks had not got to the end of their rope in the matter of concessions and that with a sufficient amount of patience still other concessions might be gained. Patience was the necessary element which Curzon lacked and now I know that without that quality it is useless to try to deal with the Turk. . .

Ismet is after all a military leader, not a diplomatist nor a politician. It has been evident throughout that he could take no step without first consulting his experts. I believe Ismet would have gone much farther in meeting the position of the Allies had it not been for Riza Nour who was obstinate from the start. On the other hand, Curzon seemed to have no understanding of the Turkish national aspirations; he did no good to the cause of the Allies by browbeating Ismet at the conference table as if the latter had been one of his "natives" in India. He assumed the attitude of a Viceroy, whereas, as a matter of fact,

[12] Bompard had just told Curzon that the Turks would not change. See Nicolson, *op. cit.,* pp. 346–48.

he was nothing but an equal.[13] But I believe that the element that contributed most to the failure of the Conference was the defection of the French; they broke the solid front, gave the Turks new strength and encouragement and ruined the chances of a successful outcome. The responsibility is theirs and Bompard's strong speeches at the end came too late; the harm had already been done by Poincaré in Paris. . . .[14]

Tuesday, February 6 [1923]

Received a telegram from the Department authorizing us to return to our respective posts if we felt that it would serve no useful purpose for the American Mission to remain at Lausanne. The Department said it considered it desirable for me to maintain contact with any members of other delegations who might remain and left it to my discretion whether this should be done by my remaining temporarily in Lausanne or keeping in touch with Lausanne from Berne.

The Childs and Amory left for Rome at noon, by the same train as Garroni and Montagna, Ismet being down at the station to see them off. Bompard left yesterday. The Admiral was to have left about the same time but could not get accommodations and decided to stay over. This greatly upset Child who jumped at the conclusion that the Admiral desired to continue negotiations with Ismet alone. In my opinion this suspicion was wholly unjustified, but Child took Ismet aside

---

[13] See *ibid.*, pp. 349–50. Nicolson maintains that Lord Curzon's work was a success. Although the second Lausanne Conference made further concessions to Turkey on the capitulations and economic clauses, "Curzon's own work at the first conference remained untouched."

[14] The element of intrigue and international rivalry which went on at Lausanne, of which I had occasion to observe many instances and illustrations, opened my eyes to the sorry state of old-world diplomacy and caused me to realize that even the plots of E. Phillips Oppenheim are not all so farfetched. During the course of the first phase of the Conference, a room of one of our secretaries was entered, his locked trunk broken open, and an envelope bearing the title and seals of the Department of State was stolen and never found. Fortunately, it contained nothing more comprehensive than the *laisser-passers* and personal accounts of the secretary in question. But from that moment we arranged to have one of our staff in the chancery day and night, without exception. — J. C. G.

at the station and told him that any further communications which he might have to make to our delegation should be made to me. Child said something to the Admiral about it too and as a result the Admiral changed his plans and left for Venice the same evening. I am quite sure that he was hurt by Child's suspicions and I regret that the breaking up of our mission should have been marred by this incident. That is Child's greatest fault — an overdeveloped sense of suspicion; it is useful within limits, but not when one continually suspects sinister motives when none are intended.

I gave a farewell dinner to the Bristols, Belins and all the remaining staff and then saw the Bristols off at the station. The Admiral and I parted with mutually good feeling. He has played the game and played it well under difficult circumstances.

Several of the Turkish and Italian staffs are remaining in Lausanne. In fact we know that Garroni and Montagna received a telegram from Rome just after they had left, instructing them to remain and sign the treaty, but it was too late. Massigli also remains. Acting under instructions from Paris he called on Ismet late tonight and stated that if the Turks would state in writing what they were willing to concede on the capitulations, as indicated in their personal conversations with Montagna and others, the Allies would be prepared to sign the treaty. The Turkish delegation withdrew and after an hour informed Massigli that they had made their reply to the Allies last Sunday and that it was now up to the Allies to inform the Turks in writing of the present Allied point of view; that everybody had "run away" from Lausanne and that they would go back to Angora and consult with their people. Ismet said he was glad that the Conference was only suspended and that after his journey to Angora he would be glad to return and resume negotiations if the Allies so desired.[15]

15 When Ismet Pasha returned to Angora, he persuaded the National Assembly to vote "for peace" provided certain modifications were made in the draft treaty. The Lausanne Conference resumed on April 23 with Sir Horace Rumbold, British High Commissioner in Constantinople, taking Lord Curzon's place.

XX

The Last Phase of the Lausanne Conference
APRIL – JULY, 1923

[No date]

The Department having directed me to be present at the reopening of the Conference of Lausanne, I proceeded there on Saturday, April 21st, and within a day or two was joined by our staff composed of Frederic Dolbeare [First Secretary of the American Embassy] from London, F. Lammot Belin [Third Secretary of the American Embassy] from Paris (as Secretary-General of the Mission), Consul Maynard Barnes from Constantinople and Edgar Turlington, Assistant Solicitor in the Department, with five clerks: Vice Consul George Fleming from Basel, Nathan Medofsky from Berne, Miss Inez Viterbo from Paris, Gray from Prague and Wylie Borum from London. We have the same offices as before, in the Beau Rivage at Ouchy. The work of decoding the very extensive telegrams from Washington, which we had begun in Berne, was carried on even in the train to Lausanne and for the first three or four days our code clerks, particularly Fleming and Medofsky, were working seventeen and eighteen hours a day, cheerfully always.

By Monday, April 23rd, the day of the reopening of the Conference, most of the other delegates had arrived: for France, General Maurice Pellé, High Commissioner in Constantinople; Great Britain, Sir Horace Rumbold, also High Commissioner; Italy, Signor Montagna, Minister in Athens; Japan, K. Otchiai, Ambassador in Rome and Haruichi Nagaoka, Minister in Prague; Turkey, Ismet Pasha, Minister for Foreign Affairs of the Grand National Assembly, Riza Nour Bey and Hassan Bey, respectively Minister of Sanitation and former Minister of Finance; Greece, Venizelos and Demetrius Caclamanos,

Minister in London; Rumania, Constantin Diamandy and Constantin Contzesco; Yugoslavia, Dr. Yovanovitch, Minister in Berne. Paternotte, Secretary of the Belgian Legation in Berne, is also present at the sessions.

On April 21st I had a long talk with Montagna; he was one of the outstanding figures of the last Conference, energetic but conciliatory in his methods, and particularly friendly toward us.[1] In strict personal confidence he gave me his views and information with regard to the Conference. The Turks, he believes, are more anxious for peace than at the time of the adjournment in February, as their army is tired and lacking in spirit, which is recognized at Angora, and as their economic situation has become worse. He believes that the British Government and people wish to have peace at almost any price and that they will make substantial concessions in order to conclude a treaty. The Italians, he says, are primarily interested in retaining the Island of Castellorizo which he says they will give up under no circumstances. This is purely a question of prestige and is neither political nor military. The Italian Government could not agree to turn back to Turkey the six or seven thousand Greeks on the island who had confided themselves to the care of Italy. Italy's interests in the financial, economic and judicial questions, he asserts, are less important

[1] He understood the mentality of the Turk and the proper method of dealing with him better than any other delegate; and not only did he bring the work of his subcommittees to a satisfactory conclusion while other committees were still deep in acrid debate, but at the critical moments of the Conference it was always he who, in a quiet and unobtrusive manner, managed to smooth matters over by his sensible and conciliatory tactics. At the end of the Conference, after Montagna had, in my opinion, contributed more than any other delegate toward reaching a final agreement, old Marquis Garroni insisted on coming up from Rome to sign the treaty for Italy, although he was the only one of the original first delegates to do this. Thus Montagna was deprived of the prestige, if it could be regarded as such, which he had earned by indefatigable work. In the darkest hours of the Conference Montagna was always optimistic, and I am convinced that on more than one occasion he personally prevented a rupture. I shall always be grateful to him for following Mussolini's policy of close co-operation with the American delegation and for keeping me intimately informed of developments and of what was going on behind the scenes. — J. C. G.

than those of other nations. (We shall see about this later.) The French, Montagna believes, will cause the most difficulty in the negotiations, especially with regard to the economic and financial clauses. He intends to urge Pellé not to raise the question of the Chester Concession [2] at Lausanne as it would complicate already difficult negotiations.

Montagna feels that Curzon and Rumbold ruined the chances of peace at the last meeting as they did not understand how to deal with the Turks; they had no knowledge of bargaining or pliability and gave away financial concessions without getting anything in return. He himself hopes to have the presidency of the committee on the judicial clauses as he knows this subject better than the others. He lent me, under a pledge of secrecy, a document recently drawn up by the British Government containing in three columns (1) the text of the original proposal of the Allies for the appointment of judicial advisers in Turkey, (2) the so-called Montagna formula, and (3) a new draft drawn up by Rumbold which will be proposed by him. Montagna considers this new draft as impractical and unacceptable to the Turks. Evidently the British have withdrawn their agreement to accept the Montagna formula, made as an eleventh-hour concession on February 5th, providing for

---

[2] The inception of the Chester project dated from the years 1908–09, when Rear Admiral Colby M. Chester began negotiations with Turkey for oil concessions in Anatolia, Syria, and Mesopotamia. Although the Grand Vizier approved the project, the Turkish parliament never officially granted the concession. The original American company which was to have taken over the concession became defunct, but a group of engineers and capitalists holding stock in the company held the project together informally. In 1920 interest revived among the group, and Admiral Chester and his partners sought the aid of the Department of State in an effort to "obtain a confirmation of his old project or rather a concession now based on the old project." At this time the American company met with the conflicting claims of other companies, particularly those of the French company. See *Foreign Relations, 1921*, II, 917–24. On May 14, 1923, Mr. Grew wrote to Thomas Sergeant Perry: "As for the Chester Concession, which at first placed us in a most unpleasant light at Lausanne, I had a short talk with Pellé and convinced him that our Government, which expects fair dealing and justice from others, is going to follow just that course itself. The murky atmosphere which surrounded us during the first ten days of the Conference has thus been considerably cleared away."

the appointment by the Permanent Court of International Justice at The Hague of judicial advisers from nationals of countries which did not participate in the war.

Montagna said he valued our friendship and would talk to me frankly throughout the Conference.

On April 22nd I called on Ismet. He said approximately the same things he had said to Admiral Bristol before leaving Constantinople with regard to the Chester Concession, concessionary negotiations at Constantinople or Angora, his doubt as to the sincerity of the Allies in desiring peace, etc.[3] He shows great eagerness to proceed immediately with negotiations for a treaty with us and maintains that the early conclusion of such a treaty would tend to hasten a settlement with the Allies. He said he considered it most desirable that the United States and Turkey should strengthen their economic relations, not only by the conclusion of a treaty, but also through economic concessions and in this latter respect Turkey had already shown her good faith by granting the Chester Concession. I asked him when he thought that such a treaty could be discussed. He replied that he would like to see negotiations begin immediately. I said that the feeling at the last meeting of the Conference was that it would complicate matters to have two treaties negotiated at the same time. But Ismet said he saw no objection to this procedure and repeated that the early signature of a treaty between Turkey and the United States would result in hastening the treaty between Turkey and the Allies. I asked him what sort of basis or form he had in mind for negotiating such a treaty. He said it should contain provisions for the resumption of diplomatic and consular relations and other matters customarily included in a treaty of amity and commerce. I alluded to the question of the protection of American religious and educational institutions in Turkey, judicial guarantees, etc. He said that the Turkish Government had already agreed to permit such institutions to carry on their activities in accordance with Turkish law and

---

[3] See *Foreign Relations, 1923*, II, 986–87, for the despatch of the High Commissioner about this talk.

that on this subject and also on the subject of judicial guarantees they would be glad to sign a definite declaration. I said that I would give the matter my attention and would talk with him further about it at a later occasion.

In the further course of the conversation I expressed my satisfaction that we were again on the road to peace and said I felt sure that Ismet realized the friendly sentiments of the United States for Turkey and that if I could ever translate these sentiments into action by helping in any proper way towards the cause of peace, he could count upon me to do so. He asked if that meant that I was willing to mediate; I said in reply that if he ever had any definite proposal to make by which I could be of any help, I should certainly give it my most careful attention and carry it out if possible. He asked me if I thought the Allies sincerely desired peace. I said that I had no doubt in my mind at all and was sure of it. He shrugged his shoulders as if in some doubt. He asked me if I was optimistic as to the outcome of this renewed conference and I replied that I was always optimistic.

Ismet Pasha said he understood that the French would bring up at the Conference their protest against the Chester Concession; that the papers were full of it and that it looked as if it would cause a lot of trouble. He asked me what our attitude would be. I said that our attitude would be in accordance with the traditional policy of the United States to protect its legitimate, natural interests and the legitimate interests of its citizens; that our Government had taken no part in negotiating the Concession and that it was now studying the facts concerning it. I might later be able to express a more definite opinion. Ismet said that the French protest was founded on no sound basis. I asked him what his attitude would be if the matter were brought up at the Conference. He said he would take the position that the question of the Concession was in no way a political matter and not subject for discussion at the Conference. I said, "Then that would seem to settle the matter." He said he feared the French would continue to press it and insist on bringing it into the negotiations. . . .

On April 23rd, I called on Sir Horace Rumbold merely to pay my respects on his arrival and in the course of conversation said to him that if I could ever be of any assistance in helping the Allies and the Turks to arrive at peace, my services would be at his disposal. I said also that our respective interests in the conventions to replace the Capitulatory regime were practically identical and that we should be disposed to co-operate with the Allies in this phase of their negotiations with the Turks. Sir Horace Rumbold thanked me.

On April 24th I called on General Pellé and in the course of informal conversation said that French and American interests with regard to the Capitulations were more or less identical and that when the proper time arrived I might be able to be of assistance to support him in the course of the negotiations. Pellé acknowledged this with evident appreciation and said smilingly that American moral support ought to count for much at the present moment, as we were on the crest of the wave in Turkey, as evidenced by the Chester Concessions which had had a great "retentissement" throughout the country. He said he had not yet received definite instructions, as his Government had not received the final text of the Concession as ratified at Angora, but that he felt the subject would have to come up at the Conference in connection with the discussion of the economic clauses. He asked me what our attitude was.

I told General Pellé that my Government had also not yet had an opportunity to study all the details of the question as the final text had not yet been received in Washington, but that our traditional policy was well-known to him, namely: the protection of the legitimate interests of our citizens and the principle of the open door. I said I felt sure that when all the factors of the matter were understood, a good many of the points at issue would probably solve themselves.

I asked him whether France regarded her rights in the matter as legal or moral or both. He replied that they were regarded as both legal and moral. The concession of the Samsoun-Sivas railway line and the development of the port of

Samsoun, in co-operation with the British, had been duly granted and signed in 1914 and work had actually begun on it, but had been interrupted by the war. In return for the concession, France had made a loan to Turkey. He said he was thoroughly familiar with the subject as he had handled much of the correspondence in the case and had protested to the Turkish Government on his own initiative. The Turkish Government has given no reply, maintaining that the protest had not come officially from the French Government itself.

I said that if at any time he desired to talk over with me the situation in detail, I should be glad to go into it with him informally. The United States Government had not negotiated the Chester Concession and was not yet familiar with all its aspects, but I felt sure that after it had been thoroughly studied, some satisfactory solution could be found.

In conversation with Joseph Sharkey of the Associated Press on the same subject yesterday he told me that a report was current to the effect that the Turks were prepared to offer some other concession to the French to replace anything that they might lose through the Chester Concession.

Ismet Pasha came to see me at his own request at 10.45 on the evening of April 26th and remained for almost an hour and a half in conversation. He began by asking me what I thought of the trend of the Conference during the last few days. I said I thought things seemed to be progressing well and that a good many points had been decided. He shrugged his shoulders, giving the impression that he was not particularly satisfied.

He then asked me what I thought about the attitude of the Allies towards the question of reparations. The Allies had today agreed to the complete suppression of Article 79 of the Economic Clauses, but did I think that they would later bring it up again under the Financial Clauses. I said I had no idea whatever as to their intentions, but that Signor Montagna had today certainly given definite assurances that Article 79 was permanently suppressed.[4] Ismet said that he had come to Lau-

---

4 Article 79 of the Economic Clauses of the Draft Treaty of Peace stated: "If the property, rights and interests of Allied nationals (excluding Greek

sanne again on the basis of the complete suppression of demands for reparations and that if the Allies persisted in these demands, he would have to go home. He stated very emphatically that he could, under no consideration, continue to negotiate on such a basis. I said that I was glad to know of his attitude on this subject and that I should take occasion to speak of it when the opportunity presented itself. . . .

Ismet then referred to my recent call upon him and said I had given him hope for the early commencement of negotiations for a treaty between the United States and Turkey (as a matter of fact I had merely listened to what he had to say and told him that I hoped to be able to talk with him further on the subject at a later occasion). Ismet asked me when we were going to be ready to begin negotiations. I told him that as I had stated at our last interview, the United States looked forward to the day when it might conclude a treaty with Turkey, but that the appropriate time for commencing negotiations for such a treaty depended upon a variety of circumstances and that for the moment I was unable to say when that time would arrive. As soon as the time had come to enter upon such negotiations, I should not fail to inform him immediately. I then said that this question of a treaty between the United States and Turkey opened up what might prove to be a difficult question, namely: the question of the Capitulations. The United States had never consented to the abrogation of the Capitulations. In our treaty of 1874 with Turkey a provision was included to the effect that our old treaties with Turkey should be revised as soon as possible. We still looked forward to such a revision and this revision would necessarily have to provide for some satisfactory regime to replace the Capitulations even if it were only to be a transitory regime. The United States

nationals) which were in territory under Ottoman sovereignty on the 1st August, 1914, no longer exist or have suffered damages resulting from acts of war, measures of requisition, measures of sequestration, transfer or confiscation or any harmful act or decision, the owner shall have the right to compensation which the Allied Powers will grant him out of the sums allocated for this object by Article 57 (Financial Clauses) and in accordance with procedure fixed by them." Great Britain, *Lausanne Conference on Near Eastern Affairs 1922–1923*, Cmd. 1814 (1923), p. 724.

and Turkey had much in common. We ourselves had struggled for our newly won independence and we sympathized with Turkey in her present national aspirations. We had our George Washington: Turkey had her Mustafa Kemal Pasha. We fully realized and appreciated the great body of opinion in Turkey which desired to throw off the old restraints. But on the other hand it must not be forgotten that we in America had a great body of public opinion which still retained the Capitulations in view. Our businessmen, our educational men and others in Turkey must be given confidence and satisfactory assurances that in carrying out their work they will have judicial safeguards. Our educational institutions must be given assurances of protection of various kinds. Our citizens must not be expected to suffer from the ancient Turkish prison regime from which some of our citizens had suffered in times past. This whole question was a very important and serious one for us and I must point out to His Excellency very clearly that we should have to maintain this position at the conference table, if occasion should arise.

Ismet spoke of the Montagna formula for the abrogation of the Judicial Capitulations as having been accepted by both parties and he asked me whether we were going to recede from the conciliatory attitude shown by our Delegation during the first meeting of the Conference. I said that our position and attitude had changed in no way whatever since Mr. Child's talks with Ismet, but that the Montagna formula by no means covered all of the question at issue. While discussing the Montagna formula, I asked Ismet whether the acceptance of the Montagna formula would in his opinion prevent the Turks from accepting other Judicial Advisers, in addition to those Advisers from neutral countries provided for by that formula. I alluded especially to the possibility of an eventual convention with the United States to cover that subject. Ismet replied that the Turkish Government would have no objection to an American Judicial Adviser, but that if such an agreement were concluded with the United States, the Allies and even Russia, would insist on having their own Judicial Advisers in Turkey. It would open the window by which the Allies and Russia would come pouring in and while an American Adviser would, he fully realized, confine himself to judicial matters, the Advisers of the other Powers would carry on political activity without any question.

Ismet said he hoped that I was not going to take any such stand at the Conference and that if he should telegraph this interview to Angora it would act like a cold "douche" on the Chester Concession. I suggested that it would be desirable to avoid crossing that bridge until we came to it and that as yet the question had not arisen. I had sincere friendship for him, the United States had sincere friendship for Turkey and I did not doubt that a satisfactory solution of all difficulties would be found. Ismet said he heartily shared my feelings.

I then referred to his remarks to me at the beginning of our conversation with regard to the question of reparations and said that since he had broached this subject which was of no direct interest to the United States and upon which I should be glad to help him if possible, I for my part, speaking entirely personally and unofficially, thought that it might be of interest to him to know that Signor Montagna had told me that the Island of Castellorizo was the great stumbling block in the path of the Italians; that they were more firmly determined on this point than any other and that he, Signor Montagna, could not be very helpful in the further negotiations, unless Castellorizo were ceded to Italy. Ismet immediately embarked on his arguments already advanced at the conference table with regard to Castellorizo being within Turkish territorial waters. I said that the matter did not concern me in any way and I merely felt he might be glad to know that Montagna, whose attitude was generally moderate and conciliatory, would probably be able to exert more influence towards arriving at peace, if this question could be settled satisfactorily to Italy. Ismet thanked me and said he believed that these informal exchanges of information would be of great use and that he counted much on me to help in bringing about peace between the Allies and Turkey. I said that the privilege was a great one and that I should be happy to do my best towards that end.

The conversation, which was cordial throughout, ended by

Ismet writing his "*hommages* to Madame Grew" in our book, commenting on the strong and splendid face of President Harding whose picture was on my table, and other personal and friendly allusions.

On April 27th, Sir Horace Rumbold called on me, in the evening, and under directions from his Government read to me an extract from an instruction received from the British Foreign Office essentially as follows: "This Government values the friendship and co-operation of the American Delegation and will be glad to learn its views and to inform it of our views during the course of the Lausanne Conference."

Rumbold then asked me whether we intended actually to join the Allies in the negotiations of the two conventions regarding the regime of foreigners and the declaration regarding judicial safeguards. I replied that I preferred to use the word "co-operate."

Rumbold said that he had placed this interpretation on my previous talk with him, but that his Government had inquired exactly how far we were prepared to go in the matter.

On April 28th, Montagna told me that in agreement with Rumbold and Pellé he had decided to postpone the discussion in the Third Committee of the economic clauses relating to concessions probably for ten days or two weeks and that he would take up all other clauses first. This would give time for the French concessionaires, who were now on their way to Constantinople, to endeavor to come to some satisfactory settlement with the Turkish Government with regard to the Chester Concession. If they failed to obtain satisfaction the subject would have to be brought up later in Lausanne.

On April 30th, Mr. Montagna called on me and asked me if I knew anything of particular interest with regard to the progress of the Conference. He said that he had talked very little with his Allied colleagues. He asked me if I approved of the postponement of the discussion in the concessionary clauses. I said that as the organization of the Conference was in the hands of the Allies, there was no reason why we, who were not negotiating the treaty, should be consulted in the matter, but that in my personal opinion the step was a wise one as it afforded an opportunity for settling these questions outside of the Conference and by direct negotiation in Constantinople or Angora. Mr. Montagna said he thought that if the direct negotiations of the concessionaires with the Turkish Government were not successful, the matter would be thrashed out through diplomatic channels between the various interested Governments. I told Mr. Montagna that I had seen General George W. Goethals quoted as having said that the Chester people desired to establish friendly relations, rather than hostility with other nations, in connection with their economic interests and that I believed that everything practicable would be done to settle this concessionary question satisfactorily to all concerned.

Mr. Montagna then said that speaking entirely from his personal point of view and without any authorization or even hints from his own Government, he hoped that Italy and the United States could work together in the Near East. I asked him to elaborate his meaning. He said that his idea was some sort of an understanding between the two Governments with a view to economic exploitation of the Near East. He said that it was no secret that Italy desired to infiltrate into Asia Minor. This was a perfectly natural and logical policy. Italy was politically weak in comparison with the other Allies, but she was militarily, sociologically and physiologically strong. France must eventually crumble away on account of her declining birth rate and the fact that she was now living on the margin resulting from the years of richness and plenty since the Revolution. In Italy, on the other hand, the birth rate was steadily increasing and instead of being a question of too few men, it was a question of too many men, therefore she must expand and overflow and if she was not permitted to do this gradually, an explosion would some day automatically occur. This is the reason why she cannot be denied her rights of infiltration into Asia Minor, together with the other nations. Her position is an extremely difficult one and Mr. Montagna implied that she receives scant consideration from England and France.

I pointed out to him that his attitude, so far as economic con-

siderations were concerned, had our full sympathy for the policy of the open door meant that the door should be open to all
on equal terms. Politically I said the United States had no
interests in Turkey. Mr. Montagna said that whatever our
interests might be now we could not avoid their becoming
political in the future. Economic infiltration implied political
infiltration. It was the logical sequence and in supporting our
economic interests, we should have to be "among those present" when the crumbling of Turkey came.

He asserted that this crumbling of the Ottoman Empire
must surely come about in the course of time. Perhaps in 25
years and during our own lifetime. In his own mind he com-
pares Turkey to a mummy which so long as it remains sealed in
its tomb retains its normal state but as soon as the tomb is
opened and it comes into contact with the outside air it immediately begins to decompose and to crumble away. Turkey's
contact with the outside nations would make her crumble away,
because she was not content to make the transition gradually
as Japan had done, but must bring it about all at once. This
very policy of immediate and complete independence would
bring about Turkey's collapse in the end. When the collapse
came, the other nations would be there to profit by it and Italy
could not be left out in the cold.

Mr. Montagna said that he would always speak his thoughts
to me with entire frankness, no matter how confidential they
might be unless they involved imparting confidences given him
by others. He believed in openness and honesty in political
matters, just as much as in personal matters between gentlemen.
He said he had always felt great friendship for the United
States and for Americans. He had worked closely with Mr.
Child, both at the former Conference in Lausanne and in
Rome afterwards. It was for our sake that he had agreed to
drop the clause requiring the Turkish Government to consult
the Ottoman Public Debt Commission before giving away concessions. He had proposed this clause exclusively for the purpose of protecting Italy against England and France in connection with concessions in the Near East. It was in no con-

ceivable manner aimed against us. He said that the Turks would have agreed to the clause and that the dropping of it was a great sacrifice for him to make, but that he had done it because we had asked it.

Mr. Montagna said he thought the French were making some kind of a private deal with the Turks, as Pellé had been much with Ismet and had now gone to Paris to report. He thought that probably this deal related to concessions, but he knew nothing about it and in any case he did not believe that any of the Allies would be willing to barter their capitulatory guarantees for economic concessions. He was to have a conference with Rumbold and Pellé this afternoon and would tell me the result of it this evening.

Montagna asked me if we were satisfied and willing to support the Montagna formula. I replied that the formula did not seem to us to give sufficient judicial guarantees, but that our attitude would depend upon circumstances and I could not yet say exactly what position we would take with regard to it. I spoke of the necessity of having the judicial advisers admitted to the Courts of Samsoun and Adana, prison inspection, etc. He said he thought all of the Allies would welcome our cooperation, in the negotiation of the conventions.

After this lengthy excerpt recounting the opening days of the second phase of the Conference, Mr. Grew was too busy to keep a daily diary. He did, however, record his most important conversations with the leading delegates, and on September 2, 1923, he summarized the key events of the Conference in the following informal talk to the American consular officials in Switzerland gathered at Interlaken.

. . . We have seen from the editorial comment at home that Ismet Pasha won a great diplomatic victory at Lausanne and stood all the Allied diplomats on their heads, to say nothing of the Americans. There is no good in denying the fact. It is perfectly true and easily explainable. It was probably the greatest diplomatic victory in history and could hardly result otherwise if we stop to consider that Ismet held all of the cards in his hands from the very start. He had his four aces at the very beginning and I think you will agree that under ordinary circumstances that is a fairly useful basis for negotiation. First, he had at his back a recently victorious army, far different from the defeated army which Turkey possessed at the time of the Treaty of Sèvres. Second, that army was in almost perfect condition and ready and eager to fight at a moment's notice. Third, not one of the Great Powers desired or intended to fight, and Ismet knew it. And, fourth, quite apart from fighting, the Allies could not present a solid front, even in the diplomatic negotiations. Instead of pooling their interests for the greater good of the greater number, each power went into the conference with its own individual interests paramount to any other consideration, each suspicious of his neighbor, and none willing to adopt a comprehensive plan and to stick to it through thick and thin. At a critical moment in the conference, one of the Great Powers showed deplorable weakness; its representative [Barrère of France] who had tried to play the game was recalled and from that moment there was no further question as to the final result. . . .

The second phase of the Conference, which began on April 23rd and ended on July 24th,[5] was in many respects far more interesting than the first phase, but I do not wish to weary you with too long an account and shall therefore limit myself to speaking of only two or three of the outstanding features. The first difficult problem we had on our hands was, strange as it may seem, the necessity of establishing friendly relations with our British colleagues. Apparently Lord Curzon had gained the impression, during the first phase of the conference, that our delegation had been distinctly pro-Turk and had aided and abetted the Turkish delegation in their alleged Machiavellian maneuvers. It is true that one or two members of our delegation, who had lived long in Constantinople, were somewhat pro-Turkish in their attitude and were perhaps seen too frequently in the company of members of the Turkish delega-

[5] The Treaty was signed at Lausanne on this date.

tion, which may have given rise to these unwarranted suspicions. But the charge that our delegation itself was pro-Turk, or took any step, or said any word contrary to the interests of the Western Powers was wholly without foundation. Throughout the entire Conference we lived up to the purpose of our mission, which was (1) to safeguard American interests and (2) to contribute in every proper way towards the conclusion of peace.[6]

Be that as it may, we learned through various channels that the British Government was not anxious that we should be present at the second phase of the Conference. The French and Italian Governments, however, took a different view of the matter and, when the notices for the second meeting were sent out by the Secretariat General, we duly received our notice with the rest, and, to my considerable apprehension, I was appointed to represent the United States alone. At the very beginning I made a point of seeing each of my Allied colleagues and telling them exactly where we stood and what we proposed to do at the Conference, and that I should take no step without giving them full information. Thereafter, whenever I saw Ismet, which was, of course, promptly known to all, I took immediate occasion to see my Allied colleagues and tell them exactly what we talked about. To make a long story short, this policy had its desired effect, because, after having strenu-

6 On April 23, 1923, Mr. Grew made the following statement to the Conference: "Permit me to speak very briefly of the position of the American representation at these resumed negotiations. We are here for the same purposes and in the same capacity as before the adjournment, participating not on the footing of a belligerent against Turkey nor as a party to the treaty of peace under negotiation between the Allied Powers and Turkey, but none the less in a fully representative capacity and with full authorization and competence to speak on behalf of the Government of the United States. In the ensuing deliberations we wish to see safeguarded the legitimate national interests of the United States, the principle of commercial opportunity for all nations, and the humanitarian considerations upon which our views have already been expressed. Should other issues arise or should amplification of these declarations prove desirable, we shall avail ourselves of the privilege of further statement or comment.

"So far as it may be within our proper functions and to the extent of our power, we wish to assist in serving the cause of peace."

ously opposed our request to be admitted to the deliberations of the various subcommittees and groups of experts, Sir Horace Rumbold, the British representative, finally withdrew his objection sometime after the Conference had started. Instead, however, of coming to me and telling me frankly of his change of attitude, as I should certainly have done in a similar case, he had to save his face at all costs and merely sent his legal expert to break the news to me. About the same time he called upon me with great ceremony and, taking a document out of his pocket, he said that he had been instructed by his Government to read to me the following message:

> His Majesty's Government values the friendship and co-operation of the American Delegation and will be glad to learn its views and to inform it of our views during the course of the Conference.

This was the only call that Rumbold made upon me during the entire three months that we were colleagues at Lausanne, although we had been young secretaries together in Cairo some twenty years ago and were again colleagues in Berlin before the war when we together sealed up the archives of the British Embassy. The French and Italian delegates, on the contrary, came to see me as often as I went to see them, and we were in the habit of dropping in on each other at any time of day or night to compare notes and discuss developments. In spite of the message from the British Government, Sir Horace Rumbold never once during the Conference consulted me or gave me his own opinion or information on his own initiative while we were in Lausanne. As a result he missed much that might have been of value to him, while the information he could have given me I was able to obtain equally well from other sources. These things count in the long run. It makes one inclined to agree with a remark made to me one day by one of my other colleagues at Lausanne that "the French are clever in little things but stupid in great ones, while the British are clever in great ones and immensely stupid in the small things."

All this sounds as if I were an Anglophobe. But I am not. I am Anglophile to the core; always have been and always shall be, and I believe that close and good relations between the United States and Great Britain are more important for the progress of civilization than any other element in the world.

The most serious development in the second phase of the Conference of Lausanne was unquestionably the Turco-Greek dispute over reparations. There is no doubt whatever that at one moment the Conference hung on the brink of rupture and Europe on the brink of war, for if the Greek army had invaded Eastern Thrace, as it was certainly on the point of doing, there would without question have been a general conflagration in the Balkans, and there is no telling how far that conflagration might have extended. The danger became evident about May 10th on which date I learned that the Greek Government was considering an ultimatum to Turkey on the following grounds: (1) maltreatment of Greek prisoners; (2) the opening by the Turks of safe deposit vaults in the Greek banks in Constantinople, and (3) the alleged expulsion of Greeks from Asia Minor. Venizelos, however, considered these points weak and recommended to his Government that the ultimatum, if issued, should be based on the Turkish claims for reparations from Greece.[7] Shortly afterwards Venizelos called on Ismet and talked to him in a most threatening and bellicose manner. Ismet said, "Do you mean you are threatening me with war?" Venizelos calmed down somewhat and offered to agree to the principle of paying reparations, but with the understanding that no cash should be paid, as Greece was incapable of doing it. Ismet proposed either arbitration or the payment of a lump sum, both of which suggestions Venizelos refused. At this stage Ismet was visibly anxious and asked permission of the Allies to send Turkish troops into Eastern Thrace to meet the

[7] Mr. Montagna advised Mr. Grew of this tense situation on May 10. According to the memorandum of the conversation: "Montagna said that after a long talk with Pellé, Montagna had won him over to his point of view and they both agreed that Venizelos' estimates with regard to the fighting power of the Greek Army were greatly overdrawn."

threat of war, which was, of course, refused. About this time Apostol Alexandris, the Greek Minister of Foreign Affairs, arrived in Lausanne and took an even more bellicose attitude than Venizelos had done. He said that Greece was absolutely determined to go to war rather than pay, and he remarked to Montagna that, as the Allies had supported the Greek offensive before, they could not now desert her. Montagna corrected him by saying "certain Allies" and added "that victory was often more costly than defeat." Alexandris said that the Greek army was the stronghold of the Allied position at the Conference and was now at the zenith of its efficiency, but that if time went by without its attacking this efficiency would decrease. Montagna indignantly refuted the suggestion that the Greek army had anything whatever to do with supporting the Allied position. Alexandris then went so far as to say that the Greek army had been deprived of victory and that its officers now demanded satisfaction by invading Eastern Thrace. There is no doubt that this whole question was one of internal Greek politics. The military party was literally champing at the bit while Venizelos' party also needed some concrete asset to retain power and they were clearly pushing him toward war.

During these days the Allies had continual meetings to determine what should be done, and it is a strange fact that throughout these meetings the British representative remained practically silent. When, finally, it was decided to make an official démarche in Athens, the British Chargé d'Affaires made his representations separate from the others.[8] They, however, did tell the Greek Government that if it went to war, it would not be permitted to enjoy the fruits of any possible victory. I called on Rumbold at this time to ascertain his opinion, and he said he considered the situation dangerous but not neces-

---

[8] On May 21, 1923, Mr. Montagna told Mr. Grew "that Rumbold's position was now very embarrassing, because he had first taken the attitude of supporting the Greeks, not so much, Montagna believed, with the intention of inciting them to war, as to exert pressure on the Turks by this method. The British had now been obliged to alter this attitude, but it made it difficult for them to act in unison with their Allies and they were therefore acting alone."

sarily critical. With the French and Italian delegates I worked in constant co-operation.

Pellé, the French representative, about this time proposed to Ismet that the Turks should accept the town of Karagatch from the Greeks in lieu of reparations. Ismet immediately demanded a further strip of territory, including the railway from Demotika, but when he was shown the weakness of this position and the fact that the Greeks could promptly put the railway out of commission with their guns, he withdrew his demand. Montagna appealed to Venizelos on the ground that if war occurred some 400,000 Greeks in Constantinople and Anatolia would probably be killed. Venizelos immediately replied that this would be met by the massacre of the same number of Mussulmans in Greece. Montagna asked Venizelos if he could countenance such terrible butchery merely to strengthen a political party now in power in Greece. When the matter was put to him in that light, Venizelos appeared ashamed of his remark. On May 24th we were all seriously disturbed by the situation. It was pointed out to Ismet (1) that the British battleship *Iron Duke* and twenty destroyers had entered the Straits; (2) that the British press was threatening war; (3) that the Greek Government and army were eager for war; (4) that Rumbold had abstained from seeing Ismet and that the British representative in Athens had made his representations alone and not in unison with the others; (5) that if war were declared, Turkey would at once be thrown out of Constantinople and Eastern Thrace, and (6) that the ability of the Turkish army to fight in Anatolia would in no way help their cause in Thrace.[9] Ismet appeared impressed by these representations and cabled the Karagatch proposal to Angora. Meanwhile every effort was made to keep Venizelos calm and to convince him that even if the Greek offensive were justified the greater good of the greater number was at stake and that Europe could not permit war.

On May 25th I called on each of the Allies on my own initia-

[9] On May 24, Mr. Montagna reported to Mr. Grew that he had just made these points to Ismet.

tive and said I could not see war intervene without exerting the influence of the United States as a totally disinterested power, and that I proposed to offer my good offices. Each of the Allies agreed heartily to this proposal. I was particularly concerned by my talk with the Yugoslav delegate, for he said that no declaration on the part of Yugoslavia was possible at the moment, as a declaration of neutrality would encourage the Turks, siding with Greece would tend to precipitate hostilities. My impression from our conversation was distinctly that Serbia would fight. Serbia was opposed to the Karagatch proposal, as she did not want to see Turkey on this side of the Maritsa. Yovanovitch also told me that Bulgaria would oppose the proposal, as this would mean two countries, instead of one, to block her outlet to the sea. I pointed out the strategic weakness of this new proposed Turkish front, but Yovanovitch said that it was more a question of propaganda in Eastern Thrace than a strategic question. Theodoroff, the Bulgarian delegate, told Ismet that he could not count on Bulgaria's support.

In spite of continual insistence on the part of Venizelos and Alexandris that a final meeting should be held, and, in spite of repeated threats on their part to leave Lausanne and to invade Eastern Thrace unless satisfaction were immediately given, every effort was made to postpone the meeting until Ismet should have had time to receive an answer from Angora regarding Karagatch. On the 25th of May it was evident that the meeting could be no longer postponed. I spent a good part of the night before the meeting with Venizelos and Ismet alternately, using every possible argument to induce a peaceful solution. Venizelos told me that he would accept the Karagatch proposal and I so informed Ismet.[10] The meeting was held

[10] Mr. Grew's conversation with Ismet Pasha was as follows: "I called on Ismet Pasha and said that we were disturbed by the rumors appearing in the Press with regard to the situation arising out of the subject of Greek reparations. Ismet affected to show surprise that any unusual situation existed. I told him approximately what I had said to Venizelos, earlier in the evening, and added that I had tried to look at the situation from both the Turkish and Greek points of view and that I was able to see it from both angles. As regards

at five o'clock with one delegate from each country present. It took place in a small room at the Château and was intensely dramatic. We all sat close together at a small table, Pellé, the President, and Ismet sitting opposite one another. Diamandy placed himself between Ismet and Venizelos with a view to separating the principals in the controversy. The meeting began with the utmost solemnity. Each delegate in turn made a speech emphasizing the seriousness of the situation and calling for conciliation and moderation on both sides. Rumbold used calm logic, Montagna made an impassioned plea, while Pellé summed up the situation in a masterful address followed by the Japanese, the Serbian, the Rumanian and myself.[11]

Ismet then began to talk and it was evident at once that in his truly Oriental way he was trying to dodge the issue. Diamandy slipped a note across the table to Pellé begging him to pin Ismet down to facts. Pellé then asked Ismet if he had

the position of the Turkish Government, I could only point out that while fully realizing its desire to build up its economic establishment, it was useless to try to do this by demanding indemnities which could probably not be paid and if the situation were allowed to drift into hostilities, Turkey would be in a much worse position than if no indemnities were paid at all. Ismet spoke at some length about the ruined homes in Anatolia always before the eyes of the public. I said that I understood that a territorial concession in place of indemnities had been proposed by the Allies. Ismet confirmed the fact that the Allies had suggested the concession of Karagatch by Greece to Turkey and said he had telegraphed the proposal to Angora, but had not yet received a reply. I asked him if he thought the reply would be favorable, but he avoided answering the question. He said it was a question in his mind whether the Greeks had not drawn up their program in advance. He said that the newspaper reports regarding a Turkish withdrawal from the Conference were devoid of foundation and that he had issued a communiqué to deny them. I said that Venizelos had told me that he would definitely accept Karagatch and would remain in Lausanne until Monday. Ismet said he expected to receive a reply from Angora by Monday. I then offered my good offices in the same way that I had offered them to Venizelos in case they could be helpful at arriving at a solution, and explained in detail why I was doing this. Ismet thanked me. I said that I was speaking personally on my own initiative and not under instructions from my Government.

"It was absolutely impossible to gather from this conversation whether Ismet expects to come to terms with the Greeks or not. His remarks and comments were all of a general nature, if not actually cryptic. It is impossible to read his mind."

11 For Mr. Grew's speech see *Foreign Relations, 1923,* II, 1011.

telegraphed the Karagatch proposal to Angora. Ismet replied in the affirmative. Pellé said, "Have you received a reply?" Ismet answered, "Yes." "Do you accept?" Ismet again tried to ramble off on tangents, but Pellé persisted and finally, after making every effort to avoid the issue, he gave a weary assent.

All this had lasted two hours during which we were all under the greatest possible strain and when it finally appeared that a solution was in sight, the psychology of human nature took its natural course and the air of solemnity changed immediately into one bordering on actual hilarity. Diamandy got up and insisted upon Venizelos moving next to Ismet. The details of the settlement were then discussed in the most amicable way; Venizelos and Ismet calling each other "mon cher ami" had their hands on each other's arms, laughed like schoolboys and appeared to be on the point of actually embracing. The Serbian danced about the room recording his protest against the cession of Karagatch, but assuring the meeting that he would not think of letting this stand in the way of peace and that he merely wished to go on record. Rumbold showed his wild enthusiasm by a contraction of the facial muscles which amounted almost to a smile and the Jap beamed benevolently through his glasses as though he had just eaten a most excellent dinner and felt at peace with the world. Just before the end of the meeting Venizelos, on behalf of Ismet and himself, thanked all those who had helped in reaching this happy solution, including the "Observer" and we all got up and shook hands all round. . . .

At the beginning of the second phase of the Conference the corridors buzzed with the Chester Concession, and it was generally believed that one of our main duties at Lausanne was to protect that undertaking. As a matter of fact, the Chester Concession, as such, was never officially mentioned at the Conference. Our fight was made on the principle of the open door and we won it on that issue.

Without going into the various developments concerning the question of concessions, I will pass directly to the point where we were suddenly confronted one day with an article which the British and French intended to incorporate in the treaty

or in a protocol to the treaty, providing that all pre-war concessionary contracts upon which work had actually begun,
or which had been the subject of negotiations, even if all the
formalities concerning them had not been fulfilled, should be
regarded by the Turkish Government as valid and maintained.
At this time I was working more or less in the dark because
these plans had been formulated by the Allies in private meetings from which I was excluded, and without full information
regarding their intentions it would have been impossible to
safeguard our interests. Fortunately, it proved possible to meet
this situation, and, from that moment, we were enabled to
keep in close touch with every step taken and every plan
formulated by our friends the enemy.[12]

It appeared that the proposed article was intended to cover

[12] Ismet Pasha informed Mr. Grew of the Allied plans on June 5. The record
of the conversation reads: ". . . He then turned to the subject of concessions
and said that the Allies were trying to force him into agreeing to a provision
in the treaty confirming pre-war concessions which had not been made legally
valid, but upon which work had commenced before the war. This he said
was directly aimed at the Chester Concession and he implied that he might be
obliged to give in to the pressure of the Allies in the cause of peace. He asked
me what I thought about it. I said: 'Do I understand that Your Excellency,
who has continually fought for the establishment of the sovereignty and legal
rights of Turkey, now contemplates abandoning those rights under pressure
from the Allies?' Ismet replied that the Allies were trying to make a political
issue of a legal question. I said that the United States had full confidence that
the Turkish Government would not yield on so important a question of principle. I said that the United States had not negotiated the Chester Concession;
that it was a purely private agreement with a private company, but that we
were very much interested in the matter of principle which appeared to be
at stake. Ismet said: 'What would be the attitude of the United States if we
should yield?' I replied: 'I fear that such a situation might have a serious
effect on the relations between the United States and Turkey.' Ismet continued
to set forth his difficult position. I said: 'I take full note of what you say.' He
replied: 'Let us talk about the matter again tomorrow night, after you have
had an opportunity to go into the matter.' I said: 'I cannot see that I shall
be able to add anything tomorrow night to what I am saying now.' I added
that if Ismet was intimating that I should bring pressure to bear on the
Allies in the matter, I must make it clear to him that I could not regard this
question as one calling for negotiations between the United States and the
Allies. On the contrary, it seemed to be purely one between the Allies and the
Turks. After some further conversation along the same lines, lasting for well
over an hour, during which I firmly maintained my attitude, Ismet took his
departure."

the interests of one French and two British companies, namely
the Régie Générale des Chemins de Fer, the Vickers-Armstrongs Company, and the Turkish Petroleum Company. With
regard to the claims of the first I had personally much sympathy.
In 1914 they had been granted by the then Turkish Government the concession of building the Samsoun-Sivas Railway
and constructing the port of Samsoun, and, on the basis of the
agreement, the French Company had begun work, while the
French Government had arranged for a considerable loan of
several million francs, the money on which had already been
advanced to Turkey before the outbreak of the war. Everything was in order except that the Turkish Parliament, although it had ratified the loan, had never actually ratified the
concession, and, therefore, while the French had every moral
and equitable right to the concession, their claim was legally
incomplete. When the Chester Concession was given at the
beginning of this year, the new Turkish Government made it
a condition of the whole concession that the American concern should take over also the contract formerly given to
France. Whether they did this with the deliberate intention
of playing us off against the French at the Conference, or
whether they did it merely because they wished to have a politically disinterested country undertake the greater part of Turkey's reconstruction, is an open question. At any rate, we could
not permit the Allies to make use of a peace treaty in order to
give legal validity to incomplete or invalid contracts in contravention to the principle of the open door.

The Vickers-Armstrongs concession was for the construction
of docks and naval arsenals and was more or less on the same
status as the alleged concession to the French company.

As for the Turkish Petroleum Company's alleged concession for the Mosul oil fields, this depended purely and simply
on a single letter from Said Halim, a former Turkish Grand
Vizier, to the British Ambassador in Constantinople in 1914,
and, far from being legally valid, could not be regarded as
having even a moral or equitable claim. For three years past
our Government had been in correspondence with the British

Government with regard to the matter and had repeatedly offered arbitration, which the British Government refused, thereby indicating the weakness of its position.

I protested in turn to each of the Allies against the proposed article.[13] Pellé, the French delegate, was frank and open about the matter and said he must fight for what France considered her legitimate rights, but that he would do nothing behind my back. Rumbold said that the provision was intended to protect the French company, and said: "How would you feel if you had paid millions of dollars on a concession and then had it taken away from you?" I replied that I should probably feel just the way the French did and that if the Turks had given away something which did not largely belong to them, they should certainly compensate the other party, but that in our opinion controversies of this kind should be settled by arbitration and not by the provisions of the peace treaty where the interests of one party to the dispute were to be left out of consideration. I asked him then if the article in question was not intended to protect certain British interests also. Rumbold replied that he was not very familiar with the subject, but that, so far as he was aware, no British interests were involved. He, however, agreed to consult his economic expert and inform me if he were mistaken. A day or two later the economic expert came to me, looking rather sheepish, and said that the interests of the Turkish Petroleum Company were to a certain extent involved in the question at issue. We smiled sweetly to ourselves and proceeded to battle. I drew up a list of fifteen arguments expressing our objections to the obnoxious clause and, in the course of further talks with the Allied delegates, I drew this pretentious-looking document from my pocket and said I regretted that it would be necessary for me to elaborate these fifteen points at the conference table and to give them immediately to the press if the Allies continued with their intention of forcing the objectionable article into the treaty. The Allies were never given a chance to see those fifteen points, but they apparently had all the effect of the proverbial sword

13 See *Foreign Relations, 1923*, II, 1021–22, for the text.

of Damocles, as a few days later one of the Allies — Montagna,
who was neutral in the dispute, came to see me, obviously at
the instigation of the others, and in the course of casual conversation inquired whether it was really my intention to use
these fifteen points in the open conference. I replied very precisely in the affirmative. A couple of days later I was informed
that the obnoxious article had been dropped.

We had, however, only just begun to congratulate ourselves
on victory when it was confidentially revealed to me that the
objectionable article had been replaced by three other articles
each aiming to cover the interests of one of the three companies
previously mentioned. Rumbold remarked that as my former
opposition had been directed exclusively against the general
principle at stake, on the ground that it was dangerously broad,
I could not now object when it was limited strictly to three
specific concerns, but he took occasion to give orders that I
was not to be shown the text of these three new articles until
they had actually been incorporated in the treaty.

I did, however, obtain the texts and went promptly to each
of the Allies and said that, whereas up until now I had merely
let Ismet talk to me and had confined my representations to
them alone, I should now actively fight with Ismet and do
everything in my power to strengthen his resistance to these
entirely inequitable provisions.[14] The Allies held another meeting and drew up a formula for the Turkish Petroleum Company which stated merely that "the rights acquired by the
Turkish Petroleum Company in 1914 shall be valid and maintained."

The new formula was conveyed to me late one evening and
I sought the opinion of Ismet and one of the Allies who was
neutral in the dispute. They both said that they and their
legal experts considered the formula wholly innocuous and
was merely to save the face of the British, because if no rights
had been legally acquired in 1914, the formula meant literally
and exactly nothing. That is the way it appeared to me and,
when I consulted my own staff, every one of them, including

14 See *ibid.*, pp. 1025–34.

our legal expert from the Solicitor's office of the Department, agreed with my opinion. It was then after midnight and we had to get a telegram off to Washington immediately. It was finished about 4 A.M. I explained the situation to the Department and added a sentence to the effect that if the Department felt that the Allies had honestly tried to meet our views and were now merely saving their faces with the Turks, I felt that we should show our appreciation by abstaining from comment at the conference table when the new formula was brought up for incorporation in the treaty. We slept on it and already in the morning began to look at the matter in another light. We said to ourselves either this new formula must have some legal significance or it is utter nonsense. By nightfall, after having discussed the subject all day, we were sure of it, and I had begun to steel myself for the blast which I felt sure would arrive from the Department on the following morning. It came, sure enough, in six sections, and began with the ominous words "I desire you," which indicated clearly the august hand which wrote it [15] and it left nothing whatever to the imagination. It said, in effect, that if this formula were incorporated in the treaty it would mean a great diplomatic victory for the British and that we were to "go to it." [16] We did. For the next week I camped on everybody's trail until I made myself about as popular as a fox in a hen roost and during the last two days and nights before the meeting I saw Ismet seven times and told him repeatedly that the United States expected every Turk to do his duty.[17] I told Ismet that at the final meeting

[15] It was from Charles Evans Hughes. — J. C. G.

[16] The Department's telegram stated: "The Turkish Petroleum Company's alleged rights have been in dispute for so long that if the British are now successful in getting them validated that success would inevitably be regarded as an important diplomatic triumph. Such victory should not be won by our own surrender, and any reservation we make should be contrived as effectively as possible." *Ibid.*, p. 1031.

[17] On July 12, 1923, Mr. Montagna, in a conversation with Mr. Grew said: ". . . see Ismet and urge him not to approach any of the Allies, but simply wait. They would not dare break the Conference on the subject of concessions as Italy would not agree and as public opinion would not approve. He said it was perfectly safe for me to tell Ismet that there was absolutely no danger of a

he must expect to be grilled and browbeaten and pulled through a sieve, but that if he stood firm he would win in the end. Ismet kept saying, "But how do I know that peace will not depend upon this issue and that the Allies will not break the Conference and declare war?" I said, "Ismet, the Allies will not go to war nor break the Conference on this issue because they know their position is unsound and because they could never go before the public opinion of the world and say that they had sacrificed peace on such a basis." [18]

The final meeting — from which I was excluded — lasted from 5 P.M. until 2 A.M. the next morning, with a short ad-journment for dinner. I received bulletins from time to time, Ismet was receiving treatment which would make the third degree in a Harlem police station seem like a club dinner. He had deep circles around his eyes, his hair was standing on end, and he looked completely worn out, but was still holding his ground manfully in spite of all assaults. The final result reached me about three in the morning. It appears that after a last onslaught at 2 A.M. the Allies capitulated and agreed to drop all mention of the Turkish Petroleum Company from the treaty and to provide for compensation for the other two com-panies in a way to which we could not possibly take exception. I saw Ismet the next morning and he looked ten years older, but we had won our fight. . . .

At the closing meeting of the Third Committee of the Con-ference on July 17, 1923, Mr. Grew made the following state-ment:

"The successful conclusion of the Lausanne Conference has now been achieved. It is too early, doubtless, and we are too

break. In any case there would be no break until an ultimatum had first been issued and he, Montagna, would advise me before any such situation arose. Ismet was very tired at the end of the meeting today and looked a broken man."

18 In a memorandum of this talk with Ismet Mr. Grew said: "Throughout all of these recent conversations with Ismet I have continually drummed into him the importance of standing firm and the danger of showing any weakness."

close to the stress and turmoil of negotiation to value the result secured at its true worth, in all its many beneficial aspects. But we need feel no hesitation in describing this result as momentous. A long period of warfare and disturbance affecting the whole of the Near East has been brought to a close; numberless problems of great difficulty and intricacy have been solved through the patience, moderation and the conciliatory spirit of the Delegations; we can now look forward with confidence to the coming period of reconstruction when the ideals of peace and tolerance which have inspired the deliberations of the Conference will receive a long and fruitful application.

"The United States welcomes today's achievement and on behalf of my Government I have the honor to express to the Delegations here assembled sincere congratulations upon the successful outcome of their labors."

XXI

The American - Turkish Treaty Negotiations
JUNE – AUGUST, 1923

The Allied-Turkish settlement at Lausanne contained a number of provisions of particular concern to the United States:
(1) The Capitulations: *The capitulations were abrogated and replaced by a system "based on respect for the independence and sovereignty of states." Non-Moslem nationals of the Allies, however, were for a period of seven years to be accorded the right to apply to courts in their own countries for the adjudication of questions involving their personal status or domestic relations. Furthermore, the Turkish Government agreed to take into its service a number of European legal advisers who would participate in the work of legislative commissions, observe and report to the Minister of Justice on the operation of the Turkish courts, receive complaints growing out of the administration of justice, the execution of sentences, and the application of the laws.*

(2) Philanthropic, Educational and Religious Institutions: *Turkey agreed to recognize the existence of such British, French, and Italian institutions as had been recognized as existing before October 30, 1914. These institutions were to be treated on a footing of equality with similar Turkish institutions in regard to fiscal charges, and they were to be subject to Turkish laws, regulations, and administrative arrangements of a public character.*

(3) The Open Door: *The Allies agreed to the principle of equality of economic opportunity, and no provisions for spheres of economic influence in Turkey were incorporated in the Treaty. The application of this doctrine to Mesopotamia, however, was left to later discussion.*

(4) Minorities: *Turkey agreed to assure full and complete protection of life and liberty to all inhabitants without distinction of birth, nationality, language, race, or religion. Turkey pledged that non-Moslem minorities should enjoy the same civil and political rights as Moslems and should have an equal right to establish and control charitable, religious, social, and educational institutions, with the right to use their own language and exercise their own religion therein. These guarantees to the non-Moslem minorities were placed under the guarantee of the League of Nations.*

(5) The Straits: *The principle of "freedom of transit and of navigation, by sea and by air, in time of peace as in time of war" was recognized subject to conformity with specific regulations prescribed in the Straits convention. The zone of the Straits was to be demilitarized. An International Straits Commission was to be established at Constantinople under the auspices of the League of Nations.*

As early as November, 1922 — during the first phase of the Lausanne Conference — informal talks had taken place between the American and Turkish delegations concerning a treaty between the two nations. The United States decided to negotiate such a treaty rather than adhere to any of the agreements in the Allied-Turkish settlement. "In the light of the traditional policy of the United States," Edgar W. Turlington, Assistant to the Solicitor, Department of State, wrote in 1924, "it was hardly to be expected that this Government would participate, either with the League of Nations or otherwise, in the guaranty of the security of the non-Moslem minorities in Turkey contemplated in the treaty of peace signed at Lausanne, or that it would agree, as the Allied Powers and Turkey did in the Straits convention, to take any measures which the Council of the League of Nations might decide upon to meet attacks upon the security of the demilitarized zone of the Straits." [1]

After a number of preliminary discussions, Ismet Pasha pro-

[1] "The American Treaty of Lausanne," *World Peace Foundation Pamphlets,* VII, 590–91.

posed to Mr. Grew on May 5, 1923, that formal negotiations for a treaty be started. Before these negotiations were started, however, Mr. Grew explained to the Allied delegates that this "would be done on the clear understanding that we would not sign such a treaty until the Turks had signed a treaty of peace with the Allies." [2]

Early in June, the American and Turkish delegations started their formal meetings although experts in each delegation had already been exchanging views. [3] *Working with Mr. Grew in the American delegation were Frederic Dolbeare, G. Howland Shaw, F. Lammot Belin, Edgar Turlington, and Maynard Barnes.*

In a letter to Allen Dulles, Chief of the Division of Near Eastern Affairs in the Department of State, Mr. Grew said of the delegation on May 14, 1923: "I do not think a more useful group could have been chosen, for each supplies something that the others lack, either in background or psychology. We hold cabinet meetings on every issue and with very few exceptions our opinions have been unanimous. In the few cases where a difference of opinion has arisen, it has later been shown that the opinion of the majority was wise and the others have freely acknowledged it. I do not think that we can go far wrong or take any unsound position when the combined judgment of these men is brought to bear on every question and I am profoundly grateful to the Department for its wisdom in selecting such a staff."

Mr. Grew was unable to keep a daily diary of the American-Turkish negotiations. He did, however, record his conversations with Ismet Pasha. These conversations reveal the major issues at conflict between the two countries, and they, also, reflect the give and take of diplomatic negotiations.

Conversation   Lausanne, June 20, 1923, 4 P.M.
                        Ismet Pasha
    I called on Ismet Pasha and took up with him the question

---

[2] Conversation with Sir Horace Rumbold, May 1, 1923.

[3] See *Foreign Relations, 1923*, II, 1076–86, for the American draft of the proposed treaty.

of his making a voluntary declaration on behalf of the Grand National Assembly to me as American Plenipotentiary embodying the provisions contained in the Minorities Clauses, Nos. 36 to 44 in the Treaty with the Allies, but omitting reference to the League of Nations. I spoke at length on the importance of favorably influencing American public opinion which would have to be reckoned with when our Treaty came up for ratification and I said that the Department of State was receiving inquiries from all over the country as to whether our treaty would provide for the protection of minorities.[4]

Ismet invoked the argument that such a declaration would be a unilateral engagement legally binding upon Turkey but subject neither to the reciprocal character of Turkey's minority agreements with the Balkan States nor to the control exercised by the League of Nations over the minority provisions in the treaty with the Allies. It appears impossible to convince him that we are not trying to bind Turkey beyond her present engagements. The argument regarding American public opinion carried little weight as Ismet invariably fell back on the assertion that Turkish public opinion must be equally considered. He referred continually to the good will if not open favoritism which Turkey has shown to the United States and clearly stated that if we were to request such a minority declaration it would create a most painful impression at Angora. He took the position that we ourselves had influenced the negotiation of the treaty with the Allies, particularly the Minorities Clauses, by our active participation and statements in the Conference and that since these clauses are aimed to protect all minorities the publication of the clauses in the United States together with a statement as to the part we took in influencing their acceptance should suffice to reassure the American public. He added that Turkey intends that her future acts shall speak even louder than her words. . . .

---

[4] Secretary of State Hughes cabled Mr. Grew on June 11, 1923: "A large part of the American public is keenly interested in provisions for the protection of minorities in Turkey, and the Department feels that this country would fail to approve an arrangement with Turkey which did not deal with this subject." *Ibid.*, p. 1087.

Conversation   Lausanne, July 20, 1923, 11 A.M.
                    Ismet Pasha

. . . Ismet Pasha came to see me by appointment at 11 o'clock
this morning and we remained in discussion until 1.15. . . .

Ismet began by referring to the six or seven matters which
have not yet been settled by the experts and asked if I thought
that they could be settled within four or five days, or whether
it might not be preferable to sign a treaty on the basis of what
had already been accomplished and to leave the other matters
for future negotiations. I replied that this was not at all our
point of view. We had both entered upon these negotiations, as
Ismet himself had pointed out in his original note, with the
intention of continuing them to a conclusion and we fully intended to remain in Lausanne as long as might be necessary
to reach this conclusion. We regarded this treaty, which was
to revise all relations between the United States and Turkey, as
an important document in which all matters pertaining to the
relations of our two countries should be dealt with and settled
as a unit, so far as it was physically possible to do so. Ismet then
said that this was also his understanding and that he had every
intention of remaining in Lausanne until a settlement was
reached. His assurances on this point appeared to me to be sincere and that he intends to act in good faith, though he might
personally prefer to postpone the negotiation of certain sections
of our treaty.

Ismet then suggested that we survey the outstanding points
and we began with:

Most Favored Nation Clause

He explained at length the objections of his Government to
most favored nation treatment as this was associated in the
Turkish mind with the Capitulations and they felt that national
treatment, being always in excess of, or equal to, most favored
nation treatment, should be fully satisfactory. He did not argue
the matter in detail or in connection with specific provisions,
but dwelt on the principle alone. I replied by citing our own
arguments and spoke of the general use of the most favored
nation clause in international agreements and the importance

which my Government attached to it as a basic principle in our present treaty. . . .

I then said that we appreciated the antipathy of the Turkish Government to the actual phrase "most favored nation treatment" and that we wished to go as far as possible in meeting the Turkish point of view in matters of this kind, for which they had such definite dislike. Therefore, in order to show our good will, we had expressed our willingness to consider a substitute phrase which would give us the principle in fact while avoiding the distasteful phrase. . . .

My Government could not consider any text which did not embody the general principle under discussion. Ismet did not reply and passed on to the next subject.

Naturalization

Ismet spoke of the Turkish law which prevented the return to Turkey of Turkish subjects who had been naturalized abroad and also of their desire to make emigration and expatriation as difficult as possible. I in turn spoke of the importance which my Government attached to this article and developed at some length our sound objection to a provision to the effect that naturalized American citizens of Turkish origin cannot return to Turkey on the basis of (A) the prejudice which such a provision would bring to bear on the right of a sovereign state to exclude from its territory, under the accepted principles of international law, persons whom it considers undesirable. The acceptance of such a provision in a treaty article would indicate that a sovereign state possesses such a right only by virtue of treaty stipulation and (B) that the inclusion of such a provision in our treaty would cause serious difficulty with a large section of our American population composed of naturalized citizens and would also undoubtedly make it impossible to secure ratification in the Senate. I spoke about our own naturalization laws and described the provision which would make it impossible for an American citizen of Turkish origin to return for any length of time to Turkey. I then spoke of our naturalization treaty of 1874 which was negotiated but on account of minor difficulties never went into effect. This treaty neverthe-

less was concluded subsequent to the Turkish law to which
Ismet Pasha referred and if a satisfactory formula had been
found at that time to obviate the difficulties it could certainly
be found now. I therefore suggested that the matter be referred
to the experts to reopen and study the subject on the basis of
our treaty of 1874 and to try to find a satisfactory formula.
Ismet concurred.

Judicial Declaration

Ismet then turned to the Judicial Declaration which he intends to address to us and explained in detail why he would
find it difficult to make any modifications in the text or to
distinguish it in any way from the declaration he is making to
the Allies. He said that the declaration was in effect addressed
to the world and applied to all countries equally. If he were
to omit the word "European" and alter the phrase "countries
who fought in the war of 1914–1918" to "countries which were
not belligerent against Turkey," it would lay Turkey open to
charges of discrimination, unless she did the same for many
other countries, including Germany and Russia, each declaration to apply to the country in question. Ismet described the
origin of the declaration which was based on the insistence of
the Allies on a transitory regime after the abolition of the capitulations. This was a very tender subject with the Turkish
Government and he had explicit instructions from Angora not
to modify or enlarge the declaration in any way.

In reply I developed the arguments which I had previously
presented to him, making it clear that this modification would
involve no real discrimination as the United States was in a
different position from the other Powers he had mentioned,
having been present at the Conference of Lausanne and having
taken an active part in the discussions, and also that it would
be taken in the United States as a discourtesy if the declaration,
when addressed to us, should not be made applicable to the
circumstances. I said we had no desire whatever to force our
advisers on Turkey; we simply wished to leave the way open.
Ismet himself had told me that Turkey would undoubtedly
desire much technical advice in the future and would undoubt-

edly turn to America on account of her political disinterestedness to supply such advice. The modifications in the declaration which we proposed would neither bind nor hamper Turkey in any way. It would leave her as free as before, but would please instead of displease the American people and Senate. My Government felt very strongly in regard to this matter. Ismet did not pursue the subject and we turned to the next point.

Capitulations

Ismet developed the Turkish viewpoint with regard to the importance of a clause in our treaty providing explicitly for the abrogation of the capitulations and spoke of the acceptance by the Allies of this point. He said that Turkey wished to begin a clean page and to eradicate the capitulations completely at this time.

In reply I pointed out that we ourselves desired to wipe the slate clean and to start afresh in all our relations and that we felt this could be best done by omitting all reference to the capitulations in our treaty. We felt that our present treaty, since it would supersede and abrogate all former treaties, would automatically abolish the capitulations without the necessity of reference thereto. We perceived serious objections to such reference and among others I mentioned the fact that it would tend to impair our capitulatory rights in other countries. Ismet asked me to explain this point, as it was not clear to him. I said that I would do so in due course, but that I first wished to develop our attitude at greater length. I said that I had encountered considerable difficulty with my own Government with regard to many of the material concessions which we had already made to meet the Turkish point of view in drafting the treaty and that certain difficulties with my Government were still to be overcome if possible. In spite of this I still desired to go even farther to meeting the Turkish viewpoint in matters to which I knew they attached great importance, and I fully realized that one of these was the capitulations. I was therefore prepared to try to help Ismet to make this treaty acceptable to his Government, but it could only be done if he would help me in other difficult matters which I would later mention. Having this in mind, I said that I was prepared to recommend to my Government, although my instructions were that no mention of the capitulations should be made in the treaty, that a formula be found to meet the Turkish point of view. In any case such a formula would have to make perfectly clear the following points:

(a) That the United States and Turkey *both* agree to the abrogation of the capitulations;

(b) That American recognition of their abolition shall have no retroactive effect;

(c) That the formula will be so phrased as not to impair our capitulatory rights in other countries.

At this point Ismet asked in what other countries we had capitulatory rights. I said I was not certain that I could mention them all offhand, but that among others were China, Egypt and Morocco. Any implication of unilateral abrogation would tend to impair those rights. I then proposed, in an entirely provisional way, and making it perfectly clear that I should first have to obtain the approval of my Government, which might prove difficult, the following formula:

The High Contracting Parties, each in so far as it is concerned, agree by common consent to the abrogation of the Capitulations.

Ismet wrote this formula down in Turkish after translation by Hussein Bey and asked if his experts had studied it. I replied that I was not aware of this. Ismet intimated that he would discuss it with them. Before leaving the subject I again pointed out quite clearly that if I obtained my Government's approval to this formula it would be a very material concession on our part and that Ismet would have to do everything in his power to make it less difficult by meeting our viewpoint in other matters.

Claims

Ismet then turned to claims and remarked that the Allies had liquidated their claims in the treaty. Turkey was willing to consider our claims prior to 1914, but could not undertake to give governmental consideration to claims subsequent to that date. [5] I immediately inquired as to the intention of his remark, since we had not been at war with Turkey and that there therefore appeared to be no reason whatever for making any discrimination in categories of claims according to date. Ismet did not reply to this inquiry but said he felt we should liquidate our own claims by sharing in the money already turned over to the Allies. I indicated marked resentment to this observation and said that we could give this proposal no consideration whatever, as we were in an entirely different position from the Allies. I then developed our argument for submitting claims to a Mixed Arbitral Tribunal and the disadvantages to both our countries of embarrassing our future diplomatic relations by saddling our next diplomatic representative with the responsibility of pressing a mass of unpaid claims. I said that this was another case of starting with a clean page. Turkey, in accepting our proposal, does not admit responsibility in all claims. She simply agrees to accept decisions of an impartial arbitral court upon which she will be equally represented with the United States. My Government stands absolutely firm on the necessity of a provision by which claims will in the last instance, at least, be referred to a mixed arbitral tribunal. As for the intermediate steps which are to lead up to that court of last instance, I desire to do everything possible to meet Ismet's views. We are willing to submit our claims to a bureau of the Turkish Government for examination. I said that this was a matter of the utmost importance to our Government and unless Ismet could meet our views in this respect, I was not optimistic of being able to persuade my Gov-

5 These were the claims of private American citizens against the Turkish Government for such things as the destruction of property. The issue was not settled in the Treaty; instead further discussion in Constantinople between representatives of the two countries led to an agreement for a mixed commission to study the claims. The mixed commission was to be established six months after the American-Turkish Treaty was ratified.

ernment to meet the Turkish views with regard to the capitulations or other matters.

Ismet observed that Turkey was not rich and that he could not subject his country to a financial burden of this kind. I replied that Turkey must certainly pay her just obligations. The method of settlement might be open to discussion.

The Straits

Ismet then turned to the Straits and said that their experts were endeavoring to find a formula which would be satisfactory. He stated that they had no objection to the United States having free passage in the Straits, but any such provision should be based on the Straits Convention with the Allies. I said I felt sure the experts would find a solution. . . .

In the intervening period from July 21 to August 1, Mr. Grew and Ismet Pasha had met regularly and discussed again and again the differences of opinion over the minorities, the capitulations, the claims of private American citizens, and the naturalization problem. On July 25 Mr. Grew cabled Secretary Hughes: "I gained hardly anything from Ismet tonight in a dispute lasting nearly four hours. . . . My feeling is that the negotiations will now develop into a test of tenacity, and will hinge upon the claims question." Foreign Relations, 1923, *II,* 1120.

Conversation   Lausanne, August 1, 1923, 7.45 P.M.
                    Ismet Pasha

After Turlington had discussed our last claims article with Munir Bey during the afternoon, I called on Ismet Pasha at 8.45 and stayed until about 9.15 P.M. I described the steps which we had taken successively to meet the Turkish point of view on claims and how at last my Government was willing to accept the principle of the two steps which Ismet had envisaged for dealing with claims, namely: (1) consideration of categories and (2) consideration of individual claims under accepted categories. I said that this final concession was an indication of great good will and conciliation on the part of the United States and that in the formula which we were now proposing we had tried simply to make the Turkish position with regard to the two successive steps more clear. I now learned, however, that Ismet desired to inject an entirely new element into the situation, namely: a provision to the effect that the nationals, companies and associations mentioned in the formula must have had American nationality according to Turkish law at the time of the origin of the claim. I said that this proposal would undoubtedly cause serious difficulty and complication, as it tended to reopen the whole controversy regarding the naturalization of Turkish citizens in the United States which, in order to make the situation easier for the Turkish Delegation, we had agreed tacitly to drop by eliminating the naturalization article.

I discussed the subject at length and finally appealed to him, for the sake of a settlement at Lausanne, not to press his point of view. Ismet said that he had no desire to bring up the question of naturalization again, but that his Government simply wished to prevent the submission of claims by persons who were not American citizens at the time the claims originated. He was acting under instructions from Angora and must insist upon the inclusion of the point. I then referred to the date of October 29, 1914 which had been included in the Turkish counter-formula and asked Ismet if this meant that Turkey recognized the American naturalization of Turkish subjects prior to that date. Ismet seemed somewhat embarrassed and replied in the negative. I said, "Then why do you put the date in the formula?" Ismet replied that it had been done in order to comply with the provision in the Allied Treaty. I pointed out that our treaty was entirely different, and after calling in Munir Bey, Ismet and he drew up another formula omitting the date in question. I examined the new formula and said that it was fully as objectionable as the first. I then spoke of our traditional view that all American citizens are equally entitled to the protection and assistance of their Government irrespective of the manner in which they acquired their American nationality and I said that I had no reason to suppose that

our Government would be prepared to consider the abandonment of its traditional view in this respect. The question
presented was one of detail which it would appear, to be in the
spirit of the formula suggested by Ismet, should be postponed
for later consideration. Any such provision in the treaty would
add greatly to the already considerable difficulties attendant
upon securing the ratification of our treaty by the Senate.

I was faced in this meeting by four members of the Turkish
Delegation, namely: Ismet Pasha, Riza Nour Bey, Munir Bey
and Hussein Bey. Munir Bey and Riza Nour Bey talked
volubly to Ismet after I had stated our point of view and gave
me the impression by their tone that they were trying to persuade Ismet to drop this question of nationality.

I also discussed with Ismet the question of "entitled" in the
first paragraph of our formula. Munir Bey in a carefully
phrased argument which seemed to me well-presented and
juridically sound explained why they objected to this word on
the ground that the standard under which categories of claims
would be entitled to consideration was not specified. He
pointed out that the phrase left the matter open to too broad
an interpretation.

I then appealed to Ismet once more to meet us in a conciliatory way by dropping the question of naturalization if we
should drop the word "entitled." Ismet who, at this time was
beginning to look at his watch and appeared ready for dinner,
said that he would discuss the matter with his experts and give
me a reply later in the evening. Munir Bey called on Turlington late in the evening and came to the provisional agreement
reported in our telegram No. 578.[6]

6 Telegram 578 in part read: "It is evident that the Turkish Government
believes that something of the sort is necessary; to us it seems innocuous,
though open to obvious objections. A statement by Ismet will read as follows:
"'From the point of view of the Turkish delegation this article implies no
obligation on the part of the Turkish Government to receive for registration
claims presented by the Government of the United States on behalf of persons
who under Turkish law are deemed to be Turkish citizens.'
"My reply will read as follows:
"'I take note of Your Excellency's declaration and I have to say that this

During the course of the discussion Ismet said that Turkish law did not necessarily prevent Turkish citizens from becoming naturalized Americans. There were cases in which the Turkish Government had given permission for them to do so. The law simply prevented their returning to Turkey.

Conversation   Lausanne, August 4, 1923, 6 P.M.
                        Ismet Pasha

After discussing the last claims formula with our staff,[7] I called on Ismet and said that in order not to overturn all our negotiations, I was now willing to adopt a previous proposal made by Mustafa Cherif Bey and Tahir Bey to the effect that all mention of claims should be omitted from the Treaty and that there should be an exchange of notes in which I should reserve for my Government full liberty of action with regard to presenting the Treaty to the Senate until the question of claims should have been settled and in which he would reply acknowledging my statement. I handed Ismet a copy of the proposed note that I should write him. Ismet left the room to consult with his experts and returned in about twenty minutes stating that he accepted this proposal and explaining approximately what he would say in his note replying to mine. As it was now too late to sign the Treaty today owing to the fact that the printing office was closed, we arranged that it should be signed on Monday afternoon. I said I had no reason to believe that my Government would disapprove of this last provisional arrangement, but that I could not guarantee to sign the Treaty until a final word was received from Washington. I told Ismet that I should proceed to Berne tonight and return on Monday morning. He said he would see that all arrangements were made and that the hour for signing should be set.

declaration does not prejudice the rights of American citizens under the laws of the United States.'

"Each of us will then observe that his Government adheres to its position." *Ibid.*, pp. 1134–35.

7 On August 4, the Turkish delegation rejected the proposal mentioned in telegram 578. The Turkish counterproposal in *ibid.*, p. 1135, was unacceptable to the United States.

When I got up to go he expressed with considerable feeling his satisfaction at the prospect of signature.

The American-Turkish Treaty regarding general relations as well as a separate extradition treaty were signed at Lausanne on August 6. A separate undertaking with respect to the treatment of American philanthropic, educational, and religious institutions in Turkey had been given to Mr. Grew on August 4. On this same day, Ismet Pasha also gave Mr. Grew a copy of the Turkish declaration concerning the administration of justice in Turkey. [8] At the meeting when Mr. Grew signed the treaties, he said:

"The Treaties which have been signed today have an important and definite purpose. They are designed to bring up to date the relations between the United States and Turkey so as to permit a close and useful co-operation between the two countries. Turkey during the past few years has been the scene of events of far-reaching significance and as a consequence her relations with other countries have been greatly modified. This alteration in Turkey's external position is closely connected with changes in her system of Government and in her political ideals. It seems fitting that these changes, which consist essentially in the adaptation and working out of ideals and principles of democracy, should furnish the occasion and the fundamental reason for the conclusion of treaties with the United States. We sincerely hope that co-operation between the two countries, which cannot but be facilitated by the present treaties, will continue to develop and will prove to be an important factor in the carrying out of those ideals.

"There is additional fitness in today's act. Not only are we establishing the relations between an older and a younger democracy on a solid foundation, but we are taking this step upon the territory of a country which has strikingly demonstrated its ability to enlist people of different language and religions in the service of the ideals of democracy and self-

8 See *ibid.*, pp. 1139–42, for the copy.

government. The hospitality which has been accorded us with such unstinted generosity by Switzerland, the Canton of Vaud and the City of Lausanne has been an inspiration throughout our negotiations and is an element inseparably associated with the results achieved.

"I cannot close without a word of cordial friendship and personal respect for His Excellency Ismet Pasha and for his colleagues. In our own country many famous soldiers have become famous statesmen and the quality that has most contributed to their success has been the quality of directness — the clear grasp of an issue, the clear presentation of a point of view. This quality on the part of Ismet Pasha has contributed to the success of our negotiations. I permit myself to say that I shall always remember with pleasure our relations at Lausanne. At the same time I should like to record my appreciation of the co-operation of the experts of the Turkish delegation and to thank them warmly for the important contribution which they have made to the success of the negotiations which we are bringing to a close today with the signature of the Treaties."

To Secretary of State Hughes, from Lausanne,
August 6, 1923

The Treaty of Amity and Commerce which we have signed today with the Turkish Delegation is far from what I should have wished to have it. It represents a considerably greater number of concessions on our part to meet the Turkish point of view than concessions on their part to meet ours. Among other concessions we have given up the articles on naturalization and claims, we have failed to obtain the desired modifications in the Judicial Declaration and we have failed to obtain any provision whatever with regard to minorities.

On the other hand, it was we who laid the original draft treaty before the Turks. Had they first submitted their own draft, the principal concessions would doubtless have been on the other side of the column. Our obtaining most favored nation treatment in the establishment articles was perhaps the most important principle gained.

Whatever may be the fate of this treaty in the Senate and however it may disappoint the American people,[9] I feel, and this feeling is shared by every member of our delegation, after careful study of the situation as it existed and has developed, that more favorable terms could not have been obtained at this time and that it is at least open to doubt whether even equally favorable terms could be obtained later.

As regards our tactics during the negotiations, it may well have seemed to the Department that at times we have appeared overimpressed by Ismet's "last words" and the indications of his early departure from Lausanne. I do not think that our anxiety was unjustified. When the date of the opening of the National Assembly was fixed for August 3rd, there is no doubt that Ismet had planned to be in Angora for that date. We were continually confronted with the possible danger to our interests of allowing him to leave before signature and the disadvantages, fully recognized by the Department, of a postponement of the negotiations. Had we not made the tentative concessions on naturalization, the judicial declaration and the capitulations article when we did, I believe he might and probably would have gone. If our negotiations were to have been a matter of "trading," it could be held that Ismet had played a subtle and clever game. But we do not and cannot feel that the question of trading entered into these negotiations at all. We can only conjecture how much importance he attached to signing the treaty here, but we are all convinced that he would not have signed it, now or later, with the inclusion of the features to which the Turkish Government objected. I therefore feel that our concessions were made at the proper moment and were essential to the conclusion of the negotiations.

Throughout our negotiations we have all felt that the Turks were essentially honest. I have this impression very strongly as a result of numerous conferences with Ismet and I find that the other members of our Delegation have the same feeling as a result of their meetings with the Turkish experts. The bar-

9 The Treaty was defeated in the Senate by six votes. See Chapter XXIII for a discussion of the issues involved.

gaining method, as I have said before, was not in evidence; the Turks were logical and frank in their methods. They knew at the start what they wanted and what they were prepared to give and we are convinced that no considerations or tactics would have led them to depart from their position in any appreciable degree. . . .

Before closing, I should like respectfully to express my full appreciation of the support and encouragement which the Department has given us throughout these negotiations and further to record in the highest terms my commendation of the efficient work, sound judgment and admirable spirit of every member of our staff throughout the Conference and our own negotiations.[10]

In 1924, Edgar W. Turlington, Assistant to the Solicitor, Department of State, summarized the American-Turkish Treaty in the following manner: "Briefly stated, the principal provisions of the arrangement constituted between the United States and Turkey by the treaty, the letters and the declaration, are as follows:

"1. The contracting parties join in declaring the régime of the capitulations in Turkey to be completely abrogated. In matters of personal status, domestic relations and personal succession, which were formerly within the jurisdiction of American consular tribunals, American citizens in Turkey are to be subject exclusively to the jurisdiction of American tribunals or authorities sitting outside Turkey. American citizens, equally with the nationals of the Allied countries, will benefit by the execution of the declaration regarding the administration of justice in Turkey.

"2. American philanthropic, educational and religious in-

[10] Secretary Hughes cabled Mr. Grew on August 7: "For Grew and staff of Lausanne Mission. I am extremely gratified with the work of the Lausanne Mission. Your telegrams have always been clear, to the point, and in sufficient detail to enable Department adequately to judge of the questions at issue. Your handling of the difficult questions which arose both in the Allied negotiations and during our own treaty negotiations has inspired the confidence of the Department in your tact, in soundness of your judgment, and in the forcefulness with which you have represented the American position."

stitutions recognized prior to October 30, 1914, will continue to be recognized by the Turkish authorities, and the situation of such institutions existing but not recognized on July 24, 1923, will be favorably examined by the authorities with a view to regularizing their position. With respect to fiscal charges these institutions will receive the same treatment as similar Turkish institutions; and in general, due regard being had to the essential conditions of their operation, they are to be, equally with Turkish institutions, subject to Turkish laws, regulations and administrative arrangements of a public character.

"3. The nationals of each of the contracting parties, subject to compliance with the local laws and regulations, including those regarding immigration, are to have complete liberty to enter and establish themselves in the territory of the other party; and while in such territory they are to enjoy the most constant protection and security for their property and their persons in accordance with generally recognized international law. They are assured, specifically, upon compliance with the local laws and regulations, complete liberty of conscience and worship; free access to courts of justice; the right to acquire, possess and dispose of movable property; the right, subject to reciprocity, to acquire, possess and dispose of immovable property so far as may be allowed by the local laws to foreigners in general; and the right to engage without hindrance 'in every kind of profession, industry or commerce not forbidden by the local laws to all foreigners.' (The last of the rights here enumerated is worthy of special note for the reason that in the Allied-Turkish 'establishment' convention, Article 4, the question of the right to engage in 'the different forms of commerce, professions and industry' was reserved for separate conventions to be concluded between Turkey and the Allies within twelve months from the coming into force of the 'establishment' convention. A similar reservation was opposed by the American plenipotentiary at Lausanne, with the result that a formula was worked out under which American citizens in Turkey will be accorded any right in this regard which may be accorded to other foreigners.)

"4. Commercial, industrial and financial concerns organized and maintaining their head offices in either country are to be recognized in the other country and to be accorded the same protection as the nationals of their country.

"5. Domiciliary visits and searches in dwellings and other buildings of citizens and concerns of either of the contracting parties may be effected only in accordance with laws, regulations and ordinances equally applicable to nationals of the country in which the buildings are situated.

"6. The nationals of each country in the territory of the other are to be exempt from military service and from contributions in lieu thereof, and both individuals and companies are to be exempt from forced loans or other exceptional levies on property.

"7. With respect to taxes the nationals of each country in the territory of the other are to be accorded the same treatment as natives of the country, and the companies of each country in the territory of the other are to enjoy the same treatment as any similar foreign companies.

"8. Most-favored-nation treatment is mutually assured as regards freedom of commerce and navigation; import and export duties; consumption and excise taxes; transit duties and drawbacks; and the protection of patent and trademark rights.

"9. Merchant and war vessels and aircraft of the United States are to enjoy complete liberty of navigation and passage in the Straits on a basis of equality with similar vessels and aircraft of the most-favored foreign nation, subject to the rules prescribed in the Allied-Turkish Straits convention. (The United States, it should be noted, assumed no obligations of a political or military character with respect to the execution of the Straits convention.)

"10. The rights and duties of consular officers are defined in accordance with international law and with provisions in existing treaties between the United States and other countries. . . ." [11]

11 "The American Treaty of Lausanne," *World Peace Foundation Pamphlets,* VII, 593–95. For the full text of the Treaty see *Foreign Relations, 1923,* II, 1153–71.

XXII

Under Secretary of State
1924 – 1925

After the arduous days of the Lausanne Conference, Mr. Grew returned to the Legation at Berne to resume the customary activities of the American Minister to Switzerland. On February 4, 1924, however, he was back in Geneva representing the United States at a four-day meeting of the Temporary Mixed Commission of the League of Nations dealing with the control of the traffic in arms and munitions of war. As has been pointed out in Chapter XVII, the United States had refused to ratify a treaty drafted at the Peace Conference of 1919 to control the arms trade. The League Assembly in 1922 asked the United States to express its objections to the 1919 Convention of St. Germain as well as to set forth any proposals it might like to make. It was over a year, however, before the Department of State replied to this request. Then, in 1924, Mr. Grew was sent to a League conference on this subject. He noted in his diary on February 4, 1924: "It was the first time that I had set foot in the League building under instructions from Washington and I felt as if I were entering a secret society for my initiation." [1] *Mr. Grew told the Commission: "I have*

[1] That first meeting of the Temporary Mixed Commission in Geneva was perhaps the most difficult I ever attended. I was the first representative of the United States to sit officially with a body of the League of Nations, which politically was anathema to the majority of Americans. The day before the meeting President Wilson died, and the initial meeting was given over to eulogistic speeches by every delegate in memory of the man who more than any other individual was the real founder of the League of Nations. Those tributes were deeply impressive to any American, but I sat there representing a Republican Administration under President Coolidge, knowing that I must make the last speech "off the cuff." The press correspondents were out in force, waiting

been instructed to attend the meetings of this Commission, in accordance with the invitation extended to my Government in December last, for the purpose of being fully advised as to any proposals that may be made and particularly to receive information respecting any draft convention which may be considered by the Commission. While I have no authority to bind the Government of the United States and while I am not here in the capacity of a technical expert, I shall be happy to transmit promptly to my Government any recommendations that may be formulated by the Commission and to say that in case any appropriate plan is devised, the question of securing the necessary legislation in the United States will have full and proper consideration."

Mr. Grew observed in his diary that the delegates "seemed a little disappointed that my instructions did not go further, allowing me to make constructive suggestions no less than to explain our objections to the Convention of St. Germain, but I left no doubt on that score and they acknowledged that this was better than nothing." On February 5, Mr. Grew noted in his diary that although the delegates "bitterly resented the attitude of the United States in not ratifying the Convention of St. Germain and in delaying for a year or more in stating our objections, they nevertheless realize that they can accomplish nothing without the United States and are now willing to regard the past as a sealed book and to try to meet our views in drawing up a new instrument."

to report to the world what I said. Norman Davis, Under Secretary of State in the Democratic Administration, sat in the front row. When my turn came I expressed, as effectively as I could, American appreciation of those tributes and then spoke briefly, but I think impressively, for I was very much moved, on what President Wilson was rather than on what he had done. Later Norman Davis and I repaired to Hugh Gibson's apartment for a much-needed drink. I saw Davis studying me and asked his reaction to what I had said about the late President. Davis answered that in a long life of considerable experience he had never seen a man so "on the spot" as I was that day. I asked him if I had gotten away with it. "Just 100 per cent," he replied. That was the beginning of a long and mutually devoted friendship. He later helped me, though without my knowing of it until much later, in securing my continuance as Ambassador to Japan in 1933. — J. C. G.

On February 6, Mr. Grew remarked in his diary: "These international conferences are really most dangerous things, for one's official reputation is often placed in jeopardy. The Department's instructions are often open to various interpretations: one may guess right, but one may also guess wrong, and a wrong guess may be very serious indeed, particularly when publicity is involved."

Before the Conference adjourned on February 8, Mr. Grew repeated the objections of the United States to the Convention of St. Germain. He pointed out that the Department of State did not believe it was drawn in a way effectually to limit armaments; that it imposed on the signatories no restrictions on the supply of arms and munitions among themselves; that the contracting powers would be prohibited from selling arms and munitions to states not parties to the Convention; that by its provisions, therefore, the United States would be required to prevent all shipment of military supplies to such countries in Latin America as had not signed or adhered to the Convention; and, finally, that its provisions relating to the League of Nations were so intertwined with the whole Convention as to make it impracticable for the United States to ratify in view of nonmembership in the League. It was also pointed out that Congress would not ratify the Convention of St. Germain, and that the American position on any new Convention would have to be reserved, until there was an opportunity to consult with the leaders of Congress.

After the conference in Geneva, Mr. Grew resumed his legation duties at Berne. On March 1, he received a personal telegram from William Phillips saying that he had just been appointed Under Secretary of State. Mr. Phillips observed that Mr. Grew would "never regret the opportunity which it gives you for personal association with such a chief, as Charles Evans Hughes." Mr. Grew remarked in his diary that day: "I am rather appalled at the prospect of the responsibility and difficult work ahead and very much surprised at the offer. It's about the last post I ever expected to be called upon to fill — or to try to fill. But it's gratifying."

Looking back on his work at Berne and the development of American relations with the League of Nations, he wrote:

"When I came we had practically no point of contact; our Government refused even to answer polite letters received from the League and its very name was anathema. Now we are co-operating in almost every non-political activity, we answer all letters, give all information asked and through my personal correspondence with Drummond and Sweetser we keep in the closest touch with all developments. I send to the Department every publication issued — sometimes ten or twenty a week. I have succeeded in making the Legation the sole channel of communication between the League and our Government, so that we can keep in the closest touch with what is going on. I should like to feel that this situation is partially due to my mission to Switzerland, for no work is nearer my heart. But we are not yet ready for membership or for participating in the political activities of Europe — I don't know that we ever shall be. We have too many discordant elements in our own country, and an American member of the Council and the Assembly could never properly represent the country as a whole. Every position he might take with regard to European politics would infuriate some national element at home, the Italians or the Irish, the Germans, Poles or Jews. This is the real and practical reason for our not joining. But so far as the League is a big international clearinghouse for nonpolitical questions — and this I conceive to be its most important function as now con-stituted — I feel that we should co-operate without restric-tions. In view of the attitude of Congress, however, our Gov-ernment is handicapped even in this."

On March 22, the Grews left Berne for Paris where Mr. Grew was to represent the United States at the First Subcom-mittee of the Temporary Mixed Commission for control of the traffic in arms. Mr. Grew noted in his diary that day: "I have never had a home that I hated so to leave for we have had our happiest times there. . . . Thus ends my mission to Switzer-land. It has been a most happy one and, I believe, not wholly negative. Certain of our interests have been advanced, the

Swiss now understand the United States somewhat better than they did before, and our Legation has acquired a prestige which I think I can safely say is second to no other. They have been profitable years."

March 29, 1924 [2]

In reporting to the Department in my despatch of March 29th from Paris, I sent a copy of the new draft convention as well as copies of all the procès verbaux of the meetings. I added:

It will be noted that the statement which I made at the opening meeting covered all the points raised in the Department's instruction relating to the traffic in arms insofar as concerned the reservations and objections of the United States. Having made this statement, as will be observed from the minutes, I purposely refrained from making any further comment on articles which concerned these objections and reservations as they came up for discussion. The views of the United States had already been made clear, and I did not wish, by any further comments, to be drawn into the debates, a circumstance which might have been construed as influencing the Subcommittee in its deliberations or as taking part in the actual drafting of the convention.[3] The only remarks which I did make subsequent to my first statement were in reply to direct questions.

The plenary session of the Temporary Mixed Commission will meet in Geneva on June 30, 1924,[4] at which meeting this draft convention, together with the opinions of the Legal Section of the League of Nations and of the Permanent Advisory Committee, to which bodies certain questions have been submitted, will be considered again and possibly further revised. Although the meeting in Geneva will technically fall within the work of the

[2] The Subcommittee for the control of traffic in arms met in Paris from March 24 to March 28. Mr. Grew summarized the work of the Subcommittee in his diary for March 29. For correspondence between Mr. Grew and the Department of State relating to the meetings of the Subcommittee, see U.S. Department of State, *Papers Relating to the Foreign Relations of the United States, 1924* (Washington: Government Printing Office, 1939), I, 17–39.

[3] The Draft Convention is included in *ibid.*, pp. 33–39.

[4] The Commission met in Geneva from July 7 to 12, 1924.

Tenth Assembly of the League of Nations, it will actually be a continuation of the labors of the Temporary Mixed Commission, to which the United States was invited to send a representative by a resolution of the Fourth Assembly.[5] Should the Department therefore desire that the United States be represented in Geneva in June, such representation would not appear to be subject to a further invitation.

Before closing this report I may say that the Agenda of the Subcommittee included the consideration of a draft convention for the control of the private manufacture of arms and munitions, prepared by Colonel David Carnegie (Canada). As certain members of the Subcommittee had urgent business calling them to other duties, at the conclusion of the meeting of Friday, March 28th, it was decided that this further convention should be referred to a small drafting committee of five members of the present Subcommittee, for consideration prior to the meeting of the T.M.C. in June. As this convention, together with the draft convention which is discussed in the body of this report, will be considered at Geneva, I thought it desirable to explain to the Subcommittee the constitutional and legislative limitations confronting the United States in the matter of the control of private manufacture. Consequently, shortly before the adjournment of the Subcommittee, I said that in view of the submission of this question to a drafting committee, I believed it might be of interest to the First Subcommittee and of possible use to the drafting committee, if I should endeavor briefly to clarify the position of the United States in the matter under discussion. The fact was that in this connection we were confronted with certain constitutional and legislative difficulties and that our Congress had no power to control mere manufacture and production within the various states of the Union. Its powers in this respect would be limited to control in the District of Columbia and in the territories and possessions of the United States. It therefore appeared to me that we were thus confronted with a serious obstacle to taking steps along the lines now under consideration.

[5] The Fourth Assembly recommended "that the Council should invite the United States Government to appoint representatives to co-operate with the Temporary Mixed Commission in preparing the draft convention or conventions." The Draft Convention adopted by the Temporary Mixed Commission for the Reduction of Armaments on July 12, 1924, was submitted to the Fifth Assembly of the League of Nations.

Following these remarks M. Dupriez [representative of Belgium], who for some years was a Professor of International Law at Harvard University, took occasion to explain in more detail these constitutional limitations. Lord Cecil [representative of Great Britain] then asked me directly whether or not there would be any constitutional difficulties which would prevent federal legislation in the United States with a view to obtaining for publication statistical information respecting production by private manufacture within the various states of the Union. I replied that in my opinion this would depend upon the interpretation of the legislation which might be enacted, but that I could not give a categorical answer and should be glad to submit the question to my Government for consideration.

Shortly thereafter the Subcommittee adjourned.

I feel that our participation in the work of the Temporary Mixed Commission and the First Subcommittee has brought about at least one important result. There is no doubt that prior to this participation a distinct feeling prevailed among the members of the League that our Government, for some reason not clearly understood, was adopting obstructionist tactics in connection with the efforts to control the traffic in arms. We have now explained not only our objections to the Convention of St. Germain, but we have indicated some of the difficulties of a constitutional or legislative nature with which we are confronted. The mere fact that we have explained these difficulties to the members of the Commission and have indicated that far from desiring to obstruct the efforts being made to control the traffic in arms, we are, on the contrary, in full sympathy with these efforts and that we ourselves should welcome any solution which might obviate the difficulties with which we were confronted, has unquestionably created a very different atmosphere in Geneva and has altered the attitude of the members of the Commission from one of tacit hostility to comprehension of our position and a sincere desire to meet our views.

The feeling in the Commission is very strong that any convention for the control of the traffic in arms must necessarily be closely associated with the League of Nations, in view of Article 24 [6] of the Covenant, and in view also of the mandate received

---

[6] Article 24 of the Covenant of the League of Nations stated that all "international bureaus and all commissions for the regulation of matters of inter-

by the Commission from the Fourth Assembly. The efforts of the First Subcommittee were largely directed towards finding a solution which would reconcile this mandate with the position of the United States, and it is felt by the Commission that this solution has been found in Lord Cecil's amendment to Article 27,[7] providing for partial or reserved adhesion. The text of this amendment, providing for reservations with the consent of the high contracting parties which would not affect the effectiveness of the control of the traffic in arms, was drawn up with a view to preventing other Powers from wrecking or weakening the effectiveness of the convention by a variety of reservations, but furnishes a loophole by which the high contracting parties could, and probably would, consent to any and all reservations on the part of the Government of the United States, in order to obtain American adhesion. The feeling is now unanimous that there would be no purpose whatever in concluding a convention to which the United States was not a party.

I frankly feel that my position in the meetings of the Temporary Mixed Commission and of the First Subcommittee has been extremely difficult owing to inadequate or conflicting instructions. In my original instructions I was authorized to point out that the Convention of St. Germain was not drawn on the theory of the limitation of armaments and that it imposed on the signatories no restriction on production or on the supply of arms among themselves. In subsequent instructions I was told that we ourselves could not restrict production in the various states of the Union owing to lack of constitutional power vested in Congress, and also that we must reserve to ourselves the right to ship arms to any government or to any belligerent recognized as such by the United States. In other words, we wanted the other powers to eliminate certain objec-

national interest hereafter constituted shall be placed under the direction of the League."

[7] Article 27 of the Draft Convention affirmed that any "State may, with the consent of the H. [igh] C. [ontracting] P. [arties] notify its partial or conditional adherence to the provisions of the present Convention, provided that such conditions or partial adherence do not affect the effectiveness of the supervision of trade in arms and ammunition."

tions to the Convention of St. Germain, but we ourselves could not eliminate the very objections that we ourselves had raised. I cannot see that these instructions are anything but radically conflicting. If we want to see an effective limitation of armaments, why do we not make some constructive suggestions instead of raising merely destructive objections. At any moment in the meetings of the Subcommittee, after I had stated our position, I expected Jouhaux [representative of France] or Jancovici [representative of Rumania] to get up and point out the confliction of my statements before the T.M.C. and the Subcommittee. What could I have said? I should have been in an awful hole. But the members of the Subcommittee seemed to understand my difficult position and were most kindly disposed. Several were good enough to say that I had handled the situation with dignity and tact, although they would have been glad of something more concrete to work on. I wrote Bill Phillips after the session of the T.M.C. in Geneva that I had never shied any job as yet, but that I should not look forward with any pleasure to participating in the sessions of the Subcommittee. After every meeting I felt as if I had spent several hours in the dentist chair and it was a profound relief when the final adjournment came. Presumably Hugh Gibson [Mr. Grew's successor as Minister to Switzerland] will have to carry on the work and if I have anything to say about it, he will be more adequately informed of our Government's attitude than I was.

In the last meeting a resolution was passed thanking me for my co-operation. . . .

On April 5, Mr. Grew sailed for America, while Mrs. Grew remained in Switzerland until their daughters had completed their school year. On April 13, Mr. Grew in Boston received a cablegram that their seventeen-year-old daughter Edith had been stricken with scarlet fever while on a trip to Venice with her schoolmates. The following day news came that Edith had died. That night Mr. Grew "sent a long telegram to Alice," and the next day he abandoned his leave of absence and left for Washington, for, as he wrote in his diary, "I must work as

*soon as possible." Mr. Hughes had considerately suggested that
he take some time off, but this he did not wish to do. He assumed office as Under Secretary of State on April 16 and immediately became Acting Secretary on his first day in office
owing to Mr. Hughes' absence from Washington.*

Thursday, April 17 [1924]

I went in to see Mr. Hughes this morning and asked him if
he wished me to come into his room informally when I had
anything to take up. He replied that we must be "thick as two
thieves" and that I always had the entrance into his room over
anybody else. . . .[8]

At 12.15 I went to the White House with Butler Wright
[Third Assistant Secretary of State]. He introduced me to Bascom Slemp [Secretary to President Coolidge] and the President's
private secretary Edward T. Clark. Slemp took me in to see
the President at once and I sat with him while a great number
of people filed by his desk, simply to have a glimpse of him.
This was the first occasion on which the daily handshaking was

[8] On one of my first days as Under Secretary of State under Mr. Hughes, he
gave me a large file of papers involving a complicated problem regarding China
and asked me to digest the material and to make recommendations for action.
Wishing to make sure of doing a good job with my first assignment I worked
most of the night going into the dossier in great detail, prepared a digest and
stated concisely what I thought ought to be done. Then the next morning I
came into Mr. Hughes' office sort of wagging like a dog who has successfully
retrieved a stick and fully expecting the accolade, "Well done thou good and
faithful servant." Alas, I had not yet fathomed the great mind, with which
from that moment I was to deal. Mr. Hughes riffled through the file, digesting
each page with almost miraculous rapidity, while I watched his expression becoming grimmer and grimmer. Finally, he put down the file, swiveled his chair
around to face me and said in the stentorian tones of which only he was
capable: "Why Mr. Grew, you have totally missed the central point of this
whole situation. Your arguments are specious from beginning to end. This is
the nub of the problem," and then he proceeded to sum up that voluminous
file in a few masterly sentences, reaching an opinion quite contrary to mine.
I took the file and slipped towards the door wholly crushed by the tirade just
received. But just as I reached the door Mr. Hughes broke into one of his
inimitable smiles and said in his most charming voice: "You understand of
course, Mr. Grew, that there is nothing personal in this." Such was the
extraordinary chief with whom I had the privilege of working during that
memorable year. — J. C. G.

abandoned and it seems an excellent solution of the question as the President is not disturbed and can continue to talk or sign papers. He was very cordial; commented on my work abroad and asked me to drop in often.

The Japanese situation is the main subject at issue. The Secretary takes the ground that Ambassador Masanao Hanihara's note was merely a statement of his understanding of the Gentlemen's Agreement and that the words "grave consequences" were not intended to convey any threat whatever.[9]

In the afternoon I accompanied the Secretary to the daily press conference in which he introduced me to the correspondents. He then told them in confidence of his attitude towards the Japanese situation. . . .

Monday, April 21 [1924]

I held my first press conference at 10.30 and told the correspondents that I was glad to take over what the Secretary, as well as I, considered the highest privilege pertaining to my office. I said that I wished to be of help so far as possible and that the correspondents could depend upon me to co-operate with them. They would probably have to bear with me until I became accustomed to the various problems before the Department, but that if I could not answer a question on the spur of the moment, I would always take it under immediate

[9] Congress in 1924 passed a new immigration law establishing the quota system for European immigrants and excluding Japanese. While the bill was being discussed, Mr. Hughes objected to Japanese exclusion on the basis that it was an insult to a sensitive people and would undo the work of the Washington Conference. The Secretary pointed out that such a law was unnecessary, since, under the Gentlemen's Agreement of 1908, Japan undertook to prevent the emigration of Japanese laborers. On April 10, 1924, Ambassador Hanihara sent a note to Mr. Hughes saying that his Government did not intend to send their nationals where they were not wanted but that Japan wanted to be treated in a self-respecting way. "I realize," he concluded, "as I believe you do, the grave consequences which the enactment of the measure retaining that particular provision would inevitably bring upon the otherwise happy and mutually advantageous relations between our two countries."

Mr. Hughes transmitted this note to Congress, although the Secretary stated that he did not think that the Japanese Ambassador had the slightest intention of making any threat.

consideration, find out if there was any information available and give it to the correspondents at the earliest possible moment. . . .

Wednesday, May 21, to Tuesday, May 27 [1924]

. . . Eliot Wadsworth, Assistant Secretary of the Treasury, called me up this week to say that at the last meeting of the Assistant Secretaries, it was decided that one Secretary from each Department would co-operate by drawing up a report of the constructive work done by his Department under the present Administration, these reports to be placed at the disposal of the Republican National Committee for use in the campaign. This immediately raised an important principle in my case and I immediately went to the Secretary to consult him. I said I wished to ask his advice on a point both of expediency and ethics; that the position of Under Secretary was generally regarded as a political post, but that I myself was a Service man and had served under many different Administrations. This applied equally to Leland Harrison [Second Assistant Secretary of State] and Mr. Wright. The question at issue was whether we should now regard ourselves as political incumbents and take an active part in the Republican Campaign, or whether we should, on the other hand, continue to maintain our nonpolitical Service status. The Secretary gave me an admirably complete and clear reply. He said he wished all Department officers to feel free to follow any course they considered best and that none of them would be dictated to. It had been a cause of great pride to him that the executive offices of the Department, and in fact nearly all the principal positions in the Department, were filled by Service men. There was only one politician in the Department and that was himself and he, Mr. Hughes said, was a very bad one. He said that we need feel under no obligation whatever to take any part in politics. Whether Mr. Coolidge or a Democrat were elected President, he felt that the new Secretary of State, who would take office on March fourth next, would be making a great mistake if he dispensed with the services of any of the present executive officers of the Department. He then said that he was immensely interested in having the constructive work of the Department during the present Administration fully recognized and that I might tell Mr. Wadsworth that the name to place on his list to submit a report from the Department of State should be that of Charles E. Hughes. In my original conversation with Eliot Wadsworth on the telephone, he seemed somewhat surprised when I mentioned my Service status and he pointed out that Henry Fletcher [Under Secretary of State, 1921–22] in the last campaign had taken a very prominent part in supporting the Republican Party.

Some criticism having been made of the speech delivered by the British Ambassador at the recent meeting of Chambers of Commerce in Cleveland, [10] he wrote a long letter to the Secretary explaining that his suggestion that we should co-operate more closely with Soviet Russia had no reference to political questions, but only to economic relations and he felt that he had therefore in no way overstepped the bounds of propriety. The Secretary told me that before the Ambassador had made his speech, he had consulted Hoover [Secretary of Commerce], who had advised him strongly to stay off of it. As a result of this conversation, the Ambassador had cut out a large part of his speech, but had, nevertheless, seen fit to dwell upon one phase of the subject. The Secretary said this looked very much as if he were acting under specific instructions from London. He drafted an admirable reply to the Ambassador in the most courteous terms, saying that the American people were very sensitive in regard to comments of foreign diplomats on questions of domestic or foreign policy concerning the United States and that he supposed the criticism of Sir Esme Howard's speech had been due to the fact that people bore in mind the recent recognition of Soviet Russia by Great Britain. The Secretary feels that the diplomats indulge in this sort of thing far too much. . . . I said that this sort of thing was seldom seen abroad, but the Secretary ascribed it to the prevalence of the custom of speech-making in America. . . .

10 Sir Esme Howard delivered the speech in Cleveland on May 6. See the *New York Times*, May 17, 1924, p. 2.

Wednesday, May 28, to Friday, June 6 [1924]

The chief subject which has concerned me this week has been the question of the administration of the Foreign Service under the provisions of the Rogers Act.[11] Two distinct plans had been formulated. One was that of Carr [Wilbur Carr, Assistant Secretary of State], who in conjunction with Tracy Lay [in charge of the Budget Office of the Department of State] has been preparing his plan during the last several years. It is based on his long experience in administering the Consular Service and from the point of view of machinery, it approaches perfection. The danger that I see in it, however, is that it would tend to bureaucratize the whole Foreign Service, which would take much of the spirit and morale out of the diplomatic branch at least. It provides for a Personnel Board, composed of the Under Secretary and two Assistant Secretaries of State, assisted by a diplomatic and a consular officer brought back from the field only for the annual or semiannual board meetings. Carr's idea would be that they would approach the questions of personnel with a fresh point of view, unobscured by the atmosphere of the Department. The routine work of personnel would be in the hands of a Personnel Bureau, composed of a Chief and Assistant Chief, representing the two branches of the Service. These men would, however, not be members of the Board itself and would have no vote. They would simply make their recommendations to the Board on the basis of their

[11] In 1919, Congressman John Jacob Rogers of Massachusetts introduced three bills to reorganize the diplomatic and consular services. He reintroduced these bills in 1921, and Mr. Hughes in 1922 submitted a draft of a bill whose main purpose was "to lay the foundation of a broader service of trained men." Mr. Rogers, then, introduced a bill containing many of Mr. Hughes' recommendations. On May 24, 1924, the Rogers bill became law. Now the Department had a Foreign Service whose members from vice consul to counselor of embassy were appointed and promoted on a merit basis and were interchangeable. A Foreign Service officer, also, could be assigned for three-year periods to the Department. In place of the Diplomatic Bureau and the Consular Bureau, the Division of Foreign Service Administration was established. Another Assistant Secretary of State was created, and on July 1, 1924, Wilbur J. Carr, formerly Director of the Consular Service, was assigned to this post. A substantial but still insufficient increase in salaries was also authorized by Congress. See Graham H. Stuart, *The Department of State* (New York: The Macmillan Co., 1949), pp. 271-75.

records of the men in the Service. Carr's feeling is that if these officers were given greater influence or prestige, their position would be precarious in the event of a political regime in the Department. I feel on the contrary that they would not have sufficient influence or prestige to justify the men in the field turning to them with their various problems, inquiries and grievances and this would throw much added labor on the Assistant Secretaries who are already overworked.

The other plan has been drawn up by Hugh Wilson [Chief of the Division of Current Information] and myself and provides for a single Director of Personnel, who shall be a member of neither branch of the Service, but a man who could command the confidence of both branches. This officer, if advisable, could be assisted by two officers from the field, who would constitute a board. With this exception, the Carr plan would be accepted and all its other machinery, including a School Board and an Examination Board, would be adopted. I submitted these two plans to the Secretary, who, after studying them, called Butler Wright, Hugh Wilson and myself into conference and with his usual clear vision and admirable powers of analysis, he pictured the situation that might arise in the Department in the case of various kinds of Secretaries of State; those who might be interested in the Service on a merit basis; those who might take no interest in it at all, and finally those who were out-and-out politicians and would look at the Service purely from the point of view of patronage. The result of this meeting was that we all agreed as to the unwisdom of appointing a Director of Personnel outside of the Service and we formulated instead a plan providing for an Executive Committee composed of three Foreign Service officers who would be members of the Personnel Board and vote thereon. This would give six votes with the Under Secretary and two Assistant Secretaries and in the event of a deadlock, matters would be referred to the Secretary of State for decision. The Secretary then saw Mr. Carr, who spoke in favor of his plan and he then asked us all to get together and try to reach an agreement.

I had several conferences with Carr and Butler Wright, but we found ourselves simply repeating the old arguments on every side and in fact going around in a circle. I, therefore, finally drew up a memorandum to Carr stating that the modified Wilson plan had been accepted and asking him to incorporate it in an Executive Order. He seemed much distressed and prophesied its failure, but drew up the Order as instructed. Hugh Wilson, Butler Wright and I think most of the diplomatic secretaries in the Department felt that the best possible plan had been evolved. When I took the Executive Order in to the Secretary, he said he thought that the provision for the Chairman of the Executive Committee ought to be so worded as to allow the appointment of some man, not necessarily a member of the Service itself, as for example, someone in the Department or someone who had formerly been in the Service and understood its problems. He brought this about by the change of a comma, so that it now reads: "There is hereby constituted an Executive Committee of the Foreign Service Personnel Board to be composed of a Chairman, and two other members who shall be Foreign Service officers of high rank representing both the diplomatic and the consular branches of the Foreign Service, to be selected by the other members of the Personnel Board with the approval of the Secretary of State." In Carr's draft, the comma, instead of coming after the word "Chairman" was placed after the phrase "two other members." Carr disapproved of this alteration and after thinking the matter over I suggested the next day that some qualifying clause might be inserted to provide that this Chairman, if not a Foreign Service officer, should have served at least five years under the Department, but Carr felt that this would simply call attention to the availability of the position outside of the Service and thought it unlikely that any future Secretary of State would be less likely to notice the comma than the proposed phrase, so the matter was left as it was. All now depends upon finding the right men to fill the positions on the Executive Committee. . . .

Tuesday, June 10 [1924]

The Republican National Convention opened today at Cleveland with Congressman Theodore Burton [of Ohio] making the keynote speech. Soon after 11.30 Margaret Castle telephoned that the speech had begun, so Bill Castle [Chief of the Division of Western European Affairs] and I hurried up to his house and heard all but the first few minutes of the speech on the radio. It lasted one hour and a half and impressed me most favorably. As a matter of fact, Castle himself had written the entire part of the speech dealing with foreign affairs and it was admirably clear and forceful. One line of Castle's, which called forth particular applause, was in connection with the opposition to our joining the Permanent Court of International Justice — "It is easier to criticize than to construct. It is easier to promise than to perform." The greatest applause of all was elicited when Congressman Burton referred to the congressional investigations against Government officials and castigated those who brought unfounded charges of corruption against innocent officials for political purposes. His remarks that the war was now over and that having brought about the downfall of the autocrats who had brought it on, we now wished to live in harmony with the people of those enemy countries and had nothing but good will towards them in working out their development in a new era, were received with stony silence, which much surprised me.

Telegrams from Tokyo today describe the disorders at the Imperial Hotel in Tokyo where a band of Japanese roughs broke up a dance. It appears that they bore banners stating that their disapproval was aimed only at the Japanese who were associating with Americans at this moment and not against the Americans themselves. Nevertheless, the feeling of hostility towards us all through Japan is apparently increasing and while the Japanese Government expresses its intention of avoiding all disorders, it does not appear to be taking any definite steps to prevent them. Three suicides have occurred as protests against the American Exclusion Act and one of those persons has been given a public funeral. A boycott against American goods is also setting in and this morning Will Hays [President of the Motion Picture Producers and Distributors of America] called me up from New York to say that the agents of the American film companies in Japan had cabled to send no more films at present as they could not be exhibited. Mr. Hays was very much upset at this blow to one of our greatest industries. . . .

Allen Dulles [Chief of the Division of Near Eastern Affairs] brought to me the draft instruction which he had prepared to Hugh Gibson for the forthcoming meeting of the Temporary Mixed Commission on the Traffic in Arms to take place in Geneva, July 7, and I spent the evening studying it. Hugh Gibson will at least go into the meeting with far more complete and explicit instructions than I had at the meetings in February and March.

The Executive Order for the administration of the Foreign Service under the Rogers Act was issued today, dated June 7. . . .

Tuesday, June 17 [1924]

Our reply to the Japanese note concerning immigration was given out this morning to the press for publicity on Thursday morning.[12] As Stephen Early and Kirke Simpson of the Associated Press desired to give the right slant to the note in sending out their stories, I had a long talk with them and pointed out its salient features, emphasizing first the very friendly and cordial feeling which pervaded it. Second, the fact that the new immigration law must be accepted as final and that only harm could be done to the interests of the two countries by cogitating on the possibility of finding some other solution which could only keep the embers of dissatisfaction burning; the sooner its

[12] The immigration law ignored Secretary Hughes' position of allowing the matter to be handled by diplomacy and imposed the exclusion of Japanese immigrants. The Secretary now had to defend a law with which he was not sympathetic. "From Japan he coveted a harvest of good will towards the United States; but he despaired of ever reaping one so long as Congress persisted in exercising the right to sow what to his eyes was an obvious variety of dragon's teeth." Samuel Flagg Bemis, *op. cit.,* p. 326.

finality was accepted, the sooner would the matter become a
dead issue to the best interests of all concerned. Thirdly, I
touched upon the argument that had been advanced in the
press to the effect that the law was in contravention to our
Treaty with Japan of 1911, the Gentlemen's Agreement and
international comity. I pointed out that in the negotiation of
the Treaty of 1911, specific reservations were made for future
legislative action, which were fully acknowledged by Japan.
So far as the Gentlemen's Agreement was concerned, this was
a unilateral act on the part of Japan and was intended to apply
to circumstances which had now terminated. As regards international comity, Japan would be the first to recognize the inherent rights of sovereignty. The correspondents expressed
much appreciation of this talk and submitted to us their story
before they sent it out. John A. MacMurray [Assistant Secretary of State], Hugh Wilson and I all went over it and made
certain suggestions. I think it is now thoroughly good. As
matter of fact, the Secretary telephoned me from Princeton
this morning and asked me to emphasize to the correspondents
of the press agencies the friendly and cordial spirit of the note
in the delivery. I did the same to the United Press correspondent this afternoon.

A strictly confidential telegram from Ambassador Herrick
in France indicates that there is much talk in France regarding
Japanese preparation for ultimate war with us.[13] I find it
difficult to attach much importance to this — at any rate under
the conditions existing in Japan at present. It seems to me
more likely that the subject will soon die a natural death and
that other things will intervene to make the Japanese people
forget it. . . .

Saturday, June 21, to Monday, June 30 [1924]
All other events this week have been overshadowed by the

---

13 The people of Japan regarded the act as a deliberate insult. Mr. Grew was
to see the reverberations, when he was Ambassador to Japan. T. A. Bailey, *A
Diplomatic History of the American People* (3d ed.; New York: F. S. Crofts &
Co., 1946), p. 706, comments: "The date on which the law became effective was
declared a day of national humiliation. Millions of Japanese could never forget."

Democratic Convention in New York. . . . The last few bal-
lots have brought about a decided swing towards Davis as one
of the dark horses and we have every hope that he may pull
it off. With the choice for President lying between two such
men as Calvin Coolidge and John Davis, we could be sure that
the country would be in good hands for the next four years.

The Secretary is making his final preparations for his European trip with the Bar Association.[14] He thinks it essential,
as he is going to London and Paris, to go to Brussels and Berlin also and if he does this, the question arises whether he
ought not also go to Rome, little as he wishes to do so in
midsummer. He told me today in confidence that the President had asked him if it were really necessary for him to go
to Rome, thereby indicating disapproval of this plan. The
Secretary thinks, although the President did not say so, that
the latter may have in the back of his mind the fact that if he
went to Rome, Mr. Hughes would have to call on the Pope as
well as the King and in view of the important part which Ca-
tholicism, on account of the Ku Klux Klan, is playing and is
going to play in the present campaign, this might well cause
embarrassment. The Secretary would like to return by the
Leviathan on August sixth and may be able to avoid Rome
simply on the ground that he has not sufficient time to make
the trip. . . .[15]

To William Phillips, June 30, 1924
Personal and Confidential

. . . This job is less appalling and even more fascinating than
I had anticipated. It is needless to tell you what an inspiration
I find in working under the Secretary. All that you were good
enough to tell me before your departure has been confirmed in
full measure, so that there is really nothing lacking in the
satisfaction in holding this position.

You will, no doubt, be interested in the decisions reached
concerning the administration of the Foreign Service under

14 Mr. Hughes was President of the American Bar Association.
15 Mr. Hughes did not visit Rome.

the Rogers Act. We had a few difficult days in lining up our respective views, but a compromise was finally reached which I think everyone now regards as satisfactory. The Personnel Board for the time being is to be composed of Carr, Wright and myself, and Consul General Charles Eberhardt, Consul Edward Norton and Hugh Wilson composing the Executive Committee which is part and parcel of the Board. We thus have six members evenly representing both branches of the Service. The Board has been sitting continuously during the last week going through the diplomatic and consular lists with a fine-toothed comb, and judging each individual on his record. A good many dead boughs have been separated from the Service through age retirement and the abolition of the unassigned list, while other men have been demoted and have been clearly given to understand that their cases will be further dealt with in the near future. In view of the short time intervening before the Act goes into effect, we felt that it would work undue hardship to dismiss any man on the spot and that they ought to be given a reasonable time to prepare for what is surely coming. I hope that many of these men will now resign on their own initiative, so that their future social and professional reputations may not be injured, as they doubtless would have been if we had insisted upon immediate dismissal. . . .

Monday, July 28 [1924]

I worked all the morning with Harrison and Doctor Young preparing a memorandum for President Coolidge on the London Reparations Conference,[16] meaning to take it over to him as soon as it was ready.[17] He was evidently still worrying

---

[16] On November 30, 1923, the Allied Reparations Commission appointed a committee, of which Charles G. Dawes and Owen D. Young were members, acting in a private capacity as Americans, to study German reparations. In July the Reparations Commission met in London to consider the Dawes Plan for a reduction in German reparations and a loan to Germany. The United States participated in the London Conference, and Secretary Hughes' presence in Europe made it possible for him to express American support for the Plan.

[17] During Mr. Hughes' absence in Europe Mr. Grew was Acting Secretary of State.

about the matter, because at 12.30, five minutes before I was ready to start, he telephoned to me and asked how soon I could give him the desired information. I went over inside of five minutes again to his personal study in the White House, as he was busy preparing his acceptance speech, and gave him a full résumé of the situation, indicating that while the three committees appeared to have reached unanimous reports, nothing could be settled until the Plenary Session this afternoon when the reports were to be presented. He read through my memorandum twice and asked me several questions and then explained confidentially why he desired the information. I told him that I would bring over the report of the Plenary Session as soon as it arrived.

The President is a man of few words. Today he sat with his feet on the desk and thought silently for several minutes before he made a remark, but each comment or question showed the careful thought that he was giving to the matter. . . .

Tuesday, July 29 [1924]

. . . I went to the President in the morning to give him the latest reports from London concerning the Reparations Conference. . . .

In the evening the President sent for me and handed me the following draft of a telegram which he wished to have sent to Ambassador Frank Kellogg in Great Britain immediately. "In case conference deadlocks finally over declaring default announce in that event to conference the President has a proposal to make. Keep conference for that and notify Department at once." This is a big proposal and one which may have far-reaching consequences. The President has not yet told me what it is, but I believe that any step in this direction on the part of our government to prevent a rupture of the conference would be received with approval, not only by our own country, but by most foreign countries and it would tend to offset the domestic criticisms of our isolation policy. As a matter of fact, our policy is less and less of isolation and we are going as far as we can in every matter without entering into European entanglements. Let us help where we can, but avoid getting mixed up in the political schemes of Europe, the extent of which I realize only too greatly after my experience at Lausanne.

It is surprising how often some newspaper offices will alter the information we give out in order to give it a more interesting aspect from the point of view of the news' publicity. We have to expect this from some of the less responsible newspapers and agencies, but the A.P. and U.P. seldom offend. This press work is one of the most difficult of my duties and I always dread the press conferences three times a week when some fifteen or twenty correspondents fire questions at me like a machine gun. Generally, however, they are pretty decent. If I say frankly that I do not wish to comment on a certain subject, they are content to drop it for the moment. . . .

Wednesday, July 30 [1924]

The President telephoned to me before I left the house this morning and asked me to send to Secretary Hughes in Paris a copy of the telegram that had gone to Ambassador Kellogg last night. When I reached the Department, I found that the London Embassy had sent a service asking us to repeat some of the phrases and words in our telegram of last night as they were not clear. I had also felt that the message was not quite clear, but did not feel in a position to tamper with the President's English. I therefore drew up a clarifying message and took it over to the President, who read it and approved. Fortunately, he did not appear to take offense at the implied slur on his own phraseology. The particular phrase the Ambassador had not understood was "keep the Conference for that" by which the President meant "hold the Conference together to receive the President's message if necessary." I sent the message to Mr. Hughes in this amplified form. The President then said he wished me to know what he had in mind, namely that in the event of a failure on the part of the Conference to agree to a method of declaring Germany in default, in case of default, he would propose that the Chief Justice of the United States would undertake to arbitrate. The President said that he had discussed the matter with the Attorney General, who saw no objection and he thought the same thing had been done by Chief Justice White in connection with a boundary dispute in Central America. I said I thought this was between Costa Rica and Nicaragua.[18] The President said he had carefully considered the matter but did not see that there would be any disadvantage in making such a proposal. I said I thought it was an admirable one and would be heartily supported by public opinion both in America and abroad; that France would find it very difficult to refuse to accept such a solution as public opinion would be entirely against her. It might be the saving of the whole situation. Later the President telephoned to say that he presumed of course that I had sent the telegram in code. I said that we had sent it in our most secret cipher; that I had taken pains to see that the fewest possible number of persons in the Department should see the message. Later in the morning, on receipt of further news from Mr. Kellogg, I went to the President again and told him that the French had now come out with their proposal foreseen on Tuesday, namely, that they did not wish to amend the Treaty of Versailles which provided that a majority vote on the Reparations Commission could declare Germany in default; that they proposed that in such a case the minority opinions should be submitted to an arbitral board composed of two Allied representatives and one American. I said that this was pretty closely in line with the President's own proposal and suggested that if he wished to create an opportunity to present his proposal and thus prevent the possibility of the acceptance by the Conference of some less satisfactory plan, it would no doubt be very easy for Ambassador Kellogg to do so through informal consultation with the members of the First Committee. I therefore suggested to the President that he might desire to take the Ambassador into his confidence and leave to his discretion the advisability of presenting the proposal in Plenary Session if a favorable

[18] Chief Justice White had arbitrated a boundary dispute between Costa Rica and Panama in 1914.

moment should occur. The President thought carefully several minutes then said that he feared that until the situation was perfectly clear-cut in an absolute deadlock over the question of determining default, it might get the Chief Justice involved in other issues and he thought it best to take no action for the moment.[19] I said I concurred and that in any case communication with London was very rapid. The President said he would like to have told the Secretary of the nature of his proposal, but that he did not dare to send it to Paris on account of the risk of a leak. He said that after all, the Secretary had left me in charge of the Department and that he must turn to me for advice.[20]

At the press conference this afternoon, the correspondents asked me if I would explain my frequent visits to the White House, at which I cheerfully smiled and said that was a subject on which I could not touch with propriety. . . .

Friday, August 15 [1924]

. . . I took up with the Secretary the appalling situation in the Passport and Visa Offices and in accordance with my recommendation, he placed Hugh Wilson in charge of both offices temporarily in order to clean out the Augean stables. The Department has been appallingly criticized for its delays in answering communications and there seems to be no system whatever in dealing with the work in those offices. Some letters I have found to have lain for several months without answers,

---

[19] The Conference came to an agreement, and there was, therefore, no need for Mr. Coolidge to offer his proposal. Ambassador Kellogg, after he became Secretary of State, asked the President what his proposal had been. According to Kellogg, "He smiled and said, 'The Conference did not break up, did it?' That is the only answer I ever got." David Bryn-Jones, *Frank B. Kellogg, A Biography* (New York: G. P. Putnam's Sons, 1937), p. 155.

[20] During 1924 I was Acting Secretary of State for sixty-nine days including six Sundays. When Acting Secretary I should properly have attended meetings of the Cabinet but not having been directly invited by President Coolidge to do so, I declined to push myself forward. Later, under the administrations of Presidents Franklin Roosevelt and Truman, I attended all Cabinet meetings while Acting Secretary, for a period of nearly six months. I occupied the chair of the Secretary of State on the President's right and was always called upon first to bring up current problems or comment. — J. C. G.

in spite of three or four periodical protests from the enraged writers. This sort of thing does the Department no good and drastic measures will have to be taken.

Before taking leave of the Secretary this evening, he was good enough to say that he had felt a great sense of security in leaving the Department in my hands while he was away and that he was greatly indebted to me. I said that I hoped he would not find too many mistakes that I had made. . . . He said that the Department work was immensely difficult and complicated at best. I said that so far as I was concerned, it was an inspiration to be with him here — a remark which he seemed highly to appreciate. He is a marvelous Chief.[21]

I cleaned up my desk and departed at 7.30 with Alice for the North Shore on a month's vacation, very glad to have the responsibility and difficult work in the last month over. . . .

[21] One day Butler Wright, who was in charge of protocol in the State Department, went in to Mr. Hughes and said, "Mr. Secretary, I have here a letter from a girls' school up in New York which says that the girls are coming to Washington next week and are anxious to pay their respects to you."

I well remember the Secretary's amazed and stentorian reaction. He shouted at poor Butler, "Girls' school! Why on earth should I waste my time receiving a girls' school! No, Mr. Wright, I will receive no girls' school. There are plenty of other officers in the Department who can attend to matters of that kind," and the Secretary again plunged into the mass of papers on his desk. Butler and I, realizing that the moment was not auspicious to pursue the matter, hastily retired.

Next week we again entered the Secretary's room. "Mr. Secretary, the girls are waiting outside in the hall."

"Girls! What girls do you refer to, Mr. Wright?"

"Why, Mr. Secretary, I told you last week about the girls' school who were coming down from New York. They merely wish to shake your hand and will take only a few minutes to file by. They will be so proud to be able to say they met our distinguished Secretary of State."

"Certainly not, Mr. Wright. Why should I waste my time receiving girls' schools? I am a busy man. I am surprised at your even suggesting such a thing. Take them away"; and again Mr. Hughes plunged into his work. But Butler was not to be easily downed and he said in his most charming and wheedling way, "Now, Mr. Secretary, you can't possibly disappoint those girls. Just see them for a moment and they will never forget it. They are right outside your door now and it will only take a minute. Why not take the bull by the horns?"

Mr. Hughes tore himself from his papers, swiveled his chair around, and broke into one of his really beatific smiles: "Don't you think you have your metaphors a little mixed, Mr. Wright? Show the ladies in." — J. C. G.

Thursday, September 18 [1924]

. . . H. Percival Dodge [American Minister to the Kingdom of Serbs, Croats, and Slovenes] at Belgrade has sent us an extremely interesting document purporting to be an instruction marked highly confidential, dated February 6, 1921, signed by Tchitcherin, Commissar for Foreign Affairs, and Karahan, Chief of the Western Section under the Soviet Government, which we have every reason to believe is authentic. Tchitcherin elaborates with great care the dissensions between various countries and indicates that the only way to attain the aims of Sovietism is for the Bolshevik representatives in foreign countries to leave nothing undone to aggravate and increase these dissensions. The most significant portion of the instruction reads as follows:

> There is no doubt that this work will sooner or later bring about favorable results but as I have mentioned the danger consists in the fact that the Great Powers will succeed in localizing the conflict. The present complete disinterestedness of Germany in the affairs of the Near East and the neutral policy pursued by the United States render our work more difficult. The latter must be directed towards the intricacy of Anglo-French and Franco-Italian interests. At present the best object for this purpose is Greece. Profiting by the confused situation in the Balkans we may succeed if not in transforming the Balkan divergencies into a European imbroglio, at least in rendering the relations between the countries of the Great Entente more tense and their interests more opposed to one another. Our representatives in Great Britain and Italy must direct their activity in view of bringing about such a result.
>
> By spreading our activity further to the East we approach new problems which increase the distance between the countries of the Great Entente. This must be always kept in mind when working in London, Paris or Rome.
>
> The interests of the Western countries have become so intricate that in present conditions it is not possible to foresee the future political combinations and alliances between them. However, we are completely aware of the fact that the creation of

partial alliances and groups more or less distant from one another may be of great profit to our interests. We draw the attention of our representatives to the following combinations:
closer connections between Great Britain and Japan as a counterpoise to America; between Great Britain and Germany as a
threat to France; between Italy and Greece as a counterpoise to
the policy of Great Britain and France in the Near East; alliance
between France and Poland as a direct threat to Germany; alliance between Czechoslovakia and Rumania as a threat to Hungary, and so forth. . . .

*By the time Mr. Hughes became Secretary of State, the United
States had inherited from the past two decades a series of
protectorates in Central and Caribbean America. The nation
had, also, acquired the widespread hatred of Latin America
for its imperialist policies. It was Secretary Hughes' policy to
liquidate American interventions in countries to the south as
quickly as political stability could be established. Mr. Hughes
declared in 1923: "Our interest does not lie in controlling foreign peoples; that would be a policy of mischief and disaster.
Our interest is in having prosperous, peaceful and law-abiding
neighbors with whom we can co-operate to mutual advantage."*

*Defense of the Panama Canal, however, he pointed out, was
essential to the security of the United States: "Disturbances
in the Caribbean region are therefore of special interest to us
not for the purpose of seeking control over others but of being
assured that our own safety is free from menace." Mr. Hughes
was not prepared, therefore, to abandon previous treaties granting the right of intervention in Panama, Cuba, the Dominican
Republic, and Haiti; nor was he willing to ignore violations
of the just rights of Americans or of other foreign nationals in
Latin American countries. "In this he did not differ from his
predecessors," S. F. Bemis has observed, "but it was his particular task, in the new frame of world politics, to convince
Latin America that the Big Stick did not really mean imperial-
ism."* The Latin American Policy of the United States *(New
York: Harcourt, Brace & Co., 1943), p. 203.*

Thursday, September 25 [1924]

The Secretary called me in this morning and said that as he expected to be absent from the Department from time to time during the next few weeks, he wished me to watch matters even more closely than usual and that while he always counted on me to feel a sense of responsibility in the Department, he wanted me during these next few weeks to feel a somewhat "heightened" sense of responsibility, especially with regard to the Central American countries. The Secretary said that no matter how much pressure should be exerted by the bankers, he had not the slightest intention of intervening in Central America. Neither the country nor Congress would support any such policy and he had no desire to create another situation such as has existed in Haiti and San Domingo.[22] We should do all we could to help the Central American Republics settle their difficulties, but only by advice and he did not wish us to make any declarations or adopt any definite lines of policy which might bind the hands of the next Administration, whether Democratic or Republican. We could not embark on any colonial policy and if these countries refused to listen to our advice they must stew in their own juice. He did not even wish to take a position which would prevent our recognizing a President in one of the Central American countries, even although he might not have fulfilled all constitutional requirements. We must be free to use our judgment and to do the best we can to aid towards stability without intervention or interference. . . .

Friday, September 26 [1924]

. . . The Secretary then showed me a letter which James J. Davis [Secretary of Labor] had handed him at Cabinet meeting this morning, enclosing a clipping which showed that Arthur Schoenfeld, our Chargé d'Affaires in Mexico, had just

[22] American Marines were landed in both Haiti and the Dominican Republic during the Wilson Administration. Mr. Hughes arranged in 1921 for the evacuation of the Marines from the Dominican Republic, which took place three years later. The Marines were not withdrawn from Haiti until 1933.

moved into the house of Seaver, who is Edward L. Doheny's representative in Mexico City. It appears that the house itself belongs to Doheny, and Seaver had been mentioned in connection with the Teapot Dome oil scandal.[23] This would open up a wonderful opportunity to our friends, the Democrats, to charge Schoenfeld with accepting favors from the oil interests and could cause the Administration much embarrassment. I am rather surprised that Schoenfeld, who is decidedly intelligent, should have let himself in for this and I prepared a telegram asking him to report at once whether the rent and conditions of his leasing of this house were in any respect more favorable than the rent and conditions of leasing of other real estate in Mexico City. It seems ridiculous that we should have to pay attention to such absurdities, but politics are politics and in campaign year every word and every action has to be considered from that point of view. . . .

I said to the Secretary today that I wanted his authority to use a little more politeness in replying to the notes received from the League of Nations. The Secretary General sent us a great many documents of interest and our form of reply was always "the Secretary of State of the United States has received from the Secretary General of the League of Nations, etc. etc." We would not use such a glacial form of acknowledgment even to a coal heaver in the United States and I suggested we might at least say that we acknowledged "with pleasure" or some phrase to that effect. The Secretary laughed and said he had no objections but feared that the Secretariat of the League, in its usual tactless fashion, would immediately announce in the press that the American Government was embarking on a policy of much closer co-operation with the League. He said that every time he tried to meet the views of the League, there had always been commotion in Geneva and long articles in the press criticizing him not for what he was

[23] The Teapot Dome scandals of the Harding period resulted in the resignation of Secretary of the Navy Denby from the Cabinet and the conviction of Secretary of the Interior, Albert Fall, for receiving bribes. Fall had secretly leased valuable naval oil reserves to the Doheny and Sinclair oil interests.

doing now but for not having done it before. He said it was always his intention to be courteous; even in the heat of political campaigning he had never had a personal quarrel with any man, and he wished to treat the League with just as much courtesy as any other organization. After he had been in the Department several months he learned quite by chance one day that a great volume of notes from the League were lying unanswered in one of the bureaus of the Department having accumulated during the latter part of Colby's administration [24] and the first part of his own. He was appalled at this lack of courtesy and immediately gave orders that every one of these notes should be answered and they were so answered in one batch. The League was almost stunned when this great volume of replies to its notes for the past year or so was suddenly received, but instead of expressing appreciation, the Secretariat let out a howl over the discourtesy of the Government in not having answered them before. The Secretary said that if there was ever a tactless position for the League Secretariat to take, it always took it. I acknowledged to the Secretary that this change in our phraseology might well expose us to the risk of charges of altering our whole policy and asked him if he were willing to take this risk. He laughed and said he would leave it to my judgment. I accordingly merely slipped in the words "with appreciation" to be used in future in our formal replies to communications received from the League and I await the result with confidence.

Yesterday, for the fun of it, I counted the number of outgoing communications which I had to sign and they totaled 90. However, I remember that during the war our Embassy on one single day sent 97 notes to the German Foreign Office. . . .

Friday, October 10 [1924]

An interesting discussion arose yesterday over the action of Argentina and Brazil in recognizing the new government in Chile.[25] William Collier, our Ambassador in Santiago, had in-

24 Bainbridge Colby was Secretary of State from March, 1920, to March, 1921.
25 Arturo Alessandri assumed the presidency of Chile on December 23, 1920. Although he maintained his personal popularity, he was unable to get Congress

quired whether we could not now follow suit. As a matter of fact most of the Great Powers of Europe and the principal South American States have granted recognition. The Secretary felt very strongly that we should not be rushed into action merely because Brazil and Argentina had acted. He agreed that the new government gave every evidence of stability and appears to have received the general acquiescence of the public, but he does not wish to show too much discrimination between our attitude towards the small States and our policy towards the larger Powers of Latin America. When a revolution occurs in one of the Central American Republics, we are generally in no hurry to extend recognition, especially if the change of government has occurred through unconstitutional means, as is the present case in Chile. . . .

I drafted the following telegram which he approved and signed:

In considering the recognition of a foreign Government this Government must, of course, first be influenced not only by the assurance that the new Government will carry out its international obligations but also that it can maintain stability and retain its power with the acquiescence of the people. In the case of the present Chilean regime the Department is hopeful that the fulfillment of these conditions may in due course be demonstrated to the satisfaction of this Government. This matter is being given most careful consideration by the Department. In the meantime, the Department does not wish to be hastened by the action of Brazil and Argentina in extending recognition to the present regime in Chile. Having all of these factors in mind, the Department desires for the present to maintain a position of reserve while leaving nothing undone to indicate friendship for the people of Chile and courtesy towards the new regime. . . .

to pass many of his plans for social and economic reform. The Army, which was in a difficult economic situation, protested against a law passed by Congress providing for parliamentary compensation, while Congress failed to pass the financial legislation needed by the Army. Alessandri called General Luis Altamirano, leader of the Army group, to head the ministry, but Alessandri felt that his position as president was now untenable, and he resigned on September 8. The military junta, headed by Altamirano, maintained itself in power until January, 1925. Luis Galdames, *A History of Chile* (Chapel Hill: The University of North Carolina Press, 1941), pp. 370–75.

Our talk also brought out the interesting fact that while in times past we have recognized de facto governments, as in the case of Venezuela and Lansing's recognition of Carranza in Mexico,[26] the policy of Secretary Hughes is that no de facto government can be recognized as such. This was clearly stated in another telegram sent to Collier today, as follows: "It is the policy of the United States either to recognize or not to recognize a new government as such. It does not recognize a regime functioning in a country as a so-called de facto government." But in view of the alteration of our policy in this respect I altered the statement to read, "It does not now recognize a regime functioning in a country as a so-called de facto government."

Another interesting discussion arose with the Secretary concerning elections in Latin America. Lately Mr. Hughes has been less and less inclined to place ourselves in a position where we should have to decline to recognize a government if it was shown that the elections were fraudulent or not constitutionally carried out. In the course of our discussion the Secretary laughed and said, "Why we have not had a fair or constitutional election in the United States for the last forty years." He was, of course, referring to the suppression of Negro suffrage in the southern States. . . .

Tuesday, October 28 [1924]

There is no use in trying to keep this diary up daily. When I arrive at my desk in the morning I am promptly swamped with business and at the end of the afternoon my brain is much too fagged to think of anything but getting home, so I can only take up the thread from time to time and try to recollect what has gone on in the meantime. . . .

On October 20 we had Kippy [S. Pinkney] Tuck and his bride, Miss Beck, the daughter of our Solicitor General James M. Beck, to lunch at Beauvoir. Tuck is going out as our

---

26 On October 23, 1892, the new government of Venezuela was recognized. On October 19, 1915, Mr. Lansing accorded formal recognition to the Carranza Government.

Consul in Geneva and we have picked him especially as the right type of man to establish useful contacts with the League of Nations and to help Hugh Gibson in that way. Gibson wrote me how difficult it was for him to keep in touch with developments in Geneva by simply sitting at the end of a telephone in Berne and I know that very well from personal experience. Gibson pointed out that at the meetings of the Assembly and Council most of the important statesmen and diplomats of Europe are gathered and that quite apart from the activities of the League there is a vast amount of valuable information to be gained if some representative of ours can mingle freely with them. He suggested that to send a Consul with diplomatic qualifications to Geneva would be at least a first step.

After the election I sincerely hope to be able to bring about a less ostrich-like attitude on our part to the League. Every day of my life confirms me in the opinion that we are well out of Leagues and should stay out of them. We can certainly be much more helpful to Europe if we do, but the League is there and doing admirable work in a variety of directions; we should regard it as a robust and growing child not as a fullfledged adult. Certainly its achievements thus far justify its recognition as a power for good in the affairs of the world. If nothing else, it has become a big clearinghouse for the exchange of views and ideas. Nothing better has yet been evolved or suggested. Therefore, let us not regard it as a perfect mechanism guaranteeing the prevention of future wars and a permanent era of peace, but at least as a step in the right direction and let us co-operate to the limit in all of its nonpolitical activities and treat it with the same courtesy and respect as we would the Standard Oil Company or any other recognized organization. Our Consul in Geneva or our Minister in Berne, or both, should be free at all times to mingle with the members of the League in Geneva to learn their views, co-operate with them and deal openly and freely to the advantage of both without fear of the newspaper correspondents or anybody else. The whole trouble in our relations with the League arises from the original Wilson-Lodge controversy and having become a political football in this country at its very inception the heat between the pro-Leaguers and anti-Leaguers has developed out of all proportions to the subject at issue. If the whole matter could be analysed dispassionately in this country we should find that the two elements of public opinion were not so very far apart. Nobody wants us to come into the League without reservations and, on the other hand, nobody wants us to abstain from co-operation with the League in its nonpolitical activities. I am hopeful that after the present election this heat will subside sufficiently to allow us to pursue a normal and reasonable course of open dealings and open co-operation without necessarily making any radical change in our basic policy. We shall see. . . .

Friday, October 31 [1924]

As the campaign draws to a close the usual last minute mudslinging has begun in earnest. A few days ago the Democratic National Committee announced the names of twenty-seven diplomatic Chiefs of Mission whom they charged with being absent from their posts and campaigning in the United States for the Republican Party while their expenses were being paid by the Government. On Wednesday evening I had undressed and was about to go to bed when the President called me up on the telephone and asked if John W. Davis when Ambassador to Great Britain in 1920 had not returned to the United States during the campaign. I said that I could not recollect this myself, but would try to get into touch with somebody who had been in the Department or the London Embassy at that time. I got Hugh Wilson and David Salmon, Chief of the Bureau of Indexes and Archives, down to the Department and after rummaging for a while through the old files we found that Mr. Davis had been in the United States from August 25 until November 2, the date of the 1920 election, and had made at least two campaign speeches in favor of the League of Nations at that time. This interesting piece of news I telephoned to Bascom Slemp who promptly gave it to Jimmy Reynolds, the

Washington manager of the Republican National Committee.
The following day we found that twenty-one diplomatic Chiefs
of Mission had been in this country in 1920 during the campaign and we also found that the list given out by the Democratic National Committee was entirely inaccurate, as many of
the men mentioned are now at their posts, so it was easy to
draw up a reply to the Democratic charges which I gave to
Slemp in the White House yesterday and it appears in the
papers this morning. The Democratic Committee had stated
with regard to myself that President Coolidge had brought me
back from my post in Switzerland and made me Under Secretary of State in order to campaign in Massachusetts and that I
was the brother-in-law of J. Pierpont Morgan. We told the
press correspondents that this statement was all right except
for three small inaccuracies, namely, that I was not absent from
my post, that I was not a brother-in-law of J. Pierpont Morgan
and that my State was not Massachusetts. Otherwise it was
perfectly correct. . . .

Monday, November 17 [1924]
    . . . On the morning of November 5th, on returning from
Boston, I went over to congratulate the President on his great
victory. He was all smiles and looked just as happy as might
be expected. The Secretary was still absent in New York,
where he had gone to vote. In the afternoon came the Serbian
Minister . . . to protest against a film entitled *Her Love Story*
with Gloria Swanson, which he regarded as a libel on the
Serbian Queen, for although Serbia itself is not mentioned,
nevertheless in one of the scenes an envelope bearing Serbian
postage stamps was shown and the name of the villain was
Duchan, which was the name of one of the greatest emperors of
Yugoslavia in the fourteenth century. According to the story,
the Queen does not behave as well as queens ought to. I got
in touch with Will Hays, the Czar of Filmdom, and within
three days he showed me a telegram from Adolph Zukor saying that the objectionable portion of the film would be
promptly deleted all over the world. It is easy to get action of

this sort through Will Hays on account of the immense power he wields as President of the Motion Picture Producers Corporation and by reason of the fact that we are continuously assisting that Corporation in preventing the piracy of American films abroad.

On November 6th, I made a half-hour's speech to the class of new Foreign Service Officers who have just passed their examinations and been assigned to posts abroad. They had had plenty of technical instructions from the various officers in the Department so I confined myself to talking to them about the great importance of courtesy both in dealing with visitors and writing letters and I developed at some length the point that with a little tact one can, as has been aptly said, tell a man he is a damn fool in such a way that he will be happy about it, and on the other hand, a tactless officer can do a service or a favor in such a grudging manner as to send the visitor away with the impression that he has been badly treated. Exactly the same principle applies in the drafting of letters, and no letter is too trivial for the writer before sending it off to put himself in the place of the recipient and imagine just what impression it would make upon himself. I also talked about the importance of the study of languages on the ground that one can never adequately get at a man's mind except in his own tongue and also the importance of cultivating a broad vision and keeping in touch with world developments, not only in the country or district in which one is stationed. . . .

The Secretary has been in splendid form since the election and I am sure is profoundly relieved to have his campaign speeches over, although there is no doubt that he probably exerted more influence on the election than any other one individual. We had a long discussion the other day about the League of Nations. I told him that we were sending Pinkney Tuck out to Geneva as Consul and that we hoped to have him establish open contact with the League by which he could be of great help to Gibson and keep us adequately informed of what was going on. The Secretary said he had no objection to this but that he wished to avoid all newspaper comment at all cost. There could be no alteration in our policy towards the League as the election had shown without the slightest doubt that the majority of the American people are against our joining it or getting mixed up in any way in European political affairs. He said that the statements in his various campaign speeches along those lines had evoked greater applause than any other topic. The correct course for us to take is to keep quietly along as we are going, co-operating in the nonpolitical activities so far as they concern our own interests, but avoiding any semblance of further rapprochement to the League. The Secretary's position is certainly sound and since Davis insisted on making the League an issue in the campaign, it is perfectly clear that the mandate of the people is unfavorable to any closer relations with the League than we have at present. . . .

Saturday, December 20 [1924]

. . . While I was with the Secretary this morning Senator Charles Curtis called him on the telephone and said that he had a splendid Kansas man in mind for some diplomatic mission. This was bad news, but after the Senator had extolled the virtues of this gentleman and the Secretary asked the Senator his name, he was quite unable to remember it. After the Secretary had hung up the receiver he laughed long and loudly. He said it reminded him of the Chairman in a public meeting who, in introducing one of the speakers highly extolled that gentleman's distinction and virtues and then leaned down and whispered to him "By the way, what is your name?"

To Secretary of State Hughes, December 30, 1924

In an endeavor to analyze the problem which you presented to me this morning, the following suggestions may be worthy of consideration:

(1) The first principle in considering possible promotions or transfers within the Service is, as you rightly pointed out, to consult the best interests of the Government before any individual claim to recognition. That principle should, of course, be the primary test of every proposed movement.

(2) Accepting that primary principle, it may then be said that every promotion or transfer of a Foreign Service officer to a better or more important post than he is now holding will unquestionably have a material effect on the esprit de corps of the whole Service as tending to encourage all ranks of the career. It would therefore seem desirable to go as far as possible in this direction so long as the action taken is not inconsistent with the first principle set forth above.

(3) So far as consistent with that principle, it may furthermore appear undesirable to promote to the grade of Minister a greater number of consular than of diplomatic officers. This point was recognized by the Personnel Board in its recent discussions as of some importance, as it was felt, even by the consular officers on the Board, that while the promotion of diplomatic officers to diplomatic missions has for some time been recognized as a normal and logical step, the promotion of consular officers to diplomatic missions is a new departure under the Rogers Act and that to develop this new principle to the detriment of the diplomatic branch would probably cause discouragement within that branch, a contingency to be avoided if possible. The list presented to you was therefore arranged in such a way that if the President should select any number of officers for promotion in the order of their presentation, the promotions from the two branches of the Service would either be equal or with the predominance in favor of the diplomatic branch. I bring forward this point in the full understanding that it should be regarded only a secondary, although still an important, consideration. . . .[27]

Saturday, January 10 [1925]

This is a very blue day for the Department. Ever since last

[27] Writing to his father-in-law, Thomas Sergeant Perry, on January 19, 1924, Mr. Grew had said about the proposal to make consular and diplomatic officers interchangeable: "Interchanges will be carried out with great discrimination and care. There will be no 'weaving back and forth' between the two branches as the Consuls wish. You can't make a carpenter out of a plumber or a sailor out of a soldier by merely labeling him as such. The two jobs are as different as that of the Army and Navy, and if you try to train a man for both he will make a success of neither."

summer the Secretary had told me that he would definitely resign on March fourth as he wished to return to private life, but I have been hoping against hope that he would reconsider. Recently, however, he has several times referred to the matter and I saw that his mind was made up. Two or three weeks ago he told me that Ambassador Kellogg was leaving London and that Mr. Houghton, our Ambassador in Berlin, would succeed him. Today the Secretary called Harrison and myself into his room and told us that his resignation had been accepted by the President and that Ambassador Kellogg would succeed him as Secretary of State on March fourth. He asked Henry Getty Chilton [Counselor of the British Embassy] to come to the Department to ask immediately for the agrément of Mr. Houghton in London and told me to inform the President immediately on Monday when the reply of the British Government should be received, as he, Mr. Hughes, was going down to Atlanta until Wednesday. Mr. Hughes said that he had spent twenty years in Government service; that he was anxious to get back to his private law practice. If he stayed on after the fourth of March, he realized it would be impossible to leave at any time during the next four years without creating the impression that there had been friction between the President and himself. At the end of another four years he would be sixty-seven years of age, which was pretty late to go back to private work. He said he felt that with Ambassador Kellogg succeeding him, very little hiatus would be created by the change as Mr. Kellogg was in close touch with foreign affairs and also with the Foreign Service. I said to the Secretary that the news of his decision was a great blow to us as it would be to the entire Department and that I felt I was expressing the views of all the officials of the Department when I said that this period of service under him had been the most inspiring in our lives. Mr. Hughes left for Atlanta shortly after three o'clock. The announcement of his resignation and of Ambassador Kellogg's forthcoming appointment was announced by the White House at five and I promptly cabled it to London and Paris for Ambassador Kellogg. . . .

To Hugh Wilson, January 19, 1925
Confidential

As you are no doubt aware, the Secretary holds that inasmuch as women are admitted to the examinations, they are entitled in the examinations to the same treatment accorded men and to certification as eligible for appointment if, apart from the question of sex, they are found to possess the qualifications for the performance of the duties of the Foreign Service.

It follows from that ruling that women are as eligible as men to the general Foreign Service provided that they fulfill the requirements of the Executive Order as to fitness (apart from the question of sex). Therefore

1. The Board has not the right to set up a separate branch of the Service for women alone.

2. If it should do so the difficulty would not be solved but the Board would merely bring upon itself the accusation of seeking to deny women entry into the regular Service by diverting them into a less attractive branch of the Service.

We might as well face the fact that women will be satisfied with nothing less than treatment on complete equality with men with respect to the Foreign Service as Clerks, Foreign Service Officers, Ministers and Ambassadors. We now admit them as Clerks without question and under the Secretary's construction of the President's Order we must certify them as eligible for appointment as Foreign Service Officers, if, apart from sex, they show the requisite qualifications. Therefore, insofar as the Board of Examiners is concerned the question of sex no longer enters into its determination of eligibility.

I can see but one course to pursue, namely, that of being so thorough in examinations, both with respect to men and with respect to women, that no one not clearly possessing fitness for the Service shall be certified as eligible. Once certified as eligible, however, I think appointments of women and their assignment to duty should proceed in the precise manner in which appointments and assignments of men are made and that we should insist upon equality of treatment throughout the career and require the same quality of performance from women as we require from men. The tendency, once women go into the field, will be to protect them, give them inside work or clerical duties and attempt to shield them from many difficulties in which their position will place them. That, in my opinion, should not be permitted to be done and every female member of the Service should be rated for her efficiency on precisely the same basis as men are rated, otherwise there would be no equality of treatment and my understanding is that first and foremost of the claims of women, with respect to Public Service, is that they shall be treated exactly as men are treated.

Friday, February 20 [1925]

The Karolyi affair is still very much to the fore. Last summer when I took the decision to admit Countess Karolyi [wife of the former President of Hungary] to this country, Széchényi [Hungarian Minister to the United States] prophesied that this would undoubtedly lead to the admission of her husband somehow or other, sooner or later. Sure enough, Countess Karolyi fell ill with typhoid fever and her physician said it was essential her husband should be here. He came after giving assurances to our Consul General in London that he wished to come merely to see his wife and would abstain from any political activities or expressions. Now the press has got hold of the story and says that when a correspondent recently asked Count Karolyi for an interview, he said he was prevented by the State Department from saying anything to the newspapers. This let out a general howl, especially in the *New York World,* charging the State Department with "muzzling." As a result of the publicity, we are informed that the Senate Foreign Relations Committee has just passed a Resolution calling on the Department for full information. The matter was discussed at Cabinet this morning and the Secretary says that the President was delightful. The Secretary explained the case and how Karolyi had been admitted on account of his wife's illness. The President said that it was a very dangerous thing to let countesses run around loose in this country. The Secretary said that we had really found no grounds upon which to exclude her; that she had not been charged with any activities or expressions which could be interpreted as subversive of this Government and that it would have been very difficult to keep her out merely to prevent her talking. "Yes," said the President. "But she might get ill." . . .[28]

Saturday, March 7 [1925]

. . . On Tuesday, March third, the Department of State gave its farewell luncheon to Mr. Hughes at which I presided. About 130 members of the Department and of the Foreign Service were present and it was a most impressive affair. I made the following address:

"Mr. Secretary, Ladies and Gentlemen:

"A colleague of ours remarked to me the other day that work in the State Department nowadays was fun. As he is one of our hardest working officials there was fortunately no necessity of reporting his remark to the Personnel Board for investigation and entry on his record. I knew just what he meant and I believe that every one of us here feels exactly as he does. Any work is fun when one has one's heart in it. . . . Our work in the State Department is all of that, because our Chief has made it so. Those of us who have had the good fortune to hear that particular peremptory note on our buzzers (I can always recognize it on mine without looking) or who have seen the glow of the little light that summoned us to headquarters will never, as long as we live, forget the thrill of satisfaction that it entailed. For it brought us into contact with a mind that tore aside the unessentials of a matter with the first thought and then penetrated to the heart of it with unerring precision; a mind that with all its logic and great wisdom still welcomed the

---

[28] After Count and Countess Karolyi had left the United States in 1924, the Count spoke slightingly of the Department of State. In 1925, when the Countess tried to return to the United States, the Department refused her a visa. Litigation followed, the Circuit Court ruling against her appeal for entry. The *New Republic* stated that Kellogg had indicated that the reasons why the Department opposed her entry were based on her husband's remarks about the Department. Stuart, *op. cit.*, pp. 282–83.

other man's point of view, still found place for humor and still more place for human sympathy. . . .

"Few chiefs fail to command the loyalty of their subordinates, but it is quite another matter to bring out and steadily maintain a feeling of genuine and deep-rooted personal affection among those who work under their leadership. Relations of this kind alter the whole complexion of the sometimes dull round of business and inspire in any organization a co-operative spirit that develops the very best it has to give. Every one of us today must be taking stock of the influence the Secretary has exerted upon our lives, influence that will be turned to account according to our several capacities. If any greater monument to his work can be erected than the specific achievements of the last four years, it may be found in the inspiring and enduring influence he has exerted upon those about him. Because of it we shall always be better servants of the Government, better men.

"During the last four years the Department of State has attained a cohesion, an enthusiasm and an esprit de corps which has never before been equalled; a Department where every man and woman works for the joy of working and knows that his work is being directed into the right channels to constructive ends. The Foreign Service has been efficiently reorganized; initial difficulties and obstacles have been overcome; encouragement throughout all ranks has been given; merit has been recognized. Neither the Department nor the Foreign Service will ever forget this record, nor will they ever forget the Secretary of State who successfully championed them throughout his term of office. . . ."

On March 4th, which turned out to be a beautiful, sunny day, Alice and I went to the Capitol, heard the closing business of the Senate and saw the Inaugural Ceremonies. . . . In the afternoon I returned to the Department while Mr. Hughes was cleaning up his desk. He fortunately changed his mind at the last moment and decided to leave in the Department all the memoranda of his private conversations with diplomats and others. We should have been seriously embarrassed had he taken them away as he intended to do, but I urged him strongly to leave them, citing to him the recent instance in which the Peruvian Government had stated that it had never requested the Secretary's good offices to arrange the boundary disputes with Colombia and Brazil. As a matter of fact, the Peruvian Ambassador had asked the Secretary to do this on behalf of his Government and the only record of the conversation was in the Secretary's private files. There was nothing else in writing on the subject. . . .

Before I left the Department I took leave of the Secretary at which time he said some very nice things which I shall never forget. I saw him later at the Inaugural Ball when he took me by both arms and said, "Well I am just through. I have just finished cleaning up my desk." He looked and seemed as happy as a boy commencing his holiday. . . .

The following afternoon, March 6th, Mr. and Mrs. Hughes left Washington, most of the Diplomatic Corps, members of the Cabinet and many others being there to see them off. It was very nearly the saddest moment of my life for when I saw him board the train it came to me as never before all that association with him had meant and what it meant to lose him. I have seldom loved a man so much and was profoundly moved and depressed. . . .

XXIII

Working with Secretary Kellogg
1925 – 1926

The appointment of Frank B. Kellogg as Secretary of State was not received with overwhelming enthusiasm by the American press. He had served as Ambassador to Great Britain for a little over two years, and he had been a one-term United States Senator from Minnesota. The press, on the whole, seemed to feel that Herbert Hoover would have been a better choice.

Mr. Kellogg proved to have a temperament far different from Secretary Hughes. Hugh Wilson, then Chief of the Division of Current Information, has written that Kellogg had "a hasty and explosive temper." If he read something irritating in the paper, he would summon everybody he could think of, and, according to Wilson, "We were greeted with a storm of rage. An immediate Council was held, Mr. Kellogg still sputtering, and out of that conference would come a calm and reasoned decision on the part of the Secretary of State. I never understood how it worked, but it seemed to." [1]

When Mr. Kellogg became Secretary of State, he told President Coolidge that he would like to appoint Dwight Morrow of J. P. Morgan and Company to the post of Under Secretary. Although Mr. Morrow was a close friend of the President's, Mr. Coolidge insisted that Mr. Grew, a diplomat with twenty years of experience, be retained. Mr. Kellogg made one political appointment in the upper level of the Department by naming his former law partner, Robert E. Olds, Assistant Secretary of State to replace John V. A. MacMurray who went as Minister to China.

[1] *Diplomat Between Wars* (New York: Longmans, Green & Co., 1941), pp. 174–75.

651

Mr. Grew served as Under Secretary for just over two years of the Kellogg administration. Unlike Mr. Hughes, who had kept the Under Secretary informed on top policy, Mr. Kellogg seldom explained to Mr. Grew the policy decisions and the discussions that the Secretary had had with the President. When both Kellogg and Coolidge were out of Washington, Mr. Grew was left with an incomplete picture of the policy that had been agreed upon between the two men. This was a serious situation in that Mr. Grew was Acting Secretary of State for fifty-four days in 1925, forty-four days in 1926, and twenty-eight days in 1927.

From his post as Ambassador to Turkey, Mr. Grew wrote, on September 11, 1928, to Assistant Secretary of State William R. Castle, Jr., explaining his relations as Under Secretary to Mr. Kellogg:

"You say that you hesitated to send me this batch of diary because it contains a remark by Mr. Kellogg about me as Under Secretary which I may not like. On the contrary, I like it very much, because he attributes my failure as Under Secretary merely to the theory that I was too much occupied with personnel matters. I personally fear, however, that the real reason is that he did not much respect my opinion. From time to time I did act as his right-hand man, particularly after periods when I had been in charge and had all the threads in my hands, as, for instance, when I had been handling the Chinese situation and met him at Swampscott in the summer of 1926 to discuss it with the President. But inevitably, in every such case, things were taken out of my hands; he stopped consulting me and left me on the sidelines, and it was not owing to personnel matters. If I had possessed the hide of a rhinoceros I might have continued to thrust myself in, but that has never been my way, or would it be yours, and it was not the way to which I had been accustomed with Mr. Hughes. From time to time he would suddenly, for no apparent reason, bring me in again and with only half the background I tried to advise wisely, but then again there would be sudden fallings off and I found myself sidetracked. No man can advise intelligently unless he is kept

*informed of every development and even at the best of times
that was never the case. Sometimes he would call me in and
read me a note or telegram on some subject with which I was
only half familiar and ask my opinion, occasionally with naval
officers or others present when it would have been embarrassing
to say that I wished to study the matter before replying. The
Under Secretary must be familiar with every subject, but he
can't be unless his chief takes pains to tell him what he has said
and thought and done. Mr. Kellogg never realized that at all.
To be suddenly sidetracked when after months of work I had
every detail of some subject, such as the Chinese situation, at
my finger tips was profoundly discouraging and naturally I lost
interest in that side of the job. I don't for a moment delude
myself by thinking that I was a successful Under Secretary, but
I sometimes wonder if anyone could be successful under those
circumstances. . . .*

*"With all that I have said, I feel a certain genuine affection
for Mr. Kellogg, for there is much in his nature that commands
affection and besides he has been most loyal to me. That is
something that overshadows everything else and I shall never
forget it."*

Sunday, March 15 [1925]

A survey of the last few weeks is interesting, especially from
the point of view of the interests of the Foreign Service. I suppose I may be regarded as the Cerberus of the Foreign Service at present — its watchdog and guardian. At any rate, it is
a great satisfaction to be able to help it along and I had
determined to leave nothing undone to secure ample recognition for it in the changes which always take place at the beginning of a new administration. I had repeatedly spoken to Mr.
Hughes of promotions and transfers that ought to be made and
had submitted the list of officers in Class I whom the Personnel
Board considered as fitted for promotion to the rank of Minister. But he continually put me off until one day he asked me
to submit a slate of changes. This I did with alacrity and my
list was incorporated in a letter to the President just as it stood.

The Secretary took an opportunity offered him by the President and talked for forty-five minutes on the subject. He took up six of my proposed changes but said he could not approach the others until the President gave him another chance. With all his force and initiative, Secretary Hughes always hesitated to bring up matters of personnel with the President until invited to do so. But before leaving office he told me that he wished to leave nothing undone in the interests of the Service and one of his last acts was to send the President his letter incorporating my list. . . .

When Mr. Kellogg took office he agreed to support the list as it stood and made it his prime interest among the many problems before him. When the resignations of John Ramer and Franklin Morales from Nicaragua and Honduras were accepted, he urged the appointments of Charles Eberhardt and George Summerlin to those posts [American Ministers to Nicaragua and Honduras] and they were promptly made. The reaction in the press was most favorable, which doubtless had its effect on the President in considering further Service nominations. Charles Kagey's resignation from Finland [as American Minister] was accepted, in return for which we appointed George L. Kreeck of Kansas to Paraguay to satisfy Senator Curtis. I informed him of the appointment by telephone and he expressed himself as thoroughly gratified. Then Finland was offered to H. Percival Dodge, who declined it on the ground of health. Hoffman Philip was transferred to Persia in accordance with the schedule and Uruguay was offered to Grant-Smith. . . .

All this time I was pushing Peter Jay [American Minister to Rumania] for Ambassador to the Argentine, as John Riddle's resignation had been accepted on the ground that his wife could not join him there — although I believe he would have been glad to stay on. Mr. Hughes had decided that point. The President however felt he must offer an Embassy to Ogden Hammond [real esate broker and Republican politician] who was being pushed by Senator Walter Edge [of New Jersey]. Edge had agreed to Morales being let out if Hammond should be given an appointment. Then Senator Edge left Washington just at the time of the vote on Charles Beecher Warren's nomination for Attorney General in the Senate (Warren was rejected by a vote of 41 to 39, Senator Lee Overman [of North Carolina], Democrat, having changed his vote after the first vote, 40 to 40, had been lost to the Republicans owing to Vice-President Charles Dawes' absence from the chair at the critical moment) and the President said that he felt no further obligation to consider Hammond for an Embassy.[2] Realizing that Peter Jay's chances were now hanging in the balance I went to the Senate to see Senator Jesse Metcalf of Rhode Island and told him that I had come not officially but as a personal friend of Jay and that it was up to him to see the President at once if he wanted the nomination to go through. I pointed out that Rhode Island had only one representative as Chief of Mission and that the Senators of other States which had several representatives were bringing all possible pressure to bear on the President for their respective candidates. Senator Metcalf promised to see the President personally the next morning. I then talked with Alfred Dennis, who had just been appointed to the Federal Tariff Commission, a personal friend both of the President and of Peter Jay, and urged him to put in a word. He went immediately to the President and spoke in high terms of Peter's ability and qualifications. I think these two steps must have swung the matter, for the following day the President authorized Kellogg to offer Jay the post. This was Friday the 13th and it proved to be a great day, for it brought forth not only Jay's appointment but the ratification of the Isle of Pines Treaty [3] as well. We did not even con-

[2] Hammond was appointed Ambassador to Spain on December 21, 1925.

[3] By the Treaty of Paris in 1898 Spain had divested herself of title to her West Indian possessions, among them the Isle of Pines, an island lying southwest of Cuba. In 1901 the Platt Amendment stated that the Isle of Pines should not be included within the boundaries of Cuba, but the ownership of the island should be determined by future negotiation. A treaty between the United States and Cuba in which the United States relinquished claim to the Isle of Pines was signed on July 2, 1903, but ratifications were not exchanged within the time limit. Another treaty without time limit was signed on March

sult Jay but merely informed him that his agrément was being asked at once; DeLancey, his brother, had told me that he would welcome it and I was sure of this myself. . . .

Monday, May 11 [1925]
. . . In the evening the monthly dinner of the Baby Cabinet at which the President was our guest and made a short address. Edward Henning [Assistant Secretary of Labor] also delivered his swan song. The President, who sat between the Chairman, Charles S. Dewey [Assistant Secretary of the Treasury] and Garrard Winston, Under Secretary of the Treasury (a somewhat close Treasury corporation) made hardly a remark throughout the evening, except when he delivered his speech, and it was uphill work for those beside him, who were apparently doing their best to entertain him. Only once in the course of the evening his face brightened and he made an amusing remark which brought a laugh. His speech related to the dignity and importance of the positions of the Assistant Secretaries and the responsibility which rested on their shoulders as trustees of the public welfare. . . .

In the decade following World War I, the Chinese revolution entered a critical stage of its development. The Washington Conference, in addition to reaffirming the policy of the Open Door and assuring the territorial integrity of China, agreed to discuss revision of the Chinese tariff rates to allow China more revenue, and to appoint a commission to investigate extraterritorial jurisdiction in China to the end that the foreign powers might be warranted "in relinquishing, either progressively or otherwise, their respective rights of extraterritoriality."

The political chaos in China, however, led to the postponement of the first meeting of this commission until January,

2, 1904. On March 13, 1925, the Senate finally consented to ratification of the treaty of 1904, by which title to the Isle of Pines was given to Cuba. U.S. Department of State, *Papers Relating to the Foreign Relations of the United States, 1925* (Washington: Government Printing Office, 1940), II, 1–14.

1926. Secretary Hughes had told the Chinese Minister in 1923, that China could hardly expect equal treatment while she exhibited "before the world inability to protect even the lives and safety of foreigners." The commission's report stated that the powers would consider abolition of extraterritoriality when China had made substantial progress in her judicial reforms.[4]

Meanwhile Chinese nationalism and antiforeignism had become acute. The authority of the internationally recognized Peking government was being challenged by war lords, and the Kuomintang forces at Canton. Nevertheless, Chinese were united in their antiforeignism, if in nothing else. National consciousness, particularly in the coastal cities, had developed to such an extent that all the treaty powers were looked upon as "obnoxious imperialists."[5] *On May 30, 1925, a Chinese mob in the International Settlement of Shanghai was fired upon by Sikh and Chinese constables. Nine Chinese were killed and Chinese protests took the form of a general strike, which brought business to a standstill for most of the summer. Antiforeign outbreaks also occurred in other areas of China, but the most serious disturbance took place at Canton. A few foreigners were killed; a successful boycott of British goods was launched; and a general strike of Chinese workmen paralyzed business in neighboring Hong Kong.*

Foreign governments demanded that China respect the sanctity of treaties and protect the lives and property of foreigners. In the midst of these difficulties the weak Peking government continued to ask for complete revision of the treaties in the name "of the legitimate national aspirations of the Chinese people."

Tuesday, July 14 [1925]

These hot summer days have seen no letup in the activity of

---

[4] U.S. Department of State, *Papers Relating to the Foreign Relations of the United States, 1926* (Washington: Government Printing Office, 1941), I, 966–83.

[5] A. Whitney Griswold, *The Far Eastern Policy of the United States* (New York: Harcourt, Brace & Co., 1938), pp. 385–86.

international affairs; in fact, just as Persia disturbed the peace-fulness of my chargéship last summer,[6] China came into it this year and actually brought the Secretary back from St. Paul after an absence of only a few days. The situation in China has been decidedly bad and has serious potentialities, but I believe we have adopted the only policy which will tend to check the disorders. The Boxer outbreak [of 1900] was based on the same underlying causes as the present movement, namely, a protest against foreign exploitation of China; but the two movements are analogous in no other respect. The Boxers were a horde of uneducated fanatics who believed that secret incantations would render them impervious to the bullets of the foreigners. Since that day, a system of education has sprung up in China based on the school system of Germany and Japan and the present movement is being carried on largely by educated students with well-defined nationalistic aspirations. This sort of movement cannot be put down by threats or force and the time seems to have come to take the first steps to meet these nationalistic aspirations of the Chinese by carrying out the commitments of the Washington Conference, namely, by calling the Tariff Conference and by appointing the Commission to study the question of extraterritoriality under Resolution V.

After the Secretary's departure for St. Paul on leave of absence on July 2, we received in succession five notes from the British Embassy stating the position of the British Government and indicating its disfavor of any step towards revision of the treaties at the present time, until China has quelled her disorders, as that would be interpreted in China as a sign of weakness.[7] We cannot agree with this position. The Japanese seem to see the situation about as we do; in fact, in MacMurray's recent talk with Shidehara [Japanese Minister for Foreign Affairs] in Tokyo, the latter said he thought the extraterritorial commission ought to function at the same time as the tariff

---

[6] Robert Imbrie, American Vice Consul in Teheran, had died from injuries received when a mob attacked him, while he was taking photographs of a sacred fountain.

[7] *Foreign Relations, 1925*, I, 770–71, 775–77.

conference. MacMurray objected to this, before knowing the attitude of the Department, and said he thought one should follow the other. Shidehara replied that this might perhaps be the best method. The Shanghai incident, in which a considerable number of Chinese were killed in attacking the Louza Police Station, has caused a good deal of complication. The legations in Peking found the Municipal Council at Shanghai guilty of negligence and recommended admonishing the Chairman and dismissing the Chief of Police. The Municipal Council, however, refused to act on these findings, holding that it is not subject to the authority of the Diplomatic Corps in Peking. This has become a moot subject and the heads of legations are appealing to their respective governments for support. The British are being pushed by the large commercial interests in China, which no doubt largely accounts for their attitude. The United States is in quite a different position from Great Britain, Japan and France which have large territories contiguous to China and large vested interests within the country and I feel very strongly that it is up to us to take the lead in insisting on carrying out the obligations of the Washington Conference.

I kept in close touch with the Secretary in St. Paul by wire, but matters finally came to a point where it seemed much better for him to return and talk to the President, who, after all, bears the responsibility for our policy. Accordingly I met the Secretary in Boston on July 11, took him to the Somerset Club for lunch and then motored down to White Court, the President's summer residence at Swampscott. We had a long conference in the afternoon and apparently persuaded the President as to the soundness of our views as he approved of the note which we had drafted to the British Embassy in reply to theirs.[8] This had been drawn up largely by Nelson Johnson,

8 The note of July 13, 1925, agreed with the British that discussions must emphasize that the Chinese had to give concrete assurances that the lives and property of foreigners in China would be protected, but the note stated that one of the best ways for outsiders to meet the national unrest in China was by a strict adherence to the agreements made at the Washington Conference. "[The] least that these Powers can do is to agree to an early calling of the

the new Chief of the Far Eastern Division, who has been a great help and knows China about as well as anyone possibly except MacMurray. After our conference, the Secretary and I dined very simply with the President and Mrs. Coolidge — a good old New England boiled dinner — while the band from the Presidential yacht, the *Mayflower,* played soft music in an adjoining room, especially the light airs that the President is very fond of. When they were playing the old Amherst song, he called my attention to it. He is not chatty at the table, but now and then makes a dry remark which is very amusing. He has a distinct sense of humor. After dinner I motored to Manchester to spend the night with Billy Chilton (Henry Getty Chilton, the British Chargé d'Affaires) as we had decided that it would be well for me to have a talk with him and explain our attitude as clearly as possible. On Sunday morning Chilton and John Balfour [Second Secretary of the British Embassy] drafted their telegram to the British Foreign Office while I took a swim on Singing Beach, after which I went to the British Chancery, read their telegram and made several suggestions for clarifying it. The telegram stated that it was based on conversations with me and that I had just spent the afternoon with the President and Secretary of State, so it was almost as if the President had been talking face to face with Sir Austen Chamberlain [Secretary for Foreign Affairs] . . . After luncheon I returned immediately to White Court. . . . The President was sitting on the piazza with his marine glasses and during the ensuing conference he used them continually to watch every ship that passed. We came to a decision on all points and the Secretary and I left for Boston in our car about 4.30. The newspapermen stopped us at the bottom of the avenue and the Secretary gave them a prepared statement in which I

Conference on Chinese tariff provided for in the Treaty of February 6, 1922." In regard to the question of extraterritoriality the "most feasible way in which the question can be approached and considered is to send to China the Commission provided for in Resolution V of the Washington Conference, in the expectation that the investigations made by that Commission will help to guide the treaty Powers as to what, if any, steps should be taken as regards the possible relinquishment of extraterritorial rights at this time." *Ibid.,* 780–83.

made one or two rapid changes at the last moment such as adding a phrase that China must live up to her responsibilities under the treaties.[9] In Boston we went to the Tennis and Racquet Club, sat there for an hour or more, had a very good dinner and then returned to Washington by the Federal. David Lawrence [President of the Consolidated Press Association] got on at the Back Bay Station and said casually that he was going to Providence, which gave him a full hour's interview with the Secretary. I noticed that he carried no bag and it was quite evident that this was a little piece of newspaper initiative. . . .

Conversation   December 19, 1925

The Italian Ambassador, Nobile Giacomo de Martino

RESOLUTION INTRODUCED BY SENATOR BLEASE REGARDING ALLEGED TRANSPORTATION TO THIS COUNTRY OF WINES AND LIQUORS BY THE ITALIAN DEBT FUNDING COMMISSION [10]

The Italian Ambassador called and said that in an entirely personal and unofficial way he wished to draw our attention to the unfortunate effect which could be caused in Italy by the resolution introduced in the Senate by Senator Blease calling for a report with regard to the alleged transportation in this country of wines and liquors by the Italian Debt Funding Commission and inquiring why the members of the Commis-

[9] The front page of the New York Times of July 13, 1925, reported Secretary Kellogg's statement to the effect that the "cornerstone" of American policy in China would be the fulfillment of the obligations to China entered into at Washington, coupled with the insistence that China take adequate steps to protect foreign lives and interests within her boundaries.

[10] On December 17, 1925, Senator Coleman Blease introduced a resolution that "the Assistant Secretary of the Treasury Hon. Lincoln C. Andrews . . . be requested to investigate immediately . . . if it is true that the recent representatives of the Italian delegation to this country in reference to the settlement of its debt to the United States were permitted to bring into this country champagne, whiskey and beer . . . and if they did, why were they not promptly arrested, as American citizens would have been?" U.S. Congress, Congressional Record, 69th Cong., 1st Sess., vol. LXVII, pt. 7 (Washington: Government Printing Office, 1926), p. 992.

sion had not been arrested as violators of the law. Mr. de
Martino said that unfortunately the news relations between
Italy and the United States were very unsatisfactory, as practically no direct press service existed and that American news
published in Italy was almost always distorted in England or
France. He said that in this particular case the French would
undoubtedly make the most of the incident in order to stir up
unfriendly feeling towards the United States in Italy. Incidentally, the Ambassador remarked that he was doing his best to
improve this press situation. He said he had cabled his Government to explain certain differences in the form of our
legislative body from the Parliaments in Europe, and that he
had advised his Government that the incident was without
importance and that no concern need be felt, but he believed
it would be very helpful if we could instruct Ambassador
Fletcher to take an opportunity in an entirely personal and unofficial way to explain that the introduction of this resolution
in Congress implied no lack of friendliness on the part of our
Government towards Italy.

I said to the Ambassador that I felt sure he would agree with
me that this sort of incident was likely to occur and frequently
did occur in any European Parliament. He assented to this,
but said that if such a resolution had been introduced in the
Italian, British or French Parliament the presiding officer
would have immediately made some remarks about the importance of courtesy to foreign Governments which would have
largely offset the effect of the resolution. He remarked that
Vice President Dawes had done nothing of this kind. I said
that I would give full consideration to what the Ambassador
had said, but could assure him in advance that Mr. Fletcher on
his own initiative would take all appropriate steps to prevent
the incident from being misunderstood in Italy. I said that
it would be very embarrassing for us to instruct one of our
diplomatic agents abroad to say to a foreign Government that
no importance need be attached to a resolution introduced
into Congress. The Ambassador readily agreed to this, but said
that all he desired to suggest was that Mr. Fletcher should take

occasion to remark that the resolution did not represent an unfriendly attitude on the part of our Government towards Italy. . . .

To Peter Jay, January 9, 1926
Personal and confidential
The Secretary has asked me to send you a line to impress upon you the great importance of maintaining the closest contact with American businessmen in the Argentine and of developing the most co-operative relations with them. The importance of the Argentine as a field of commercial expansion cannot be overestimated and the Secretary desires that nothing be left undone to cultivate and foster American trade throughout Latin America especially. The personal relationships which you can establish with representatives of American business throughout the Argentine and especially in Buenos Aires will, we feel, prove helpful in many ways and I know that you will leave nothing undone in that direction. To so experienced an officer as yourself, it is hardly necessary to say this, and the purpose of this letter is merely to lay particular emphasis on one phase of your work which is becoming and will continue to become of ever-increasing importance in your present bailiwick. . . .

Conversation   January 11, 1926
Rev. Fr. John J. Burke, General Secretary of the National
Catholic Welfare Conference

COMMITTEE ON INTELLECTUAL CO-OPERATION, LEAGUE OF
NATIONS

Father John J. Burke called and said that his organization had been requested to send a representative to sit with the Committee on Intellectual Co-operation of the League of Nations at Geneva, but before assenting they desired to consult the Department and to know if any reason were perceived why such a step would be undesirable from the point of view of the Government. Fr. Burke said that while his organization was essentially a Catholic body it was first of all American and that it would not wish to take any step which could possibly embarrass the Administration or which could have any adverse effect on the fate of the World Court resolution now pending in Congress. He said that there was no present intention, even if they should send a representative to Geneva, to have him become a permanent member of the Committee, but merely to sit in as an observer for the time being and to report on its work. Fr. Burke mentioned the American National Committee of the Committee on Intellectual Co-operation of the League of Nations and left with me a list of its members, containing such names as those of Elihu Root, Charles W. Eliot, Herbert Putnam, et al. He also said that there were also several American citizens who are members of the Geneva Committee. He realized that if the great Catholic organization of the United States should be represented there would be publicity and comment and therefore they wished to consult the Department before proceeding.

I thanked Fr. Burke for his courtesy in consulting us in the matter and told him that as a general rule, when consulted, we had expressed no disapproval of private American organizations or citizens participating in the nonpolitical activities of the League of Nations. I said that the Government itself had been represented in many of these activities, notably in questions relating to narcotics, traffic in arms, etc. But that when the question had arisen as to Government participation in the Geneva Committee on Intellectual Co-operation it had been found that a representative unofficial American committee had already been formed and as this Government had no Ministry of Education there had seemed to be no good reason for us to participate officially. I said that I would bring his inquiry to the attention of the Secretary and would give him a reply in due course.

I called Fr. Burke on the telephone and informed him that while the Secretary much appreciated his courtesy in consulting the Department in the foregoing matter the Secretary did not desire to comment in any way.

Conversation   January 25, 1926
    The Honorable H. W. Brooks, First Secretary, British
                            Embassy

RECOGNITION OF GENERAL CHAMORRO OF NICARAGUA [11]

Mr. Brooks of the British Embassy called and said that he had cabled to the British Government what I had told him in our last conversation — on January 23 — regarding our policy of supporting the Central American Treaty of 1923 and of our intention on that basis to refuse to recognize General Chamorro in Nicaragua. In the meantime, he said, a telegram had been received from the British Government, which had apparently been sent before the arrival of the telegram from the Embassy, stating that according to reports received by the British Government Chamorro was the only strong man in Nicaragua who could be expected to hold the country together and inquiring whether this fact was being given consideration in the formulation of our policy. Mr. Brooks therefore said he felt he ought to inquire whether there was anything to add to what I had told him the other day.

I said to Mr. Brooks that we had given full consideration to the personal strength of General Chamorro, but that this could make no difference in our policy. If we were to deviate from our support of the Central American Treaty and deal with each case on its individual merits, recognizing those who came into power by unconstitutional means if we felt they had sufficient strength, on that very day the open season for revolutions in Central America would commence because each revolutionist would consider himself the strong man of the country

[11] The United States withdrew its Marines from Nicaragua in 1925. Shortly thereafter General Chamorro executed a coup d'état and forced a subservient Congress to declare him President. The Central American Powers in 1923 had signed a treaty agreeing that they would "not recognize any other Government which may come into power in any of the five Republics through a coup d'état or a revolution." The United States and the four remaining Central American states, therefore, refused to recognize Chamorro. The United States landed troops, dictated an armistice between contending factions, and organized a provisional government.

and would conduct his revolution in the belief that he would obtain recognition from our Government if he succeeded. I gave as an example the situation in Honduras last year and explained how Carias had been deterred by the certainty that he would not be recognized by this Government under any circumstances if he should come into power by unconstitutional means.[12]

Mr. Brooks said that he would simply cable his Government that there was nothing to add to the statement I had made to him in our last conversation.

February 1, 1926

The outstanding points of interest to the State Department during the last several months have been four in number, namely, Tacna-Arica, Mexico, Nicaragua and the Preliminary Arms Conference called by the League of Nations.

The Tacna-Arica Arbitration has been a source of great worry. . . . General Pershing has been working under the greatest difficulties in his preparations. The strain finally reacted on his health to such an extent that he was obliged to leave Arica and General Lassiter has been appointed in his place, at least temporarily. There had been some talk of other Latin American countries, notably Argentina and Uruguay, offering their good offices for diplomatic settlement which would envisage giving a portion of the disputed territory and a port on the sea to Bolivia. This, however, has not materialized.[13]

---

[12] In the presidential elections in Honduras in October, 1923, no candidate received a majority of the votes, and when the Congress failed to elect a president, López Gutiérrez, the President since 1920, established a dictatorship, proposing to maintain power, until a special assembly could meet to establish a new government. Tiburcio Carias, one of the recent candidates, organized a revolt against Gutiérrez, and the United States suspended its relations with his Government. American Marines were landed, and under the guidance of the United States the rival groups reached an agreement for choosing a new president. Barahona, a conservative, was chosen President.

[13] For over fifty years the area of Tacna-Arica had been in dispute between Chile and Peru. In 1922, the United States offered its good offices, and President Coolidge as arbitrator on March 5, 1925, called for a plebiscite in the

The Mexican Congress has passed two bills — the Land Law, interpreting Article 17 of the Constitution and the Petroleum Law, which, if applied retroactively will seriously jeopardize vested American rights. We have adopted a patient policy and have corresponded with the Mexican Government in the most friendly terms in the hope that the President will, on his own initiative, issue regulations so that these laws shall not be applied retroactively. Ambassador James Sheffield had a talk with Plutarco Calles the other day which seems to promise well, but the Mexican Government has taken the stand that they are going to show the United States that she cannot interfere in Mexican domestic affairs and a virulent press campaign has been conducted against us.[14] In Sheffield's talk with the President, the latter let slip a remark to the effect that he had given orders that this campaign should cease, which was a pretty clear indication that he himself had first instigated it. We are cordially hated there and it is not easy to foresee what the final outcome will be. . . .

In Nicaragua, General Chamorro has finally seized the presidency, having first driven the Liberals from Congress, then seized the Loma Fortress overlooking Managua, having him-

area. After a short time, General William Lassiter replaced General Pershing as President of the plebiscite commission. In June, 1926, General Lassiter recommended that the plebiscite be abandoned, because Chile's attitude rendered a free and fair plebiscite impossible. Finally when President-elect Hoover visited South America, he was able to bring the nations together for a plebiscite which settled the controversy. See W. J. Dennis, *Tacna and Arica* (New Haven: Yale University Press, 1931).

14 Relations with Mexico deteriorated under Secretary Kellogg. In 1923, Mr. Hughes had worked out agreements which averted for the moment the confiscation of American agricultural holdings and the nationalization of the subsoil deposits. Then, the United States Government recognized the Government of Mexico, and President-elect Calles was warmly welcomed in a visit to Washington. In 1925, however, the Mexican Congress passed laws which threatened American property rights. Kellogg issued a statement that the United States would support the Mexican Government "only so long as it protects American lives and American rights and complies with its international engagements and obligations. The Mexican Government is now on trial before the world." Although some Americans demanded intervention in Mexico, Kellogg was widely criticized in the American press. The *Macon Telegraph,* for instance, said the statement was the "worst diplomatic blunder in American history."

self appointed Commander in Chief of the Army and then driving Vice-President Juan Sacasa in flight from the country. We have consistently stated that our policy would be in strict accordance with the Treaties of 1923 and although General Chamorro apparently thought, or pretended to think, that we were bluffing, he has definitely been informed that we cannot and will not recognize him and all of the Central American States have acted likewise. I have often wondered whether our policy in this respect is right, because from time to time a good and strong man, such as Porfirio Díaz in Mexico and General Chamorro in Nicaragua will prove to be the only men capable of holding their countries together. But if we let down the bars at all and recognize anyone who comes to power by unconstitutional means, there will be many an open season for revolutions, the national sport in Central America, and people like Carias in Honduras will say what fools they were for being deterred by the United States from seizing the power that was so easily within their grasp. . . .

The Secretary has been under a terrible strain lately and a day or two ago he said to me rather pathetically that he had altogether too much to do, so today I called in the Chiefs of the Geographical Divisions and asked them to try to keep everything except matters of prime importance away from the Secretary and bring them to me first. A great many things come to the Secretary's desk which there is no need whatever for him to consider, but whatever he sees he goes into with the utmost thoroughness. After hesitating for a long time, he finally today agreed to the appointment of an administrative assistant to take over the whole administration of the Department, thereby relieving Butler Wright and the rest of us from a mass of administrative work which we ought never to have to do. The plan is that this man, who will be Donald Evans of the Bureau of Efficiency, will be a sort of super-Chief Clerk and will be supposed to decide all but the most important questions of administration on his own initiative without bothering anybody. It is a trial step but I profoundly hope it will prove successful. . . .

Tuesday, February 2 [1926]

William Walker Smith [former Foreign Service officer] came in today to introduce Mr. Howard T. Oliver and the following astonishing conversation ensued: Oliver said that there were several revolutionary groups organizing in Mexico which were being given moral support by various groups in the United States and he wanted the Department's advice in regard to co-ordinating these various groups into one large movement. He said that he spoke with authority for a number of Americans interested in Mexico as he was chairman of the Executive Committee of an organization in New York known as "The Mexico Pilgrims." Not wishing to be outnumbered in a conversation of this nature, I called in Richard Tanis [Assistant Chief of Division of Mexican Affairs] and repeated what Oliver had said and then told Oliver very emphatically and definitely that not only would this Government not listen to or consider for a moment the question of fomenting revolutions in a country with which we maintained friendly relations, but if any facts concerning such movements came to our attention we should in good faith bring those facts to the attention of the government concerned. After this statement Oliver had not much further to say. As regards the Land and Petroleum Laws, I told him that the application of these measures would depend on the administrative measures issued by the President of Mexico and that until these regulations were issued, we could not foresee what the effect upon American interests would be. . . .

To Alexander Weddell, American Consul General
at Mexico City, February 6, 1926
Confidential

We have read your letter of January fourteenth with much interest and fully recognize the weight of the considerations which you advanced. There is no doubt that a great deal of misinformation concerning Mexico gets into the American press and that the tone of the editorials in American newspapers frequently indicates that the authors are not informed of the true conditions prevailing in Mexico. Your suggestion that the Department should take the steps which are open to it to inform more fully our editors and our people of the elementary facts existing in Mexico today is steadily in the Department's mind and we shall act in that direction whenever it seems to us that this can wisely and safely be done.

There is another side to the picture, however, which must not be left out of consideration. You know the tendency of certain elements of the American press as well as of the press of other countries to create sensation where no cause therefor exists. If we, no matter how discreetly, begin to feed the American correspondents with facts and opinions concerning the situation in Mexico and the injurious tendencies of actual and proposed legislation, this can easily turn the whole press of the United States overnight to a position of active opposition and antagonism to the Mexican Government. A movement of this kind, once started, often assumes the proportions of a snowball running downhill, gathering momentum as it goes, and while the more conservative press would doubtless confine itself to the actual facts and sane comment thereon, other elements, ever on the lookout for sensation, would soon be calling upon this Government to take steps varying from a diplomatic rupture to armed intervention. It is much less injurious to let our press follow its present line than to have it adopt an attitude of open hostility which would immediately be reflected in the Mexican press and would result in an exchange of vituperations tending to inflame public opinion on both sides of the border.

Of course we cannot foresee what is going to happen in future. Much will apparently depend upon the regulations to be issued by the President for the interpretation and application of the land and petroleum laws. Our policy for the present is to take no step which will render it difficult for President Calles to meet our views concerning the dangers of retroactive legislation. There is no use in being anything but courteous and patient unless or until the legislation is applied in such a way as adversely to affect vested American interests in a retroactive manner. We wish carefully to avoid placing President

Calles in a position where he must act ruthlessly in order to save his face. Certainly no word has been said or written up to the present to the contrary. We hope that things may work out in a way to avoid the necessity of acrimonious correspondence in the future. This remains to be seen.

I hope that I have made our position clear and that I have been able to show you the pitfalls which would be encountered if we were to try to steer the American press into the channels which you have in mind.

There is one further point which might be mentioned, namely, that the articles from the American press which you see in Mexico are those chosen for publication in Mexico because they express friendship to Mexico's cause. They represent only a small minority of the press of the United States and in most instances only those papers which are politically opposed to the present Administration. Do not therefore accept the idea that because these articles are reproduced they represent anything like a real picture of the opinion of the American press on this question which has been overwhelmingly favorable to our position.

By way of illustrating what I have written in the second paragraph of this letter I may say that a few weeks ago the Division of Current Information of the Department informed the press agencies of the background of the Land Law and of the Petroleum Law and articles were written by the agencies on both subjects, so that as a result every editor in the United States has had a carefully compiled article which he knows, although not so labeled, to be from official sources and which in the great majority of cases he has clipped and filed for future reference. The ground is therefore prepared and we shall not be faced with amazement on the part of the press in case of a future change of policy. We can plant and reap what sort of crop we desire. However, during the days succeeding the publication of these articles, the Division of Current Information was swamped with special writers, all of them or the great majority of them, desiring to write stories about the recall of the Ambassador, rupture of diplomatic relations, intervention and what not. It was with the utmost difficulty and by endless persuasion that the Chief of that Division was able to hold the newspapermen down to a great extent, so that only the most extreme elements of the press came out with matters of this nature. We could not hold the press down if we were to continue to feed it with material of this kind. The matter is really mathematical. Each reporter who writes on a given story must go a little further than the preceding writer and when you have, first, the agencies, then the special correspondents, and add to that the free lances, you can invariably expect a story much stronger and more radical than the original.

Conversation   March 5, 1926
            Rear Admiral Andrew T. Long, U.S.N.

JAPANESE POLICY TOWARDS MANCHURIA AND
PROPAGANDA AGAINST THE UNITED STATES

Rear Admiral Long informed me that a person in close touch with Japanese affairs in whom Admiral Long has confidence and who has frequently in times past given him information which has proved accurate (as, for instance, the policy of the Japanese Delegation to the Disarmament Conference at Washington) has now informed him that the Japanese Government has every intention of occupying Manchuria permanently and that the step will be taken some time this spring, probably between the middle of May and the middle of June. Furthermore, the Japanese Government expects to renew its treaty of alliance with Great Britain. At the same time the Japanese Government intends to start a campaign of propaganda against the United States in order to render this country unpopular with foreign nations and to minimize the weight of any opposition it may raise to the carrying out of Japanese policy in Manchuria. This campaign would commence in Europe, particularly in France, and would later extend into the United States and then to the Far East. As corroboration of this, Admiral Long showed me an article recently published in France of a nature decidedly uncomplimentary to the United States which had been sent him by his correspondent as evidence of the accuracy of his report.

Conversation   April 2, 1926
    The Italian Ambassador, Nobile Giacomo de Martino

PRESENT: The Secretary and the Under Secretary
SUBJECT: REMARKS OF SENATOR MCKELLAR PUB-
         LISHED ON PAGE 6503 IN THE CONGRES-
         SIONAL RECORD, APRIL 1, 1926

The Italian Ambassador, having previously talked with Mr. Grew, brought to the Secretary's attention the statement of Senator McKellar published on page 6503 in the *Congressional Record* of April 1, 1926, to the effect that the King of Italy had been bribed by Mussolini to capitulate at the time of the march on Rome. The Ambassador said that up until now he had been content to draw the attention of the Department informally to the various insults which had been directed at Italy in the Senate in connection with the discussions of the Italian Debt Settlement but that now the honor of his Sovereign was involved and as he was the personal representative of his Sovereign he must lodge a formal protest and inform his Government that he had done so. He talked at length concerning the serious offense which this particular statement would give to the Italian nation. The Secretary asked the Ambassador what he felt should be done about it and the Ambassador said he felt that the Secretary of State should make an official expression of regret in the press. The Secretary said he considered the statement in the Senate an outrage but was uncertain as to what steps he could properly take in the matter. Mr. Grew suggested that while the Executive branch of the Government deplored any statements in Congress which might tend to injure the friendly relations between the United States and another country, official comment by the Secretary of State upon any point of the debate in the Senate at this juncture would probably have an adverse effect on the vote on the Italian debt settlement and might be used with effect by the opposition Senators.[15] The Ambassador concurred in this view, but said that the matter was too serious to let pass without some public statement. The Secretary asked Mr. Grew to ascertain whether there was any precedent for action by the Secretary of State in a similar case. The Ambassador asked that he be informed as soon as possible of any decision that might be reached and was promised by Mr. Grew that this would be done.

The Ambassador then took occasion to inform the Secretary that his predictions as to the effect of the anti-Fascist propaganda directed from Paris were now being proved accurate because the New York newspaper *Nuevo Mundo* which was the official organ of the anti-Fascist organization today referred to this insult to the King and asked in a sarcastic tone what Mussolini was going to do about it.

In his previous conversation with Mr. Grew the Ambassador remarked that such an insult to a foreign Sovereign in a legislative body was unprecedented. Mr. Grew, while personally deploring the incident, felt obliged to draw the Ambassador's recollection to the vilification of President Wilson which took place in Italy at the time of the Fiume incident in 1919.[16]

The Treaty which Mr. Grew had signed with Turkey at Lausanne was defeated in the United States Senate on January 19, 1927, when the Senate failed by a margin of six votes to reach the necessary two-thirds majority. Among the three most commonly cited arguments against the Treaty were that it failed to provide for Wilson's plan to establish a free and independent Armenia, that it contained no guarantees for the

[15] On November 14, 1925, at Washington an agreement for settlement of the Italian war debt, based on sums lent by the United States to Italy during the war period, had been reached.

[16] At the Peace Conference in Paris in 1919 the Italians had put forward their claim to Fiume, as a compensation for Dalmatia which it appeared would be given to Yugoslavia. A deadlock ensued. To expedite a solution to the problem of Fiume, Wilson had taken the unusual step of appealing directly to the Italian people. This appeal precipitated from Italy a torrent of abuse of the President and his efforts.

*protection of Christians and non-Moslems, and that it did not
provide for Turkish recognition of the American nationality of
former subjects of Turkey. Leaders in opposition to the ratification of the Treaty were Bishop Manning, James Gerard,
David Hunter Miller, Oscar Straus, Chauncey Depew, and Senators Robinson, King, and Swanson. Mr. Grew on February
24, 1926, had cabled the American High Commissioner in
Constantinople:*

*"Department informed that a canvass of the Senate shows
that there are not sufficient votes at the present time to ratify
the Turkish treaty and that there will be a very large Democratic vote against it as well as possibly some Republican opposition. The policy of those in charge of the treaty in the Senate
is to be patient in the hopes of eventually securing sufficient
votes for ratification. Any further representations by Americans
in Turkey setting forth the importance of ratification in American interests might be helpful at this juncture. The foregoing
is for your information and discreet use."*

To Charles Slattery, Bishop Co-Adjutor of
Massachusetts, April 7, 1926

I note that your name appears among the one hundred and
ten Bishops who signed a petition against the ratification of the
American-Turkish Treaty.[17] Relying therefore upon our
friendship and upon your interest in the present situation in
Turkey and our relations with that country I venture to ask
your consideration of one particular point raised by the protest.
There cannot be and there never has been any question that

---

[17] The American Committee Opposed to the Lausanne Treaty, headed by
David Hunter Miller, published articles and books advocating that the United
States reject the Treaty. Among other less dramatic statements of why the
United States should oppose the settlement made at Lausanne were such paragraphs as "Christian girls are being bought at $5 a head by missions to save
them from the horrors of becoming prisoners in Turkish harems. Thirty
thousand girls at least are captive . . . girls are branded on the face to stamp
them as fugitives who must be returned to their owners if they escape." Bishop
Ethelbert Talbot and Thomas Gailor had said that ratification of the Lausanne
Treaty would be the same as approving "of the monstrous wrongs inflicted by
the Turkish Government" upon the innocent women and children of Turkey.

"we should be as solicitous for the performance of our moral duty as for protection of our material rights." I take it that the signers of the protest would define our moral duty in Turkey as twofold: first of all a duty to afford proper assistance and protection to American institutions engaged in religious, philanthropic and educational work in Turkey and, secondly, a duty to do what we can for the Minorities. The first of these duties is recognized and effect is given to it by the letter on institutions which Ismet Pasha addressed to me at Lausanne and which is an integral part of the Treaty settlement. That there has been no neglect of duty on our part in this respect is clearly shown by the fact that all of the Americans directing or participating in this kind of work in Turkey strongly favor the ratification of the Treaty and have said so collectively and individually on many occasions. In this connection I am enclosing herewith a copy of a petition addressed to the Secretary of State and to Senator Borah [Chairman of the Senate Foreign Relations Committee] and signed by 106 Americans in Constantinople. This petition has just been given to the press.

As to a moral duty which the Bishops may consider that we have towards the Minorities, I cannot but feel that this is a matter to be examined in a practical rather than in an abstract manner. The question is what we *can* do for the Minorities in Turkey at the present time. I think you will agree with me that we will not wage war against Turkey in behalf of the Minorities and, if such is the case, then all solutions of the Minorities question which cannot be attained with the consent of Turkey are automatically excluded. The setting up of an Armenian Home is clearly one of the solutions which cannot be attained without the use of force. Moral support in some appropriate form would appear to be the most that we can do for the Minorities and, if so, it is desirable that by ratifying the Treaty and resuming regular diplomatic relations with Turkey, we should place ourselves in a position to act effectively if in the future an occasion presents itself for exerting this moral support.

I believe that consideration of this point of view will convince you that we have not been unmindful of our moral duty in elaborating our relations with Turkey. The important question at issue, I think, is this: Are we going to permit our righteous indignation over past injuries to exclude us effectively from opportunities to extend future help?

I do not know Bishop Manning [of New York] personally but I wish he might be made aware of these considerations. I even wish more heartily that there could be a reconsideration of his position and yours in the matter, for unwittingly the signers of the petition may, I fear, seriously harm the very Minorities whom they wish to serve. . . .[18]

To Thomas Sergeant Perry, April 10, 1926

You will be interested to know that Howland Shaw, who has recently returned from Constantinople to take charge of our Division of Near Eastern Affairs, took my letter personally to Bishop Slattery, lunching with him yesterday, and that the Bishop immediately wrote to Senator Borah that he desired to withdraw his name from the petition opposing ratification of the Lausanne Treaty. It is gratifying to find an honest and courageous man who is big enough to admit his error when he is wrong and Slattery has so proved himself. He told Shaw that he had received a two-page telegram from Bishop Manning asking if he would join him in signing the petition and, while at first doubtful, he thought it over all day and finally decided to do it, largely out of regard, I imagine, for Bishop Manning. I am calling on Bishop Freeman [of Washington] today with the same purpose in view and the Secretary is sending to each of the signers of the petition the resolutions passed by the American religious, philanthropic, educational and busi-

[18] I was openly accused in the Senate of having "sold my nation's birthright for a mess of pottage" because I had not obtained in this treaty a home for Armenians. When deputations of Americans of Armenian origin came to see me in Washington, I sometimes said to them: "Gentlemen, I would have been delighted to get you a home in Armenia, if you had not overlooked one little detail." "What was that?" they asked. "Simply that you failed to send over an American army of 300,000 men to take the territory by force." Those deputations had very little sense of humor. — J. C. G.

ness organizations in Constantinople, merely for their information and consideration. I hear from Senator Borah that the petition of the Bishops has helped rather than hurt the chances of the Treaty and if we can get a few more of the Bishops to desert the ship on the ground that they were not aware of the facts when they signed the petition, the effect will be immense.[19] We were afraid of a solid Democratic bloc on account of the plank in the last Democratic platform opposing ratification,[20] but some of them are already beginning to wobble and I am more optimistic now than I have been at any time. The Treaty may come up next week. . . .

Nine years after the defeat of the Lausanne Treaty, Mr. Grew wrote the following explanation of the defeat to his daughter, Mrs. J. Pierrepont Moffat:

"First, if you ever have another talk with Senator King, or if you ever find a chance for a talk, you might ask him why the Senate, having defeated our Lausanne Treaty with Turkey, gave its advice and consent, without even a debate, to the two treaties which I subsequently negotiated and concluded with Turkey in Angora, covering part of the ground of the treaty signed at Lausanne but whose general tenor and provisions were much, very much, less favorable to American interests than our Lausanne treaty, and which still didn't mention the Armenians, although at that date they were the most favorable that we could possibly have put across. In other words, our Lausanne treaty, if ratified, would have given us very much more favorable treatment — in fact more favorable than was given to any other country — than could possibly have been obtained seven years later. The only way to secure an independ-

19 As a result of Mr. Grew's letter to Bishop Slattery and others among the 110 Bishops who had signed Bishop Manning's petition to the Senate, several of the signers withdrew their names from the petition.

20 The Democratic platform stated that we "condemn the Lausanne Treaty. It barters legitimate American rights, and betrays Armenia, for the Chester Oil Concession.

"We favor the protection of American rights in Turkey, and the fulfillment of President Wilson's arbitral award respecting Armenia."

*ent Armenia, or any of the other things desired for the Arme-
nians, would have been to send a big American army over to
Anatolia to subjugate Turkey.*

*"But there is really no use whatever in trying to discuss or
argue the point with Senator King, because the issue was purely
a question of domestic Democratic politics at the time — the
Armenian element in New York having been strong enough to
get their case included in the Democratic platform and to enlist the support, undoubtedly by copious funds to the Democratic campaign, of a small but aggressive group of American
senators and bishops. Senators King and Swanson were not
open to argument, and Borah, leading the defense, was not
sufficiently interested to fight with his usual fire; he merely read
long excerpts from printed reports and everybody went to
sleep, while Swanson and King used all the oratory at their
command to persuade the Senate that I had bartered away the
interests of the United States for a mess of pottage in a 'nefarious'
treaty, and they won by 6 votes which swung to them at the
last moment."*

To Senator Charles Curtis May 20, 1926
Urgent

In accordance with your request, I am sending you enclosed
a statement of the outstanding reasons why we believe the
Treaty with Turkey should be ratified. I have endeavored to
make it as brief as possible without sacrificing a clear presentation of the situation.

If you desire to have this statement mimeographed and will
send me a telephone message as to how many copies you wish,
I can have them struck off and sent to you immediately.

The Outstanding Reasons Why the Treaty with Turkey Should Be Ratified

1. Our old treaties with Turkey do us no good now. They
cannot be effectively invoked to protect our interests in Turkey at the present time. They are incomplete and out of date.

Every American working in Turkey knows this and has said so.

2. There is no use talking about retaining the Capitulations unless we are willing to go to war with Turkey to enforce them. Their abolition has been recognized by all the other countries which have concluded treaties with the present Government of Turkey, including all of the Great Powers except the United States.

3. All the Americans in Turkey, representing religious, philanthropic, educational and business interests want the new treaty ratified. They see no reason why the work to which they and their predecessors have given many years of effort should be lightly thrown overboard by the failure of ratification.

4. The rejection of the treaty will not help the Greeks and Armenians in Turkey. On the contrary, it will simply mean that American influence in Turkey will be reduced to zero and any opportunity to exert moral support in behalf of the Minorities will be entirely lost.

5. It is impossible, except by going to war, to detach from Turkey any territory for an Armenian home and we are under no obligations, legal or moral, to do so. The Treaty of Sèvres was never ratified and we were not even a signatory. President Harding, according to the American Committee Opposed to the Lausanne Treaty, said no more than "What may be done (for the Armenian cause) will be done." The Committee has never given out the full text of the Letter.

6. Our new treaty with Turkey gives to Americans and their interests in Turkey exactly as favorable treatment as is accorded to any other foreigners the Governments of which have concluded treaties with the present Turkish Government. Twenty-seven Powers have concluded such treaties.

7. Opinions regarding modern Turkey may differ but this has nothing to do with ratification of the Treaty. If there was no ethical impropriety in our having formal treaty and diplomatic relations with the Governments of Abdul Hamid and of the Young Turks, why should this impropriety be considered to exist now? Certainly, the Turkey of Mustafa Kemal Pasha is not worse than the Turkey of Abdul Hamid and of the

Young Turks. Even Henry Morgenthau [American Ambassador to Turkey, 1913–16] as late as April 5, 1917, urged that diplomatic relations with Turkey should not be severed.

Conversation   September 7, 1926
The Mexican Ambassador, Señor Don Manuel C. Téllez
MEXICAN PROPAGANDA IN THE UNITED STATES

In the course of a visit from the Mexican Ambassador today I told him that I understood that he had on his own initiative been good enough to inform Mr. Kellogg that the Mexican consular officers in the United States would indulge in no propaganda of any kind. In that connection I showed him a clipping from the *New York Times* of September 5 from which it appeared that Consul General Elias had issued a statement criticising in somewhat forcible terms the representations which had been made to the President by the Knights of Columbus concerning the religious situation in Mexico.[21] The Ambassador said that it was true that he had assured the Secretary that his consular officers, all of whom were under his direct instructions, were indulging in no propaganda on their own initiative. He wished also to say that the Mexican Govern-

21 The Calles Government passed a number of laws curbing the power of the Catholic Church. The Knights of Columbus in early August, 1926, passed a resolution at their Supreme Convention asking the State Department to "put an end to this ignominious contempt which has been shown by Calles for Americans' appeal and to resolutely demand protection for American citizens." On September 1, a group of the Knights led by James A. Flaherty met with President Coolidge to request that the United States use its good offices to ameliorate the conditions in Mexico. Consul General Arturo M. Elias said of the action and statements of the Knights: "Here at last the people of the United States have the story of what has been called 'the Mexican religious question' in all its baldness. No subterfuge; no claim that the property interest of any citizen of the United States has been jeopardized, but the Chief Executive of the United States is deliberately asked by the representative of the Catholic hierarchy to interfere with the acts of the Chief Executive of another sovereign Government who is insisting that the representatives of an ecclesiastical establishment obey the sovereign law of the land as laid down in its constitution.

"The immense effrontery of such an act surely needs no comment to a people with such traditions as those of the United States."

ment maintained no publicity bureau and controlled no newspaper in the United States and no efforts whatever were made
to spread Mexican propaganda in this country. The Ambassador felt, however, that when a statement appeared in the American press concerning Mexican affairs which was contrary to
the facts it was entirely legitimate and proper for the Mexican representatives in the United States to rectify the misstatements. He said that the President of the Knights of Columbus
when in Mexico had carefully refrained from issuing statements there, but as soon as he came to the United States he
immediately took every occasion to talk to the public about the
internal affairs of Mexico. The Ambassador considered his
statement to the President both inaccurate and unjustified and
the statement of the Consul General was merely for the purpose
of rectifying these misstatements. I said to the Ambassador that
I would report to the Secretary what he had been good enough
to tell me and that he should consider my observations as informal.

To Dr. Endicott Peabody, Headmaster of Groton
School, September 21, 1926
    Thank you for your letter of September eighth and for your
courtesy in sending me your article in favor of debt cancellation which I have read with interest. . . .[22]
    To sum up, the situation seems to me to be this: The Gov-
ernment has no right to cancel the debts unless or until the
majority of the people of the United States demand it. But
even if this demand should come, either spontaneously or as a

    [22] The question of American cancellation of Allied debts was a troublesome
one in world politics. The United States Government during the war and
shortly after it had lent the Allies over ten billion dollars. The debtor nations
argued that the money was America's contribution to the general cause. Most
of the money, they pointed out, had been left in the United States to buy supplies and had made American business extremely prosperous. Furthermore, the
debtor nations contended that they did not have enough gold to pay the debt,
and that the United States by its high tariffs was preventing payment in
goods. The charge was common that the United States by its attitude of
insisting that the debts be paid had become Uncle Shylock rather than Uncle
Sam.

result of propaganda, it is very questionable whether such cancellation would be in the interests of the debtor countries themselves. I personally believe that it would be the worst thing that could happen to them. And, finally, the argument that because we profited by the war we are adopting a Shylock-like policy. We lost heavily by the war. Our present prosperity is due to the determined, practical and scientific efforts of our people to overcome these losses. The very fact that in spite of our contribution to the war we are now prosperous should be a cause for rejoicing rather than of envy on the part of Europe, because the greater our prosperity the more will Europe profit and without our prosperity European reconstruction would be a vastly slower process than it has been and is going to be. The thinking European welcomes our prosperity and does not desire the cancellation of the debts. Therein England showed her foresight, for look at her financial stability today. I wish that our people could understand these facts and see this situation clearly, for there is danger that their vision may be obscured by fallacious arguments, unsound theories and a failure to comprehend the situation as it exists. . . .

To a Colleague in the Foreign Service,
October 25, 1926

The *New York Times* of October 22 carries the following statement: "Contributions to Senator Wadsworth's campaign in New York were reported as $1,000, all given by [the recipient of this letter]. . . . "

This report may of course be inaccurate, but assuming that it is true I think I ought to point out to you just what this means. Of course we do not for a moment wish to interfere in anything which may be regarded as a purely personal matter, but this is not entirely personal, because owing to the publicity which must legally be given to every such contribution it has a distinct reflection on the whole Foreign Service. I may say at the start that the sympathy manifested by you in the election campaign of Senator Wadsworth is shared by a great many of the Senator's admirers in the Foreign Service. There is no implication in what I say that the contribution, if made at all, was not made in an entirely deserving direction. A great many Foreign Service officers, whatever their politics, would like to see Jim Wadsworth re-elected.

The aspect of the matter which I have in mind is just this. The Rogers Act and previous legislation have aimed to take the Foreign Service out of politics and have effectively done so. The whole spirit of this legislation aims at continuous tenure of office regardless of political considerations. Foreign Service officers are to be retained and promoted on the basis of efficiency without regard to the Party in power. However, the moment a Foreign Service officer publicly and materially supports a political candidate of one party as opposed to the candidate of the other Party, he places not only himself but the whole Foreign Service, of which he is a member, in an anomalous position. He furnishes opponents of Civil Service principles in the Foreign Service with a perfectly logical argument for returning to the principle of political patronage within the Foreign Service. He robs the proponents of Civil Service principles of one of their soundest contentions, namely, that Foreign Service officers in accepting office are tacitly pledged to abstain entirely from domestic political activities in order that they may serve under successive administrations, whether Republican or Democratic, while retaining the confidence of both. It is manifestly unlikely that a Foreign Service officer who has shown active political partisanship by contributing to a Republican campaign fund could possess the complete confidence of a future Democratic administration. Such a step as you are reported to have taken therefore not only may impair your own future usefulness but it leaves the whole Service open to the charge that while enjoying the advantages of Civil Service principles, its members are nevertheless unwilling to undertake Civil Service obligations.

There is another aspect of the matter which one cannot avoid taking into consideration. Whatever the purpose of a political campaign contribution may be — and in this case we have no doubt that your purpose was to assist the election of the candidate whom you considered to be best fitted for the position — the impression is bound to be made on the Foreign Service, rightly or wrongly, that the contributor has at least as a secondary object the securing of senatorial support in connection with his own future advancement and that the contributor is thus taking an advantage over his colleagues who, either on principle are unwilling or from necessity are unable to make similar contributions. The unfortunate effect of such an impression on the morale of the Service is obvious.

This letter is written in the friendliest spirit and I am sure I can depend upon you to receive it in a similar spirit. It is prompted by the fact that all the members of the Personnel Board feel very strongly concerning the point at issue and they have requested me as chairman to bring their point of view to your attention in this informal way.

To Thomas Sergeant Perry, November 8, 1926

. . . I am glad to know of the two books you recommend. My time for reading is unfortunately pretty short and I still have a mass of interesting books ahead of me which I am longing to get at. I enjoy biography and autobiography most of all and I found Sir Edward Grey's book one of the most fascinating, as well as Rennell Rodd's.[23] Speaking of Rodd, it appears that he has developed into a somewhat pompous martinet and that his secretaries were none too fond of him. When recently serving on some delegation to the League of Nations one of his staff composed the following:

> We think it exceedingly odd,
> That our eminent delegate Rodd,
> Spells his name, if you please,
> With a couple of d's,
> While one is sufficient for God. . . .

Some time in December, I am going off on a ten days' speak-

[23] Edward Grey, *Twenty-Five Years, 1892–1916* (New York: Frederick A. Stokes Co., 1925); James Rennell Rodd, *Social and Diplomatic Memories, 1884–1893* (London: E. Arnold & Co., 1922), and *Social and Diplomatic Memories, 1894–1901* (London: E. Arnold & Co., 1923).

ing trip through the southern states to tell the great American public something about our Foreign Service and what it can do for them. The trip is to be arranged by the United States Chamber of Commerce, which suggested it. I have always wanted to see some of those southern states and while it will be a strenuous journey, I think there will be many elements of interest in it. . . .

To Frank B. Kellogg, November 29, 1926

In accordance with your instructions, I respectfully lay before you the following considerations regarding the situation concerning our Chiefs of diplomatic missions abroad.

The present Administration has followed the wise policy of not disturbing Chiefs of Mission, even though political appointees, merely because they were appointed by a previous administration and have served more than the traditional term of four years. With this policy, those of us in the Department who have to do with personnel matters are in entire sympathy. So long as an Ambassador or Minister is rendering efficient service and is a fit representative of the Government, he should not be moved merely to make way for a new appointee.

When, however, it is conclusively shown that an Ambassador or Minister has not rendered efficient and effective service, or is not a fit representative of this Government abroad, then it is felt that after a reasonable term of office a change is both desirable and logical and certainly in accordance with long established custom. There are many Chiefs of Mission in the Service today, political appointees, who have not rendered efficient and effective service, who are not fit representatives of the Government and whose terms of office have been extended to five and six years or more. It is felt that changes in these positions would be in the best interest of the Government.

There is another important element to be considered. During the last thirty years efforts have been made by successive administrations to develop an efficient Foreign Service in order to carry out effectively the increasing demands of American business and of our steadily increasing interests abroad.

President Cleveland in 1895, President Roosevelt in 1905, President Taft in 1909 and President Coolidge in 1924 successively endorsed these efforts by approving legislation and issuing Executive Orders with a view to taking the Diplomatic and Consular Services out of politics and applying Civil Service principles by providing for permanent tenure of office and promotion exclusively for merit. In the Rogers Act of 1924 the importance of promoting efficient Foreign Service officers to. the position of Chief of Mission was definitely recognized and a moral obligation was placed upon the Administration to consider the names of efficient Foreign Service officers for such promotions.

The present Administration has gone far in this direction, having filled six of fourteen vacancies of that nature by career men. Nevertheless, of these six appointments, four were made to small Central American posts while only one Robert Skinner [Minister to Greece] was sent to a European post. At present of 50 Ambassadors and Ministers only 19, or 40 per cent, are career men.

The situation in the Service today is as follows: Every year a considerable class of young men is taken into the Service. This year there were twenty. Class I of the Service is filled with twenty-three men who have had from fifteen to forty years experience in the Service. A large proportion of these officers, are fully equipped, competent and fitted in every way to represent the United States as Minister or Ambassador. If experience continues to show that only an infinitesimal proportion of these officers can ever hope to become Chiefs of Mission, and that very few of even that small number can ever hope to be sent to desirable posts where their wives can live in healthful and cultural surroundings and where their children can obtain their normal education, the incentive to the best young men of the country to adopt the Foreign Service as a career and the morale of the Service through all its ranks are bound to suffer. That feeling is very marked in the Service today and has come to me from many sources. There is much discouragement.

I am not sure that the President appreciates this situation nor am I sure that he has ever been given a clear comprehension of what we are trying to accomplish with the Foreign Service and what it is going to mean to the country in future and what it means today. If the morale and therefore the effectiveness of the Foreign Service are to be sacrificed to temporary political expediency, I do not think that we can look to the future with equanimity. The American people are essentially practical and businesslike. They demand the most efficient service that the Government can render and they cannot fail to approve and support the application to our Foreign Service of the principles which make successful business houses, namely, the practical recognition of ability. No business house is going to succeed if the majority of its vice presidents are appointed for political considerations rather than for ability, experience and familiarity with the work. The large business organizations and chambers of commerce of the country solidly supported the Rogers Act and are solidly behind us in what we are trying to accomplish.

It therefore seems to all of us that the time has come to put the matter up squarely to the President. I believe that the resignations of several of the Chiefs of Mission, political appointees, who have served more than their traditional terms without rendering the highest type of service can with all propriety be requested, and I think that to the vacancies thus created a considerable number of efficient, able and deserving Foreign Service officers of Class I with long experience should be promoted. Such a step would encourage all the ranks of the Service, would give an added incentive to the best young men in the country to come forward for the Service, would meet with high approval from the public, business organizations and chambers of commerce throughout the country and would at the same time be serving the best interests of the Government. . . .

XXIV

Completion of Service as Under Secretary of State

1927

While Secretary Kellogg was on a brief vacation just before Christmas, 1926, the turbulent situation in North China approached near chaos. The Peking Government possessed little authority and almost no power. The rival war lords General Feng, the Christian General, and Chang Tso-lin, Manchurian war lord, were struggling for control of the area about Tientsin. Their military operations threatened to close the road to Peking. The Boxer Protocol of 1901 had stated:

"Article VIII

"The Chinese Government has consented to raze the forts of Taku and those which might impede free communication between Peking and the sea; steps have been taken for carrying this out.

"Article IX

"The Chinese Government has conceded the right to the Powers in the protocol annexed to the letter of the 16th of January, 1901, to occupy certain points, to be determined by an agreement between them, for the maintenance of open communication between the capital and the sea." [1]

Mr. Grew, as Acting Secretary of State and with the President's authorization, although Coolidge knew little about the subject, sent an ultimatum to the opposing Chinese forces warning them that the road to Peking must be kept open, and he, also, issued orders that American destroyers were not to allow a blockade of the Taku channel below Tientsin.

[1] U.S. Department of State, *Foreign Relations of the United States, 1901. Appendix* (Washington: Government Printing Office, 1902), p. 316.

When Mr. Kellogg returned, he nearly repudiated Mr. Grew's actions. In 1937, after a conversation with John V. A. MacMurray, who had been Minister to China in 1926, Mr. Grew wrote of the incident:
"Saturday, November 20.

" . . . MacMurray and I spent much of the afternoon talking. He went over the situation in 1926 when he was Minister to China and I was Under Secretary of State and said that if I had not supported him against Kellogg, then Secretary of State, he would certainly have had to resign. As a matter of fact, Mac-Murray knew definitely that my stand had brought about my 'downfall' as Under Secretary and that from the moment of my action as Acting Secretary of State at Christmas, 1926, in issuing orders that the American destroyers were to keep the Taku channel open under the terms of the Boxer Protocol when the hostilities between the Christian General Feng and Chang Tso-lin threatened to close it, Kellogg had determined to get me out. I sent that instruction while Kellogg was absent for a brief Christmas vacation and when he returned he called me into his office and said very angrily: 'I understand, Mr. Secretary, that during my absence you have declared war on China.' In my opinion it was the only thing to do, because if we hadn't done it, the British would have been let down, the Boxer Protocol would have become a dead letter and Peking might again have been endangered. Kellogg was under great pressure from the missionaries who espoused the cause of that crafty brigand, Feng, just because he was a Christian and my action tended to enrage them. Later the President called me over to the White House where he had the morning paper on his desk; he waved it at me and said very angrily: 'What does all this mean?' I reminded him of our previous talk. Coolidge swung his swivel chair around and looked out on the White House lawn for several minutes. Then, having thought it out, he turned back to me, merely remarked 'All right, Mr. Secretary' and went on with his work. . . ."

The Chinese situation remained turbulent throughout the closing months of Mr. Grew's service as Under Secretary of

State. In 1926, the Kuomintang Government in Canton launched a military campaign northward. Within less than a year the armies of Chiang Kai-shek were masters of half of China including the vital Yangtze area.

Conversation   February 3, 1927
    Mr. Sao-Ke Alfred Sze, Chinese Minister
    Mr. J. C. Grew, Under Secretary of State

PRESENT: Mr. N. T. Johnson, Chief of the Division of Far Eastern Affairs
SUBJECT: THE CHINESE SITUATION

The Chinese Minister called upon Mr. Grew this morning and stated that he had seen a report from London to the effect that we were increasing our naval forces in Chinese waters; that he had understood the Secretary to say that we had not increased our forces and that he would like very much to have some information on the matter so that he could reassure his own people. Mr. Grew informed the Chinese Minister that he was not able to comment on statements made to the Minister by the Secretary, but that we had not increased the number of our naval vessels in Chinese waters except to send some additional destroyers from Manila to Shanghai and places on the Yangtze where the lives of Americans had been threatened. Mr. Grew stated he did not see how any Government could make any statement as to what it might do in case of any contingency. Mr. Johnson explained that the Asiatic Fleet, which was based at Manila, consisted of two sections, one section remaining at Manila most of the year, while the other section, mostly made up of small river gunboats, were more or less permanently in Chinese waters. The Secretary had stated to the Minister that American naval vessels were in these waters for the protection of American life and property only; that the Asiatic Fleet had not been increased by one ship so far as the Department knew, although several destroyers had been sent from Manila to Shanghai and the Yangtze Valley, and that the Admiral had gone from Manila to Shanghai with his Flagship. Mr. Johnson added that the newspapers reported that marines formerly at

Guam had been shifted from Guam to Manila, to be held there for emergency and some other marines had been concentrated at San Diego, eventually to be sent to Guam to replace the marines formerly at Guam. The newspapers also reported that three cruisers had been ordered to Honolulu. The Chinese Minister referred to the fact that the Secretary had promised him a memorandum regarding this Government's policy of sending its naval forces to Asiatic waters, which he had not received, thus being unable to keep his Government informed or to prevent misunderstandings. Mr. Johnson stated that he did not know exactly in what form the Secretary intended to make this memorandum but that he understood the Secretary intended to make a little memorandum stating just what vessels we had and where. The Chinese Minister stated that it was very difficult for him to keep his people informed unless he knew exactly what was going on, that he had informed them that we were not sending more vessels but that more vessels had arrived. Mr. Johnson had explained that these additional vessels were merely part of the fleet in Asiatic waters. The Minister made some remark about not being able to understand the subtleties of the English language. Mr. Grew said that we did not deal in subtleties but we dealt openly and frankly to the point; that no Government could engage not to send vessels to protect its citizens, that we could only tell him what had been done at the time we spoke and that we could not speak for the future. . . .

In the Far East, the United States Government was not only concerned over China. Relations with Japan, as well, had become increasingly tense. Ever since 1924, the tension that had developed between Japan and the United States focused attention upon the problem of naval armaments. The Washington Conference had established limitations on the building of battleships and aircraft carriers by the major powers, but, by 1927, a new race had developed in the construction of cruisers, submarines, and other smaller vessels. The United States, however, had failed to keep up with the other powers in building

*its navy and had not maintained the battleship strength allowed
under the Washington Treaty.*

*President Coolidge in his message to Congress in January,
1927, proposed that the signatories to the Washington Treaty
should meet to extend limitations to other categories of naval
armaments. On February 10, he issued a call for such a conference at Geneva.[2] France and Italy, however, refused to take
part. Great Britain, Japan, and the United States met at Geneva from June 20 to August 4, 1927, but the Conference broke
up in complete failure.[3]*

Conversation   February 24, 1927
The Italian Ambassador, Nobile Giacomo de Martino
ITALIAN NOTE ON REDUCTION OF NAVAL FORCES

The Italian Ambassador referred to the Italian note declining
to accept our proposal for a discussion at Geneva of naval armament limitation and read to me portions of two telegrams
which he had received from Mussolini to the effect that if this
Government would agree to "appuyer" — support — the thesis of parity between Italy and France he, Mussolini, would re-
examine our proposal. I said to the Ambassador that it was
obviously out of the question for us to do anything of this kind,
as we had very carefully abstained in our note from making any
concrete suggestions concerning the relative positions of Italy
and France which might give offense to one or the other and
for that very reason we had left the matter entirely open and
unprejudiced for discussion at the conference table. I said that
we recognized Italy's particular geographic situation and that
this was another reason for our avoiding any concrete proposals which might prejudice the case in advance. The Ambassador then asked me to comment on the phrase "far-reaching
building programs" and asserted that this could not be taken
to apply to Italy which had embarked on no such program. I

2 U.S. Department of State, *Papers Relating to the Foreign Relations of the
United States, 1927* (Washington: Government Printing Office, 1942), I, 1–5.

3 See B. H. Williams, *The United States and Disarmament* (New York:
Whittlesey House, 1931), pp. 175–76, 183–84.

replied that the phrase was not intended to apply to any in-dividual country, but was used in a general sense. The Ambassador then said that he had been instructed by Mussolini to endeavor to avoid any comment in the American press concerning Italian militarism and he asked me if I could not say a word to the press correspondents to the effect that Italy was not a militaristic nation. I replied that I thought that any statement of this kind would come better from the Ambassador than from the Department. . . .

Conversation   March 5, 1927
The President

CONFERENCE FOR LIMITATION OF NAVAL ARMAMENTS

Accompanied by William Castle [Chief of the Division of Western European Affairs], I called on the President and said that in view of the acceptance of Great Britain and Japan and the refusal of France and Italy to attend the Naval Limitation Conference at Geneva which had been proposed by the President, it now became necessary to decide what our next steps should be. I explained Italy's position, namely, that she desired to enter no such conference unless assured in advance of parity with France and that if such a conference were held Italy thought that some of the smaller Powers, such as Yugoslavia, Greece, etc., should be invited to participate, as she feared their encroachments in case her own naval equipment should be limited. Mr. Castle pointed out that if the five larger Powers should come to an agreement this very fact would remove the fear which is the basis of all naval building on the part of the smaller Powers, that if in spite of this the smaller Powers should embark on large building programs the other Powers would be in much stronger position to insist on their calling a halt. I showed the President various telegrams which indicated that if a naval conference were actually held Italy would probably be reluctant to abstain. I therefore suggested that I see the British and Japanese Ambassadors and state to them that this Government desired to proceed with the proposed conference on a Three-Power basis and to ask them to ascertain the views of their respective Governments in this respect. If their replies were favorable, I then suggested that we write notes to France and Italy and express the hope that they would see their way clear to be represented at least by observers in the discussions. The President concurred in this proposal. Before leaving the room Mr. Castle said, "Mr. President, do you not think it would be advisable for Mr. Grew to call in the British and Japanese Ambassadors at once and communicate this proposal to them informally instead of writing notes?" The President answered in the affirmative.

Conversation   March 5, 1927
The British Ambassador, Sir Esme Howard, and the Japanese
    Ambassador, Mr. Tsuneo Matsudaira

LIMITATION OF NAVAL ARMAMENTS

The British and Japanese Ambassadors called separately at my request and I said to them, after discussing the matter with the President, that in spite of the refusal of France and Italy to take part in the proposed naval limitation discussions at Geneva we hoped that these conversations could at least be held by Great Britain, Japan and the United States and I inquired whether this procedure was satisfactory to their respective Governments. Both Ambassadors intimated that in their private opinion such procedure would be agreeable to their Governments, but that they would telegraph to ascertain and would let me know in due course. I said that we proposed to reply to the French and Italian notes expressing regrets that they had found it impossible to participate and expressing also the hope that they might find it possible at least to be represented by observers at the proposed conference. Both Ambassadors thought well of this procedure. Mr. Matsudaira asked me whether we had any reason to believe that either France or Italy would reconsider its refusal. I said that we have no official grounds for such a belief, but as the subject was one of vital importance I hoped that those two Powers would at least find it desirable to send observers to follow the discussion.

In informal conversation I spoke of Italy's desire for some concrete assurances in advance of the conference that Franco-Italian parity would be maintained and that also that some of the smaller naval Powers, such as Yugoslavia, Greece, et cetera, would be included in the conference. I said it was obviously impossible for us to say in advance that we would support any particular thesis in the conference and that our whole purpose has been to leave the matter absolutely open and unprejudiced for free and friendly discussion at the conference table. As regards the smaller Powers it seems to us that if the larger Powers should agree to limitation, the international fear which was the basis of all naval building by the smaller Powers would be obviated and that there would then be no purpose for them to proceed with extensive building. If they should do so, the Greater Powers would then be in a far stronger position to protest. Sir Esme Howard and Mr. Matsudaira both concurred in these views.

Conversation   March 8, 1927
                    The President
             LIMITATION OF NAVAL ARMAMENTS

I called on the President this morning and told him that the press had received a report from London that we had proposed to Great Britain and Japan a three-Power Naval conference in view of the refusal of France and Italy to participate and I said to the President it seemed to me better to state to the press frankly that this proposal had been made in an informal way rather than to refuse to comment which would result in idle speculation. The President asked me to what proposal I referred. I said I referred to the proposal which he had instructed me on Saturday to make to the British and Japanese Ambassadors. The President said, "I recollect giving you no such instructions, Mr. Grew. I understood that you were going to write notes to France and Italy to try to get them to come in and I telephoned you yesterday morning to ask if there had been any developments." I then repeated to the President the nature of our conversation on Saturday and said that Mr. Castle and I had both returned to the Department with the clear understanding that the President had authorized the proposal in question. I said it was our understanding that the notes to the French and Italian Governments were to be written only after Great Britain and Japan had answered the proposal for a three-Power conference and that I did not see that it would be in any way possible to get France and Italy to change their attitude at least until a three-Power conference had been definitely arranged. I said that when the President telephoned to me yesterday morning there had at that time been no further development as I had not yet heard from the British and Japanese Ambassadors with regard to the reaction of their Governments to our proposal. I then showed to the President the telegrams from London and Tokyo intimating that the British and Japanese Governments were favorably disposed to such a three-Power conference and also the recent despatch from Mr. Herrick explaining the underlying reasons for France's abstention. . . . When he had read them I said, "Mr. President, I am appalled to think that there has been a misunderstanding of your wishes." The President said, "It's all right; I think you are on the right track and you had better go ahead and see what happens." [4] On returning to the Department I consulted Mr. Castle who was entirely clear in his mind that the President had definitely authorized me to make the proposal to the British and Japanese Ambassadors.

Conversation   April 6, 1927
The Japanese Ambassador, Mr. Tsuneo Matsudaira
CONFERENCE FOR THE LIMITATION OF NAVAL ARMAMENTS

The Japanese Ambassador left with me the . . . note [5] stating that the Japanese Delegation to the proposed conversations at

---

[4] Although President Coolidge occasionally seemed to forget his authorizations for action, whenever I refreshed his memory he always supported my action. — J. C. G.

[5] *Foreign Relations, 1927*, I, 33.

Geneva concerning the limitation of naval armament would leave Japan about April 24 and expected to arrive in Geneva about June 8, so that the Japanese Government requested that the conversations open after June 11. The Ambassador asked that the text of this note not be made public but he had no objections to informing the press of the plans of the Japanese Delegation. The Ambassador furthermore said that he did not expect a reply to this note unless we desired to make one.

The Ambassador then said that while the Japanese delegates had not yet been officially appointed, he was able to inform me that the chief delegate would be Viscount Makoto Saito, Governor General of Korea and the second delegate would be Viscount Kikujiro Ishii, Ambassador to France. His Government wished him to point out to the Department the high rank of these two delegates as an indication of the importance they attached to the meeting. He said that Viscount Saito, who was an expert on naval affairs, was one of the highest ranking Japanese statesmen and in fact was senior to Admiral Tomosaburo Kato who headed the Japanese delegation to the Washington Conference and that Viscount Ishii was the ranking officer in the Japanese Foreign Service.

Mr. Grew's last weeks as Under Secretary were strenuous and difficult. On February 16, 1927, Congressman Charles Edwards from Georgia introduced a resolution calling for all information about appointments to the Foreign Service. On March 18, 1927, a feature writer for the N.E.A. service stated that "promotion and plums are being dealt out to diplomatic officers on the basis of social position and wealth, whereas consular officers are neglected and robbed of decent prospects for retirement in spite of an average greater maturity, ability, and experience." [6]

The Personnel Board of which Mr. Grew was chairman included Assistant Secretary of State W. J. Carr, formerly director of the consular service, Assistant Secretary of State J. Butler Wright, career diplomat, and three Foreign Service officers, one of whom had been a consular officer. According to the N.E.A. article, "Grew and Wright are accused of being the heads of

6 See, for instance, the Frederick, Maryland, *News.*

the inner circle of social diplomats which has set the well-to-do
diplomats over the hard-working consul . . . the men who are so
sore at the 'system' in the department contend that the spirit
of the Rogers Act is being violated and perverted to the end
that the tea-hounds of the service are getting all the breaks."

To Arthur Bliss Lane, First Secretary of the
American Embassy at Mexico City, May 3, 1927
. . . Bill Castle and Howland Shaw have been appointed to
the Personnel Board, and we are now having our last few meetings with the members of both the old and new Boards. You
probably know the principal problem which confronts us.
When the Rogers Act went into effect we adopted two separate
efficiency lists for the purposes of promotion, one diplomatic,
and one consular. It was not then thought feasible to do anything else, as the records of the work of diplomatic officers were
very incomplete and there was no ground for figuring out ratings of diplomatic and consular officers on the same basis.
Therefore, whenever a vacancy occurred in the diplomatic
branch in any class a diplomat was promoted to fill it, and the
same thing on the consular side. This resulted in a great many
more promotions of diplomats than consuls according to their
relative proportion in the Service. In fact, about ten diplomatic officers have been promoted twice since the Rogers Act
went into effect, but no consular officers have had two promotions. This has resulted in much criticism and dissatisfaction in the consular ranks, and the inevitable explosion occurred this spring in the form of a resolution by the House of
Representatives, introduced by Congressman Edwards, calling
on us for all the facts in the matter, as well as a great deal of
unfortunate publicity in the press. The Personnel Board discussed the matter at great length and was divided in its opinion
as to whether we should now adopt a single promotion list.
The responsibility for a decision was, however, taken off our
shoulders by an opinion of the Solicitor that a single list was
mandatory under the provisions of the Rogers Act, and therefore a single list will be used in the future.
The next problem before us was what, if any, reparation

should be made for the loss of deserved promotions by consular officers. Many officers in that branch maintain that in order to make just reparation we should figure the promotions on the basis of the relative proportion of consular and diplomatic officers. In other words, that the consuls should have had promotions since July 1, 1924, at approximately three and one-half to one. The Board, however, considered that this would not be at all fair, because if there had been a single list since the beginning, and if officers had been promoted from both branches according to their relative efficiency, the promotions might not have been at all in proportion to the number of officers in each branch. Therefore, we adopted the only logical method of reparation, namely, to go back and examine every officer's record, both diplomatic and consular, in order to try to adjust the matter purely on the basis of relative efficiency. If we had adopted the proportionate system we would now have to make about eighty-eight promotions of consular officers before any more diplomats were promoted. By the system adopted we have found, after the most complete and conscientious study, that forty-four consular promotions are due and probably would have been made if we had used a single list from the beginning. We shall therefore now proceed to make these forty-four consular promotions by way of reparation before any further diplomatic promotions are made. We fortunately have money enough to do this all at once, and possibly even to include a few diplomatic promotions in the normal course shortly thereafter. In other words, these forty-four consular promotions, and possibly one or two diplomatic promotions, will be announced separately as reparation. We shall then adopt a single list, which is already being completed, dovetailing the diplomats and consuls together on the basis of co-related efficiency ratings, and then proceed to make as many further promotions from the tops of the lists of the various classes as we have money for. All this will be duly explained to the field by a circular instruction which will also be given to the press and communicated to Congress. in order that Congress, the public, and the consuls may know that the Personnel

Board has made logical and just reparation for errors arising out of a system which for the last three years we have had to follow, contrary to the intentions of the Rogers Act, owing to the lack of adequate data concerning the efficiency of officers in the diplomatic branch. During the last three years we have acted to the best of our judgment on the situation which we inherited, and I do not see now that we could have done anything else. Every member of the Board agrees to this. Nevertheless, it is clear that this system resulted in unjustly penalizing consular officers, or in favoring diplomatic officers, whichever way you look at it, and it is equally clear that due reparation must be made as a matter of simple justice. The Personnel Board is unanimous about this too, and when explained to the field I hardly see how anyone can question the logic of our action. Many consuls, and possibly Congress, will feel that we have not gone far enough by way of reparation, and some diplomatic officers may feel that no reparation should have been made at all. I suppose it will be impossible to please everybody. This is the most difficult personnel problem that has come up since I have been in the Department, and it has caused every one of us a great deal of anxiety and a great deal of thought. The action taken yesterday in agreeing to promote forty-four consuls by way of reparation was concurred in by the members both of the old Board and the new Board, and there was no dissenting voice.

All this will be explained, as I say, in a circular instruction, but I am telling you of it in advance as I know your keen interest in all these problems.[7]

---

[7] In his *Diplomat Between Wars*, pp. 171–72, Hugh Wilson, who was one of the three Foreign Service officers on the Board at this time, wrote that the disparity in promotion could not have been avoided in the early years. He, also, stated that "I do not remember a single incident in which the decision of the board was taken other than by unanimity. The presence on the board of Wilbur Carr and of Edward Norton, both of them deeply interested in the consular service, would seem to be a sufficient guaranty that they were adequately protected." Mr. Wilson further commented that, although the Board was labeled as a "Harvard clique," he was from Yale, Wright from Princeton, and Norton was from no university. Carr was a graduate of the Commercial College of Kentucky University.

The stir over the promotion system failed to subside. The Senate Foreign Relations Committee investigated the situation and revealed that, in the 214 promotions during the first two and one-half years of the Rogers Act, 63 per cent of all the diplomatic officers were advanced, while only 37 per cent of the consular officers had been promoted.[8]

When the Washington Merry-Go-Round *was published in 1931, the authors charged that Mr. Grew and the other diplomats on the Board "picked their friends for the best foreign posts and saw to it that the amenable Mr. Kellogg got them approved at the White House." This book, also, stated that although Mr. Grew had made an excellent record as a Foreign Service officer, as Under Secretary of State he was "in constant hot water."*[9]

After reading this book, Mr. Grew reviewed the issue in his diary entry for September 7, 1931: "As for its comments on the old Personnel Board, it's rather a pity that history will never be allowed to know the facts but, as I wrote to Hugh Wilson and Butler Wright, I am proud to be in the same boat with such other good 'Harvard' men as themselves. Somebody with a sense of humor might at least point out that the so-called Harvard clique in the Department was largely made up of representatives of Yale, Princeton and a smattering of other colleges. The acts, policy and reputation of the old Personnel Board will never, presumably, be set right before the public simply because the senatorial investigating committee, composed of Senators George Moses, David Reed and Pat Harrison, was neither impartial nor fair; it desired and intended to condemn the Board and to find in favor of the consuls regardless of the evidence or the truth; the consular malcontents alone were allowed to testify; no diplomatic officer was heard and the evi-

---

[8] U.S. Congress, Senate, Committee on Foreign Relations, *Reorganization and Improvement of the Foreign Service*, Sen. Report 1069, 70th Cong., 1st Sess. (Washington: Government Printing Office, 1928), p. 3; Stuart, *op. cit.*, pp. 287–88.

[9] Drew Pearson and Robert S. Allen, *Washington Merry-Go-Round* (New York: Horace Liveright Inc., 1931), pp. 140–41.

dence of Mr. Kellogg and Mr. Carr, both of whom were fair, was largely ignored. Yet Senator Moses, when I briefly discussed the matter with him last year, had the face to tell me that the findings had been strictly in accord with the evidence — and then returned to the floor of the Senate before I could reply. I may have been, as the book implies, a rotten Under Secretary of State — it would have been impossible to be a good one under Kellogg — but as chairman of the Personnel Board the record of our meetings will show a clean bill of health which the most carping critic could find no fault with. These records are unfortunately confidential and cannot now be divulged, since they deal in detail with personalities and the faults and failings of individuals. But if the consular malcontents had made their charges in the open, or directly to the Board which they were afraid to do in spite of my written request for constructive criticism, instead of sneaking up to the Hill behind our backs and carrying on their subversive propaganda under cover like contemptible moles, there might have been a happier outcome for everyone. But history, alas, will never record and never know the truth. Anything that redounds to the discredit of the old Diplomatic Service and the members thereof is grist to the mill of Congress, the public, the press and the editorial writers; we shall always be associated with pink tea and spats (which many a good congressman wears, by the way) and the public would be bitterly disappointed if they thought we weren't living up to our character as painted. The consuls, meanwhile, whatever their faults or failings, will always be the hard-working, efficient fair-haired boys. 'Give a dog an ill name, and hang him.' . . ."

In addition to the criticism that diplomats had been favored for promotion over consuls, it was also charged in 1927 that members of the Personnel Board gave themselves choice posts overseas. The critics noted that in the spring of 1927 J. Butler Wright and Hugh Wilson were appointed to Hungary and Switzerland, and, that on May 19, 1927, Mr. Grew was appointed Ambassador to Turkey.

Secretary Kellogg, however, stated that he was responsible for recommending to the President Mr. Wright and Mr. Grew. Furthermore, Mr. Kellogg said that the original recommendation for Mr. Wilson had come from Hugh Gibson, who had just been promoted from Minister to Switzerland to Ambassador to Belgium.

When Mr. Kellogg met Mr. Grew in Paris on April 11, 1931, Mr. Kellogg explained to Mr. Grew how he had made it clear to members of the Senate, that Mr. Grew had not promoted himself and that the Turkish post had been accepted by Mr. Grew because the President felt that he was the one man who could negotiate a treaty with Turkey. After this conversation, Mr. Grew noted in his diary: "I know that Kellogg was glad to have a change in the undersecretaryship, but I was even gladder than he was. Still, I have a lot of affection for the old man." On November 20, 1937, after Mr. Grew and John V. A. Mac-Murray had discussed their experiences with Secretary Kellogg, Mr. Grew wrote in his diary: "Kellogg often did behave like a petulant child and in those moods it was quite useless to try to argue or talk logic with him but, as Jack agreed with me, no man could be more kindly or charming in his gentler moods and we both feel nothing but affection for him. Once he had gotten me out of the Department he was perfectly delightful to me and in our subsequent meetings and correspondence there had always been a note of genuine friendship."

The appointment of Mr. Grew as Ambassador to Turkey on May 19, 1927, received a great deal of praise in the press. The New York Times *declared, for instance, on May 20: "The appointment of Mr.* JOSEPH C. GREW, *Under-Secretary of State, to be Ambassador to Turkey returns to the field a professional diplomat who has had wide experience. Thanks to his participation in the conferences that led to the formulation of the Lausanne treaties, he is particularly well versed in the complicated questions involved in Turkey's new international status, and in her relations with the United States. The failure of the Senate to ratify this treaty left the situation somewhat anomalous. Doubtless Mr.* GREW *will turn his past experience to good use in arranging satisfactory methods for settlement of the issues still pending between the two countries. . . ."*

To Alexander C. Kirk, Assistant to Under Secretary Grew, July 15, 1927

. . . Now just a word about my leaving the Department. It is always more agreeable to be missed than not. Such is human nature and I appreciate what you say about it a lot, although I think the adjustment to new conditions won't come very hard. But I gather from what you say that in the back of your mind is a feeling that I am sort of quitting the ship. You know I did not ask for Constantinople. I received distinct impressions that the Administration wanted me to go and were only delaying the appointment because some time previously I had expressed reluctance to leave Washington. That reluctance gradually disappeared and I thought it was up to me to let that fact be known. Some time before, the Secretary had asked me whether I would like to go to Brussels or Ottawa and I had replied that if agreeable to him I would prefer to remain in the Department. However, he wouldn't have inquired if he had not been quite ready for a change, nicht wahr? Then there was another element. I wanted Constantinople above everything but I should not have said so if I had felt that I was further needed in the Department. As a matter of fact I think a change was clearly indicated. Robert E. Olds was to all intents and purposes Under Secretary so far as political matters were concerned.[10] As for personnel matters, new blood was clearly needed on the Board, both from the point of view of Congress and certain sections of the field. So it was not wholly a question of having earned what meant most to me. I frankly feel that the time had come. . . .

10 The lack of consultation on policy matters between Mr. Kellogg and Mr. Grew had been mentioned in the press before Mr. Grew had been appointed Ambassador to Turkey. A feature article by the N.E.A. Service on March 19, 1927, stated: "One of the most interesting bits of gossip about the State Department tells of a feud between Secretary of State Kellogg and Under Secretary Joseph C. Grew. When Kellogg is away, Grew takes charge, but when Kellogg returns to his job he totally ignores Grew, according to some members of the department personnel." The Frederick, Maryland, *News.*

END OF VOLUME I